Praise for
Faith of My Fathers

"A serious, utterly gripping account of faith, fathers, and the military."

—*Publishers Weekly* (starred review)

"A remarkable personal history . . . unconventional and interesting."
—*The Washington Post Book World*

"McCain's character has withstood tests the average politician can only imagine. . . . He may be the last of his kind."

—*Newsweek*

"A good read . . . engaging, sometimes funny, and often profoundly moving . . . The family stories, the naval history, the fighter-jock anecdotes, and the stoic bravery of the POWs make for a large, almost unwieldy, and sublimely American story. . . . If you are yourself a patriot and you find yourself stirred by stories of honest patriotism, then you will surely find *Faith of My Fathers* irresistible."

—*National Review*

"Hard to top and impossible to read without being moved."

—*USA Today*

"A testament to the martial values of honor and patriotism . . . lively and readable."

—*The New York Times*

"Eloquent and honest."

—*The New York Review of Books*

"A fascinating history of a remarkable military family . . . [McCain] gets to the core of those ineffable qualities of wartime brotherhood and self-sacrifice that are so far beyond common notions of 'patriotism.' *Faith of My Fathers* does this better than any other book by a Vietnam vet."

—*The Christian Science Monitor*

"A candid, moving, and entertaining memoir . . . impressive and inspiring, the story of a man touched and molded by fire, who loved and served his country in a time of great trouble, suffering, and challenge."

—*Kirkus Reviews*

"*Faith of My Fathers* is the powerful story of a war hero. In it we learn much of what matters most. As prisoner (and later Senator) McCain instructs us: Glory is not an end in itself, but rather a reward for valor and faith. And the greatest freedom and human fulfillment comes from engaging in a noble enterprise larger than oneself. *Faith of My Fathers* teaches deep truths that are valid in any age but that warrant special attention in our own."

—WILLIAM J. BENNETT

By John McCain and Mark Salter

*Character Is Destiny: Inspiring Stories Every Young Person
Should Know and Every Adult Should Remember*

Faith of My Fathers: A Family Memoir

Why Courage Matters: The Way to a Braver Life

Worth the Fighting For: A Memoir

13 Soldiers: A Personal History of Americans at War

FAITH OF MY FATHERS

RANDOM HOUSE – NEW YORK

Faith of My Fathers

John McCain

with Mark Salter

2016 Random House Trade Paperback Edition

Copyright © 1999 by John McCain and Mark Salter

Published in the United States by Random House,
an imprint and division of Penguin Random House LLC, New York.

RANDOM HOUSE and the HOUSE colophon are
registered trademarks of Penguin Random House LLC.

Originally published in hardcover in the United States by Random House,
an imprint and division of Penguin Random House LLC, in 1999.

All photographs are from the McCain family collection.

LIBRARY OF CONGRESS CATALOGING-IN-PUBLICATION DATA

McCain, John.
Faith of my fathers: a family memoir / John McCain with Mark Salter.
p.   cm.
ISBN 978-0-399-59089-4
Ebook ISBN 978-0-375-50458-7
1. McCain, John, 1936—Religion.   2. McCain, John, 1936—Family.
3. Legislators—United States—Biography.   4. United States.   Congress.
Senate—Biography.   5. McCain, John S. (John Sidney), 1911–1981.
6. Fathers—United States—Biography.   7. McCain, John Sidney, 1884–1945.
8. Grandfathers—United States—Biography.   9. United States.   Navy—
Biography.   I.   Salter, Mark. II.   Title.
E840.8.M467   A3   1999   973.9'092'2—dc21   99-13496
[B]
Printed in the United States of America on acid-free paper

randomhousebooks.com

2 4 6 8 9 7 5 3 1

For Doug, Andy, Sidney,
Meghan, Jack, Jimmy, and Bridget

A survivor of Auschwitz, Viktor Frankl wrote movingly of how man controls his own destiny when captive to a great evil. "Everything can be taken from man but one thing: the last of human freedoms—to choose one's own attitude in any given set of circumstances, to choose one's own way."

I have spent much of my life choosing my own attitude, often carelessly, often for no better reason than to indulge a conceit. In those instances, my acts of self-determination were mistakes, some of which did no lasting harm, and serve now only to embarrass, and occasionally amuse, the old man who recalls them. Others I deeply regret.

At other times, I chose my own way with good cause and to good effect. I did not do so to apologize for my mistakes. My contrition is a separate matter. When I chose well I did so to keep a balance in my life—a balance between pride and regret, between liberty and honor.

My grandfather was a naval aviator, my father a submariner. They were my first heroes, and earning their respect has been the most lasting ambition of my life. They have been dead many years now, yet I still aspire to live my life according to the terms of their approval. They were not men of spotless virtue, but they were honest, brave, and loyal all their lives.

For two centuries, the men of my family were raised to go to war as officers in America's armed services. It is a family history that, as a boy, often intimidated me, and, for a time, I struggled halfheartedly against its expectations. But when my own time at war arrived, I realized how fortunate I was to have been raised in such a family.

From both my parents, I learned to persevere. But my mother's extraordinary resilience made her the stronger of the two. I acquired some of her resilience and her felicity, and that inheritance made an enormous difference in my life. Our family lived on the move, rooted not in a location, but in the culture of the Navy. I learned from my mother not just to take the constant disruptions in stride, but to welcome them as elements of an interesting life.

The United States Naval Academy, an institution I both resented and admired, tried to bend my resilience to a cause greater than self-interest. I resisted its exertions, fearing its effect on my individuality. But as a prisoner of war, I learned that a shared purpose did not claim my identity. On the contrary, it enlarged my sense of myself. I have the example of many brave men to thank for that discovery, all of them proud of their singularity, but faithful to the same cause.

First made a migrant by the demands of my father's career, in time I became self-moving, a rover by choice. In such a life, some fine things are left behind, and missed. But bad times are left behind as well. You move on, remembering the good, while the bad grows obscure in the distance.

I left war behind me, and never let the worst of it encumber my progress.

This book recounts some of my experiences, and commemorates the people who most influenced my choices. What balance I have achieved is a gift from them.

— Acknowledgments —

I could not have written this book without the encouragement and assistance of many people to whom I am greatly indebted. My mother, a natural storyteller if ever there was one, reminded me of a great many family stories I had either forgotten or had never heard before. She was quite generous with her time despite her initial suspicion that I was "just trying to show off." My brother, Joe McCain, keeper of family papers and legends, was an invaluable help in organizing and fact checking.

My father's dear friend Rear Admiral Joe Vasey (ret.), who time and again interrupted his busy schedule to answer at length my many queries, gave me the best sense of my father as a submarine skipper and a senior commander. Moreover, he directed me to a wonderful website, hometown.aol.com/jmlavelle2, the work of Admiral Vasey and Jim Lavelle, which is a fountain of information about the experiences of the officers and crew of the USS *Gunnel*, one of the submarines my father commanded during World War II. I cannot praise or thank them enough for keeping the memory of their service alive and on-line.

Many thanks are due as well to Admiral Eugene Ferrell, my old skipper, who reminded me of how proud I was, so many years ago, to have learned from a master ship handler how to be a sailor. Veteran war correspondent Dick O'Malley, a friend and keen observer of my grandfather during the war, told me many good tales about the old man in his last days at sea.

My old friend and comrade Orson Swindle reviewed the manuscript and kindly marked for excision anything that smacked of self-aggrandizement. Keeping me honest is a role he has often played in my life and will, I hope, continue to play for a good while longer. My Academy roommate Frank Gamboa resurrected a few stories from our misspent youth that I had managed to bury years ago. Lorne Craner, son of my dear friend Bob Craner, shared many of his father's memories of our time in prison, and was a great help in sorting out times and places that I had gotten thoroughly confused.

Dr. Paul Stillwell, director of the Oral History Project at the Naval Institute, kindly allowed me to read the interviews of my father and many of my father's and grandfather's contemporaries, a wonderful resource for anyone interested in learning about the men who made the modern U.S. Navy. I am grateful for the assistance of Chris Paul, who spent a part of his vacation sorting through volumes of my father's papers. Thanks also to Joe Donoghue for successfully tracking down information and photographs that had eluded me.

Three others deserve special recognition and gratitude. Academy graduate, Vietnam veteran, and gifted reporter Bob Timberg, who often gives me the unsettling feeling that he knows more about me than I do, was a great source of encouragement and guidance. Just as important, Bob suggested that I meet with his agent, and now mine, Philippa (Flip) Brophy, who succeeded where others had failed by convincing me that Mark Salter and I could write a good story. She was a patient, steady influence throughout the drafting of the manuscript, as was my editor, Jonathan Karp. Although Jon is the only editor I have ever worked with, I cannot imagine how anyone could have done a better job. He and Flip kept us on track and calm, a tough assignment when working with a couple of amateur writers.

Finally, both Mark and I would like to thank our wives, Cindy McCain and Diane Salter, and our children for tolerating yet another demand on our time that kept us from our more important, and better loved responsibilities. Any merit in this book is due in large part to the help of the kind souls named above.

John McCain
Phoenix, Arizona

I

Faith of our fathers, living still,
In spite of dungeon, fire and sword;
O how our hearts beat high with joy
Whenever we hear that glorious word!

Faith of our fathers, holy faith!
We will be true to thee till death.

—Frederick William Faber,
"Faith of Our Fathers"

CHAPTER 1

In War and Victory

I have a picture I prize of my grandfather and father, John Sidney McCain Senior and Junior, taken on the bridge of a submarine tender, the USS *Proteus*, in Tokyo Bay a few hours after the Second World War had ended. They had just finished meeting privately in one of the ship's small staterooms and were about to depart for separate destinations. They would never see each other again.

Despite the weariness that lined their faces, you can see they were relieved to be in each other's company again. My grandfather loved his children. And my father admired my grandfather above all others. My mother, to whom my father was devoted, had once asked him if he loved his father more than he loved her. He replied simply, "Yes, I do."

On the day of their reunion, my father, a thirty-four-year-old submarine commander, and his crew had just brought a surrendered Japanese submarine into Tokyo Bay. My grandfather, whom Admiral Halsey once referred to as "not much more than my right arm," had just relinquished command of Halsey's renowned fast carrier task force, and had attended the signing of the surrender aboard the USS *Missouri* that morning. He can be seen in a famous photograph of the occasion standing with his head bowed in the first rank of officers observing the ceremony.

My grandfather had not wanted to attend, and had requested permission to leave for home immediately upon learning of Japan's intention to capitulate.

"I don't give a damn about seeing the surrender," my grandfather told Halsey. "I want to get the hell out of here." To which Halsey replied, "Maybe you do, but you're not going. You were commanding this task force when the war ended, and I'm making sure that history gets it straight." In his memoir, Halsey described my grandfather "cursing and sputtering" as he returned to his flagship.

To most observers, my grandfather had been as elated to hear of Japan's decision to surrender as had the next man. Upon hearing the announcement, he ordered the doctor on his flagship to break out the medicinal brandy and passed cups around to all takers. He was a jocular man, and his humor could at times be wicked. He told a friend, as they prepared for the surrender ceremony, "If you see MacArthur's hands shaking as he reads the surrender documents it won't be emotion. It will be from too many of those mestiza girls in the Philippines."

In the days immediately following the announcement that Emperor Hirohito had agreed to surrender, a few of the emperor's pilots had either not received or not believed the message. Occasionally, a few Japanese planes would mount attacks on the ships of my grandfather's task force. He directed his fighter pilots to shoot down any approaching enemy planes. "But do it in a friendly sort of way," he added.

Some of his closest aides sensed that there was something wrong with the old man. His operations officer, Commander John Thach, a very talented officer whom my grandfather relied on to an extraordinary extent, was concerned about his health. Thach went to my grandfather's cabin and asked him if he was ill. In an account of the exchange he gave many years later, Thach recalled my grandfather's answer: "Well, this surrender has come as kind of a shock to all of us. I feel lost. I don't know what to do. I know how to fight, but now I don't know whether I know how to relax or not. I'm in an awful letdown."

Once on board the *Missouri*, however, he was entirely at ease. Rushing about the deck of the battleship, hailing his friends and reveling in the moment, he was the most animated figure at the ceremony. He announced to Admiral Nimitz, Commander in Chief, Pacific, that he had invented three new cocktails, the July, the Gill, and the Zeke, each one named for a type of Japanese plane his task force had fought during the war's last hard months. "Each time you drink one you can say 'Splash one July' or 'Splash one Zeke,' " he explained.

After the surrender, Halsey reports, my grandfather was grateful for having been ordered to join the others on the *Missouri*. "Thank God you made me stay, Bill. You had better sense than I did."

Immediately after father and son parted company that day, my grandfather left for his home in Coronado, California. Before he left, he issued his last dispatch to the men under his command.

> I am glad and proud to have fought through my last year of active service with the renowned fast carriers. War and victory have forged a lasting bond among us. If you are as fortunate in peace as you have been victorious in war, I am now talking to 110,000 prospective millionaires. Goodbye, good luck, and may God be with you.
>
> McCain

He arrived home four days later. My grandmother, Katherine Vaulx McCain, arranged for a homecoming party the next day attended by neighbors and the families of Navy friends who had yet to return from the war. Standing in his crowded living room, my grandfather was pressed for details of the surrender ceremony, and some of the wives present whose husbands were POWs begged him for information about when they could expect their husbands' return. He responded to their inquiries courteously, seemingly content, as always, to be the center of attention.

Some of the guests remembered having observed that my grandfather seemed something less than his normally ebullient self; a little tired from his journey, they had thought, and worn out from the rigors of the war.

In the middle of the celebration my grandfather turned to my grandmother, announced that he felt ill, and then collapsed. A physician attending the party knelt down to feel for the admiral's pulse. Finding none, he looked up at my grandmother and said, "Kate, he's dead."

He was sixty-one years old. He had fought his war and died. His Navy physician attributed his fatal heart attack to "complete fatigue resulting from the strain of the last months of combat." Halsey's chief of staff, Admiral Robert Carney, believed he had suffered an earlier heart attack at sea and had managed to keep it hidden. According to Carney, the admiral "knew his number was up, but he wouldn't lie down and die until he got home."

My grandfather had made his way to the *Proteus* to join my father immediately after the surrender ceremony. During a luncheon aboard ship hosted by the commander of U.S. submarines in the Pacific, father and son retreated to a small stateroom for a private conversation. In an interview my father gave thirty years later for the Naval Institute's Oral History Project, he briefly described their last moment together. Nothing in my grandfather's manner gave my father reason to worry about the old man's health. "I knew him as well as anybody in the world, with the possible exception of my mother. He looked in fine health to me," my father recalled. "And God knows his conversation was anything but indicative of a man who was sick. And two days later he died of a heart attack."

Little else is known about their last conversation. To the best of my knowledge, my father never talked about it to anyone except the Naval Institute interviewer. And the only detail he offered him, besides the description of my grandfather's apparent well-being, was a remark my grandfather had made about how dying for your principles and country was a privilege.

His obituary ran on the front page of the *New York Times* as it did in many major metropolitan papers. My grandmother received condolences from the nation's most senior military and civilian commanders, including President Truman, General MacArthur, and Admirals Nimitz and Halsey. Navy Secretary Forrestal wrote her that "the entire Navy mourned."

In the Naval Academy yearbook for 1906, the year my grandfather graduated, the editors chose quotations from the classics to describe each member of the class. For my grandfather, the choice was prophetic, a line from Milton: "That power which erring men call chance."

He was laid to rest in Arlington National Cemetery following a Washington funeral attended by Forrestal and the Chief of Naval Operations, Fleet Admiral Ernie King. Among his pallbearers was General Alexander Vandergrift, who had commanded the Marines on Guadalcanal, and Vice Admiral Aubrey Fitch, the Superintendent of the United States Naval Academy. He was awarded a fourth star posthumously.

My father, who had left for the States immediately upon receiving word of the admiral's death, arrived too late to pay his respects. My mother found him standing on the tarmac at San Diego when she returned from Washington. He was in the throes of deep grief, a grief that took years to subside. He told my mother he was relieved to have missed the funeral. "It would have killed me," he explained.

There was, however, an event near the end of my grandfather's life that no one discussed. In none of the published accounts of my grandfather's death nor in any of the many tributes offered by his contemporaries was mention made of the incident that had cost my grandfather his command just one day before the war's end.

Less than three months earlier, he had been ordered by Nimitz to resume command of Task Force 38, which at that time constituted almost the entire Third Fleet as it provided air support to the American invasion of Okinawa. One week after he resumed command, my grandfather and Halsey received the first reports from search planes of a tropical storm south of Okinawa that was fast becoming a typhoon.

When the first reports of the June typhoon were received, the fleet meteorologists advised Halsey not to move the fleet. But Halsey, fearing that the typhoon would drive him westward and in range of Japanese planes based in China, ordered his task groups to sail southeast in an attempt to get around the storm. My grandfather was aboard his flagship, the *Shangri-La*. Puzzled by his instructions, he turned to his friend, a war correspondent for the Associated Press, Dick O'Malley, and said, "What the hell is Halsey doing, trying to intercept another typhoon?" His observation was a reference to Halsey's actions during a typhoon that had struck the fleet in December 1944, sinking two destroyers. According to John Thach, my grandfather had recommended a heading for the fleet that would have avoided the earlier storm, as had Admiral Nimitz. But Halsey had insisted on another course, a course that tragically failed to take his ships out of harm's way.

A little less than six months later, at one o'clock on the morning of June 5, Halsey received a late report from an amphibious command ship that this latest storm was too far to the south for the fleet to get safely around it. Halsey attempted to get out of its way by reversing course from southeast to northwest, greatly surprising the commanders of his task groups, who were now in imminent peril.

At four o'clock, one of those commanders, Admiral J. J. Clark, signaled my grandfather (to whom Halsey had given tactical command of the fleet's race to safer waters) that their present course would bring his task group directly into the storm. A few minutes later he signaled, "I can get clear of the center of the storm quickly by steering 120. Please advise."

My grandfather consulted Halsey, who advised against a course change. He then signaled Clark for an updated report of the position and bearing of the storm's eye before ordering Clark to use his best judgment. After communicating with Halsey and Clark, my grandfather could have spent only a few minutes considering the matter before deciding to reject Halsey's advice. But it was a few minutes too long. His order came twenty minutes after Clark signaled for advice and too late for his task group to escape the worst of the storm.

Although none of Clark's ships sank, many of them were damaged, including four carriers. One hundred and forty-two aircraft were lost. Six men from Clark's task group and a nearby fueling group were swept overboard by the storm-tossed seas and drowned. Four others were seriously injured.

A few days after Task Force 38 resumed operations off Okinawa, my grandfather and Halsey were ordered to appear before a court of inquiry on June 15. In the court's opinion, the fleet's encounter with the typhoon was directly attributable to Halsey's order to change course and my grandfather's failure to instruct Clark for twenty minutes.

Upon receiving the court's report, Secretary Forrestal was prepared to relieve both Halsey and my grandfather. But Admiral King persuaded Forrestal that Halsey's relief would be too great a blow to the Navy's and the country's morale.

Two months later, my grandfather was ordered to relinquish his command.

Professional naval officers constitute a small community today. It was a much smaller one in the years when my father and grandfather made their living at sea. Yet I only learned of the episode that closed my grandfather's career when, many years later, I read an account of the typhoon in E. B. Potter's biography of Admiral Halsey.

My father never mentioned it to me.

CHAPTER 2

Slew

In his memoirs, Admiral Halsey makes brief mention of the typhoon, blaming his task group's encounter with it on late warnings and erroneous predictions of the storm's course, but he offers no description of my grandfather's role in the disaster.

My grandfather's request to return home rather than witness the drama of Japan's surrender was a measure of his despair over losing his command. Halsey did write of his subordinate's outrage at being relieved of his command, describing him as "thoroughly sore."

I once suspected, as my father probably had, that the court's findings had hastened my grandfather's death. But as I grew older, it became easier to dismiss my suspicion as the dramatization of the end of a life that needed no embellishment from a sentimental namesake. My grandfather had not been banished into retirement after losing his command. President Truman had ordered him to Washington to serve under General Omar Bradley as the deputy director of the new Veterans Administration to help integrate back into civilian society the millions of returning American veterans, a prestigious and important appointment.

I doubt any assignment would have eased immediately the indignation he must have felt over losing his last wartime command. But by all accounts, my grandfather was a tough, willful, resilient man who, had he lived, would have resolved to serve with distinction in his new post as the surest way to put a great distance between himself and that fateful storm.

I was a few days shy of my ninth birthday when my grandfather died. I had seen very little of him during the war, and most of those occasions were hurried affairs. I remember being awakened in the dead of night on several occasions when he dropped in unannounced on his way from one assignment to another. My mother would assemble us on the parlor couch and then search the house for her camera, to record another brief reunion between her children and their famous grandfather. Even before the war, my father's career often kept a continent or more between my grandparents and me. And the recollections I have of him have dimmed over the half century that has elapsed since I saw him last.

The image that remains is that of a rail-thin, gaunt, hawk-faced man whose slight build was disguised by a low-timbered voice and a lively, antic presence. It was fun to be in his company, and particularly so if you were the primary object of his attention, as I remember being when we were together.

He rolled his own cigarettes, which he smoked constantly, and his one-handed technique fascinated me. While the skill was anything but neat (Admiral Halsey once ordered a Navy steward to follow him around with a dustpan and broom whenever he was aboard the admiral's flagship), that it could be accomplished at all struck me as praiseworthy. He would give me his empty bags of Bull Durham tobacco, which I valued highly, and which deepened my appreciation of the performance.

In today's slang, he lived large. He was called Sid by his family and Slew by his fellow officers, for reasons I never learned. He liked to take his shoes off when he worked and walk around the office in his

stocking feet. He smoked, swore, drank, and gambled at every opportunity he had. His profile in the 1943 *Current Biography* described
him as "one of the Navy's best plain and fancy cussers."

Rear Admiral Howard Kuehl served on my grandfather's staff as
a young lieutenant during the campaign for the Solomon Islands,
when my grandfather commanded all land-based aircraft in the South
Pacific. In an article he wrote about his wartime experiences, he affectionately recounted an example of his boss's colorful idiosyncrasies.

In addition to his other duties, Kuehl served as the wine mess
treasurer, an assignment that obliged him to maintain a meager inventory of liquor for the officers' recreational use and to obtain from my
grandfather and his staff officers adequate funds for that purpose.
When an officer received transfer orders, he was entitled to a refund
of his wine mess share. In September 1942, after my grandfather had
received orders reassigning him to Washington, Kuehl visited him on
the afternoon before his scheduled departure. Dutifully attempting to
return my grandfather's share of the kitty, he was momentarily taken
aback when my grandfather ordered that it be returned "in kind."
Summoning considerable courage, Kuehl informed his boss that because liquid spirits were a precious commodity aboard ship it was
an unofficial but scrupulously observed custom that an officer returning to the States would not take any with him. Assuming no further
admonishment was necessary, Kuehl then handed over to my dis-
gruntled grandfather the money owed to him.

The next morning, my grandfather's staff lined up at the gang-
way to shake his hand and bid him an affectionate farewell. When he
reached his intrepid wine mess treasurer, he shot him a look of affected displeasure and said, "Kuehl, goddammit, you're a crook."

My mother often recounts the occasions when her father-in-law
would order her to accompany him on a long night of carousing in his
favorite gambling den of the moment. He seemed to have one in every
place he was stationed. He also managed to spend considerable time
at horse tracks, where his enthusiasm for the sport was evident in the
sums of money he spent to make it interesting. As commanding offi-

cer of the aircraft carrier USS *Ranger*, he would order his yeoman into the first boat headed ashore whenever the *Ranger* came into home port, tasking him with the urgent business of placing his bets with the local bookie.

A young ensign, William Smedberg, fresh from the Naval Academy, reported for duty to the USS *New Mexico*, where my grandfather was serving as executive officer. An hour after he arrived he was summoned to my grandfather's cabin. Apparently, the ship's home port hosted a rowing regatta among the officers and enlisted men of the various ships stationed there, and my grandfather, being a sporting man who enjoyed a good wager, had taken a keen interest in the event. He had examined Ensign Smedberg's record at the Academy and discovered he had been coxswain on an Academy crew. Smedberg recounted their exchange:

"Young man, I understand that you were a coxswain at the Naval Academy?"

"Yes, sir, I was coxswain of the hundred-and-fifty-pound crew."

"Well, that's good, because you're going to be coxswain now of the officers' crew and the enlisted crew. You're to take them both out every morning we're in port at five o'clock. And you're to win both those races."

They won both races, making my grandfather a happy and somewhat more prosperous man. (Ensign Smedberg would eventually reach flag rank, serve as Superintendent of the Naval Academy when I was a midshipman there, and retire a vice admiral.)

My grandmother once informed my grandfather of a new treatment for ulcers she had just read about in a magazine. Pounding his fist on a table, he shouted, "Not one penny of my money for doctors. I'm spending it all on riotous living." My grandmother was reported to have given him an adequate allowance for that purpose while retaining unchallenged control over the rest of the family's finances.

While serving as a pallbearer for one of his Naval Academy classmates on a cold, rainy day at Arlington National Cemetery, my grandfather listened to a young officer suggest that he button up his raincoat to protect himself from the elements. The old man, raincoat flapping in the wind, looked at his solicitous subordinate and said, "You don't think I got where I am by taking care of my health, do you?"

My mother, who was enchanted by him, keeps in her living room a large oil portrait of the admiral, distinguished and starched in his navy whites. In reality he was a disheveled-looking man with a set of false teeth so ill-fitting that they made a constant clicking noise when he moved his jaw and caused him to whistle when he spoke.

Admiral Halsey and he were such good friends that even in the strain of war, when my grandfather was Halsey's subordinate, theirs was a relaxed and open relationship marked by mutual respect and candor. They delighted in ribbing each other mercilessly and playing practical jokes on each other. On the evening before a trip to Guadalcanal together, my grandfather had spent the night in Halsey's quarters. He had absentmindedly left his teeth sitting on a bureau in Halsey's bathroom. Halsey saw the teeth sitting there and, delighted by an opportunity to discomfit his old friend, slipped them into his shirt pocket. One of my grandfather's aides recalled the scene that followed as the party was departing for Guadalcanal, my grandfather frantically searching for his missing teeth while Halsey badgered him to hurry up.

"Can't go, I can't go. I've lost my teeth," he implored. To which the much-amused Halsey responded, "How do you expect to run naval aviation if you can't take care of your own teeth?"

After another fruitless search, and a few more minutes of Halsey poking fun at him, and my grandfather hurling insults right back, my grandfather resigned himself to going to Guadalcanal toothless. At the plane, a grinning Halsey handed the teeth back to him, and caught, I am sure, a torrent of abuse from my grandfather.

When in combat, he dispensed with all Navy regulations governing the attire of a flag officer. Disheveled, stooped, weighing only 140 pounds, and looking many years older than his age, he was, nevertheless, unmistakably Navy. Sailors who served under him called him, behind his back but affectionately, "Popeye the sailor man." He wore a ratty, crushed green cap with its frame removed from the crown and an officer's insignia sewn onto the visor. Halsey once described it as "unique in naval costume." Like most sailors, my grandfather was a superstitious man, and he treasured his "combat cap" as a good luck talisman. So did everyone else on his flagship, fearing that any misfortune that befell the old man's hat was a sign of approaching calamity. Whenever the wind blew the hat from its perch, men would dive to the deck and frantically scramble for it lest it be blown overboard. My grandfather, who was aware of the crew's shared regard for the supernatural powers of his unorthodox headgear, watched in amused silence and grinned broadly when a relieved sailor handed it back to him.

The cap was a gift from the wife of a naval aviator. My grandfather was much admired by the aviators under his command and by their families, who knew how deeply he grieved over the loss of his pilots. I have heard from colleagues of my grandfather that he would cry routinely when he received casualty reports. "Whenever a pilot was lost," John Thach said of him, "it was not just a sad thing, but it seemed like a personal loss to him and it took a lot out of him." He loved life, and lived his as fully as anyone could. It is easy to understand how greatly it must have pained him to see any man, especially someone under his command, lose his life prematurely.

Commander Thach recalled how my grandfather liked to talk to the pilots just after they returned from a strike. Thach would select those pilots whose experiences he knew would most interest the old man and bring them immediately to the admiral's cabin. My grandfather would give them a cup of coffee and listen intently as his young flyers described the details of their mission, always asking them at the end of the interview, "Do you think we're doing the right thing?"

The pilots loved these exchanges, recognizing in my grandfather's genuine interest in their views a regard for them that was not always apparent in the busy, distracted mien of other senior commanders. My grandfather valued the interviews as well. He believed an able commander profited from the insights of the men under his command and should always take care to see that his own decisions were informed by the assessments of those who were charged with executing them. "He never quit learning," Thach observed. "He didn't have complete and abiding faith in his own judgment, and I don't think anyone should."

Cecil King, a retired chief warrant officer, had served under my grandfather's command at the naval air station in Panama in 1936. My grandfather had ferociously chewed him out once for writing false dispatches as a practical joke, one of which reported a Japanese attack on an American embassy. Although he gave the young sailor the tongue-lashing of his life, he didn't have him court-martialed or even seriously discipline him. Eight years later, when my grandfather was commanding the fast carriers in the Pacific in the last year of the war, King happened to be standing in a crowd of sailors in New Guinea when my grandfather and several of his aides walked by. A few paces after he passed King and his buddies, my grandfather stopped and turned around. Pointing his finger at King, he said, "You're the son of a bitch who almost started World War Two by yourself," and laughed.

That he would remember so many years later, with his mind preoccupied with the demands of a wartime command, one of the tens of thousands of sailors he had commanded over his career is a remarkable testament not only to his memory, but to his devotion to his men. Certainly King thought so. "Every skipper's a legend to his people. And he was a legend to us. The fact that he smoked Bull Durham cigarettes, rolled them himself; the fact that he didn't wear shoes; the fact that he was just a giant of a guy. Everything he did was first-class."

An aviator under my grandfather's command was believed to have been drunk when he crashed his airplane and died. According to King, for the benefit of the dead man's family, my grandfather kept the suspected cause of the accident from coming to light in an official inquiry. "I was so struck by his compassion and understanding," King remarked. "The common conception was that he would go the last mile and some more too [for his men]."

James Michener knew my grandfather, and wrote briefly about him in the preface to his famous work *Tales of the South Pacific*: "I also knew Admiral McCain in a very minor way. He was an ugly old aviator. One day he flew over Santo and pointed down at the island wilderness and said, 'That's where we'll build our base.' And the base was built there, and millions of dollars were spent there, and everyone agrees that Santo was the best base the Navy ever built in the region. I was always mighty proud of McCain, for he was in aviation, too."

My father believed him to be the most exemplary leader in the United States Navy. "My father," he said, "was a very great leader, and people loved him. . . . My mother used to say about him that the blood of life flowed through his veins, he was so keenly interested in people. . . . He was a man of great moral and physical courage."

In pictures of him from the war you sense his irreverent, eccentric individualism. He looked like a cartoonist's rendering of an old salt. As a boy and a young man, I found the attitude his image conveyed irresistible. Perhaps not consciously, I spent much of my youth—and beyond—exaggerating that attitude, too much for my own good, and my family's peace of mind.

Of more lasting duration, and of far greater consequence, was the military tradition he bequeathed to my father and me; the tradition he was born to, the latest in a long line of my ancestors who had worn the country's uniform.

He was the first McCain to choose the Navy. Until he entered the Academy in 1902, the men of his family had served in the Army; his brother, William Alexander, a cavalry officer who was known in the Army as "Wild Bill," was the last. Bill McCain had chased Pancho Villa with Pershing, served as an artillery officer in World War I, and later been a brigadier general in the Quartermaster Corps. He was the last McCain to graduate from West Point.

No one in my family is certain if we are descended from an

unbroken line of military officers. But you can trace that heritage through many generations of our family, finding our ancestors in every American war, in the War for Independence, on the side of the Confederacy in the Civil War. One distinguished ancestor served on General Washington's staff. Camp McCain in Grenada, Mississippi, is named for my grandfather's uncle Major General Henry Pinckney McCain, a West Pointer, and reputedly a stern autocrat who was known as the father of the Selective Service for organizing the draft in World War I.

We trace our martial lineage through two families, the McCains and the Youngs. My great-grandfather, yet another John Sidney McCain, married Elizabeth Young in 1877. Both were descendants of Scots Presbyterians who, in the aftermath of Queen Mary's death at the hands of her royal English cousin, suffered the privations that were the fate of those who had remained loyal to the Scottish crown.

The McCains, bred to fight as Highland Scots of the Clan McDonald, arrived in the New World shortly after America gained her independence, when Hugh McCain settled his wife and six children in Caswell County, North Carolina, and built his estate, Lenox Castle.

Hugh's grandson, William Alexander McCain, died while serving in the Mississippi cavalry during the Civil War. William's oldest son, Joseph Watt McCain, also fought for the Confederacy. In his first battle he passed out at the sight of blood and was mistakenly left for dead by his comrades. William's third son, the aforementioned father of the Selective Service, Henry Pinckney McCain, was the first to serve the flag of the restored Union.

William McCain's second son, my great-grandfather, barely fourteen years old at the end of the Civil War, offered to enlist as well, giving his age as eighteen. He was rejected, but later in his life would express his patriotism by serving as sheriff of Carroll County, Mississippi, and inspiring his sons, my grandfather and great uncle, to pursue careers as professional officers. His wife's family, however, claimed a more distinguished and ancient military history.

The Youngs, of the Clan Lamont from the Firth Cumbrae Islands, arrived in America earlier than the McCains, having first fled to Ireland during England's "Great Rebellion." In 1646, Mary Young Lamont and her four sons crossed the Irish Sea in open boats after her husband and chief of the clan, Sir James Lamont, and his clansmen were defeated in battle by the forces of Archibald Campbell, the eighth Duke of Argyle.

The long-feuding clans had fought on different sides in the civil war, the Campbells for Cromwell, and the Lamonts loyal to Charles I. After surrendering to the Campbells, two hundred Lamont men, women, and children had their throats cut by the villainous duke, and Sir James and his brothers spent five years in a dungeon.

Fearing further reprisals, Sir James's wife and sons wisely fled their hostile native land, adopted Mary's maiden name, Young, and settled quietly in County Antrim, Ireland. Two generations later, the family immigrated in the person of Hugh Young to Augusta County, Virginia.

In 1764, Hugh's sons, John, a captain in the Augusta County militia, and Thomas, fought a brief skirmish with Indians in the Battle of Back Creek. Thomas was killed and scalped. Like his descendants, Captain Young was not one to suffer such an insult quietly. He tracked the killers for three days, fought them again, killed a number of them, and recovered his brother's scalp, burying it with Thomas's body.

It was John Young who, as a militia captain during the Revolutionary War, caught the attention of George Washington, joined the infantry, and was welcomed to the general's staff. Valorous and exceedingly diligent about safeguarding his family's honor, John Young set an example emulated by generations of Youngs and McCains who eagerly reinforced the family reputation for quick tempers, adventurous spirits, and love for the country's uniform.

John Young's three elder sons all died in childhood. His fourth son, David Young, held the rank of captain in the United States Army and fought in the War of 1812. David's son, Samuel Hart Young, moved the family to Mississippi, where Samuel's eldest son, Dr. John William Young, fought for the Confederacy.

The fifth of Samuel Young's eight children, Elizabeth Ann, united the McCain and Young families by her marriage to my great-grandfather, and their union gave life to two renowned fighters, my great-uncle Wild Bill and my grandfather Sid McCain.

Wild Bill joined the McCain name to an even more distinguished warrior family. His wife, Mary Louise Earle, was descended from royalty. She claimed as ancestors Scottish kings back to Robert the Bruce. But her family took their greatest pride in their direct descent from Emperor Charlemagne.

Although it was his brother's children who extended the Charlemagne line, I suspect my grandfather felt justified in borrowing the distinction for the rest of the family. He took considerable pride in the McCains' association with the distinguished conqueror, thinking it only fitting that his descendants share in the reflected glory.

As a boy and young man, I may have pretended not to be affected by the family history, but my studied indifference was a transparent mask to those who knew me well. As it was for my forebears, my family's history was my pride. When I heard my father or one of my uncles refer to an honored ancestor or a notable event from our family's past, my boy's imagination would conjure up some future day of glory when I would add my own paragraph to the family's legend. My father was a member of the Society of the Cincinnati, an association of direct descendants of General Washington's officers. His evident pride in claiming such distinguished ancestry gave me the sense not only that I had a claim on my country's history, but that it would fall to me to represent the family when the history of my generation was recorded. As a teenager, I would occasionally show my closest friends the picture of the surrender ceremony aboard the USS *Missouri* and point with pride to the McCain who stood among the conquerors.

At a point early in my own naval career, I was stationed as a flight instructor at McCain Field, an air station in Meridian, Mississippi, named for my grandfather. One day, as I made my approach to land, I was waved off. Radioing the tower, I demanded, "Let me land, or I'll take my field and go home," earning a rebuke from the commanding officer for disrespectfully invoking the family history.

It is a formidable history, not easily escaped even today by descendants who might wish to pursue some interest outside the family business.

My grandfather was born and raised on his father's plantation in Carroll County, Mississippi. The property had been in our family since 1848, when William Alexander McCain moved there from the family estate in North Carolina. My great-grandmother had named the place Waverly, after Walter Scott's Waverly novels, but it was always called Teoc, after a Choctaw Indian name for the surrounding area that meant "Tall Pines."

I spent some time there as a boy and loved the place. The house, which had once belonged to a former slave, became the family's home after their first manor burned down, and was a more modest structure than the white-columned antebellum mansions of popular imagination. But I spent many happy summer days in outdoor recreation on the property in the congenial company of my grandfather's younger brother, Joe, who ran the plantation. The house still stands, I have been told, uninhabited and dilapidated, with no McCain in residence since my Uncle Joe died in 1952.

I have been told that the McCains of Teoc were clannish, devoted to one another and to their traditions. They never lamented the South's fall, although they had been loyal to its flag, nor did they discuss the war much, even among themselves. Neither did they curse the decline in the family's fortunes, the lot they shared with many plantation families in the defeated South. By all accounts, they were lively, proud, and happy in their world on the Mississippi Delta. Yet my uncle and grandfather left the comfort of the only world they knew, never to be rooted to one location again.

I am second cousin to the gifted writer Elizabeth Spencer. She is the daughter of my grandfather's sister and was raised in Carrollton, Mississippi, near the family estate. In her graceful memoir, *Landscapes of the Heart,* she wrote affectionately of her two uncles and the first stirring of their lifelong romance with military adventures.

> What could they do around farms and small towns in an impoverished area, not yet healed from a civil war? The law? The church? Nothing there seemed to challenge them.
>
> I wonder if their dreams were fed by their reading. They favored bold adventure stories and poems—Kipling, Scott, Stevenson, Henty, Macaulay, Browning. Stuck away in trunks in the attic in Carrollton, school notebooks I came across when exploring were full not only of class notes but also of original verses that spoke of heroism and daring deeds. Their Latin texts with Caesar's *Gallic Wars* were in our bookshelves. They were cavalier. . . .
>
> I thought of my uncles years later, when I read in Henry James' *The Bostonians* how Basil Ransom of Mississippi had gone to Boston in the post–Civil War years because he was bored sitting around a plantation.

After two years at "Ole Miss," my grandfather decided to follow his older brother to West Point. At his brother's urging, my grandfather prepared for the exacting entrance exams by taking for practice the Naval Academy exams that were given some weeks earlier at the post office in the state capital. His scores were high enough to earn him an appointment to Annapolis, which, with little reflection, he accepted.

He was a popular midshipman but a less than serious student, graduating in the bottom quarter of his class. That rank, however, exceeded the grasp of his son and grandson, who graduated well beneath it and were lucky to receive their commissions at all.

In his third year at Annapolis, he failed his annual physical. In a report to the Academy Superintendent, the examining medical officer rejected him for further service "on account of defective hearing." The superintendent responded by noting the "great need of officers at the present time, and the fact that this Midshipman has nearly completed his course at the Naval Academy at great expense to the Government," and recommended to the Surgeon General that "this physical disability be waived until the physical examination, prior to graduation, next year." The Surgeon General approved the waiver.

Whether or not his hearing recovered by the time he graduated is unknown. I can find no record of his last physical examination at the Academy. I can only assume that if the hearing defect persisted the following year, the examining physician overlooked it. In his quarterly fitness report of June 30, 1906, all that is noted on the single line describing the midshipman's health is "very good."

My grandfather's undistinguished record at the Academy did not affect his subsequent career in the Navy. In those days, an Academy graduate was not immediately commissioned an ensign, but was required to serve for two years as a "passed midshipman." Following graduation, he saw action on the Asiatic Station in the Philippines, serving first on the battleship *Ohio* and then on the cruiser *Baltimore*.

He caught the approving eye of his first commanding officer, Captain L. G. Logan, skipper of the *Ohio*, who filed laudatory quarterly fitness reports, remarking that "Midshipman McCain is a promising officer, and I commend him for favorable consideration of the Academic Board." Six months later, a more skeptical CO, Commander J. M. Helms, skipper of the *Baltimore*, reserved judgment about the young officer, noting, "I have not been acquainted with this officer long enough to know much about him."

By his next fitness report, my grandfather had apparently run afoul of his new skipper, who had by that time become acquainted enough with him to fault him as "not up to the average standard of midshipmen" and to advise that he "not be ordered to any ship as a regular watch officer until qualified."

While giving him mostly good marks for handling the various duties of a junior officer, Commander Helms apparently found my grandfather's discipline wanting. He noted that he had suspended him "from duty for three days for neglect of duty." While standing as the officer of the watch, he had allowed officers who had attended a party in the navy yard to return to ship and continue to "get drunk." The next quarter, Commander Helms again reported that my grandfather was "not up to the average standard of midshipmen."

Shortly thereafter, my grandfather was spared further reproaches from the disapproving Commander Helms. He was ordered to serve on the destroyer *Chauncey*, where he was highly regarded by his new commanding officer. Six months later, he reported for duty as executive officer to the great Chester Nimitz, then a young ensign, on a gunboat captured from the Spanish, the USS *Panay*, and had, by all accounts, the time of his life sailing around the southern islands of the Philippine archipelago.

Their mission allowed them to sail virtually wherever they pleased, call on whatever ports they chose, showing the flag, in essence, to the Filipinos at a time when the United States feared a Japanese challenge for control of the Philippines. The *Panay* was less than a hundred feet long and had a crew of thirty, handpicked by Nimitz. They cruised an immense expanse of the archipelago, putting in for fresh water and supplies at various ports, arbitrating minor disputes among the locals, and generally enjoying the exotic adventure that had come their way so early in life. Both Nimitz and my grandfather remembered the experience fondly for the rest of their lives. Nimitz once said of it, "Those were great days. We had no radio, no mail, no fresh food. We did a lot of hunting. One of the seamen said one day he 'couldn't look a duck in the beak again.' "

His tour in Asia ended in late 1908, when, after being commissioned an ensign, he sailed for home on the battleship USS *Connecticut*, the flagship of Teddy Roosevelt's Great White Fleet, then en route home from its famous world cruise.

In the First World War my grandfather served as an engineering officer on the armored cruiser *San Diego*, escorting wartime convoys across the Atlantic through schools of German U-boats and learning how to keep his composure in moments of great peril and stress.

In 1935, Captain McCain enrolled in flight training, complying with a new Navy regulation that required carrier skippers to learn to fly. Unlike many of his contemporaries, whose flight training was more verbal than practical, my grandfather genuinely believed that flight instruction would be indispensable to him if he was to command a carrier competently. Recognizing its potential importance, he had begun to study naval aviation as early as 1926. "I was stubborn about it," he said. But that did not mean he felt it necessary to become a skilled pilot. Cecil King remarked that in Panama, "the base prayed for his safe return each time he flew."

He would never enjoy the reputation of an accomplished pilot. According to the superintendent of training at the naval flight school in Pensacola, Florida (where I would learn to fly twenty-three years later), in the last two weeks of his training, my grandfather "cracked up five airplanes." Reportedly, before he soloed for the first time, he told his instructor, "Son, the Bureau of Navigation sent me down here to learn to fly. Now, you do it." Nevertheless, he did solo, and he completed a full course at the naval flight school. He was fifty-two years old when he earned his wings, among the oldest men ever to become Navy pilots.

If he never felt obliged to learn how to fly well, he did love the sensation of flying. He had interrupted his training to spend time on the carrier *Ranger*, to observe how the ships he longed to command worked. He told the skipper that he wanted to spend all his time flying in the backseat of the carrier's planes. The pilot designated to fly him on these excursions recounted the experience many years later, admitting the *Ranger*'s skipper had mischievously told him to give the old man "the works."

At fifteen thousand feet, the pilot began a simulated dive-bombing run on the *Ranger*. He threw the plane into a vertical dive, straight down and at full throttle, toward the pitching carrier. By the time the pilot pulled out of the dive they had approached the carrier so closely and at such a high speed that they "blew the hats off the people on the *Ranger* bridge."

As they began their ascent, the pilot turned around to see how his passenger was doing. Instead of finding a frightened old man in his backseat, the pilot was pleased to see my grandfather with "a grin up around both ears and shaking his hands like a boxer." Taking this as an indication that my grandfather wouldn't object to a repeat performance, the pilot dove on the carrier again. This time, however, my grandfather's ears failed to pop during their steep descent, and when the pilot turned to check on him after pulling out of the second dive he saw that my grandfather was suffering considerable pain from the pressure in his head. The pilot signaled that he wanted to come in, and landed the plane safely on the carrier deck. The ship's doctor rushed to attend my grandfather and in short order managed to equalize the pressure in my grandfather's ears.

The pilot didn't know what kind of reception he would get from my grandfather after the doctor had finished treating him. He worried that the pleasure my grandfather had expressed in the thrill of their first dive might have been replaced by annoyance at having been put through the rigors of a second dive without giving his express consent. The concern was unnecessary. My grandfather simply thanked him "for a very swell ride."

"I liked the old boy from then on. So did most of the rest of the gang. They weren't worried about him. He could take it."

CHAPTER 3

Gallant Command

For five months, early in the Second World War, my grandfather commanded all land-based aircraft operations in the South Pacific, and he was serving in that capacity during the first two months, August through September 1942, of the battle for Guadalcanal in the Solomon Islands.

Lasting from August 1942 to February 1943, the Guadalcanal campaign, in the words of historian Samuel Eliot Morison, was "the most bitterly contested in American history since the Campaign for Northern Virginia in the Civil War," comprising "seven major naval engagements, at least ten pitched battles, and innumerable forays, bombardments and skirmishes."

On August 7, in the first amphibious operation conducted by American forces since the Spanish-American War, the 1st Marine Division landed on Guadalcanal to prevent the Japanese from using a nearly completed airfield for their land-based bombers. Simultaneously, three thousand Marines landed on nearby Tulagi Island to seize its harbor and the Japanese seaplane base there. Despite being harried by Japanese bombers, the landings were astonishingly successful.

The Marines, encountering ineffective opposition on the ground, had secured all beachheads on the two islands as well as the air base on Guadalcanal by the evening of August 8. They renamed the captured base Henderson Field.

Whatever relief American commanders may have felt over the initial success of the operation was soon forgotten in the disaster that occurred forty hours after the first Marines had waded ashore. Shortly after midnight on August 9, a task group from the Japanese Eighth Fleet surprised the divided Allied naval force protecting the landings. The ensuing Battle of Savo Island, named for a small volcanic island several miles off Guadalcanal, ended in what Morison accurately termed "the worst defeat ever inflicted on the United States Navy in a fair fight." By the time the Japanese admiral in command of the enemy force called off the attack for fear of being counterattacked by American carrier planes, his ships had sunk four heavy cruisers and one destroyer, killing 1,270 men.

Fortunately, the Japanese, having gained by their victory command of the sea, failed to land adequate reinforcements on the islands. Thus the Allied defeat was not a decisive event in the battle for the Solomon Islands. It was, however, a bloody defeat, giving a name to the water between Savo and Guadalcanal islands—Ironbottom Sound. Worse, the surviving Allied ships that had been forced from the area had not completed off-loading the landing force's food and arms. Sixteen thousand Marines were left stranded with only half their weapons and supplies on the densely forested, mountainous island. They were forced to live on reduced rations and whatever rice they could scrounge. Consideration was given to withdrawing them, but the value of the easily taken Henderson Field, with sufficient space and level ground for large bombers and poorly defended by a small Japanese garrison, motivated Allied commanders to continue the campaign.

On August 15, my grandfather ordered the first Marine Corps planes to land at Henderson. Supplies and reinforcements arrived the same day by sea. On August 18, the Japanese landed a small, inadequate force of a thousand men. The Marines destroyed them two days later. More Japanese reinforcements were under way, arriving almost nightly. By mid-September, six thousand Japanese were ashore, still not a sufficient number to dislodge the Marines, but battles raged daily throughout most of the month. In the Battle of Bloody Ridge a thousand Japanese were killed at a cost of forty Marines. Nevertheless, the Japanese managed to continue reinforcing their garrison, and the most serious land battles for Guadalcanal would not begin until October, after my grandfather had been ordered to Washington by President Roosevelt to serve as Chief of the Bureau of Naval Aeronautics and Deputy Chief of Naval Operations.

In the early weeks of the campaign, Japanese planes and ships made up for lack of progress on the ground by pounding Guadalcanal daily with shells and bombs. My grandfather rushed planes, fuel, and ammunition to the island and organized air strikes against the enemy. Gasoline was in terribly short supply on the island, and extraordinary heroics were performed by the skippers and crews of seaplane tenders, their ships overloaded with drums of fuel, who sailed through exceedingly dangerous waters and under skies thick with enemy planes to carry gasoline to Guadalcanal. He spoke often and gratefully of the courage of the crews that brought gasoline to his dry planes at Henderson.

He also became emotional, often crying, when he recalled the faces and spirit of the Marines and pilots defending the airfield in those exhausting, dangerous early weeks of the campaign. He spoke of his young pilots who "took a beating unequaled in the annals of war. Without relief, they fought day after day, night after night, for weeks."

In September he twice flew to Guadalcanal in a B-17, leading large contingents of fighter planes to Henderson, "slipping them in at dusk when the Japs couldn't see us." He stayed ashore, under fierce bombing from Japanese aircraft.

He later told one of his air commanders that the pilots he met there had resigned themselves to die for their country and had shaken his hand with the attitude of men "taking a last farewell." For the rest of the war, the loss of a single pilot would distress him terribly. I suspect every casualty report he read must have summoned up the faces of those fatalistic pilots on Guadalcanal who were ready to die at his command.

There was one story from his experiences on Guadalcanal that he always delighted to tell. One night after he had gone to sleep, a wave of Zeros attacked, and a Marine lieutenant escorted him to a trench, where he took cover with a crowd of tired Marines. One sergeant, particularly weary of this nightly ritual, expressed his displeasure by shouting a string of profanities over the noise of the attacking planes. The lieutenant yelled at him, "Pipe down! We've got an admiral in here." The offending Marine paused for a moment and then loudly sighed, "I'll be good and almighty damned," causing the admiral in question to laugh heartily, grateful to be so amused at a moment of peril.

My grandfather was awarded the Distinguished Service Medal for his leadership during the early days of the Solomon Islands campaign. The citation commended his "courageous initiative," "judicious foresight," and "inspiring devotion to duty."

As Chief of the Bureau of Naval Aeronautics, he made one last visit to Guadalcanal in January 1943. Halsey, Nimitz, and my grandfather flew to Guadalcanal together to inspect the airfield and the condition of the men still fighting what remained of the enemy garrison.

Bull Halsey had assumed command of the South Pacific fleet in October. After a series of legendary sea battles during which Halsey had secured his reputation as a daring and determined commander, culminating in the Battle of Guadalcanal from November 12 to the 15th, Japanese hopes of retaking the island became futile. Over a period of six days beginning on October 20, significantly reinforced Japanese troops were defeated in fierce jungle fighting by the now battle-hardened Marine defenders. Their grim, bloody battles ensured Guadalcanal's vaunted place in American military lore. By the middle of November, Japan's defeats on land and sea had guaranteed that the island would remain in American hands. Yet they fought on for nearly three more months.

My grandfather, returning to the island in the last days of the campaign, was impressed by what he found, relieved to see fit, vigorous, well-supplied, and confident Marines mopping up the last of the enemy. The valiant 1st Marine Division had by this time been relieved by fresh reinforcements. And he went to sleep that night in a small hut near the airfield, happy and confident that the long, difficult struggle was nearly won.

Halsey's biographer, E. B. Potter, wrote: "There were few wiser or more competent officers in the navy than Slew McCain, but whenever his name came up, somebody had a ridiculous story to tell about him—and many of the stories were true." Potter was right. Even today, I receive letters from men who served with my grandfather and want to share an anecdote about him. Among my favorites is the story of his last night on Guadalcanal.

After he, Halsey, and Nimitz had retired for the night, at about ten-thirty, Japanese bombers attacked. The admirals had just survived an attack the day before, while they were conferring at the naval base on Espíritu Santo. With the evening attack at Henderson, it was clear that Japanese intelligence had learned of the presence of three admirals in the field, and that they were the target of the attack. Halsey and my grandfather left their huts as the first bombs struck, each diving for cover into a different trench. As legend has it, my grandfather's trench was a latrine ditch—the latrine had been moved that morning, but the trench had not yet been filled in with dirt. My grandfather is said to have spent the rest of the raid there shivering in foul conditions and the mosquito-infested night air.

As the Chief of the Bureau of Naval Aeronautics, he coordinated the design, procurement, and maintenance of naval aircraft. Coming late to naval aviation made him suspect in the eyes of career aviators, who would have preferred one of their own in command. But his success at Guadalcanal convinced Roosevelt and Forrestal that he was the right man for the job. He would rather have stayed in the Pacific. Administrative work did not suit his restless nature. A subordinate remarked that he was "an excellent fighter, but a poor planner and administrator." Whenever he could, he avoided the interminable meetings of the various production boards he served on, Allied conferences, and other planning discussions, designating a subordinate to attend in his place. He was, it was said, a frequent figure at the Army-Navy Club, where he indulged his love of pinochle. But if deskwork and its attendant bureaucracies bored him, he was, nevertheless, a man who took pride in accomplishing the objective of his mission. He showed, if not great attention to detail, his usual abundant energy in pursuit of his chief objective, to procure the world's greatest naval air force.

His experiences at Guadalcanal had taught him what the Navy needed in the Pacific. Too few planes and too few men to fly them had forced the pilots under his command to fly constantly, and they had been reduced to a state of near lifelessness by the strain. When he arrived in Washington, he declared, "I want enough planes for the United States Navy and enough pilots to fly them." He wanted two crews for every plane in the Navy. And he charged ahead procuring aircraft and personnel at a lightning pace. One observer likened him to a "little fighter plane trying to get at the enemy, darting and sweeping through the rambling Navy building."

He ordered the production of Wildcats and Avengers accelerated, confident of the planes' value as indispensable new instruments of war. "[They] prevented the invasion of Australia. They stopped the enemy at Guadalcanal and destroyed his airplanes at a ratio of several to one. They helped to drive him off at Midway and thus prevented the invasion of the Hawaiian Islands." My grandfather knew how to fight the Japanese, and he outfitted the Navy for the task.

An approving Roosevelt appointed him to a newly created post,

Deputy Chief of Naval Operations for Air. He was the Navy's air boss, responsible for every aspect, human and material, of naval aviation (often catching hell from a quarrelsome Halsey for his personnel decisions). He served in that command until the pace of war in the Pacific accelerated as the war in Europe approached its end.

In August 1944, he returned to the Pacific to temporarily command Task Group 38.1, one of the fast carrier groups in the Third Fleet's powerful Task Force 38, in preparation for assuming command of the entire task force a few months later. This was the command my grandfather had aspired to above all others; the moment, I suspect, he had waited for all his life. An obituary writer for the *New York Herald Tribune* wrote of my grandfather's return to the Pacific, "In September, 1944, a minor newspaper item revealed that Admiral McCain was off to sea again. The assignment was undisclosed, but the Japanese, and then America, had not long to wait before they knew."

He was a born leader, fit for command not because of an imposing physical presence, but because he possessed an easy, natural authority with his men, whom he seemed to understand as if he had known them all their lives. Dick O'Malley, a veteran war correspondent, considered him one of the finest, most effective leaders in the Pacific Theater. With his reporter's practiced eye for character details, Dick was struck by the unaffected qualities that made my grandfather such a gifted commander. "Admiral John S. McCain was a very quiet-spoken man but when he gave an order in his soft, clear voice, there was never any doubt there was command in it. I always remember that Admiral McCain seemed to get his orders carried out more promptly than others and there was a puzzling feeling that those doing his bidding didn't feel pushed by authority so much as persuaded by reason. . . . I remember a day when we had a hell of a time with both kamikazes and land-based fighter planes. We were on the bridge after it was over and he smiled at a young lieutenant. 'Well done,' he said. 'I'm putting you in for a citation. It was a very busy day.' That was his style: relaxed, muted and soft-voiced, but when you heard it, it made your heart beat a little faster."

He had been in command of the task group for barely two months when the long-awaited campaign to liberate the Philippine Islands began, leading to the largest naval battle of World War II, the Battle of Leyte Gulf. A week before the campaign began, my grandfather would prove himself as brave and resolute a fighter as any of his illustrious forebears had been. And although circumstances kept him away from most of the action during the Battle of Leyte Gulf, before the guns were silent he would demonstrate again that like his old friend Halsey, he was a daring and resourceful commander, and perhaps the better tactician of the two.

In preparation for the assault, my grandfather's fast carriers launched strikes against Japanese airfields on Formosa on October 12. Their mission was to destroy the enemy's airpower available to defend against an attack on the Philippines. This they accomplished quite successfully, although they met with stiff resistance. Over the next two days, 520 Japanese planes were destroyed and considerable damage was inflicted on Japanese installations ashore.

The Japanese did manage a counterstrike, fiercely attacking the ships of Task Group 38.1. On October 13, an enemy torpedo plane penetrated the task group's defense screen of fighter planes and hit the cruiser *Canberra*. The torpedo hit flooded the *Canberra*'s engine rooms, rendering her dead in the water. Rather than sink the wounded cruiser, my grandfather ordered another cruiser, the *Wichita*, to take her in tow while two destroyers circled them. He then assembled a covering force composed of destroyers and cruisers from three task groups to protect the *Canberra* as she was towed to port.

The next day and night, Japanese planes attacked in large numbers. The cruiser *Houston* was torpedoed. Badly damaged, without power, and listing seven degrees to starboard, the cruiser was in dire straits. The *Houston*'s skipper believed she was breaking up, and many of her crew jumped overboard. My grandfather told him to abandon ship, and ordered several destroyers to help rescue her crew. He gave orders to sink the cruiser once her crew was safe, but when he received word that her skipper thought she could be salvaged he ordered the cruiser *Boston* to tow the crippled *Houston* to safety.

Admiral Mitscher commanded the task force at the time. He had ordered my grandfather to save the cruisers if he could. In Commander Thach's words, "Mitscher took the other task groups and got the hell out of there, leaving McCain with Task Group 38.1 alone to do the job."

Using most of the entire task group as a protective screen, my grandfather had his ships steam ahead of the "crippled division," which included the two damaged cruisers and their cruiser and destroyer escorts. They endured repeated fierce attack from enemy sorties, but ships' guns and fighters from two of the task group's light carriers managed to destroy most of the attackers. My grandfather wrote in his battle action report that until seven o'clock that evening "there were almost always bandits overhead." All the while, planes from his heavy carriers continued to strike their targets on Formosa.

On the 15th, enemy planes again attacked, and one managed to hit the *Houston* with another torpedo. My grandfather had risked much to salvage the cruisers. It had taken almost eight hours to get the two ships under tow, and once that was accomplished the task group had been able to make a top speed of only two or three knots as it ran a gauntlet of Japanese air attacks. Wave after wave of Japanese planes were determined to make my grandfather's decision to save the ships cost him dearly. Had they succeeded in finishing off either of the two cruisers, or worse, had they sunk any of his other ships, the decision to save the ships would have been regarded as a terribly costly mistake.

Battle action reports, with their dry, matter-of-fact recitation of successive events, portray little of the intense anxiety my grandfather must have felt during those five October days. An action of this complexity requires the commander to make hundreds of instant decisions, anticipating the extent and location of enemy assaults, positioning his ships accordingly, evaluating reports from anxious subordinates, and answering their urgent requests for instructions. Whatever strain he felt throughout this arduous battle was not apparent in my grandfather's report.

In one sentence he notes a second hit on the *Houston* and the damage it inflicted. In the sentence below he reports "little activity on 17 October, routine Combat Air and anti-submarine patrols being maintained." In the next sentence he signals the success of his venture and the relief he must have experienced by reporting simply, "At the end of the day, Task Group 38.1 turned to course 250, and headed back toward the Philippines on a high speed run at 25 knots."

The author of a book on the fast carrier battles in the Pacific disparaged my grandfather, dismissing him as nothing more than a deputy to Halsey who was never given tactical command of his task force. Furthermore, the author alleged that my grandfather had relied completely on John Thach for tactical innovations. My grandfather did give enormous responsibilities to his operations officer and had always taken care to credit Thach with many of the task force's innovations. When he hired Thach for the job, having never met him prior to that, Thach had asked him why he had selected him. "I've heard you're not a yes man," my grandfather answered, "and I don't want any yes man on my staff."

Thach, who admired my grandfather greatly, strongly disputed the author's harsh criticism and insisted that "he had command *all* the time."

He was a brave man, and he commanded with courage. Dick O'Malley, who observed him closely in the last, strenuous days of his command, said, "There wasn't anything that could put the wind up in him." In a letter Dick wrote to me, he recalled my grandfather's courage under fire. "One day a kamikaze came out of the sun heading either for us or the *Essex*, which was close behind. [McCain] just stood leaning on the rail, watching. 'They'll get him with those five-inchers,' he said calmly. They did."

A little over three months after my grandfather brought the crippled cruisers safely to port, Admiral Halsey decorated him with the Navy Cross. Had the enterprise turned out differently, my grandfather might have been relieved of his command.

––––––––

The Battle of Leyte Gulf began on October 23, 1944, when two U.S. submarines patrolling waters off Palawan Island in the southeastern tip of the Philippine archipelago encountered elements of an enormous Japanese battleship force under the command of Vice Admiral Takeo Kurita. Over the next three days, four separate battles would be fought pitting a Japanese carrier fleet and two battleship forces against elements of the U.S. Third and Seventh fleets. When the last battle ended, the Japanese Navy was finished as an effective fighting force for the remainder of the war, but not before the United States Navy had nearly suffered a defeat of catastrophic dimensions.

On October 20, under the overall command of General Douglas MacArthur, the Sixth Army, commanded by Lieutenant General Walter Krueger, had staged amphibious landings on the beaches of Leyte Island in the middle of the archipelago, escorted and protected by the Seventh Fleet, commanded by Vice Admiral Thomas Kinkaid. The operation was hugely successful. By the end of the day, seventy to eighty thousand troops were ashore.

Halsey's Third Fleet, under the overall command of Admiral Nimitz, was ordered to cover and support the Seventh Fleet. Nimitz had added a clause to Halsey's orders instructing his subordinate to seize an opportunity to destroy a major portion of the Japanese fleet if one arose in the course of the battle, giving Halsey, who had dreamed all his life of commanding an epic battle at sea, leave to fulfill his lifelong ambition. Nimitz's failure to place both U.S. fleets under one naval command inevitably led to poor communications between the two fleets. When Halsey perceived an opportunity to take offensive action against the enemy and seized it, the dual command structure nearly resulted in strategic disaster.

On October 22, Halsey ordered my grandfather's task group, the strongest carrier force in his fleet, to detach from the fleet and sail 660 miles to Ulithi Island to refuel. Even after the two American submarines discovered Kurita's force in the Palawan Passage and destroyed three of its heavy cruisers, Halsey still saw no reason to order my grandfather to return. It was a decision that both Halsey and my grandfather would soon regret.

The Japanese knew that the loss of the Philippines would destroy any hope that Japan could yet prevail against its vastly superior enemy. They devised a desperate gamble to destroy the invading American force, risking virtually all that remained of the Japanese Navy in the attempt. A Northern Force with four carriers serving as a decoy was ordered to entice the offensive-minded Halsey into giving chase, leaving the Seventh Fleet exposed in Leyte Gulf.

Meanwhile, two Japanese battleship forces, Kurita's powerful Center Force and a Southern Force, sailed for the central Philippines. The Southern Force would enter south of Leyte through the Surigao Strait. If Halsey fell for the decoy and left his station off the San Bernardino Strait, Kurita's Center Force would force the unprotected strait from the north, sail down the coast of Samar Island, converge with the Southern Force, and destroy the unsupported American invasion fleet.

On the 23rd, Third Fleet aircraft located the Center Force, and Halsey prepared to do battle. The next day, he recalled my grandfather, but it was too late for him to get within range of the enemy, and Halsey was deprived of 40 percent of his air strength as he fought what is known as the Battle of the Sibuyan Sea.

In Leyte Gulf, Admiral Kinkaid was readying his Seventh Fleet to do battle with the small Japanese Southern Force. Lacking the big carriers of the Third Fleet, the Seventh Fleet had only eighteen small, unarmored escort carriers to provide airpower with lightly armed planes and poorly trained pilots. Nevertheless, Kinkaid knew his fleet, 738 ships in all, was more than a match for the enemy force approaching from the south.

The Japanese Northern Force had gone undetected until seventy-six of its aircraft attacked one of Halsey's carrier groups late in the Battle of the Sibuyan Sea. Now aware that Japanese carriers were in the area, Halsey's blood was up; he believed that "an opportunity to destroy a major portion of the enemy fleet" was at hand. He broke off the attack on Kurita's force and ordered all of his carrier groups north to seek and annihilate Ozawa's carriers. The decoy had succeeded. Halsey left the Seventh Fleet unguarded, vulnerable to and unaware of the threat approaching from the north.

Halsey had not even bothered to inform Kinkaid that he had left the strait. Before he ordered his forces north, he had signaled Nimitz that he intended to form three groups of his fast battleships into a new, powerful surface task force, Task Force 34. Kinkaid had intercepted the signal and assumed that the "three groups" were carrier groups that would be left behind to guard the strait. In fact, Halsey's decision to attack the decoy force had preempted the formation of Task Force 34, and all the ships that would have constituted it were now steaming away from the strait.

As Kinkaid had expected, the Seventh Fleet's cruisers, destroyers, and battleships quickly and effectively destroyed the Japanese Southern Force. But a few minutes after the last shots were fired, at dawn on October 25, Kurita's ships began shelling one of the Seventh Fleet's three escort carrier groups operating just north of the entrance to Leyte Gulf. This group, known by its radio call sign, "Taffy Three," was seriously overmatched by the powerful enemy force now descending upon it. Nevertheless, the unit fought valiantly, losing one carrier, two destroyers, and one destroyer escort in the ensuing Battle of Samar Island.

As he raced toward the Northern Force, Halsey finally formed Task Force 34, and ordered the battleships to steam ahead of the carriers. Third Fleet aircraft began attacking the Japanese carriers at eight o'clock on the morning of the 25th, and continued until evening.

When the second strike of the day was under way, Halsey

received an urgent message from Kinkaid informing him that the Seventh Fleet's small carriers were under attack off Samar Island by a superior enemy force and pleading for assistance from Halsey's carriers. Halsey ignored the message and continued north. He received several successive messages from Kinkaid, the last warning that Kinkaid's battleships were running out of ammunition. At nine-thirty, Halsey signaled back, informing Kinkaid that my grandfather's task group was on the way.

At ten o'clock, Halsey received a message from Admiral Nimitz: WHERE IS, REPEAT, WHERE IS TASK FORCE THIRTY FOUR? THE WORLD WONDERS. The message infuriated Halsey, who interpreted the sentence "The world wonders" as an insulting rebuke. He threw his cap to the deck after reading it.

Clearly, Nimitz was alarmed about the Seventh Fleet's precarious situation and wanted Halsey's battleships to defend the battered escort carrier units off Samar Island and prevent the enemy from entering Leyte Gulf. The success of the invasion hung in the balance. But the message to Halsey had been a mistake. The last three words had been included as padding to confuse enemy decoders. The signal clerk who received the message before it was handed to Halsey should have deleted them. The irate Halsey considered his response for an hour before signaling Nimitz, I HAVE SENT MCCAIN.

My grandfather was already on the way before Halsey recalled him to the battle. He had intercepted Kinkaid's messages to Halsey and had made the decision to render whatever assistance he could to the outgunned escort carriers without waiting for orders from the fleet commander. He turned his task group around and raced downwind at a speed of thirty knots toward the battle.

At the time, he had two squadrons of dive-bombers in the air that had not returned from scouting patrols. Carriers have to turn into the wind before aircraft can land on them. In order not to slow down the entire task group while the returning scouts landed, he ordered his carriers to race ahead of the rest of the task group at a top speed of thirty-three knots. When six or more of their planes returned they approached upwind to begin their landing patterns. The carriers whipped around into the wind and took them aboard. Once the planes landed, the carriers turned sharply downwind again and resumed their thirty-three knots until the next planes returned, and the maneuver was repeated. Thus, the carriers were able to take on their planes without impeding the forward movement of the entire task group, which maintained an overall speed of thirty knots. It was a very difficult maneuver that had never been attempted before, nor since to the best of my knowledge. It required split-second timing on the part of the carrier skippers and the returning pilots, and steel nerves on the part of the commander who ordered its execution.

Halsey had also dispatched his battleships and one of his carrier groups to join the fight. But Halsey's response had come too late to inflict much additional damage on the main Japanese force.

My grandfather was now steaming toward the battle, but he was still nearly 350 miles to the east. He went to his cabin for a few minutes to consider the situation and decide what to do. A short time later, at ten-thirty, he emerged from his cabin, gave the order for his carriers to "turn into the wind," and launched his aircraft. He knew that at such a distance from their targets, they would burn all their fuel reaching the battle and would have to land on other carriers or in the Philippines if they didn't run out of fuel while striking the enemy force. It was a daring move, and one of the longest-range carrier strikes of the Pacific war.

By the time Task Force 34 and the accompanying carriers arrived off Samar Island, Kurita had broken off his attack and turned north, fearing that he faced a much larger fleet than the greatly outnumbered Taffy Three. At the time of his withdrawal, his ships were within forty miles of the invasion force. He initially intended to reassemble his disorganized force and resume the attack on Leyte Gulf. But the Japanese commander suddenly lost his nerve and made for the San Bernardino Strait. The commander of Taffy Three, Vice Admiral

Clifton Sprague, who had commanded his ships with courage and re-sourcefulness during the fierce attack, credited the battle's abrupt end to divine intervention.

John Thach credited Kurita's unexpected retreat to intelligence the Japanese commander had received that warned him of the ap-proaching strike from my grandfather's planes. Thach had read an interview Kurita had given after the war. The old admiral explained his decision to withdraw from the battle by recalling information he had received of a large air strike coming from an unknown loca-tion. Kurita's chief of staff gave the same explanation for the force's withdrawal.

According to Thach, until Kurita received the intelligence that precipitated his decision to run, he "thought the whole task force was up there, and he didn't know about McCain. As a matter of fact, nei-ther did Halsey and Mitscher know what McCain was doing at the time."

Kurita's forces escaped through the strait, despite being harried by my grandfather's planes. In several accounts of the Battle of Leyte Gulf, historians praised my grandfather for understanding the predicament confronting Kinkaid's carriers and the stakes at risk in the battle better than had the other commanders of Task Force 38. They also judged him a much better tactician than his old friend and commander, Halsey.

Halsey had glimpsed the prospect of a moment of glory and hur-ried recklessly toward it. He had not fought at the battles of Midway and the Coral Sea, and he was hell-bent to seize this opportunity to destroy the last of the enemy's once mighty carrier force. In fact, he managed to sink four carriers and one destroyer. But his disregard for the Seventh Fleet's situation had jeopardized the entire invasion and had allowed the main Japanese battleship force to escape.

My grandfather, grasping the size of the threat that Halsey had so badly underestimated, had risked his planes in a desperate attempt to fill the gap left by Halsey's run for glory.

A few days after the Battle of Leyte Gulf, my grandfather relieved Admiral Mitscher and assumed command of the entire Task Force 38. He directed its operations until the Philippine Islands were retaken, and then, after a four-month interval, until the war's end. In that command he directed assaults against Japanese strongholds in Indochina, Formosa, China, and the Japanese home islands. By the war's end, his ships were "steaming boldly within sight of the Japanese mainland."

At his death, he was a leading figure in naval aviation, credited with devising some of the most successful innovations in the use of attack carriers. "Give me enough fast carriers," he said, "and let me run them, and you can have your atom bomb."

Near the end of the Battle of Leyte Gulf, the Japanese introduced their last desperate offensive measure to prevent the inexorable Allied advance to the Japanese homeland—the kamikaze attack. Throughout the rest of the Philippines campaign, kamikaze assaults wreaked horrible damage on the Third and Seventh Fleets.

In December, my grandfather and John Thach devised an innovation to keep Japanese planes based on Luzon from attacking the invasion convoy or joining the terrifying suicide missions. He called it the "Big Blue Blanket." He had his planes form an umbrella that flew over Luzon's airfields twenty-four hours a day, destroying over two hundred Japanese planes in a few days. In a series of Japanese raids on ships participating in the invasion of Mindoro, not one plane had flown from Luzon. My grandfather's pilots had kept them all grounded.

He increased the striking power of his carriers by reducing the number of dive-bombers by half and doubling the number of fighters, fitting them with bombs so that they could serve, as circumstances warranted, as both fighter and bomber.

He also concentrated his antiaircraft fire by reducing his four task groups to three. He dispatched "picket" destroyers to patrol waters sixty miles from the flanks of his force to warn him of an approaching strike. He assigned his pickets their own patrol aircraft. When his planes returned from a strike they were ordered to circle designated pickets so that the patrol aircraft could identify them as friendly and pick out any kamikazes that had attempted to slip past the force's defenses in company with the returning planes.

In a strike on Saigon, his pilots attacked four Japanese convoys and destroyed or damaged sixty-nine enemy ships in a single day, a record that endures to this day. During a three-month period, in preparation for the invasion of the Japanese home islands, my grandfather's task force sank or damaged 101 cruisers, destroyers, and destroyer escorts and 298 merchant ships. During that same period they destroyed or damaged 2,962 enemy planes. Japanese ships were no longer safe even in the waters off the Japanese mainland. Throughout this last campaign, which ended when atomic bombs dropped on Hiroshima and Nagasaki, my grandfather lost only one destroyer.

He was awarded his second Distinguished Service Medal for his "gallant command" of fast carriers from October 1944 through January 1945. The citation praised his "indomitable courage" as he "led his units aggressively and with brilliant tactical control in extremely hazardous attacks." He received a third DSM, posthumously, for his service in the last three months of the war, when he "hurled the might of his aircraft against the remnants of the once vaunted Japanese Navy to destroy or cripple every remaining major hostile ship by July 28."

Under my grandfather's command, TF 38 was considered the most powerful naval task force ever assembled for combat. Following his death, Secretary Forrestal stated: "His conception of the aggressive use of fast carriers as the principle instrument for bringing about the quick reduction of Japanese defensive capabilities was one of the basic forces in the evolution of naval strategy in the Pacific War."

An officer who served with him said it more succinctly: "When there isn't anything to be done, he's the kind of fellow who does it."

The night after my grandfather died, Paul Shubert, a radio network commentator, talked about the controversial wartime decision allowing men of advanced years like Halsey and my grandfather to hold strenuous combat commands, while younger, fitter officers remained in subordinate roles. Shubert took no side in the dispute, but he spoke of my grandfather, of his age and "frail physique." Despite his condition, my grandfather "had his will," Shubert allowed. Whether younger officers could have accomplished what he had or not, "John Sidney McCain did what his country called on him to do—one of those intrepid seafarers who refused to accept the traditional devotion to the past . . . who learned to fly when he was past fifty, and went on to high rank in the Navy skies—one of the world's greatest carrier task force commanders, an outstanding example of American manhood at sea."

Eight years after my grandfather's death, I watched Admiral Halsey deliver the main address at the commissioning of the Navy's newest destroyer, the USS *John S. McCain*, in Bath, Maine. Halsey was an old man then. I remember he wore thick glasses and appeared very frail as he stood to make his remarks. As he began to talk about his friend of so many years, his eyes welled up with tears, and he began to sob. Barely a half minute had passed before he announced he was unable to talk anymore, and sat down.

Plainly, Halsey deeply mourned my grandfather's loss. But the audience sensed that the old admiral was overcome that day by more than sadness at his friend's passing. Many years had passed since my grandfather's death, and surely Halsey had gotten over his grief by then. I suspect that the commissioning had prompted a great tide of memories that overwhelmed the admiral. As old men do, Halsey could not think of a departed friend without evoking the memory of all they had gone through together. For Halsey, the memory of my grandfather's friendship conjured up all the grim trials and awful strain of combat, the losses they had endured, and the triumphs they had celebrated together as leading figures in a great war that had changed the world forever. The recollection had stunned the old man and left him mute.

I met Halsey that evening, at a reception after the ceremony. He asked me, "Do you drink, boy?"

I was seventeen years old, and had certainly experienced my share of teenage drinking by then. But my mother was standing next to me when the admiral made his inquiry, and I could do nothing but nervously stammer, "Well, no, I don't."

Halsey looked at me for a long moment before remarking, "Well, your grandfather drank bourbon and water." Then he told a waiter, "Bring the boy a bourbon and water."

I had a bourbon and water, and with his old commander watching, silently toasted the memory of my grandfather.

CHAPTER 4

An Exclusive Tradition

In 1936, while commanding the naval air station in Panama, my grandfather was introduced to me, his first grandson and namesake. My father was stationed in Panama at the same time, serving aboard a submarine as executive officer. He had brought his young, pregnant wife with him. I was born in the Canal Zone at the Coco Solo air base hospital shortly after my grandfather arrived there. My father was transferred to New London, Connecticut, less than three months later, so I have no memory of our time in Panama.

My mother has fond memories of the place despite the rough living conditions that junior officers and their families suffered in prewar Panama. Among those memories is an occasion when my parents left me in my grandfather's care while they attended a dinner party. My mother, mindful of my father's concerns about coddling infants, instructed my grandfather to put me to bed in my crib, and not to mind any protest I might make. When they returned they found me sleeping comfortably with my grandfather in his bed. Admonished by my mother for pampering me, he gamely insisted that the privilege was only fitting. "Dammit, Roberta, that boy has the stamp of nobility on his brow." Had he lived longer, he might have puzzled over my adolescent misbehavior, lamenting the decline of his once noble grandson.

My parents were married in 1933 at Caesar's Bar in Tijuana, Mexico. They had eloped. My mother's parents, Archibald and Myrtle Wright, objected to the match. For months prior to their elopement, my grandmother had forbidden my father to call on my mother, believing him to be associated with a class of men—sailors—whose lifestyles were often an affront to decent people and whose wandering ways denied their wives the comforts of home and family.

My mother, Roberta Wright McCain, and her identical twin, Rowena, were the daughters of a successful oil wildcatter who had moved the family from Oklahoma to Los Angeles. Wealthy and a loving father, Archie Wright retired at the age of forty to devote his life to the raising of his children. The Wrights were very attentive parents. They provided their children a happy and comfortable childhood, but they took care not to spoil them. And in their care, my mother grew to be an extroverted and irrepressible woman.

My parents met when my father, a young ensign, served on the battleship USS *Oklahoma*, which was homeported at the time in Long Beach, California. Ensign Stewart McAvee, the brother of one of my Aunt Rowena's boyfriends and an Academy classmate of my father's, also served on the *Oklahoma*. At his brother's urging, he had called on Rowena, and soon became a frequent visitor at the Wright home.

Eventually, Ensign McAvee developed a crush on my mother. He took her out on several occasions and often invited her to visit the *Oklahoma*. On one of those visits she met my father, who was dressed in his bathrobe when McAvee introduced them. My mother only remembers thinking how young my father looked, and small, with cheeks, she said, like two small apples. My father, however, was infatuated at once.

Until my parents' courtship, my mother had, in her words, "never teamed up with any man." She was, she confesses, immature and unsophisticated, possessing no serious aspirations, but cheerfully open to life's varied experiences. Her mother frequently complained to her, "If a Japanese gardener crossed the street and asked you to go to Chinatown, you would go." To which my mother always responded, "Why, sure I would." When she met my father, she was a beautiful nineteen-year-old student at the University of Southern California. But unlike her twin sister, she had never fallen in love nor shown more than a casual interest in dating.

As my mother describes it, she would typically go out in large groups where the boys always outnumbered the girls. When a young man asked her for a date, she would reply by inquiring what he had in mind. If he proposed to escort her to the Friday-night dance at the Biltmore Hotel, or the Saturday-afternoon tea dance at the Ambassador Hotel, or the Saturday-evening dance at the Roosevelt Hotel, she consented, believing any other assignation to be a poor use of her time. But even obliging dates were rewarded with nothing more than my mother's charming company and had to content themselves with membership in her wide circle of frustrated suitors.

A short time after being introduced to my mother, my father appeared on her doorstep and asked her to accompany him the following Saturday to the Roosevelt Hotel. She agreed, assuming he was acting on behalf of Ensign McAvee. But McAvee would not be among the young naval officers consorting with my mother's crowd that evening. Instead, my mother found herself having "more fun than I had ever had in my life" with the diminutive, youthful Jack McCain.

Their romance progressed for over a year, despite my grandmother's growing anxiety and the aggrieved McAvee's angry reproaches. When my grandmother finally ordered an end to the relationship and banished my father from the Wright home, my mother prevailed on former suitors to call on her and take her surreptitiously to meet my father.

Until confronted with maternal opposition, my mother "had never planned on marrying anyone." By her own admission, she was a willful, rebellious girl. Her attraction to my father was only strengthened by her mother's disapproval, and when my father proposed marriage she consented. They eloped on a weekend when my grandmother was in San Francisco. Just before they departed for Tijuana, my mother informed her softhearted father of her intention. Despite his misgivings, he did not stand in her way.

My father had asked one of his shipmates to explain to the executive officer on the *Oklahoma* that he had gone off to get married, but the friend had thought my father was joking. That Saturday, during the ship's inspection, the captain asked, "Where's McCain?" My father's friend responded, "He said he was going to get married or something." When my father returned to the *Oklahoma* that Sunday, having dropped his new bride at home, he was confined to the ship for ten days with a stern censure from the captain for failing to ask leave to get married.

The bond between my mother and her parents was a strong one, and my grandparents' alarm at losing their daughter to the itinerant life of a professional sailor was understandable. It took several years for them to grow accustomed to the idea. But, in due course, they accepted the marriage and shared with my father the deep affection that distinguished their family.

Captain John S. McCain, Sr., thought the match to be an excellent one from the start. He was as charmed and amused by his new daughter-in-law as she was by him. Six months after my parents married, my father was suspected by the ship's physician of having contracted tuberculosis, and was admitted to a Navy hospital because he had suddenly lost a great deal of weight. When the doctors there asked if my father could explain his dramatic weight loss, he attributed it to his recent marriage.

Sometime later, my grandfather was in Washington, where he went to Navy Records and asked to see his son's latest fitness report. There he read of my father's condition and his response to the doctor's inquiries: "My wife doesn't know how to cook, and my meals are very irregular." Much amused, my grandfather kept a copy of the report, and delighted in showing his friends how his "son couldn't wait to get married, and within six months the girl had nearly killed him."

Stationed in San Diego at the time of my parents' elopement, my grandfather had traveled to Tijuana with them to attend the ceremony and stand at his son's side. Theirs was also an exceptionally close relationship.

The relationship of a sailor and his children is, in large part, a metaphysical one. We see much less of our fathers than do other children. Our fathers are often at sea, in peace and war. Our mothers run our households, pay the bills, and manage most of our upbringing. For long stretches of time they are required to be both mother and father. They move us from base to base. They see to our religious, educational, and emotional needs. They arbitrate our quarrels, discipline us, and keep us safe. It is no surprise then that the personalities of children who have grown up in the Navy often resemble those of their mothers more than those of their fathers.

But our fathers, perhaps because of and not in spite of their long absences, can be a huge presence in our lives. You are taught to consider their absence not as a deprivation, but as an honor. By your father's calling, you are born into an exclusive, noble tradition. Its standards require your father to dutifully serve a cause greater than his self-interest, and everyone around you, your mother, other relatives, and the whole Navy world, drafts you to the cause as well. Your father's life is marked by brave and uncomplaining sacrifice. You are asked only to bear the inconveniences caused by his absence with a little of the same stoic acceptance. When your father is away, the tradition remains, and embellishes a paternal image that is powerfully attractive to a small boy, even long after the boy becomes a man.

This is the life to which my older sister, Sandy, my younger brother, Joe, and I were born. It was the life my father was born to as well. And it was the life that adopted my mother, substituting its care for that of a loving and protective family.

CHAPTER 5

Small Man with the Big Heart

My father was born in Council Bluffs, Iowa. In several profiles and obituaries, he is described as a native of that Midwestern town, but he was no more a native of Council Bluffs than I am a native of Panama. My grandmother had gone into labor when visiting family in Council Bluffs while my grandfather was at sea.

His boyhood withstood the strain of the frequent interruptions, upheavals, travel, and separation that the Navy imposed on the lives of its officers' families. He would never know any other life. From early childhood, he understood he would share his father's vocation.

People who grow up without such expectations might think that anticipating so young the general course of your life would make a child self-assured. That may be the case for some. But I think for most of us our strong sense of predestination made us prematurely fatalistic. And while that condition gave us a kind of confidence, it was often a reckless confidence. We started with small rebellions against the conventions of our heritage. And as we grew older and coarser, our transgressions became more serious.

We often exceeded the limits of our parents' patience and earned the displeasure of educators. There were times in my youth when I harbored a secret resentment that my life's course seemed so preordained. I often wondered if my father had ever felt the same way. Neither of us ever misbehaved by design, or purposely threw some insurmountable obstacle in the path of our expected naval careers. Our antics were much more spontaneous than that. But did he, like me, occasionally speculate that his troublemaking might disrupt his family's plans for him, and was he as surprised as I was to discover that the thought did not fill him with dread? I don't know. But I do know that when both of us reached the end of our naval careers, we could not imagine finding a greater measure of satisfaction than we had found in a life at sea in our country's service. Neither of us ever sinned so grievously that we altered our fate. The Navy did not banish us. And years later, we realized we had mistaken our reaction to the Navy's forbearance for disappointment. In memory, it appears as relief.

My father was a slight boy, even smaller than his father. He never grew taller than five feet six, and near the end of his life he weighed no more than when he left the Naval Academy, 133 pounds. His irregular childhood, the constant disruptions occasioned by his father's transfers, were a challenge to him, as, I suspect, was his small stature. It intensified an adolescent compulsion to prove his courage and daring to his peers in whatever new social circumstances he found himself in. The quickest way to do so was to exhibit a studied indifference to the established order, devise imaginative circumventions of the rules, take your punishment, show no remorse, and fight at the drop of a hat.

He was only sixteen years old when his father delivered him to the United States Naval Academy for his plebe summer in June 1927; by his own admission, he was too young for the challenges of such a rigid institution and the highly competitive nature of the place. He had been included on President Coolidge's list of appointees that year, passed his preliminary physical in March, and completed the entrance exams in April.

His nervous father was at sea at the time, serving as executive officer aboard the USS *New Mexico*. When the ship made port in Panama on April 26, a fellow officer on the *New Mexico* sent a letter to a friend who was associated with the Naval Academy in some capacity and asked if he could find out if my father had passed the exams. "Our exec . . . is very anxious to know if the boy made it." One month later, my grandfather's helpful friend received a brief telegram from an officer on the Academy Academic Board: JOHN S MCCAIN JUNIOR PASSED APRIL EXAMINATION STANDING SEVENTH ON PRESIDENTIAL LIST.

Shortly before my father entered the Academy, my grandfather, whose ship was being overhauled in the navy yard in Bremerton, Washington, invited him to spend two weeks aboard ship. They were two weeks my father treasured all his life. He referred to them as a "final and farewell gesture before I went into the Naval Academy" and began his own life at sea.

It is difficult to imagine my grandfather being too concerned with my father's performance at the Academy, considering his own less than commendable record there. He was, however, a watchful father.

In April 1928 he was detailed as an instructor to the Naval War College in Newport, Rhode Island, and upon arrival he cabled a request to the Academy Superintendent that all reports on Midshipman McCain be sent to him there. Those reports, sent at the end of every term, were not encouraging. Had the old man been more of a spit-and-polish type, he might have reconsidered the career choice he had made for his son. As it was, while he might have been uneasy about the difficulty his son had staying out of trouble at the Academy, he would have become really alarmed only if it appeared that my father's shortcomings might result in his dismissal.

My father was constantly in trouble at the Academy. His grades were poor, his discipline worse. By the end of his first term his grades hovered barely above the lowest acceptable marks, where they would remain for four years. His class standing in his first term was 557 out of 601 midshipmen. That was his high-water mark for his first two troubled years at Annapolis. The next term, he stood 537 out of 549. The following year, he had dropped to 498 out of 504.

Unimpressive as they were, his grades seldom slipped below the minimum satisfactory level. The ever shrinking aggregate number of his classmates indicates the number of midshipmen whose performance was considered so deficient that they were expelled.

My father approached catastrophe on three occasions, in his first, third, and fourth years. On all three occasions he was warned that "the Superintendent notes with concern that you are unsatisfactory in your Academic work . . . and he wishes to take this opportunity to point out that unless you devote your entire effort to improve your scholastic work you are in grave danger of being found deficient at the end of the year." "Copy to Parent" was written on the bottom left-hand corner of each notice.

The only consistently good marks my father received were for Seamanship and Flight Tactics, and Ordnance and Gunnery. These courses were taught only in the last three terms, and my father earned the equivalent of a B in both courses every term. In the first term of a midshipman's last year, his personal hygiene is graded. Here again my father, whom my mother once called "the cleanest man I've ever known," received an above-average mark. These were the only bright spots in an otherwise dismal academic performance.

My father was an intelligent man, and quite well read as a boy. His low grades as a student cannot be credited to a poor intellect. Rather, I assume they were attributable to his poor discipline, a failing that was almost certainly a result of his immaturity and the insecurity he must have felt as an undersized youth in a rough-and-tumble world that had humbled many older, bigger men.

"I went in there at the age of sixteen," he once told an interviewer, "and I weighed one hundred and five pounds. I could barely carry a Springfield rifle."

Even as an upperclassman, my father struggled to meet the robust physical standards imposed on midshipmen, who were expected to take athletics as seriously as their scholastic endeavors. In my father's third year, the superintendent informed him that he was "deficient in physical training for the term thus far completed." Consequently, my father's Christmas leave was canceled that year, and he was "required to remain at the Naval Academy for extra instruction during that period."

My father's roommates, two of whom were linemen on the varsity football team, treated him like a little brother and went to great lengths to protect him. They helped him through the relentless hazing of his plebe year, took the blame when they could for his infractions of Academy regulations, and made it clear that they would deal with any midshipman who thought to abuse him. However, when they were plebes, despite their formidable size, they could not prevent upperclassmen from physically disciplining my father. My father hated the hazing he was subjected to—some of it quite severe, even by the standards of his day—and forever after questioned the custom's usefulness to the task of making officers.

Even after my father graduated, he inspired almost paternal affection in many of his peers. A shipmate who occupied the bunk below my father on the *Oklahoma*, a huge man who had also played varsity football at Annapolis, would routinely wake up in the middle of the night to replace the blanket my father had kicked off in his sleep.

As hard as they tried, my father's friends could not spare him the consequences of his own natural rebelliousness. His report cards for every term, save one, list a staggering number of demerits for bad conduct—114 in his first term, an astonishing 219 his second. Except for the first term of his last year, my father never accumulated fewer than a hundred demerits a term, and usually he was closer to two hundred.

I, too, was a notoriously undisciplined midshipman, and the demerits I received were almost enough to warrant my expulsion. But I never racked them up as prodigiously as my father had. And when I read the accounts of his "unmilitary conduct" today, and the scores of demerits it earned him, I am little short of astonished by the old man's reckless disregard for rules. His offenses were various: talking in ranks; using obscenity; absent without leave; fighting; disrespect shown to an upperclassman. They ran the entire gamut of what the Academy considered serious offenses, and the punishments he received were onerous.

Typically, he found some value in his troublemaking and in the punishment he earned for it. "You get to know people that you don't ordinarily know if you're one of the good boys. And sometimes the world's not always made up of all the good boys, either, not by a long shot," he said.

"I was known as a 'ratey' plebe, and that's the plebe who does not conform always to the specific rules and regulations of the upperclassmen," my father explained in his interview for the Naval Institute. "Some of these upperclassmen would come up and make some of these statements to you, and required you to do such things which only incited rebellion and mutiny in me. And although I did them, the attitude was there, and they didn't like that. But it was a fine institution."

In his last year, my father was removed from the watchful care of his concerned roommates. He was expelled from the dormitory, where his rebelliousness might have infected good order and discipline in the ranks, and exiled to quarters and a hammock for a bed aboard the *Reina Mercedes*, a ship seized from the Spanish during the Spanish-American War and kept moored at the Academy.

First classmen in my father's time were not allowed to exceed 150 demerits. During his final term, my father came perilously close to exceeding the number, and was informed by his battalion commander that his graduation from the Academy was anything but certain. "If we get one more demerit on you, McCain," he warned, "we're either going to turn you back into the next class, or you'll be dropped from the muster roll. I can't tell you which will happen. But you can rest assured one of the two will."

From that moment on, my father remembered, "I shined my shoes and everything else and did everything right. When it came time for me to graduate, I took my diploma, and I went. I think that was the closest call I had."

My father was reported to have suffered his punishments without complaint. He would have disgraced himself had he done otherwise. He was a principled young man. Strict obedience to institutional rules was not among his principles, but manfully accepting the consequences of his actions was.

Neither would my father have considered for a moment committing a violation of the Academy's honor code. Honor codes were something he had been raised from birth to respect, and I truly believe he would have preferred any misfortune to having his honor called into question for an offense he committed. He was a small man with a big heart, and the affection in which he was held by his peers was attributable in part to his unquestioning allegiance to the principles of honorable conduct. His profile in the Class of 1931 yearbook commended his character with the following inscription: "Sooner could Gibraltar be loosed from its base than could Mac be loosed from the principles which he has adopted to govern his actions."

The memory of his frequent clashes with its regulations and authorities never diminished my father's abiding reverence for the Academy's traditions and purpose, although he also never lost his realistic appreciation of a typical midshipman's many shortcomings. He once served for two years as an instructor at the Academy, and he boasted that "the lads learned soon enough never to try to hoodwink an old hoodwinker." And he looked back on his Academy days, as he looked back at most of his life, with a satisfaction that was remarkably free of nostalgia.

He remained until the end of his life one of the Academy's most steadfast defenders. In 1964, when my father had attained the rank of vice admiral, he got in a public dispute with one of the Navy's most prominent leaders, Hyman Rickover, the father of the nuclear submarine. In testimony before Congress reported in the Annapolis newspaper, Rickover had "blasted the Academy for everything from the quality of its teaching to the hazing of plebes and the relative competence of ROTC and Academy officers."

Rickover, an Academy graduate himself, had long complained to the Navy hierarchy that the Naval Academy was not turning out qualified officers for his nuclear submarines. This he attributed to the Academy's antiquated curriculum and traditions, which he derided as nothing more than quaint and anachronistic customs of an institution focused on the past. He believed it neither grasped nor concerned itself with the imperatives of leadership in the modern, nuclear Navy that he had, with peerless tenacity, set about creating.

My father understood that technological advances and the nature of Cold War rivalry necessitated innovations and profound changes in his beloved submarine service. Although he and Rickover were not friends and Rickover's cold, imperious personality made him difficult to like, my father admired Rickover's ability, intelligence, and vision, and he supported Rickover's efforts to revolutionize seapower.

Nevertheless, he strongly objected to Rickover's assault on the Naval Academy and to his call for systemic change in the way the Navy trained its future leaders. He felt that Rickover's remedies abandoned proven leadership principles. The primary mission of the Academy was to strengthen the character of its officers. Without good character, my father believed, all the advanced instruction in the world wouldn't make an officer fit for service.

As long as human nature remained what it was, the Academy's traditions were, by my father's lights, more effective at imparting the cardinal virtues of leaders than the methods devised by any other human institution. Rickover, he argued, was more interested in turning out technicians than officers whose worth would ultimately be measured by how well they inspired their subordinates to risk everything for their country.

My father called a press conference aboard his flagship the day after Rickover's testimony to rebuke his fellow admiral and reject the argument that naval officers were better trained in private institutions. "The Naval Academy is designed to make sure an officer is well founded in the sciences and liberal arts. But there's something else," he said. "In leadership there's no such thing as a master's degree. We've got to develop that type of officer who has the tools to develop his own leadership capabilities. I won't talk about Rickover except to say he may have overlooked this aspect."

This was not my father's first dispute with the irascible and solitary genius. Rickover had made admiral before my father, but not before being passed over for promotion on several occasions. Rickover was Jewish, and some felt that he was the victim of the anti-Semitism harbored by many among the Navy's leadership. Others believed that Rickover, who professed no concern for the affection of his brother officers, was repaid for his indifference with the active dislike of a good many admirals. Whatever the reason, the Navy Selection Board had for several years unfairly left him off its list of flag rank recommendations to the Secretary of the Navy, which, for all practical purposes, determined who would and would not wear an admiral's star.

Rickover did have a number of supporters in the Navy, my father among them, who may have been as put off by Rickover's personality as was the Selection Board, but who recognized his genius and devotion to the Navy. He also had considerable political support in both the legislative and executive branches of government.

After several flag lists failed to reward Rickover's indisputable accomplishments, the Secretary of the Navy passed word to the Selection Board that he would refuse to accept any flag list that didn't include Rickover's name. Thus admonished, the Selection Board finally recommended that Rickover be made a rear admiral.

Shortly after Rickover's promotion, my father, still a captain, called to congratulate his new superior. An embittered Rickover responded to my father's courtesy by declaring curtly that he had made admiral without "the help of any damn officer in uniform."

"That's a damn lie, Admiral," my offended father replied before hanging up on the surprised Rickover. My father could never tolerate officers whose resentment over personal disappointments made them contemptuous of the service. Rickover, he felt, had earned his promotion, had deserved his stars earlier than he received him. But that didn't mean he had accomplished the feat entirely on his own. My father believed that the Navy, for all its faults, took care of its own, sometimes acting later than it should have, but eventually according all their due.

Their relationship didn't improve much after that angry exchange, and their dispute over the Academy only exacerbated the tension between them. Yet, near the end of their lives, they had a reconciliation of sorts, although neither of them would have characterized it as such because neither was the type who would have accorded incidental professional rancor the status of a personal animosity.

After my father had retired, and very late in Rickover's unusually long career, both men became quite ill and were admitted to the Naval Medical Center in Bethesda, Maryland. They were given rooms on the same floor. Both were expected to remain hospitalized for some time, and as there were no other Navy legends in residence at the time, they began spending a good part of every day together.

Perhaps they saw in each other qualities they had overlooked earlier. Perhaps they talked about the only thing they had in common, the Navy, the only thing either of them ever talked about. They may have simply enjoyed reminiscing, as old sailors are apt to reminisce, about their experiences and the vicissitudes of long Navy careers. Or perhaps, as old men, they recognized that they had each devoted every particle of their being to their shared cause, and were, for their devotion, more alike than not.

They left the hospital as friends, and remained so for the little time that remained to them.

———

My father suffered a serious disappointment his last year at Annapolis. In the same year that my grandfather was earning his naval aviator wings, my father was judged "not physically qualified" for aviation school. I suspect this was a hard blow to my father. His lifelong ambition was to emulate the man he most admired, and being deprived of this opportunity to follow in the old man's footsteps must have shaken his resolve considerably.

After graduating, barely, standing eighteenth from the bottom, my father was assigned to the *Oklahoma*. Before he left, he requested permission to attend the naval optical school in Washington, D.C. Dejected after being denied pilot training, he temporarily wavered in his desire to immediately commence building a successful naval career, preferring to spend a pleasant year enjoying the attractions of the nation's capital (where he had attended high school).

The request was routed through the Academy Superintendent, who offered his opinion that "young officers just graduated from the Naval Academy should join the ships of the Fleet as soon as possible." Two weeks later my father received his answer from the Bureau of Navigation. He was ordered to consider himself released from his current occupation or any other duty that he may have received earlier orders for and report without further delay to the commanding officer of the USS *Oklahoma*.

As he would throughout his career, he made the most of his opportunity. His father's career guidance to him had been limited to impressing on his son the importance of command. "It doesn't make any difference where you go," his father often said, "you've got to command." With that in mind, my father entered the submarine service after his tour on the *Oklahoma*. His father approved of the decision and told him "to make a good job of it," which my father did in his relentless pursuit of a command.

CHAPTER 6

Mr. Seapower

I hesitate to write that my father was insecure, but he was thrust into difficult circumstances at such a young age that it would have been very hard to resist some self-doubt. He was an aspiring man whose ambition to meet the standard of his famous father might have collided with his appreciation for the implausibility of the accomplishment. Nevertheless, he would succeed, and become the Navy's first son of a four-star admiral to reach the same rank as his father.

The Navy consumed nearly his every thought. He had few aspirations for success outside its narrow confines. Whatever other interests engaged his mind were in some way associated with the Navy, including his preferences in literature, history, philosophy, and the study of military tactics and strategy. He attended every Army-Navy football game he could, not because he loved football, but because it involved the Navy. It could have been the Army-Navy tiddlywinks championship and he still would have wanted to attend it.

He did not fish or hunt or share his father's fondness for gambling or my enthusiasm for sports. He played tennis often, and kept to a daily regimen of rope-jumping and sit-ups, not because he particularly enjoyed exercise, but because he intended to keep himself fit for combat command. During one of his tours in Washington, D.C., a local paper observed that he was "a familiar sight to Washington commuters who frequently see him stride across the 14th Street Bridge, walking the four miles between his Capitol Hill home and the Pentagon."

He worked ceaselessly. Lacking the gregariousness and easy charm of his father, he was less comfortable in social situations, a failing that can be an obstacle to an officer's advancement. He wasn't withdrawn or unapproachable, and he didn't shrink from social obligations. He just didn't seem entirely at ease when his career required something more than strict, tireless dedication to the task at hand.

My mother was indispensable to my father. She had adapted to Navy life with few regrets, and acquired an abiding affection for the whole of the culture she had entered upon marriage, once remarking that she was "tailor-made" for the Navy. Her vivacious charm, beauty, and refinement assured her success in the social aspect of Navy life and more than compensated for my father's weaker possession of those graces. Her complete devotion to my father and his career contributed more to his success than anything else save his own determination.

The Navy in the years before the Second World War, the Navy my mother married into, was a small, insular world where everyone knew everyone else. "We were all in the same boat," my mother says of those days. "There wasn't any point for anyone to put up a false front." She means, of course, that few Navy families lived beyond their means. But they did live graciously, as graciously as circumstances allowed, assisting each other in a common effort to preserve the exacting social standards that were appropriate for an officer and his family in the small, prewar Navy.

Most families of naval officers lived on modest resources, a condition attributable to the meager salaries paid to officers in those days. Although my mother came from a wealthy family, our family lived, in accordance with my father's wish, on his income alone. Yet we never wanted for anything, and we believed we lived within a privileged society where refined manners made the relative poverty that most families shared inconspicuous.

In 1934, my father, a young ensign, was ordered to Hawaii to serve as a junior officer on a submarine. He brought his new bride with him, to what my mother called "paradise." Home to America's Pacific Fleet, Hawaii in the 1930s was the heart of Navy culture, where singular standards of social etiquette and personal and professional ethics were rarely breached.

Newly arrived officers, dressed in white uniforms, took their wives, who were attired in white gloves and hats, to call on the families of fellow officers every Wednesday and Saturday between four and six o'clock. The husband laid two calling cards on the receiving tray, one for the officer in residence and the other for the lady of the house. His wife offered a single card for her hostess, as it was inappropriate for an officer's wife to call on another officer. The visits never exceeded fifteen minutes. Within ten days, the officer and his wife who had been paid this homage returned the compliment by calling on the newly arrived couple at their home. The commanding officer was always called on first, followed by the executive officer. Their rank excused them from paying a return call.

When an officer had finished his tour he would complete another round of calls to bid good-bye, leaving his card with its upper left-hand corner turned down as a signal of his imminent departure.

Every Saturday night, my father and mother, dressed in formal attire, attended a party at the Pearl Harbor Submarine Club, after spending their afternoon at the Royal Hawaiian Hotel's four o'clock tea dance. The Beach Club at Waikiki, with its five-dollar monthly dues, was another venue for stylish socializing among the officers and their families. Though the exacting formality of this society seems pompous and excessive today, few who lived within its rules then thought it anything other than normal and appropriate. Even when they dined alone at home, my father dressed in black tie and my mother in a long evening gown.

One aspect of my parents' social life was unique to my father's branch of the service. The submarine service was a small component of the Navy and even more insular than the Navy at large. Small ships manned by small crews, submarines hosted a more intimate fraternity, less socially segregated by rank than those found aboard battleships and carriers. My parents were on familiar terms with the families of enlisted men on his submarine; officers and men attended parties at one another's homes and celebrated weddings and christenings together.

Submarine officers, like all naval officers, faithfully observed the professional distinctions governing their relationship to enlisted men, upon which the good order and discipline of the service depended. But living aboard ship in such small quarters bred an off-duty informality among officers and their enlisted shipmates. They were friends, and my father, like his father, valued those friendships highly.

More than the manners of polite society distinguished the life of a naval officer. His character was expected to be above reproach, his life a full testament to the enduring virtues of an officer and a gentleman. Those virtues were not necessarily as many as those required of clergy. An officer's honor could admit some vices, and many officers, my father and grandfather included, indulged more than a few. But honor would not permit even rare or small transgressions of the code of conduct that was expected to be as natural a part of an officer's life as was his physical description.

An officer must not lie, steal, or cheat—ever. He keeps his word, whatever the cost. He must not shirk his duties no matter how difficult or dangerous they are. His life is ransomed to his duty. An officer must trust his fellow officers, and expect their trust in return. He must not expect others to bear what he will not.

An officer accepts the consequences of his actions. He must not hide his mistakes, nor transfer blame to others that is rightfully his.

He admits his mistakes openly, and accepts whatever sanction is imposed upon him without complaint.

For the obedience he is owed by his subordinates, an officer accepts certain solemn obligations to them in return, and an officer's obligations to enlisted men are the most solemn of all. An officer must not confer his responsibilities on the men under his command. They are his alone. He does not put his men in jeopardy for any purpose that their country has not required they serve. He does not risk their lives and welfare for his sake, but only to answer the shared duty they are called to answer. He will not harm their reputations by his conduct or cause them to suffer shame or any penalty that only he deserves. My father once said, "Some officers get it backwards. They don't understand that we are responsible for our men, not the other way around. That's what forges trust and loyalty."

An officer accepts these and his many other responsibilities with gratitude. They are his honor. Any officer who stains his honor by violating these standards forfeits the respect of his fellow officers and no longer deserves to be included in their ranks. His presence among them is offensive and threatens the integrity of the service.

Even in the small Navy world that disappeared with the Second World War, some officers fell short of the demands of honor. If they did so grievously, or repeatedly, or without remorse and requital, they were, if not thrown out of the service, so completely ostracized, so bereft of respect, that they would usually leave of their own accord. If the Navy tolerated their conduct, it would shame everyone in the service.

My parents arrived in Hawaii in the aftermath of the infamous Massie scandal, which had deeply shaken prewar Hawaiian society and the entire Navy community there. A young lieutenant, Thomas Massie, who some time earlier had served on my father's submarine, had committed an unpardonable breach of the code. He was, reportedly, an intemperate and unlikable man, and his petulant and difficult wife, Thalia Massie, one of three daughters of a Kentucky bluegrass family of aristocratic pretensions, was even less likable.

One evening, Massie and his wife drove with a few other officers and their wives to a nightclub in a rough part of Honolulu. There the officer and his wife became very drunk. What happened next and why has never been determined with certainty. What is known is that at some point the wife had left the nightclub without her husband. Her husband located her at home later that evening, bruised and frightened and claiming to have been abducted and raped by as many as six native Hawaiian boys. She identified five boys who had been arrested that same evening for a traffic altercation as her assailants, and they were subsequently put on trial for the crime.

The evidence against the boys was far from conclusive. The jury was unable to reach a verdict, and a mistrial was pronounced. The accused were released on bail pending retrial. One month later, Lieutenant Massie persuaded two enlisted men from the submarine base to help him and his blue-blooded mother-in-law apprehend and murder one of the defendants. A short time later, Massie, his mother-in-law, and one of the enlisted men were stopped by police while racing through town in their car, curtains covering the windows, with the body of one of the boys wrapped in a tarp on the floor of the backseat.

The conduct of this officer shocked and outraged the rest of Hawaii's naval community, but not because the man had exacted mortal vengeance for his wife's rape. That showed poor judgment, perhaps, but given the nature of the alleged crime, the act was forgivable. What was unforgivable was that the officer had involved enlisted men in his crime, placing them in great jeopardy to help him avenge an offense that concerned only him and his wife. That was a grave breach of an officer's duty to his men.

There was a trial, and Massie, his mother-in-law, and the two enlisted men were convicted of manslaughter even though the famous defense attorney Clarence Darrow had defended them. They escaped justice, however. The Navy had intervened in the case to help in their defense, and, after their conviction, to help persuade the governor of Hawaii to commute their sentence from ten years to one hour. After the convicted vigilantes had served their hour in the governor's office, the Navy quickly sent them and Thalia Massie back to the States.

Many of his fellow officers felt shamed by Massie's conduct, and by the Navy's intervention in the matter. Initially, most officers believed the allegation of rape and their fellow officer's subsequent explanation of the killing as self-defense. They found it hard to believe an officer would lie. But most soon came to believe that he had indeed lied about the killing, and that he and his wife had probably lied about the rape as well. The discovery made the Navy's intervention on his behalf as unpardonable as the officer's use of enlisted men.

When my parents arrived, the scandal still dominated all conversation in every officer's home. The entire community seemed distressed over this singular violation of the standards they had always accepted as an unquestioned, ennobling way of life. And it was a long time before they recovered from the shock of it all.

My mother said that on the ship that returned him to the States, the disgraced Massie was observed to be frequently drunk and "making a natural fool of himself." She claims that some years later, he was incorrectly reported to have killed himself—an act that most of his fellow officers and their wives who had known of his crime and the damage it had done to the Navy's honor thought appropriate.

This was the Navy in which my father and grandfather felt so at home. They had entered its ranks already imbued with the notions of honor that distinguished a good officer. They were the standards passed down from one generation to another in their family. As boys, no less than as men, they did not lie, steal, or cheat, and they never shirked their duty. My brother once said that our father's word "had the constancy of Newtonian laws of physical motion." He added, "I have never met a more honest man than my father. I literally cannot think of a single time he did not tell the truth about something, as best he knew it."

My mother recalls playing gin rummy with my father once when she jokingly accused him of cheating. He reacted so strongly to the accusation, with such evident distress over the charge, admonishing her to "never say such a thing again," that she never did. Not even in jest.

The Navy revered my father's and grandfather's shared ideals and offered them adventure. It promised them the perfect life, and they were grateful to their last breath for the privilege.

Happy in his profession, my father worked every day, without exception. On Christmas morning, after we had opened our presents in front of the Christmas tree, he would excuse himself, change into his uniform, and leave for his office. I cannot recall a single instance when he came home from work earlier than eight o'clock in the evening.

As any other child would, I resented my father's absences, interpreting them as a sign that he loved his work more than his children. This was unfair of me, and I regret having felt that way. The most important relationship in my father's life had been his bond with my grandfather. That cherished bond influenced every major decision my father made throughout his life. Yet my grandfather had been absent from his family at least as often as my father was away from us, probably more often. He had done his duty as his country had asked him to, and his family understood, and admired him for it.

My father felt no shame in attending just as diligently to the responsibilities of his office, nor should he have. I am certain that he wanted to share with me the warm affection that he and his father had shared. But he wanted me to know also that a man's life should be big enough to encompass both duty to family and duty to country. That can be a hard lesson for a boy to learn. It was a hard lesson for me.

He worked hard to please his superiors and accepted every assignment as an opportunity to prove himself. Even when he viewed a new assignment as sidetracking him from his pursuit of important commands, he never betrayed the slightest hint of bitterness. "No matter what job you get," he told my mother, "you can make a good one out of it."

He once helped a friend get a prestigious position on an admiral's staff. My father thought him to be a born leader and expected great things from him in the Navy. But the man didn't like the long hours associated with the job. Nor did his wife, who openly resented the demands placed on young officers and their families.

Late one Sunday night, the admiral on whose staff my father's friend served called him to get the combination for a safe that contained classified documents he wanted to review. The young officer started to give him the combination over the phone, and the admiral cut him off abruptly. "Don't you dare give me that combination over the phone," he admonished his aide. Both my parents were shocked at their friend's careless regard for his professional responsibilities. My mother remarked, "Had it been Jack, he would have said, 'Sir, I'm on my way.' " It would never have occurred to my father to respond in any other way.

My father was devout, although the demands of his profession sometimes made regular churchgoing difficult. His mother, Katherine, was the daughter of an Episcopal minister, and she had ably seen to her son's religious instruction, no small feat in a home where the head of the household happily indulged a variety of vices.

My father didn't talk about God or the importance of religious devotion. He didn't proselytize. But he always kept with him a tattered, dog-eared prayerbook, from which he would pray aloud for an hour, on his knees, twice every day.

He drank too much, which did not become him. And I often felt that my father's religious devotion was intended in part to help him control his drinking. In the Navy in which my father came of age, men relaxed by drinking. The greater the burdens a man bore, the more he drank to relieve himself of them.

During the Second World War, when exhausted submarine crews finished a combat patrol in the Pacific, which typically lasted from six weeks to two months, they would come into port at Midway Island or Freemantle, Australia, for a month's "rest camp." These remote locations offered few natural or cultural distractions from the terrors of war. Midway's sole distinction was its claim to be home to a third of the world's population of gooney birds, large, awkward, and odd-looking fowl. Visiting sailors named the island Gooneyville. There is little else memorable about the place. To compensate for barren land-scapes and somber circumstances, the Navy would see to it that the men had someplace to drink when the pleasure of playing baseball and horseshoes wore thin. In Freemantle, the Navy rented houses for the men and stocked them with cases of beer and liquor. The men, most of them kids in their teens and twenties, lacking anything better to do, would drink themselves senseless until their next patrol.

During one typically intoxicated evening while on leave at Midway, the officers of a recently arrived submarine tore up the officers' club when the bartender refused to serve them. For a time, they kept their destruction within reasonable limits. Then they discovered a plaque dedicated to the club that had been commissioned by the officers of an-other submarine in the days before submariners were banished from the place. Seeing this, and deeply aggrieved that the submariners' courtesy had been repaid with such a gross discourtesy, they took the plaque and tore the cabinet that contained it from the wall.

A short time later, a young ensign from the shore patrol arrived to restore order. After repeated unsuccessful attempts to ascertain which officer was in charge of the marauders, the ensign left to call for help. As he was placing the call a group of the officers walked over to him. One of them announced, "I'm in charge. Jack McCain, skipper of the *Gunnel*."

In a report the young ensign filed with the base commander the following day, he described how my father and his officers continued to ransack the officers' club until they were eventually persuaded to leave by the duty officer, who had arrived on the scene carrying his side arm. They took the offending plaque and the cabinet that had housed it along with several other pieces of furniture and drove off in a jeep and a weapons carrier they had stolen earlier in the evening. My father drove the jeep back to the old, dilapidated "Gooneyville Hotel," where he and his officers were quartered. He was accompanied by his executive officer, Joe Vasey, who recalled that when they arrived at their destination, my father "abruptly decided to drive through the main entrance into the lobby, overestimating by only an inch or so the width of the entrance."

My father then retired to his room. When the rest of the *Gunnel*'s officers arrived in the stolen weapons carrier, Vasey instructed them to return the confiscated furniture to the officers' club, which they did, heaving the large cabinet into a hallway and leaving it there in pieces.

The next morning, the Navy commodore in command at Midway called my father to his office and chewed him out for some time. Afterward, my father ordered his men to return the confiscated plaque to the officers' club.

During another leave, this time in Freemantle, my father and some of the men under his command barely escaped death after one of them had drunk himself so thoroughly witless that he threw a box of bullets into the fireplace of the house where they were drinking. The rounds cooked off and fired into walls and furniture as my father and his friends dove for cover.

When spirits were in short supply, submariners often drank the alcohol that was used to fuel torpedoes. My father once served as engineering officer on a submarine. His first day on the job, he discovered that his predecessor had drunk nearly all the torpedo alcohol aboard. His submarine was scheduled to stand for inspection that day, and he had to borrow a quantity of the alcohol from other submarine commanders to cover up the embarrassing deficit.

There was one rule about drinking that most submariners, my father included, considered inviolate. A submariner never drank aboard ship. Submarine warfare is as treacherous and mentally exacting as any form of warfare can be. It requires the combatants to be in full possession of their faculties at all times while under way. Accordingly, no matter how excessive their binge drinking was when ashore, my father and his crew stayed sober at sea.

My father returned from war with a great appetite for drink, which he overindulged until the very last years of his life. He didn't drink at work, and was never completely incapacitated by his weakness. But he would often ease his way into social settings by drinking too much. And, as with most people, drinking changed his personality in unattractive ways. When he was drunk, I did not recognize him.

On occasions, friends cautioned him that his drinking was harming his career, but he never let it get so out of hand that it ruined his fitness for command. His aspirations were dear to him, and his determination to achieve them more formidable than the allure of any vice.

Like his father, my father swore a lot, and subordinates often referred to him as "Good Goddam McCain." Also like his father, he was a chain-smoker, although he preferred enormous cigars to my grandfather's roll-your-own cigarettes.

As an ensign, he had served on a submarine commanded by Captain Herman Saul, whom my father regarded as an exemplary officer, and whose leadership style he tried to emulate. Saul taught my father the difficult technique of keeping a submerged submarine perfectly level, a skill my father mastered. Saul also introduced his protégé to the pleasure of smoking stogies, and my father, like his mentor, was seldom without one. The cigars performed an additional function later in his life, often serving as pointer and exclamation point for his well-regarded lectures on the history and importance of seapower.

As a submarine skipper, my father often let junior officers bring the ship into port so they could gain the experience necessary to operate a submarine competently. On one occasion, while my mother, sister, brother, and I watched from the pier, a young officer struggled to navigate my father's submarine through the strong river current coming into port at Groton, Connecticut. My father was standing in the conning tower, a cigar in his mouth, talking to his executive officer. He was not paying sufficient attention to his ship's progress.

It was clear to all of us watching onshore that the young ensign piloting the sub was going to drive her directly into the pier. When, at the last moment, my father finally recognized the approaching catastrophe, he turned excitedly to give the order "All engines stop." Unfortunately, as he drew a breath to bark out the order he inhaled his cigar and choked. A moment later, the submarine crashed into the pier, knocking down a lamppost, which landed on our car. My father calmly ordered the ensign to back the ship out and bring it in again, which he did without incident.

With his ship safely in port, my father went home with us and began a long and difficult argument with his insurance company over the credibility of his insurance claim for a car destroyed by a submarine.

My father developed his seapower lecture in midcareer, when he served as the Navy's first Chief of Information, and later as the Navy's senior liaison officer to the United States Congress. Both posts helped to broaden his circle of acquaintances outside the Navy. He became a frequent witness before congressional committees, experiences that he used to improve his lecture and polish his delivery. He acquired some of the skills of an accomplished military historian who moonlighted as a stage actor. Appreciative audiences gave him the nickname "Mr. Seapower."

My parents kept a house on Capitol Hill, where they entertained leading political and military figures. My mother's charm proved as effective with politicians as it was with naval officers. The political relationships my parents forged during this period contributed significantly to my father's future success. Among their friends was Carl Vinson, chairman of the House Armed Forces Committee. At my father's invitation, he ate his breakfast, prepared by my mother, at my parents' home on many if not most mornings when Congress was in session.

My father was not, however, a political admiral—a term of derision accorded to successful officers whose records lacked combat experiences comparable to those of the war fighters who disapproved of them. Moreover, my father, who surely valued the patronage of civilian commanders as necessary to his single-minded pursuit of four stars, nevertheless harbored a little of the professional military man's dislike for the sail-trimming and obfuscation of politics.

He was, as his father had been, a man of strong views who spoke his mind bluntly. This is as risky a habit in Navy politics as it is in civilian politics, and it often caused him trouble. Both McCain Senior and Junior believed war to be a ruthless endeavor, the purpose of which was to annihilate your enemy. A wise combat commander keeps a wary respect for his enemy's abilities, but neither my father nor my grandfather let his prudence temper his contempt for his country's enemies.

My grandfather's frequent insulting references to the personal qualities of the Japanese enemy were in accord with the conventions of the time, although when I read them today I wince at their racist overtones. I don't believe they were intended as racist screeds. But war, which occasions much heroism and nobility, also has its corruptions. That's what makes it so terrible, a thing worth avoiding if possible.

My grandfather, as combatants often do, needed to work up a powerful hate for his enemy. He once recommended of the Japanese "killing them all—painfully." Hate is an understandable reaction to the losses and atrocities suffered at the hands of the enemy. But hate also sustains the fighter in his devotion to the complete destruction of his enemy and helps to overcome the virtuous human impulse to recoil in disgust from what must be done by your hand.

My father rose to high command when communism had replaced fascism as the dominant threat to American security. He hated it fiercely and dedicated himself to its annihilation. He believed that we were locked inescapably in a life-and-death struggle with the Soviets. One side or the other would ultimately win total victory, and seapower would prove critical to the outcome. He was outspoken on the subject.

When he attained commands that required diplomatic skills, his candor occasionally lacked the rhetorical courtesies that attended the first attempts at détente. This often caused anxiety in the State Department, prompting complaints in cable traffic about Admiral McCain's indiscretion. It concerned some of his civilian and military commanders in the Pentagon as well, but it won him both admirers and detractors, despite the prominent antiwar sentiment in 1960s America. I imagine it also fortified that sense of himself that, as a boy, he derived from flouting conventions. Addressing the Naval Academy Class of 1970, he commented on the popular antiwar slogan "Make love, not war" that naval officers "were men enough to do both."

Few successful naval officers crest the heights of command without making enemies as well as friends along the way. My grandfather and father had their detractors in the Navy, some of whom may have disliked their highly personalized style of leadership, others their grasping ambition. But they were well respected by most of their fellow officers as resourceful, resilient, and brave commanders.

It was, however, the regard in which they were held by the enlisted men who served under them that gave them the greatest satisfaction. They both had great empathy for the ranks and went out of their way to show it.

An aide to Admiral Elmo Zumwalt, commander of U.S. naval forces in Vietnam, once recounted many years later an incident that typified my father's concern for his sailors. My father, who was Zumwalt's boss at the time, was in Vietnam on one of his regular visits to the field. Zumwalt decided to host a dinner for my father and several other senior American officials and ordered his young aide to arrange it. During the dinner, a Navy steward who was serving my father tipped a platter of roast beef au jus, and the juice spilled onto my father's head and shirt. "I got up in great embarrassment," the aide remembered, "to try to help Admiral McCain." But the admiral politely refused the young man's assistance as well as his offer of a clean shirt. "If I use your shirt, you'll just frame it," my father joked, "and tell everybody that this is a four-star admiral's shirt that you've been wearing. I can wear my own."

The next morning, as my father was preparing to leave the country, he called Admiral Zumwalt to instruct him not to punish the steward. "That was an accident last night and absolutely no fault of his. I know you won't let anything happen, but I just wanted to affirm my intent in the matter." The aide, who monitored Zumwalt's calls, never forgot the concern my father showed that morning for the welfare of a worried Navy steward. "It takes a very large man," he observed, "to remember something that small at six-thirty the next morning and to make sure that people didn't overreact. I was impressed."

To some of his most senior subordinates, my father could be a difficult and demanding boss. He kept his own counsel and would sometimes leave his subordinates in the dark about matters that directly concerned them. A few of them felt, perhaps with cause, that he did not treat them fairly. But his closest aides, men who worked with him and for him more than once during his career, loved him. And he was almost universally revered by those whose rank was the farthest beneath his own. They knew he held them in high esteem, and they returned the compliment.

To this day, several times a year I receive letters from men who once served in the ranks under my father's or grandfather's command. Some are from aides, who closely observed them for long periods of time under conditions of great stress. Others are from men who write to tell me of an occasion when my father or grandfather had boarded a ship commanded by a subordinate, and had ignored the welcoming party of ship's officers to walk immediately over to them and inquire after their welfare and that of their shipmates. I value these testimonials as much as my father and grandfather did. They are from men who at one time risked death at the order of the John McCain they wrote to praise.

CHAPTER 7

The *Gunnel*

The day the Japanese sank the fleet in Pearl Harbor is one of my earliest memories. I was five years old. We were living in New London at the time. It was a Sunday morning, and my entire family was—for reasons I cannot recall—standing in the front yard of our small house. A black car passing our house slowed down and the driver, a naval officer, rolled down his window and shouted, "Jack, the Japs have bombed Pearl Harbor." My father left for the base immediately. I saw very little of him for the next four years.

He commanded three submarines during the war. The first command he held just briefly before being ordered on his first combat patrol. The second, the USS *Gunnel,* served as a reconnaissance and beacon ship for Operation Torch, the American invasion of North Africa. The *Gunnel* was ordered to leave New London at midnight on October 18 and proceed to waters off Fedala, French Morocco, about fifteen miles north of Casablanca, arriving there five days in advance of the invasion. Under strict orders to remain undetected at all costs, the *Gunnel* was to make landfall submerged, a dangerous and exacting maneuver, and, once there, to reconnoiter and photograph the beaches to determine the best landing sites.

By means of infrared searchlights invisible to the unaided eye, the *Gunnel* served as a lighthouse for the invading armada, keeping the ships on course for the landing beaches. An hour before midnight on November 7, the *Gunnel*'s signalman sighted the huge fleet cresting the horizon exactly on schedule. The *Gunnel* began flashing its designated signal, and throughout the night American ships took up their positions off the Moroccan coast and lowered their landing craft.

At dawn, the *Gunnel*'s secret mission complete, my father was ordered to fly the American flag, illuminate it with a spotlight, and proceed on the surface at top speed out of the congested area to safer waters near the Canary Islands.

Friendly fire, a misfortune of war today, was a much more frequent occurrence in earlier wars. In their first combat patrol, the crew of the *Gunnel* had a number of close calls when friendly ships and planes, in the fog of war, mistook my father's submarine for a German sub, as American submarines in war zones were an unfamiliar sight in 1942.

On their passage out of the invasion area, my father allowed his crew to stand topside in shifts to watch the naval barrage directed at the fortifications at Fedala and Casablanca. As my father and some of his crew stood mesmerized, watching the spectacular assault, the booming guns of American battleships firing one-ton shells toward the outgunned enemy, an American P-40 plane dropped out of the clouds and began strafing the *Gunnel*. My father ordered the sub to dive, and he and the other men on deck scrambled down the conning-tower hatch.

Fifteen minutes later, the *Gunnel* surfaced and was signaled by an American seaplane. "Good morning, sallow face, I am here to protect you." The plane escorted the *Gunnel* to safety for some time until it broke off to chase an approaching French plane away from the sub.

A little after noon that same day, an American bomber was spotted approaching the *Gunnel*. When the plane ignored the sub's signal, dipped a wing, and turned as if preparing for a dive-bombing, the executive officer, standing on the *Gunnel*'s bridge, ordered a crash dive. The sub descended at a dangerously steep angle as the bomb exploded so close that some of the crew were struck by flying paint chips knocked loose from inside the sub's conning tower by the force of the blast.

When the *Gunnel* reached its assigned station and patrolled waters off the Canaries, it was hunted for four days by German subs. On November 13, my father was ordered to make for a British submarine base at Roseneath, Scotland. En route three days later, the *Gunnel* was spotted and chased by a U-boat. Later that same day, one of the *Gunnel*'s four main engines broke down. Over the next nine days, the three remaining main engines stopped working.

When the last of its four engines gave out, the *Gunnel* was still a thousand miles from Scotland and sailing in extremely hazardous waters infested with German subs and patrolled by German aircraft. My father ordered his engineers to convert the auxiliary engine, normally used to power the sub's lights and air-conditioning, for propulsion.

Under full power, the *Gunnel* could make twenty knots on the surface and nine knots submerged. Powered by its auxiliary engine, the sub could make only five knots at best as it limped slowly toward Scotland, submerged by day and on the surface by night.

My father radioed his condition to naval authorities, and the *Gunnel* was redirected to a closer naval base, at Falmouth in southern England. The British offered to send an escort or a tug to tow the *Gunnel* to safety. According to the *Gunnel*'s torpedo officer, "Both offers were promptly and unequivocally declined by Captain McCain as he chomped down hard on his cigar."

Were the overworked auxiliary engine to break down, the *Gunnel* would be dead in the water. Use of the sub's lighting and fans was reduced to bare minimum. One of the machinist's mates placed a small statue of Buddha in front of the small engine and ordered passing crewmen to bow respectfully.

On November 19, still a week's voyage from Falmouth, my father sighted through the sub's periscope several ships' masts on the horizon. As three ships, antisubmarine escorts serving as a screen for an advancing convoy, drew closer, my father ordered battle stations. The *Gunnel*'s communications officer searched the ship recognition manuals but could find nothing that would identify the approaching ships as friendly.

At about three thousand yards, the three ships detected the *Gunnel*, and they advanced toward her. My father prepared his crew to fight. One of his officers recalls him declaring, "If those bastards drop depth charges we are going to give it to them." But just before the fight commenced my father recognized a British ensign flying on the closest ship.

My father ordered a red smoke-signal rocket launched from an underwater tube. The lead British warship ordered my father to surface with the *Gunnel*'s torpedo tubes pointed away from the ships. When he did so, the *Gunnel* found itself in the center of a triangle with the guns of all three British ships pointing at it. One of the British commanding officers hailed my father through a megaphone and announced, "Good thing you fired that red smoke. We were about to blast you out of the water."

Six days later, on Thanksgiving Day, the *Gunnel* reached Falmouth. After repairs, the sub proceeded to Roseneath. After further repairs, the *Gunnel* returned to the States, where it was outfitted in Portsmouth, New Hampshire, for combat duty in the Pacific.

Upon completion of his first combat mission, the thirty-one-year-old submarine skipper was commended by the Atlantic Fleet Commander in Chief. "Commander John S. McCain, by extremely skillful and daring handling of his ship, performed special missions which contributed materially to the successful execution of an extremely difficult landing of a large expeditionary force on a strange and poorly charted coast."

Although he had initially wanted to be an aviator, in later years my father would remark that his disqualification as a pilot had been a lucky twist of fate. He was proud to be a skipper in a service that was then and is now a select branch of the Navy. The submarine service places a high premium on the individual initiative of its commanders, especially in war. Long patrols, inconsistent communications with base command, battles often fought alone, fateful decisions left entirely to the skipper—the service suited my father's personality completely. "It's a unique life in submarines," he gratefully recalled. "You're on your own . . . completely detached from the world."

He was a resourceful skipper, adept at devising imaginative improvements to his sub's war-fighting capabilities. He worked out a formula for targeting torpedoes at unseen enemy ships while submerged. He did it by taking sound bearings of the other ship and comparing his sub's course and speed to his estimate of the target's speed, thereby deriving the enemy's range and course. It was a remarkably accurate system, and my father credited a great many sunken enemy ships to its effectiveness.

He invented an electric firing device for the ship's guns. Until he improved the firing mechanism, the firing pin of submarine guns was released by depressing a foot pedal on the gun mount. The gunner had to apply a considerable amount of pressure to the pedal to get it to release the pin and fire a shell. Often the exertion by the gunner threw his aim off. My father rigged up a handheld firing button. All the gunner had to do was press a button held in his right hand, enabling him to keep a steadier aim while firing.

The officers and crew of the *Gunnel* called him Captain Jack. In the words of his executive officer, and friend of many years, retired Rear Admiral Joe Vasey, the men of the USS *Gunnel* "would do anything for their skipper."

My father made a point of knowing all about the personal lives of the men under his command. He daily wandered through the submarine's compartments, greeting and joking with his subordinates. He paused here and there to have a cup of coffee with the men, and to have them bring him up to date on the details of their lives back home.

There were eight officers and seventy-two enlisted men on board the *Gunnel*. My father knew the first names of every one of them. He knew who was married and who was single; how many kids they had; whose wives were pregnant and whether they were hoping for a boy or a girl. He knew what sports they favored; what they had done for a living before the war; what they wanted to do when they returned home. He knew what scared them and what made them angry. After the war, when any one of them contacted him for assistance, he did all he could to provide it.

Admiral Vasey, who worked for my father again when he reached the pinnacle of his career as Commander in Chief, Pacific, calls him "the greatest leader of men I have ever known."

My father and a few of his officers returned to the *Gunnel* one morning much the worse for wear after a long, raucous night ashore in Freemantle, Australia. The *Gunnel* was to leave on combat patrol that day. As they boarded the sub, my father turned to his exec and said, "Joe, muster the crew. I want to talk to these guys."

My father paced in front of the assembled crew, an unlit cigar protruding from the corner of his mouth, and exhorted them to martial glory. "Fellows, we're going off to fight the goddam Japanese. We're gonna find 'em and fight 'em wherever the hell they are. We're gonna fight these bastards, and we're gonna lick 'em. We're not gonna let these Japs hide from us. We'll fight 'em even if we have to go into their harbors to find them, and they're gonna be goddam sorry we did, I'll tell you that. Now, every man who wants to go with me, take one step forward, and anyone who doesn't, stay right where you are."

Laughing and roaring approval, every man of the *Gunnel* stepped forward and signaled his pride in following Captain Jack wherever he chose to lead him.

Many years later, in a commencement address he gave at the Naval Academy, he spoke of the all-important relationship between a skipper and the enlisted men under his command, the bluejackets, who were, he often said, the "backbone of the Navy." "When you step aboard ship and stand in front of your first division of bluejackets," he said, "they will evaluate you accurately and without delay. In fact, there is no more exacting method of determining an officer's worth. Furthermore, you can't fool bluejackets. They are quick to recognize the phony. If you lose the respect of these men, you are finished. You can never get it back."

My father never lost the respect of the men who sailed under his command. He taught them their duty, as they taught him his, and made them proud to carry it out. And he looked after them.

Heading for Fremantle, Australia, for fuel during one patrol, the *Gunnel*'s officer of the deck sighted a bomber overhead. Knowing it was either an American or Australian plane, the officer exchanged prescribed recognition signals with the bomber indicating they were friendly.

A few moments after the plane passed overhead, it turned and made a run on the *Gunnel*. My father was on the bridge. As the plane menacingly approached, my father gave the order to dive. As his ship submerged, the plane released two bombs, which fell close by, shaking the *Gunnel* violently.

A few hours later, the *Gunnel* reached port. After the *Gunnel* tied up to the dock, my father asked the officer of the deck if he was sure he had given the bomber the right recognition signal. The young officer replied that he had. Angrily, my father had Joe Vasey bring him the two largest ensigns on board, one of whom had been an intercollegiate heavyweight wrestling champion. "Men, I want you to go find the bastards who did this to us, and take care of them. You got that?"

"Aye, aye, sir," the two hulking ensigns shouted, and then took off at a brisk pace to execute their skipper's order.

Some hours later, my father heard some kind of commotion on the dock and came up on deck to see what was happening. There he found the two ensigns he had ordered to avenge the *Gunnel*'s honor stumbling toward the ship, amid a crowd of Australian Army officers, all of whom were drunk, carrying beers in their hands and singing "Waltzing Matilda" loudly and off-key.

The two ensigns had apparently inquired of the Australians who were now escorting them back to ship where they might locate the offending bomber crew. Judging that the two men might come to more harm than good, the Australians pleaded ignorance about the crew's whereabouts, but promised to look into the matter if the ensigns would join them for a drink. The ensigns decided they surely had enough time to suspend their search briefly for a quick beer, and a good many beers later they found themselves part of the roving, boisterous chorus that now stood in the gaze of the much-amused skipper of the *Gunnel*.

My father was never one to begrudge any man under his command a much-deserved respite from war, and he gladly wrote off the ensigns' failure to carry out his orders to the greater good of improving Allied relations. No one laughed harder than he did at the drunken spectacle on the Fremantle dock. Long after the event, he would still joke with the wayward ensigns about how they had let their Australian brothers-in-arms get the better of them.

Patrolling the waters between Midway and Nagasaki on their second combat patrol, the crew of the *Gunnel* had their greatest success under my father's command as well as their first encounter with Japanese depth charges, one of the most harrowing experiences in naval warfare.

In the early evening of June 18, while hunting on the surface in the East China Sea just south of the Korean peninsula, the *Gunnel* sighted the masks and smokestacks of seven large Japanese freighters and two smaller vessels. The smaller boats, one a fishing trawler and the other probably a small destroyer, were serving as escorts. The ships were making full speed and changing course by forty to sixty degrees every ten minutes. By plotting their base course, the *Gunnel*'s navigation officer determined that the convoy was heading for Shanghai.

Unable to close with the fast-moving convoy while his submarine was submerged and making a top speed of only nine knots, my father decided to surface and, traveling at seventeen knots, get ahead of the convoy during the night. Over the next several hours the *Gunnel* raced to cut off the Japanese ships. By midnight it had reached its intended patrol site but had lost sight of the convoy.

Around five-thirty the morning of the 19th, the sub's radar picked up an enemy plane patrolling eight miles away. My father gave the order to submerge. When the *Gunnel* surfaced an hour later, the convoy was on the horizon, now steaming slowly. The *Gunnel* dove again and proceeded to close with the enemy at full speed, taking periscope observations every five minutes.

An hour and a half later, the *Gunnel* was within firing range of the freighters. My father fired three torpedoes from his bow tubes at the nearest ship, an old freighter of about eight thousand tons. A minute later, he fired three more from the bow at a second freighter. The first freighter was hit, and it sank within a few minutes while the *Gunnel* reached for the bottom.

At eighty feet the men of the *Gunnel* heard another torpedo explode. It had missed the second freighter but struck a third ship two thousand yards on the port side of the intended target. A moment later one of the convoy's two escort ships dropped the first of seven depth charges, each one detonating closer than the preceding one.

Joe Vasey described what it was like to be depth-charged: "You usually first heard the click of the detonator through the hull. But the explosion was the worst. It was like being in a steel container with someone hitting a giant sledgehammer against it. It can shake the whole bloody sub." Submarine crewmen prepared by bending their legs to absorb the impact. As Joe Vasey explained, many a submariner "had fractured legs from the shock of the deck plates and standing too rigidly."

The *Gunnel* had submerged 150 feet when the last of the seven depth charges exploded. One of the escorts, probably the trawler, was directly overhead. It dropped a grapnel over the side to try to hook the sub, a favorite tactic of commercial fishing vessels that were pressed into war service. The grapnel's chain dragged along the port side of the *Gunnel*, "rattling slowly and excruciatingly," my father recorded in his log, adding that "the chains of Marley's ghost sounded very much like that to old Scrooge."

My father ordered the *Gunnel* to descend to a depth of three hundred feet. The sub ran at that depth for four hours. Twice my father heard the enemy escort pass directly overhead. After an hour had passed without hearing anything from the enemy ship that was searching, its depth charges ready, for the *Gunnel*, my father came up to periscope depth. He sighted a Japanese warship about three thousand yards to his starboard, and immediately submerged again to three hundred feet.

A large Japanese naval base was located at Sasebo, less than a hundred miles to the east of the *Gunnel*'s position. In response to the *Gunnel*'s attack on the convoy, three destroyers had been sent out of Sasebo to hunt down and destroy the American sub. The approaching ship was one of them.

During its deep dive, it was necessary for the *Gunnel* to allow some water to flood in, making the sub heavier and enabling it to remain submerged at such a great depth. The *Gunnel* ran in this heavy condition for several hours, while the three destroyers hunted the sub with their sonar. When they were close, my father and his crew could hear distinctly through the sub's hull the destroyer's sonar pinging incessantly. The air was growing foul and the crew's nerves were strained to the breaking point. One of the *Gunnel*'s signalmen, Charles Napier, recalled fifty years later: "The Catholics were fingering their rosaries, other religious sailors were praying, and some were simply trying to figure how to get out of the situation."

Around nine o'clock that night, the *Gunnel*, its batteries dangerously low and its air banks nearly depleted, surfaced. The weary and frightened crew gasped clean air for the first time in sixteen hours.

Water from a leak in the conning tower had flooded the pump

room and grounded out an air compressor and the air-conditioning plant. Intending to run on the surface while the crew made repairs, my father took the sub close to the area where he had sunk the freighter.

It was a cloudless night with bright moonlight and calm seas. At nine-thirty, a lookout spotted one of the Japanese destroyers 5,800 yards away. My father put the destroyer astern of the sub and gave the order for battle stations. He ordered every man off the bridge except for the quartermaster and himself and told the crew to make ready two of the stern torpedo tubes. He ran the *Gunnel* at full speed, making eighteen knots, but the destroyer made thirty knots, and closed rapidly.

At a little less than three thousand yards, the destroyer's guns opened up on the *Gunnel,* firing fused projectiles that passed over and on either side of the sub.

My father had ordered Joe Vasey, the *Gunnel*'s torpedo officer, to work out a firing solution for all four of the stern torpedo tubes. With shells fired from the destroyer's guns "getting uncomfortably close," exploding overhead and missing barely to the *Gunnel*'s port and starboard sides, my father yelled, "Goddammit, shoot, Joe, shoot." Vasey fired the two operable torpedoes "down the throat" of the destroyer as my father sounded the diving alarm.

When the *Gunnel* reached thirty-five feet, the first torpedo hit the destroyer. A few seconds later, five depth charges detonated simultaneously off the *Gunnel*'s stern. My father recorded the moment in his log, breaking his usual habit of restricting his official record to a dry recitation of the facts and avoiding dramatic embellishment: "The awesome sounds of exploding depth charges and collapsing bulkheads as the warship rapidly sank close astern of *Gunnel* was an unforgettable experience for all hands."

My father leveled the sub off at two hundred feet. When he picked up the two remaining destroyers on his sonar rapidly approaching, he took the *Gunnel* down to three hundred feet and commenced evasive tactics. The destroyers dropped eight more depth charges off the sub's stern. After six hours, the *Gunnel* surfaced very briefly to charge its batteries and air banks. Spotting the destroyers, my father took it down again. He remained submerged for the next eighteen hours with all auxiliary engines turned off, keeping the sub's noise at a minimum to avoid detection by sonar.

Running silent for such a long period was a perilous predicament for a submarine crew. You ran the risk of losing all power as the batteries, which could be charged only when the submarine was surfaced, ran down completely. The air grew unbreathable as the submarine's carbon dioxide absorbent was used up. This was the situation my father and his crew faced on the evening of June 20.

The air became so foul that crew members not needed at battle stations were ordered to rest in their bunks, where they would consume less oxygen. Earlier, the crew had felt a sense of hopelessness when the grapnel chain had scraped against the *Gunnel*'s side, knowing that if the hook grabbed onto something, depth charges would immediately be dropped directly onto the sub. Most of the crew, terrified, soaked with perspiration, had managed to control their emotions, and they responded to their skipper's orders. Some of the younger crew members had wept, facedown in their bunks. Fear and poor air made a few men delirious, and one of them had to be strapped down.

The anxiety of those who were still in possession of their faculties after many hours submerged was growing into frantic desperation. Over the last two days they had endured the excitement of the chase and attack on the convoy, a hair-raising close call in a surface battle with an enemy destroyer, and the terror of repeated depth charge attacks. Now they were sweating out endless hours fathoms down, exhausted, slowly suffocating while their sub faced the imminent prospect of lying dead in the water.

The temperature inside the sub had reached 120 degrees. The humidity was 100 percent. Above them, two destroyers constantly patrolled, determined to locate and destroy the American submarine that had sunk their sister ship.

At eight-thirty that night, my father called all his officers to the wardroom. There the chief of the boat and chief electrician's mate informed them that the batteries would last only thirty to sixty minutes more, and that all the sub's good air was gone. The *Gunnel* would have to surface as quickly as possible. After receiving this discouraging report, my father informed his officers of his intentions.

The sub would surface slowly to reduce the likelihood that the blowing of its ballast tanks would be detected by the enemy's sonar. As soon as it surfaced, the ship's guns would be immediately manned and readied for battle. If either of the destroyers was in range, the *Gunnel* would shoot it out, and charge its batteries and air banks on the run.

My father offered one other course of action to his officers, a course he strongly opposed. If his officers did not unanimously concur with his decision to fight, he would order all classified information and materials destroyed, surface the sub, and scuttle her. All hands would jump overboard and hope for rescue, a remote hope at best, given that the Japanese skippers whom they would rely on for rescue were undoubtedly bent on vengeance and unlikely to be sympathetic.

To a man, my father's officers shouted their preference for a fight.

When they surfaced, they sighted the destroyers at a considerable distance and steaming away from the *Gunnel.* They gave no indication that they spotted the sub. My father reversed course and hurried away. The batteries for two of his diesel engines were recharged, and fresh air filled the ship.

Ten days after my father's submarine eluded the destroyers, it reached Midway. I suspect the men of the USS *Gunnel* were never so happy to see that desolate, uninteresting island.

My father received the Silver Star for this action. The citation praised his "conspicuous gallantry, . . . bravery under fire and aggressive fighting spirit."

After five combat patrols aboard the *Gunnel*, my father, now Commander McCain, took command of the USS *Dentuda*, which completed one patrol in the South China Sea before the war's end. During its only patrol, the *Dentuda* fought a gun battle with two Japanese patrol craft and an inconclusive submerged battle with a Japanese submarine.

It was as commander of the *Dentuda* that my father entered Tokyo Bay, exhausted from the strain of command in one of the more terrifying forms of combat, to enjoy his last reunion with the father whose example had led him to this life.

CHAPTER 8

Four Stars

In 1965, my father reported for duty in New York, to serve as vice chairman of the delegation to the United Nations Military Staff Committee and as Commander of the Eastern Sea Frontier and the Atlantic Reserve Fleet.

He had distinguished himself in other commands since the Second World War and had enjoyed a notably successful career. He had commanded two submarine divisions. During the Korean War, as a captain, he served as second in command on the destroyer USS *St. Paul*. He was well regarded by influential leaders in Washington and had been given several important commands, the last being command of the Atlantic Fleet's Amphibious Force, when he directed the American invasion of the Dominican Republic.

In 1965, violent clashes between warring factions, one of which was believed to be a Communist front, had brought the Dominican Republic to the verge of civil war. President Johnson ordered my father to command the amphibious assault of Operation Steel Pike 1, the invasion and military occupation of the Caribbean nation. The operation was controversial. Critics judged it, with good reason, to be an unlawful intervention in the affairs of a sovereign nation. My father, typically, was undeterred by domestic opposition. "Some people condemned this as an unwarranted intervention," he observed, "but the Communists were all set to move in and take over. People may not love you for being strong when you have to be, but they respect you for it and learn to behave themselves when you are."

The operation was a success, and, at the time, it constituted the largest amphibious operation ever undertaken in peacetime. After its completion, he was awarded the Legion of Merit for attracting "worldwide attention to the highly mobile and devastating might" of the Navy and Marine Corps.

His subsequent assignment at the United Nations, however, was regarded by the Navy as a dead end and was expected to be his last. He was a three-star admiral, and the prospects for a fourth star were remote. But two years later he was ordered to London to assume command of all U.S. naval forces in Europe. A fourth star came with the job. He relieved the renowned Admiral John Thach, my grandfather's old operations officer and friend.

Within a year, he was given command of all U.S. forces in the Pacific, the largest operational military command in the world. The dominion of the Commander in Chief, Pacific Command (CINCPAC) is geographically immense, encompassing 85 million square miles, extending from the Aleutian Islands to the South Pole and from the west coast of North and South America to the Indian Ocean.

CINCPAC, Admiral Nimitz's wartime command, remains the U.S. Navy's second most prestigious office. Only the office of Chief of Naval Operations is a greater privilege, and, if truth be told, a good many officers would prefer running the Pacific Command to running the entire Navy. My father had achieved prominence in his beloved Navy that surpassed his father's storied career. The *Washington Post* reported his triumph under the headline NAVY CHEERS APPOINTMENT OF MCCAIN.

Shortly after his new assignment was made public, my father received a letter from a retired sailor who had known my grandfather during the war. He wrote of how highly regarded my grandfather had been by the enlisted men under his command.

Dear Admiral,

Maybe I shouldn't be sending this to you, but I had to when I saw your name in this morning's paper. <u>Commander of United States Forces in the Pacific.</u> I am an ex–carrier man, 1943–1946. Was Admiral John S. McCain your dad? I was a plank owner on the *Wasp*, and Admiral McCain was at our commissioning. . . . We had admirals on board before and after but Admiral McCain was liked by all the ship's company. It was a privilege to have served under him. They all speak of Admirals Halsey, Nimitz, Sprague, Spruance, Mitscher, and Bogan. But Admiral John S. McCain was tops with us. Every night about 8 P.M. he would walk around the flight deck with that salty-looking admiral's cap of his in his hands. He would stop and talk to us on our gun mount. Maybe you won't have time to read this. I don't send letters at all but when I heard of you and your command I just had to.

I imagine the old sailor's note, rejoicing in the professional triumph of the son of a Navy legend, must have moved my father very much. Though I was not privileged to witness his change-of-command ceremony, I have always believed that for that one moment, my father, so hard driven by his often oppressive desire to honor his father's name, looked on his career with tranquillity and satisfaction. He must have felt the old man's pride as he took his first salute as commander of the greatest military force in the world, with dominion over the waters where the answer "I've sent McCain" had once relieved an anxious predecessor.

Over a million soldiers, sailors, and airmen now answered to my father's orders. As CINCPAC, my father had command over the war in Vietnam. General Creighton Abrams, then commanding U.S. forces in Vietnam, was his subordinate; as was I, a lieutenant commander, held as a prisoner of war in Hanoi.

II

I heard the old, old men say,
'All that's beautiful drifts away
Like the waters.'

> —William Butler Yeats,
> "The Old Men Admiring
> Themselves in Water"

CHAPTER 9

Worst Rat

I was not quite two years old when my parents felt it necessary to instill in me a little self-restraint and my instruction in some of the colder realities of life began in earnest. During an otherwise tranquil early childhood, I had quite unexpectedly developed an outsized temper that I expressed in an unusual way. At the smallest provocation, I would go off in a mad frenzy, and then, suddenly, crash to the floor unconscious. Alarmed at this odd behavior and worried that I was suffering from a strange and possibly serious illness, my parents consulted a Navy physician for an explanation. The doctor assured them that the malady was not serious. It was self-induced. When I got angry I held my breath until I blacked out.

The doctor prescribed a treatment that seems a little severe by modern standards of child care. He instructed my parents to fill a bathtub with cold water whenever I commenced a tantrum, and when I appeared to be holding my breath to drop me, fully clothed, into it.

I do not recall at all these traumatic early encounters with the harsh consequences of my misbehavior, buried, as they must be, deep in my subconscious. But my mother assures me that they occurred, and went on for some time until I was finally "cured." Whenever I worked myself into a tiny rage, my mother shouted to my father, "Get the water!" Moments later I would find myself thrashing, wide-eyed and gasping for breath, in a tub of icy-cold water. Eventually, I achieved a satisfactory (if only temporary) control over my emotions. And as a side benefit, the treatment apparently instilled in me an early reverence for the principle of equal justice under the law. After my first few experiences with the dreaded immersion therapy, I would shout, "Get the water! Get the water!" whenever my older sister, Sandy, momentarily lost control of her temper.

My mother often despaired over the quality of our education. When asked today how her children were educated she is apt to respond that we were "raised to be completely ignorant."

The frequent relocations imposed on Navy families were the chief obstacle to a decent education. As soon as I had begun to settle into a school, my father would be reassigned, and I would find myself again a stranger in new surroundings forced to establish myself quickly in another social order. I was often required in a new school to study things I had already learned. Other times, the curriculum assumed knowledge I had not yet acquired.

Many of the base schools I attended were substandard institutions. Sometimes the school building was nothing more than a converted aircraft hangar. The classes mixed children of varying ages. We might have one teacher on Monday and a different one on Tuesday. On other days, we lacked the services of any teacher at all. My first purpose during my brief stay in these schools was to impress upon my classmates that I was not a person to suffer slights lightly. My second purpose was to prove myself as an athlete. When I was disciplined by my teachers, which happened regularly, it was often for fighting.

My parents worried a great deal about our irregular schooling. Once, when we were transferred to Long Beach, California, my father resolved to improve upon the educational circumstances to which we had grown accustomed. He drove to the rectory of a Catholic parish and pleaded with the monsignor to allow us to attend the parish school. He even offered to convert to Catholicism if that was necessary. The good monsignor admitted us without obliging my parents to abandon their church.

My mother's complaint not withstanding, I enjoyed my early education. I enjoyed it for the very quality that caused my parents to despair—its informality. Until I was sent at fifteen to a boarding school, I relied on the members of my family to be my principal instructors. My mother assumed most of this responsibility, and she proved to be an imaginative and amusing educator.

Like wealthy parents who "finish" their children's education with a tour of the European continent, my mother saw our frequent cross-country trips to join my father as an opportunity to supplement our irregular schooling. She was forever routing our journeys through locations that offered a site of historical significance or a notable institute of the arts or sciences.

When we passed through cities we searched for whatever the locals considered their most prominent attraction—art galleries, museums, churches, buildings designed by celebrated architects, natural phenomena, and the homes of historical figures. I recall being greatly impressed with Carlsbad Caverns, the Grand Canyon, the Petrified Forest, the high bluffs and Civil War history of Natchez, Mississippi, and the venerated shrines of American heroes, especially Washington's Mount Vernon and Andrew Jackson's Hermitage. They were all memorable events in my childhood, and I recall them today with gratitude.

We once spent a night in El Paso, Texas, so that my mother could take us across the border to Juárez, Mexico, the next day. She wanted us to see a cathedral that her father had taken her to see when she was a young girl; he had regaled her with stories of its difficult construction, how its enormous wooden beams had to be floated down the Colorado River. We arrived in Juárez to find the city much changed from my mother's recollection of it. She could not locate the cathedral, which she said had dominated the town when she saw it last. We became lost, and when we found ourselves in a rough neighborhood where the men were all dressed in zoot suits, she sensibly called off the search and beat a hasty retreat for the border.

My mother went about these tours with her usual direct, enthusiastic approach to life and her extraordinary self-confidence. The difficulties we encountered en route seldom proved superior to her problem-solving skills. And when her children posed a problem to her progress, we too proved inferior to her resolve.

I earned my reputation as a "hell-raiser"—my mother's term—in high school and at the Naval Academy. But, appropriately, it was in my mother's mobile classroom that I gave the first indication that I was headed in a troubling direction. On an exhausting trip from Washington to Coronado, my mother had become exasperated with Sandy and me. We had been quarreling for hours on end. Reaching back from the front seat to throw a banana at me for making a smart-aleck reply to her most recent rebuke, she accidentally hit Sandy. When I laughed at her for missing her target, my mother grabbed the first object in reach, an empty aluminum thermos, and flung it at me, hitting me on the brow, knocking me temporarily mute, and denting the thermos.

Having now reached the end of her maternal patience, she resolved to hasten our arrival in Coronado. We diverted from our course so that we could stop in College Station, Texas. Upon arriving there, my mother located the dean of students at Texas A&M and appealed to him to help her find a student who was in need of transportation to California and would agree to travel with us and share the driving. We checked into a hotel that evening, and my mother wrote to my father to inform him that for the first time in my life I had been "a real pain in the neck." Apparently she had forgotten by this time my brief period of defiance as a two-year-old, which had ended in complete surrender to parental authority. After the cold-water treatment had subdued my incipient rebelliousness, I possessed for the next ten years a rather meek disposition.

The next morning two students arrived to take my mother up on her offer. As the trip progressed, my mother charmed our new companions. One of them remarked how fortunate we were to have such an attractive and clever mother. The compliment was too much for me, as I was still angry over the previous day's swift and unexpected punishment. Holding up the damaged thermos and pointing to my head, I replied, "Oh yeah, you think she's so great. Look what she did to me." My denunciation prompted gales of laughter from my mother. She laughed about it intermittently for most of the remainder of the trip, as did our new traveling companions. And she still laughs when reminded of the incident today.

I became my mother's son. What I lacked of her charm and grace I made up for by emulating and exaggerating other of her characteristics. She was loquacious, and I was boisterous. Her exuberance became rowdiness in me. She taught me to find so much pleasure in life that misfortune could not rob me of the joy of living. She has an irrepressible spirit that yields to no adversity, and that part of her spirit she shared with us was as fine a gift as any mother ever gave her children. My father, as she will admit if asked, always came first with her. She loved him deeply, and made his life whole, mending as best she could the breaches in his life, the times when doubt and insecurity would cloud his sense of his destiny. Even today, many years after his death, my mother still keeps a card on which, after his passing, she wrote down a list of the things my father had found pleasure in, from his favorite meal to his favorite music, as well as a list of the things he had disliked. But although there was never any doubt about the primacy my father enjoyed in my mother's affections, her heart has always been large enough to encompass her children with as much love and care as any mother's child has ever enjoyed.

When I was young, similarities between my mother and me were more apparent than were those between my father and me. My father and I probably seemed in many respects, at least superficial ones, very different people. My keen-eyed brother in his observations on our family's domestic life often remarked on our father's and my contrasting dispositions in those long-ago days. We were, he thought, mirror opposites. My father was taciturn, while I was noisy. My father was shy, while I "loved working a crowd." My father "was often quiet at the dinner table, while the rest of us raised hell, argued, until Dad would intervene—always on my mother's behalf. John was either fiercely immersed in the squabble or the root cause of it."

My father was a more learned man than his grades at the Naval Academy indicated. He taught physics at the Academy for two years and was regarded as an able instructor. He had many intellectual interests, but he especially loved history and English literature. An "outstanding command of the English language," he often remarked, "will stand you in good stead as time moves on." He was an avid reader of Toynbee and Spengler. He could recite great lengths of poetry from memory. He loved Edgar Allan Poe, Kipling, Dante, Tennyson, and Lewis Carroll. But his favorite poem was Oscar Wilde's ode to the British Empire, "Ave Imperatrix," which he quoted from at length in his lectures on seapower:

> *The fleet-foot Marri scout, who comes*
> *To tell how he hath heard afar*
> *The measured roll of English drums*
> *Beat at the gates of Kandahar.*

He was a great admirer of the British Empire, crediting it with keeping "a relative measure of peace" in the world for "someplace in the neighborhood of two centuries."

He read and reread the biographies of historical figures whose lives, he felt, would always be an inspiration to others. "I heard some man make a statement one time not so long ago," he once recalled of a popular futurist, "that reading the lives of great men was somewhat a waste of time because this was past history. Well, this is stupid on the face of it, because one of the real factors of life is what you learn from reading about the lives of great men, because there are certain fundamentals of human relationships that never change."

Alfred Thayer Mahan, the great naval historian, author of the seminal work on the importance of naval expansion, *The Influence of Sea Power upon History,* was my father's inspiration and his passion. He quoted from Mahan's book often and at length, not only in his seapower lectures but to almost anyone he thought could profit from Mahan's wisdom. He talked about Mahan to me quite often, during his occasional attempts to help steer me toward a successful naval career.

My paternal grandmother was a well-educated woman of gifted intellect and refined manner. She had been an instructor of Latin and Greek at the University of Mississippi, where she taught my grandfather. Bookish and eight years his senior, she won the devotion of the much coarser but widely read naval officer. Throughout their union, they indulged together their shared love of literature, reading aloud to each other whenever time allowed. That my father was well versed in the classics is undoubtedly a tribute to both his parents: his mother, the scholarly taskmaster; his father, the rough adventurer who in glamour resembled the fictional heroes who had enlivened the provincial world of his Mississippi childhood. Together they instilled in my father their love of literature and learning, encouraged his imagination, gave him responsibilities early in life, and fortified him with their values. As a schoolboy, he got in trouble once for telling his classmates a tall tale about having seen a bear on the way to school. His mother excused the lapse, remarking, "All little boys must have an imagination. Don't worry, he'll know about honesty and the truth."

It was while I was in my grandmother's care that I began to develop my own interest in literature. I spent the summer of 1946 with my widowed grandmother and her daughter, my Aunt Katherine, at their house in Coronado. My grandmother was a composed, straight-laced woman who kept a formal house. I still recall quite vividly their maid summoning me to tea and supper every day, at precisely four and seven, by ringing a bell. If I lingered too long at whatever activity I was preoccupied with and arrived a minute or two past the appointed hour, my grandmother would dismiss me very politely from her presence. She would observe that she had looked forward to dining with me, but as I had failed to arrive promptly, she would have to forgo the pleasure of my company until the next meal. She never yielded to any of the elaborate excuses I devised to coax her into allowing an exception to her daily routine.

The room I occupied in my grandmother's house was furnished with my father's boyhood belongings. It contained a substantial collection of the authors he had favored as a boy. I spent most of the summer reading one volume after another. Among the authors who most impressed me in that summer of unsupervised study were Mark Twain, Robert Louis Stevenson, James Fenimore Cooper, Edgar Rice Burroughs, and Booth Tarkington. I was also taken with the tales of King Arthur's court. These works instilled in me a lifelong love of reading. And, with their straightforward moral lessons, they reinforced my sense of right and wrong and impressed upon me the virtue of treating people fairly.

Among the Stevenson volumes was a collection of his poetry. It included the poem he wrote for his own epitaph, "Requiem."

> Under the wide and starry sky
> Dig the grave and let me lie:
> Glad did I live and gladly die,
> And I laid me down with a will.
>
> This be the verse you grave for me:
> Here he lies where he longed to be;
> Home is the sailor home from the sea,
> And the hunter home from the hill.

In his brief life, Stevenson had been quite an adventurer, wandering the continent of Europe, and later the Americas and the South Pa-

cific. He had lived in the capitals of Europe, in the Adirondacks of up-
state New York, and in Monterey, California. He spent the last years
of his life in a house he had built in Western Samoa, a location as remote from the cold austerity of his native Scotland as could be imagined. He is buried there on a low hill overlooking the Pacific.

Stevenson is recalled in biographies as a restless, striving man.
Crediting a tropical grave as the place "he longed to be" struck me as
a brave declaration of self-determination. I thought the poem the perfect motto for all who lived a life according to their own lights, and a
moving tribute to the lives of strong-willed, valorous men like my
grandfather and father. I read it as an exhortation to "be your own
man." It influenced my childhood aspiration to find adventures, pursue each one avidly, and, when it had run its course, find another.

Like my father and grandfather, I lacked as a boy the physical size
to appear imposing on first acquaintance. Together with the challenges of my transient childhood, my small stature motivated me to
prove quickly to new schoolmates that I could stand up for myself.
The quickest way to do so was to fight the first kid who provoked me.

Whether I won or lost those fights wasn't as important as establishing myself as someone who could adapt to the challenges of a new
environment without betraying apprehension. I foolishly believed
that fighting, as well as challenging school authorities and ignoring
school regulations, was indispensable to my self-esteem and helped
me to form new friendships.

The repeated farewells to friends rank among the saddest regrets
of a childhood constantly disrupted by the demands of my father's career. I would arrive at a new school, go to considerable lengths to
make new friends, and, shortly thereafter, be transplanted to a new
town to begin the process all over again. Seldom if ever did I see again
the friends I left behind. If you have never known any other life, these
experiences seem a natural part of existence. You come to expect
friendships to last but a short time. I believe this breeds in a child a
desire to make the most of friendships while they last. The relation-

ships make up with intensity what they lack in length. That's one of the benefits of an itinerant childhood.

On the other hand, you never lose the expectation that friendships come and go and should not be expected to do otherwise. That fatalistic expectation is reinforced later in life when war imposes a sad finality on relationships grown extremely close under difficult conditions. Even when you are an adult, when passing time and changing circumstances separate you from old friends, their absence seems unremarkable and in accord with the normal course of things.

This is not to say that I value my friends less than other people value theirs. On the contrary, I have made friends with many people over the years, and whether I see them or not, whether they are still living or not, their friendship honored me, and honors me still. Many of my friendships exist only in memory. But they are memories I cherish for the lessons they taught me and the values they imparted to me, gifts that proved invaluable in later years.

At each new school I arrived eager to make, by means of my insolent attitude, new friends to compensate for the loss of others. At each new school I grew more determined to assert my crude individualism. At each new school I became a more unrepentant pain in the neck.

These are the attitudes I brought to Episcopal High School in Alexandria, Virginia, when I enrolled there, Class of '54. My parents had resolved to put an end to our haphazard education and arranged for my sister, my brother, and me to attend private boarding schools. I was sent to Episcopal to prepare for my unavoidable appointment to the United States Naval Academy three years later.

———————

I liked EHS more than I liked my previous schools. No doubt my memory of it has softened over time as it became mixed with nostalgia for the pleasurable vanities of youth—vanities that the Naval Academy worked hard to suppress in its resolve to make a man of me. I did not at first acquaintance recognize Episcopal and its antique traditions as hospitable. Unlike my classmates, I arrived without any allegiance to those traditions, having had no share of them in my roving childhood. The traditions in which I was raised were peculiar to military families, and the dimensions of my small Navy world had mapped the limits of experience for most of my earliest friends.

When I entered Episcopal I encountered another small world, but one so unfamiliar to me that I thought it exotic. The Episcopal High School Class of 1954 was all male and all white. But more than the racial bigotry and gender segregation of the times distinguished the class from the rest of our generation. Most of the students came from families who lived south of the Mason-Dixon line and east of the Mississippi River, and their fathers, grandfathers, and great-grandfathers had preceded them at the school. Almost all were sons of wealthy men. None but me were sons of professional officers in the armed services.

The Navy has, of course, its own aristocracy, but not one that seemed to me as exclusive, mannered, and fixed as the aristocracy from which EHS drew its ranks. Most of my classmates were so settled in their society that they had an air of serenity uncommon in the young. They were not snobs. But they had envisaged the whole of their futures before they came to EHS, and what they had foreseen was so pleasant an existence that the certainty of it made them very self-assured young men.

After graduation, about half of my class would enroll in the University of Virginia, an arcadia of genteel Southern learning. The other half would venture north to one or another Ivy League school where wealthy children from North and South mixed and the friction of differing regional cultures was eased by their common appreciation for refined living. When they had completed their education, many of my classmates returned to their families and settled into careers in their fathers' businesses, law firms, and medical practices.

I, too, had a clear sense of how my life would unfold after I left Episcopal. I, too, was destined to join my father's business. But I knew my life would diverge from those of my classmates as sharply as my childhood had differed from theirs. I was on leave from the Navy while I attended high school. And the Navy expected me to return when I graduated.

I cannot recall any other student at EHS who expected to enter military service. Some would be drafted into the Army. I am sure they accepted that responsibility without complaint, and served honorably. But no one in the Class of '54 except me anticipated a career in the armed forces.

The most pervasive military influence at the school was the heroic legends taken from the annals of Civil War history. More precisely, they were the stories of Confederate heroes. There is a memorial at the school that commemorates those students who were among the fallen in the Civil War. It's a long list. You would be hard-pressed to find among those honored dead the name of anyone who gave his last full measure of devotion to the Union. More Episcopal graduates died in the Civil War than in any subsequent war in our nation's history.

EHS gave me a sense of what life could be like were I somehow to elude a Navy career. On a school holiday, some friends and I visited Princeton University. Long afterward, I would daydream about enrolling at Princeton, joining one of its stately eating clubs, and sharing in the romance of a place that seemed to me to offer equal parts of scholastic excellence and gracious leisure. But I was never so enthralled by the attraction of such a life that I deluded myself into sincerely believing it would be mine. I was bound for the Naval Academy, and while I seldom discussed with my high school friends the fate that awaited me, I knew that were we ever to meet again, they would find me in uniform.

My father never ordered me to attend the Naval Academy. Although I am sure we must have talked about it from time to time, I cannot recall the conversations. There are no scenes in my memory of sitting in my father's study listening to him expound on the virtues of an Academy education, or explain the reasons why I must follow him to Annapolis as he had followed his father. Neither do I recall any arguments with my parents about my wanting to consider an alternative future. I remember simply recognizing my eventual enrollment at the Academy as an immutable fact of life, and accepting it without comment.

I remember my parents frequently commenting on it to their friends. "He's going to the Naval Academy," they would casually remark, not with the evident satisfaction one derives from a welcome discovery of a child's potential, but as if they were discussing an inheritance that had been marked for my eventual possession. It was as if they were saying, "Someday this house will be Johnny's"—which, in a way, was what they meant.

My father and grandfather believed they had discovered the perfect life for a man. To them, the Navy was the most accommodating profession for good men who craved adventure. They never imagined possessing a greater treasure than a life at sea, and they regarded it as a legacy they were proud to bestow on their descendants, who, they assumed, would be appropriately grateful.

EHS offered me more than a glimpse at a different culture. It shared certain aspects of service academies. Life there was regimented. Jackets and ties were worn at all times. Students attended chapel every morning. On Sundays, we held morning services at the church on Seminary Hill and evening services at the chapel. The academics were superb and serious. But athletics were accorded equal importance in our education. Classes were held in the morning, including Saturday morning. We broke for lunch at twelve-thirty. The afternoons were devoted to athletic training.

Demerits were handed out for every infraction, large and small, of school regulations, and I piled them up. I was chronically late for class. I kept my room in a near permanent state of disorder and filth. I mocked the dress code by wearing a ratty old jacket and tie with a pair of infrequently laundered Levi's. And I despised and resisted the caste system that first-year students were obliged to endure with good humor.

EHS was not a military academy, but it borrowed a few traditions from Southern service academies. Like the Virginia Military Institute and the Citadel, Episcopal imposed on first-year students the designation "rats." Rats were expected to submit to a comparatively mild form of hazing. Mild or not, I resented the hell out of it. And my resentment, along with my affected disregard for rules and school authorities, soon earned me the distinction of "worst rat."

My hazing increased to correspond to the disrespect with which I treated school customs, and my ever-lengthening catalog of demerits was addressed with ever-longer punishments. But neither my offenses nor their consequences were so serious that they caused a permanent estrangement to develop between me and the staid society that I imposed upon.

My initial entry into EHS society was rough. I was one of the smaller boys in my class, a fact that upperclassmen, annoyed by my obdurate refusal to show a rat's humility, took to be further evidence of arrogance on my part, or arrogance that was all the more insufferable to them because neither social connections nor physical stature justified it. Despite my Confederate ancestors and my family's Southern origins, my heritage was perceived as rootless and not particularly distinguished—a perception confirmed by my conspicuous lack of a Southern accent.

These circumstances might have made for a lonely three years, but I managed to make friends and find a place for myself without pretending to share in the culture from which EHS students were drawn. I was good at sports, and athletics were my passage through my difficult first weeks at the school. I played football in the fall. I wrestled in the winter. I played tennis in the spring. I wasn't an exceptional athlete, but I was good enough to earn the respect of my teammates and coaches.

Eventually, I would use my reputation both as a credible athlete and as a troublemaker to earn a modest distinction as a leader of sorts at Episcopal—a leader of a few troublemakers, but a leader nonetheless. I was part of a small cadre of students who satisfied our juvenile sense of adventure by frequently sneaking off-campus at night to catch a bus for downtown Washington, and the bars and burlesque houses on 9th Street.

Our exploits there were tame compared to my more reckless conduct at the Naval Academy. But because we exaggerated them for the benefit of our rule-abiding classmates we were granted some prestige for our daring, and for the welcome fallacy that our excursions were somehow leading us to romantic opportunities that were only imagined in our all-male society.

The school hosted two dances a year, and for most students these were the only opportunities during the school year to enjoy the company of girls. To give the impression that you were regularly pursuing liaisons outside the school's walls with women you were unlikely to meet at a school dance was a sure route to notoriety on campus. That the impression was, for the most part, contrived did not overly concern us. We deluded ourselves into believing the most salacious rumors about our behavior.

I had good friends at Episcopal. Memory often accords our high school years the distinction of being among the happiest, most relaxed of our lives. I remember Episcopal in that light, and the friendships I formed there make up the better parts of my remembrance. But there was one unexpected friendship that enriched my life at EHS beyond measure.

Were William B. Ravenel the only person I remember from high school, I would credit those days as among the best of my life. His influence over my life, while perhaps not apparent to most who have observed its progress, was more important and more benevolent than that of any other person save members of my family.

Mr. Ravenel headed the English department at EHS, and he coached the junior varsity football team, on which I played. He had been a star running back at Davidson College and had a master's degree in English from Duke University. Stocky and compact, he still had the appearance and manner of an athlete but without the callowness that often marks men who live in the shadow of their long-ago successes on the playing field.

Like most men of his generation, Mr. Ravenel had known far greater danger than that posed by a tough defensive line. He had served in Patton's tank corps during the Third Army's aggressive advance across Europe and had survived its hard encounters with Hitler's panzer divisions. He was a lieutenant colonel in the Army Reserve, the only master at the school who still served in the military.

With his craggy face and athlete's build, he was a rugged-looking man. He seemed to his students to be as wise and capable as any man could expect to be. He loved English literature, and he taught us to love it as well. He had a way of communicating with his students that was uniquely effective and personal. He made us appreciate how profound were the emotions that animated the characters of Shakespeare's tragedies. *Macbeth* and *Hamlet*, in his care, were as compelling and revealing to boys as they are to the most learned and insightful scholar. He wasn't Mr. Chips, but he was as close to that ideal teacher as anyone is ever likely to find. No other master had half as much of our respect and affection. My class dedicated our senior yearbook to him. He was, simply, the best man at the school; one of the best men I have ever known.

Demerits required the offender to march ceaselessly around the long circle drive in the front of the school or to tend the yard of a master's house. It was my good fortune to have received for my many transgressions assignment to work in Mr. Ravenel's yard. Perhaps the school authorities knew they were doing me a favor—knew that Mr. Ravenel was best able to repair the all too evident flaws in my character.

I don't know if it was their benevolence or providence that brought me to his attention. Neither do I understand why it was that Mr.

Ravenel took such an interest in me, seeing in me something that few others did. But that he did take an interest in me was apparent to all. And as he personified the ideal of every student, Mr. Ravenel's regard for me signaled my classmates that I had some merit despite the fact that they and I had to strain to see it.

I discussed all manner of subjects with him, from sports to the stories of Somerset Maugham, from his combat experiences to my future. He was one of the few people at school to whom I confided that I was bound for the Academy and a Navy career, and to whom I confessed my reservations about my destiny.

In the fall of my senior year, a member of the junior varsity football team had broken training and been found out. I cannot recall the exact nature of the offense, but it was serious enough to merit his expulsion from the team. Mr. Ravenel called a team meeting, and most of the players argued that the accused be dropped from the team. I stood and offered the only argument for a less severe punishment.

The student in question had, in fact, broken training. But unlike the rest of us, he had chosen at the start of the year not to sign a pledge promising to abide by the training rules faithfully. Had he signed the pledge, he would have been expelled from school, because violating the pledge constituted an honor offense. Had he signed it, I wouldn't have defended him. But he had not. Moreover, he had not been caught breaking training, but had confessed the offense and expressed his remorse freely, without fear of discovery. I thought his behavior was no less honorable than that of a student who signed the pledge and adhered to its provisions.

So did Mr. Ravenel. But he kept his own counsel for most of our discussion, preferring, as was his way, to let his boys reason the thing out for ourselves.

At the start, most of my teammates wanted to hang the guy. But I argued that he had made a mistake that he sincerely regretted, and, uncoerced, had admitted the infraction. His behavior warranted no further disciplinary action. As I talked, I noticed Mr. Ravenel nodding his head. When some of the other guys started to come around to my point of view, Mr. Ravenel closed the discussion by voicing support for my judgment. The team then voted to drop the matter.

After the meeting broke up, Mr. Ravenel approached me and shook my hand. With relief evident in his voice, he told me we had done the right thing, and thanked me for my efforts. He allowed that before the meeting he had been anxious about its outcome. He had hoped the matter would be resolved as it had been, but was uncertain it would. Still, he had not wanted to be the one who argued for exoneration; he wanted the decision to be ours and not his. He said he was proud of me.

I have never forgotten the confidence his praise gave me. Nor have I ever forgotten the man who praised me. Many years later, when I came home from Vietnam, Mr. Ravenel was the only person outside of my family whom I wanted to see. I felt he was someone to whom I could explain what had happened to me, and who would understand. That is a high tribute to Mr. Ravenel. For I have never met a prisoner of war who felt he could explain the experience to anyone who had not shared it.

I regret that I was never able to pay him that tribute. Mr. Ravenel had died of a heart attack two years before my release. He lived for only fifty-three years. His early death was a great loss to his family, friends, and students, and to everyone who had been blessed with his company; a loss I found difficult to accept.

I was often accused of being an indifferent student, and given some of my grades, I can appreciate the charity in that remark. But I was not so much indifferent as selective. I liked English and history, and I usually did well in those classes. I was less interested and less successful in math and science. My grades at Episcopal were divided along those lines. Overall, my academic record there could be fairly described as undistinguished, but acceptable. I graduated a member in adequate if not good standing of the Class of 1954. One of my closest friends at the school, Rives Richey, said later, "If they'd rated everybody in the class for likely to succeed, I guarantee you he'd have been in the bottom ten, without any question."

A few months prior to graduation, I had taken the Naval Academy entrance exams. I had applied myself, after having been enrolled by my father in a course at an Academy preparatory school, and did surprisingly well, even on the math exam. At graduation there was no longer even the slightest doubt that I would follow my father and grandfather to Annapolis. And on June 28, after a short vacation with some friends at Virginia Beach, my father drove me to the Academy to begin my plebe summer.

In those days an officer escorting his son to the Naval Academy was thought to be an event charged with symbolic importance, a solemn rite of passage. Yet I don't remember it so. I had so long expected the day, so often envisioned the drive, that the actual event seemed more familiar than remarkable. I remember being nervous, and my father offering me typical words of encouragement. But nothing occurred in that one-hour trip that affected my long-held paradoxical image of the Academy, a place I belonged at but dreaded.

CHAPTER 10

Plebe

To my surprise, I liked it at first. I liked almost every minute of it until that time when my education at the Naval Academy began in earnest. I liked it until plebe summer concluded with the return of the upperclassmen from their vacations, eager to commence their campaign to humiliate, degrade, and make miserable me and every other plebe they encountered.

During plebe summer, Academy life had been sort of a highly organized camp: sports, pleasant company, and, compared to what awaited us after Labor Day, rather benign leadership from the few upperclassmen and junior officers who supervised us. I made friends easily. I boxed, wrestled, ran the obstacle course, and marched in formation. I did well enough in all of these activities that I briefly showed an enthusiasm for the place that my superiors mistook for an indication that I was an emerging class leader. They made me a company commander that summer. It was one of the very few occasions when I distinguished myself in a positive way at the Academy.

Coming out of plebe summer, I had, in Academy parlance, good grease, which meant I showed a natural aptitude for the service and possessed embryonic leadership qualities. The grease would last about a week past summer's end. For a short time in my last year at the Academy, I would again possess good grease. But that was to be an anomaly in a long history of transgressions and improprieties.

The Academy that welcomed the Class of '58 was essentially unchanged from the days of my father's and grandfather's classes. The Academy prided itself on the continuity of its traditions, linking tomorrow's officers with the heroes of an honored past. It wasn't until the 1970s that the Academy, at the prodding of the influential Admiral Rickover, agreed to substantive changes in its core curriculum and even some of its more venerable customs.

When I arrived there, the *Reina Mercedes,* where my father had been obliged to reside his last year, was still visible in the Yard. The curriculum was the same. There were no electives. Everyone took the same courses, which included a good number of rather outdated offerings such as a stupefyingly dull class in Navy boilers, the purpose of which was lost on midshipmen living in the nuclear age.

Every plebe was issued a copy of *Reef Points,* a book of Navy legends and maxims that plebes were expected to quickly memorize. The first passage I was expected to commit to memory, as it had been expected of my father and grandfather, was John Paul Jones's "Qualifications of the Naval Officer":

> It is by no means enough that an officer of the Navy should be a capable mariner. He must be that, of course, but also a great deal more. He should be as well a gentleman of liberal education, refined manners, punctilious courtesy, and the nicest sense of personal honor.
>
> He should be the soul of tact, patience, justice, firmness and charity. No meritorious act of a subordinate should escape his attention or be left to pass without its reward, even if the reward is only a word of approval. Conversely, he should not be blind to a single fault in any

subordinate, though at the same time, he should be quick and unfailing to distinguish error from malice, thoughtlessness from incompetency, and well meant shortcoming from heedless or stupid blunder.

In one word, every commander should keep constantly before him the great truth, that to be well obeyed, he must be perfectly esteemed.

In this well-ordered, timeless world, with its lofty aspirations and grim determination to make leaders and gentlemen of schoolboys, plebes who possessed minor eccentricities might be tolerated somewhat, but arrogant nonconformists encountered open hostility. Recognized as belonging in the latter category, I soon found myself in conflict with the Academy's authorities and traditions. Instead of beginning a crash course in self-improvement so that I could find a respectable place in the ranks, I reverted to form and embarked on a four-year course of insubordination and rebellion.

Once the second and first classes returned, the unexpected happiness I had experienced in my first weeks at Annapolis rapidly disappeared in the strain of surviving the organized torment that is plebe year. From that moment on, I hated the place, and, in fairness, the place wasn't all that fond of me, either.

Now, more than forty years after my graduation from the Naval Academy, I understand the premise that supported the harsh treatment of plebes. I may have even grasped it at the time I experienced it, but was simply reluctant to accept its consequences personally. Service academies are not just colleges with a uniform dress code. Their purpose is to prepare you for one profession alone, and that profession's ultimate aspiration is a combat command. The Academy experience is intended to determine whether you are fit for such work, and if you are, to mold your natural ability into the attributes of a capable officer. If you aren't, the Academy wants to discover your inaptitude as quickly as possible. The period of discovery is your plebe year, when you are subjected to as much stress as the law and a civilized society will allow. The agents of the Academy's will are the upperclassmen, most of whom relish the assignment.

One-quarter of the plebes who entered the Academy with me had decided or were told to find another line of work by the time our class graduated. Most of them left during our plebe year, unable to cope with the pressures, having failed to lose their individuality in the corporate identity. Upperclassmen had driven them out.

Of course, nothing in peacetime can replicate the dire experiences of war. But the Academy gives it a hell of a try. The workload imposed on you by instructors is daunting but by itself is probably not enough to break all but the least determined plebe. It is the physical and mental hazing by upperclassmen that makes the strain of plebe year so excruciating. It seems mindless and unrelenting.

We were expected to brace up, sit or stand at rigid attention with our chins tucked into our neck, whenever upperclassmen came into view. Our physical appearance was expected to conform to a code with rules so numerous, esoteric, and pointless that I thought them absurd. We were commanded to perform dozens of menial tasks a day, each one intended to be more demeaning than the last, and made all the more so by the heap of verbal abuse that would accompany it. We were ordered to supply encyclopedias of obscure information to any silly son of a bitch who asked a question. When we did not know an answer, which, of course, our interrogators hoped would be the case, we were made to suffer some further humiliation as punishment for our ignorance.

As bad as my plebe year seemed, it was a considerably more civilized experience than it had been for my grandfather and father. My father, who was two years younger and much smaller than I when he entered the Academy, had been hazed cruelly and suffered much worse treatment than that which awaited me twenty-seven years later. But he accepted his trial with better humor and more courage than would I. Even as a boy, my father exhibited a fierce resolve to prove himself the equal of any man.

Rear Admiral Kemp Tolley, who was an upperclassman at the

Academy when my father was a plebe, described the merciless treatment accorded my father by Tolley's roommate. He explained the "preferred method" used by "sadistically inclined" midshipmen to punish plebes—a broom with its bristles cut to just below its stitching. "A man pulled that thing back as hard as he could, like a baseball bat, and whacked you with it when you were bent over. The first time it hit you, you just couldn't believe that a broom could do that. It jolted your backside right through the top of your head."

Kemp had a roommate, "one of these sadists," who delighted in using the broom on my father whenever my father was unable to recite one or another of the "utterly useless things" a plebe was supposed to have memorized, things like the day's lunch menu or the names of various British battleships. As pictured in Kemp's account, my father was a pathetic physical specimen, a "little runt" who "looked like a wretched little animal that had just got out of the water with its fur still wet." But he compensated for his lack of stature with extraordinary courage. "In order to protect himself," Kemp said, "he was tougher than hell.

"[O]ld Jack would bend over, and my roommate would hit him—three or four or five times. Then he would say, 'Do you want another one? Are you going to learn it the next time?'

"And Jack would say, 'Hit me again, sir. I can take it.' And he would tell him that until my roommate would give up, even though tears were coming out of his eyes. That was the kind of guy he was. Jack McCain was not, in my personal opinion, one of the brightest naval officers that ever lived, but he certainly was one of the guttiest."

The practices of plebe year described in Admiral Tolley's account of my father's ordeal exceed the severity of my experience, but I despised my upperclass tormentors nonetheless. And although I lacked my father's courage, I tried in my own way not to yield my dignity to their abuse.

It was a trying time. That was the point, of course. Though I may now understand the purpose of that punishing year, even grant the necessity of learning to tolerate the barely tolerable, I neverthe-less hated every minute of it. And I resented everyone who inflicted it on me. I dislike even the memory of it. But, like most graduates of the Academy, my hate for the experience does not constitute regret. It rests in memory, paradoxically, with my appreciation, gratitude really, for the privilege of surviving it, and for the honor of that accomplishment.

At moments of great stress, your senses are at their most acute; your mind works at a greatly accelerated pace. That's the purpose, I take it, of plebe year—not simply to test your endurance, but to show that you can function exceptionally well, as a leader must function, in concentrated misery. I began to glimpse this truth about midway through my plebe year when added to contempt for imperious upper-classmen was my burgeoning pride in not succumbing to their design to see me bilge out.

I resisted not by refusing the hazing but by letting my resentment show, and by failing to conform fully to the convention of a squared-away midshipman. I tried to balance my insolence on just the other side of intolerable, but I worked hard to expose a trace of my resis-tance. I wanted the lords of the first and second class to know my compliance was grudging and in no way implied my respect for them. I did not accept that they were entitled to my deference, as Academy custom held, for the minor accomplishment of having lived for a year or two longer than I had. Nor did I accept that the abuse they had suffered in their plebe year now gave them the moral authority to abuse me. The Academy granted them that authority, and I wanted to remain at the Academy. I did not want to break. So I suffered their tyranny to the extent necessary to avoid bilging out. But no more than that.

A civilian observer might have judged my appearance to be as neat as that of any other midshipman, but by the exacting standards of the Academy I was a slob. My roommates and I kept our personal quarters in less than acceptable order. My ritual obedience to an upperclassman's commands was perfunctory, or, at least, I hoped there was something in my manner that gave the impression that I lacked proper enthusiasm for the task. These are small rebellions, to be sure. But they were noted, and I was pleased that they were.

One second classman in particular tested my self-control, and I had a hard time suppressing the urge to respond to his assaults on my dignity in a way that would have hastened my departure from the Academy.

Henry Witt (false name) was the son of a chief petty officer. I was a captain's son. Witt never tired of reminding me that our respective stations at the Academy reversed the order of our fathers' relationship in the Navy. "My father is a chief, and yours is a captain. Isn't that strange, McCain," he observed as I discharged the commission he had given me at the start of the year. He had instructed me to enter his room every morning at five-thirty, close the window he left open at night, turn up his radiator, and perform various other small tasks to make comfortable the advent of his day.

There was in Witt's edgy hostility resentment not evident in the affected disdain upperclassmen typically held for plebes. He had a bitterness about him that apparently stemmed from an imagined injustice. Perhaps he admired his father very much, and resented the officers whom his father was obliged to obey, thinking them lesser men, and perceiving in the exercise of their authority a self-importance that demeaned his father's dignity. Maybe he had felt ill at ease his plebe year among so many officers' sons, and his insecurity had embittered him. Or he might have just been a jerk who enjoyed humiliating people.

I never learned what experience lay at the heart of Witt's contempt for me, but whatever it was, I hated its expression like hell, because I believed it implied an assumption that my grandfather and father were the kind of shallow officers who let rank determine their regard for sailors. They were not that kind of officer. They took great care with their men. They often put more faith in the judgment of their chiefs than in that of their fellow officers. They were fair judges of character, good commanders who measured their respect for a man according to his merit and not his station. And had they ever seen me locate my self-regard in class distinctions, they would have quickly expressed their disappointment in me.

Witt did not know my father or grandfather, and he should not have assumed anything about their character. Nor, for that matter, should he have assumed anything about mine. Also implicit in his scorn was an assumption that he had merited his appointment to the Academy, while I was merely the Navy's version of a fraternity legacy. Had my father and grandfather been accountants, it is unlikely I would have sought appointment to the Academy. But it was their example, and my father's expectation, that led me there, not their influence in the Navy. I had passed the same exams as Witt had.

I disliked him intensely, as did my friends. "Shitty Witty the Middy," we called him, and behind his back we ridiculed his pretensions, which was, he probably assumed, exactly how we would have reacted had he treated us decently.

The following year, Witt's last at the Academy, my friends and I, still resentful of his mistreatment of us during plebe year, seized opportunities to avenge our injured pride. The reprisals amounted to nothing serious, small inconveniences really. But we felt they balanced the book with Witt, and recovered whatever degree of our self-respect had been a casualty in the previous year's encounters with him.

After graduation, the second most anticipated event of a midshipman's last year at the Academy was the first class's training cruise. In June, eager midshipmen would embark, sometimes in barely seaworthy ships, for a six-week cruise to exotic ports. During the cruise, it was presumed, they would learn the essentials of life at sea, though often they only acquired a taste for the excesses of leave in foreign ports.

Every midshipman was assigned a cruise box to stow his gear in during the summer cruise. At graduation, the box was sent to his first duty station. My friends and I got hold of Witt's cruise box and changed the address to a fraternity at an Ivy League school, where it arrived some days later, never to be recovered by its puzzled owner.

It's hard to credit our trivial revenge on Witt as anything more than the sort of puerile mischief that kids often aggrandize as acts of justice. We took the pranks more seriously than their effects warranted, just as I accorded far more gravity to Witt's assaults on my dignity than they warranted. Had I really possessed the sturdy sense of honor I prided myself on, I would have suffered his harassment with equanimity.

I made this observation only a few years after my first encounter with Witt, when I learned he had been killed. He was serving as a flight instructor at a naval air station in the South and had flown his T-28 to the town where his father had retired from the Navy. As he flew in front of his parents' house and unwisely attempted a dangerous maneuver, he lost control of his plane and crashed while his parents watched.

Considering all the adversity that a human being confronts in a lifetime, what had passed between Witt and me was nothing. I was embarrassed that I had taken his abuse so seriously. My animosity dissolved into regret after I learned of his death. I assumed his death had been caused by an impulse to impress his father. It was an impulse a great many other midshipmen and I understood.

CHAPTER 11

Low Grease

Although my friends and I seethed at the treatment we received from upperclassmen, our main nemesis was our company officer, Captain Ben Hart (false name), a red-faced, muscular, bullnecked Marine who had played on the Academy football team some years earlier. His father was a Marine colonel, and Captain Hart had been raised to revere the protocols of command.

He was probably in his late twenties when we knew him, although he seemed much older to us. He was tightly wound, the kind of guy who never appeared relaxed. I don't think he possessed even an anemic sense of humor. It was hard to imagine him out of uniform. He was a stickler for rules and regulations and exhibited the overeagerness of a junior officer trying too hard to allay his own insecurities. Every day when his wife dropped him off at work, he bade her goodbye with a crisp salute while standing at attention.

Hart wasn't highly regarded by the other officers at the Academy, but he was fiercely determined to command respect from his subordinates. He intended to bring any miscreant in his company quickly to heel. I was one of the miscreants he had in mind.

A group of midshipmen who shared a common conceit that we were rebels against the established order had formed a small club and anointed ourselves the Bad Bunch. My roommates Frank Gamboa, Jack Dittrick, and I were the chief instigators of the group's mischief, but membership often included a few conspicuously squared-away midshipmen. Chuck Larson, one of my best friends at the Academy, was a member who joined in many of our misadventures. In the fall semester of our last year, he was selected brigade commander, the top leadership post for midshipmen, and president of our class. He went on to a spectacularly successful career in the Navy, wearing four stars as Commander in Chief, Pacific (my father's last command), and as Superintendent of the Naval Academy.

Our exploits were well known to most midshipmen, as well as to Academy authorities. We were hardly as daring as we regarded ourselves, but we managed to defy most of the rules without committing any breach of the honor code. We were in search of a good time, which led us over the Academy walls on many an evening.

Nothing serious ever occurred in our nightly revels outside the Yard. Mainly we drank a lot of beer, occasionally we got in fights, and once in a while we found girls willing to give us the time of day. However, most of our activities were proscribed by the Academy, and the fact that we were never caught in the act only intensified the anger of our superiors. It drove Captain Hart crazy.

Failing to apprehend us in the commission of a serious offense, but aware of the notoriety we enjoyed in our class, Captain Hart scrupulously called us to account for smaller infractions of Academy regulations and punished us more severely than required. By so doing, he hoped to prove to the rest of our company that we had not escaped justice for our more egregious threats to the brigade's good order and discipline. I spent the bulk of my free time being made an example of, marching many miles of extra duty for poor grades, tardiness, messy quarters, slovenly appearance, sarcasm, and multiple other violations of Academy standards.

My reputation as a rowdy and impetuous young man was not, I am embarrassed to confess, confined to Academy circles. Many upstanding residents of lovely Annapolis, witnesses to some of our more extravagant acts of insubordination, disapproved of me as thoroughly as did many Academy officials. Neither did I often find more appreciative audiences on the road.

During my second year at the Academy, I met and began dating a girl from a Main Line suburb of Philadelphia. The following summer, she called me at my parents' house on Capitol Hill, where I was spending my leave, and invited me to visit her family for a few days. I instantly accepted the invitation, grateful for a little relief from what had been a pretty monotonous leave.

On the agreed-upon day, I bade good-bye to my parents for the weekend and departed Washington's Union Station on the train to Philadelphia. Some hours later, I arrived at Philadelphia's 30th Street Station, where I was supposed to catch the next commuter train for her town. I had a few minutes to kill before my train left, so I decided to have a quick beer in the station's bar.

As I settled on a bar stool, dressed in my white midshipman's uniform, I drew the attention of several friendly, inebriated commuters, who graciously offered to buy me a beer. I welcomed the offer and their company. We chatted amiably as I, eager to be on my way, quickly drained my glass. Not wishing to appear discourteous, however, I cheerfully consented when they pressed me to accept another drink, and several others after that.

I missed the first train, and then two others, before I politely refused my new friends' entreaties to continue drinking and made my way unsteadily through the station to catch the last train of the evening that would carry me to my girlfriend's hometown. After arriving there, I hailed a cab, and finally I arrived, several hours behind schedule, at my destination.

As I ascended the long staircase that led to the front door of her house I was aware that I was probably not in ideal condition to be introduced for the first time to her family. Nevertheless, I believed I could manage the task without betraying the extent of my insobriety.

At the top of the stairs, I noticed that the front door was open. Knocking on the screen door, I was beckoned inside as my girlfriend and her mother and father rose from their chairs to greet me. When I reached for the door handle, I lost my balance and fell through the screen and into a heap on the floor of the entry hall. My startled hosts helped me to my feet, and after I spent a few moments dusting myself off and clumsily straightening my uniform, they led me into the living room.

My unorthodox entry must have aroused her father's suspicions that I was perhaps not the suitable escort for their daughter they had expected the United States Naval Academy to provide. I cannot recall much of the conversation that ensued in their warm and brightly lighted living room. Whatever I said, and the manner in which I said it, apparently confirmed my host's suspicions. After little more than a quarter hour of their hospitality, he abruptly thanked me for paying them a visit and wished me a safe journey home.

I took this gesture as an indication that my weekend visit was to be substantially abbreviated. Politely, I asked if someone would be kind enough to call me a cab, and a few minutes later I was on my way back to Philadelphia to catch a late train for Washington.

When I arrived in the early morning of the next day, my surprised mother greeted me with: "What happened? I thought you were going away for the weekend."

"Mother, I don't want to talk about it," I replied sullenly, and headed for my room, and a few hours' sleep.

I never saw the girl or her family again.

A combination of academic performance and grease grade determined a midshipman's class standing. The company officer assigned your grease grade. Hart considered my aptitude for the service to be the poorest in the company. In fact, by Hart's reckoning I possessed no aptitude at all. He never failed to give me the low grease, which, combined with my spotty academic record, always kept me some-where near the very bottom of the class standings.

I must take most of the responsibility for my poor relationship with my company officer. We were a poor match from the start: Hart was a meticulous, by-the-book junior officer who was unfailingly def-erential to his superiors, and I was an arrogant, undisciplined, insolent midshipman who felt it necessary to prove my mettle by challenging his authority. In short, I acted like a jerk, and gave Hart good cause to despise me.

The encounter that set the stage for our four years of discord occurred early in my plebe year. My roommates and I had returned to our room late one morning to find my bed (or "rack," in Academy jargon) unmade, the sheets and cover balled up in the center of the mattress. That was not the condition I had left it in when earlier that morning I had gone to my first class. I might not have been scrupulous about obeying many Academy regulations, but I usually managed to make my bed in the morning. Apparently, Captain Hart considered the manner in which I performed this morning ritual to be below Academy standards, and had stripped my bed to show his dissatisfaction.

I don't recall which disturbed me more, the fact that he had stripped my bed or simply the idea of Hart prowling around in my room when I was not there. Whatever the cause, I instantly lost my temper and what little self-restraint I possessed in those days. Dis-regarding my roommates' pleas to forget the insult, I marched im-mediately to Hart's office to confront him. I knocked on his door, and entered before he gave me leave to do so. Without any prefa-tory remark, and with only the sloppiest of salutes, I declared my indignation:

"Captain, please don't do that again. I am too busy to make my bed twice a day."

My honor avenged, I turned on my heel and left his office before I had been dismissed or reprimanded by my shocked company officer.

My behavior was inexcusable. Such impertinence was not tolerated at the Academy, least of all when the offender was nothing more than a troublemaking plebe. I should have paid a terrible price for my outburst. But Hart took no action and never said a word to me about it. I am sure it intensified his contempt for me and steeled his determination to purge me from his company. Today, when I remember this incident, I am ashamed of myself, but at the time, Hart's failure to respond immediately and forcefully to my insubordination caused me to respect him even less.

It is fair to say that Hart hated us. He had acute tunnel vision as he focused, often to the exclusion of all else, on our flawed characters. He knew what we were doing, and he was consumed by an intense desire to apprehend us in midcrime. With any luck, he would rid the Academy of our odious presence. He couldn't stand the sight of us, and believed me to be the worst of a very bad lot. At times, his loathing was comical.

Every company officer was obliged to host the members of his company in their last year, inviting them in small groups to dine at his quarters. The implicit purpose of the custom was to provide us with a little practical training in the social graces before we began our careers as officers who would be expected to know our salad fork from our soup spoon.

No doubt Hart had by this time wearied somewhat of chasing us, but his contempt for Frank, Jack, and me was still palpable. Nevertheless, he couldn't contrive a legitimate reason to refuse us our moment at the Hart dinner table. Accordingly, the three of us and our other, more respectable roommate, Keith Bunting, were invited to join Captain and Mrs. Hart for dinner on a pleasant spring evening in 1958. We anticipated the experience with a mixture of amusement and dread. We did not find very appealing the prospect of spending several hours awkwardly pretending to enjoy the company of a man who clearly despised us. But on the other hand we expected the evening to have enough entertainment value to provide material for a few jokes when it was over.

Before the event we laughed while conjuring up the image of our earnest company officer temporarily suspending his blind hatred of us to help us grasp the rudiments of gentlemanly deportment; watchfully presiding over the table; fussing over deficiencies in our table manners; noting whether we navigated the cutlery correctly and whether we paid the lady of the house the proper amount of formal deference; weakly attempting clever repartee; raising his glass aloft and booming, "Gentlemen, the Academy," or "the Corps." As it turned out, the captain had planned a considerably less ostentatious affair than we had imagined.

At the appointed hour, Captain Hart picked us up at Bancroft Hall, and drove us in silence to his home, where we presumed Mrs. Hart awaited our presence at her table. When we arrived at his quarters, we naturally headed toward the front door. Hart commanded us to stop. "No, gentleman, come around here," he ordered. He led us around the house to the backyard, where a picnic table had been set for dinner. The grill had been lighted. Hart entered his kitchen through the back door. He returned a moment later with hot dogs, beans, and a few bottles of Coca-Cola. We ate the meal in silence, quickly. No formalities were observed. No toasts to the Academy or the Corps. No strained attempts at witty dinner conversation. No Mrs. Hart. A half hour after we arrived, he loaded us back into his car and returned us to Bancroft. Quite an etiquette lesson.

To Hart's severe disappointment, I managed to remain at the Academy despite what he perceived as my seditious intentions. For all my antics, I avoided accumulating the number of demerits required to discharge a midshipman from further service. My grades were usually poor, but, as I had at Episcopal, I showed greater aptitude for English and history, subjects I enjoyed.

The eminent naval historian E. B. Potter was one of my professors, and I liked him and his classes very much. For my term paper in one of Professor Potter's classes, I chose to write about my grandfather. In preparing the research for the paper, I had written Admiral Nimitz to ask for his impressions of him.

I received a very prompt and generous response from the then elderly national hero. He wrote me that my grandfather had been a great man who had contributed significantly to our victory in the Pacific, but he devoted most his letter to a detailed account of the days he and my grandfather had sailed around the Philippines on the *Panay* as very young men at the beginning of their long and distinguished careers.

I recall the term paper only with embarrassment for its clumsy prose and poor scholarship. But I still feel pride when I remember the kind and generous regard that the old admiral lavished on my grandfather's memory, and that I faithfully recorded for Professor Potter, who had written extensively about both men and knew more about my grandfather's career than I did.

Unfortunately, the curriculum at the Academy was weighted preponderantly toward math and the sciences. Indeed, in those days, all midshipmen were obliged to major in electrical engineering. I struggled with it, possessing no special calling to the trade. Nevertheless, as I was adept at cramming for exams, and blessed with friends who did not seem to mind too much my requests for urgent tutorials, I managed to avoid complete disaster. I got by, just barely at times, but I got by.

CHAPTER 12

Fifth from the Bottom

I am sure my disdainful contemporaries and disapproving instructors believed I would become a thoroughly disreputable upperclassman were I somehow to escape expulsion during my plebe year. Most of the time, my behavior only confirmed their low regard for me. For a moment, though, I came close to confounding their expectations. That moment began when I boarded the USS *Hunt* to begin my first-class cruise to Rio de Janeiro in June of 1957.

The *Hunt* was an old destroyer. It had seen better days. It seemed to me a barely floating rust bucket that should have been scrapped years before, unfit even for mothballing. But I was ignorant, a sailor's son though I was, and I overlooked the old ship's grace and sea-worthiness. I assumed the *Hunt* was suitable only for the mean task of giving lowly midshipmen a rustic experience of life at sea. I was wrong.

We lived in cramped quarters in the aft of the ship. We kept the hatch open to cool our quarters with the breeze blowing off the Chesapeake Bay. Once the *Hunt* left the bay and entered the Atlantic, the seas grew heavier and seawater washed in through the hatch. We lived in the pooled water for several days. The rough seas sent a good number of us running for the lee side to vomit. We had restricted water hours on the cruise, which meant there was only enough water to allow us to drink from the ship's water fountains during a three-hour period every day. We took saltwater showers.

We spent a third of the cruise in the engineering plant, a grim place that seemed, to the untrained eye, a disgrace. The boilers blew scorching hot air on us while we spent long hours in misery learning the mysteries of the ship's mechanics. That the ship sailed at all seemed to us a great testament to the mechanic's mates' mastery of improvisation. It was a hell of a vessel to go to sea in for the first time.

We spent another third of the cruise learning ship's navigation, and the last third on the bridge learning how to command a ship at sea.

The skipper was Lieutenant Commander Eugene Ferrell. He seemed to accord the *Hunt* affection far out of proportion to her virtues. More surprisingly, he seemed to have some affection for me. He expressed it in eccentric ways, but I sensed his respect for me was greater than I had lately been accustomed to receiving from officers. I appreciated it, and I liked him a lot.

I spent much of the cruise on the bridge, where the skipper would order me to take the conn. There is a real mental challenge to running a ship of that size, and I had little practical experience in the job. But I truly enjoyed it. I made more than a few mistakes, and every time I screwed up, the skipper would explode, letting loose an impressive blast of profane derision.

"Dammit, McCain, you useless bastard. Give up the conn right now. Get the hell off my bridge. I mean it, goddammit. I won't have a worthless s.o.b. at the helm of my ship. You've really screwed up this time, McCain. Get the hell out of here!"

As I began to skulk off the bridge, he would call me back. "Hold on a second. Come on back here, mister. Get over here and take the conn." And then he would begin, more calmly, to explain what I had done wrong and how the task was done properly. We would go along pleasantly until I committed my next unpardonable error, when he would unleash another string of salty oaths in despair over my unfitness for the service, only to beckon me back for a last chance to prove myself worthy of his fine ship.

It was a wonderful time. I enjoyed the whole experience. As I detected in Ferrell's outbursts his sense that I showed some promise, I worked hard not to disappoint him, and I learned the job passably well. I was rarely off his bridge for much of the cruise. No other midshipman on the *Hunt* was so privileged.

Inspired by the experience, I began to consider becoming an officer in the surface Navy, with the goal of someday commanding a destroyer, instead of following my grandfather into naval aviation. I told Ferrell of my intentions, and he seemed pleased. Fine gentleman that he is, he never rebuked me after I abandoned my briefly held aspirations for a destroyer command and returned to my original plan to become an aviator. Many years later, he wrote me, and recalled a chance encounter we had sometime in the early sixties. "I was surprised but pleased to see that you were wearing two stripes and a pair of gold wings. Your grandfather would have been very proud of you."

Years later, while serving as a flight instructor in Meridian, Mississippi, I realized that I had adopted, unintentionally, Lieutenant Commander Ferrell's idiosyncratic instruction technique. I took pride in the fact.

When a Navy ship at sea needs to refuel or take on supplies and mail, it must come alongside and tie up to a refueling or replenishing ship while both vessels are under way. The maneuver is difficult to execute even in the calmest seas. Most skippers attempt it cautiously, bringing their ship alongside the approaching vessel very slowly.

But the most experienced ship handlers are bolder, and pride themselves on their more daring form. They come alongside at two-thirds or full speed, much faster than the other ship. At precisely the right moment they throw the engines in reverse, and then ahead again at one-third speed. It's a spectacular thing to see when it's done right. An approximate image of the maneuver is a car traveling at sixty miles an hour as it approaches a parallel parking space; the driver slams on the brakes and pulls cleanly, without an inch to spare, into the spot.

Eugene Ferrell was a gifted ship handler, and he never considered coming alongside another ship in any other fashion, unless, of course, a green midshipman had the conn. I had watched him perform the task several times, and had admired his serene composure as he confidently gave the orders that brought the rushing *Hunt* abruptly but gracefully into place, moving at exactly the same speed as her sister ship. A seaman would fire a gun that shot a line to our bow. Soon the two ships, several lines now holding them in harness, would sail the ocean together for a time, never touching, but in perfect unison. It was a grand sight to behold.

One beautiful afternoon, the flagship of the destroyer division to which the *Hunt* was attached, flying the ensign of the commanding admiral, approached us for the purpose of replenishing the *Hunt*'s depleted stores. Lieutenant Commander Ferrell gave me the conn, and without a trace of apprehension, bade me bring her alongside the admiral's flagship.

Ferrell told me to bring her up slowly, but offered no rebuke when I gave the order "All engines ahead two-thirds." At precisely the right moment, I ordered, "All engines back full." A few moments later, again well timed, I ordered, "All engines ahead one-third." Thrillingly and to my great relief, the *Hunt* slipped into place so gracefully that any observer would have thought the skipper himself, master ship handler that he was, had the conn.

Ferrell was proud of me, and I was much indebted to him. He had given me his trust, and I had had the good fortune to avoid letting him down. After the two ships were tied up, he sent a message to the admiral. "Midshipman McCain has the conn." The impressed admiral sent a message to the Superintendent of the Naval Academy, informing him of my accomplishment.

Many years later I learned that Ferrell had been a student and admirer of my father's. Perhaps that explains his kindness toward me. Whatever the reason for the care he took with me, I was grateful for it. His confidence in me gave me more confidence in myself, and greater assurance that I belonged at sea than I had ever experienced in the rigid, disapproving world of the Academy. Eugene Ferrell was the man who taught me the craft of my father and grandfather. He gave me cause to love the work that they had loved. Debts such as that you incur for life. I sailed for Rio de Janeiro a more contented young man than I had ever been before.

Liberty in Rio. My imagination could not have embellished the good time we made of our nine days in port, indulging in the vices sailors are infamous for, as if we had been at sea for months instead of weeks. After some excessive drinking, nightclubbing, and little or no sleep, I had exhausted my appetite for the joys of liberty and intended to return to ship. Chuck Larson persuaded me to accompany him to a party at a grand house on Sugarloaf Mountain. There I met and began a romance with a Brazilian fashion model, and gloried in the envy of my friends.

We danced on the terrace overlooking the bay until one o'clock in the morning, when I felt her cheek was moist.

"What's the matter?" I asked.

"I'll never see you again," she replied.

I told her that we would remain in town for eight more days, and that I would gladly spend as much time in her company as she would grant me. But she rebutted my every assurance with "No, I can never see you again."

"Are you engaged?"

"No."

"Look, I'm going to be down at the gate of the shipyard at one o'clock tomorrow afternoon. I'll be there, and I want you to be there, too."

She said nothing in reply, and an hour later she left the party with her aunt, who served as her constant companion and chaperone.

The next afternoon, I left the ship at about twelve-thirty and waited for her at the place I had designated. An hour passed, and she had not arrived. Another hour and still she had not appeared. An hour after that, I forlornly prepared to abandon all hope. Just as I was preparing to return to the ship in a state of deep despondency, she pulled up in a Mercedes with gull-wing doors. She honked the horn, and I jumped in, ecstatic.

I spent every free moment with her for the rest of my stay in Rio. She was very beautiful, stylish, and gracious—common attributes in her wealthy and socially prominent family. She took me to dinners and receptions where I toasted my extraordinary good fortune in the company of cabinet members, generals and admirals, wealthy aristocrats, and, on one occasion, the president of Brazil.

We spent my last evening on liberty together. She drove me to my ship the next morning. I emerged from under the open gull-wing door and kissed her to a chorus of rowdy cheers from my shipmates. I accepted their approval with an affected sheepish humility.

When we returned to Annapolis, I had a few weeks' leave, which I used to fly right back to Rio to continue my storybook romance. By the following Christmas, the distance between us, and our youthful impatience and short attention spans, brought an end to our affair. But it resides in my memory, embellished with age, of course, among the happier experiences of my life.

On the return cruise we made port in the Virgin Islands and at Guantanamo Bay, Cuba, where we received further instruction in the rituals of shore leave. Guantanamo in those pre-Castro days was a wild place. Everyone went ashore and headed immediately for huge tents that had been set up on the base as temporary bars, where great quantities of strong Cuban beer and an even more potent rum punch were served to anyone who professed a thirst and could afford a nickel a drink.

The officers' club boasted the same menu in slightly more comfortable surroundings. We drank there for a good while, serenaded by a Pat Boone record. A music lover had evidently come ashore and filled the O club's jukebox with as many nickels as he could scrounge, choosing but one selection, "Love Letters in the Sand," which played over and over again. Returning to the ship, my friends and I were delighted to discover that the throng of sailors and Marines crowding the landing had taken a dislike to one another and had begun fighting. The shore patrol arrived and waded into the riot of whites and khaki vainly trying to separate the opposing forces. It was bedlam. We loved it.

On the cruise back to Annapolis I returned to my place on the bridge and happily resumed my one-on-one tutorial in the elements of expert ship handling. Two officers who were attached to the Academy but were not officers in my company had been assigned to the cruise to evaluate our performance. They gave me the best marks, reporting that I had shown a very high aptitude for the service. I had the high grease.

Captain Hart was astonished. He was convinced there had been a terrible error, perhaps a case of mistaken identity. First-class cruise had turned out to be the best time of my young life.

Inspired by my success on the USS *Hunt*, I resolved to make something of myself in my last year at the Academy. I studied hard and maintained a respectful attitude toward my superiors. I set up a tutoring system for plebes who were struggling academically. I managed the battalion boxing team, which won the brigade championship. My grades were improving, and I stayed well out of trouble. I had become, for a brief time, a squared-away midshipman whom any company officer could be proud of—any company officer save mine.

In January, I went to Captain Hart's office to receive my grease grade, which I was confident would elevate me for the first time from the bottom regions of the class standings where I had dwelled in infamy for three years. Hart began by noting my improved behavior. "Keep this up, son, and you'll have something to be proud of." When I asked where he had placed me in the company, he mumbled an answer that I couldn't make out.

"Where, sir?"

"At the bottom," he whispered.

"Where?"

"At the bottom."

Rising from my chair, I glared at Hart, who remained seated. "You can expect nothing more from me, Captain," I said as I left his office, slamming the door so hard behind me that I thought its opaque glass window would break.

Any other officer would have shouted at me, "Get back in here and sit down, mister! Where do you get off barking at me like that?" Not Captain Hart. He never spoke of the interview. He knew he had wronged me. For the first time, I had wanted something from him, had felt I'd earned it. And he, dogged to the end, had gotten his revenge.

True to my word, I returned to the habits of my first three years, accumulating demerits by the dozen, waiting out, indifferently, my last few months at the Academy.

A month after my interview with Hart, my room was chosen for a surprise inspection. It didn't pass. Only one roommate is responsible for keeping the room in some semblance of order, the job rotating among four roommates on a monthly basis. The surprise inspection occurred on my watch.

"Room in gross disorder" was the charge. The customary punishment for such an offense was fifteen demerits and three hours of extra duty. I received seventy-five demerits. A midshipman was allowed only 125 demerits his last year. Any more and he bilged out. I was already carrying forty demerits when the inspector arrived. It was a practical impossibility to last more than three months without collecting another ten. The slightest mistake, the most insignificant oversight, would get me kicked out in the last few weeks before graduation. My fate, I thought, was sealed.

I telephoned my parents. My father was at sea, so I informed my mother that I was coming home. I explained the circumstances, and that my expulsion was imminent. I might as well come home now, I argued, and not waste a few days or weeks waiting for the ax to fall.

My mother wisely cautioned me not to make an irrevocable decision until I had an opportunity to talk to my father. In the meantime, she advised me to talk things over with my wrestling coach, Ray Schwartz, a friend of my parents and a good man. Mr. Schwartz commiserated with me about my difficult predicament, and agreed that I had been punished excessively for a minor infraction. But he, too, advised me to withhold any decision until I had discussed the situation with my father. A day or two later, I received a summons from the Commandant of the Naval Academy, Captain Shin. My mother had called him.

"What's this I hear about you leaving?" he asked.

"I have too many demerits, sir," I replied.

"Why?"

"Because I have been punished unfairly, sir."

I then explained how the sentence had far exceeded the prescribed penalty, and that I thought the action was unjust. My complaint seemed only to irritate him. He said I was spoiled, a charge that I greatly resented.

"Whatever you say, sir, but it's still not fair."

He leveled a scornful gaze at me and told me to leave.

The commandant was neither the first nor the last person to accuse me of being spoiled, implying that my parents had greased my way in the world. Witt had been the first to do so when he derided me for being a captain's son. Later in my career, as I rose through the ranks, some would attribute my advance to my admiral father's benefaction. I suppose it is an accusation that many children of successful parents learn to ignore. I never did, however. I grew red-faced and angry every time some know-it-all told me how easy a life my father had made for me. The life my father led me to has been a richly rewarding one, and I am grateful to him for it. But "easy" is not the first adjective that comes to mind when describing it.

My father was only a captain when I was at the Naval Academy, a rank that surely didn't grant him the influence to compensate for my shortcomings. Later in my life, when my father wore stars on his shoulder, he would, indeed, influence my career, but in ways my detractors did not appreciate. He had met the standard his father had set. It was my obligation and my privilege to try to uphold it.

A week or two after Captain Shin instructed me to leave his presence, I was informed that the punishment for my disordered room had been reduced to thirty demerits and seven days of confinement. I was relieved to comply with the order.

A month or so after the room inspection incident, I had yet another close brush with disaster. The ever vigilant Captain Hart believed he had at last discovered a violation that would result in my swift expulsion from the Academy.

In September of my last year, my roommates and I, along with four roommates in the room next to ours and two other midshipmen on our floor, chipped in to buy a television set. In those days, Academy regulations enjoined midshipmen from keeping electrical appliances of any kind in their rooms. Even hot plates were considered contraband. I remember a few midshipmen would take back to their rooms bread and cheese from the mess hall after the evening meal, and sell cheese sandwiches to the rest of us. It was a thriving industry, much appreciated by me and every other hungry midshipman who was denied the convenience of devices to store or prepare food.

Mindful of but undeterred by the regulation, our small syndicate had decided we would risk the wrath of our superiors for the pleasure of watching the Friday-night fights on our own television. We each pitched in ten dollars and bought a used black-and-white television with a twelve-inch screen. We kept the set hidden in a crawl space in our room, located behind a wooden panel. The panel could be easily removed by hand, and we would bring the set out to watch the fights on Friday, *Maverick* on Sunday, and other popular television programs of the time.

We lived in Bancroft Hall, the Academy's only dormitory, which at the time had not been changed in any of its particulars since the turn of the century. The floors in Bancroft Hall were referred to, in ship nomenclature, as decks. We lived on the top deck, the fourth. We soon drew considerable numbers of top-deck residents to our room to join our forbidden television viewing. On Friday nights, it was standing room only.

In every hall of every deck, a third-year midshipman served as the mate of the deck. The mate's job was to receive and deliver messages to the midshipmen in residence there and, generally, to stand as a sentinel for his part of the deck to ensure that nothing untoward happened on his watch. The mate on our hall stood at a podium directly across the hall from my room. We pressed him into service as our lookout on evenings when we were crowded around our television set. He kept an eye out for company officers who would have loved to discover our blatant disobedience and rapped a warning on my door when one approached.

As upperclassmen, we no longer had to worry about being disciplined or harassed by other midshipmen as we had been during our plebe year. We also took comfort in knowing that our indiscretions would be kept confidential within the brigade and not reported to unsuspecting officers. The most sacrosanct principle governing a midshipman's behavior was the unwritten rule "Never bilge a classmate," which required midshipmen to overlook any violation of the rules by a fellow midshipman short of honor code violations.

Brigade discipline was supervised by four authorities, the most senior being the officer of the watch, an office that was rotated monthly among company officers. Those midshipmen with the highest grease in the brigade rotated daily as the midshipman of the watch, while a group of the more promising plebes served as their assistants.

My pal Chuck Larson, whose exemplary scholastic record and obvious aptitude for command had won him the highest office a plebe could hold, brigade commander, was serving as the midshipman of the watch. Academy officials would have been disappointed to discover their prized midshipman among those gathered around the television in my room to watch a boxing match, shirking the duties of his office to enjoy a few minutes of illicit fun with some of the more disreputable midshipmen at the Academy.

In the middle of our viewing, the mate of the deck rapped on my door to warn us that the officer of the watch was approaching. We quickly returned the television set to its hiding place and stuffed the midshipman of the watch, dressed in his formal blue uniform and wearing his sword, along with his startled plebe, into my closet. The rest of us opened up textbooks and earnestly affected the appearance of dutiful midshipmen gathered together in a study group. Fortunately, the officer never bothered to enter our room. Had he done so, our atypical studiousness surely would have aroused his suspicion.

A few days later, when I returned to my room after classes had ended for the day, I found a message on my desk ordering me to report to Captain Hart. Hart's office was five doors down from my room. Responding to my summons, I knocked on his door, entered, stood at attention, and announced myself: "Midshipman McCain, First Class, sir."

Sitting there with a look of considerable satisfaction, Hart allowed himself a rare smile as he threw a Form 2 across his desk to me and inquired, "Do you want to sign this now?" A Form 2 was the standard notification that a midshipman had been put on report. A midshipman was required to sign the form acknowledging his offense.

I picked up the form and read the line where the offense was reported: "electrical equipment, unauthorized use of," and on the line below, "television set."

While all the midshipmen on the fourth deck were at class, Hart had taken the opportunity to closely inspect our quarters. So thorough was the inspection that Hart had entered the rooms' crawl spaces, which adjoined each other. When he reached our room and discovered the contraband hidden in our crawl space, he must have silently exulted in his good fortune, believing that the day of judgment was finally at hand for the sorriest midshipman in his company.

The penalty for the offense was thirty demerits and seven days' confinement. The demerits I had already accumulated took me perilously close to the limit, and again I faced certain expulsion. I thought over my situation for a moment while Hart waited contentedly for my response.

"Sir, this isn't necessarily mine," I finally replied.

"What do you mean?" he asked.

"The television, it isn't necessarily mine."

"Whose is it?" the now less content and incredulous Captain Hart responded.

"I'll let you know in a very short time."

A puzzled look overtook the captain's smile, and he dismissed me with an order to report back quickly with an answer.

I returned to my room and called the television's ten owners together. I explained the situation, and that I had to bring Hart an answer right away. "Only one of us is going to get the demerits," I said, "and we have to choose who, right now." We settled the question as we always settled things in those days, with a "shake around." Over my objection, my friends, aware of my perilous situation at the Academy, excused me from participating.

In unison, each man hit his right fist three times into the palm of his other hand. On the third strike, each stuck out some of the fingers of his right hand. We then counted off the sum of the nine men's extended fingers, one number per man, with the last number falling on the man who would confess ownership of the television. As luck and fate would have it, the man turned out to be Henry Vargo.

Henry Vargo was a model midshipman. Studious, disciplined, respectful, Henry hardly ever bothered to watch the television. He had joined in its purchase only to help us out, to be one of the guys. Henry did not possess very many demerits, so the punishment he was about to receive wouldn't pose much of a problem for him. As added compensation, we magnanimously said that Hart would have to give the television back at the end of the year and Henry could keep it.

Smiling with satisfaction and relief, I returned to Hart's office to reveal the culprit.

"Midshipman McCain, First Class, sir."

"Well?"

"Sir, the television set belongs to Midshipman Vargo."

"Midshipman Vargo!" he bellowed in disbelief.

"Yes, sir, Midshipman Vargo."

Fighting to stop from smiling, I watched Hart's face flush red with anger. Finally, he dismissed me—"Get out of here, McCain."

I left him and walked back to my room, much relieved to have evaded, for the last time, Hart's wrath and his four-year quest to bring me to justice.

———

A few months later I sat amid a sea of navy whites, fifth from the bottom of my class, listening to President Eisenhower confer our degrees, exhort us to noble service on behalf of the Republic, and commission me an ensign in the United States Navy.

Eisenhower's remarks were not particularly memorable, owing to a combination of his flat delivery and our impatience to begin celebrating our liberation. Although he wasn't much of a speaker, we all admired the President. I remember wishing at one point during commencement that my dismal performance at the Academy had earned me an even lower place in the class standings.

In those days, only the first one hundred graduates in the class were called to the dais to receive their diplomas from the President. Graduation was conferred on the rest of us by company. John Poindexter graduated first in our class, an honor he had well earned. He walked proudly to the podium to receive his diploma and a handshake from the President of the United States, which the President bestowed on him with a brief "Well done and congratulations."

The midshipman who graduates last in his class is affectionately called the anchorman. When the anchorman's company was called, he was cheered by the whole brigade and hoisted onto the shoulders of his friends. Eisenhower motioned him up to the dais, and to the crowd's loud approval personally handed him his diploma; both President and anchorman smiling broadly as the President patted him on the back and chatted with him for a few minutes. I thought it a fine gesture from a man who understood our traditions.

I was proud to graduate from the Naval Academy. But at that moment, relief was the emotion I felt most keenly. I had already been accepted for flight training in Pensacola. In those days, all you had to do was pass the physical to qualify for flight training, and I was eager to embark on the life of a carefree naval aviator.

My orders left me enough time to take an extended holiday in Europe with Jack, Frank, and another classmate, Jim Higgins. We bummed a ride to Spain on a military aircraft from Dover Air Force Base in Delaware. We spent several enjoyable days in Madrid, then boarded a train for Paris. Four days after we arrived, my friends left Paris for Copenhagen and the World's Fair. I remained behind, waiting to meet my new girlfriend, the daughter of a tobacco magnate from Winston-Salem, North Carolina. We were in Paris during the summer of de Gaulle.

At the time, France was fighting a war to hold on to its Algerian colony, and its conspicuous lack of military success had caused the collapse of the French Fourth Republic. Terrorist bombings and other unpleasantness associated with the war had driven many Parisians out of the city to seek refuge in the French countryside. We had the city to ourselves, and we enjoyed it immensely.

Near the end of our stay, we stood in a throng of cheering Parisians along the Champs Elysées as two long, noisy lines of motorcycle policemen led the way to the Arc de Triomphe for de Gaulle's motorcade. The general and now president of the infant Fifth Republic stood erect in the backseat of his convertible limousine nodding at the overwrought crowds as they chanted, "Algerie Française, Algerie Française."

Four years after returning to power, and despite his solemn promise that Algeria would be forever French, de Gaulle granted the colony's independence. Nevertheless, he cut a hell of a figure that day, standing there so impassive and noble-looking while his nation's adoration washed over him. I was a kid at the time, and the general's grandeur made a great impression on me. In truth, I remain just as impressed four decades later.

I suppose to most people who knew me at Annapolis, my entire career at the Naval Academy is aptly summarized by the anecdotes I have recorded here. Most of my reminiscences feature the frivolous escapades with which I once established my reputation as a rash and prideful nonconformist.

In truth, I was less exceptional than I had imagined myself to be. Every class has its members who aspire to prominence by unconventional means. My father and grandfather had enjoyed only slightly less tarnished reputations at the Academy. My father, perhaps mindful of his own performance, rarely chastised me for falling well short of an exemplary midshipman's standards. In fact, I don't recall the subject of my record at the Academy ever being extensively discussed by either of my parents.

There was one occasion when my father registered his disapproval over my conduct at the Academy. One evening in our second year, my roommates and I were in the middle of a water balloon fight, adding to our room's usual disarray. We suspended our activity when someone knocked on the door. Frank opened the door to find an officer facing him with a disdainful look on his face as he appraised our room's unacceptable condition and the four of us standing in our skivvies soaking wet. My roommates greeted our unexpected guest by briskly standing at attention. I greeted him by saying, somewhat quizzically, "Dad?"

After an awkward second or two, he ordered, "As you were,

gentlemen," and as my roommates began to exhale, he added, "This room is in gross disorder. John, meet me downstairs in five minutes." With that, he turned on his heels and left. I met him less than five minutes later, and he proceeded to lecture me, observing, "You're in too much trouble here, Johnny, to be asking for any more." That single incident is the only time I can remember my father upbraiding me for my dismal performance as a midshipman.

My behavior was not something that particularly worried my father. I believe he assumed that, like him, I would be absorbed into the traditions of the place whether I wished to or not, and that when the time arrived for me to face a real test of character, I would not disappoint him. He had seen many an officer who enjoyed the reputation of a rake—indeed, he had been one himself—rise to the occasion in the most dire situations, and exhibit courage and resourcefulness that confounded earlier detractors. He expected no less from me.

Even as I spent my years as a junior officer in the same profligate manner I had spent my Academy years, I cannot recall his severely rebuking me. America had fought two wars during his career, and he was certain there would soon be another one. He knew I would fight, and I think he trusted me to do my duty when my moment arrived. I don't know if I deserved his trust, but I am proud to have had it.

If I had ignored the less important conventions of the Academy, I was careful not to defame its more compelling traditions: the veneration of courage and resilience; the honor code that simply assumed your fidelity to its principles; the homage paid to men who had sacrificed greatly for their country; the expectation that you, too, would prove worthy of your country's trust.

Appearances to the contrary, it was never my intention to mock a revered culture that expected better of me. Like any other midshipman, I had wanted to prove my mettle to my contemporaries, and to the institution that figured so prominently in my family history. My idiosyncratic methods, if you can call them that, amounted to little more than imaginative expressions of the truculence I had used at other schools and in other circumstances to fend off what I had identified, often wrongly, as attacks upon my dignity.

The Academy, despite the irritating customs of plebe year and the encumbrances it placed on the individualist, was not interested in degrading my dignity. On the contrary, it had a more expansive conception of human dignity than I possessed when I arrived at its gates. The most important lesson I learned there was that to sustain my self-respect for a lifetime it would be necessary for me to have the honor of serving something greater than my self-interest.

When I left the Academy, I was not even aware I had learned that lesson. In a later crisis, I would suffer a genuine and ruthless attack on my dignity, an attack that, unlike the affronts I had exaggerated as a boy, left me desperate and uncertain. It was then I would recall, awakened by the example of men who shared my circumstances, the lesson that the Naval Academy in its antique way had labored to impress upon me. It changed my life forever.

— CHAPTER 13 —

Navy Flyer

My early years as a naval officer were an even more colorful extension of my rowdy days at the Academy. At flight school in Pensacola, and then at advanced flight training with my pal Chuck Larson in Corpus Christi, Texas, I did not enjoy the reputation of a serious pilot or an up-and-coming junior officer.

I liked to fly, but not much more than I liked to have a good time. In fact, I enjoyed the off-duty life of a Navy flyer more than I enjoyed the actual flying. I drove a Corvette, dated a lot, spent all my free hours at bars and beach parties, and generally misused my good health and youth.

At Pensacola, I spent much of my off-duty time at the legendary bar Trader John's. On Friday and Saturday nights, after happy hour at the officers' club had ended, almost every unmarried aviator in Pensacola headed for Trader John's. It was a vast, cavernous place that was packed shoulder to shoulder on the weekends, as was the back room where local girls, trained as exotic dancers, entertained rowdy crowds of aviators. Pensacola has since designated the place a historic landmark in recognition of its former infamy when it was the scene of some of the wildest revelry the state of Florida had ever experienced.

After graduation from the Academy, our class was divided between those newly commissioned ensigns who intended to extend their carefree bachelorhood and those who had left the commencement ceremony to immediately enter the blessed state of matrimony. A good number of my classmates, including several of my closest friends, had married their girlfriends before taking up their first duty assignment, and this difference in our married status unfortunately created a social division between us.

At Pensacola, married ensigns and their wives mostly socialized together. Married couples had to rent homes off base and had less disposable income than their unmarried friends. I and the other residents of the base's bachelor officers' quarters, with more money to waste and mindful that the amusements we sought were likely to offend the sensibilities of our married friends' respectable young wives, kept largely to ourselves.

Walt Ryan was one of my closest friends from the Academy, a charter member of the Bad Bunch. He, too, had been accepted into pilot training at Pensacola, but because he had married after graduation, I saw less of him than I would have preferred. His wife, Sarah, was a lovely, well-mannered girl whom I liked very much. I saw them both occasionally, and always enjoyed their company, but on most weekends I kept less civilized company.

At some point during my time at flight school, I had begun dating a local girl whom I had met at Trader John's. She made her living there, under the name Marie, the Flame of Florida. She was a remarkably attractive girl with a great sense of humor, and I was quite taken with her. Since her work kept her busy on Friday and Saturday nights, our dates occurred on Sunday evenings when the bar was closed.

Most Sundays we went to the movies and had a nice dinner afterward. One Sunday, however, on our way downtown we passed Walt Ryan's house, where I recognized the cars of several other married friends. I impulsively decided to pull over and join the party uninvited, telling Marie that I wanted to introduce her to some of my friends. Always a good sport, Marie agreed to my suggestion.

Most of my friends' wives were from privileged families and had been educated at distinguished Eastern schools. Marie, the Flame of Florida, had a more interesting biography, more in the "graduated from the school of hard knocks" genre. The young wives she was about to meet would be decorously attired and unfailingly genteel. Marie was dressed somewhat flamboyantly that evening, as was her custom.

Walt and Sarah greeted our surprise visit with their usual graciousness, inviting us in without too much hesitation, offering us drinks, and introducing us to the six or so other couples gathered in their home. After the introductions and a few inane pleasantries were exchanged, the conversation seemed to become a little awkward, at times lapsing into long silences.

Marie sensed that the young wives, while certainly not rude to her, were less than entirely at ease in her presence. So she sat silent, not wishing to impose on anyone or intrude in the conversations going on around her. After a while, she must have become a little bored. So, quietly, she reached into her purse, withdrew a switchblade, popped open the blade, and, with a look of complete indifference, began to clean her fingernails.

My startled hosts and their guests stared at her with looks that ranged between disbelief and alarm. Marie seemed not to notice, and concentrated on her task. A short time later, recognizing that our presence had perhaps subdued the party, I thanked our hosts for their hospitality, bid good-bye to the others, and took my worldly, lovely Flame of Florida to dinner.

I crashed a plane in Corpus Christi Bay one Saturday morning. The engine quit while I was practicing landings. Knocked unconscious when my plane hit the water, I came to as the plane settled on the bottom of the bay. I barely managed to get the canopy open and swim to the surface. After X rays and a brief examination determined I had not suffered any serious injury, I returned to the quarters Larson and I shared. I took a few painkillers and hit the sack to rest my aching back for a few hours.

My father learned of the accident immediately and asked a friend, the admiral in charge of advanced flight training, to check on me. Chuck Larson and I had adjoining rooms in the bachelor officers' quarters. We had moved both our beds into the same room and used the second room to entertain in. The room was, of course, in a constant state of "gross disorder."

When the admiral contacted by my father arrived, I was asleep and Chuck was shaving. He pounded on the door while Chuck, unaware that a distinguished visitor was at our door, shouted at him to "hold his horses." He opened the door to our guest, snapped a salute, and stood nervously while the admiral surveyed the wreckage that was our quarters. Groggily, I thanked the admiral for his concern. Neither he nor my father needed to have bothered. I was out carousing, injured back and all, later that evening.

I began to worry a little about my career during my deployments on several Mediterranean cruises in the early sixties. I flew A-1 Skyraiders in two different squadrons on carriers based in Norfolk, Virginia: on the USS *Intrepid* for two and a half cruises in the Mediterranean; and on the nuclear-powered USS *Enterprise* for one short and one long Mediterranean cruise.

The A-1 was an old, propeller-driven plane; it was a very reliable aircraft and a lot of fun to fly. We would sometimes take them on twelve-hour flights that were quite enjoyable, flying low, and admiring the changes of scenery over the long distances we flew.

The pilots in the squadrons were a close-knit group. We enjoyed flying together, as well as one another's company while on shore leave in Europe. I found plenty of time to revel in the fun that European ports offered a young, single flyer; spending holidays on Capri, risking my wages in the casinos of Monte Carlo. However, by my second cruise on the *Intrepid*, I had begun to aspire to a reputation for more commendable achievements than long nights of drinking and gambling. I had started to feel a need to move on, a natural impulse for me, born of the migrant's life I had led since birth.

Like my grandfather and father, I loved life at sea, and I loved flying off carriers. No other experience in my life so closely approximated the exploits of the brash, daring heroes who had captivated my schoolboy's imagination during those long afternoons in my grandmother's house. Ever since reading about the storied world of men at arms, I had longed for such a life. The Navy, especially with a war on, offered the quickest route to adventure if I could manage to avoid committing some career-ending mistake.

Once, when I thought I was about to flunk out of the Academy, I had contemplated joining the French Foreign Legion. I wrote to an address in New Orleans for information about how to join the legendary force. I received a nice brochure. While reading it, I discovered that the Legion required nine years of obligated service. I decided to try to stick it out in the Navy. Now I accepted that any adventure that might come my way would almost surely be found while I wore a Navy uniform. The Navy was stuck with me, and I with it, and I decided to make the best of my circumstances.

Remembering the satisfaction of my days on Commander Ferrell's bridge, I volunteered for bridge watches and qualified as an "officer of the deck under way," proving capable of commanding a carrier at sea. Already enjoying a reputation for large living as colorful as that of my legendary forebears, I began to give my superiors some reason to think I might eventually prove myself, if not as gifted an officer as my father and grandfather, perhaps competent enough not to squander my legacy.

As I was one of the few bachelors in my squadron, I volunteered on three occasions to spend my leave attending escape and evasion school to prepare myself for the possibility of being shot down in combat. I also volunteered because I found the course to be a pretty good time.

One course took place during a large Army exercise in Bavaria, Germany. A number of other pilots and I were released at night in the middle of the Black Forest. We wore our flight suits and were allowed only those belongings that a pilot would normally possess when he ejected during a combat mission, which amounted to a few C rations.

We were given a map and instructed to find our way, undetected, to a designated safe area. Soldiers participating in the exercise were ordered to hunt us down. The Army also broadcast over the radio a reward offer to any German civilians who found us and reported our whereabouts to the authorities. An Air Force pilot and I teamed up and began a careful trek through woods filled with eager soldiers.

It took five days to reach the safe area. There was plenty of water around, and although we were hungry, we enjoyed ourselves. The forest was beautiful, and the summer weather was pleasant. Several mornings we awoke under the shelter of a large fir tree to the sound of German families out for an early-morning stroll through the woods (Germans are great walkers). We hustled quickly and quietly away lest some lucky, unsuspecting German seize the opportunity to add to the family's wealth.

My Air Force friend and I were the only pilots to avoid capture and reach our designation. When we arrived, Special Forces soldiers picked us up and took us to a lovely inn on a lake in a small German village called Unterdeisen, where we remained until the exercise was completed two days later. The inn was run by a former Luftwaffe pilot, who took us flying in glider planes. We whiled away the rest of the time drinking beer, admiring the scenery, and watching deer come down to the lake to drink.

As we had not been captured (nor was I captured during two other similar exercises I participated in), we were not subjected to simulated interrogations or any other unpleasantness associated with being captured in war. When the exercise was over, we were taken to

Special Forces headquarters in Bad Tolz, where we were debriefed and attended lectures and films about what we might expect were we ever to have the bad luck to be prisoners of war.

In those days, the military emphasized escape and evasion more than it dwelled on life in a prison camp. However, an Air Force major who had been a POW in Korea was brought in to brief us on his experiences, and I shared quarters with him for the two days I remained at Bad Tolz. He told us that while he had not experienced a great deal of torture as a POW, American prisoners in Korea had been kept isolated, and on near-starvation rations.

What I remember most from my conversations with him was my astonishment at learning that this congenial, well-adjusted former POW had been kept in solitary confinement. I commended him for his physical and mental courage, and remarked that I seriously doubted I could have survived such a long stretch in solitary. He told me I would be surprised what suffering a man could endure when he had no alternative.

While at Bad Tolz, I and the pilot I had escaped and evaded with met two college girls from the States who were spending the summer in Europe. Since the *Intrepid* wasn't due in port for another ten days, we joined them on their drive through southern Germany to Italy, ending our brief time as fugitives with a very pleasant holiday. There was little we had experienced during our Bavarian excursion that approximated the experiences of pilots who were hunted and captured in a real war.

There were occasional setbacks in my efforts to round out my Navy profile. My reputation was certainly not enhanced when I knocked down some power lines while flying too low over southern Spain. My daredevil clowning had cut off electricity to a great many Spanish homes and created a small international incident.

While I was stationed at Norfolk during my service on the *Intrepid* and *Enterprise,* a few pilots in my squadron and I lived in Virginia Beach in a beach house known far and wide in the Navy as the infamous "House on 37th Street." We enjoyed a reputation for hosting the most raucous and longest beach parties of any squadron in the Navy. On the whole, however, I made steady, if slow, progress toward becoming a respectable officer.

In October 1962, I was just returning to home port at Norfolk after completing a Mediterranean deployment aboard the *Enterprise.* The air wing of a carrier always leaves the ship just before she comes into home port. My squadron had flown off the *Enterprise* and returned to Oceana Naval Air Station while the ship put in at Norfolk. While at Oceana we would train out of land bases until the *Enterprise*'s next deployment.

A few days after our return, we unexpectedly received orders to fly our planes back to the carrier. Our superiors explained the unusual order by informing us that a hurricane was headed our way. The explanation only aroused our curiosity further, since none of us had heard any forecast of an approaching storm, nor did putting to sea strike us as a reasonable course of evasion.

Nevertheless, we flew all our planes back to the carrier within twenty-four hours and headed out to sea. In addition to our A-1s, the *Enterprise* carried long-range attack planes, which typically had a hard time managing carrier takeoffs and landings. We embarked on our mysterious deployment without them.

As the *Enterprise* passed Cherry Point, Virginia, a Marine squadron of A-4s approached and attempted to land. I watched the scene from up in the air tower. Several of the Marine pilots experienced considerable difficulty trying to land. Our air boss turned to a representative of the Marine squadron and said we didn't have time to wait for all their planes to land; some of them would have to return to their base. The Marine replied that his planes were already below bingo fuel, which meant that they did not have sufficient fuel to return to base and had to land on the *Enterprise*.

I was quite puzzled by the apparent urgency of our mission— we'd been hustled back in one day, leaving some of our planes behind;

the Marine squadron had been ordered to join us with only enough fuel to land or ditch. The mystery was solved a short while later when all pilots were assembled in the *Enterprise*'s ready room to listen to a broadcast of President Kennedy informing the nation that the Soviets were basing nuclear missiles in Cuba.

The *Enterprise,* sailing at full speed under nuclear power, was the first U.S. carrier to reach waters off Cuba. For about five days, the pilots on the *Enterprise* believed we were going into action. We had never been in combat before, and despite the global confrontation a strike on Cuba portended, we were prepared and anxious to fly our first mission. The atmosphere aboard ship was fairly tense, but not overly so. Pilots and crewmen alike adopted a cool-headed, business-as-usual attitude toward the mission. Inwardly, of course, we were excited as hell, but we kept our composure and aped the standard image of a laconic, reserved, and fearless American at war.

After five days the tension eased, as it became apparent the crisis would be resolved peacefully. We weren't disappointed to be denied our first combat experience, but our appetites were whetted and our imaginations fueled. We eagerly anticipated the occasion when we would have the chance to do what we were trained to do, and discover, at last, if we were brave enough for the job.

We remained in the Caribbean for another two or three months. We did a lot of heavy flying, landing at various Caribbean nations, and our accident rates began to increase. Our commanders arranged for the pilots to get some R&R, and I soon found myself boarding a carrier Onboard delivery plane for four days of fun in Montego Bay, Jamaica.

Shortly after I got back to the ship from my Jamaican holiday, the *Enterprise* left the Caribbean and returned to port in Norfolk. A little while later, I embarked on my last Mediterranean cruise, an event that marked the end of my days as a completely carefree, unattached, and less than serious Navy flyer.

My newly formed professional aspirations were not as far-reaching as were my father's as he diligently pursued flag rank, single-minded in his intention to emulate his famous father. Certainly I would have been proud to achieve the feat myself, but I doubt I ever allowed myself to daydream about someday wearing an admiral's stars.

I had, by this time, begun to aspire to command. I didn't possess any particular notion of greatness, but I did hold strong notions of honor. And I worried that my deserved reputation for foolishness would make command of a squadron or a carrier, the pinnacle of a young pilot's aspiration, too grand an ambition for an obstreperous admiral's son, and my failure to reach command would dishonor me and my family.

Despite my concerns, I resolved to follow the conventional course to command. With the country at war, that course led to Vietnam. The best way to raise my profile as an aviator, perhaps the only way, was to achieve a creditable combat record. I was eager to begin.

More than professional considerations lay beneath my desire to go to war. Nearly all the men in my family had made their reputations at war. It was my family's pride. And the Naval Academy, with its celebration of martial valor, had penetrated enough of my defenses to recall me to that honor. I wanted to go Vietnam, and to keep faith with the family creed.

When I was a young boy, I would often sit quietly, unobserved, and listen to my father and his friends, who had gathered in our home for a cocktail or dinner party, reminisce about their wartime experiences. They talked about battles on sea and land, kamikaze attacks, depth-charge attacks, Marine landings on fiercely defended Pacific atolls, submerged battles between submarines, gun battles between ships of the line—all the drama and fury of war that most kids went to the movies to experience.

But the men in my house who spoke about war did so with an unstudied nonchalance, a style reserved for commanders who had long ago proved whatever martial virtues their egos required them to possess. They did not bluster or brag or swap war stories to impress each other. They talked about combat as they talked about other experiences in the service. They talked about the lessons of leadership they learned and how they could apply them to current situations.

They talked about how their commanding officers had performed in battle, who had been the most capable and steady leaders, and who had not measured up to the demands of their offices. It was evident in the way my father's friends talked about my father, especially those who had served on submarines with him, that they revered him as a fighting commander. They treated him differently, more respectfully, than they did one another. They often regaled a party with descriptions of my father biting down hard on an unlit cigar in the middle of a fight, unafraid and intensely focused on destroying the enemy.

They talked about how the men under my father's command had been affected by combat, and how my father had inspired their confidence in his leadership. They remembered how my father had quieted his crew's fear by making clear to them that he cared about them, respected them, and would show them the way to fight the Japanese without getting them all killed. They made military life seem more exciting and attractive to me.

They were proud veterans of an epic war, and they never felt the need to exaggerate their experiences. They took dramatic license only with stories about their days away from combat, when they were sent to distant, sometimes exotic, more often bleak refuges for a few weeks' respite from war. Midway Island loomed large in their personal folklore of war, and they seemed to take a curious pride in having endured its charmless environs, a pride they displayed more openly than their pride as conquerors of a formidable enemy. My father often sang to us, and sometimes quietly to himself, the ditty he had sung so often in war, "Beautiful Midway," seeming to recall in its incantation some memorable irony of battle.

> Beautiful, beautiful Midway,
> Land where the gooney birds play.

We're proud of our predecessors,
Who kept the Japs at bay.

We live in the sand and skavole,
Down where the sea breezes blow.
There will always be a Midway,
The goddammdest place I know.

He also often recounted, with more humor than embarrassment, an occasion early in the war when he and my grandfather were both briefly on leave and had accepted my invitation to address the students at my grade school in Vallejo, California. Both men liked the idea of appearing before a group of admiring kids as father and son warriors and bringing tales of courage and adventure to impressionable schoolkids. My grandfather spoke first, my father in the front row watching him. He had become accustomed during the war to public speaking and had inspired a number of audiences with stories from the Solomon Islands campaign. He would bring them to their feet with tales about great naval battles; about the gallant Marines who held their ground and beat the Japanese in the enemy's preferred form of warfare, jungle fighting; and about his intrepid pilots at Henderson Field, who persevered through savage bombing and shelling.

This time, however, was different. The tender youth of his audience seemed to distract him, and rendered his usually robust delivery a little flat. His found it difficult to give his usual rousing call to arms, filled as it was with ridicule and scorn for the enemy, and laced extensively with profanity for punctuation and emphasis. He had always prided himself on his rough ways, as a man for whom salty language had always been a perfectly serviceable means of communication. Now he was knocked off his stride as he searched for ways to commend to a group of children their fathers' courage in language their mothers would approve.

My father watched his father's discomfort with obvious amusement, at times laughing out loud as the old sailor struggled to find some way to hold his audience's attention without resorting to impolite language. Further confounded by his son's delight in his dilemma, he abruptly ended his remarks without ever having hit his high notes. But his wit had not entirely deserted him. He concluded his speech by gesturing toward my father, who had expected to give the audience a riveting description of his battles beneath the sea. "Now, children, my son will sing 'Beautiful Midway' for you," my grandfather said as he grinned and winked at my father.

Crestfallen, my father did as he was instructed and sang to my schoolmates his favorite tune, but in a soft, low voice and with none of his usual enthusiasm. We all watched with puzzled looks on our faces. I perked up a little at the end when I thought I heard my father change the last line of the song from "the goddammdest place I know" to the "gosh-darnedest place I know." After he finished, he hurried away, escorted by his grinning father, who clapped him on the back and complimented him on his performance.

My father never had to sit me down and explain the nature of an officer's life to me, to spell out the demands and expectations that came with the uniform. As the son of a professional officer, I had abundant opportunity to observe the long absences, hard work, and frequent upheavals that attended a military career. I knew firsthand the dominance the Navy's priorities held over family considerations.

But it was war, the great test of character, that made the prospect of joining my father's profession attractive, and I was very curious about my father's knowledge of it. I listened intently to every conversation about war that my father and his friends had in my presence. I admired them as they relaxed with drinks in hand, their thoughts turned again to the days when their dreams of adventure had become harshly real and the last attributes of their youth had been lost in the noise and gun smoke of battle. I hoped that I, too, would know days when I would learn that courage was finding the will to act despite the fear and chaos of battle.

One summer, on leave from the Academy, I went to see my father in his study in our house on Capitol Hill and asked him to tell me about his experiences in the Second World War. He set aside what he was reading and described in detail, but in a very businesslike manner, his war.

He began with his combat patrol in the Atlantic, when the *Gunnel* had reconnoitered the North African coast. He told me about losing power in all his ship's engines, save the auxiliary engine, and how nerve-racking was the *Gunnel*'s slow progress to Scotland and safety. He described bleak Midway Island, and how ironic it seemed that men were sent to such a desolate, inhospitable place to recover from the hardships of war. He recounted the terrifying hours he had spent submerged as exploding depth charges unrelentingly shook his submarine. He talked about his narrow escape after sinking the destroyer, how they had been hunted relentlessly by its sister ships. He described how badly his crew had been affected by the experience, and the measures he had taken to prevent them from wasting oxygen and losing their minds. He talked warmly about the friendships he had formed during the war, and how important they were to enduring the strain and deprivations that war imposes on a commanding officer.

He told me all about his war, letting the facts speak for themselves. My father respected the facts of war. He felt no need to embellish them to make a point or to make any obvious pronouncements like "Let this be a lesson to you, boy." He assumed his story, briefly but honestly told, would answer my curiosity, and that I would derive from it what lessons I should.

Implicit in his assumption was his respect for me, and I was grateful to have it. I was not a member of the audience attending his seapower lectures. I was the son and grandson of Navy officers, and I had his trust that I would prepare myself for my turn at war.

I had known less of my father's attention than had many of my friends whose fathers were not as deeply involved in their work or absent as often as my father was. My father could often be a distant, inscrutable patriarch. But I always had a sense that he was special, a man who had set his mind to accomplishing great things, and had ransomed his life to the task. I admired him, and wanted badly to be admired by him, yet indications of his regard for me were more often found in the things he didn't say than in the things he did.

He wasn't purposely sparing with praise or encouragement, but neither did he lavish such generous attention on his children. He set an example for us, an example that took all his strength and courage to live. That, I believe, is how he expressed his devotion to us, as his father had expressed his devotion to him.

He assumed that I had the qualities necessary to live a life like his; that I would be drawn by some inherited proclivity to a life of adventure. He trusted that when I met with adversity, I would use the example he had set for me just as he had relied all his life on his father's example.

The sanctity of personal honor was the only lesson my father felt necessary to impart to me, and he faithfully saw to my instruction, frequently using my grandfather as his model. All my life, he had implored me not to lie, cheat, or steal; to be fair with friend and stranger alike; to respect my superiors and my subordinates; to know my duty and devote myself to its accomplishment without hesitation or complaint. All else, he reasoned, would be satisfactorily managed were I to accept, gratefully, the demands of honor. His father had taught him that, and the lesson had served him well.

"There is a term which has slipped somewhat into disuse," he remarked late in his life, "which I always used till the moment I retired, and that is the term 'an officer and a gentleman.' And those two imply everything that the highest sense of personal honor implies."

———

For nine months after leaving my squadron on the *Enterprise,* I served on the staff of the Chief of Air Basic Training in Pensacola. A job on an admiral's staff is considered a plumb assignment for an ambitious junior officer, and I was lucky to have it. But I was more eager to build my reputation as a combat pilot, and I looked for any opportunity to hurry the day when I would deploy to Vietnam.

One day, I got word that Paul Fay, Undersecretary of the Navy at the time, was coming to visit. After a round of meetings, Fay wanted to play a little tennis to relax. I was asked to play with him. After tennis, we went swimming at the officers' club. I took the opportunity to ask the undersecretary if he could help get me a combat tour in Vietnam.

Navy pilots rotate tours of sea and shore duty. I had left my squadron immediately after my last deployment in the Mediterranean. Fay knew that I had just begun my rotation on shore duty, but he promised to see what he could do. A few weeks after Fay returned to Washington, I got a call from one of his aides informing me that I would be sent to Vietnam, but not before I had finished my current rotation. I decided to put in for a transfer to Meridian, Mississippi, where, as a flight instructor at McCain Field, I could fly more in preparation for my combat tour.

Because Meridian was a remote, isolated location that offered few obvious attractions for pilots at play, I was reasonably serious about my work, and I became a better pilot. My fitness reports began to reflect these first signs of maturity. My superiors began to notice in me faint traces of qualities associated with capable officers. They once selected me as instructor of the month.

We worked long hours at Meridian, twelve or more hours a day. Every day began with the morning briefing at five-thirty, followed by the first of three training flights. After our third flight, we ended the long day with a debriefing. Meridian was a dry town at the time, and besides the officers' club, the only place where alcohol could be found was at an old roadhouse located outside the city limits. The county sheriff had come to the base one day, announcing at the gate that he had come to demand that alcohol no longer be served at the O club. He was refused entry. It was, as one pilot put it, "a hard town to have any fun in."

Given the challenge that our colorless circumstances posed to our imaginations, however, my fellow officers and I expended considerable energy devising entertainments to make time pass quickly and pleasantly. We organized a number of legendary bacchanals that abide, fondly, in the memory of many middle-aged, retired, and nearly retired Navy and Marine officers under the name of the legendary Key Fess Yacht Club.

Early in my time at McCain Field, a base beautification project had been launched by our well-intentioned commanding officer, at the behest of his wife and the wives of other senior officers. The plan to improve our plain surroundings included the construction of several man-made lakes. Bulldozers dug large holes in the base's clay soil, which stood empty until enough rainfall filled them with water to give them, it was hoped, a natural appearance. Sadly, they looked more like swamps than lakes, and they stank like a swamp as well.

One particularly unattractive and malodorous lagoon, called Lake Helen in honor of the CO's wife, lay just off the back of the BOQ, a prospect most of us regarded with bemusement as we walked along the outdoor corridors along which the doors to our rooms were located. Living among us at the time was a Marine captain who worked in an administrative capacity at the base. He was a man with a great thirst, which he attempted to slake virtually around the clock. He set up a bar on a card table in his room, and day and night we would hear him beckon any passerby, from young ensigns to room stewards, into his quarters for "a drink before din-din."

Late in the evening, we would often find him outside his room, leaning precariously on the balcony railing, cursing the eyesore that was Lake Helen. He had taken an intense dislike to the offending lagoon and would rage at it profanely for hours. Refusing to acknowledge its given name, he called it Lake Fester. Planted in the middle of the lake was a small island, nothing more than a little mound of dirt with a few spindly trees perched there pathetically. Our hard-drinking Marine neighbor called it Key Fess. And soon most of the residents of the BOQ referred derisively to the lake and its ridiculous island by those names.

One evening, several of us were bemoaning the sorry condition of our social life when someone came up with the brilliant idea of forming the Key Fess Yacht Club. The next weekend, attired in yachting dress of blue jackets and white trousers, we commissioned the club. We had strung lights on the trees of Key Fess and draped banners and flags over the BOQ's railings. We elected the club's officers, choosing Lake Fester's chief critic, the Marine captain, as the club's first commodore. I was elected vice commodore. We christened an old aluminum dinghy the *Fighting Lady,* and as "Victory at Sea" blasted over loudspeakers, we launched her ceremoniously on her maiden voyage to Key Fess, with the new commodore standing comically amidships, hand tucked inside his jacket like Washington crossing the Delaware.

Over the next several months, the weekend revels of the Key Fess Yacht Club became famous in Meridian and throughout the world of naval aviation. Huge throngs of people could now be found every Saturday night on the shores of Lake Fester, throwing themselves wholeheartedly into the evening's festivities. We held a toga party in the officers' club one night, replacing all its furniture with the mattresses from our rooms, which I still remember as one of the most exhausting experiences of my life. We often paid bands to come in from Memphis and entertain us.

Some of the club's members dated local girls, who spread the word in sleepy Meridian about our riotous activities, and soon a fair share of the town's single women were regular guests at our parties. One Sunday morning, BOQ residents were awakened by cries of help coming from Key Fess. Someone had rowed a few young ladies out to Key Fess the night before and stranded them there. We rowed the *Fighting Lady* out to rescue them. Despite their weariness, they still managed to give full vent to their anger, complaining bitterly about the mosquito bites that covered them.

Aviators from both east and west coasts began showing up for the fun. An admiral even flew in from Pensacola one Saturday to see for himself what all the fuss was about. Eventually, our commodore received orders to transfer to another base. I was elected the new commodore. Aviators flew in from everywhere to attend the huge party celebrating the change of command. We had put Naval Air Station, Meridian, on the Navy's map.

Despite the demands of my office as commodore of the Key Fess Yacht Club, I managed to devote at least as much energy to my job as I did to my extracurricular activities. Correspondingly, my reputation in the Navy improved. Anticipating my forthcoming tour in Vietnam, and confident that I could perform credibly in combat, I had begun to believe that I would someday have command of a carrier or squadron. I finally felt that I had settled into the family business and was on my way to a successful career as a naval officer.

I was also in the middle of a serious romance with Carol Shepp of Philadelphia, a relationship that added to my creeping sense that I might have been put on earth for some other purpose than my own constant amusement.

I had known and admired Carol since Academy days, when she was engaged to one of my classmates. She was a divorced mother of two young sons when we renewed our acquaintance shortly before I left for Meridian. She was attractive, clever, and kind, and I was instantly attracted to her, and delighted to discover that she was attracted to me.

Carol would occasionally visit me at Meridian and good-naturedly join in the weekend's festivities. But most weekends during our brief courtship, I abjured the social activities at Meridian, preferring Carol's company to the usual revelry at the Key Fess Yacht Club. On Friday afternoons, I would take a student pilot on a four-hour training flight to Philadelphia, refueling at Norfolk on the way. I would arrive at seven or eight o'clock in the evening. Carol would be waiting at the airfield to pick me up, and we would go out to dinner.

Connie Bookbinder, whose family owned Bookbinder's Restaurant, had been Carol's college roommate, so every evening we dined there on lobster and drank with friends. On Saturdays we would go to a football game at Memorial Stadium or a college basketball game at the Pallestra. We would enjoy some other entertainment on Sunday before I flew back to Meridian on Sunday night.

We had been dating for less than a year when I realized I wanted to marry Carol. The carefree life of an unattached naval aviator no longer held the allure for me that it once had. Nor had I ever been as happy in a relationship as I was now. I was elated when Carol instantly consented to my proposal.

We married on July 3, 1965. My marriage required that I relinquish my office as commodore of the yacht club, which I did without regret. The party held to celebrate my retirement was a memorable one.

Carol's two sons, Doug and Andy, were great kids, and I quickly formed a strong affection for them. I adopted them a year after our marriage, and I have been a proud father ever since. A few months later, Carol gave birth to our beautiful daughter, Sidney.

That December, I flew to Philadelphia to join my parents at the Army-Navy football game. My mother had brought Christmas presents for Carol and the kids, and I stowed them in the baggage compartment of my airplane on the return flight to Meridian. Somewhere between the Eastern Shore of Maryland and Norfolk, Virginia, as I was preparing to come in to refuel, my engine flamed out, and I had to eject at a thousand feet. The Christmas gifts were lost with my airplane.

This latest unexpected glimpse of mortality added even greater urgency to my recent existential inquiries and made me all the more anxious to get to Vietnam before some new unforeseen accident prevented me from ever taking my turn in war.

So it was with some relief that I received my orders at the end of 1966 to report to Jacksonville, Florida, where I would join a squadron on the USS *Forrestal* and complete Replacement Air Group (RAG) training. I trained exclusively in the A-4 Skyhawk, the small bomber that I would soon fly in combat missions. Later that year, we sailed through the Suez Canal, on a course for Yankee Station in the Tonkin Gulf and war.

III

In me there dwells
No greatness, save it be some far-off touch
Of greatness to know well I am not great.

—Alfred, Lord Tennyson,
"Lancelot and Elaine"

CHAPTER 14

The *Forrestal* Fire

Tom Ott had just handed me back my flight helmet after wiping off the visor with a rag. Tom was a second-class petty officer from Hattiesburg, Mississippi, and a fine man. He had been my parachute rigger since I came aboard the USS *Forrestal* several months earlier to begin RAG training off Guantanamo Bay. A parachute rigger is responsible for the maintenance and preparation of a naval aviator's equipment. Tom had heard me complain that I often found it difficult to see through my visor. So he always came on deck before launch to clean it one last time.

I was a thirty-one-year-old A-4 pilot, and like most pilots I was a little superstitious. I had flown five bombing runs over North Vietnam without incident, and I preferred that all preflight tasks be performed in the same order as for my previous missions, believing an unvarying routine portended a safe flight. Wiping off my visor was one of the last tasks executed in that routine.

Shortly before eleven on the morning of July 29, 1967, on Yankee Station in the Tonkin Gulf, I was third in line on the port side of the ship. I took my helmet back from Tom, nodded at him as he flashed me a thumbs-up, and shut the plane's canopy. In the next instant, a Zuni missile struck the belly fuel tank of my plane, tearing it open, igniting two hundred gallons of fuel that spilled onto the deck, and knocking two of my bombs to the deck. I never saw Tom Ott again.

Stray voltage from an electrical charge used to start the engine of a nearby F-4 Phantom, also waiting to take off, had somehow fired the six-foot Zuni from beneath the plane's wing. At impact, my plane felt like it had exploded.

I looked out at a rolling fireball as the burning fuel spread across the deck. I opened my canopy, raced onto the nose, crawled out onto the refueling probe, and jumped ten feet into the fire. I rolled through a wall of flames as my flight suit caught fire. I put the flames out and ran as fast as I could to the starboard side of the deck.

Shocked and shaking from adrenaline, I saw the pilot in the A-4 next to mine jump from his plane into the fire. His flight suit burst into flames. As I went to help him, a few crewmen dragged a fire hose toward the conflagration. Chief Petty Officer Gerald Farrier ran ahead of me with a portable fire extinguisher. He stood in front of the fire and aimed the extinguisher at one of the thousand-pound bombs that had been knocked loose from my plane and were now sitting in the flames on the burning deck. His heroism cost him his life. A few seconds later the bomb exploded, blowing me back at least ten feet and killing a great many men, including the burning pilot, the men with the hose, and Chief Farrier.

Small pieces of hot shrapnel from the exploded bomb tore into my legs and chest. All around me was mayhem. Planes were burning. More bombs cooked off. Body parts, pieces of the ship, and scraps of planes were dropping onto the deck. Pilots strapped in their seats ejected into the firestorm. Men trapped by flames jumped overboard. More Zuni missiles streaked across the deck. Explosions tore craters in the flight deck, and burning fuel fell through the openings into the hangar bay, spreading the fire below.

I went below to help unload some bombs from an elevator used to raise the jets from the hangar to the flight deck and dump them over the side of the ship. When we finished, I went to the ready room, where I could check the fire's progress on the television monitor located there. A stationary video camera was recording the tragedy and broadcasting it on the ship's closed-circuit television.

After a short while, I went to sick bay to have my burns and shrapnel wounds treated. There I found a horrible scene of many men, burned beyond saving, grasping the last moments of life. Most of them lay silently or made barely audible sounds. They gave no cries of agony because their nerve endings had been burned, sparing them any pain. Someone called my name, a kid, anonymous to me because the fire had burned off all his identifying features. He asked me if a pilot in our squadron was okay. I replied that he was. The young sailor said, "Thank God," and died. I left the sick bay unable to keep my composure.

The fires were consuming the *Forrestal*. I thought she might sink. But the crew's heroics kept her afloat. Men sacrificed their lives for one another and for their ship. Many of them were only eighteen and nineteen years old. They fought the inferno with a tenacity usually reserved for hand-to-hand combat. They fought it all day and well into the next, and they saved the *Forrestal*.

The fire on the flight deck was extinguished that first afternoon, but the last of the fires still burned belowdecks twenty-four hours later. By the time the last blaze was brought under control, 134 men were dead or dying. Dozens more were wounded. More than twenty planes were destroyed. But the *Forrestal*, with several large holes in its hull below the waterline, managed to make its way slowly to Subic Naval Base in the Philippines.

It would take almost a week for the *Forrestal* to reach Subic, where enough repairs would be made to the ship to enable it to return to the States for further repairs. It would take two more years of repairs before the *Forrestal* would be seaworthy enough to return to duty. All the pilots and crew who were fit to travel assumed we would board flights for home once we reached the Philippines. It appeared that my time at war was to be a very brief experience, and this distressed me considerably.

Combat for a naval aviator is fought in short, violent bursts. Our missions last but an hour or two before we are clear of danger and back on the carrier playing poker with our buddies. We are spared the sustained misery of the infantrymen who slog through awful conditions and danger for months on end. Some pilots like the excitement of our missions, knowing that they are of short duration, but most of us concentrate so fiercely on finding our targets and avoiding calamity that we recall more vividly our relief when it's over than we do our exhilaration while it's going on.

I did not take a perverse pleasure in the terror and destruction of war. I did not delight in the brief, intense thrill of flying combat missions. I was gratified when my bombs hit their target, but I did not particularly enjoy the excitement of the experience.

Nevertheless, I was a professional naval officer, and the purpose of my years of training had been to prepare me for this moment. As the crippled *Forrestal* limped toward port, my moment was disappearing when it had barely begun, and I feared my ambitions were among the casualties in the calamity that had claimed the *Forrestal*.

A distraction from my despondency appeared on the way to Subic in the person of R. W. "Johnny" Apple, the *New York Times* correspondent in Saigon. Serving as a pool reporter, he arrived by helicopter with a camera crew to examine the damaged ship and interview the survivors. When he finished collecting material for his report, he offered to take me back to Saigon with him for the daily press briefing irreverently referred to as the "Five O'Clock Follies." Seeing it as an opportunity for some welcome R&R, I jumped at the invitation. I passed a few days there pleasantly, wondering about my future, and beginning a lifelong friendship with Johnny.

Shortly after I returned to the *Forrestal*, an officer from the carrier USS *Oriskany* addressed my squadron to ask if any of us would consider volunteering for combat duty aboard his ship. The *Oriskany* had lately lost a number of pilots, and the squadron was considerably undermanned. A few others and I signed up.

The year before the *Forrestal* fire, the *Oriskany* had also suffered a terrible disaster at sea when a magnesium flare had ignited a blaze that nearly destroyed the ship. The *Oriskany* fire was not as great a holocaust as the fire that had engulfed the *Forrestal*. Ordnance had not exploded in the blaze, and the fire was brought under control in four hours. But it was nevertheless a terrible calamity for the pilots and crew. Forty-four men had been killed. In addition, the carrier was suffering high casualties in 1967. The *Oriskany* was regarded as a dangerous place to live.

I was relieved at this unexpected change in my fortunes. The *Oriskany* was coming off Yankee Station for a few weeks, and my services would not be needed until it returned. I met Carol and the kids in Europe and spent a pleasant family holiday, visiting my parents in London and relaxing on the French Riviera. I was still waiting for my final orders when we returned to Orange Park, Florida, which was near my last squadron's home base in Jacksonville, and where my family would await my return from combat duty. In September, my orders came through. I was an eager thirty-one-year-old lieutenant commander in the Navy, no longer worrying excessively about my career.

Many of my parents' friends wrote to them after the *Forrestal* fire to express their concern for my welfare. My father wrote a brief response to all, informing them, "Happily for all of us, he came through without a scratch and is now back at sea."

CHAPTER 15

Killed

On September 30, 1967, I reported for duty to the *Oriskany* and joined VA-163—an A-4 attack squadron nicknamed the Saints. During the three years of Operation Rolling Thunder, the bombing campaign of North Vietnam begun in 1965, no carrier's pilots saw more action or suffered more losses than those on the *Oriskany*. When the Johnson administration halted Rolling Thunder in 1968, thirty-eight pilots on the *Oriskany* had been either killed or captured. Sixty planes had been lost, including twenty-nine A-4s. The Saints suffered the highest casualty rate. In 1967, one-third of the squadron's pilots were killed or captured. Every single one of the Saints' original fifteen A-4s had been destroyed. We had a reputation for aggressiveness, and for success. In the months before I joined the squadron, the Saints had destroyed all the bridges to the port city of Haiphong.

Like all combat pilots, we had a studied, almost macabre indifference to death that masked a great sadness in the squadron, a sadness that grew more pervasive as our casualty list lengthened. But we kept our game faces on, and our bravado became all the more exaggerated when the squadron returned to ship after a mission with one or more missing pilots. We flew the next raid with greater determination to do as much damage as we could, repeating to ourselves before the launch, "If we destroy the target, we won't have to go back."

We had one of the bravest, most resourceful squadron commanders, who was also one of the best A-4 pilots in the war, Commander Bryan Compton. In August, six weeks before I reported for duty, Bryan had led a daring raid on a thermal power plant in Hanoi. For the first time the Saints had been equipped with Walleye smart bombs, and their accuracy reduced the risk of killing great numbers of civilians when striking targets in densely populated areas. The Hanoi power plant was located in a heavily populated part of Hanoi and had consequently been off-limits to American bombers. Contrary to North Vietnamese propaganda and the accusations of Americans who opposed the war, the bombing of North Vietnam was not a campaign of terror and wanton destruction against innocent civilians. Pilots and their military and civilian commanders exercised great care to keep civilian casualties to a minimum. With the introduction of smart bombs, militarily significant targets that had previously been avoided to spare innocent lives could now be attacked.

Bryan Compton successfully petitioned for his squadron to receive smart bombs. Once the Saints were equipped with the new ordnance, he sought and received permission to bomb the power plant. He took just five other pilots from the squadron with him on the mission. Diving in from different points on the compass, through a terrible barrage of antiaircraft fire and surface-to-air missiles, five of the six A-4s hit their target. The mission was a huge success, but rather than leaving off the attack as soon as the bombs had struck their target, Bryan flew two more passes over the power plant, taking pictures of the bomb damage. For his courage and leadership of the raid, Bryan received the Navy Cross.

I was third pilot on another raid Bryan led, this time over Haiphong. During the raid, the plane of the number two pilot was shot down. None of us saw him eject. Bryan wanted to determine whether or not the missing pilot had managed to escape his destroyed aircraft and parachute safely to ground. He kept circling Haiphong at an extremely low altitude, about two thousand feet, searching in vain for some sign that the pilot had survived. We were taking a tremendous pounding from flak and SAMs. I was scared to death waiting for Bryan to call off the search and lead us back to the *Oriskany* and out of harm's way. To this day, I will swear that Bryan made at least eight passes before he reluctantly gave up the search. Bryan has since dismissed my account of his heroism as an exaggeration, claiming, "You can't trust a politician. They'll lie every time." But I remember what I saw that day. I saw a courageous squadron commander put his life in grave peril so that a friend's family might know if their loved one was alive or dead. For his heroics and his ability to survive them, the rest of the squadron regarded Bryan as indestructible. We were proud to serve under his command.

In the early morning of October 26, 1967, I prepared for my twenty-third bombing run over North Vietnam. President Johnson had decided to escalate the war. The *Oriskany*'s pilots were on line twelve hours a day, flying raids from midnight to noon or from noon to midnight. We would rest for twelve hours while another carrier took up the battle, and then return to combat for another twelve-hour shift. The Saints were now dropping on Vietnam 150 tons of ordnance a day. Until this moment we had found Johnson's prosecution of the war, with its frustratingly limited bombing targets, to be maddeningly illogical.

When I was on the *Forrestal*, every man in my squadron had thought Washington's air war plans were senseless. The night before my first mission, I had gone up to the squadron's intelligence center to punch out information on my target. Out came a picture of a military barracks, with some details about the target's recent history. It had already been bombed twenty-seven times. Half a mile away there was a bridge with truck tracks. But the bridge wasn't on the target list. The target list was so restricted that we had to go back and hit the same targets over and over again. It's hard to get a sense that you are advancing the war effort when you are prevented from doing anything more than bouncing the rubble of an utterly insignificant target. James Stockdale, the air wing commander on the *Oriskany* who had been shot down and captured in 1965, aptly described the situation as "making gestures with our airplanes."

Flying missions off the *Oriskany*, I often observed Soviet ships come into Haiphong harbor and off-load surface-to-air missiles. We could see the SAMs being transported to firing sites and put into place, but we couldn't do anything about them because we were forbidden to bomb SAM sites unless they were firing on us. Even then, it was often an open question whether we could retaliate or not.

We lost a pilot one day over Haiphong. Another pilot released his bombs over the place he thought the SAM had been fired from. When we returned to the *Oriskany*, the pilot who had avenged his friend was grounded because he had bombed a target that wasn't on Washington's list. We all squawked so much that our commanders relented and returned the enterprising pilot to flight status. But the incident left a bad taste in our mouths, and our resentment over the absurd way we were ordered to fight the war grew much stronger, diminishing all the more our already weakened regard for our civilian commanders.

In 1966, Defense Secretary Robert Strange McNamara visited the *Oriskany*. He asked the skipper for the strike-pilot ratio. He wanted to make sure the numbers accorded with his conception of a successful war, and he was pleased with the figures he received from the skipper. He believed the number of missions flown relative to the number of bombs dropped would determine whether or not we won the war in the most cost-efficient manner. But when President Johnson ordered an end to Rolling Thunder in 1968, the campaign was judged to have had no measurable impact on the enemy. Most of the pilots flying the missions believed that our targets were virtually worthless. We had long believed that our attacks, more often than not limited to trucks, trains, and barges, were not just failing to break the enemy's resolve but actually having the opposite effect by boosting Vietnam's confidence that it could withstand the full measure of American airpower. In all candor, we thought our civilian commanders were complete idiots who didn't have the least notion of what it took to win the war. I found no evidence in postwar studies of the Johnson administration's political and military decision-making during the war that caused me to revise that harsh judgment.

When the orders came down to escalate the bombing campaign, the pilots on the *Oriskany* were ecstatic. As the campaign heated up, we began to lose a lot more pilots. But the losses, as much as they hurt, didn't cause any of us to reconsider our support for the escalation. For the first time we believed we were helping to win the war, and we were proud to be usefully employed.

Today's attack on Hanoi was to be an Alpha Strike, a large raid on a "militarily significant" target, involving A-4s from my squadron and our sister squadron on the *Oriskany*, the "Ghost Riders," as well as fighter escorts from the carrier's two F-8 squadrons. It would be my first attack on the enemy capital. The commander of the *Oriskany*'s air wing, Commander Burt Shepard, the brother of astronaut Alan Shepard, would lead the strike. Our target was the thermal power plant, located near a small lake almost in the center of the city, that the Saints had destroyed two months earlier; it had since been repaired.

The day before, I had pleaded with Jim Busey, the Saints' operations officer, who was responsible for putting the flight schedule together, to let me fly the mission. The earlier raid on the power plant was the pride of the squadron, having earned Navy Crosses for Bryan and Jim. I wanted to help destroy it again. I was feeling pretty cocky as well. The day before, we had bombed an airfield outside Hanoi, and I had destroyed two enemy MiGs parked on the runway. Jim, who called me "Gregory Green-Ass" because I was the new guy in the squadron and had flown far fewer missions than had the squadron's veteran pilots, consented, and put me on the mission as wingman.

I was still charged up from the previous day's good fortune, and was anticipating more success that morning despite having been warned about Hanoi's extensive air defense system. The *Oriskany*'s strike operations officer, Lew Chatham, told me he expected to lose some pilots. Be careful, he said. I told him not to worry about me, that I was sure I would not be killed. I didn't know at the time that downed pilots imprisoned in the North referred to their shootdowns as the day they were "killed."

Hanoi, with its extensive network of Russian-manufactured SAM sites, had the distinction of possessing the most formidable air defenses in the history of modern warfare. I was about to discover just how formidable they were.

We flew out to the west of Hanoi, turned, and headed in to make our run. We came in from the west so that once we had rolled in on the target, released our bombs, and pulled out we would be flying directly toward the Tonkin Gulf. We had electronic countermeasure devices in our planes. In 1966, A-4s had been equipped with radar detection. A flashing light and different tone signals would warn us of imminent danger from enemy SAMs. One tone sounded when a missile's radar was tracking you, another when it had locked onto you. A third tone signaled a real emergency, that a launched SAM was headed your way. As soon as we hit land and approached the three concentric rings of SAMs that surrounded Hanoi, the tone indicating that missile radar was tracking sounded. It tracked us for miles.

We flew in fairly large separations, unlike the tight formations flown in World War II bombing raids. At about nine thousand feet, as we turned inbound on the target, our warning lights flashed, and the tone for enemy radar started sounding so loudly I had to turn down the volume. I could see huge clouds of smoke and dust erupt on the ground as SAMs were fired at us. The closer we came to the target the fiercer were the defenses. For the first time in combat I saw thick black clouds of antiaircraft flak everywhere, images familiar to me only from World War II movies.

A SAM appears as a flying telephone pole, moving at great speed.

We were now maneuvering through a nearly impassible obstacle course of antiaircraft fire and flying telephone poles. They scared the hell out of me. We normally kept pretty good radio discipline throughout a run, but there was a lot of chatter that day as pilots called out SAMs. Twenty-two missiles were fired at us that day. One of the F-8s on the strike was hit. The pilot, Charlie Rice, managed to eject safely.

I recognized the target sitting next to the small lake from the intelligence photographs I had studied. I dove in on it just as the tone went off signaling that a SAM was flying toward me. I knew I should roll out and fly evasive maneuvers, "jinking," in fliers' parlance, when I heard the tone. The A-4 is a small, fast, highly maneuverable aircraft, a lot of fun to fly, and it can take a beating. Many an A-4 returned safely to its carrier after being badly shot up by enemy fire. An A-4 can outmaneuver a tracking SAM, pulling more G's than the missile can take. But I was just about to release my bombs when the tone sounded, and had I started jinking I would never have had the time nor, probably, the nerve, to go back in once I had lost the SAM. So, at about 3,500 feet, I released my bombs, then pulled back the stick to begin a steep climb to a safer altitude. In the instant before my plane reacted, a SAM blew my right wing off. I was killed.

CHAPTER 16

Prisoner of War

I knew I was hit. My A-4, traveling at about 550 miles an hour, was violently spiraling to earth. In this predicament, a pilot's training takes over. I didn't feel fear or any more excitement than I had already experienced during the run, my adrenaline surging as I dodged SAMs and flak to reach the target. I didn't think, "Gee, I'm hit—what now?" I reacted automatically the moment I took the hit and saw that my wing was gone. I radioed, "I'm hit," reached up, and pulled the ejection seat handle.

I struck part of the airplane, breaking my left arm, my right arm in three places, and my right knee, and I was briefly knocked unconscious by the force of the ejection. Witnesses said my chute had barely opened before I plunged into the shallow water of Truc Bach Lake. I landed in the middle of the lake, in the middle of the city, in the middle of the day. An escape attempt would have been challenging.

I came to when I hit the water. Wearing about fifty pounds of gear, I touched the bottom of the shallow lake and kicked off with my good leg. I did not feel any pain as I broke the surface, and I didn't understand why I couldn't move my arms to pull the toggle on my life vest.

I sank to the bottom again. When I broke the surface the second time I managed to inflate my life vest by pulling the toggle with my teeth. Then I blacked out again.

When I came to the second time, I was being hauled ashore on two bamboo poles by a group of about twenty angry Vietnamese. A crowd of several hundred Vietnamese gathered around me as I lay dazed before them, shouting wildly at me, stripping my clothes off, spitting on me, kicking and striking me repeatedly. When they had finished removing my gear and clothes, I felt a sharp pain in my right knee. I looked down and saw that my right foot was resting next to my left knee, at a ninety-degree angle. I cried out, "My God, my leg." Someone smashed a rifle butt into my shoulder, breaking it. Someone else stuck a bayonet in my ankle and groin. A woman, who may have been a nurse, began yelling at the crowd, and managed to dissuade them from further harming me. She then applied bamboo splints to my leg and right arm.

It was with some relief that I noticed an army truck arrive on the scene to take me away from this group of aggrieved citizens who seemed intent on killing me. Before they put me in the truck, the woman who had stopped the crowd from killing me held a cup of tea to my lips while photographers recorded the act. The soldiers then placed me on a stretcher, loaded me into the truck, and drove me a few blocks to an ocher-colored, trapezoid-shaped stone structure that occupied two city blocks in the center of downtown Hanoi.

I was brought in through enormous steel gates, above which was painted the legend "Maison Centrale." I had been shot down a short walk's distance from the French-built prison, Hoa Lo, which the POWs had named "the Hanoi Hilton." As the massive steel doors loudly clanked shut behind me, I felt a deeper dread than I have ever felt since.

They took me into an empty cell, in a part of the prison we called the Desert Inn, set me down on the floor still in the stretcher, stripped to my underwear, and placed a blanket over me. For the next few days I drifted in and out of consciousness. When awake, I was periodically taken to another room for interrogation. My interrogators accused me of being a war criminal and demanded military information, what kind of aircraft I had flown, future targets, and other particulars of that sort. In exchange I would receive medical treatment.

I thought they were bluffing, and refused to provide any information beyond my name, rank, serial number, and date of birth. They knocked me around a little to force my cooperation, and I began to feel sharp pains in my fractured limbs. I blacked out after the first few blows. I thought if I could hold out like this for a few days, they would relent and take me to a hospital.

For four days I was taken back and forth to different rooms. Unable to use my arms, I was fed twice a day by a guard. I vomited after the meals, unable to hold down anything but a little tea. I remember being desperately thirsty all the time, but I could drink only when the guard was present for my twice-daily feedings.

On about the fourth day, I realized my condition had become more serious. I was feverish, and was losing consciousness more often and for longer periods. I was lying in my own vomit, as well as my other bodily wastes. Two guards entered my cell and pulled the blanket down to examine my leg. I saw that my knee had become grossly swollen and discolored. I remembered a fellow pilot at Meridian who had broken his femur ejecting from his plane. His blood had pooled in his leg, and he had gone into shock and died. I realized the same thing was happening to me, and I pleaded for a doctor.

The two guards left to find the camp officer, who spoke some English. He was short and fat, with a strangely wandering right eye that was clouded white by a cataract. The POWs called him "Bug." He was a mean son of a bitch.

Desperate, I tried to bargain with him. "Take me to the hospital and I'll give you the information you want." I didn't intend to keep my word, reasoning that after my injuries had been treated, I would be strong enough to deal with the consequences of not holding up my end of the bargain.

Bug left without replying, but returned a short while later with a medic, a man the POWs called Zorba. Zorba squatted down and took my pulse. He turned to Bug, shook his head, and uttered a few words.

"Are you going to take me to the hospital?" I asked.

"No," he replied. "It's too late."

I appealed, "Take me to the hospital and I'll get well."

"It's too late," he repeated.

He and the doctor left my cell, and panic that my death was approaching briefly overtook me.

There were few amputees among the POWs who survived their imprisonment. The Vietnamese usually refused treatment to the seriously injured. I don't know whether they were negligent for purposes of cost efficiency, reasoning that Americans, unused to unsanitary conditions, were likely to develop fatal infections following an amputation, or if they refused us treatment simply because they hated us. Whatever the reason, a lot of men died who shouldn't have, the victims of genuine war crimes.

I lapsed into unconsciousness a few minutes after Bug and Zorba left me to my fate, a condition that blessedly relieved me of the terrible dread I was feeling. I was awakened a short while later when an excited Bug rushed into my cell and shouted, "Your father is a big admiral. Now we take you to the hospital."

God bless my father.

My parents were in London when I was shot down. They were dressing for a dinner party when my father received a telephone call saying that my plane had been shot down over Hanoi. My father informed my mother what had happened. They kept their dinner engagement, never mentioning to any of the other guests the distressing news they had just learned.

When they returned home, my father got a call from his boss, Admiral Tom Moorer, Chief of Naval Operations. Admiral Moorer was a friend and had decided to break the sad news to my father himself. "Jack, we don't think he survived."

My parents then called Carol, who had already been notified of my shootdown by the Navy. My mother told her to prepare for the worst: that I was dead, and they would have to find a way to accept that. My father, very matter-of-factly, said, "I don't think we have to."

After speaking with Carol, my parents placed calls to my sister and brother to break the bad news to them. Joe was working as a reporter for the *San Diego Tribune* at the time. He knew something was wrong when he answered the phone and both our parents were on the line.

Without any preliminaries, my mother said: "Honey, Johnny's been shot down."

"What happened?"

"He was hit by a missile and went down."

My brother's question hung in the air unanswered for a moment until my father explained: "His wingman saw his plane explode. They don't think he got out."

Joe began to cry, and then asked my father, "What do we do now?" He recalled my father answering in a soft, sad voice, "Pray for him, my boy."

The next day, October 28, Johnny Apple wrote a story that appeared on the front page of the *New York Times*: ADM. MCCAIN'S SON, *FORRESTAL* SURVIVOR, IS MISSING IN RAID.

I was moved by stretcher to a hospital in central Hanoi. As I was being moved, I again lapsed into unconsciousness. I came to a couple of days later and found myself lying in a filthy room, about twenty by twenty feet, lousy with mosquitoes and rats. Every time it rained, an inch of mud and water would pool on the floor. I was given blood and glucose, and several shots. After several more days passed, during which I was frequently unconscious, I began to recover my wits. Other than the transfusion and shots, I received no treatment for my injuries. No one had even bothered to wash the grime off me.

Once my condition had stabilized, my interrogators resumed their work. Demands for military information were accompanied by threats to terminate my medical treatment if I did not cooperate.

Eventually, I gave them my ship's name and squadron number, and confirmed that my target had been the power plant. Pressed for more useful information, I gave the names of the Green Bay Packers' offensive line, and said they were members of my squadron. When asked to identify future targets, I simply recited the names of a number of North Vietnamese cities that had already been bombed.

I was occasionally beaten when I declined to give any more information. The beatings were of short duration, because I let out a hair-raising scream whenever they occurred. My interrogators appeared concerned that hospital personnel might object. I also suspected that my treatment was less harsh than might be accorded other prisoners. This I attributed to my father's position, and the propaganda value the Vietnamese placed on possessing me, injured but alive. Later, my suspicion was confirmed when I heard accounts of other POWs' experiences during their first interrogations. They had endured far worse than I had, and had withstood the cruelest torture imaginable.

Although I rarely saw a doctor or a nurse, I did have a constant companion, a teenage boy who was assigned to guard me. He had a book that he read at my bedside every day. In the book was a picture of an old man with a rifle sitting on the fuselage of a downed F-105. He would show me the picture, point to himself, and then slap me.

I still could not feed myself, so the boy would spoon-feed me a bowl of noodles with some gristle in it. The gristle was hard to chew. He would jam three of four spoonfuls in my mouth before I could chew and swallow any of it. Unable to force any more into my mouth, he would finish the bowl himself. I got three or four spoonfuls of food twice a day. After a while I really didn't give a damn, although I tried to eat as much as I could before the boy took his share.

After about a week in the hospital, a Vietnamese officer we called Chihuahua informed me that a visiting Frenchman had asked to look in on me, and had volunteered to carry a message back to my family. I was willing to see him, assuming at the time that my family probably believed I was dead.

As I later learned, the Vietnamese, always delighted when a propaganda opportunity presented itself, had already announced my capture, and helpfully supplied quotes from the repentant war criminal commending the Vietnamese people's strong morale and observing that the war was turning against the United States. And in an English-language commentary broadcast over the Voice of Vietnam, entitled "From the Pacific to Truc Bach Lake," Hanoi accused Lyndon Johnson and me of staining my family's honor.

Adding to the ever longer list of American pilots captured over North Vietnam was a series of newcomers. John Sidney McCain was one of them. Who is he? A U.S. carrier navy lieutenant commander. Last Thursday, 26 October, he took off from the carrier *Oriskany* for a raiding mission against Hanoi City. Unfortunately for him, the jet plane he piloted was one of ten knocked out of Hanoi's sky. He tried in vain to evade the deadly accurate barrage of fire of this city. A surface-to-air missile shot down his jet on the spot. He bailed out and was captured on the surface of Truc Bach Lake right in the heart of the DRV capital.

What were the feats of arms which McCain achieved? Foreign correspondents in Hanoi saw with their own eyes civilian dwelling houses destroyed and Hanoi's women, old folks and children killed by steel-pellet bombs dropped from McCain's aircraft and those of his colleagues.

Lt. Com. John Sidney McCain nearly perished in the conflagration that swept the flight deck of the U.S. carrier *Forrestal* last July. He also narrowly escaped death in Haiphong the Sunday before last but this time what must happen has happened. There is no future in it.

McCain was married in 1965 and has a ten-month-old daughter. Surely he also loves his wife and child. Then why did he fly here dropping bombs on the necks of the Vietnamese women and children?

The killing he was ordered to do in Vietnam has aroused indignation among the world's peoples. What glory had he brought by his job to his father, Admiral John S. McCain Jr., commander in chief of U.S. Naval Forces in Europe? His grandfather, Admiral John S. McCain, commander of all aircraft carriers in the Pacific in World War II, participated in a just war against the Japanese forces. But nowadays, Lt. Com. McCain is participating in an unjust war, the most unpopular one in U.S. history and mankind's history, too. This is Johnson's war to enslave the Vietnamese people.

From the Pacific to Truc Bach Lake, McCain has brought no reputation for his family in the United States. The one who is smearing McCain's family honor is also smearing the honor of Washington's United States of America. He is Lyndon B. Johnson.

Prior to the Frenchman's arrival, I was rolled into a treatment room, where a doctor tried to set my broken right arm. For what seemed like an eternity, he manipulated my arm, without benefit of anesthesia, trying to set the three fractures. Blessedly, the pain at its most acute rendered me unconscious. Finally abandoning the effort, he slapped a large and heavy chest cast on me, an act I can hardly credit as considerate on the part of my captors. The cast did not have a cotton lining, and the rough plaster painfully rubbed against my skin. Over time, it wore two holes in the back of my arm down to the bone. My other arm was left untreated.

Exhausted and encased from my waist to my neck in a wet plaster cast, I was rolled into a large, clean room and placed in a nice white bed. The room contained six beds, each protected by a mosquito net. I asked if this was to be my new room, and was told that it was.

A few minutes later, a Vietnamese officer, a Major Nguyen Bai, paid me a visit, accompanied by Chihuahua. He was the commandant of the entire prison system, a dapper, educated man whom the POWs had nicknamed "the Cat." The Cat informed me that the Frenchman who would arrive shortly was a television journalist, and that I should tell him everything I had told my interrogators. Surprised, I told the Cat I didn't want to be filmed.

"You need two operations on your leg, and if you don't talk to him, then we will take your cast off and you won't get any operations," he threatened. "You will say you are grateful to the Vietnamese people, and that you are sorry for your crimes, or we will send you back to the camp."

I assured him that I would say nothing of the kind, but believing that the Cat would send me back to Hoa Lo, and worrying that I could not endure the truck ride back, I agreed to see the Frenchman.

A few minutes later, François Chalais entered the room with two cameramen. He questioned me for several minutes, asking about my shootdown, my squadron, the nature of my injuries, and my father. I repeated the same information about my ship and squadron and told him I was being treated well by the doctors, who had promised to operate on my leg. Off camera, the Cat and Chihuahua were visibly displeased with my answers. Chihuahua demanded that I say more.

"I have no more to say about it," I replied.

Both Vietnamese insisted that I express gratitude for the lenient and humane treatment I had received. I refused, and when they pressed me, Chalais said, "I think what he told me is sufficient."

Chalais then inquired about the quality of the food I was getting, and I responded, "It's not like Paris, but I eat it." Finally, Chalais asked if I had a message for my family.

"I would just like to tell my wife that I'm going to get well. I love her, and hope to see her soon. I'd appreciate it if you'd tell her that. That's all I have to say."

Chihuahua told me to say that I could receive letters and pictures from home. "No," I replied. A visibly agitated Cat demanded that I say on camera how much I wanted the war to end so I could go home. Again, Chalais stepped in to help me, saying very firmly that he was satisfied with my answer, and that the interview was over. I appreciated his help.

Although I had resisted giving my interrogators any useful information and had greatly irritated the Cat by refusing his demands during the interview, I should not have given out information about my ship and squadron, and I regret very much having done so. The information was of no real use to the Vietnamese, but the Code of Conduct for American Prisoners of War orders us to refrain from providing any information beyond our name, rank, and serial number.

When Chalais had left, the Cat admonished me for my "bad attitude" and told me I wouldn't receive any more operations. I was taken back to my old room.

Carol went to see Chalais after he returned to Paris, and he gave her a copy of the film, which was shown in the States on the CBS evening news a short time later.

My parents saw it before it was broadcast nationally. A public affairs officer, Herbert Hetu, who worked for my father when my father was the Navy chief in Europe, had a friend who was a producer at CBS. His friend informed him that CBS had the film of my interview, and he offered to screen it for my parents. Hetu and my parents were in New York at the time. My father was scheduled to give a speech on the emerging strength of the Soviet Navy to the prestigious Overseas Press Club. It was an important and much-anticipated speech that he had been preparing for weeks.

Hetu viewed the film and decided not to show it to my father before he delivered his speech, fearing it would "uncork him." Instead, he persuaded his friend at CBS to hold the film until the morning, when my parents could view it. He then contacted my father's personal aide and told him: "After the speech, get with the admiral and tell him about this film. They're going to hold it and we'll take him over to CBS tomorrow. I'm sure he'll want to see it."

Hetu accompanied my parents to CBS the next day. He remembered my father reacting very emotionally to the film. "We took him over with Mrs. McCain, and I think I said to the admiral, 'I think you and Mrs. McCain ought to see this by yourselves. You don't want anybody else in there.' So that's the way they watched it, and it was a very emotional piece of film. . . . I think Admiral McCain and his wife looked at the film twice. His reaction afterward was very emotional, but he never talked to us about it. Some things are just too painful for words."

It was hard not to see how pleased the Vietnamese were to have captured an admiral's son, and I knew that my father's identity was directly related to my survival. Often during my hospital stay I received visits from high-ranking officials. Some observed me for a few minutes and then left without asking any questions. Others would converse idly with me, asking only a few innocuous questions. During one visit, I was told to meet with a visiting Cuban delegation. When I refused, they did not force the issue, either out of concern for my condition or because they were worried about what I might say. One evening, General Vo Nguyen Giap, minister of defense and hero of Dien Bien Phu, paid me a visit. He stared at me wordlessly for a minute, then left.

Bug arrived one day and had me listen to a tape of a POW denouncing America's involvement in the war. The POW was a Marine, a veteran who had flown in the Korean War. The vigor with which he criticized the United States surprised me. His language did not seem stilted, nor did his tone sound forced.

Bug told me he wanted me to make a similar statement. I told him I didn't want to say such things.

He told me I shouldn't be afraid to speak openly about the war, that there was nothing to be ashamed of or to fear.

"I don't feel that way about the war," I replied, and was threatened for what seemed like the hundredth time with a warning that I would be denied an operation because of my "bad attitude."

In early December, they operated on my leg. The Vietnamese filmed the operation. I haven't a clue why. Regrettably, the operation wasn't much of a success. The doctors severed all the ligaments on one side of my knee, which has never fully recovered. After the war, thanks to the work of a kind and talented physical therapist, my knee regained much of its mobility—enough, anyway, for me to return to flight status for a time. But today, when I am tired or when the weather is inclement, my knee stiffens in pain, and I pick up a trace of my old limp.

They decided to discharge me later that December. I had been in the hospital about six weeks. I was in bad shape. I had a high fever and suffered from dysentery. I had lost about fifty pounds and weighed barely a hundred. I was still in my chest cast, and my leg hurt like hell.

On the brighter side, at my request, the Vietnamese were taking me to another prison camp. Bug had entered my room one day and abruptly announced, "The doctors say you are not getting better."

The accusatory tone he used to relay this all too obvious diagnosis implied that I was somehow responsible for my condition and had deliberately tried to embarrass the Vietnamese medical establishment by refusing to recover.

"Put me with other Americans," I responded, "and I'll get better."

Bug said nothing in reply. He just looked at me briefly with the expression he used to convey his disdain for an inferior enemy, then withdrew from the room.

That evening I was blindfolded, placed in the back of a truck, and driven to a truck repair facility that had been converted into a prison a few years earlier. It was situated in what had once been the gardens of the mayor of Hanoi's official residence. The Americans held there called it "the Plantation."

To my great relief, I was placed in a cell in a building we called "the Gun Shed" with two other prisoners, both Air Force majors, George "Bud" Day and Norris Overly. I could have asked for no better companions. There has never been a doubt in my mind that Bud Day and Norris Overly saved my life.

Bud and Norris later told me that their first impression of me, emaciated, bug-eyed, and bright with fever, was of a man at the threshold of death. They thought the Vietnamese expected me to die and had placed me in their care to escape the blame when I failed to recover.

Despite my poor condition, I was overjoyed to be in the company of Americans. I had by this time been a prisoner of war for two months, and I hadn't even caught a glimpse of another American.

I was frail, but voluble. I wouldn't stop talking all through that first day with Bud and Norris, explaining my shootdown, describing my treatment since capture, inquiring about their experiences, and asking for all the details of the prison system and for information about other prisoners.

Bud and Norris accommodated me to the best of their ability, and were the soul of kindness as they eased my way to what they believed was my imminent death. Bud had been seriously injured when he ejected. Like me, he had broken his right arm in three places and had torn the ligaments in his knee—the left knee in his case. After his capture near the DMZ, he had attempted an escape, and had nearly reached an American airfield when he was recaptured. He was brutally tortured for his efforts, and for subsequently resisting his captors' every entreaty for information.

First held in a prison in Vinh before making the 150-mile trip north to Hanoi, Bud had experienced early the full measure of the mistreatment that would be his fate for nearly six years. His captors had looped rope around his shoulders, tightened it until his shoulders were nearly touching, and then hung him by the arms from the rafter of the torture room, tearing his shoulders apart. Left in this condition for hours, Bud never acceded to the Vietnamese demands for military information. They had to refracture his broken right arm and threaten to break the other before Bud gave them anything at all. He was a tough man, a fierce resister, whose example was an inspiration to every man who served with him. For his heroic escape attempt, he received the Medal of Honor, one of only three POWs in Vietnam to receive the nation's highest award.

Because of his injuries, Bud was unable to help with my physical care. Norris shouldered most of the responsibility. A gentle, uncomplaining guy, he cleaned me up, fed me, helped me onto the bucket that served as our toilet, and massaged my leg. Thanks to his tireless ministration, and to the restorative effect Bud and Norris's company had on my morale, I began to recover.

I slept a lot those first weeks, eighteen to twenty hours a day. Little by little, I grew stronger. A little more than a week after I had been consigned to his care, Norris had me on my feet and helped me to stand for a few moments. From then on, I could feel my strength return more rapidly each day. Soon I was able to stand unaided, and even maneuver around my cell on a pair of crutches.

In early January, we were relocated to another end of the camp, a place we called "the Corn Crib." We had neighbors in the cells on either side of ours, and for the first time we managed to establish communications with fellow POWs. Our methods were crude, yelling to each other whenever the turnkeys were absent, and leaving notes written in cigarette ash in a washroom drain. It would be some time before we devised more sophisticated and secure communication methods.

One day a young English-speaking officer escorted a group of older, obviously senior party members into our cell. Their privileged status was evident in the quality of their attire, which, although perhaps not elegant by Western standards, was far better than that worn by most Vietnamese of our acquaintance.

For a few moments after entering, the entire group just stared at me. Finally, the young officer began asking me questions in English, translating my answers for the assembled dignitaries.

"How many corporations does your family own?"

Puzzled by the question, I looked at him for a moment before asking, "What do you mean?"

"How many corporations does your family own? Your father is

a big admiral. He must have many companies that work with your government."

Laughing at the absurd premise of the question, I replied, "You've got to be putting me on. My father is a military officer whose income is confined to his military salary."

When my answer had been translated, the crowd of high-ranking officials, all of whom had thrived in a system of government infamously riddled with corruption, smiled and nodded at each other, dismissing my protest as unimaginative propaganda. In their experience, admirals and generals got rich. Surely in a country as wealthy and undisciplined as the United States, military officers used their influence to profit themselves and their families.

Around that time, we began to notice that the Vietnamese were showing us unusual leniency. Our diet improved a little. For a few days we received large bunches of bananas. The Cat would often visit us and inquire about our health and how we were getting along.

No one invested much effort in interrogating us or getting us to make propaganda statements. Once we were instructed to write summaries of our military histories. We invented all the details. Mine contained references to service in Antarctica and as the naval attaché in Oslo, two places, I am sorry to say, I had never visited.

We were suspicious of the Vietnamese's motives, as we doubted that they had begun to take seriously their public commitments to a policy of humane treatment of prisoners. But initially we were at a loss to figure out their purpose.

We weren't in the dark for long. One evening in early February, Norris told us that the Vietnamese were considering releasing him along with two other prisoners. For a couple of weeks, the Vietnamese had regularly interrogated Norris. Unbeknownst to us, they had been quizzing Norris to determine whether he was willing and suitable to be included in their first grant of "amnesty." Bud advised him to reject the offer. The Code of Conduct obliged us to refuse release before those who had been captured earlier had been released.

The next day, Norris was removed from our cell. The day of his release, February 16, I was carried on a stretcher with Bud walking beside me to a room where we were to bid Norris good-bye. A crew was filming the departure ceremony. Bud asked if he had been required to make any propaganda statement or do anything else he might later on regret. Norris said that he had not, and we let the matter drop.

Some of the prisoners were pretty hard on Norris and the other two prisoners for taking early release. Norris had taken very good care of me. He had saved my life. I thought him a good man then, as I do today. I feared he had made a mistake, but I couldn't stand in judgment of him. I thought too well of him, and owed him too much to stand between him and his freedom. I wished him well as he departed, carrying a letter from me to Carol in his pocket.

CHAPTER 17

Solitary

Bud and I remained roommates for about another month. When the Vietnamese observed that I could get around on my crutches, they moved Bud to another cell. In April 1968, Bud was relocated to another prison, and I was moved into another building, the largest cellblock in the camp, "the Warehouse." I cannot adequately describe how sorry I was to part company with my friend and inspiration. Up until then, I don't believe I had ever relied on any other person for emotional and physical support to the extent I had relied on Bud.

Although I could manage to hobble around on my crutches, I was still in poor shape. My arms had not yet healed, and I couldn't pick up or carry anything. I was still suffering from dysentery, a chronic ailment throughout most of my years in prison, and I weighed little more than a hundred pounds. The dysentery caused me considerable discomfort. Food and water would pass immediately through me, and sharp pains in my stomach made sleeping difficult. I was chronically fatigued and generally weak from my inability to retain nourishment.

Bud, whose injuries were nearly as debilitating as mine, helped me enormously by building my confidence in my eventual recovery.

He joked often about our condition, and got me to laugh about it as well. When other POWs teased us as they observed us hobbling along to the showers, no one laughed harder than Bud.

Bud had an indomitable will to survive with his reputation intact, and he strengthened my will to live. The only sustenance I had in those early days I took from the example of his abiding moral and physical courage. Bud was taken to a prison, "the Zoo," where the conditions and the cruelty of camp authorities made the Plantation seem like a resort. He would suffer terribly there, confronting the full force of man's inhumanity to man. But he was a tough, self-assured, and amazingly determined man, and he bore all his trials with an unshakable faith that he was a better man than his enemies. I was distraught when he left, but better prepared to endure my fate thanks to the months of his unflagging encouragement. I bid good-bye to him warmly, trying not to betray the sadness I felt to see him go. I would remain in solitary confinement for over two years.

It's an awful thing, solitary. It crushes your spirit and weakens your resistance more effectively than any other form of mistreatment. Having no one else to rely on, to share confidences with, to seek counsel from, you begin to doubt your judgment and your courage. But you eventually adjust to solitary, as you can to almost any hardship, by devising various methods to keep your mind off your troubles and greedily grasping any opportunity for human contact.

The first few weeks are the hardest. The onset of despair is immediate, and it is a formidable foe. You have to fight it with any means necessary, all the while trying to bridle the methods you devise to combat loneliness and prevent them from robbing your senses.

I tried to memorize the names of POWs, the names and personal details of guards and interrogators, and the details of my environment. I devised other memory games to keep my faculties sound. For days I tried to remember the names of all the pilots in my squadron and our sister squadron. I also prayed more often and more fervently than I ever had as a free man.

Solitary —

Many prisoners spent their hours exercising their minds by concentrating on an academic discipline or hobby they were proficient in. I knew men who mentally designed buildings and airplanes. I knew others who spent days and weeks working out complicated math formulas. I reconstructed from memory books and movies I had once enjoyed. I tried to compose books and plays of my own, often acting out sequences in the quiet solitude of my cell. Anyone who had observed my amateur theatrics might have challenged the exercise's beneficial effect on my mental stability.

I had to carefully guard against my fantasies becoming so consuming that they took me permanently to a place in my mind from which I might fail to return. On several occasions I became terribly annoyed when a guard entered my cell to take me to the bath or to bring me my food and disrupted some flight of fantasy where the imagined comforts were so attractive that I could not easily bear to be deprived of them. Sadly, I knew of a few men in prison who had grown so content in their imaginary worlds that they preferred solitary confinement and turned down the offer of a roommate. Eventually, they stopped communicating with the rest of us.

For long stretches of every day, I would watch the activities in camp through a crack in my door, grateful to witness any unusual or amusing moment that broke the usual monotony of prison administration. As I began to settle into my routine, I came to appreciate the POW adage "The days and hours are very long, but the weeks and months pass quickly."

Solitary also put me in a pretty surly mood, and I would resist depression by hollering insults at my guards, resorting to the belligerence that I had relied on earlier in my life when obliged to suffer one indignity or another. Resisting, being uncooperative and a general pain in the ass, proved, as it had in the past, to be a morale booster for me.

Hypochondria is a malady that commonly afflicts prisoners held in solitary confinement. A man becomes extremely conscious of his physical condition and can worry excessively over every ailment that plagues him. After Bud and I were separated, I struggled to resist concern bordering on paranoia that my injuries and poor health would eventually prove mortal.

I received nothing in the way of medical treatment. Three or four times a year, Zorba, the prison medic, would drop by for a brief visit. After a quick visual appraisal of my condition he would leave me with the exhortation to eat more and exercise. That I often could not keep down the little food allowed me after the guards had taken their share did not strike Zorba as paradoxical. Nor did Zorba bother to explain how I might manage to exercise given my disabling injuries and the narrow confines of my cell. I was routinely refused permission to spend a few minutes a day out of doors where I might have had the space necessary to concoct some half-assed exercise regimen.

I did try, despite my challenging circumstances and uncooperative guards, to build up my strength. In the summer of 1968, I attempted to do push-ups, but lacked the strength to raise myself once from my cell floor. I was able to perform a single standing push-up off the wall, but the experience was so painful that it only served to exacerbate my concern about my condition.

By late summer in 1969, my dysentery had eased. The strength I gained from holding down my food enabled me to begin exercising my leg. Whenever possible, I limped around my cell on my stiff leg, and I was greatly cheered when I noticed the limb slowly becoming stronger.

My arms were another matter. Over a period of two years, I began to regain some use of them, but even then exercise occasionally resulted in my arms' total immobility for a period that could last up to a month. After I returned to the States, an orthopedic surgeon informed me that because the fracture in my left arm had not been set, using my arm as much as I had during my imprisonment had worn a new socket in my left shoulder.

In the last two years of my captivity, prisoners were quartered together in large cells. Because of the improvement in our food and living conditions, I was strong enough to perform a rigorous daily exercise routine. Lopsided push-ups and a form of running in place that resembled hopping more than it did running gave my daily workout a comical aspect. But in addition to endlessly amusing my roommates, the routine considerably strengthened both my mental and physical reserves.

Left alone to act as my own physician, I made diagnoses that were occasionally closer to hysterical than practical. Among its many unattractive effects, dysentery often causes rather severe hemorrhoids. When this affliction visited me, I became morose, brooding about its implications for my survival. After some time, it finally occurred to me that I had never heard of a single person whose hemorrhoids had proved fatal. When this latest infirmity disappeared after a couple of months, I made a mental note to stop acting like an old man who stayed in bed all day fussing about his angina.

There is little doubt that solitary confinement causes some mental deterioration in even the most resilient personalities. When in 1970 my period of solitary confinement was finally ended, I was overwhelmed by the compulsion to talk nonstop, face-to-face with my obliging new cellmate. I ran my mouth ceaselessly for four days. My cellmate, John Finely, who had once been held in solitary himself and understood my exuberant reaction to his company, listened intently, frequently nodding his head in assent to my rhetorical points even though he could not possibly have taken in more than a fraction of my rambling dialogue.

I have observed this phenomenon in many other men when they were released from solitary. One of the more amusing spectacles in prison is the sight of two men, both just released from solitary, talking their heads off simultaneously, neither one listening to the other, both absolutely enraptured by the sound of their voices. Most "solos" settled down after spending a few days with a roommate and recovered the strength and confidence of men who were sound in both mind and body.

We had a saying in prison: "Steady strain." The point of the re-mark was to remind us to keep a close watch on our emotions, not to let them rise and fall with circumstances that were out of our control. We tried hard to avoid seizing on any small change in our treatment as an indication of an approaching change in our fortunes.

We called some POWs "gastro politicians," because their spirits soared every time they found a carrot in their soup. "Look at this. They're fattening us up," they would declare. "We must be going home." And when no omen appeared in the next day's meal, the gastro politician's irrational exuberance of the previous day would disappear, and he would sink into an equally irrational despondency, lamenting, "We're never getting out of here."

Most of the prisoners considered it unhealthy to allow themselves to interpret our circumstances like tea leaf readers divining some se-cret purpose in the most unremarkable event. Prison was enough of a psychological strain without riding an emotional roller coaster of our own creation. Once you began investing meals or an unexpectedly civil word from a guard with greater meaning than it merited, you might begin to pay attention to the promises or threats of your cap-tors. That was the surest way to lose your resolve or even your mind.

"Steady strain, buddy, steady strain," we cautioned each other whenever we began to take a short view of our lives. It was best to take the long view. We would get home when we got home. There wasn't anything we could do to hasten that day's arrival. Until then we had to manage our hardships as best we could, and hope that when we did get home we would have been a credit to ourselves and to the country.

When you're left alone with your thoughts for years, it's hard not to reflect on how better you could have spent your time as a free man. I had more than a normal share of regrets, but regret for choosing the career that had landed me in this place was not among them.

I regretted I hadn't read more books so I could keep my mind bet-ter occupied in solitary. I regretted much of the foolishness that had characterized my youth, seeing in it, at last, its obvious insignificance.

I regretted I hadn't worked harder at the Academy, believing that had I done so, I might have been better prepared for the trial I now faced.

My regrets were never so severe that they made me despondent, but I did experience remorse to an extent I had never known in the past, an emotion that helped mature me. I gained the insight, common to many people in life-threatening circumstances, that the trivial pleasures of life and human vanity were transient and insignificant. And I resolved that when I regained my freedom, I would seize opportunities to spend what remained of my life in more important pursuits.

"All that's beautiful drifts away/Like the waters," lament Yeats's old men. Except, I discovered, love and honor. If you valued them, and held them strongly, love and honor would endure undiminished by the passing of time and the most determined assault on your dignity. And to hold on to love and honor I needed to be part of a fraternity. I was not as strong a man as I had once believed myself to be.

Of all the activities I devised to survive solitary confinement with my wits and strength intact, nothing was more beneficial than communicating with other prisoners. It was, simply, a matter of life and death.

Fortunately, the Vietnamese—although they went to extraordinary lengths to prevent it—couldn't stop all communication among prisoners. Through flashed hand signals when we were moved about, tap codes on the wall, notes hidden in washroom drains, and holding our enamel drinking cups up to the wall with our shirts wrapped around them and speaking through them, we were able to communicate with each other. The whole prison system became a complex information network, POWs busily trafficking in details about each other's circumstances and news from home that would arrive with every new addition to our ranks.

The tap code was a simple device. The signal to communicate was the old rhythm "shave and a haircut," and the response, "two bits," was given if the coast was clear. We divided the alphabet into five columns of five letters each. The letter K was dropped. A, F, L, Q,

and V were the key letters. Tap once for the five letters in the A column, twice for F, three times for L, and so on. After indicating the
column, pause for a beat, then tap one through five times to indicate
the right letter. My name would be tapped 3-2, 1-3, 1-3, 1-1, 2-4, 3-3.

It was an easy system to teach the uninitiated, and new guys
would usually be communicating like veterans within a few days. We
became so proficient at it that in time we could communicate as effi-
ciently by tapping as we could by speaking through our drinking cups.
But I preferred, whenever circumstances allowed, to speak to my
neighbors. The sound of the human voice, unappreciated in an open
society's noisy clutter of spoken words, was an emblem of humanity to
a man held at length in solitary confinement, an elegant and poignant
affirmation that we possessed a divine spark that our enemies could
not extinguish.

The punishment for communicating could be severe, and a few
POWs, having been caught and beaten for their efforts, had their spirits broken as their bodies were battered. Terrified of a return trip to
the punishment room, they would lie still in their cells when their
comrades tried to tap them up on the wall. Very few would remain un-
communicative for long. To suffer all this alone was less tolerable than
torture. Withdrawing in silence from the fellowship of other Americans and the doggedly preserved cohesion of an American military
unit was to us the approach of death. Almost all would recover their
strength in a few days and answer the summons to rejoin the living.

In October 1968, I heard the guards bring a new prisoner into the
camp and lock him into the cell behind mine. Ernie Brace was a decorated former Marine who had flown over a hundred combat missions
in the Korean War. He had been accused of deserting the scene of an
aircraft accident, court-martialed, and discharged dishonorably from
the service. Determined to restore his good name, he had volunteered
as a civilian pilot to fly supply missions in Laos for the United States
Agency for International Development, and, when asked, to secretly
supply CIA-supported military units in the Laotian jungle.

During one such operation, Communist insurgents, the Pathet Lao, overran the small airstrip where he had just landed and captured him. His captors handed him over to soldiers in the North Vietnamese Army, who marched him to a remote outpost near Dien Bien Phu. He was imprisoned for three years in a bamboo cage with his arms and legs bound. He attempted three escapes. He was brutally tortured, held in leg stocks, and tethered to a stake by a rope around his neck. After his last failed escape attempt, the Vietnamese buried him in a pit up to his neck and left him there for a week.

In 1968, he was brought to Hanoi. Uncertain whether the United States government was aware he had been captured alive, he was greatly relieved to realize that he was now in the company of American POWs whose captivity was known to our government.

When the commotion in the cell behind me died down as the guards left Ernie alone in his new home, I tried to tap him up on the wall. In terrible shape, and fearful that the knocks he heard in the cell next door were made by Vietnamese trying to entrap him in an attempted violation of the prohibition against communicating, he made no response. For days I tried in vain to talk to him.

Finally, he tapped back, a faint but audible "two bits." I put my drinking cup to the wall and spoke directly to my new neighbor.

"Do you have a drinking cup?"

No response.

"Tap twice if you have a drinking cup and once if you don't."

No response.

"I'm talking through my cup. Do you have a drinking cup? If you have a cup, wrap your shirt around it, hold it up to the wall, and talk to me."

No response.

"You want to communicate, don't you?"

No response.

I continued at some length, vainly trying to get him to talk to me. But as he had just been given a drinking cup, his suspicion that he was being set up by the Vietnamese intensified as I urged him to make illicit use of it.

A few days later, the possibility that he could talk with another American for the first time in three years overrode his understandable caution. When I asked him if he had a cup, he tapped twice for yes.

"I'm Lieutenant Commander John McCain. I was shot down over Hanoi in 1967. Who are you?"

"My name is Ernie Brace," came the response.

"Are you Air Force? Navy? Marine?"

"My name is Ernie Brace."

"Where were you shot down?"

"My name is Ernie Brace."

To my every query, Ernie could only manage to say his name before he broke down. I could hear him crying. After his long, awful years in the jungle, the sound of an American voice, carrying with it the promise of fraternity with men who would share his struggle, had overwhelmed him.

It took some time before Ernie could keep his composure long enough to engage in informative conversation. But once he did, he became a tireless talker, hungry for all information about his new circumstances and eager to provide me with all the details of his capture and captivity.

I was somewhat surprised to learn he was a civilian. I assumed he was CIA, but refrained from asking him. As a civilian, Ernie was under no obligation to adhere to the Code of Conduct. The United States expected him not to betray any highly sensitive information, the disclosure of which would endanger the lives of other Americans. But other than that, he was not required to show any fidelity to his country and her cause beyond the demands of his own conscience.

But Ernie's conscience demanded much from him. He kept our code faithfully. When the Vietnamese offered to release him, he declined, insisting that others captured before him be released first. No one I knew in prison, Army, Navy, Marine, or Air Force officer, had greater loyalty to his country or derived more courage from his sense of honor. It was an honor to serve with him.

Incongruous though it must seem, early on, POWs could be better informed about the circumstances of other prisons and the men held there than we were about the population of our own camp. Many cells at the Plantation were uninhabited when I first came there, and we had a hard time establishing a camp-wide communications network. Some prisoners were located in other buildings or in cells some distance away and separated by empty rooms from mine. Most of our senior officers at the Plantation were kept in isolated cells. They were out of reach of our tapping, and we did not walk by their cells when we were taken to the washroom and the interrogation room.

New arrivals who had been placed in cells within my communications bloc brought us information about the men held at Hoa Lo, the Zoo, and other prisons in and around Hanoi. But we often puzzled over the identity of men held a short distance from us in different parts of the camp. A tough resister, Ted Guy, an Air Force colonel, was living in a different building. Unable to communicate with him, the men in my block assumed for several months that the senior officer nearest to us, Dick Stratton, a Navy commander, was the senior ranking officer for the whole camp. Ernie Brace informed us of our error. He had learned about Colonel Guy's presence in our ranks in a conversation with another POW.

There were about eighty Americans held at the Plantation during my first years in prison. Eventually I would come to know many of the men at the Plantation. Keeping an ever-lengthening account of the men we learned were prisoners was the solemn responsibility of every POW. We would fall asleep at night while silently chanting the names on the list. Knowing the men in my prison and being known by them was my best assurance of returning home. Communicating not only affirmed our humanity. It kept us alive.

CHAPTER 18

The Plantation

The walls of the Plantation enclosed what had once been a lovely estate. Numerous trees were all that remained of the gardens, but the large mansion that had formerly housed Hanoi's mayor when Vietnam was a French colony still stood in reasonably good repair. We called it "the Big House," and we were taken there for initial interrogation. It also provided receiving rooms for American peace delegations, who arrived with great fanfare to affirm how well we were being treated despite the terrible crimes we had committed against the Vietnamese people.

Several warehouses surrounded the mansion. They were divided into cells and housed the POW population. Various other smaller buildings dotted the estate and served as quarters for the guards and other prison workers. After Bud Day and I were separated, I was kept alone in Room 13 West at the south end of the Warehouse. Directly across the courtyard from my cell was the interrogation room, where I would often reside during periods of attitude adjustment.

The cells in the Plantation were large compared to those at other prisons. Mine was approximately fifteen by fifteen feet. Each cell had a wooden board for a bed and a naked lightbulb dangling on a cord in the center of the ceiling. The light was kept on twenty-four hours a day. I got used to it after a while. It didn't bother me much in the winter, but in the summer heat, when most prisoners were suffering miserably from heat rash and boils, the extra warmth from the light made our discomfort all the harder to bear. Adding to the intensity of our discomfort was the building's tin roof, which must have increased the summer heat by ten or more degrees.

The cell windows were boarded up to prevent us from seeing out and from communicating with one another, blocking all ventilation except for some small holes near the top of wall. Every door had a peephole that turnkeys used to look in on us. Every door also had cracks in it through which we could observe our turnkeys and the daily activities of camp personnel.

The daily routine was simple and excruciatingly dull. The guards struck a gong at six in the morning, signaling the start of a new day. We rose, folded our gear, and listened from the loudspeakers in our cells to Hanoi Hannah, the "Voice of Vietnam," a half hour of witless propaganda, rebroadcast from the night before. For most POWs, Hannah was a pretty good source of entertainment.

"American GIs, don't fight in this illegal and immoral war," Hannah pleaded, before reporting the latest victories of the heroic people's liberation forces. She brought us the news from home, which was, of course, limited to updates on antiwar activities and incidents of civil strife. She often played recordings of speeches by prominent American opponents of the war. In 1972, she unwittingly informed us that an American had landed on the moon by playing a portion of a campaign speech by George McGovern chastising Nixon for putting a man on the moon but failing to end the war. The musical interlude was a mix of Vietnamese patriotic songs and a few American songs, usually some scratchy old Louis Armstrong records that some fleeing Frenchman had left behind when France relinquished its Indochinese colony.

During the Tet Offensive, in 1968, Hannah couldn't restrain her patriotic ardor as she gleefully regaled us with news of "many heroic victories" over the American imperialists and their puppet regime in the South. The guards shared her enthusiasm. On the night Tet began, they were all fired up, racing around the camp, yelling and shooting their rifles into the night air. The POWs were clueless about the cause of the commotion until Hannah brought us the news the next evening.

Hannah was especially excited about the siege of the American Marine base at Khe San, confidently predicting, night after night, its imminent surrender. Six weeks after she first alerted us to the siege, Hannah stopped updating us on the progress of the people's heroic liberation of Khe San. Evidently the Marines defending Khe San had proved heroic as well.

About an hour after Hannah's morning rebroadcast, the turnkeys opened each cell door, and, one at a time, each prisoner brought his waste bucket out, set it down, and stepped back into his cell. After all the waste buckets were placed outside and the guards had locked the prisoners back in their cells, two POWs were assigned the task of collecting the buckets, dumping their contents into a large hole in the back of the camp, washing them out, and returning them to their owners. For a brief while, the prisoners used this daily chore to pass notes on cigarette paper and other scraps of paper. The Vietnamese soon discovered our treachery and kept a closer eye on the unfortunate POWs who drew this duty.

After the buckets were returned, the guards filled our teapots. If it was a wash day, they would then take us to bathe. In winters, when water was plentiful, we would often bathe twice a week. In summer, when water was scarce, we would sometimes go weeks without bathing. After we had hung our wet clothes and washrag out to dry and returned to our cells, each prisoner was taken back out, one at a time, to pick up his breakfast, usually a piece of bread and a bowl of soup made by boiling something that vaguely resembled a pumpkin.

Each prisoner was then returned to his cell and locked in before the next prisoner was allowed to collect his morning meal.

The food at the Plantation was notoriously bad, and, as the old joke goes, the portions were too small. Discipline among the Plantation's guards was poor, and we suffered from a high rate of food thievery. The pots in which our meals were prepared were never washed, and the guards who served us were only slightly cleaner. I never enjoyed a reputation for cleanliness, but my frequent bouts of dysentery brought on by my filthy living conditions greatly increased my appreciation of the virtue, and I cringed whenever I watched our food being prepared.

After we finished eating, the process was repeated in reverse as we returned our empty bowls. There were no other activities after breakfast until we were brought out for the afternoon meal. On wash days we collected our dry clothes with the afternoon meal.

Shortly after lunch, around noon, they rang the gong again to signal the afternoon nap, which lasted until two. Until the gong sounded we weren't allowed to lie down unless we were ill. On some afternoons they piped in additional propaganda broadcasts over the loudspeakers, occasionally playing them all afternoon. Other times we went for weeks without afternoon tributes to the great patriotic struggle, although Hannah never missed an evening or morning broadcast.

Our boredom was periodically alleviated by the provision of reading materials. The camp literature offered little in the way of a rewarding read. Most often, I was given a copy of the *Vietnam Courier,* a propaganda rag full of decidedly tendentious news accounts of the war and current events.

Reading the *Courier,* I was always amused by its descriptions of Ho Chi Minh's many remarkable attributes, powers normally associated with the Divinity. If a certain province reported a poor rice harvest one year, Uncle Ho would arrive on the scene, and, bingo, next year's harvest set a record. Got a problem with your tractor, call Uncle Ho for an illuminating lecture on tractor maintenance. If air pirates were bombing your village, Uncle Ho would teach the village idiot how to target a surface-to-air missile and in no time at all he would be destroying whole squadrons. No task was too small for Ho. He would always take a few minutes from his busy administration of the war to cure whatever ailed you.

Other times, I received awkwardly written books boasting of extraordinary Vietnamese war victories, whole battalions of American infantry annihilated by a few determined peasants, grandmothers shooting down American aircraft. Of course, all our literary diversions required us to endure a fulminating condemnation of American war crimes.

We were also read aloud to quite often. Works by prominent American authors who were opposed to the war and by other, less distinguished pamphleteers were haltingly, and some times unintelligibly, broadcast throughout the camp. Dr. Spock's works, sadly not his texts on child care, were a popular form of political enlightenment.

Sometimes we were made to watch movies in which Vietnamese nationalism was accorded even greater supernatural powers than it was in books and newspapers. A tank division or several American battalions were never a match for one lightly armed, gallant, kind-to-women-and-children Vietnamese fighting man. Of course, the Vietnamese took elaborate precautions when taking us to the movies, lest we hopelessly inferior Americans pull some kind of trick on our virtuous, all-knowing guards. Each prisoner watched the movies from a separate cubicle made with blankets or mosquito netting hung over a line.

Although I suppose I should have been insulted by such heavy-handed propaganda, it was so clumsy and so absurd that it seldom failed to amuse me. I came to welcome most of it as a reliably entertaining diversion, but it also exacerbated my yearning for a world in which all information was not portioned out sparingly and in disguise to advance someone's military or political objectives.

We were deprived of even the most basic comforts. It would be too time-consuming a task to list all the things I missed in prison. I missed the staples of life, of course, good and plentiful food, a comfortable bed, being out of doors. But the thing I missed most was information—free, uncensored, undistorted, abundant information.

When we were released from prison in 1973, the first thing most of us did after arriving at Clark Air Base in the Philippines was order a steak dinner or an ice cream sundae or some other food we had longed for in prison. But I was as hungry for information as I was for a decent meal, and when I placed my dinner order I asked also for newspapers and magazines. I wanted to know what was going on in the world, and I grasped anything I could find that might offer a little enlightenment.

Every night at the Plantation, except Saturday night, all the camp personnel would attend what we derisively referred to as "revival" meetings. We would lie on our hard bunks and listen to the Vietnamese fervently cheer, clap, and shout expressions of nationalism and simplistic slogans epitomizing their national ideology. Each one would take a turn reading from a tract of anti-American propaganda.

At nine o'clock every evening, the guards rang the evening gong instructing us to go to sleep, and, shivering in the cold or sweating in the stifling heat, beset by mosquitoes, and in the glare of a naked lightbulb, we tried to escape to our dreams. That was our day.

The only thing that changed my daily regimen was an interrogation. Interrogations were irregular events. Three or four weeks could pass before I was subjected to one. Other times I was interrogated twice in one day, sometimes by senior officers, sometimes by lower-ranking officers or enlisted personnel whom we called "quiz kids." The sound of jangling keys and fumbling with locks at night or at other irregular times had the effect of unexpected gunfire. I shot bolt upright the moment I heard it, gripped by terror, my heart beating so loud I thought it would be audible to the approaching guard. In the years after I came home, I never suffered from flashbacks or posttraumatic stress syndrome, as it is clinically termed. But for a long time after coming home, I would tense up whenever I heard keys rattle, and for an instant I would feel the onset of an old fear come back to haunt me.

They never interrogated or tortured us in our cells. They always took us to the interrogation rooms, spartan cells with bare walls, furnished with just a wooden table, a chair behind the table, and a stool in front of it, lower than the chair, for the prisoner to sit on.

Some interrogations were comparatively benign. Sometimes they were little more than training sessions for a new interrogator who was trying to learn English. The interrogators would demand information, or order me to confess my crimes into a tape recorder. When I refused, they would make a perfunctory threat to persuade me to reconsider. When I refused again, they just sent me back to my cell, the threatened beating forgotten.

Once I was instructed to draw a diagram of an aircraft carrier. I decided to comply with the order, but took considerable artistic license in the process. I drew a picture of a ship's deck with a large swimming pool on the fantail, the captain's quarters in a chain locker, and various other imagined embellishments.

Vietnamese propaganda about the soft, luxurious life that upper-class Westerners (a social class to which military officers were naturally thought to belong) led made the interrogators easy marks for a lot of the b.s. we devised to avoid giving them any useful information. My fantastic rendering of an American carrier didn't arouse my gullible interrogator's suspicions until I noted its keel was three hundred feet deep. Unfortunately, he knew that the shallow waters of the Tonkin Gulf couldn't accommodate a ship that drew this much water. He denounced me as a liar and ordered me punished.

After a couple of physically intense interrogations, my captors forced me to read the "news" a few times over the camp loudspeakers. On each occasion, I managed to badly fracture the syntax of the prepared text and affect a goofy, singsong delivery. The Vietnamese, observing that my prisonmates laughed whenever my voice came over the speakers, soon despaired of my qualities as a broadcaster. One of my interrogators informed me that "the other prisoners say you make fun of us," and soon my brief career as the Plantation's Walter Cronkite was over.

One spring, a young interrogator I had not seen before decided to practice his English by chatting amiably with me about Western religious customs. "What is Easter?" he asked me. I told him that it was the time of year we celebrated the death and resurrection of the Son of God. As I recounted the events of Christ's passion, His crucifixion, death, resurrection, and assumption to heaven, I saw my curious interrogator furrow his brow in disbelief.

"You say He died?"

"Yes, He died."

"Three days, He was dead?"

"Yes. Then He came alive again. People saw Him and then He went back to heaven."

Clearly puzzled, he stared wordlessly at me for a few moments, then left the room. A short time later, he returned, his friendly manner gone, an angry resolve replacing it.

"Mac Kane, the officer say you tell nothing but lies. Go back to your room," he ordered, the mystery of my faith proving incomprehensible to him.

On other occasions the interrogators were deadly serious, and if they threatened to beat you into cooperation, you were certain they would give it a hell of a try.

Often we knew how difficult things were likely to become by the identity of the interrogator. We called one interrogator "the Soft Soap Fairy," for his delicate manners and the solicitous good-cop routine he employed in well-spoken English to plead with prisoners for their cooperation. "How are you, Mac Kane," he would greet me. If another interrogator who lacked Soft Soap's gentility had recently roughed me up, he would tell me how sorry he was. "This terrible war," he would say. "I hope it's over soon."

"Me too," I would reply.

After these preliminary courtesies were concluded, Soft Soap would start questioning me with a schoolboy's curiosity about life in the States, and American movie stars.

Soft Soap was a political officer, and theoretically he had authority at least commensurate with the camp commander's. But he was never around for the less pleasant aspects of an interrogator's work. He never threatened to torture us, but would advise us that our lack of cooperation was likely to incur the camp commander's displeasure and warn us that the commander could be a harsh and unforgiving man. Whenever we personally experienced just how harsh and unforgiving, Soft Soap always claimed that he had been away from the camp at the time and unable to prevent our punishment from getting out of hand.

"I'm sorry, Mac Kane, I was not here. The camp commander sometimes cannot control himself."

"No problem."

Regrettably, I didn't always draw Soft Soap as my interrogator. In the later years of my captivity, I sometimes sat on the stool looking into the cockeyed stare of the Bug. If I refused Bug's demands or gave him any lip, he would order the guards to knock me around until I at least stopped trading insults with him. The Bug was a sadist. Or at least his hate for us was so irrational that it drove him to sadism. He was famous for accusing prisoners, when our recalcitrance had enraged him, of killing his mother. Given the wildness of his rage, I often feared that we had.

On occasions when he was particularly determined, I would find myself trussed up and left for hours in ropes, my biceps bound tightly with several loops to cut off my circulation and the end of the rope cinched behind my back, pulling my shoulders and elbows unnaturally close together. It was incredibly painful.

However, even during these difficult encounters I realized my captors were more careful not to permanently injure or disfigure me than they were with other prisoners. When they tied me in the ropes, they rolled my sleeves up so that my shirt served as padding between my arms and the ropes, a courtesy they seldom granted their other victims. The Vietnamese also never put me in ankle stocks or leg irons, a punishment they inflicted on many POWs.

With the exception of a rough time I would experience in the summer of 1968, and a few other occasions when a guard or interrogator acted impulsively out of anger, I always sensed that they refrained from doing their worst to me. The realization that my captors accorded me different treatment than the other prisoners made me bolder and at times more reckless than I should have been. It also made me feel guilty to know that my courage and loyalty had not been put to the test with the same cruelty and tenacity that marked our captors' attempts to destroy the resolve of other prisoners.

There were others who, like Bug, seemed to enjoy their work. But many of the interrogators were bureaucrats who mistreated us simply because they had been ordered by their superiors to extract certain information from us. For them, it was a job, less dangerous than other jobs, to be sure, but not particularly pleasant. The word would come down from the ministry to get more war crimes confessions, and, dutiful to a fault, the interrogators would set about getting war crimes confessions by whatever means necessary.

We could always tell when new orders had arrived and things were about to take a turn for the worse. Prisoners would start disappearing from their cells, some for hours, others for days. When they returned to their cells they would start tapping, telling us they had been tortured, how bad it was, and what the Vietnamese were after. The rest of us sat in our cells, sometimes listening to the screams of a tortured friend fill the air, sweating out the hours until the guards came for us.

They never seemed to mind hurting us, but they usually took care not to let things get so out of hand that our lives were put in danger. We strongly believed some POWs were tortured to death, and most were seriously mistreated. But the Vietnamese prized us as bargaining chips in peace negotiations, and, with tragic exceptions, they usually did not intend to kill us when they used torture to force our cooperation.

In my case, I felt pretty certain that no matter how rough my periodic visits to the interrogation room were, my father's rank gave me value as a potential propaganda opportunity and as a proffer in peace negotiations, and thus restrained my captors from killing me.

Authority was apportioned among four categories of prison authorities. The senior officers and interrogators occupied the top of the pecking order. The camp commander, a regular army officer, was nominally in charge of the prison. But it was obvious to all prisoners that the camp political officer, drawn from the ranks of the political bureau of the army, was the man in charge. He had responsibility for all matters involving prisoner indoctrination and behavior, interrogations, confessions, and propaganda displays.

The relationship between camp commander and political officer varied somewhat from camp to camp. At the Plantation, Soft Soap Fairy was the political officer, and he always referred to "Slopehead," the camp commander, as the officer responsible for torture and punishment. Slopehead did most of the dirty work, but Soft Soap, for all his protestations of innocence, was responsible for getting the information from prisoners that Slopehead would eventually try to beat out of us.

Next in line were the turnkeys who supervised our daily routine. They let us out of our cells to collect our meals and to bathe, locked us back in when we had finished, monitored us constantly to prevent communication, and, if so disposed, responded when we called *"Bao cao"* to get their attention.

The turnkeys were younger than the interrogators; many of them were still in their teens. Some of them treated us no worse than their job description obliged, but others harbored considerable animosity toward us and seemed to relish opportunities to degrade us. Being so young, most turnkeys, when they first took up this line of work, were curious about the strange Americans they guarded. But in time, increasingly irritated by our evident disrespect for their authority, many of them grew to despise us, and they would go out of their way to give us a hard time.

For a time, I had a turnkey who ritualistically expressed his intense dislike of me. We called him "the Prick." He would enter my cell and order me to bow. Our captors believed that their advantage over us entitled them to formal displays of deference. They expected us to bow whenever they approached us. We believed otherwise. When the Prick ordered me to bow, I would refuse, and he would respond to the discourtesy by smashing his fist into the side of my head and knocking me down. On a few occasions when I just didn't feel up to the confrontation and bowed, he hit me anyway. These encounters were not episodic. They occurred every morning for nearly two years.

The Prick had other, less violent means of harassing me. He would often intentionally spill my food, trip me when I walked to the showers, or take me to the shower on a hot summer day and laugh when I discovered there was no water in the tank. But he seemed to regard his morning visitations as the most satisfying form of self-expression.

Occupying the last station in the camp hierarchy were the Vietnamese we called "gun guards." These were young soldiers who wandered around the camp carrying a rifle on their shoulder. Many had physical handicaps or other limitations that made them unfit for jungle fighting. Most gun guards were largely indifferent to us. Their duty was certainly preferable to fighting at the front, wherever that might be on a given day, and I'm sure they appreciated the relative security of their work. But few ever displayed a particular zeal for lording their authority over the prisoners. They just did their job, in six-hour shifts, and counted their blessings.

After one difficult interrogation, I was left in the interrogation room for the night, tied in ropes. A gun guard, whom I had noticed before but had never spoken to, was working the night shift, 10:00 P.M. to 4:00 A.M. A short time after the interrogators had left me to ponder my bad attitude for the evening, this guard entered the room and silently, without looking at or smiling at me, loosened the ropes, and then he left me alone. A few minutes before his shift ended, he returned and tightened up the ropes.

On Christmas Day, we were always treated to a better-than-usual dinner. We were also allowed to stand outside our cells for five minutes to exercise or to just look at the trees and sky. One Christmas, a few months after the gun guard had inexplicably come to my assistance during my long night in the interrogation room, I was standing in the dirt courtyard when I saw him approach me.

He walked up and stood silently next to me. Again, he didn't smile or look at me. He just stared at the ground in front of us. After a few moments had passed he rather nonchalantly used his sandaled foot to draw a cross in the dirt. We both stood wordlessly looking at the cross until, after a minute or two, he rubbed it out and walked away. I saw my good Samaritan often after the Christmas when we venerated the cross together. But he never said a word to me nor gave the slightest signal that he acknowledged my humanity.

An Air Force major lived in the cell next to me at the Plantation. Bob Craner and I were indefatigable communicators. We talked endlessly through our cups or by tap code on any subject that came to mind.

Bob was a naturally taciturn fellow. He had a roommate for a time, Guy Gruters, another Air Force officer. Had I also had a roommate, Bob might have been less inclined to talk to me as much as he did. But I was alone, and I needed to talk as much as possible with my neighbor to keep from lapsing into despair. So Bob kept up his end of our ceaseless conversation to get me through my years in solitary. We talked at great length every day about our circumstances, our families, and our lives back in the States.

He loved baseball and revered Ted Williams. Bob could recite

Williams's batting average in every year he had played in the major leagues. He was never more animated than when arguing over who was the better ballplayer, Williams or Stan Musial. In high school, Bob had developed a crush on a young girl. After admiring her from afar for many months, he worked up the nerve to ask her out. When he arrived at her home to collect her for their first date, they somehow fell into a conversation about baseball, during which the young lady ventured an opinion on the Williams-Musial dispute. She thought Musial the better player. From that moment on, Bob would have nothing to do with her.

He had grown up in a family of modest means and after high school had entered the cadet program started by the Air Force, which at that time didn't have an academy of its own. He eventually earned a college degree while serving in the Air Force. He was a naturally gifted pilot, and, recognizing his talent, the Air Force had sent him to fighter weapons school at Nellis Air Force Base in Nevada, which only the best pilots were permitted to attend.

Air Force pilots were allowed to fly only one hundred combat missions in Vietnam. When Bob had completed his hundredth mission, he requested and was denied another tour by his commanding officer. He went to Saigon to argue his case with the Air Force command in Vietnam. After a long campaign, his superiors relented and granted him another tour. He was shot down on his 102nd mission.

He never complained about his misfortune nor regretted having prevailed on the Air Force to let him fly another combat tour. He joked when he told me about it, laughing when he remarked, "Well, I guess I got my wish." But I never observed a trace of bitterness or self-reproach in Bob. We both were doing what we wanted to do, what we had so long prepared to do, when our luck turned for the worse. We chose our lives and were grateful for their rewards, and we accepted the consequences without regret.

He was my dear friend, and for two years I was closer to him than

I had ever been to another human being. Bob spoke for both of us when, months after we were released from prison, he described how completely we had relied on each other to preserve our humanity.

> McCain and I leaned on each other a great deal. We were separated by about eighteen inches of brick, and I never saw the guy for the longest time. I used to have dreams . . . we all did, of course, and they were sometimes night-mares . . . and my world had shrunk to a point where the figures in my dreams were myself, the guards and a voice . . . and that was McCain. I didn't know what he looked like, so I could not visualize him in my dreams, be-cause he became the guy—the only guy—I turned to, for a period of two years.
>
> We got to know each other more intimately, I'm sure, than I will ever know my wife. We opened up and talked about damn near everything besides our immediate problems—past life, and all the family things we never would have talked to anybody about. We derived a great deal of strength from this.

A great deal of strength indeed. And I am certain I derived more strength from our friendship than he could possibly have derived from it. Bob Craner kept me alive. Without his strength, his wisdom, his humor, and his unselfish consideration, I doubt I would have sur-vived solitary with my mind and my self-respect reasonably intact. I relied almost entirely on him for advice and for his unfailing ability to raise my spirits when I had lost heart.

He was a remarkably composed man with the courage to accept any fate with great dignity. There were times when I would start to lose my nerve. I would detect some sign that another camp purge was coming, and my dread of another beating would start to get the better of my self-control. Anticipating a beating could often prove more un-nerving than the beating itself.

"Bob, I think it's coming again, and I don't think they'll miss us."

"If it comes, it comes," he counseled me. "If it doesn't, it doesn't, and there isn't a damn thing we can do about it."

It may strike others as odd that such fatalism could have comforted us, but it did. It was the best attitude you could hold under the circumstances. It steeled me when I was weak, and made me feel better about myself. Worrying about a beating was pointless. There wasn't much I could do to prevent it, save disgrace myself, and disgrace hurt more than the worst beating.

Whenever I was plagued by doubts about my situation or my own conduct, I turned to the voice on the other side of my wall. And it was to Bob I went for guidance one June evening in 1968, after the Vietnamese had offered me my freedom.

--- CHAPTER 19 ---

The Fourth of July

For months, I had received conspicuously lenient treatment. By the time Bud and I were separated, I was able to walk for short distances, and the Vietnamese decided I was fit enough to withstand interrogations, or "quizzes," as the POWs called them. The Vietnamese had caught me communicating several times, and I was forever displaying a "bad attitude" toward my guards. During this period, I possessed the camp record for being caught the most times in the act of communicating, yet the Vietnamese often only punished my offenses with threats. Sometimes they withheld my daily cigarette ration or my bathing privileges, a punishment that served to make me even surlier toward my guards. Once in a while they would cuff me around, but not often, and they never seriously hurt me.

In my first return to the interrogation room after being left alone for many weeks, Soft Soap had asked me if I would like to go home. I had replied that I would not go home out of turn. To this, and with uncharacteristic churlishness, Soft Soap had said, "You are all war criminals and will never go home."

After I went back to my cell, I relayed Soft Soap's offer up the communication chain to Hervey Stockman, an Air Force colonel who was our senior ranking officer at the time. Offers of early release were a fairly common practice at the time, and we regarded them as nothing more than psychological torture. So neither the SRO nor I took Soft Soap's inquiry very seriously.

Sometime in the middle of June 1968, I was summoned to an interview with the Cat. His interpreter was an English-speaking officer we called "the Rabbit," an experienced torturer who enjoyed his work. I had been brought to the large reception room in the Big House, the room they often brought visiting peace delegations to for their clumsily staged propaganda displays. The room was furnished with upholstered chairs, a sofa, and a glass coffee table supported by two decorative ceramic elephants. An inviting spread of tea, cookies, and cigarettes had been laid out on the table.

The Cat began telling me about how he had run the prison camps during the French Indochina War, and how he had given a couple of prisoners their liberty. He said he had seen the men recently, and they had thanked him for his kindness. He told me Norris Overly and the two Americans released with him had gone home with honor.

After about two hours of circuitous conversation, the Cat asked me if I wanted to go home. I was astonished by the offer and didn't immediately know how to respond. I wasn't in great shape, was still considerably underweight and miserable with dysentery and heat rash. The prospect of going home to my family was powerfully tempting. But I knew what the Code of Conduct instructed, and I held back from responding, saying I would have to think about it. He told me to go back to my cell and consider his offer carefully.

The Vietnamese usually required prisoners who were released early to make some statement that indicated their gratitude or at least their desire to be released. They viewed such expressions as assurances that the released prisoner would not denounce his captors once he was back home, and spoil whatever propaganda value his release was intended to serve. Accordingly, they would not force a prisoner to go home.

As soon as I could, I raised Bob Craner and asked for his advice.

We talked the offer over for a while and speculated about what I might be asked to provide in exchange for my release. After a considerable time, Bob told me I should go home. I had hoped he would advise me not to take the offer, which would have made my decision easier. But he argued that the seriously injured should be excused from the Code's restrictions on accepting amnesty and should take release if offered. He said I should go home, as my long-term survival in prison was in doubt.

Close confidants though we had been for months, Bob and I had never really seen any more of each other than a couple of brief glimpses when the turnkeys took one or the other of us to the interrogation room or to the showers. Bob had never observed my physical condition and had only reports from other prisoners and my own occasional references to the state of my health upon which to base his judgment about my fitness for prolonged imprisonment. Yet this good man, who revered our Code of Conduct, and who braved the worst adversity with dignity, offered me a rationale to go home, out of turn, while others in at least as bad shape as I was in remained behind.

"You don't know if you can survive this," he argued. "The seriously injured can go home."

"I think I can make it," I replied. "The Vietnamese tell me I won't, but if they really thought that I'm in such bad shape they would have at least sent a doctor around to check on me."

"You can't be sure you're up to this. What do they want from you in return?"

"They didn't say."

"Well, when you go back, just play along with them. See what they want to let you go. If it's not much, take it."

"I don't think I should go down that road. I know and you know what they want, and we won't let it go any further. If I start negotiating with them, it's a slippery slope. They'll tell me they don't want anything, but they'll just wait until the day I'm supposed to go, and then tell me what they want for it. No matter what I agree to, it won't look right."

I wanted to say yes. I badly wanted to go home. I was tired and sick, and despite my bad attitude, I was often afraid. But I couldn't keep from my own counsel the knowledge of how my release would affect my father, and my fellow prisoners. I knew what the Vietnamese hoped to gain from my release.

Although I did not know it at the time, my father would shortly assume command of the war effort as Commander in Chief, Pacific. The Vietnamese intended to hail his arrival with a propaganda spectacle as they released his son in a gesture of "goodwill." I was to be enticed into accepting special treatment in the hope that it would shame the new enemy commander.

Moreover, I knew that every prisoner the Vietnamese tried to break, those who had arrived before me and those who would come after me, would be taunted with the story of how an admiral's son had gone home early, a lucky beneficiary of America's class-conscious society. I knew that my release would add to the suffering of men who were already straining to keep faith with their country. I was injured, but I believed I could survive. I couldn't persuade myself to leave.

Bob still counseled me to take the offer if the Vietnamese were willing to let me go without getting any antiwar propaganda from me. So I spelled out the reasons why I should not do it.

"Look, just letting me go is a propaganda victory for them. I can tell they really want me to do this. I mean, they really want me to go. And if they want something that much it's got to be a bad thing. I can't give them the satisfaction, Bob.

"Second, I would be disloyal to the rest of you. I know why they're doing this—to make every guy here whose father isn't an admiral think the Code is shit. They'll tell all of you, 'We let McCain go because his father's an admiral. But your father's not and nobody gives a damn about you.' And I don't want to go home and see my father, and he wouldn't want to see me under those conditions. I've got to say no."

Bob didn't say much after that. He just wished me well, and then we dropped the matter. Several days later, I went to tell the Cat I wouldn't accept his offer.

I sat for some time in the same well-furnished room with the Cat and the Rabbit, exchanging pleasantries and helping myself to their cigarettes. Eventually, again using the Rabbit to interpret, the Cat asked me if I had considered his offer. "I have," I answered.

"What is your answer?"

"No, thank you."

"Why?"

"American prisoners cannot accept parole, or amnesty or special favors. We must be released in the order of our capture, starting with Everett Alvarez"—the first pilot captured in the North.

He then suggested that my physical condition made my long-term survival doubtful. "I think I will make it," I replied. He told me the doctors believed I would not survive without better medical care. His response amused me, and I smiled when I told him that I found that hard to believe, since I never saw a doctor except the indifferent Zorba, whose only prescribed treatment for my condition had been exercise and the consumption of my full food ration.

Cat, who evidently did not share my sense of irony, then tried to convince me that I had permission from my Commander in Chief to return home.

"President Johnson has ordered you home."

"Show me the orders."

"President Johnson orders you."

"Show me the orders, and I'll believe you."

He handed me a letter from Carol in which she expressed her regret that I had not been released earlier with Norris and the other two prisoners. It was the kind of thing you expect your wife to say. I didn't believe that Carol wanted me to dishonor myself, and the fact that the Vietnamese had kept her letter from me until now angered me, an emotion that usually serves to stiffen my resolve. I was dismissed with an order to reconsider my answer, and returned, holding my wife's letter, to my cell.

A week later, I was summoned to a third interview, much weakened by dysentery, which had worsened since our last meeting. The interview was shortened by the effect of my illness. Shortly after I arrived, I asked permission to return to my cell to relieve myself. The request greatly irritated the Cat, who accused me of being "very rude." "I'm sorry, but I have to go," I responded. He angrily terminated the interview, and I was returned to my cell.

During these sessions, the Cat had promised me that I would not be required to make any propaganda statements in return for my release. I had no doubt that he was lying. I knew that once I agreed, the Vietnamese would exert enormous pressure on me to record a statement, and I worried that my resolve would dissipate as I faced the imminent prospect of homecoming.

On the morning of the Fourth of July, Soft Soap entered my cell and mentioned that he knew I had received a generous offer to go home. "You will have a nice family reunion, Mac Kane," he suggested.

"Yes," I acknowledged, "but I can't accept it."

A few hours later, I faced a solemn Cat. That morning, the camp loudspeakers broadcast the news that three prisoners had been chosen for early release. The Cat had summoned me to offer me one last chance to accept his offer. This time I was not taken to the large reception room but to an interrogation room. There were no cookies or cigarettes offered. The Rabbit spoke first.

"Our senior officer wants to know your final answer."

"My final answer is no."

In a fit of pique, the Cat snapped the ink pen he had been holding between his hands. Ink splattered on a copy of the *International Herald Tribune* lying on the table, opened to a column by Art Buchwald.

He stood up, kicked over his chair, and spoke to me in English for the first time.

"They taught you too well, Mac Kane. They taught you too well," he shouted as he abruptly left the room.

Yes, they had.

The Rabbit and I sat there for a few moments staring at each other in silence before he angrily dismissed me.

"Now it will be very bad for you, Mac Kane. Go back to your room."

I did as instructed and awaited the moment when the Rabbit's prediction would come true.

That same day my father assumed command of all U.S. forces in the Pacific. I wouldn't learn of my father's promotion for nearly a year, when two recently captured pilots were brought to the Plantation. A few months after they arrived, one of them managed to get a one-sentence message to me:

"Your father assumed Commander in Chief in the Pacific, July 4, 1968."

CHAPTER 20

Lanterns of Faith

At the end of the Korean War, America was shocked when a number of American prisoners of war chose to live in China rather than be returned to the United States. Reports about the brainwashing of POWs were publicly disclosed, along with even more disturbing accounts of some POWs who had treated their comrades inhumanely. Consequently, the military began to instruct American servicemen about what they could expect should they be captured and, more important, about what was expected of them. Toward that end, the Code of Conduct for American Prisoners of War was drafted. It reads as follows:

I

I am an American, fighting in the forces which guard my country and our way of life. I am prepared to give my life in their defense.

II

I will never surrender of my own free will. If in command, I will never surrender the members of my command while they still have the means to resist.

III

If I am captured, I will continue to resist by all means available. I will make every effort to escape and aid others to escape. I will accept neither parole nor special favors from the enemy.

IV

If I become a prisoner of war, I will keep faith with my fellow prisoners. I will give no information or take part in any action which might be harmful to my comrades. If I am senior, I will take command. If not, I will obey the lawful orders of those appointed over me and will back them up in every way.

V

When questioned, should I become a prisoner of war, I am required to give name, rank, service number, and date of birth. I will evade answering further questions to the utmost of my ability. I will make no oral or written statements disloyal to my country and its allies or harmful to their cause.

VI

I will never forget that I am an American, fighting for freedom, responsible for my actions, and dedicated to the principles which made my country free. I will trust in God and in the United States of America.

Although the experiences of prisoners in the Korean War had necessitated this formal declaration of an American prisoner's responsibilities, the military did not anticipate how the North Vietnamese would regard POWs. Unlike the Japanese and Germans, and more insistently than the North Koreans and Chinese, the Vietnamese considered prisoner-of-war camps to be an extension of the battlefield.

Ho Chi Minh had declared that the war would be won on the streets and campuses of American cities, and the Vietnamese were determined that we would serve that end. With the exception of incidents of arbitrary cruelty, many features of our treatment—forced confessions and antiwar declarations, meetings with peace delegations, early releases—were intended to help sway American public opinion against the war. Since the Vietnamese invested so much time and energy in coercing our cooperation, our fidelity to the Code was almost constantly challenged. Yet its principles remained the most important allegiance of our lives.

———————

The days dragged on as I waited for the Cat to make good on his threat. I knew a bad time lay ahead, and that I would soon confront a greater measure of my enemy's cruelty, an experience many of my comrades had already endured but I had been spared. I had seen the Cat's fury, and it had made a deep impression on me. I tried to be fatalistic, and prepare myself to suffer the inevitable without dishonoring myself.

For almost two months nothing happened. Three prisoners had been released in early August. Their departure had been delayed for several weeks, and I assumed the Vietnamese had neglected my punishment to avoid complicating the release. Treatment for all prisoners in the camp was lax in advance of the event. I assumed that the Vietnamese were worried that if word got out that I had been tortured for refusing to leave, the prisoners who had accepted release might change their minds.

Then one evening in late August, several guards came and announced that the camp commander, the rough customer we called Slopehead, wanted to see me. They took me to a large room, a theater that had been used for Christmas services the year before.

Speaking through an interpreter, Slopehead accused me of committing "black crimes against the people" and violating all of the camp's regulations. He told me the time had come for me to show gratitude to the Vietnamese people and sorrow for my war crimes. Knowing that I was in serious trouble and that nothing I did or said would make matters any worse, I replied:

"Fuck you."

"Why do you treat your guards disrespectfully?"

"Because they treat me like an animal."

Hearing this, Slopehead gave an order, and the guards lit into me. Shouting and laughing, they bashed me around the room, slamming their fists into my face and body, kicking and stomping me when I fell. Lying on the floor, bleeding, I heard Slopehead speak to the interpreter.

"Are you ready to confess your crimes?"

"No."

With that, the guards hauled me up and set me on the stool. They cinched rope around my biceps, anchored it behind my back, and then left the room. The rope hurt and restricted my circulation, but, again, they had not tied it as tightly as they had on others, and I knew I could tolerate it. I remained there for the rest of the night.

In the morning, three guards came in, removed the rope, and took me to an interrogation room, where the deputy camp commander, a dull-witted man we called "Frankenstein" for his bulging forehead and numerous facial warts, waited for me. When I refused his order to confess, I was dragged to the room behind my cell where some time later Ernie Brace would be held.

The room was empty of any furnishings save a waste bucket. I had no bedding or personal belongings. The room didn't have a door, only a louvered window large enough to pass through. I was kept there for four days.

At two-to-three-hour intervals, the guards returned to administer beatings. The intensity of the punishment varied from visit to visit depending on the enthusiasm and energy of the guards. Still, I felt they were being careful not to kill or permanently injure me. One guard would hold me while the others pounded away. Most blows were directed at my shoulders, chest, and stomach. Occasionally, when I had fallen to the floor, they kicked me in the head. They cracked several of my ribs and broke a couple of teeth. My bad right leg was swollen and hurt the most of any of my injuries. Weakened by beatings and dysentery, and with my right leg again nearly useless, I found it almost impossible to stand.

On the third night, I lay in my own blood and waste, so tired and hurt that I could not move. The Prick came in with two other guards, lifted me to my feet, and gave me the worst beating I had yet experienced. At one point he slammed his fist into my face and knocked me across the room toward the waste bucket. I fell on the bucket, hitting it with my left arm, and breaking it again. They left me lying on the floor, moaning from the stabbing pain in my refractured arm.

Despairing of any relief from pain and further torture, and fearing the close approach of my moment of dishonor, I tried to take my life. I doubt I really intended to kill myself. But I couldn't fight anymore, and I remember deciding that the last thing I could do to make them believe I was still resisting, that I wouldn't break, was to attempt suicide. Obviously, it wasn't an ideal plan, but it struck me at the time as reasonable.

Slowly, after several unsuccessful attempts, I managed to stand. I removed my shirt, upended the waste bucket, and stepped onto it, bracing myself against the wall with my good arm. With my right arm, I pushed my shirt through one of the upper shutters and back through a bottom shutter. As I looped it around my neck, the Prick saw the shirt through the window. He pulled me off the bucket and beat me. He called for an officer, who instructed the guards to post a constant watch on me. Later I made a second, even feebler attempt, but a guard saw me fumbling with the shutter, hauled me down, and beat me again.

On the fourth day, I gave up.

"I am a black criminal," the interrogator wrote, "and I have performed the deeds of an air pirate. I almost died and the Vietnamese people saved my life. The doctors gave me an operation that I did not deserve."

I had been taken back to the theater after telling my guards I was ready to confess. For twelve hours I had written out many drafts of the confession. I used words that I hoped would discredit its authenticity, and I tried to keep it in stilted generalities and Communist jargon so that it would be apparent that I had signed it under duress.

An interrogator had edited my last draft and decided to rewrite most of it himself. He then handed it to me and told me to copy it out in my own hand. I started to print it in block letters, and he ordered me to write in script. He demanded that I add an admission that I had bombed a school. I refused, and we argued back and forth about the confession's contents for a time before I gave in to his demand. Finally, they had me sign the document.

They took me back to my room and let me sleep through the night. The next morning, they brought me back to the theater and ordered me to record my confession on tape. I refused, and was beaten until I consented.

I was returned to my cell and left alone for the next two weeks.

They were the worst two weeks of my life. I couldn't rationalize away my confession. I was ashamed. I felt faithless, and couldn't control my despair. I shook, as if my disgrace were a fever. I kept imagining that they would release my confession to embarrass my father. All my pride was lost, and I doubted I would ever stand up to any man again. Nothing could save me. No one would ever look upon me again with anything but pity or contempt.

Bob Craner tried to reassure me that I had resisted all that I was expected to resist. But I couldn't shake it off. One night I either heard or dreamed I heard myself confessing over the loudspeakers, thanking the Vietnamese for receiving medical treatment I did not deserve.

Many guys broke at one time or another. I doubt anyone ever gets over it entirely. There is never enough time and distance between the past and the present to allow one to forget his shame. I am recovered now from that period of intense despair. But I can summon up its feeling in an instant whenever I let myself remember the day. And I still wince when I recall wondering if my father had heard of my disgrace. The Vietnamese had broken the prisoner they called the "Crown Prince," and I knew they had done it to hurt the man they believed to be a king.

The following month, Averell Harriman, then serving as President Johnson's emissary to the fruitless peace negotiations in Paris with the North Vietnamese, sent the following cable to Secretary of State Dean Rusk:

1. At last tea break Le Duc Tho attended, he mentioned that DRV had intended to release Admiral McCain's son as one of the three pilots freed recently, but he had refused. According to Tho, Commander McCain feared that if he was released before the war is over, President Johnson might "cause difficulties" for his father because people will wonder if McCain had been brainwashed.

2. We said that in past cases pilots had been reluctant to accept release because they did not want to feel that they were given preference over their fellow pilots. In McCain's case, perhaps it was he did not want people to think he had been released because of his father's position. Tho said that we were reversing what the pilot actually thought and that he feared difficulties would be created for his father. However, Tho added, this was only hearsay which he had picked up when he was back in Hanoi. We replied it would be difficult to understand McCain's attitude as described by Tho, and that in past cases of this kind the pilot had wanted to be loyal to his comrades. In any event, we wished the DRV would release more pilots and that way we would know what they think. We agree with Tho that ending the war is the best way of securing pilot releases, but pending that we hope DRV will release more of them.

They came back at the end of two weeks for another statement. I didn't give it to them. I had recovered enough to resist. The next year and a half would be the hardest months of my captivity.

―――――――

The severe treatment of prisoners lasted until the end of 1969. During this period, we were beaten for communicating with one another, for declining to meet with visiting American "peace delegations," for refusing to make statements and broadcasts, and for mouthing off to our guards. I had a hard time suppressing the urge to verbally assault my captors as they went about the business of humiliating me. Acts of defiance felt so good that I felt they more than compensated for their repercussions, and they helped me keep at bay the unsettling feelings of guilt and self-doubt that my confession had aroused.

Whenever I emerged from the interrogation room after a few hours or a few days of punishment, I tried to make a show of my indifference to my circumstances. Whether I walked of my own accord or was dragged by guards back to my cell, I always shouted greetings to the prisoners whose cells I passed, smiled, and flashed a thumbs-up. In the years since I came home, I have occasionally been embarrassed to hear some of my fellow POWs commend me for those attempts at good cheer. They believed they were intended to boost their spirits. In truth, they were mostly intended to boost my own.

On Christmas Eve in 1968, about fifty of us were taken to the theater where a few months earlier the events leading to my humiliation had begun. There the Vietnamese intended to film a religious service that they could use to demonstrate their humane treatment of us. I was placed next to a young apprentice seaman, Doug Hegdahl, who had fallen off his ship in the Tonkin Gulf during an evening artillery barrage.

I had often watched through cracks in my door as he swept the camp courtyard. The guards assigned Doug this enviable duty because they thought he was a harmless idiot. Doug possessed neither the survival training nor the familiarity with the Code of Conduct that captured pilots had.

Yet this teenage farm boy from North Dakota had devised a ploy to convince the Vietnamese that he was dim-witted, unthreatening, and without propaganda or military value. Given what the Vietnamese perceived as his low station in the Navy, they believed breaking him wouldn't have any useful effect on the morale of the other prisoners either.

Doug convincingly played the role of an uneducated peasant who didn't have the foggiest notion of what he was doing in this strange place. The Vietnamese left him alone and allowed him out of his cell to work at menial tasks. So engaged, Doug would serve as a conduit for communications from one part of the camp to the other, sweeping up in his pile of debris notes we had written on toilet and cigarette paper. He also seized opportunities for a little small-scale sabotage, pouring dirt into the gas tanks of trucks and making other clever minor assaults on the Vietnamese war effort.

Standing next to Doug, and realizing that the guards, knowing they were on camera, were restrained from forcing our cooperation, I began talking to Doug in a loud voice and recounting my recent experiences. Soft Soap Fairy motioned to me and in a stage whisper ordered, "Mac Kane, be quiet." I responded by raising my middle finger for the camera and profanely telling him and the other guards present to leave us be. Soon almost all the other prisoners attending the service began talking and flashing hand signals to one another. Even the three-man prisoner choir joined in, smiling and laughing as they entered the general exchange of information. The guards hustled around vainly trying to get us to quiet down.

Trying to be heard above the commotion, a Vietnamese pastor offered a sermon in which he compared Ho Chi Minh to Jesus Christ and Lyndon Johnson to King Herod. Soon one very angry guard, forgetting that cameras were rolling, began making threatening gestures at me. I called him a son of a bitch and other less flattering things. He charged toward me, but other guards pulled him back. On the whole, it was a rejuvenating experience.

The service concluded, and I returned to my cell possessing a little bit more of the holiday cheer than I had expected to feel on my second Christmas in captivity. I expected to be beaten for interfering with the propaganda pageant. Two days later, I was.

The arrogance I sometimes displayed to my captors contradicted the humility I felt around other prisoners who were routinely and severely tortured. Dick Stratton had suffered horribly under torture. He had huge, infected scars on his arms from rope torture. His thumbnails had been torn off, and he had been burned with cigarettes. By such means, they had forced him to attend a "press conference." When they ushered him into the room, Dick affected the vacant stare of a catatonic and bowed deeply in four directions toward his surprised captors, thereby signaling to the Americans who would see the broadcast that the POWs were obviously being tortured.

In May 1969, two Air Force officers, John Dramesi and Ed Atterbury, who had been captured a few months before my shootdown, managed a daring escape from the Zoo, the prison in the southwest of the city, where conditions were awful. For nearly a year, they had planned and physically trained for the escape. On a rainy Saturday night, their faces darkened, wearing conical Vietnamese hats and carrying knives they had fashioned from bits of metal they had found, they slipped through tiles they had loosened in the roof of their cellblock and climbed over the prison wall. They made for the Red River, intending to steal a boat and be well downriver before daylight. They were recaptured at dawn the next day, before they reached the river. They were cruelly tortured for their courage. Ed Atterbury was beaten to death. But John, one of the toughest men I have ever known, survived.

I did not learn of the escape attempt until I had been moved back to Hoa Lo, where I met men who had been held at the Zoo with John and Ed. Nevertheless, those of us held at the Plantation surmised that something had happened. Our room inspections became more frequent and more thorough. Our interrogations became considerably more intense. One of the Plantation POWs had been severely tortured for information about suspected escape plans at the Plantation, his tormentors refusing to believe his protestations that there were none. These developments, together with the general worsening of our conditions, alerted us that someone had probably attempted to escape.

Incidents of surpassing courage and defiance were commonplace in those worst days of captivity, and they made my own attempts at rebellion seem minor in comparison. I derived my own resolve from the example of Bud Day, who, although seriously wounded, had valiantly attempted to evade capture, and from countless other examples of resistance that had been carried, flashed, and tapped from cell to cell, camp to camp. They were a lantern for me, a lantern of courage and faith that illuminated the way home with honor, and I struggled against panic and despair to stay in its light. I would have been lost without their example. In recurring moments of doubt and fear, I concentrated on their service, and on the service of my father, and his father, and I accepted my fate.

Of all the many legends of heroic devotion to duty I had come in this strange place to know as real, and to seek strength and solace from, none was more inspiring that the story of Lance Sijan. I never knew Lance Sijan, but I wish I had. I wish I had had one moment to tell him how much I admired him, how indebted I was to him for showing me, for showing all of us, our duty—for showing us how to be free.

He was gone before I heard of him. But Bob Craner and Guy Gruters had lived with Lance for a time, and Bob had told me his story very early in our friendship.

Air Force Captain Lance Sijan was shot down near Vinh on November 9, 1967. For a day and a half, he lay semiconscious on the ground, grievously injured, with a compound fracture of his left leg, a brain concussion, and a fractured skull. He made radio contact with rescue aircraft, but they were unable to locate him in the dense jungle. On November 11, they abandoned the search.

Crawling on the jungle floor at night, Lance fell into a sinkhole, further injuring himself. For six weeks he evaded capture. On Christmas Day, starved, racked with pain, he passed out on a dirt road, where a few hours later the North Vietnamese found him. Thus began the most inspiring POW story of the war, a story of one man's peerless fidelity to our Code of Conduct. To Lance Sijan, the Code was not an abstract ideal, but the supreme purpose of his life.

The Code is a straightforward document. Its simply worded assertions might strike cynics as posturing, a simplistic and chauvinistic relic of a time when Americans carried with them to war a conceit that they were stronger, better, and more virtuous than any enemy they would face. In truth, few prisoners could claim that they never came close to violating one or more of its principles. But the Code had its appeal, and almost all of us were mindful not to take its demands lightly.

The Code instructs every prisoner to evade capture, and when captured, to seize opportunities for escape. Most of us imprisoned in Hanoi knew that escape was almost certainly impossible. The guards never seemed to be unduly worried about preventing escape because they knew we would have to escape from a city as well as a prison. Had we been able to slip out of camp undetected, our identity would have been impossible to disguise in an isolated Asian population of a million people. Few of us ever seriously contemplated escape, and our senior officers never encouraged it. A few truly brave men tried. All were caught and tortured.

Neither did every prisoner refrain from providing information beyond the bare essentials sanctioned by the Code. Many of us were terrorized into failure at one time or another.

But Captain Sijan wasn't. He obeyed the Code to the letter.

A short time after he was captured, he overpowered an armed guard and managed to escape, taking the guard's rifle with him. Recaptured several hours later, he was tortured as punishment for his escape attempt and for military information. He refused to provide his captors anything beyond what the Code allowed. By the time he reached Hanoi, he was close to death.

Over six feet tall, he weighed less than a hundred pounds when he was placed in a cell with Bob Craner and Guy Gruters. He lived there barely a month. In and out of consciousness, often delirious, he would push on the walls of his cell and scratch on the floor searching vainly for a way out. When he was lucid and not consumed with pain, he would quiz his cellmates about the camp's security and talk with them about escaping again.

Interrogated several times, he refused to say anything. He was savagely beaten for his silence, kicked repeatedly and struck with a bamboo club. Bob and Guy heard him scream profanities at his tormentors, and then, after he had endured hours of torture, they heard him say in a weak voice: "Don't you understand? I'm not going to tell you anything. I can't talk to you. It's against the Code."

Bob and Guy tried to comfort him during his last hours. Working in shifts timed to the tolling of a nearby church bell, they cradled his head in their laps, talked quietly to him of his courage and faith, told him to hang on. Occasionally he shook off his delirium to joke with his cellmates about his circumstances.

Near the end, the guards came for him. Lance knew they were taking him away to die. As they placed him on a stretcher, he said to his friends, "It's over . . . it's over." He called to his father for help as the guards carried him away.

A few days later, the Bug told Bob Craner what he already knew, that his friend was dead. And Bob, a good and wise man, resolved to share with any prisoner he could reach the legend of Lance Sijan so that all of us could draw strength from the example of a man who would not yield no matter how terrible the consequences. A few weeks later, when I was moved into the cell next to Bob's, he told me the story of Lance Sijan: a free man from a free country, who kept his dignity to the last moment of his life.

To maintain our unity, prisoners relied heavily on the senior ranking officers to promulgate policies for the camps. The primary reason the Vietnamese worked so hard to disrupt our communications was to prevent any form of military unit cohesion from strengthening our resistance. Toward that end, they segregated senior officers from the rest of the prison population, making communication with them difficult, and they kept many of the most determined and inventive communicators in solitary confinement.

Contact with senior officers is a very important element of an effective campaign of resistance, and we worked as hard to maintain communications with them as the guards worked to prevent them. If we couldn't communicate, we couldn't organize, and if we couldn't organize, the Vietnamese would pick us off one by one.

We relied on senior officers for more than affirmations or interpretations of the Code of Conduct. Frequently we needed little more than a word of encouragement from our commander to firm up our own resolve when we were preparing to endure the latest round of interrogations. Although there were periods, some quite long, when the Vietnamese succeeded in truncating our chain of command, we would eventually invent some way to restore our communication links to the SROs.

Our senior officers always stressed to us the three essential keys to resistance, which we were to keep uppermost in our mind, especially in moments when we were isolated or otherwise deprived of their guidance and the counsel of other prisoners. They were faith in God, faith in country, and faith in your fellow prisoners.

Were your faith in any of these three devotions seriously shaken, you became much more vulnerable to various pressures employed by the Vietnamese to break you. The purpose of our captors' inhumanity to us was nothing less than to force our descent into a world of total faithlessness; a world with no God, no country, no loyalty. Our faith would be replaced with simple reliance on the sufferance of our antagonists. Without faith, we would lose our dignity, and live among our enemies as animals lived among their human masters.

There were times in many a prisoner's existence when the Vietnamese came close to robbing his faith; when a prisoner felt abandoned, left to cling to faith in himself as his last strength, his last form of resistance. Certainly this had been my experience when I was broken in the fall of 1968.

Ironically for someone who had so long asserted his own individuality as his first and best defense against insults of any kind, I discovered that faith in myself proved to be the least formidable strength I possessed when confronting alone organized inhumanity on a greater scale than I had conceived possible. Faith in myself was important, and remains important to my self-esteem. But I discovered in prison that faith in myself alone, separate from other, more important allegiances, was ultimately no match for the cruelty that human beings could devise when they were entirely unencumbered by respect for the God-given dignity of man. This is the lesson I learned in prison. It is, perhaps, the most important lesson I have ever learned.

During the worst moments of captivity, keeping our faith in God, country, and one another was as difficult as it was imperative. When your faith weakened, you had to take any opportunity, seize on any sight of it, and use any temporary relief from your distress to recover it.

POWs often regard their prison experience as comparable to the trials of Job. Indeed, for my fellow prisoners who suffered more than I, the comparison is appropriate. Hungry, beaten, hurt, scared, and alone, human beings can begin to feel that they are removed from God's love, a vast distance separating them from their Creator. The anguish can lead to resentment, to the awful despair that God has forsaken you.

To guard against such despair, in our most dire moments, POWs would make supreme efforts to grasp our faith tightly, to profess it alone, in the dark, and hasten its revival. Once I was thrown into another cell after a long and difficult interrogation. I discovered scratched into one of the cell's walls the creed "I believe in God, the Father Almighty." There, standing witness to God's presence in a remote, concealed place, recalled to my faith by a stronger, better man, I felt God's love and care more vividly than I would have felt it had I been safe among a pious congregation in the most magnificent cathedral.

The Vietnamese also went to great lengths to sow doubts in our minds about our country and one another. They threatened us constantly that we would never again be free. They taunted us with insults, disparaged our loyalty to a country they claimed never asked about us or made our return the subject of negotiations. We were abandoned, they insisted, by a country busy with a war that wasn't going well and too torn apart by widespread domestic turmoil to worry about a few forgotten pilots in Hanoi.

During the long pause between bombing campaigns in the North, while the months and years dragged on, it was hard to take our interrogators' ridicule of our conviction that our loyalty to America was returned, measure for measure, by our distant compatriots. But we clung to our belief, each one encouraging the other, not with overexuberant hopes that our day of liberation was close at hand, but with a steady resolve that our honor was the extension of a great nation's honor, and that both prisoner and country would do what honor asked of us.

In prison, I fell in love with my country. I had loved her before then, but like most young people, my affection was little more than a simple appreciation for the comforts and privileges most Americans enjoyed and took for granted. It wasn't until I had lost America for a time that I realized how much I loved her.

I loved what I missed most from my life at home: my family and friends; the sights and sounds of my country; the hustle and purposefulness of Americans; their fervid independence; sports; music;

information—all the attractive qualities of American life. But though I longed for the things at home I cherished the most, I still shared the ideals of America. And since those ideals were all that I possessed of my country, they became all the more important to me.

It was what freedom conferred on America that I loved the most— the distinction of being the last, best hope of humanity; the advocate for all who believed in the Rights of Man. Freedom is America's honor, and all honor comes with obligations. We have the obligation to use our freedom wisely, to select well from all the choices freedom offers. We can accept or reject the obligation, but if we are to preserve our freedom, our honor, we must choose well.

I was no longer the boy to whom liberty meant simply that I could do as I pleased, and who, in my vanity, used my freedom to polish my image as an I-don't-give-a-damn nonconformist. That's not to say that I had shed myself entirely of that attribute. I had not, and have not yet. But I no longer located my self-respect in that distinction. In prison, where my cherished independence was mocked and assaulted, I found my self-respect in a shared fidelity to my country. All honor comes with obligations. I and the men with whom I served had accepted ours, and we were grateful for the privilege.

When my interrogators played tapes to me of other POWs confessing to war crimes, expressing their gratitude for lenient treatment, or denouncing our government, I did not silently censure my comrades. I knew that they had made those statements under the most extreme duress, and I told the Vietnamese so.

"No, they are their true feelings," the interrogator would rebut, "and you should not be ashamed to state your true feelings. We will not tell anyone if you do. No one would know."

"I would know. I would know," I responded.

In these instances when the enemy entreated me to betray my country by promising to keep my disloyalty confidential, my self-regard, which had for so long been invested with an adolescent understanding of my father's and grandfather's notions of character, obliged me to resist. But there was another force now at work to brace my resolve, and to give me insight into the essence of courage in war.

Tom Kirk, a fellow prisoner whom I hold in high regard, once explained, simply and exactly, the foundation of our resistance. "You live with another guy, and you go over there and you're tortured and you're brought back in that room and he says: 'What happened?'

" 'They did this.'

" 'What'd you tell them?'

". . . You've got to face this guy; you're going to have to tell him the truth. I wanted to keep faith so that I knew that when I stood up at the bar with somebody after the war, that, by God, I could look him in the eye and say, 'We hacked it.' "

We were told to have faith in God, country, and one another. Most of us did. But the last of these, faith in one another, was our finai defense, the ramparts our enemy could not cross. In prison, as in any of war's endeavors, your most important allegiance is to the men you serve with. We were obligated to one another, and for the duration of our war, that obligation was our first duty. The Vietnamese knew this. They went to great lengths to keep us apart, knowing we had great strength in unity.

A few men lost their religion in prison or had never been very devout. A few men were not moved by appeals to patriotism or to written codes of conduct. Almost all of us were committed to one another. I knew what the others were suffering. Sitting in my cell, I could hear their screams as their faith was put to the test. At all costs, I wanted, as Bob Craner often put it, "to hold up my end of the bargain."

My first concern was not that I might fail God and country, although I certainly hoped that I would not. I was afraid to fail my friends. I was afraid to come back from an interrogation and tell them I couldn't hold up as well as they had. However I measured my character before Vietnam no longer mattered. What mattered now was how they measured my character. My self-regard became indivisible from their regard for me. And it will remain so for the rest of my life.

Had I accepted that many of the others had surrendered their dignity voluntarily, had agreed to live with such reproachful self-knowledge, I doubt I would have resisted to the extent that I did, and thus I would probably not have recovered from the shame I felt when I was broken.

This is the truth of war, of honor and courage, that my father and grandfather had passed on to me. But before my war, its meaning was obscure to me, hidden in the peculiar language of men who had gone to war and been changed forever by the experience. So, too, had the Academy, with its inanimate and living memorials to fidelity and valor, tried to reveal this truth to me. But I had interpreted the lesson, as I had interpreted my father's lesson, within the limits of my vanity. I thought glory was the object of war, and all glory was self-glory.

No more. For I have learned the truth: there are greater pursuits than self-seeking. Glory is not a conceit. It is not a decoration for valor. It is not a prize for being the most clever, the strongest, or the boldest. Glory belongs to the act of being constant to something greater than yourself, to a cause, to your principles, to the people on whom you rely, and who rely on you in return. No misfortune, no injury, no humiliation can destroy it.

This is the faith that my commanders affirmed, that my brothers-in-arms encouraged my allegiance to. It was the faith I had unknowingly embraced at the Naval Academy. It was my father's and grandfather's faith. A filthy, crippled, broken man, all I had left of my dignity was the faith of my fathers. It was enough.

CHAPTER 21

Commander in Chief

As my days in captivity lengthened, the man whose example had led me to Vietnam stood at the summit of his long naval career. I have heard several accounts of how my father managed to attain command of the Pacific. The most credible is the account provided by Admiral Tom Moorer, who, as Chief of Naval Operations, was my father's boss. Although the Pacific Command is traditionally reserved for the Navy, all services vie for it, as it is one of the military's most prestigious commands. Many months before a CINCPAC retires, jockeying begins among the services to get the President to appoint one of their own to the post. The Navy usually prevails, but the competition is intense, and the outcome is seldom certain from the outset.

In 1968, when Admiral U. S. Grant Sharp was scheduled to retire as CINCPAC, Admiral Moorer not only wanted to retain the command for the Navy, but wanted my father, to whom he was very close, to get the job. My father was not considered the most likely candidate for the post by many of his contemporaries. They had been surprised when he was appointed Commander of U.S. Naval Forces in Europe. His detractors in the Navy had attributed the promotion to his political connections and his assiduous cultivation of friendships with the most senior Navy brass. They would attribute his promotion to CINCPAC to those same relationships. There is some truth to their speculation, though not enough to justify their derision of my father's success.

Both my father and my mother worked hard to build relationships with people who could help advance his career, but social networking was mainly my mother's domain. She had the charm required for success in that field. My father won the regard of his superiors, military and civilian, by proving himself useful to them. He was a competent, reliable, often innovative, and always indefatigable subordinate who could be relied upon to accept any job without complaint and to make the most of it. Additionally, he had the gift of being able to articulate his and his superiors' views with clarity and force.

My father worked awfully hard for his success, and by so doing rendered his country many years of good and faithful service. He had earned whatever help he was provided by powerful friends. In an interview for the Naval Institute's Oral History Project, Admiral Moorer's account of how my father got the Pacific Command reveals both the influence his patrons wielded on his behalf and how he came to enjoy their patronage.

Shortly before the Joint Chiefs of Staff were to meet to decide which service would assume command in the Pacific, with each service ready with its own nominee, Admiral Moorer, as luck would have it, was scheduled to attend a ceremony at the White House welcoming the king of Nepal. That morning, General Earl Wheeler, the Chairman of the Joint Chiefs of Staff, had informed Moorer that the President was unlikely to consent to my father's appointment and that he should select another nominee for the post. Moorer, however, knew that Ellsworth Bunker, the American ambassador to Vietnam, whose wife happened to be ambassador to Nepal, would also be attending the welcoming ceremony that afternoon. Bunker and my father had worked closely together during the U.S. intervention in the Dominican Republic in 1965. Moorer knew my father had made a great impression on the ambassador, and he viewed the White House event as an opportunity to make the case for my father directly to the President and to enlist Bunker, whose judgment the President respected, in the cause.

Right after the conclusion of the ceremony, President Johnson indicated he wished to speak to Admiral Moorer. "Do you really think McCain should be CINCPAC?" the President asked. To which the admiral responded, "If I didn't think Jack McCain would be a fine CINCPAC, I would never have nominated him in the first place." Gesturing toward Bunker, Moorer suggested to the President that he solicit the ambassador's views on the appointment. As Moorer knew he would, Bunker "just went into extremes of enthusiasm about McCain." Persuaded by his trusted adviser's unqualified endorsement, Johnson immediately called a press conference and announced my father's appointment as Commander in Chief, Pacific, depriving the Joint Chiefs of the opportunity to formally consider and recommend a candidate.

"I stacked the deck and I've never regretted it," Moorer remembered. "I've had many people work with me and for me, and I've worked for many people myself, but I've never known anyone as loyal as Jack McCain was."

After his appointment as CINCPAC was announced, my father received a great many congratulatory notes. Several stand out. Among them was a letter from a chief bosun's mate who had once served under my father:

> At last, a fighting admiral in a fighting command. All that you have said has come to pass. Though history and the politicians will not give you credit for it, and you cannot say, I told you so, there are many of us who can and do. In the eyes of every professional man-of-wars man, you are the greatest admiral of our time. . . .

I am afraid I have been too personal and I mean no disrespect, but Admiral I felt I would burst if I did not let you
know of my feelings. . . . Give 'em Sea Power, sir.

A "fighting admiral in a fighting command," my father was respected by his brother officers but loved by the bluejackets, the enlisted men who knew his respect for them was genuine and who
returned his respect many times over.

He assumed command of the Pacific in the last year of the Johnson administration and held it until July 1972, the last year of Richard
Nixon's first term. My wife, mother, sister, and brother attended his
change-of-command ceremony, which, at his request, was held aboard
the *Oriskany*, the carrier I was flying off the day I was shot down.

Henry Kissinger once told me that whenever he suspected President Nixon's resolve to make difficult decisions about the war was wa-
vering, he arranged for my father to brief the President. My father's
no-nonsense determination, Dr. Kissinger claims, was infectious and
served as a tonic for the President's flagging spirits.

My father wasn't much of a believer in fighting wars by half
measures. He regarded self-restraint as an admirable human quality,
but when fighting wars he believed in taking all necessary measures
to bring the conflict to a swift and successful conclusion. The Vietnam War was fought neither swiftly nor successfully, and I know this
frustrated him greatly. In a speech he gave after he retired, he argued that "two deplorable decisions" had doomed the United States
to failure in Vietnam: "The first was the public decision to forbid
U.S. troops to enter North Vietnam and beat the enemy on his home
ground. . . . The second was . . . to forbid the [strategic] bombing of
Hanoi and Haiphong until the last two weeks of the conflict. . . .
These two decisions combined to allow Hanoi to adopt whatever
strategy they wished, knowing that there would be virtually no re-
prisal, no counterattack."

For the rest of his life, he believed that had he been allowed to wage total war against the enemy, fully employing strategic airpower, mining Vietnamese ports early on, and launching large-scale offensives in the North, he could have brought the war to a successful conclusion "in months, if not weeks." He was exaggerating, I'm sure, to make a point. Given the resilience of the enemy, and their fierce willingness to pay a very high price and resolve to prevail over time, I doubt the war could have been wrapped up as quickly as my father envisioned even had we escalated our campaign to the extent he deemed necessary. But, given the dismal consequences of our haphazard, uncertain prosecution of the war, with its utterly illogical restraints on the use of American power, his frustration was understandable and appropriate.

Like other senior commanders, he believed the United States had squandered its best opportunity to win the war in the aftermath of the Tet Offensive, "when we had destroyed the back of the Viet Cong. . . . And when we had finally drawn North Vietnamese troops out into the open."

He recalled with resentment Washington's refusal to accede to the military's plans for a major offensive to be launched from the old imperial capital, Hue. The plan called for an amphibious assault on Hue to spearhead a drive around the flanks of the North Vietnamese Army and across the country to the border, cutting the enemy's supply lines from the North. "Permission for this operation was refused," he lamented, "because Washington was afraid that the Red Chinese might then enter the war. It was a ridiculous conclusion based on no evidence. Just fear and anxiety."

Even before he assumed command in the Pacific, when he was still the Navy chief in Europe, he had prepared and delivered a briefing to the Joint Chiefs of Staff on the feasibility and necessity of mining the port of Haiphong. Like any other capable military strategist, he knew that the support the North Vietnamese and the Vietcong received from the Soviet Union and China was critical to their ability to simply outlast us. They hoped to suffer whatever losses were inflicted on them by their vastly more powerful adversary until they had exhausted America's patience and will to see the war through to a successful conclusion. Without the massive support of their allies they would fail.

What my father didn't share with his civilian commanders and many of his fellow military commanders was an overly acute fear that doing something about Chinese and Soviet support would involve us in a wider, perhaps global war. He doubted either country would be provoked to the point of war if we rightly decided to disrupt their efforts to aid our enemy, efforts that, after all, resulted in the deaths of many thousands of Americans. Indeed, he interpreted Soviet and Chinese actions as a far more reckless provocation of a great power than any response on our part was likely to be.

Like the men who flew missions to the North, he knew the enemy's resolve was greatly strengthened by the material assistance their allies provided them, and he wanted to do something about it. As a submarine commander he had executed his country's policy of total war, a policy that attacked the sources of the enemy's material support just as vigorously as it attacked the enemy's armed forces. He had sunk a great many merchant ships on his patrols in the Pacific. He couldn't believe that the United States would simply leave unchallenged this clear threat to the war effort that he was now commanding.

Most of the arms and supplies used by North Vietnam's armies entered the country through the port of Haiphong, with lesser amounts entering through the smaller ports of Cam Pha and Hong Gai. Thanks to the strategic foresight of Admiral Moorer, the Navy was well prepared to conduct mining operations in the enemy's ports, and my father and other senior commanders repeatedly urged their civilian commanders to order the action. Washington invariably rejected their appeals on the grounds that the mining would probably result in damage to Soviet and Chinese merchant ships, and thus would seriously escalate the war by involving those countries further in the hostilities, and possibly even provoke a global war.

As early as 1966, military commanders began urging Washington to approve a mining operation, but they could not overcome Defense Secretary McNamara's and President Johnson's apprehension that the action entailed too great a risk of a wider war.

When the North Vietnamese launched a major offensive in December 1971, at a time when U.S. forces in Vietnam had been reduced to 69,000 men, President Nixon finally directed my father to mine Haiphong and other northern ports immediately. The Nixon administration had dispensed with much of the micromanaging of the war that had so ill served the Johnson administration, particularly the absurd target restrictions imposed on American bomber pilots. Relations between military commanders and their civilian superiors improved when President Nixon and Defense Secretary Melvin Laird entered office. The new administration was clearly more interested in and supportive of the views of the generals and admirals who were prosecuting the war. My father had a good relationship with both Nixon and Laird, as well as with the President's National Security Adviser, Henry Kissinger.

President Nixon had continued and even accelerated the drawdown of American forces in country begun by his predecessor, while seeking a negotiated end to the war. But he resolved to apply greater military pressure on the enemy while negotiations and "Vietnamization," the name given to the strategy of preparing South Vietnam to ultimately fight the war on its own while simultaneously drawing down American forces, were under way. In the interim, Nixon intended to escalate hostilities, both to hasten his diplomacy's successful conclusion and to strengthen the South Vietnamese regime.

In May 1970, with my father and General Abrams strongly urging it, the administration had authorized an incursion into Cambodia by U.S. and South Vietnamese forces. The enemy had used the sanctuary of the neighboring country to establish formidable military positions, especially along the border, from which they threatened much of the South, including Saigon. The incursion was of brief duration, and it was based on sound military reasoning. Nevertheless, given the considerable growth in domestic opposition to the war at the time, the decision provoked a firestorm of criticism. Neither the President nor his advisers nor his senior commanders wavered in their support for the action.

When North Vietnam launched its offensive in late 1971, Washington was very receptive to the requests of my father and his fellow commanders to respond to the North's aggression decisively. The administration authorized the immediate use of B-52 bombers, for the first time, to strike North Vietnamese targets.

The following May, the administration ordered my father to commence mining operations in North Vietnamese harbors. The President announced to the nation his conclusion that "Hanoi must be denied the weapons and supplies it needs to continue the aggression."

Most of the mining was conducted by carrier-based A-6 Intruders. The operation was a resounding success. Casualties were minimal. Twenty-seven foreign merchant ships remained trapped behind the blockade for the nine months the mining campaign was in effect. Almost all other ships were prevented from entering North Vietnamese ports. The flow of foreign arms and supplies to the North was abruptly and completely halted.

Neither did the war's escalation, so long anticipated as the unavoidable result of mining the harbors, occur. The administration's opening to China and its policy of détente with the Soviets were by this time well established and contributed significantly to the response of the Soviets and the Chinese to the mining of their client's harbors. Their reaction to what was once feared as a casus belli was remarkably muted.

The reaction in both the higher and lower reaches of the United States military was relief. The men charged with fighting the war believed that for the first time a rational policy to undercut the enemy's critical lifeline was in effect. Thus, they and their civilian bosses reasoned, the war's end would be hastened.

The reaction among the Americans held as prisoners in Hanoi, who learned of the actions from new arrivals to our ranks, was unanimous approval.

Despite their approval of the administration's more aggressive approach to the war, General Abrams and the other commanders in the field, including my father and most of the military establishment, doubted the efficacy of the administration's overall strategy to Vietnamize the war while seeking a negotiated conclusion in Paris. Abrams had profound misgivings that the South Vietnamese could develop the military capability the administration assumed possible. My father concurred, and strongly supported his subordinate's concerns.

Admiral Vasey, whom my father appointed as head of strategic plans and policies for the Pacific Command, told me that my father "fired some tough messages to Washington." His most frequent back-channel correspondents were the Chairman of the Joint Chiefs and the Secretary of Defense. Henry Kissinger and Secretary of State William Rogers were also recipients of my father's appeals to rethink their strategy. However, his arguments, while fairly considered, were not successful in persuading them of the necessity of the reevaluation he and Abrams believed was necessary. The drawdown of American forces continued, while the progress of the peace talks in Paris waxed and waned, and South Vietnam reluctantly and without adequate resolve or preparation approached nearer the day when it would stand alone. The American public grew ever more impatient for the war to end. The administration, even after the President was reelected in a landslide, did not possess enough political strength to oppose the people's will. Washington did what it could to ensure "peace with honor," but the country's priority was to get out of Vietnam, and get out we would.

By the time the end did come, with the signing in Paris of the peace accords, my father had retired from active duty. No longer restrained by his role as a subordinate to civilian superiors, he dismissed the agreement. "In our anxiety to get out of the war, we signed a very bad deal." This he offered even though the "very bad deal" would bring his son home. He was an honest man, with an exacting sense of duty.

Long after the war, I once rashly remarked that the entire senior command of the armed forces had a duty, which they shirked, to resign in protest over Washington's management of the war, knowing it as they did to be grievously flawed. Obviously, my father was implicitly included in my indictment. It was a callous remark that I probably should have refrained from offering, but I felt strongly about the obligation of military leaders to place the country's welfare before their own careers. So did the men whom I criticized. They were honorable people, including, certainly, my father. Their opposition to the war's course, which in many of their cases they pressed in the strongest possible terms to the politicians who designed it, almost surely led many of them to consider resigning. But their country was at war. And I am sure that their sense of duty to help see the thing through to the end, a value first embraced in a great war thirty years before, far more than any career consideration, prevailed over a conscientious contemplation of a principled resignation.

Having once served as the Navy's liaison officer to Congress and enjoying several close friendships with members of Congress, my father was quite familiar with the character of politicians. But he was puzzled and troubled by widespread and mounting congressional opposition to the war. Likewise, he was astonished at the breadth of opposition among the American people. He was, of course, respectful of the subordinate relationship of the military to the people of a democracy and their elected representatives. But it is fair to say that he believed something had gone badly wrong in a country that did not, by his lights, stand behind the men it had sent into harm's way to fight for it.

As CINCPAC, my father was expected to testify periodically before the committees of the House and Senate that authorized and appropriated the Defense Department's budget. The Pacific Command's vast expanse, including all of the Pacific and Indian oceans, from the West Coast of the United States to the Persian Gulf, encompassed a number of highly charged security situations in addition to the ongoing hostilities in Vietnam. Although our forces in Vietnam were progressively reduced during my father's watch, tensions on the Korean peninsula and in the Taiwan Strait were always a danger, and there was fear that the Soviets might generate a major crisis in the region while we were preoccupied with the war. It was the Pacific Command's responsibility to safeguard the shipping lanes and air traffic of half the world.

Accordingly, it was necessary for the United States, as the only military guarantor of regional stability, to maintain a large and expensive presence in Asia while executing the endgame of an unpopular war in Indochina. And my father was not one to subordinate his responsibilities to the prevailing political sentiments of the time, which assumed that our presence in the Pacific should be accorded lesser significance once the unfortunate war in Vietnam was finally ended. Even if the region's other tinderboxes were to become unexpectedly tranquil, my father's long-standing apprehension of the emerging Soviet naval threat was enough to persuade him that Pacific Command should retain its priority for American military planners. Thus, he could not countenance on his watch force reductions that he believed would jeopardize our supremacy in the area whether we were engaged in open hostilities or not.

In his opening statement to a Senate committee in 1971, my father gave his projection of the necessary force requirements for the Pacific, after first assessing the state of the war and the various security threats in the region confronting the United States. Many of the senators in attendance were familiar with my father and his views. Some of them he considered friends. They listened respectfully to my father's presentation, even if one or another of them had doubts about the size of the force level my father was advocating.

One senator, an outspoken opponent of the war, was not an intimate of my father's, nor, apparently, was he familiar with my father's ethics. When his turn came to question my father, he immediately took issue with his central argument, that we needed to increase our presence in the Pacific, and he did so in the one manner that anyone familiar with my father's reputation for probity knew better than to pursue. In effect, he accused him of lying.

He callously implied that my father had intentionally exaggerated his threat assessments to justify force levels that were excessively large and unnecessary. To this senator, my father was an archetype, the old military hawk used to getting his way from unquestioning legislators who had always left military decisions to the military. But times had changed. The World War II–vintage military brass were no longer accorded automatic respect by younger members of Congress, who, though they may have lacked much if any military experience themselves, prided themselves on their modern sensibility and ability to see through an old hawk's con. To this particular senator, men like my father had gotten us into an unwinnable, unpopular, and probably immoral war. They were not to be trusted.

This was not, of course, the first time my father had testified before a congressional committee. Nor was it the first time my father had encountered a quarrelsome legislator. He had forged personal relationships with a good many politicians and over the years had had any number of spirited debates with them on all manner of military subjects. It was, however, the first time any member of Congress had challenged his honesty, and that was an injury he would accept from no one.

Once the insult was offered, my father forgot all thought of the purpose of his testimony. Neither did he particularly give a damn about disputing the senator's view of our force requirements. All that mattered to him was that he respond to the attack on his good name, which he did instantly and forcefully.

According to Admiral Vasey, who had accompanied my father to the hearing room and was seated right behind the witness table, the moment the senator finished making the offensive remark, my father jumped to his feet. Red-faced, and jabbing his finger in the direction of his accuser, he proceeded to deliver a heated and sarcastic lecture on strategy and the responsibilities of the Commander in Chief, Pacific. "I don't remember his specific words," Admiral Vasey recounted in a letter to me, "but he made it crystal-clear that he was an officer of the highest integrity, as was his father before him, and he strongly objected to any insinuation that reflected on the moral character of himself or his testimony, or of the United States military."

When it appeared that my father was not about to let up on the offending senator, Admiral Vasey discreetly grasped the bottom of my father's coat and pulled him down into his seat, "but not before observing the sly smiles on the faces of other committee members."

Such outbursts were rare in those days in the ostentatiously formal precincts of Capitol Hill. They are even rarer today. There were few things in his life my father valued more dearly than his career. But his good name was one of them. He would have sacrificed anything to defend it, as the errant senator found out that day.

Of course, my father was at the end of his career, and already wore four stars. He had achieved his life's ambition, and there was nothing an antagonistic member of Congress could do about it. My father did have hopes of extending his tour as CINCPAC, and that, of course, could have been put at risk by his publicly upbraiding a sitting member of Congress. I am confident, however, that my father did not give a damn about the risks involved in what some might have viewed as his astonishingly rash behavior. I doubt he believed any job was worth having if it required him to suffer such an insult in silence.

My father prided himself on being a strategic thinker. Obviously, the war consumed most of his time, but, as he had for most of his career, he focused much of his attention on the future threats to American naval supremacy in the Pacific. He had long been concerned about the growing strength of the Soviet Navy, and he believed one of his most important duties as CINCPAC was to ensure that the United States was prepared to contain the emerging Soviet naval threat. Toward that end, my father worked not just to maintain the Navy's military advantage in the Pacific, but to strengthen the United States' relationships with the countries in the region.

Needless to say, American diplomats in Asia were not always delighted to share their responsibilities with a naval officer, especially one as outspoken and often unpredictable as my father. But my father enjoyed warm, personal relationships with many Asian leaders and could speak to them more forthrightly and often to better effect than could a good many American ambassadors in Asia. Many Asian heads of state had come to power as military leaders. Many were not philosophically well disposed toward the virtues of democracy. They were often more comfortable in the company of a senior American military official who wished to talk with them only about questions of regional security and military power, and in a language familiar to them, than they were in the company of our diplomats.

My father's reputation as a frank, gruff, and engaging American military representative was widespread throughout Asia. Most, if not all, of the Asian heads of state whose countries were either allies of the United States or officially nonaligned with either superpower considered him a personal friend. He was accorded extraordinary courtesies whenever he paid official visits to their countries.

A few years ago, I met with Lee Kuan Yew, who as Singapore's "senior minister" has governed the city-state for decades and is considered by many to be the elder statesman of Asia. My visit was an official one, but Lee began our conversation by reminding me that he had been a friend of my father's. He went on to talk at great length about my father, in a tone suffused with fond regard for his memory. He paid polite but rather less close attention to the official subjects I had come to discuss. Throughout our discussion, he kept returning to my father, and repeating how highly he had valued my father's friendship and counsel. That was fine with me.

On another official visit, this time to Taiwan, I was invited to be the guest of honor at a luncheon banquet hosted by most of the Taiwan military command. The affair lasted over two hours, and considerable quantities of a Chinese rice wine that tastes more like whiskey than wine were consumed by the twenty or more aging generals in attendance. Every ten minutes or so, one or another of the generals rose to his feet and reverently offered a toast to the memory of my father, "the great American admiral, John McCain."

Joe Vasey accompanied my father on his official visits to Asian capitals. He tells a humorous story about a trip they made to Indonesia during which they paid a call on President Suharto, who, until very recently, was one of Southeast Asia's most durable dictators. The story illustrates my father's diplomatic style and the respect accorded him by Asian leaders.

My father and Suharto enjoyed each other's company, and the meeting lasted much longer than planned. Near the end of their conversation, my father surprised his host and the American diplomats who accompanied him to the meeting by commenting on Indonesia's recent purchase of Soviet ships. "Why in the hell did you accept motor torpedo boats and submarines from the Soviets? Our intelligence reports indicate they are a bunch of junk." Before Suharto could respond, my father asked his permission to visit one of the subs. After briefly consulting with an aide, Suharto agreed, and the next day my father and Admiral Vasey were flown to a naval base at the other end of Java.

When they arrived, they instantly confirmed the opinion of naval intelligence that the submarines in question were junk. They were freshly painted and immaculate, and the officers and crew were well turned out. But the two veterans of the American submarine service knew an antiquated ship when they saw one. It was clear to both of them that the sub had never been submerged or even under way since it had arrived some months earlier. Nevertheless, my father wanted to make a complete inspection. He asked the Indonesian admirals accompanying them to permit them to continue their inspection belowdecks, which, after a brief delay to prepare the crew, they were allowed to do.

When he reached the forward torpedo room, my father asked his host to fire a water slug, a standard test routinely performed by all navies. The outer door of the tube is opened, and after the tube fills with water a blast of air blows the water back out. The Indonesians agreed, assuring my father that the test was performed weekly on all their submarines. However, it seemed to take an inordinate amount of time for the demonstration to be performed, and it was obvious the Indonesians were uncertain how to proceed. When at length they attempted to fire the slug, the procedure was done in reverse. My father and Vasey were standing just a few feet behind the tube when high-pressure air blew open the tube's heavy bronze inner door. The door narrowly missed Admiral Vasey, he recalled, and the "great whoosh of high pressure air and oily vapor immediately engulfed the entire torpedo room in a dark cloud as our Indonesian friends scrambled up the vertical ladder to safety." As they gasped for air, Vasey guided my father to the ladder and out of harm's way. Although much amused by the mishap, my father never remarked on it in subsequent meetings with his hosts.

Few, if any, American diplomatic or military officials could have expected such elaborate courtesies from the government of a country that was not an ally of the United States. But because of the respect Asian leaders had for my father he could use his influence to obtain important diplomatic and intelligence opportunities for the United States, always thinking ahead to future challenges to our security. He would even do his own intelligence work when the opportunity arose, as was the case on this occasion.

Admiral Vasey put the incident in a strategic perspective, observing that Washington was preoccupied with Vietnam and less concerned with Soviet overtures to Indonesia that were intended to promote political entente between the two nations. But Indonesia's proximity to vital sea-lanes concerned my father very much. He feared that Indonesia's drift into the Soviet sphere of influence would "drastically change the strategic face of Southeast Asia." According to Vasey, after my father's visit, "no further Russian military assistance was provided."

In time, I think the State Department came to value my father's somewhat unorthodox diplomacy, recognizing the opportunities his familiar relations with Asian rulers provided to U.S. statecraft. He was the first CINCPAC to be a regular participant in the annual conference of American ambassadors in Asia. Admiral Vasey observed that the ambassadors initially viewed my father "with great apprehension, but once they knew him and understood his style, they looked forward to his visits. His close rapport with and the confidence in him by Asian leaders always resulted in handsome dividends, insights and information." I know that President Nixon and Dr. Kissinger valued his influence in the region, for in later years they told me so.

He flew to Vietnam about once a month to confer with General Creighton Abrams and assess the war's progress. He held Abrams in very high regard, and I believe Abrams reciprocated his admiration. Their appointments were announced by the President in the same press conference. But where my father's appointment had come as something of a surprise to official Washington, Abrams's appointment had been expected. He had been his predecessor's second in command, in which capacity he had acquitted himself well. My father outranked him, and Abrams was expected to report through my father to the Joint Chiefs. But as a practical matter, his opinion was expected to hold greater sway with Washington than my father's, at least to the extent that any military commander's could influence an administration that was so directly involved in both strategic and tactical decision making. And my father was a firm believer in giving his commanders in the field the full support they sought from CINCPAC, a policy he insisted on to his staff at Camp Smith, CINCPAC headquarters.

Disagreements and hard feelings within the Military Assistance Command in Vietnam, MACV, about Washington's management of the war abated somewhat with the inauguration of the Nixon administration, but that is not to say that they disappeared altogether. No military operation, before or since, experienced the extraordinarily close involvement of political decision makers in day-to-day military decisions. But then no war since the Civil War was as politically controversial as Vietnam. MACV relied on my father to pass on its views and concerns to Washington, and he did not let MACV down. After every visit to the field, he dutifully passed up the line, unvarnished and with his full concurrence, whatever was bothering General Abrams and the other commanders of MACV.

Understandably, my father's appointment initially occasioned some apprehension in the field. He was, after all, an admiral. Vietnam was essentially a ground war, and most of its commanders were generals. It was, I'm sure, MACV's hope that my father would confine his visits to a few routine briefings and not attempt to impose a sailor's views on the infantry's war. But although he ably supported his commanders, he was not content to supervise the war from a distance. The war was his responsibility, and he never ducked his responsibilities. He quickly proved himself an astute commander and an important resource for MACV. He won the respect of Abrams and the other senior officers in Vietnam, who came to welcome his frequent visits as opportunities not just to vent their frustrations with Washington but to take advantage of the old man's counsel.

My mother accompanied him on all his trips to Vietnam. Frequently, my mother's sister, Rowena, joined them. My father's contemporaries often kidded him for having two wives, a reference to the fact that my mother and aunt were identical twins and to their constant presence at his side. He delighted in amplifying the joke himself. Whenever anyone asked him how he managed to tell his wife and sister-in-law apart, he would gruffly respond, "That's their problem."

In truth, my father was delighted and flattered by the attention his wife and sister-in-law received. He was, in his way, as devoted to his wife and sister-in-law as they were to him. He enjoyed being constantly attended by two beautiful women, and what contentment he knew in his life, which was less, I think, than other men knew, he usually found in their company. My mother always traveled with my father. Had the Navy allowed it, I am sure she would have accompanied him on sea duty, and found in the alternately exciting and dull world of men at sea some useful and interesting way to occupy her time.

My father seldom went to Vietnam simply to receive official briefings. On most of his visits, after conferring with Abrams and senior officers, he would go into the field to talk with the younger officers and enlisted men who were doing the fighting. While he was in the field, my mother and Aunt Rowena remained in Saigon, shopping, sightseeing, visiting, and waiting for his return.

My father did not affect a regard for the opinion of his soldiers in a transparent attempt to boost their morale. He genuinely believed that their views about how the war was going were just as important as the views of their commanders in Saigon. Like his father before him, he believed that the men who executed combat orders were the best judges of their soundness. He wanted to know what they thought about operations that had been completed and about those that were imminent or in the planning stages. He wanted to know how news from home was affecting their morale. He wanted to know if they thought we would win the war. He based his own opinions on the war's conduct in large part on what he learned from the colonels, captains, lieutenants, sergeants, and privates who were conducting it.

A participant in one of my father's field briefings described the experience in a letter to me. In the summer of 1968, my father and General Abrams unexpectedly arrived at a battalion base camp in the Mekong Delta. There they received an improvised briefing on the battalion's operations from the battalion commander. My correspondent, Randy Carpenter, was then a twenty-two-year-old draftee who had through attrition been made a platoon leader. He had been asked to present my father with a captured AK-47 rifle. He recounted what happened after the brief ceremony concluded.

> Your father, smoking a very large cigar, in a rough voice politely thanked everyone and asked if he and General

Abrams could talk to me in private. He excused the three of us and we went to a small isolated area. Your father asked all of the questions. He wanted to know how much and what kind of action my platoon had seen. He asked general questions about the morale of my men and my morale. What kind of news we were getting from the states and how we were getting it? Had I been inside Cambodia on any operations? Did we have any men missing in action? Would I or my men have any problem expanding the operation into neighboring countries? What would the men's reaction be if we were asked to go into North Vietnam? . . . The meeting lasted about fifteen minutes and at the end I was ordered not to discuss any of what we talked about with anyone.

He was the commander my grandfather surely had hoped he would become: forceful, determined, clear thinking, and respectful of his men. Had my grandfather held the post, I believe he would have commanded in the same way. I like to believe my father recognized this, and that the recognition strengthened his confidence, and brought him a good measure of satisfaction.

Late in the war, my father would give the order that sent B–52s to rain destruction upon the city where I was held a prisoner. That was his duty, and he did not shrink from it.

While I was imprisoned, he never spoke about me at length to anyone other than my wife and mother. When friends offered their sympathy, he would thank them politely and change the subject.

He received hundreds of letters from members of Congress, dignitaries, fellow officers, enlisted men, family friends, and acquaintances offering their sympathy and prayers for my return. He politely and briefly replied to each one.

His responses were almost always written in the same style. The first paragraph of each began with an expression of his appreciation for the correspondent's sympathy, and closed, almost unvaryingly, with the line "God has a way of solving problems and we have great faith in the future." The next paragraph would address another subject, often extending an invitation to visit my parents in London.

Copies of his letters are kept with my father's official papers. There are only three I have reviewed that differ substantially from the others. The first is a letter my father wrote to the wife of Colonel John Flynn. John was the most senior American officer in captivity. He had been shot down the day after I was captured and taken to the same hospital where I was held. We never saw each other in the hospital, although one day Cat, in his usual bragging mood, had shown me his identity card. For the first three years of his captivity, John, like the other higher-ranking officers, was kept segregated from the rest of us and out of our communication chain.

My father wrote empathetically to Mrs. Flynn, commiserating with her that they must resign themselves to trusting in God and the courage of their loved ones as the only assurance that they would come home. "There is little anyone can say and even less they can do when personal tragedy strikes," he wrote. "Our hearts are with you."

The second letter was a reply to the friend with whom I had completed the escape and evasion course in Germany. He had written my parents to share his observations of me, assuring them that I had been well prepared for my present adverse circumstances and possessed the ability to "come away from this situation in good condition, and to be an example to others." My father wrote back that he and my mother had "derived much reassurance from the account of your experiences [with John]."

The last letter was a reply to Admiral B. M. "Smoke" Strean, who was the Deputy Chief of Navy Personnel and had approved my transfer to the *Oriskany* after the *Forrestal* fire. Admiral Strean had "hesitated to write because I feel I had a part in this—in helping him get what he wanted—and thus a feeling of some blame in the outcome." Strean assured my father that his normal practice was to go slowly when considering requests for "unscheduled assignments which carry some hazard. . . . [But] your son badly wanted this assignment."

My father quickly wrote back to reassure his apologetic friend: "I deeply appreciate your letter. You are a great man in every respect. You should have no regrets. I have no regrets. John wanted to go back and I know he would not have been happy otherwise. I am proud of him."

Few close observers of my father ever detected that my captivity caused him great suffering. He never let his concern affect his attention to duty or restrain him from prosecuting the war to the greatest extent his civilian commanders allowed.

However, his closest aides knew he kept a personal file containing all reported information about the POWs, the location and conditions of the camps, and every scrap of intelligence about me that could be obtained. Included in my father's file were copies of the letters I had written to Carol, as well as some copies of letters that other prisoners had written to their wives.

During my first months of captivity I was allowed to write several letters to Carol, a privilege I attributed to the publicity surrounding my capture. Eventually, the Vietnamese withdrew the privilege and restricted me to one or two letters a year. Not until late in 1969 would prisoners be allowed to write home on a monthly basis.

Carol wrote me every month. The Vietnamese withheld all but a few of her letters from me. She also sent me many packages, few of which I received, and none of which contained all the items she had sent. With the exception of 1971 and 1972, I would usually receive a package at or sometime after Christmas.

It was always clear that the guards had taken most of the contents as their share before passing a package on to me. Sometimes I received candy, instant soup, socks, and underwear. Once I received pipe tobacco but not the pipe that had been included with it. One package contained only a single pair of skivvies and a bottle of vitamins. The

Vietnamese had neglected to remove the shipping receipt that indicated the package had originally contained five pounds of material.

That I received so few of Carol's letters and packages is probably attributable to Carol's refusal to send them through the offices of the antiwar organization COLIAFAM, the Committee of Liaison with Families of Servicemen Detained in North Vietnam. COLIAFAM had arranged with the Vietnamese government to be exclusively authorized to process letters and packages to the POWs. Many families, including mine, refused to sanction this abridgment of a prisoner's right under the Geneva Convention to receive mail without interference from his captors or any agency working on his behalf.

One Christmas, Carol received a letter from COLIAFAM denouncing the resumption of the bombing campaign in the North and demanding an immediate and total withdrawal of American forces from Vietnam. A postscript contained a none too veiled threat, warning her that letters that were not delivered by COLIAFAM "will not be accepted and . . . may jeopardize [the prisoner's] mail rights."

When I was a prisoner of war I resented the antiwar activists who had visited Hanoi and, wittingly or unwittingly, made our life in prison more miserable than it already was. Today I no longer bear any ill will for most of these people. I have made far too many mistakes in my own life to forever disparage people, most of whom were very young at the time, who long ago, and in the name of peace, made a bad mistake. I have not yet, however, managed to relinquish my resentment of COLIAFAM.

To exploit the anguish of families for the purpose of propagandizing and giving aid and comfort to the enemy is an offense so grievous that it merits denunciation even today, many years after the fact. Had COLIAFAM not intervened, the Vietnamese, for their own sake, would have eventually allowed us to send and receive mail without insisting that it serve the antiwar cause at home. Although I would have dearly loved to receive more mail, I was proud of Carol for refusing to cooperate in a plan to dishonor me. It took courage and wisdom on her part not to be enticed by COLIAFAM's "humanitarian gesture" into aiding my enemies.

My father never wrote me a letter during the war. He knew that the Vietnamese would have regarded a missive from him as a propaganda bonanza. He did try once to secretly pass a message to me.

Prisoners were required to write letters home on a preprinted six-line form. We were instructed to write only on the lines provided, to write legibly, and to restrict our message to comments about our health and family. Many POWs, however, managed to exceed our captors' instructions and pass encoded messages in their letters home.

For example, after my years in solitary ended, my first cellmate, John Finley, wrote a letter to his wife that asked her to say "hi to cousin King Mc, Abel and his brother." His wife was puzzled by the request, as she knew no one by the name of Mc or Abel. Naval intelligence analyzed the letter, interpreted "Abel and his brother" as an allusion to Cain, and thus concluded that the writer was making a reference to McCain.

Two months later, John wrote another letter to his wife in which he very subtly distinguished certain letters. When the letters were read together they spelled MCCAIN MY MATE.

I, too, tried to pass hidden messages in my letters. Lacking John Finley's ingenuity, I was considerably less subtle in the means I used. Vietnamese writing makes frequent use of accent marks. I borrowed the fashion for my letters to Carol, placing marks above certain letters to spell out my secret message.

My technique was quite obvious, and Carol noticed it immediately. In the first letter in which I attempted covert communication, the marked letters spelled out LCOL GUY, a reference to Ted Guy, who was then my senior at the Plantation. In another I passed on that CRANERMATE [Craner and Gruters] WELL. In another, I informed her that I GET NO MAIL I AM OK.

After reading these letters, Carol, properly, sent them on to naval intelligence, where my lack of sophistication in encryption aroused considerable concern. An intelligence officer wrote my father's aide to apprise him of my efforts, and of their concern that my messages were so indiscreet that it was "hard to see how they passed even basic censorship."

The officer asked my father's permission to use one of Carol's letters to me to transmit a carefully hidden caution. My father agreed and ordered the message to read, JUNIOR URGES CAUTION PLEASE STOP THIS.

I would have been surprised to receive the message, for I thought I was a fairly clever communicator, or, more honestly, I trusted in the dull wits of the Vietnamese censors to compensate for my indiscretion. As it turned out, my trust was well placed. I never received my father's warning, because the Vietnamese withheld Carol's letters from me. So I kept on sending messages in my letters. The Vietnamese never caught me.

Had I received the old man's message, I might have been a little put out, but I think I also would have appreciated the indication of his concern. I would have taken some comfort in the knowledge that he was, as best he could, watching out for me.

The Navy did manage to get one message through to me. Some weeks after my transfer to Hoa Lo in late 1969, the Vietnamese gave me a package from Carol that they had been holding for a while. It had survived inspection with a few of its original contents intact: a few cans of a vitamin-rich baby formula, a bottle of vitamins, several handkerchiefs, and one tin of candy.

Carol hoped the baby formula would compensate for the nutrition-free diet the Vietnamese provided us. It was intended to be mixed with milk. Lacking any, I had to mix it with water. The result was so unpalatable that despite my chronic hunger, I simply couldn't stomach the stuff, and I threw the rest away.

The candy was another matter. The can contained about twenty pieces of chocolate with vanilla centers. They were such a prized treat that I decided to ration them, savoring one piece each day. On the fourth or fifth day, as I was rejoicing in the pleasure of eating my daily ration, chewing it slowly and deliberately, I felt a foreign particle in the center of the chocolate. I spit it on the ground and finished eating.

A few moments later, thinking it strange that the manufacturers of the candy would have tolerated such poor quality control, I picked the object up to inspect it. It was a tiny plastic capsule. Excitedly, I moved into the shadows in a corner of my cell, where I tried to open the capsule. Although a naked lightbulb lit my cell twenty-four hours a day, it was of such low wattage that it only dimly illuminated a small area. Almost no natural light infiltrated my cell, and I was free to work on the capsule unseen even in daylight hours.

The capsule was fitted very tightly, and I had a difficult time prying it open. I spent a long time working at it unsuccessfully. Finally I found a sliver of bamboo and used it to push the capsule apart. Inside was a small, folded, incredibly thin piece of plastic. I unfolded it and read the message that the Navy had written on it.

The message read something like:

I HOPE YOU ARE WELL. YOUR FAMILY IS FINE. THE LINER OF THIS CAN WORKS LIKE INVISIBLE INK. PLACE IT OVER YOUR LETTERS. PRESS A HARD OBJECT ON IT. IT WILL WRITE SECRET MESSAGE.

I was elated and very encouraged. The Navy was trying to communicate with me, a clear sign that our country had not forgotten about us. I extracted the white paper liner from the can, inspected it to see if I could detect the invisible residue that coated it, and impatiently waited for my first opportunity to put the thing to good use.

Unfortunately, the Vietnamese chose this particular time to change their normal practice of supervising the prisoners' letter writing. Over the last year, they had allowed me to write home once every few months. They would give me the form, and I would write my few lines, which they then took away and inspected. If it met with their approval, they would return with it and tell me to copy it word for word on a second form. Up until this time, I had always been left alone in my cell to transcribe the letter onto the second form.

The next time they gave me leave to write home, I hurriedly scribbled a few lines on the first form and anxiously awaited the guards' return with the second. To my great disappointment, after my letter passed inspection, the guards took me to the interrogation room to copy it while they watched. I have no idea what precipitated this change in the routine. Perhaps they had begun to suspect that I was writing in some kind of code. Or perhaps they had discovered another prisoner using a device to pass hidden messages in his letters home. I never learned what had aroused their suspicions. But whatever it was, it effectively prevented me from ever using the device the Navy had hoped would enable me to pass messages by less obvious means than I had been employing.

After this latest letter, the Vietnamese curtailed my letter-writing privilege for a long time. When many months later they restored the privilege, they never again allowed me to write a single word outside the presence of guards. I was never able to use the liner.

Despite my disappointment, the experience, on the whole, was an uplifting one. The attempt to facilitate communication with naval intelligence was welcome evidence of the Navy's concern and its desire to gain a fuller understanding of our situation, information I assumed it would use to our benefit. I was cheered and gratified by the effort even though it was unsuccessful.

My father did not meet with any of the prisoners who had been released early. But his file contained all their debriefing reports and reports from officers who had talked with them about me.

In a conversation that was reported to my father, a prisoner, one of the August 1968 releases whom I had been invited to join, informed his debriefing officer that according to camp rumor I had refused release.

Doug Hegdahl and two other prisoners were released in August

1969. An intelligence officer who interviewed Hegdahl asked them for information about me, and cabled my father the following report:

YOUR SON WAS SERIOUSLY WOUNDED WHEN SHOT DOWN IN HANOI BUT HAS MADE FINE RECOVERY AND NOW, ACCORDING THIS GROUP, LOOKS "QUITE WELL." HE HAS BEEN EVERYTHING YOU WANT YOUR SON TO BE AND HAS STOOD UP MANFULLY AGAINST ALL EFFORTS TO PERSUADE HIM TO UTTER TRAITOR- OUS STATEMENTS.

In a subsequent report from Hegdahl, my father was informed about my efforts to disrupt the Christmas service in 1968. Hegdahl also remarked that "John is known in the camp as a daredevil. He frequently gets caught attempting to communicate with other PWs." Hegdahl thoughtfully concluded his report with the observation that the other prisoners respected me for refusing to cooperate with the North Vietnamese.

As grateful as the old man must have been to receive this information, the men providing it had been released nearly a year after I had been broken and made my confession. The knowledge of this diminished considerably the satisfaction I otherwise would have derived from knowing my father had, at last, received a report that his son had good grease.

Hegdahl and the others knew I had been offered release, and they were also certainly aware of the events that occurred after my refusal. I had told Hegdahl at the Christmas service that I had been beaten for turning down the Vietnamese offer. And had the Vietnamese played over the camp loudspeakers a tape of my confession, as I believed happened, they would have heard it. But they made no mention of this in their report, or, if they had, the reporting officer failed to pass it on to my father.

They need not have bothered. A month before my father was apprised of their debriefing, he had received a report that a heavily edited propaganda broadcast, purported to have been made by me, had been analyzed, and the voice compared to my taped interview with the French journalist. The two voices were judged to be the same. In the anguished days right after my confession, I had dreaded just such a discovery by my father.

After I came home, he never mentioned to me that he had learned about my confession, and, although I told him about it, I never discussed it at length. I only recently learned that the tape I dreamed I heard playing over the loudspeaker in my cell had been real; it had been broadcast outside the prison and had come to the attention of my father.

If I had known at the time my father had heard about my confession, I would have been distressed beyond imagination, and might not have recovered from the experience as quickly as I did. But in the years that have passed since the event, my regard for my father and for myself has matured. I understand better the nature of strong character.

My father was a strong enough man not to judge too harshly the character of a son who had reached his limits and found that they were well short of the standards of the idealized heroes who had inspired us as boys. And I am strong enough now to know that my father had sufficient faith in me to assume I had done the best I could, and that learning I had been broken would only have aroused in him an increased concern for my welfare.

On the one occasion when I briefly recounted the experience for him, he listened impassively until I finished, put his hand on my shoulder, and said, "You did the best you could, John. That's all that's expected of any of us."

My mother knew that my father suffered from the burden of commanding a war in a country where his son was imprisoned. She believes the strain aged him considerably. She told me later of how she would hear him in his study, praying aloud on his knees, beseeching God to "show Johnny mercy." He continued to politely rebuff all attempts by friends to discuss with him what he considered to be his personal misfortune. To the world, he was, as ever, a competent, tireless naval officer, strictly devoted to his duty. Whatever private anguish he suffered, he suffered in silence.

I received a letter once from a retired Army colonel who had been a Cobra helicopter platoon commander in Vietnam. He recounted for me a New Year's Day he had spent unhappily at Quang Tri, having flown a fire team north to guard against violations of the holiday cease-fire. As he ate his lunch and waited miserably for nightfall, a Navy helicopter unexpectedly landed near his Cobra. An officer stepped out of the helicopter, walked to the end of the strip, and remained there for a while.

"One of his pilots came over to us to look at our ships and visit, and one of my warrants remarked, 'Who's that?'—referring to the officer about fifty yards from us. The Navy pilot said, 'That's Admiral McCain. He has a son up north and this is as close as he can get to him.' "

Every year he was CINCPAC, my father spent the Christmas holidays with troops near the DMZ. The letter quoted above represents dozens of reports I have received over the years that mentioned my father's custom of withdrawing from his company at the end of the meal, walking north, and standing alone for a long time, looking toward the place where he had lost his son.

My father served two tours as CINCPAC. During his second tour, he suffered a mild stroke. Admiral John Hyland, who commanded the Pacific Fleet at the time, and with whom my father had a somewhat difficult relationship, remembered being told by my father's executive assistant that the old man would "never be able to come back. He's finished." But my father had other plans. According to Hyland, "Things just continued to run. . . . We'd all go down . . . to see him every day or so and talk with him and so on. But, not very long after that, he came back to duty, and he was fine."

As the end of his second tour approached, my father lobbied

Washington to extend his tenure for another year so that he could continue in command until the war ended. His request was turned down. President Nixon flew to Honolulu to attend the ceremony that officially ended my father's command in the Pacific. Two months later, after forty-one years on active duty, he retired from the Navy.

Despite his apparent recovery, he was never again a well man after his stroke. He lived for nearly nine years after he retired. But, in truth, he had, like his father before him, sacrificed his life to hold a command in his country's war.

CHAPTER 22

The Washrag

Our treatment reached its nadir after the Atterbury and Dramesi escape attempt. Reprisals were ordered at every camp. Many prisoners were tortured to reveal other escape plans. Beatings were inflicted for even minor infractions of prison rules. The food was worse. Security was tightened and our cells were frequently and thoroughly inspected. Many of us suffered from boils—in the sweltering heat, our lymph glands clogged up and baseball-sized boils developed under our arms. All we had to treat them with was small vials of iodine. The guards took them away from us because Ed and John had used iodine to darken their faces the night of their escape.

During that spring and summer, I was caught communicating several times. Sometimes I earned a beating for my efforts, but other times I was just made to sit on a stool in the corner for a day or two like a disobedient schoolboy. Once I was ordered to stand facing the wall for two days and two nights. On the second day, exhausted, I sat down. A guard discovered me, mistook my weariness for insolence, and, in a rage, beat and jumped on my bad leg. The resulting pain and swelling in my leg forced me to use a crutch again. Surprisingly, camp officials chastised the guard for physically abusing me without their approval.

During another of my punishments, a severe one, I again complained that I was being treated like an animal. My guards were then ordered to feed me like an animal. Every day for a week, they brought me a bowl of soup with a piece of bread thrown in it and ordered me to eat it with my hands.

The summer of 1969 was a long, difficult time. But as autumn arrived, our treatment began to improve. By the end of the year, the routine beatings had all but stopped. Prisoners were still physically mistreated as punishment for communicating or other violations of camp regulations. But beatings to extract propaganda information all but ceased. We occasionally received extra rations of food. For a brief period, the guards came to my cell every night and removed the boards blocking the transom over my cell to let in the evening breeze. At times, some of the guards were almost pleasant in their dealings with us. We had hard times ahead of us, but from October of that year until our release, our circumstances were never as dire as they had been in those long early years of captivity.

This welcome change in our treatment coincided with the death of Ho Chi Minh, leading many POWs to think that old Uncle Ho must have had a less than avuncular affection for the air pirates occupying his prisons. A funereal dirge was broadcast over loudspeakers everywhere in Hanoi on the morning of September 4, and the black-and-red mourning patches worn by the guards that day aroused our suspicion that old Ho had passed on to his eternal reward.

I don't know for certain whether the terrible summer of 1969 was partly a consequence of Ho's animosity to us, and the change in our fortunes explained by the fact that death had finally silenced his exhortations to the people to treat us like criminals. What we learned from new shootdowns late in the war was that word of our treatment had finally reached the rest of the world, and the discovery that there was a darker side to the plucky North Vietnamese nationalists had begun to cloud Hanoi's international horizons.

In August 1969, the Vietnamese released, to an American antiwar delegation, Doug Hegdahl, Wes Rumble, and Robert Frishman. Defense Secretary Melvin Laird had showed photographs of Hegdahl and Frishman to members of the Vietnamese delegation in Paris and demanded their release. All of them were in bad shape. Frishman had no elbow, just a limp, rubbery arm. Rumble had a broken back. Hegdahl had lost seventy-five pounds. Dick Stratton and our senior ranking officer, Ted Guy, had ordered him to accept the release. He had memorized the names of most of the POWs held in the North.

In a change from Johnson administration policy, the Nixon administration allowed the three returned POWs to publicly reveal details of torture and deprivation. The ensuing public fury, led by the newly organized National League of Families of POWs and MIAs in Southeast Asia, of which my brother, Joe, was an active member, began to turn world opinion against Hanoi. And the Vietnamese, ever mindful of their reliance on international goodwill, decided to suspend their campaign to beat and starve us into submission.

The first indication that the Vietnamese had revised their "humane and lenient" policy was evident in changes in the way we were exploited for propaganda purposes. We were no longer threatened or tortured to make us confess war crimes or renounce our country. The Vietnamese were now extremely anxious to convince the world that we were well treated.

POWs were filmed playing cards and other games, reading their mail, attending religious services, and opening packages from home. Fewer and fewer prisoners were kept in solitary confinement, although I remained alone for several more months. The Vietnamese more often dispensed with physical intimidation to extract statements from us and instead appealed to our thoughts about our families, or tried to plant doubts about the progress of the war or our government's good faith to win our cooperation.

Their present public relations dilemma was much on our captors' minds. "The whole world supports us" was Hanoi's proudest boast, parroted by politburo member and lowly prison guard alike. They were clearly exasperated by this setback in their design to win the war on America's campuses and streets, and at odds over what to do about it.

Soft Soap burst into my cell once, highly agitated, and complained, "Even the Russians criticize us. You tell lies about us. You say we pull out your fingernails and make you live in rooms with no ventilation." That Soft Soap made this complaint while I languished in the suffocating environment of my unventilated cell made the experience only slightly less surreal than listening to the loudspeaker in my cell inform me that the American government was lying about Vietnam's mistreatment of prisoners.

There were, at this time, various personnel shake-ups among camp authorities that were evidently related to our change in treatment. My turnkey, the Prick, who had started every day by attempting to humiliate me, disappeared from the prison's guard roster. I derived considerable satisfaction from imagining him humping it down the Ho Chi Minh Trail cursing his bad luck and carrying an impossibly heavy burden, or sweating out a night firefight with a company of better-armed Marines.

The Cat may have suffered the most from the bad turn in Vietnam's public relations. He was relieved as commander of all the camps and thereafter seemed to function as the senior officer of one part of the Hanoi Hilton. He was still accorded the deference due a senior officer, but he was no longer the highest authority.

From this period on, he seemed almost solicitous of the prisoners' well-being. He often appeared nervous and distressed. He was observed complaining that prisoners should not be badly mistreated, and, reportedly, he would grow quite agitated upon discovering that a guard had discharged too enthusiastically the responsibilities of his office.

Later on, I learned from another POW that the Cat had been obliged to denounce himself in front of the party for mistreating prisoners in violation of Vietnam's policy of "humane and lenient" treatment for all prisoners.

On a bitter cold Christmas night in 1969, after I had been transferred from the Plantation back to Hoa Lo, the prison where I had spent my first days of captivity, I received an unexpected visitor. Moments after the last Christmas song had played over the camp loudspeakers, my cell door burst open, and to my complete surprise, the Cat entered my room, dressed in suit and tie, and began to chat with me about home and Christmas. Unlike our previous encounters, he had no need of an interpreter. He spoke English well enough. He offered me cigarettes, which I smoked one after the other. He talked about his experiences in the war, and in the French Indochina War before it. He talked about his family, showing me a diamond tie pin his father had given him. He asked about my family, and expressed his regret that I could not be with them this holiday.

At one point he told me about a particularly beautiful part of Vietnam, near the Chinese border, Ha Long Bay, famous for the thousands of volcanic islands that rise dramatically from its waters. He mentioned that Ho Chi Minh loved the place, and had occasionally enjoyed resting in an old French villa on one of the bay's islands. Not long ago I visited Ha Long Bay, and I can attest to Ho's good taste in vacation spots.

As he got up to leave, he reminded me that had I accepted release the year before, I would be enjoying a far more pleasant holiday this evening.

Without rancor, he remarked, "You should have accepted our generous offer. You would be with your family tonight."

"You will never understand why I could not," I responded.

"I understand more than you think," he shot back as he left my cell.

I didn't know what to make of this unusual encounter at first, fearing that it was the precursor to another attempt to release me. After a while, however, it occurred to me that the Cat was simply in an expansive holiday mood, and being a man who evidently possessed some Western tastes, he had wanted to affect the image of a courtly enemy enjoying a brief Christmas truce with a fellow officer. I didn't mind. I enjoyed the cigarettes.

Despite our improved fortunes in the fall and winter of 1969, we continued to suffer moments of despair, occasioned by grim misfortune, and sometimes by less serious experiences.

Keeping a sense of humor was indispensable to surviving a long imprisonment without losing our minds, and most of us looked hard to find some humor in our experiences. Many greeted the most difficult moments with a dark gallows humor, and we were always grateful for occasions to laugh about the embarrassments and absurdities of daily prison life. When we are asked today about our years in prison, many of us are apt to include in our account, "We had a lot of fun, too."

As implausible as that glib response is—and surely it is exaggerated—we did manage to have some fun despite our dreary, often depressing existence. And the prisoners whose company we valued the most were those who could make the rest of us laugh at our circumstances and ourselves.

Bob Craner had a ready wit, and he favored a droll, ironic brand of humor that never failed to cheer me up when I was down. When the death of seventy-nine-year-old Ho Chi Minh and the appointment of his seventy-six-year-old successor was announced, Bob commented, "Ah, the Young Turks are taking over." Our daily dose of propaganda often included tributes to the skilled marksmen who defended North Vietnam from American bombers. Hannah's frequent reports of downed American aircraft invariably claimed that the plane had been destroyed "with the very first round." Bob often responded to Hannah's familiar boast by speculating that the Vietnamese must have a warehouse somewhere where thousands of crates of shells were stored, each one labeled "Very First Round."

Although we were neighbors during the worst years of my imprisonment, we managed to make light of our conditions whenever we could, and to laugh about the peculiar predicaments we frequently found ourselves in as we tried to make the most of our dismal existence.

Queenie was a pretty, slender young girl with lovely long hair. She worked as a secretary at the camp and occasionally helped out in the kitchen. We would see her when the guards brought us out to collect our bowls of soup, and Bob Craner and I would look through cracks in our cell doors to see her float around the camp, giggling and tossing her ponytail. All the guards mooned over her, but child though she was of a classless society, she only had eyes for the camp officers.

There were only two other women in the camp, a kitchen worker we called "Shovel" for her unusually flat profile, and the cook, "Mammy Yokum," a wizened old crone who chewed betel nut and screamed bloody murder at any guard who had the temerity to enter her kitchen unbidden.

Inevitably, we began to have fantasies about Queenie, which she kindled with shy smiles when she caught either of us gazing at her. Bob and I would joke about plans for the day we won the war, when we would forsake family and country to live quietly with Queenie in Thailand. But our love was unrequited.

One terrible day, my ardor got the better of me. A guard had taken me, hobbling on my crutches, to the stall where we were allowed to bathe and wash our clothes by taking water from a tank, a cup at a time, and pouring it on ourselves and our belongings. The stalls the prisoners used were directly across the open courtyard from a washroom the Vietnamese used. They had old, splintered wooden doors. When we were inside, the guard would place a steel bar in brackets across the door to prevent our escape, then wander away to chat with his friends.

The door had cracks in it, which I would look through to observe the daily activities in camp. On this day, I was thrilled to discover that Queenie had decided to take a turn at the washroom; I saw her carrying a load of her clothes in that direction. I suspended my bath to watch her while she washed her clothes, holding each article up to closely inspect her progress. As I maneuvered for a better view, I lost my balance and fell against the door. The guard had decided he didn't need to lock me in, as I was unlikely to get very far on crutches, and had set the bar next to the door. The door flew open, and I fell, naked and noisily, onto the bricks in front of the washroom.

Because of my bum leg, I couldn't stand up, and I thrashed around on the ground frantically trying to scramble back into the stall. Startled, Queenie briefly appraised my humiliating situation, then demurely covered her eyes. My guard, hearing the commotion, rushed back, saw what had happened, cuffed me around a bit, and threw me back in the stall, where I finished cleaning up in abject misery. From that moment on, whenever Queenie saw me she would shoot me a look of utter disdain. I suffered her contempt in agony. My kind friend Bob Craner commiserated with me, but did not bother to restrain his laughter over my misfortune, and by so doing turned my embarrassment into a welcome source of amusement for both of us.

I was, and remain, deeply indebted to Bob for his warm fellowship and for the humor he used so effectively to brighten our small, hostile world. So it was with deep guilt, second only to the guilt I felt over my confession, that I discovered I had done Bob a grave injustice. That the experience concluded humorously is a testament to the kind of guy Bob was, and how important his friendship was to me.

The Vietnamese allowed us certain amenities. We all received one short-sleeved shirt, one long-sleeved shirt, one pair of pants, and one pair of rubber sandals fabricated from old tires. We each had a drinking cup, a teapot, a toothbrush, toothpaste, and a bar of soap stamped "37%" (37 percent of what we never learned). We received a daily ration of three cigarettes (often withdrawn as punishment). But our most prized possession was a small, coarse square of cotton rag that served as both washcloth and towel.

I appreciate how difficult it must be for the reader to understand the inflated value of such an unremarkable article. But to a man who is deprived of almost all material possessions, who lies day after day in a dirty, oppressively hot cell, glazed in sweat and grime, a washcloth, no matter how undistinguished, is an inestimable comfort.

On wash day, when we were brought out to collect our first meal of the day, we would each hang our wet clothes and our washrag to dry on a wire strung in the courtyard. We would retrieve the articles as we brought back the afternoon meal.

On one such day in the fall of 1968, between our two meals, the guards hauled me out of my cell and took me to a punishment room for ten days of attitude adjustment. This was during a time when my attitude was frequently adjusted. As I was being transported, I noticed my belongings drying nicely in the sun and immediately began to long for the comfort of my cherished washrag.

Ten days later, my attitude well adjusted, I returned to my cell, and to my intense sorrow found that my washrag was no longer on the wire. Nor was it anywhere else to be found. I was beside myself, and, I am ashamed to admit, I began to feel resentful of the good fortune of my fellow POWs, who were not suffering the deprivation I was then experiencing. Some POWs in the camp had roommates, each with his own washrag—two and three washrags to the cell! Surely, I rationalized, three men could make do with two washrags.

When next I saw a rag hanging on the line, I took it, and joyfully used it for days, although I had to suppress incipient feelings of remorse to sustain my joy.

Some months later, on my way back to my cell, I spied my old washrag drying on the line. I recognized it as my long-lost rag by a distinctive hole in its center. With a sigh of relief, I retrieved it and hung the stolen rag in its place.

That evening Bob Craner tapped me up on the wall. He was enraged.

"Dammit, the worst thing ever has happened to me," he exclaimed. "A couple of months ago some rotten bastard stole my washrag, and I went for weeks without one. One day when I was sweeping leaves in the courtyard, I found an old rag in the dirt. I spent a long time cleaning it up. I never hung the thing on the wire because I was afraid some jerk would steal this one too. But today was such a nice, sunny day, I couldn't resist, and I hung it out to dry. And can you believe it, some son of a bitch stole it. Dammit. I can't believe it. Again I have no washrag."

I said nothing as he poured out his troubles. When he finished, I sank to the floor, feeling as remorseful as I ever have, but I was not brave enough to confess my crime.

Every day, I heard Bob yell, *"Bao cao, bao cao"*—the phrase we used to summon the guards—"Washrag, washrag, give me a washrag, goddammit." They ignored him.

On Christmas Day, after a good meal and a few minutes spent outside, Christmas carols played from the camp loudspeakers. They were a welcome relief to the atonal patriotic hymns the Vietnamese favored most other days, trying to crush our resolve with "Springtime in the Liberated Zone" and "I Asked My Mother How Many Air Pirates She Shot Down Today."

That evening, listening to "I'll Be Home for Christmas" on a full stomach, longing for home, and feeling the spirit of Christmas, I resolved to confess my crime to Bob. I tapped him up on the wall, reminded him that Christmas was a time for forgiveness, and explained what I had done. When I finished, he made no response. He just thumped on the wall, which was our sign for approaching danger and the signal to cease communicating.

Later in the evening, he called me.

"Listen. In the Old West the worst thing you could do to a man was steal his horse. In prison the worst thing you can do to a man is steal his washrag. And you stole my washrag, you son of a bitch." Although he intended his complaint to be humorous, I still felt terribly guilty.

Bob remained without the comfort of a washrag for quite a while after my confession, and he would often decry the injustice of it to me. "I get so sick of drying my hair with my pants," he would lament as pangs of guilt stabbed at my conscience. I felt bad about the injury I had done Bob throughout the remainder of our captivity, finally relieving my guilt on our first Christmas as free men by sending Bob a carton of five hundred washrags as a Christmas present.

CHAPTER 23

Hanoi Hilton

By next Christmas, in 1969, Bob and I were no longer neighbors. On December 9, another prisoner and I were moved to Hoa Lo, where most of our most senior officers were held. Loaded into the back of a truck, we were blindfolded during the short ride to the Hilton. Unaware of who my traveling companion was, I placed my hand on his leg and tapped: "I am John McCain. Who are you?" He tapped back a reply: "I am Ernie Brace."

Ernie and I were taken to a section of the prison the POWs called "Little Vegas," where each building was named after a different casino. We were locked in "the Golden Nugget." We were given cells near each other, with only one other cell between us, and we were able to communicate with each other with little difficulty. Our cells faced the bath area, and by the end of my first day in Vegas I was able to contact many of the men in the camp.

I occupied three different rooms in Little Vegas that year. All of them offered excellent opportunities for communication, and I formed many close friendships with men whom I greatly admired. Treatment continued to improve, although we were periodically subjected to physical abuse for communicating.

I remained alone in the Golden Nugget until March, when my period of solitary confinement was finally ended with the arrival of John Finley, whom I was relieved to welcome as my new roommate.

That first Christmas in the Golden Nugget, while I was puzzling over my surprise social visit from the Cat, my wife was hovering between life and death in the emergency room of a Philadelphia hospital.

Carol had taken the kids to her parents' house for the holidays. After dinner on Christmas Eve, she drove to our friends the Bookbinders' to exchange gifts. It had begun to snow by the time she started back to her parents, and the roads were icy. She skidded off the road and smashed into a telephone pole, and was thrown from the car. The police found her some time later in shock, both legs fractured in several places, her arm and pelvis broken, and bleeding internally.

Several days passed before she was out of immediate danger. It would be six months and several operations before she was released from the hospital. Over the next two years, she would undergo many more operations to repair her injured legs. By the time the doctors were finished she would be four inches shorter than she was before the accident. After a year of intensive physical therapy she was able to walk with the aid of crutches.

Carol has a determined spirit. Had she less courage and resolve, I doubt she would have walked again. Her injuries had been so serious that at first the doctors had considered amputating her legs, but she had refused them permission. With her husband in prison on the other side of the world and three small children to raise alone, she now faced a long, painful struggle to recover from her nearly fatal injuries, resisting the prospect of having to live the remainder of her life in a wheelchair. I've known people with better odds who gave in to despair and self-pity. Not Carol. She suffered her hardships with courage and grace. She persevered, brave and hopeful, confident that our luck would turn and all our lives would somehow work out all right.

When the doctors told her they would attempt to notify me about her accident, she told them not to; she didn't wish to add to my burdens. She would see her way through her misfortune without even the small comfort she might have derived from a few words of concern from me. I've never known a braver soul.

My family was often on my mind. I spent a part of each long day wondering and worrying about them. I didn't worry about their material well-being. I knew they were receiving my pay. But I worried, as all POWs worry, about the psychological burden my long absence imposed on my wife and children.

My children were so young when I had left for war. Sidney had not yet reached her first birthday. I feared my absence, and the uncertainty about my ever coming home, would rob them of part of the joy of living that children from happy homes naturally possess. I had to fight back depression sometimes, thinking that they might have become sullen, insecure kids.

Not too long after my capture, Sidney's memories of me had faded. To her I had become an object of curiosity, a man in a photograph whom her mother and brothers talked about a lot. She did not remember me so much as anticipate me, praying at night and on holidays with the rest of the family for the long-awaited reunion with a father she did not really know. In the years I was away, Carol allowed the children to accumulate a menagerie of pets—dogs, cats, fish, and birds. In 1973, when my release from prison had been announced and Carol informed the kids that I would be home soon, Sidney was confused.

"Where will he sleep?" she asked.

"With me," Carol answered.

"And what will we feed him?"

In prison, I pictured my family as they had been when I last saw them: my wife healthy and happy; my sons, not much older than toddlers, rambunctious and curious; my daughter a contented, beautiful infant; all of them safe and sound and carefree. So few of Carol's letters ever reached me that I had little detailed knowledge of how they were all getting along. I didn't know how Carol was managing to raise the kids alone or how the children's personalities were developing. The boys were now old enough to take an interest in sports, but I couldn't think of them as budding athletes. I had a hard time even picturing them at their current age. Sidney was no longer a baby, but I couldn't imagine what she looked like. When I closed my eyes, I just saw the small faces I had bid good-bye to, and I worried that the calamity that had befallen us might have touched them with a sadness they were too young to sustain.

I derived much comfort, however, from knowing that the Navy takes care of its own. Growing up in the Navy, I had known many families that had met with misfortune, the man of the house having gone off to war and not returned. And I had seen the Navy envelop them in a supportive embrace, looking after their material needs, the men from other Navy families helping to fill the void in fatherless households. I knew that the Navy was now looking after my family, and would, to the best of its ability, see to their needs and happiness, trying to keep the disruption caused by our misfortune from devastating their lives.

Our neighbors in Orange Park, many of whom, but not all, were Navy families, were extraordinarily kind and generous to my family while I was in Vietnam. They were the mainstay of my family's support, and I owe them a debt I can never adequately repay. They helped with the maintenance of our home, took my kids to sporting events, offered whatever counsel and support were needed, and generally helped my family hold together, body and soul, until I could get back to them. During Carol's long convalescence and therapy they were nothing less than an extended family to my family, and their love and concern was as much a mark of their good character as it was a blessing to the people they helped.

Today, at odd times, I find myself becoming quite sentimental about America. In the distant past, that was not how my patriotism typically found expression. I attribute much of my emotion to the good people of Orange Park, Florida. I no longer think of the country's character in abstract terms. Now, when I think about Americans, and how fortunate I am to be included in their number, I see the faces of our neighbors in Orange Park, and give thanks that by a lucky accident of birth, I was born an American.

The Cat came to see me one day and asked that I meet with a visiting "Spanish" delegation. I told him that it would not be worth his while, because I wouldn't make any antiwar or pro-Vietnam statements or say anything positive about the way prisoners were being treated. To my surprise, he said I would not be asked to make such statements.

I consulted Commander Bill Lawrence, the SRO of the Golden Nugget and "the Thunderbird," another nearby building. He told me to go ahead. That night I was taken to a hotel to meet the delegation, which turned out to be one man, Dr. Fernando Barral, a Cuban propagandist masquerading as a psychiatrist and moonlighting as a journalist. He interviewed me for half an hour, asking rather innocuous questions about my life, the schools I had attended, and my family. When he asked me if I hoped to go home soon, I replied, "No. I think the war will last a long time, but the U.S. will eventually win."

He then asked me if I felt remorse for bombing the Vietnamese. "No, I do not." The interview was published in a Cuban publication, *Gramma*, and later broadcast over the Voice of Vietnam. In it my interviewer observed that I had the attributes of a psychopath, as I showed no remorse for my crimes against the peace-loving Vietnamese people. Near the end of the interview, Barral offered his professional opinion of my personality:

> He showed himself to be intellectually alert during the interview. From a morale point of view he is not in traumatic shock. He is neither dejected nor depressed. He was able to be sarcastic, and even humorous, indicative of psychic equilibrium. From the moral and ideological point of

view he showed us he is an insensitive individual without human depth, who does not show the slightest concern, who does not appear to have thought about the criminal acts he committed against a population from the almost absolute impunity of his airplane, and that nevertheless those people saved his life, fed him, and looked after his health, and he is now healthy and strong. I believe that he bombed densely populated places for sport. I noted that he was hardened, that he spoke of banal things as if he were at a cocktail party.

During the interview he quietly drank three cups of coffee and smoked one of the cigarettes the Vietnamese had placed on the central table.

After I returned to my cell, I reported the interview to Bill Lawrence and to Commander Jeremiah Denton, the SRO of Little Vegas. Bill thought I had handled the situation appropriately, but something about it must have troubled Jerry. He made no comment immediately, but a little while later, he issued a new policy, that prisoners were to refuse all requests to meet with "visitors." Given that our enemies made some use of every such exchange, Jerry's order was certainly a sound one, even though it deprived me of further opportunities to demonstrate my "psychic equilibrium" to disapproving fraternal socialists, not to mention the extra cigarettes and coffee.

About a month later, both John Finley and I declined to meet with another peace delegation. That afternoon I was taken to a courtyard of the prison and ordered to sit on a stool for three days and nights. I was not beaten, although Bug checked in periodically to threaten me. After my punishment had ended, I was taken to the Cat's office, where I was puzzled to hear him apologize for my three days on the stool. He claimed he had been absent from the camp when the punishment was ordered. "Sometimes," he allowed, "my officers do the wrong thing."

In April, John and I were moved to a cell in Thunderbird, and were delighted to receive news that the POWs in Little Vegas would be allowed out of their cells for a period each day to play pool and Ping-Pong on tables set up in an empty cell. Our new recreation period, besides being a welcome distraction from prison drudgery, provided an excellent opportunity to improve communications between different parts of the camp.

I was designated as the Thunderbird "mailman," responsible for carrying notes to and from Stardust, where Jerry Denton was held. Air Force Major Sam Johnson, a great friend and an imaginative and always cheerful resister, was the mailman for Stardust. We hid encoded notes behind a wooden light switch in our new recreation room and thus managed to disseminate Jerry Denton's policies to all the parts of the camp under his command.

In June, I was involuntarily relieved of my duties as mailman. I was caught trying to communicate with Dick Stratton, who was held at that time in a cell in "the Riviera," next door to the pool room. I declined when ordered to confess my crime, and spent a night sitting on the stool.

The next day, I was taken to "Calcutta," a filthy punishment room, six feet by three feet, with only a tiny louvered window for ventilation. I would be confined there for three months.

Prior to my arrival, Bill Lawrence had been languishing in Calcutta for weeks. He had been shot down four months before me, taken to Hoa Lo, and locked in a torture room, known only by its number, Room 18. There he suffered five days of beatings and rope torture. From his cell he could hear the screams of his backseater, Lieutenant j.g. Jim Bailey, who was being tortured in a nearby room.

Bill Lawrence was a natural leader. He had already had a remarkable Navy career. He had been brigade commander at the Naval Academy, a four-letter man, and president of the Class of 1951. After graduation, he was asked to remain at the Academy to rewrite the honor code. He was sent to test pilot school, where he graduated first in his class, and went on to fly the new F-4 Phantom. He had been one of the first members of his class, if not the first, to be selected early for lieutenant commander.

While commanding a squadron in Vietnam, Bill received word that Admiral Tom Moorer, the Chief of Naval Operations, wanted him to serve as his aide, the most prestigious assignment that a young officer could be offered. Bill asked that he be allowed to remain in Vietnam to finish his squadron command tour.

When I was moved to Little Vegas, many of our most senior officers were kept isolated from the rest of us. Bill was my immediate superior. He was a model commander, steady as a rock, always in control of his emotions, never excited, never despairing or self-consumed. Several guys in Vegas had been Bill's classmates. Because he had been promoted early, he outranked them. Thus, Bill had to provide leadership not only to junior guys like me, but to his peers. He had to tell his classmates what to do. That is a challenging assignment, but I never heard a single man reject, dispute, or resent Bill's commands. He was universally respected.

I used to tap him up on the wall for guidance all the time. I shared with Bill every question or concern I had. He had a way about him, very calm and reassuring, that put you at ease and inspired confidence in his judgment.

Some guys, burdened with despair, needed to be fired up. Bill would do it, convincing them that they were more than a match for their antagonists. Rambunctious and impatient, I needed a commander with quiet resolve who could help rein in my impulsiveness.

"Take it easy, John. Do the best you can, John. Resist as much as you can. Don't let them break you completely," Bill would caution me, gently warning me not to be so reckless that I plunged headlong into trouble. He was a remarkable commander.

Calcutta had space enough for only one prisoner. My dread of being confined in squalid, isolated Calcutta was alleviated a bit by the knowledge that my bad luck would liberate Bill. When I returned from Calcutta, considerably the worse for wear, Bill cheerfully thanked me for going to so much trouble to get him out.

I was a fairly skillful communicator, adept at tapping and better than average at recognizing and seizing unexpected opportunities for passing messages. I was not, I'm sorry to say, a very cautious one, and I often had reason to regret it. As was the case at the Plantation, the guards frequently apprehended me in the act.

Most of the punishments I received from 1969 on, some tolerable, others less so, were a result of my repeated indiscretions. Calcutta was one of the less tolerable punishments. I had been roughed up a few times, but not severely. Nor was the prospect of a few months' solitary confinement particularly terrifying to me. I certainly didn't welcome it, but I had survived worse before.

What made Calcutta so miserable was its location, at least fifty feet from the next occupied cell. It was impossible to communicate with anyone. Communicating was the indispensable key to resistance. Without that, it was hard to derive strength from others. Absent the counsel of fellow prisoners, I would begin to doubt my own judgment, whether I was resisting effectively and appropriately. If I was in communication only for a brief moment once a day, I would be okay. When I was deprived of any contact with my comrades, I was in serious trouble.

Calcutta was the first time since I had been released from the hospital that I was unable to communicate with anyone for an extended period of time. My isolation was awful, worse than the beatings I had been sentenced to for communicating. Compounding my misery was the cell's poor ventilation, and I suffered severe heat prostration in the extreme warmth of a Vietnamese summer, one of the effects of which was a constant buzzing in my ears that nearly drove me crazy. I was seldom allowed to bathe or shave. The quality of my food rations worsened. I became ill with dysentery again, and started to lose weight.

During my confinement in Calcutta, I was periodically taken to an interrogation room for quizzes. Unlike the bad old days, quizzes were now comparatively benign events. We were seldom beaten for information. My Calcutta quizzes were usually pro forma attempts to persuade me to meet with delegations. Mindful of Jerry Denton's order, I refused them.

On one occasion, an interrogator we called "Staff Officer" told me, "Everybody wants to see Mac Kane. They all ask about Mac Kane. You can see anybody you want."

"Well, I hate to disappoint them," I replied, "but I have to."

I had become very accustomed to close contact with my fellow prisoners since I had been released from solitary confinement. My state of mind had become so dependent on communicating with them that I worried my spell in isolation would fill me with such despair that I might break again. Blessedly, my fears were unfounded.

I had been greatly strengthened by the company of the good men of Little Vegas, and my resolve was firmer than it had ever been. I was sustained by the knowledge that the others knew where I was and were concerned about me. I knew they were demanding my release. And, most important, I knew they would be proud of me when I returned if I successfully resisted this latest tribulation. This was especially comforting to me because I suffered still from the knowledge that I had usually been better treated by the Vietnamese than had most of my comrades.

I was finally released from Calcutta in September and moved with John Finley to a cell in the Riviera, two doors down from Air Force Colonel Larry Guarino, with whom we immediately established good communications. I also managed to cut a small hole in the louvers above our cell door. Standing on my upended waste bucket, I could talk to a great many prisoners from different parts of the camp who were, by this time, allowed outside for a few moments to exercise. In retaliation for my various offenses, I was denied this privilege and allowed outside only once a week to bathe.

In what had now become a routine occurrence, I was again caught communicating, and once more confined for a period in an interrogation room. There I encountered the only two prisoners of my acquaintance who had lost their faith completely. They had not only stopped resisting but apparently crossed a line no other prisoner I knew had even approached. They were collaborators, actively aiding the enemy.

I do not know what caused these men to forsake their country and their fellow prisoners. Maybe they had despaired of ever being released, fearing the war wouldn't end before they were old men. They might have eventually fallen for routine Vietnamese denouncements of the "criminal American government," and grown to resent their civilian commanders for leaving them in this godforsaken place. Maybe they bought the whole nine yards of Vietnamese propaganda, that the war was unjust, their leaders warmongers, and their country a craven, imperial force for evil. Or maybe they were that rarest breed of American prisoners in Vietnam, POWs who, in exchange for certain comforts and privileges, had surrendered their dignity voluntarily and agreed to be the camp rats.

Whatever the cause, it cannot excuse their shameful conduct. I cannot say I ever observed any trace of shame in them as they whiled away the months and years in their unique circumstances. Indeed, during the time I closely observed them, they seemed to thrive, apparently undisturbed by the contempt of the rest of us.

When I encountered them, they had been kept away from the other POWs for some time. The interrogation room I had been taken to was located close to their cells. To pass the time until I was returned to the Thunderbird, I would stand on my waste bucket and look out through the louvered window at the top of my cell door. From my vantage point I could watch the two spend what in Hoa Lo amounted to fairly pleasant days.

The guards would bring them eggs, bananas, and other delicacies to eat. They were on quite friendly terms with the guards, who spoke to them politely and seemed almost solicitous about their comfort. They spent most of every day in a small courtyard back of the washroom where bamboo mats had been erected to screen them from observation by the rest of us. But from my elevated position standing on top of my bucket, I could see over the mats, and I watched them as they sunned themselves, read their mail, and talked to each other, apparently entirely at ease.

I had a nearly devout belief in the restorative power of communicating, as my recurring detentions for violating the camp rule indicate. I assumed, wrongly in this instance, that any American who was in regular communication with his superiors and other prisoners would, by and large, adhere to the Code of Conduct. Even when broken, a man could recover his dignity if he was able to contact his friends for support. Certainly that had been my experience when, my defenses shattered, I had relied on Bob Craner to bring me back from the dead.

But my two new neighbors waged the first assault on my until-then unassailable regard for communications as the force that bound us together and gave us the courage and strength to resist.

One morning as I set my bowl outside my cell after finishing breakfast, the guard walked away from me for some reason without locking me back in and was briefly out of sight. For a moment, I was at liberty. I decided to make good use of the unexpected privilege to establish contact with the two men, who were in their usual place of recreation.

I hustled over to the courtyard and pulled down the bamboo mat. "Hey, guys, my name's McCain. Who are you?"

I did not intend to chastise them for their disloyalty or even encourage them to start acting like officers and recover their dignity. I only hoped that I could briefly establish contact, and by taking that risk motivate them to try to keep in communication with me, reasoning that a few days' contact with another prisoner might bring them back to their senses. I was wrong.

Startled by my greeting, they looked at me for a second as I grinned back at them, and then, to my intense disappointment, they began shouting *"Bao cao"* to summon the guard. I was stunned, and the few blows I received for my audacity from the annoyed turnkey were insignificant compared to the melancholy I felt after discovering that there were at least two men who were indifferent to my evangelical zeal for communicating.

The two men who had betrayed my concern by ratting me out to the guard remained segregated from the rest of us for the duration of the war. They never attempted, as far as I know, to atone for their disloyalty and regain their self-respect. When we were all released, the two were brought up on charges. The charges were dropped, but they were dismissed from the service. Their superiors, like the rest of the country, wanted to put the war and all its bitter memories behind them. I wasn't disappointed in the decision. The two have to live with the memory of their treachery. I suspect that is punishment enough.

Not long after that discouraging experience, in early December, I was moved to another cell next door to my dear friend Bob Craner. A couple of weeks later, I was allowed outside half of each day. Prison life was improving, and it was about to get a whole lot better.

CHAPTER 24

Camp Unity

Christmas, 1970. The most welcome event of my imprisonment. I was transferred with a great many other prisoners to large rooms in an area we called "Camp Unity." Camp Unity had seven cellblocks with, initially, thirty to forty prisoners held in each. Ultimately, after captured B-52 pilots and crewmen began to arrive and more prisoners from other camps were brought in, our total number would reach over 350.

In the center of each room was a concrete pedestal on which we all slept. A few of the badly injured POWs and our senior ranking officers were kept in different cells. The Vietnamese refused to recognize rank and never allowed our seniors to speak for us. This angered us greatly and worked to the disadvantage of our captors. Had they worked through our SROs, they would have found it a little easier to deal with us.

At Camp Unity I was reunited with many old friends, including Bob Craner and my first roommate, Bud Day. I was moved there when many of the toughest men in prison were moved into the camp. Jerry Denton, Jim Stockdale, Robbie Risner, Dick Stratton, George

Coker, Jack Fellowes, John Dramesi, Bill Lawrence, Jim Kasler, Larry Guarino, Sam Johnson, Howie Dunn, George McKnight, Jerry Coffee, and Howie Rutledge, all legendary resisters, were relocated in Unity's cellblocks. We were overjoyed to be in one another's company, and a festival atmosphere prevailed.

If you have never been deprived of liberty in solitude, you cannot know what ineffable joy you experience in the open company of other human beings, free to talk and joke without fear. The strength you acquire in fraternity with others who share your fate is immeasurable.

That first night, when so many of us were unexpectedly allowed one another's company, not a single man slept. We talked all night, and well into the next day. We talked about everything. What might this change in our fortunes mean? Were we going home soon? Had the Vietnamese some public relations reason for putting us together? Had they been embarrassed by some new disclosure of their abusive treatment of us? We talked about what we had endured at the hands of the enemy; about the escapes some men had attempted and the consequences they suffered as a result. We talked about news from home. We talked about our families, and the lives we hoped to return to soon.

No other experience in my life could ever replicate my first night in Camp Unity, and the feeling of relief that overcame me to be living among my friends. I have lived many happy years since, and am a blessed and contented man. But I will never experience again the supreme happiness I felt my fourth Christmas in Hanoi.

POWs who had been lately held at camps outside Hanoi had learned of a recent, nearly successful American rescue attempt at a camp twenty miles outside Hanoi called Son Tay. The attempt had scared the hell out of the Vietnamese, and they had begun to bring prisoners from all outlying camps into prisons in Hanoi. Many of the Son Tay prisoners had been moved into Camp Unity a couple of weeks before the rest of us were.

In Camp Unity our SROs ordered us to form into a cohesive military unit—the Fourth Allied POW Wing. The wing's motto was "Return with Honor." Colonel Flynn would soon end his long years of isolation when he was moved into a room with the other Air Force colonels and assumed command of the wing.

Each room served as a squadron, with the senior ranking officer in each room in command. Each squadron was broken into flights of about six men, each with a flight commander. We were organized to continue resisting. It was a lot easier to defy your enemy when you are surrounded by fellow resisters.

Among my closest friends was Orson Swindle, one of the Son Tay prisoners, a tough, good-natured Marine pilot from Georgia. In our first months in Unity, he lived in the room next to mine, and we first met by tapping through the wall that separated our rooms. Orson had been shot down near the DMZ on November 11, 1966. He had been beaten and rope-tortured repeatedly during the thirty-nine days it took his captors to reach Hanoi. From the beginning of his captivity, Orson had impressed the Vietnamese as a hard man to crack.

In August 1967, Orson was held at "the Desert Inn" with three other determined resisters, George McKnight, Wes Schierman, and Ron Storz. One night an enraged Vietnamese officer accompanied by several guards burst into their cell accusing the Americans of various infractions of camp regulations. They locked Ron Storz in leg stocks, roped his arms behind him, and stuffed a towel down his throat. When George McKnight screamed at them to stop, they did the same to him.

Orson and Wes were also put in the stocks and rope-tortured, but not gagged. When the guards began savagely beating McKnight and Storz, the two ungagged men screamed, "Torture!" The guards turned to Orson and Wes and began beating them, trying to force gags into their mouths. Twisting their heads to avoid the gags, the two kept shouting, "Torture, torture," until all the prisoners in Little Vegas began screaming with them.

The beatings continued mercilessly until the men were an unrecognizable bloody mess. McKnight had nearly suffocated to death before his gag was removed. Eventually the four were led through a crowd of cursing, spitting, striking Vietnamese to separate stalls in the washroom. There they were beaten all night long.

The next morning, shortly after several American planes had flown over the city, the guards rushed at Orson, kicking him repeatedly in retaliation for the appearance of American airpower. The four spent the rest of the day in separate interrogation rooms, enduring long hours of continued torture until they were all forced to make a confession.

Later that day, Orson, George, and Wes were transferred to a prison they called "Dirty Bird," for its exceptionally filthy conditions, and kept, shackled, in solitary confinement. The prison was nothing more than a single building. The Vietnamese had decided to convert it into a jail because of its advantageous location. It was adjacent to an important target for American bombers, and the Vietnamese hoped that the presence of American prisoners in the vicinity would dissuade American military commanders from ordering any air strikes on it. The target was a thermal power plant—the target I had attempted to bomb in my last moment of freedom. Orson would joke later that "as scared as I was when they bombed the power plant, I would have really been scared had I known John was on the way, knowing he'd hit everything around the target except the power plant itself."

McKnight, along with another inmate, George Coker, eventually managed to free themselves from their leg irons and make a daring escape from Dirty Bird. They were recaptured the next day.

Ron Storz had not been taken with his cellmates to Dirty Bird. After they tortured him to the point of submission, the Vietnamese intended to use Ron to inform on his SRO, Jim Stockdale. Attempting to kill himself, Ron used an ink pen to cut his wrists and chest. He was eventually taken to a place its inhabitants called "Alcatraz," located behind the defense ministry a short distance from Hoa Lo. He was one of eleven men kept there, among them several high-ranking

Americans including Jim Stockdale and Jerry Denton, and McKnight and Coker, who had been taken there after their failed escape.

The Alcatraz Eleven had distinguished themselves as die-hard resisters. Their new prison, situated across the courtyard from an open cesspool, reflected their distinction as special cases. The cells were tomblike, windowless, and measuring four feet across. They were locked in leg irons at night.

Ten of the men kept there, most of them for over two years, would remember the place as the worst of many difficult experiences. The eleventh, Ron Storz, would never leave Alcatraz. He had been physically and mentally abused for so long that he had lost either the will or the ability to eat, and had slowly wasted away. The Vietnamese kept Ron behind when they released the others from Alcatraz, claiming he was too sick to move. He died there, alone.

Orson had been spared the deprivations of Alcatraz. He had been taken from Dirty Bird to Little Vegas shortly after we bombed the power plant. In November 1968, he was transferred to the prison at Son Tay, where his captors ordered him to write approvingly to prominent American politicians who opposed the war. He refused.

His steadfastness earned Orson a trip to the punishment room, where he was seated on a low stool and locked in leg irons. The guards were ordered to prevent him from sleeping. Whenever he nodded off, a guard slapped him awake. After several days and nights, Orson began to suffer from hallucinations. Still he would not write. During one particularly vivid hallucination, Orson became violent. After subduing him, the guards relented and let him sleep. He was given food and allowed to rest for three days.

On the third day, he was again ordered to write. Refusing, he was subjected to further mistreatment. Chained to his stool and denied sleep for another ten days and nights, he finally relented.

After Orson's ordeal, another prisoner who had refused to write was given the same punishment. He broke after a day. The guards told him, "You're not like Swindle."

Although I did not meet Orson Swindle until I was moved into Unity, I, like most other prisoners, had heard of him. His reputation for being as stouthearted as they come was a camp legend by the time I met him.

As a resistance leader, Jim Stockdale had few peers. He was a constant inspiration to the men under his command. Many of his captors hated him for his fierce and unyielding spirit. The Rabbit hated him the most. One day, the Rabbit ordered Jim cleaned up so that he could be filmed for a propaganda movie in which he would play a visiting American businessman. He was given a razor to shave. Jim used it to hack off his hair, severely cutting his scalp in the process and spoiling his appearance, in the hope that this would render him unsuitable for his enemies' purpose. But the Rabbit was not so easily dissuaded. He left to find a hat to place on Jim's bleeding head. In the intervening moments, Jim picked up a wooden stool and repeatedly bashed his face with it. Disfigured, Jim succeeded in frustrating the Rabbit's plans for him that evening.

On a later occasion, after being whipped and tied in ropes at the hands of the demented Bug, Jim was forced to confess that he had defied camp regulations. But Bug was not through with him. He informed Jim that he would be back tomorrow to torture him for more information. Jim feared he would be forced to give up the names of the men he had been communicating with. In an effort to impress his enemies with his determination not to betray his comrades, he broke a window and slashed his wrist with a shard of glass. For his extraordinary heroism, Jim Stockdale received the Medal of Honor when he returned home, a decoration he had earned a dozen times over.

Robbie Risner was another of my Camp Unity cellmates whose reputation preceded him. Air Force Lieutenant Colonel Robinson Risner commanded a squadron in Vietnam. He had also been a much-decorated pilot in the Korean War. Early in 1965, *Time* magazine had featured the air ace on its cover, praising Robbie as one of America's greatest combat pilots.

Several months later, on September 16, 1965, Robbie was shot down ninety miles south of Hanoi. When he arrived at Hoa Lo two days later, he was taken to an interrogation room. There the Rabbit, seated at a table with a copy of the aforementioned issue of *Time* in full view, greeted him: "Ah, Colonel Risner, we've been waiting for you."

I can only imagine the sinking feeling Robbie must have had as he discovered the Vietnamese were regular readers of American periodicals. Nevertheless, from the first moment of his imprisonment to the last, Robbie Risner was an exemplary senior officer, an inveterate communicator, an inspiration to the men he commanded, and a source of considerable annoyance to his captors. Among the longest-held prisoners, he suffered the appalling mistreatment regularly inflicted on POWs during the brutal early years of imprisonment. Throughout his trials, he gave the Vietnamese good cause to appreciate the physical courage and strength of character that had landed him on the cover of *Time*.

In my first cellblock in Unity, Building Number 7, I lived with many of the more senior prisoners. Air Force Colonel Vernon Ligon was the senior ranking officer. Robbie Risner, Jim Stockdale, and Jerry Denton were his deputies. Near the end of 1971, I would be moved into another cellblock, Number 2, with Orson. Bud Day, the ranking officer in Number 3, assumed command of our squadron.

Until we were all moved into Unity, I had not had the pleasure of Bud's company since we had parted at the Plantation three years earlier. Bud had been held at Hoa Lo while I was living in Little Vegas, but out of reach of my communication chain. For most of the years preceding our reunion, Bud had suffered awful conditions and monstrous cruelty at the Zoo, where mass torture was a routine practice. For a time, the camp personnel at the Zoo included an English-speaking Cuban, called "Fidel" by the POWs, who delighted in breaking Americans, even when the task required him to torture his victim to death.

Bud was the third-ranking officer at the Zoo, after Larry Guarino and Navy Commander Wendell Rivers. When Larry and Wendy were moved to Vegas, Bud became the SRO. To the poor souls who shared the misfortune of being imprisoned in the Zoo, Bud was as great an inspiration as he had been to me during our few months together.

I doubt I will ever meet a tougher man than Bud Day. After the Dramesi-Atterbury escape, treatment worsened in all the camps, but it reached an astonishing level of depravity in the camp they had escaped from—the Zoo. Men were taken in large groups to various torture rooms where they were beaten, roped, stomped on, and struck with bamboo clubs. Their wrists and ankles were shackled in irons. Few were gagged. The Vietnamese wanted the others to hear the screams of the tortured. This new terror campaign was intended to destroy any semblance of prisoner resistance. It lasted for months.

The Vietnamese introduced a new torment to their punishment regime—flogging with fan belts. Prisoners were stripped and forced to lie facedown on the floor. Guards would take turns whipping them with fan belts, which unlike ropes and cords would only raise welts on the sufferer's back and not tear his flesh. They would not relent until their victim had mumbled his assent to whatever statement their torturers demanded he make. The senior officers were spared this treatment for some time. The Vietnamese wanted them to witness the suffering of their subordinates before turning the full brunt of their malevolence on them.

Guarino was the first senior to be taken. He was rope-tortured, sleep-deprived, clubbed, and whipped for weeks, until at long last he broke and gave the Vietnamese an acceptable confession.

Bud was next. His arms were still useless from the rope torture he had experienced after his capture. This time they would flog him nearly to death before he relented. They made him confess to knowledge of elaborate escape planning in the camp, planning that John or Ed would have been grateful for had it truly existed. The Vietnamese wanted names. Bud would only give them his. They flogged him some more until to his great sorrow he gave them two more names. When they stopped, he took it back, claiming that the men he named were innocent, as indeed they were.

They resumed the torture, demanding that Bud inform on another prisoner, Wendy Rivers. Bud refused, and was whipped again. After six weeks his ordeal finally ended.

Nothing that happened to me during my time in prison approximated the suffering that these men, who had steeled themselves with an unyielding devotion to duty, survived. That they had survived was itself an act of heroism. I had experienced a few rough moments, and, out of spite for my enemies as much as from my sense of duty, I had tried to fight back. But these men, and the many other prisoners whose heroism made them legends, humbled me, as they humble me today whenever I recall what they did for their country and for those of us who were once privileged to witness their courage.

CHAPTER 25

Skid Row

In February 1971, we began a dispute with the Vietnamese over their refusal to allow us to conduct religious services in a manner we thought fitting. The Church Riot began when the camp edict against POWs gathering in groups larger than six and against one man addressing large groups was used to forbid us to hold services. Our SRO ordered us to challenge the prohibition. On Sunday, February 7, we held a church service. We had informed our warden, Bug, of our intentions. George Coker began the service, and Rutledge gave the opening prayer. Robbie Risner read the closing prayer. A four-man choir sang hymns.

Soon Bug arrived and yelled at us to stop. He ordered the choir to cease singing. He was ignored, and the service continued. In a rage, Bug had the guards haul Risner, Coker, and Rutledge out into the courtyard. As they were led out, Bud Day started singing "The Star-Spangled Banner," and soon every man in every cellblock joined in. When we finished the anthem, we started on a succession of patriotic tunes. The whole prison reverberated with our singing, and the wild applause that erupted at the end of every number. It was a glorious moment.

Finally, the Vietnamese managed to disrupt our fun when they marched in en masse, arrayed in full riot gear, and broke up the party.

Risner, Rutledge, and Coker were taken to a punishment cell in the part of the Hilton we called "Heartbreak Hotel." Our SRO, Vernon Ligon, warned Bug that we would hold church services next Sunday, and every Sunday after that.

Bud Day, Jim Kasler, and I were among a number of POWs ordered out of the room to be interrogated and harangued by camp authorities for our criminal behavior. We were taken out separately, and the expression on the guards' faces as they escorted us at bayonet point indicated the seriousness of the situation.

A number of senior Vietnamese officers from various camps were standing together in the courtyard, officers who had been responsible for the brutality we had endured in the bad old days. But they were no longer permitted to use torture as a first resort to coerce our submission, and they appeared anxious and uncertain about how to cope with our new assertiveness.

When we were returned to our room, Bud, Bill Lawrence, and I discussed our captors' predicament, and how at odds they all seemed. We were emboldened by their confusion. The guards placed ladders against our building and stood on the rungs to peer into our window and scribble notes about our behavior. Their notes were used by the camp officers to determine which POWs should be moved to other cells and camps. The quality of the food declined from bad to awful. Jerry Denton ordered us to begin a hunger strike until our grievances were settled and Risner, Rutledge, and Coker were returned to us.

One evening, a few nights after the riot, one of the two collaborators at Hoa Lo who had ratted on me for trying to talk to them read a poem over the camp loudspeakers that he had written about the riot. The poem was titled "Cowards Sing at Night." It scorned us for raising our voices in protest to sing the national anthem.

By this time, the poem's author did not have any friends in camp besides the Vietnamese and his fellow collaborator. Most of us pitied him more than we hated him. That night, however, after he finished his poetry reading, there were any number of prisoners who would have killed him had they had the opportunity to do so.

At week's end, Soft Soap Fairy announced that it had always been the policy of camp authorities to permit religious expression. Therefore, we would be allowed to hold brief religious services as long as we didn't abuse their tolerance to further our "black schemes."

As part of Vietnamese efforts to convince the world that we were being well treated, they had recently stopped using letter-writing privileges as a tool to force our cooperation and begun encouraging us to write home often. It occurred to me that this change in prison policy offered an excellent opportunity to take advantage of our enemy's eagerness to improve their public image. I thought it fitting to use a privilege that had often been denied us to suit Hanoi's war ends as a means to suit our own.

I proposed to our senior officers that we begin a letter-writing moratorium until our treatment and conditions were improved. If men were physically abused for refusing to write home, I suggested we write honestly about our mistreatment. I was confident the Vietnamese would never let such letters reach our worried families.

After some discussion our senior officers agreed, but, wisely, made the no-letter policy voluntary. Some men had not communicated with their families for years and were understandably anxious to let their families know they were all right. By summer, however, nearly everyone was refusing to write home.

On the evening of March 17, less than three months after we had begun living in large groups, Bud Day, Orson Swindle, and I were taken from our rooms. Along with twenty-four others, several men from each room in Camp Unity, we were blindfolded, loaded into trucks, and driven to a punishment camp ten miles outside Hanoi, a place we called "Skid Row."

During the trip, some of the prisoners tried to fix the location of our destination. It was a common practice for POWs to keep a mental record of directions and distance when we were being relocated. One man was designated to control the vectors by memorizing each turn of the truck in sequence while another silently counted the time that elapsed between turns.

The exercise required extraordinary concentration, but usually yielded a remarkably accurate estimate of our location. It was not something that I was very good at it, however, and so I never seriously attempted to join in the exercise. Wherever we were heading, we would still be prisoners of war in North Vietnam when we arrived there. While I was as curious as the next guy about our destination, I knew that those basic facts of our existence would not be affected by a change of scenery. So that night I bounced along in the back of the truck, blindfolded and tied in ropes, silently cursing my bad luck, while my friends concentrated on their labors.

We had been singled out for our bad attitude, which I somewhat regretted, for it had cost me the open society of Camp Unity. But punishment wasn't the only purpose of our exile from Camp Unity. The Vietnamese had decided to round up all the troublemakers whose influence with the other prisoners made it difficult to maintain order and discipline in the new living arrangements at Hoa Lo. Thus, though we were not happy about our relocation, we all took a certain pride in our distinction as the camp's hard cases. The POWs who remained at Camp Unity called us the "Hell's Angels."

We were kept in solitary confinement in small cells, six by four feet, each with a narrow wooden bunk. The cells had no ventilation and were without lights or bathing facilities. The camp had a stinking well with human waste floating in its dank water. My morale sank.

Bud Day remained our SRO. He was kept in one of the cells in the back of the building, while I occupied one in the front. Miserable, we took to insulting and arguing with our guards. Bud ordered us to knock it off, believing that beatings were unlikely to improve our wretched circumstances. His order was occasionally disobeyed, as our anger undermined our discipline. Frustrated, Bud kept insisting that while we should not accept mistreatment without complaint, we should also refrain from unnecessarily provoking the guards.

Bud himself had been beaten and threatened with a fan belt a few weeks after our arrival at Skid Row, and had for a few days been locked on his bunk in stocks. He wanted to spare the rest of us such abuse if it could be avoided without compromising our principles. Overall, when we left the guards alone, they left us alone, satisfied that leaving us to suffer in such squalor was adequate punishment for our crimes. But Bud had a hard time keeping control over several of us. I regret that I occasionally added to my dear friend's burden. My temper, worsened by my return to solitary confinement in this dismal camp, occasionally got the better of me.

A small space separated the cells in the front of the building from a brick wall. The upper part of each cell door was barred, but otherwise uncovered. Wooden shutters that could have been used to cover the bars were kept open for those of us in the front, while the windows in the back cell were usually kept closed. The Vietnamese routinely tried to undermine our solidarity by according some prisoners a privilege of open shutters while denying it to others. I was pleased to receive this particular privilege, as it mitigated the effect solitary confinement had on my morale.

During our first days in Skid Row, we communicated freely with each other through our barred windows, talking constantly and loudly, our voices bouncing off the wall in front of us. Initially the guards didn't seem to mind our ceaseless chattering. Occasionally they warned us not to talk so loudly, but they made no other objection to our conversations.

After a week or so, senior prison authorities must have reminded our guards that Skid Row was meant to be a punishment camp for recalcitrant prisoners and instructed them not to show any leniency to us. One morning, as soon as we resumed our conversations of the previous day, the guards appeared, shouting, "No talking. No talking."

"Bullshit," I yelled back. "I'm going to talk." Too accustomed now to unconstrained conversation, and still angry over our expulsion from Unity, I was in no mood to be silenced.

"No talking, Mac Kane!"

"Bullshit. I'm going to talk. You bastards kept me in solitary for years. You're not going to shut me up now."

One of the guards, intending to terminate any further protest on my part, slammed and locked the wooden shutter over the bars of my door, leaving me fuming in my darkened cell.

Refusing to back down, my anger now completely beyond control, I screamed at the guards, "*Bao cao, bao cao.* Open it up. *Bao cao, bao cao.* Open it up, you bastards, open it up." The guards scurried off to find an officer. When they located one, they led him back to my cell and opened up the shutter, finding me red-faced and glaring at them through the bars.

"What's wrong with you, Mac Kane?" the officer inquired.

"I'm not putting up with this shit anymore. That's what's wrong with me," I answered. "I want to talk, and you're not going to shut me up."

The officer left without responding to my declaration, the guards hurrying after him. Ten minutes later, the guards returned and instructed me to roll up my sleeping mat and other belongings. I did as instructed. They escorted me from my cell and chucked me into the cell next door, which was occupied by Navy Lieutenant Pete Schoeffel.

This new arrangement suited me fine, and I quickly cooled off. But I doubt Pete welcomed the idea of sharing quarters as much as I did. The cells were hardly suited to cohabitation, measuring little larger than a cardboard box. Two men could barely stand shoulder to shoulder. Nevertheless, Pete took it all in good humor, graciously giving me leave to sleep in his bunk because of my bad leg, while he found what little comfort he could on the concrete floor.

In August, monsoon rains threatened to flood the Red River and Skid Row, and we were transferred back to Hoa Lo. For a brief moment we held out hope that we were being returned to Camp Unity.

Our hope was crushed when were marched into Heartbreak Hotel, where we were kept four and five to a room. The rooms were small and the conditions miserable. Many of the men became ill; a few were suffering from hepatitis. Tempers were frayed, and morale sank even lower. A couple of months later we were taken back to Skid Row, which, given the awful conditions at Heartbreak, was almost a relief. While conditions remained miserable, the Vietnamese lightened up on the discipline, and we were allowed to talk among ourselves without fear of further punishment.

We were released from Skid Row in three groups. Bud, Orson, and I, our bad attitudes uncorrected by our time in exile, were in the last group to leave. In November 1971, we were finally reunited with our friends at Camp Unity and put into a cellblock together, our morale restored.

CHAPTER 26

Pledge of Allegiance

During the last fourteen months at Camp Unity, I served as entertainment officer, appointed to the post by Bud Day. In this capacity I was ably assisted by a number of my roommates, most notably Orson Swindle and Air Force Captains Jim Sehorn and Warren Lilly. We enjoyed the work.

Bud designated me room chaplain, an office I took quite seriously even though I lacked any formal training for it. Orson and I also served as the communication officers for the room, charged with maintaining regular contact with the other rooms in Unity. We both had plenty of experience for the work, and despite my reputation for recklessness, I prided myself on the job we did.

We never let a holiday or a birthday pass without arranging a small, crude, but welcome celebration. Gifts fashioned out of odd scraps of material and our few meager possessions were bestowed on every prisoner celebrating a birthday. A skit, always ribald and ridiculous, was performed to commemorate the occasion by embarrassing the celebrant. Marine Corps, Navy, and Air Force anniversaries were also formally observed.

Both an avid reader and a movie fan, I took great pride in narrating movies and books from memory. With a captive audience, I would draw out the telling of a novel, embellishing here and there to add length and excitement, for hours before I lost the audience's interest. Among the texts both the audience and I enjoyed most were works of Kipling, Maugham, and Hemingway.

Our most popular entertainments, however, were our productions of Sunday, Wednesday, and Saturday Nights at the Movies. I told over a hundred movies in prison, some of them many times over. I tried to recall every movie I had ever seen from *Stalag 17* to *One-Eyed Jacks* (a camp favorite). Often running short of popular fare, I would make up movies I had never seen. Pilots shot down during air raids in 1972 were a valuable resource for me. They had seen movies that I had not. Desperate for new material, I would pester them almost as soon as they arrived and before they had adjusted to their new circumstances. "What movies have you seen lately? Tell me about them." On first acquaintance, they probably thought prison life had seriously affected my mind. But they would give me a few details, and from that I would concoct another movie for Saturday night. Movies had become a lot more risqué in the five years I had been away. I narrated a few of these as well, and my audience was all the more attentive.

My performance was usually well received, although on occasion some of the men's interest flagged when watching a repeat performance for the fourth or fifth time. However, I always enjoyed the undivided attention of one inveterate movie fan.

Air Force Major Konrad Trautman, a reserved, precise son of German immigrants, never missed a performance. He would take his seat early and wait patiently for the movie to begin. With a pipe filled with cigarette tobacco clenched tightly between his teeth, he sat impassively, never making a sound. He listened intently to every word I uttered. No matter how many times he had seen a movie or how crude the production, Konrad never betrayed the least hint of disappointment. Fans like that are hard to come by for even the most celebrated actor, and I always took great encouragement from Konrad's evident appreciation of my qualities as a thespian.

During the Christmas season we performed a different skit and sang carols in our crudely decorated room every night for the five nights before Christmas. A longer production was saved for Christmas night. Orson Swindle and I, with a few other guys, staged a mangled production of Dickens's *A Christmas Carol.* We livened up the venerable tale with parody, most of it vulgar, to the great amusement of our howling audience. Jack Fellowes played Tiny Tim, attired in nothing but a makeshift diaper. Another, not known for his particularly feminine appearance, was chosen to play Bob Cratchit's wife.

A week before, Bud had asked Bug for an English-language Bible. Bug initially dismissed the request with a lie, claiming that there were no Bibles in North Vietnam. A few days later, perhaps remembering that his interference with the practice of our religion had resulted in the Church Riot earlier that year, Bug announced that a Bible, "the only one in Hanoi," had been located. One prisoner was to be designated to copy passages from it for a few minutes.

As room chaplain, I was given the assignment. I collected the Bible from where it had been left by a guard, on a table in the courtyard just outside our cell door. Hastily, I leafed through its tattered pages until I found an account of the Nativity. I quickly copied the passage, and finished just moments before a guard arrived to retrieve the Bible.

On Christmas night we held our simple, moving service. We began with the Lord's Prayer, after which a choir sang carols, directed by the former conductor of the Air Force Academy Choir, Captain Quincy Collins. I thought they were quite good, excellent, in fact. Although I confess that the regularity with which they practiced in the weeks prior to Christmas occasionally grated on my nerves.

But that night, the hymns were rendered with more feeling and were more inspirational than the offerings of the world's most celebrated choirs. We all joined in the singing, nervous and furtive at first, fearing the guards would disrupt the service if we sang too loudly. With each hymn, however, we grew bolder, and our voices rose with emotion.

Between each hymn, I read a portion of the story of Christ's birth from the pages I had copied.

" 'And the Angel said unto them, Fear not: for, behold, I bring you good tidings of great joy, which shall be to all people. For unto you is born this day, in the city of David, a Savior, which is Christ the Lord.' "

The night air was cold, and we shivered from its effect and from the fever that still plagued some of us. The sickest among us, unable to stand, sat on the raised concrete sleeping platform in the middle of the room, blankets around their shaking shoulders. Many others, stooped by years of torture, or crippled from injuries sustained during their shootdown, stood, some on makeshift crutches, as the service proceeded.

The lightbulbs hanging from the ceiling illuminated our gaunt, unshaven, dirty, and generally wretched congregation. But for a moment we all had the absolutely exquisite feeling that our burdens had been lifted. Some of us had attended Christmas services in prison before. But they had been Vietnamese productions, spiritless, ludicrous stage shows. This was our service, the only one we had ever been allowed to hold. It was more sacred to me than any service I had attended in the past, or any service I have attended since.

We gave prayers of thanks for the Christ child, for our families and homes, for our country. We half expected the guards to barge in and force us to conclude the service. Every now and then we glanced up at the windows to see if they were watching us as they had during the Church Riot. But when I looked up at the bars that evening, I wished they had been looking in. I wanted them to see us—faithful, joyful, and triumphant.

The last hymn sung was "Silent Night." Many of us wept.

We held a Christmas dinner after the service. We had arranged our room to resemble a "dining-in," a much-loved military ritual, in which officers, attired in their best uniforms, sit at table according to rank, to dine and drink in elaborate formality. Lacking most of the necessary accouterments, we nevertheless made quite an evening of it. The senior officers sat at the head of the table, while numerous speeches and toasts to family, service, and country were honored. All of us were proud to have the opportunity to dine again, even in our less than elegant surroundings, like officers and gentlemen.

After dinner we exchanged gifts. One man had used his cotton washcloth and a needle and thread he had scrounged somewhere to fashion a hat for Bud. Other men exchanged dog tags. Most of us exchanged chits for Christmas gifts we wished each other to have. We all gave one man who had been losing at poker lately an IOU for another $250 in imaginary chips.

Back from Skid Row that Christmas, we were overjoyed to entertain ourselves again in the company of men who had managed through all those years to retain their humanity though our enemies had tried to turn us into animals. From then on, with brief exceptions, our existence in Hanoi was as tolerable as could be expected when you are deprived of your liberty.

The Vietnamese had given us several decks of cards, and we played a lot of bridge and poker. My luck at the table usually ran bad, to the endless amusement of Orson, who liked to taunt me for what he considered my unskilled approach to the games. Almost every Sunday afternoon, we held a bridge tournament that included six tables of players.

We had more profitable uses for our time as well, which made our days pass just as quickly as did our reproductions of various popular entertainments. An education officer was designated and classes were taught in almost every imaginable subject, all the POWs called on to share their particular field of learning. Language classes were popular and to this day I can read more than a few words in several languages. The guards frequently confiscated our notes, however, an impediment that greatly complicated our grasp of foreign languages. Other subjects ranged from quantum physics to meat-cutting.

Lectures were held on the four nights when we were not required to stage a movie reproduction. Orson and I taught classes in literature and history, and I took as much pride in my history lectures as I did in my movie performances, calling our tutorial "The History of the World from the Beginning."

Our classes and amateur theatrics made time, the one thing we had in abundance, pass relatively pleasantly and helped temper the small conflicts that inevitably arise when men are confined together in close quarters. No matter how irritated we occasionally felt over slight grievances with one another, nothing could ever seriously detract from the pleasure we took from our own company in the last full year of our captivity.

Our situation improved even more in April 1972, when President Nixon resumed the bombing of North Vietnam and, on my father's orders, the first bombs since March 1968 began falling on Hanoi. Operation Linebacker, as the campaign was called, brought B-52s, with their huge payload of bombs, into the war, although they were not used in attacks on Hanoi.

The misery we had endured prior to 1972 was made all the worse by our fear that the United States was unprepared to do what was necessary to bring the war to a reasonably swift conclusion. We could never see over the horizon to the day when the war would end. Whether you supported the war or opposed it—and I met few POWs who argued the latter position—no one believed the war should be prosecuted in the manner in which the Johnson administration had fought it.

No one who goes to war believes once he is there that it is worth the terrible cost of war to fight it by half measures. War is too horrible a thing to drag out unnecessarily. It was a shameful waste to ask men to suffer and die, to persevere through awful afflictions and heartache, for a cause that half the country didn't believe in and our leaders weren't committed to winning. They committed us to it, badly misjudged the enemy's resolve, and left us to manage the thing on our own without authority to fight it to the extent necessary to finish it.

It's not hard to understand now that, given the prevailing political judgments of the time, the Vietnam War was better left unfought. No other national endeavor requires as much unshakable resolve as war. If the government and the nation lack that resolve, it is criminal to expect men in the field to carry it alone. We were accountable to the country, and no one was accountable to us. But we found our honor in our answer, if not our summons.

Every POW knew that the harder the war was fought the sooner we would go home. Long aware of the on-and-off peace negotiations in Paris, we were elated when the Nixon administration proved it was intent on forcing the negotiations to a conclusion that would restore our freedom.

As the bombing campaign intensified, our morale soared with every sortie. It was after one raid, and our raucous celebration of its effect, that the guards dragged Mike Christian from our room.

Mike was a Navy bombardier-navigator who had been shot down in 1967, about six months before I arrived. He had grown up near Selma, Alabama. His family was poor. He had not worn shoes until he was thirteen years old. Character was their wealth. They were good, righteous people, and they raised Mike to be hardworking and loyal. He was seventeen when he enlisted in the Navy. As a young sailor, he showed promise as a leader and impressed his superiors enough to be offered a commission.

What packages we were allowed to receive from our families often contained handkerchiefs, scarves, and other clothing items. For some time, Mike had been taking little scraps of red and white cloth, and with a needle he had fashioned from a piece of bamboo he laboriously sewed an American flag onto the inside of his blue prisoner's shirt. Every afternoon, before we ate our soup, we would hang Mike's flag on the wall of our cell and together recite the Pledge of Allegiance. No other event of the day had as much meaning to us.

The guards discovered Mike's flag one afternoon during a routine inspection and confiscated it. They returned that evening and took Mike outside. For our benefit as much as Mike's, they beat him severely, just outside our cell, puncturing his eardrum and breaking several of his ribs. When they had finished, they dragged him bleeding and nearly senseless back into our cell, and we helped him crawl to his place on the sleeping platform. After things quieted down, we all lay down to go to sleep. Before drifting off, I happened to look toward a corner of the room, where one of the four naked lightbulbs that were always illuminated in our cell cast a dim light on Mike Christian. He had crawled there quietly when he thought the rest of us were sleeping. With his eyes nearly swollen shut from the beating, he had quietly picked up his needle and thread and begun sewing a new flag.

I witnessed many acts of heroism in prison, but none braver than that. As I watched him, I felt a surge of pride at serving with him, and an equal measure of humility for lacking that extra ration of courage that distinguished Mike Christian from other men.

CHAPTER 27

Release

The bombing of North Vietnam was halted in October when peace talks resumed in Paris. By December, it was clear that the talks had stalled because of North Vietnamese intransigence. On December 18, at around nine o'clock in the evening, it was renewed with a vengeance as Operation Linebacker II commenced and the unmistakable destructive power of B-52s rained down on Hanoi.

Despite our proximity to the targets, we were jubilant. We hollered in near euphoria as the ground beneath us shook with the force of the blasts, exulting in our guards' fear as they scurried for shelter. We clapped each other on the back and joked about packing our bags for home. We shouted "Thank you!" at the night sky.

No prisoner betrayed the slightest concern that we were in any danger. I didn't hear anyone say, "We might be hit." We just cheered the assault on and watched the show. Once in a while a guard came by and yelled at us to shut up, to which we responded by cheering even louder.

When a Vietnamese SAM hit a B-52, as, regrettably, happened on several occasions, the explosion and burning fuel would illuminate the whole sky, from horizon to horizon, a bright pink-and-orange glow. In this unnatural light, we could see the Vietnamese gasping at the strange sight and tearing around the camp in a panic.

Some of the gun guards had responded to the shriek of the air raid sirens by manning their defense stations slowly, joking and laughing with each other, apparently indifferent to the coming assault. They probably believed it to be only a drill. Now they were racing around trying to figure out how to defend themselves from this unexpected, massive bombardment. Terrified, some of them fired their rifles into the sky at targets that were miles above them.

For many of our guards this was their first taste of modern warfare, and their confidence in the superiority of their defenses was visibly shaken. Many of them cowered in the shadows of our cellblocks, believing, correctly, that the B-52 pilots knew where Americans were held in Hanoi and were trying to avoid dropping their bombs near us.

It was quite a spectacular show. Antiaircraft guns booming, bombs exploding, fires raging all over the city. It is sinful to take pleasure in the suffering of others, even your enemies, and B-52s can deliver a lot of suffering. But the Vietnamese had never before experienced the full extent of American airpower. They believed that the airpower they had previously witnessed was all we were capable of delivering, and that their formidable air defenses were more than a match for it. Now they stood in awe and terror of the real thing, the full measure of conventional American power.

Before the B-52 raids, the Vietnamese had always stepped up the pressure on us whenever the United States escalated the air campaign. They knocked us around a little more often and a little more enthusiastically, just to make the point that they were still confident of victory. In the aftermath of the B-52 raids, some of the guards who had treated us the most contemptuously became almost civil when speaking to us. Some of them even began to smile at us, almost comically. It was impossible for us not to feel pride and relief as we watched people who had badly mistreated us recognize, at long last, how powerful an enemy we represented.

The first raid lasted until four-thirty in the morning. As the raids continued over the following nights, we could see that the Vietnamese air defenses were diminishing. They had few missiles left to fire, and the antiaircraft guns fell silent. Bridges were destroyed, arsenals blown up, the city's defense infrastructure devastated. They were being beaten, and they knew it.

The day after the first bombing raid, one of the officers burst into our room and screamed hysterically, "We are not afraid! We are not afraid!" He added that the Vietnamese were certain to win the war, thereby convincing us that, for the moment at least, he thought they were losing. After the last raid, an officer entered our cell smiling broadly as he informed us that they had destroyed all the B–52s. I was standing with Bud Day and Jack Fellowes when we received this distressing news. Bud looked at the officer for a moment, then laughed and said, "Bullshit."

In the bad old days, Bud would have been dragged out of there and tied in ropes for such defiance. Now all the officer was disposed to do was argue with Bud. "Look, no more bombs. We destroyed all your bombers."

I've often thought that the more perceptive Vietnamese must have realized, as we did, that the raids would shorten the war, and though they were distressed by the ferocity of the attacks, they might have regarded them as a harbinger of peace.

During one raid that did not involve B–52s, a bomb fell so close to us that shrapnel sprayed the camp courtyard. Our momentary apprehension that the pilot's targeting was not so accurate that our safety was guaranteed did not dampen our high spirits. We took what shelter we could, of course, just in case. But we greeted the low distant grumble of every approaching sortie like a long-lost friend.

We knew that the peace talks were entering their last phase. With the encouragement of the B–52s, we were confident they would be concluded in short order. We all believed, for the first time, that this would be our last Christmas in prison, and we were drunk with the thought of going home.

The B-52s terrorized Hanoi for eleven nights. Wave after wave they came. During the days, while the strategic bombers were refueled and rearmed, other aircraft took up the assault. The Vietnamese got the point. The Paris peace talks resumed on January 8, 1973, and were swiftly concluded. The accords were signed on the 27th, but we were not informed of the event until the next day, when we were ordered to form in the courtyard for an important announcement.

As a Vietnamese officer read the full text of the peace agreement, including the part that provided for the release of prisoners of war, we stood silently at attention. Our senior officers, knowing that this moment was imminent, had warned us not to demonstrate our emotions when the agreement was announced. They suspected that the Vietnamese intended to record the event for its propaganda value and broadcast pictures of jubilant POWs celebrating peace to a worldwide audience.

They were right. Film crews were on hand for the ceremony, with their cameras rolling. Not a single POW betrayed the slightest emotion as the accords were read and we were informed we would all be released in two months. When the ceremony concluded we broke ranks and walked quietly back to our cells, seemingly indifferent to the news we had just received. Back in our cells, we waited for the disappointed film crew and the other assembled Vietnamese to disperse before we began to embrace one another and express our unrestrained joy.

By this time I had been transferred back to the Plantation, where I remained until my release. The guards left us alone for the remaining weeks, and we walked about the courtyard freely, played volleyball, and talked with whomever we pleased. We were not yet at liberty, but we were beginning to remember what it felt like to be free.

Henry Kissinger arrived in Hanoi to sign the final agreement. Near the end of his visit, the Vietnamese offered to release me to him. He refused the offer. When I met Dr. Kissinger back in the States some weeks later and he informed me of the Vietnamese offer and his response, I thanked him for saving my honor.

The prisoners were released in four increments in the order in which we had been captured. On March 15, the Rabbit called my name off the roster of POWs to be released that day. A few days earlier we had received, for the first time, Red Cross packages. The night before, we were given a large dinner, complete with wine, our first substantial meal in a long time.

On the day before my release, I had been ordered to see the camp commander and a high-ranking political officer who spoke English. The political officer told me that he had recently seen the doctor who had operated on my leg, and that he had expressed his concern about my condition.

"Would you like to write a note to your doctor or see him to tell him how you are, and to thank him for your operation?"

Noticing a tape recorder sitting on the table, I answered in the negative.

"Why not?"

"Well, I haven't seen the asshole in five years and I wonder why he should have his curiosity aroused at this point. I know he's been very busy."

Dressed in cheap civilian clothes, we boarded buses for Gia Lam airport on the outskirts of Hanoi. As I stepped off the bus at the edge of the airport tarmac, I saw a big, green, beautiful American C-141 transport plane waiting to take us to Clark Air Force Base in the Philippines. I nearly cried at the sight of it. At the airport, lined up in formation according to our shootdown date, we maintained our military bearing as a noisy crowd of Vietnamese gawked at us. I could hear cameras whirring and shutters clicking. Vietnamese and American officers were seated at a table, each holding a list of prisoners. When it was time for a prisoner to step forward, representatives of both militaries called off his name. An officer from his service then escorted each prisoner across the tarmac and up the ramp into the plane. When my name was called, I stepped forward. The American officers seated at the table outranked me, so I saluted them.

Just prior to my departure, the Vietnamese had supplied me with another pair of crutches, even though I had been getting along fine without any. I decided to leave them behind. I wanted to take my leave of Vietnam without any assistance from my hosts.

Three days before my release, the *Los Angeles Times* had run a huge banner headline proclaiming: HANOI TO RELEASE ADMIRAL'S SON. My father had been invited to join his successor as CINCPAC, Admiral Noel Gaylor, at the welcoming ceremony at Clark. He asked if the parents of other POWs had been invited. Told they had not, my father declined the offer.

CHAPTER 28

Free Men

We cheered loudly when the pilot announced that we were "feet wet," which meant that we were now flying over the Tonkin Gulf and in international airspace. A holiday atmosphere prevailed for the rest of the flight. We were served sandwiches and soft drinks, which we hungrily consumed. We clowned around with each other and with the military escorts and nurses who accompanied us and seemed as happy to see us as we were to see them. Our animated conversations rose above the droning of the aircraft's engines.

Although I am sure I celebrated my liberation with as much exuberance as the next man, I recall feeling that the short flight to Clark lacked the magnitude of drama I had expected it to have. I had envisioned the moment for many years. The event itself seemed somewhat anticlimactic. I enjoyed it, but before we arrived at our destination I was thinking ahead to the next flight, the flight home. The flight to Clark resides in my memory as an exceptionally pleasant ride to the airport.

I felt a little different when we left Clark for home and I bade farewell to men with whom I had formed such strong bonds of affection and respect. We sent one another off with best wishes and promises to reunite soon. But the sudden separation hurt a little, and on the flight home a strange sense of loneliness nagged me even as my excitement to see my family became more intense as every passing hour brought me closer to them.

Bud Day and Bob Craner were on my flight to Clark. They and Orson Swindle had become the closest friends I had ever had. We were brothers now, as surely as if we had been born to the same parents. Even after we resumed our crowded, busy lives as free men, we remained close. I still see Bud and Orson often, and I am most at ease in their company. Bob Craner died of a heart attack in 1981, too young and too good to have left this earth so long before the rest of us. I have never stopped missing him.

In an interview he gave not long after our homecoming, Bob explained, as well as anyone could explain, how regret mixed with happiness on the day when our dreams came true. "It was with just a little melancholia that I finally said good-bye to John McCain," he remembered. "Even at Clark, we were still a group . . . and the outsiders were trying to butt in, but we weren't having too much of that. . . . On the night before I was to get on an airplane at eight o'clock the following morning, I could sense that here was the end. Now this group is going to be busted wide open and spread all over the United States. It may be a long time, years, before we rejoin, and when we do, it won't be the same."

I flew to freedom in the company of many men who had suffered valiantly for their country's cause. Many of them had known greater terror than I had; resisted torture longer than I had held out, faced down more daunting challenges than I had confronted, and sacrificed more than had been asked of me. They are the part of my time in Vietnam I won't forget.

Bob was right—it was an end, and it would never again be quite the same. But the years that followed have had meaning and value, and I am happy to live in the present.

Prior to the pilot's announcement that we had left Vietnamese airspace, most of us were restrained, having not quite shaken off the solemn formality with which our departure ceremony was conducted.

Of course, we expected it would take much longer to shake off entirely the effects of our experiences in prison. Many of us were returning with injuries, and at best it would take some time for our physical rehabilitation to make satisfactory progress. I worried that my injuries might never heal properly, having been left untreated for so many years, and that I might never be allowed to fly again or perhaps even remain in the Navy. I faced a difficult period of rehabilitation, and I was for a long time uncertain that I would ever recover enough to regain flight status. Although I never regained full mobility in my arms and leg, I did recover, thanks to my patient family and a remarkably determined physical therapist, and I eventually flew again.

Neither did we expect to soon forget the long years of anguish we had suffered under our captors' "humane and lenient" treatment. A few men never recovered. They were the last, tragic casualties in a long, bitter war. But most of us healed from our wounds, the physical and spiritual ones, and have lived happy and productive lives since.

We were all astonished at the reception we received first at Clark and later when we stopped at Hickham Air Force Base in Hawaii en route to our homes. Thousands of people turned out, many of them wearing bracelets that bore our names, to cheer us as we disembarked the plane. During our captivity, the Vietnamese had inundated us with information about how unpopular the war and the men who fought it had become with the American public. We were stunned and relieved to discover that most Americans were as happy to see us as we were to see them. A lot of us were overcome by our reception, and the affection we were shown helped us to begin putting the war behind us.

I once heard the Vietnam War described as "America's fall from grace." Disagreements about the purpose and conduct of the war as well as its distinction of being the first lost war in American history left

some Americans bereft of confidence in American exceptionalism—
the belief that our history is unique and exalted and a blessing to
all humanity. Not all Americans lost this faith. Not all Americans who
once believed it to be lost believe it still. But many did, and many
still do.

Surely, for a time, our loss in Vietnam afflicted America with a
kind of identity crisis. For a while we made our way in the world
less sure of ourselves than we had been before Vietnam. That was a
pity, and I am relieved today that America's period of self-doubt has
ended. America has a long, accomplished, and honorable history. We
should never have let this one mistake, terrible though it was, color
our perceptions forever of our country's purpose. We were a good
country before Vietnam, and we are a good country after Vietnam. In
all of history, you cannot find a better one.

I have often maintained that I left Vietnam behind me when I arrived
at Clark. That is an exaggeration. But I did not want my experiences
in Vietnam to be the leitmotif of the rest of my life. I am a public figure now, and my public profile is inextricably linked to my POW experiences. Whenever I am introduced at an appearance, the speaker
always refers to my war record first. Obviously, such recognition has
benefited my political career, and I am grateful for that. Many men
who came home from Vietnam, physically and spiritually damaged, to
what appeared to be a country that did not understand or appreciate
their sacrifice carried the war as a great weight upon their subsequent
search for happiness. But I have tried hard to make what use I can of
Vietnam and not let the memories of war encumber the rest of my
life's progress.

In the many years since I came home, I have managed to prevent
the bad memories of war from intruding on my present happiness. I
was thirty-six years old when I regained my freedom. When I was
shot down, I had been prepared by training, as much as anyone can be

prepared, for the experiences that lay ahead. I wasn't a nineteen- or twenty-year-old kid who had been drafted into a strange and terrible experience and then returned unceremoniously to an unappreciative country.

Neither have I been content to accept that my time in Vietnam would stand as the ultimate experience of my life. Surely it was a formative experience, but I knew that life promised other adventures, and, impatient by nature, I hurried toward them.

Vietnam changed me, in significant ways, for the better. It is a surpassing irony that war, for all its horror, provides the combatant with every conceivable human experience. Experiences that usually take a lifetime to know are all felt, and felt intensely, in one brief passage of life. Anyone who loses a loved one knows what great sorrow feels like. And anyone who gives life to a child knows what great joy feels like. The veteran knows what great loss and great joy feel like when they occur in the same moment, the same experience.

Such an experience is transforming. And we can be much the better for it. Some few who came home from war struggled to recover the balance that the war had upset. But for most veterans, who came home whole in spirit if not body, the hard uses of life will seldom threaten their equanimity.

Surviving my imprisonment strengthened my self-confidence, and my refusal of early release taught me to trust my own judgment. I am grateful to Vietnam for those discoveries, as they have made a great difference in my life. I gained a seriousness of purpose that observers of my early life had found difficult to detect. I had made more than my share of mistakes in my life. In the years ahead, I would make many more. But I would no longer err out of self-doubt or to alter a fate I felt had been imposed on me. I know my life is blessed, and always has been.

Vietnam did not answer all of life's questions, but I believe it answered many of the most important ones. In my youth I had doubted time's great haste. But in Vietnam I had come to understand how brief a moment a life is. That discovery did not, however, make me overly fearful of time's brisk passing. For I had also learned that you can fill the moment with purpose and experiences that will make your life greater than the sum of its days. I had learned to acknowledge my failings and to recognize opportunities for redemption. I had failed when I signed my confession, and that failure disturbed my peace of mind. I felt it blemished my record permanently, and even today I find it hard to suppress feelings of remorse. In truth, I don't even bother to try to suppress them anymore. My remorse shows me the limits of my zealously guarded autonomy.

My country had failed in Vietnam as well, but I took no comfort from its company. There is much to regret about America's failure in Vietnam. The reasons are etched in black marble on the Washington Mall. But we had believed the cause that America had asked us to serve in Vietnam was a worthy one, and millions who defended it had done so honorably.

Both my confession and my resistance helped me achieve a balance in my life, a balance between my own individualism and more important things. Like my father and grandfather, and the Naval Academy, the men I had been honored to serve with called me to the cause, and I had tried to keep faith with them.

I discovered I was dependent on others to a greater extent than I had ever realized, but that neither they nor the cause we served made any claims on my identity. On the contrary, they gave me a larger sense of myself than I had had before. And I am a better man for it. We had met a power that wanted to obliterate our identities, and the cause to which we rallied was our response: we are free men, bound inseparably together, and by the grace of God, and not your sufferance, we will have our freedom restored to us. Ironically, I have never felt more powerfully free, more my own man, than when I was a small part of an organized resistance to the power that imprisoned me. Nothing in life is more liberating than to fight for a cause larger than yourself, something that encompasses you but is not defined by your existence alone.

When I look back on my misspent youth, I feel a longing for what is past and cannot be restored. But though the happy pursuits and casual beauty of youth prove ephemeral, something better can endure, and endure until our last moment on earth. And that is the honor we earn and the love we give if at a moment in our youth we sacrifice with others for something greater than our self-interest. We cannot always choose the moments. Often they arrive unbidden. We can choose to let the moments pass, and avoid the difficulties they entail. But the loss we would incur by that choice is much dearer than the tribute we once paid to vanity and pleasure.

During their reunion aboard the *Proteus* in Tokyo Bay, my father and grandfather had their last conversation. Near the end of his life, my father recalled their final moment together:

"My father said to me, 'Son, there is no greater thing than to die for the principles—for the country and the principles that you believe in.' And that was one part of the conversation that came through and I have remembered down through the years."

On that fine March day, I thought about what I had done and failed to do in Vietnam, and about what my country had done and failed to do. I had seen human virtue affirmed in the conduct of men who were ennobled by their suffering. And "down through the years," I had remembered a dying man's legacy to his son, and when I needed it most, I had found my freedom abiding in it.

I held on to the memory, left the bad behind, and moved on.

PACHINKO

PACHINKO

Min Jin Lee

GRAND CENTRAL
PUBLISHING

NEW YORK   BOSTON

Copyright © 2017 by Min Jin Lee
Cover design by Anne Twomey
Cover image by Tom Hallman
Cover copyright © 2017 by Hachette Book Group, Inc.

Grand Central Publishing
Hachette Book Group
1290 Avenue of the Americas
New York, NY 10104
grandcentralpublishing.com
twitter.com/grandcentralpub

First Edition: February 2017

Grand Central Publishing is a division of Hachette Book Group, Inc.
The Grand Central Publishing name and logo is a trademark of Hachette Book Group, Inc.

The publisher is not responsible for websites (or their content) that are not owned by the publisher.

The Hachette Speakers Bureau provides a wide range of authors for speaking events. To find out more, go to www.hachettespeakersbureau.com or call (866) 376-6591.

Library of Congress Cataloging-in-Publication Data
Names: Lee, Min Jin, author.
Title: Pachinko / Min Jin Lee.
Description: First edition. | New York : Grand Central Publishing, 2017.
Identifiers: LCCN 2016023353| ISBN 9781455563937 (hardcover) | ISBN
   9781455569496 (large print) | ISBN 9781478907121 (audio download) | ISBN
   9781478967439 (audio book) | ISBN 9781455563913 (ebook)
Subjects: LCSH: Families—Korea—Fiction. | Domestic fiction. | BISAC:
   FICTION / Literary. | FICTION / Cultural Heritage. | FICTION / Family
   Life. | FICTION / Historical.
Classification: LCC PS3612.E346 P33 2017 | DDC 813/.6—dc23 LC record available at
https://lccn.loc.gov/2016023353

ISBN: 978-1-4555-6393-7 (hardcover); 978-1-4555-6391-3 (ebook); 978-1-4789-7088-0 (signed edition); 978-1-4555-6949-6 (large print)

LSC-C

10 9 8 7 6 5 4 3 2 1

For Christopher and Sam

Gohyang/Hometown

1910–1933

Home is a name, a word, it is a strong one; stronger than magician ever spoke, or spirit answered to, in strongest conjuration.

—Charles Dickens

I

Yeongdo, Busan, Korea

History has failed us, but no matter.

At the turn of the century, an aging fisherman and his wife decided to take in lodgers for extra money. Both were born and raised in the fishing village of Yeongdo—a five-mile-wide islet beside the port city of Busan. In their long marriage, the wife gave birth to three sons, but only Hoonie, the eldest and the weakest one, survived. Hoonie was born with a cleft palate and a twisted foot; he was, however, endowed with hefty shoulders, a squat build, and a golden complexion. Even as a young man, he retained the mild, thoughtful temperament he'd had as a child. When Hoonie covered his misshapen mouth with his hands, something he did out of habit meeting strangers, he resembled his nice-looking father, both having the same large, smiling eyes. Inky eyebrows graced his broad forehead, perpetually tanned from outdoor work. Like his parents, Hoonie was not a nimble talker, and some made the mistake of thinking that because he could not speak quickly there was something wrong with his mind, but that was not true.

In 1910, when Hoonie was twenty-seven years old, Japan annexed Korea. The fisherman and his wife, thrifty and hardy peasants, refused to be distracted by the country's incompetent aristocrats and corrupt rulers, who had lost their nation to thieves. When the rent for their house was raised again, the couple moved out of their bedroom and slept in the anteroom near the kitchen to increase the number of lodgers.

The wooden house they had rented for over three decades was not large, just shy of five hundred square feet. Sliding paper doors divided the interior into three snug rooms, and the fisherman himself had replaced its leaky grass roof with reddish clay tiles to the benefit of his landlord, who lived in splendor in a mansion in Busan. Eventually, the kitchen was pushed out to the vegetable garden to make way for the larger cooking pots and the growing number of portable dining tables that hung on pegs along the mortared stone wall.

At his father's insistence, Hoonie learned to read and write Korean and Japanese from the village schoolmaster well enough to keep a boarding-house ledger and to do sums in his head so he couldn't be cheated at the market. When he knew how to do this, his parents pulled him out of school. As an adolescent, Hoonie worked nearly as well as a strong man twice his age with two well-shaped legs; he was dexterous with his hands and could carry heavy loads, but he could not run or walk quickly. Both Hoonie and his father were known in the village for never picking up a cup of wine. The fisherman and his wife raised their surviving son, the neigh-borhood cripple, to be clever and diligent, because they did not know who would care for him after they died.

If it were possible for a man and his wife to share one heart, Hoonie was this steady, beating organ. They had lost their other sons—the youngest to measles and the middle, good-for-nothing one to a goring bull in a pointless accident. Except for school and the market, the old couple kept young Hoonie close by the house, and eventually, as a young man, Hoonie needed to stay home to help his parents. They could not bear to disap-point him; yet they loved him enough not to dote on him. The peasants knew that a spoiled son did more harm to a family than a dead one, and they kept themselves from indulging him too much.

Other families in the land were not so fortunate as to have two such sensible parents, and as happens in countries being pillaged by rivals or nature, the weak—the elderly, widows and orphans—were as desperate as ever on the colonized peninsula. For any household that could feed one more, there were multitudes willing to work a full day for a bowl of barley rice.

In the spring of 1911, two weeks after Hoonie turned twenty-eight, the red-cheeked matchmaker from town called on his mother.

Hoonie's mother led the matchmaker to the kitchen; they had to speak in low tones since the boarders were sleeping in the front rooms. It was late morning, and the lodgers who'd fished through the evening had finished their hot suppers, washed up, and gone to bed. Hoonie's mother poured the matchmaker a cup of cold barley tea but didn't break from her own work.

Naturally, the mother guessed what the matchmaker wanted, but she couldn't fathom what to say. Hoonie had never asked his parents for a bride. It was unthinkable that a decent family would let their daughter marry someone with deformities, since such things were inevitable in the next generation. She had never seen her son talk to a girl; most village girls avoided the sight of him, and Hoonie would have known enough not to want something he could not have—this forbearance was something that any normal peasant would have accepted about his life and what he was allowed to desire.

The matchmaker's funny little face was puffy and pink; black flinty eyes darted intelligently, and she was careful to say only nice things. The woman licked her lips as if she was thirsty; Hoonie's mother felt the woman observing her and every detail of the house, measuring the size of the kitchen with her exacting eyes.

The matchmaker, however, would have had great difficulty in reading Hoonie's mother, a quiet woman who worked from waking until bed, doing what was needed for that day and the next. She rarely went to the market, because there was no time for distracting chatter; she sent Hoonie for the shopping. While the matchmaker talked, Hoonie's mother's mouth remained unmoving and steady, much like the heavy pine table she was cutting her radishes on.

The matchmaker brought it up first. So there was that unfortunate matter of his foot and broken lip, but Hoonie was clearly a good boy—educated and strong as a pair of oxen! She was blessed to have such a fine son, the matchmaker said. She deprecated her own children: Neither of her boys was dedicated to books or commerce, but they were not

terrible boys. Her daughter married too early and lived too far away. All good marriages, the matchmaker supposed, but her sons were lazy. Not like Hoonie. After her speech, the matchmaker stared at the olive-skinned woman whose face was immobile, casting about for any sign of interest.

Hoonie's mother kept her head down, handling her sharp knife confidently—each cube of radish was square and certain. When a large mound of white radish cubes formed on the cutting board, she transferred the load in a clean swipe into a mixing bowl. She was paying such careful attention to the matchmaker's talking that privately, Hoonie's mother feared she would begin to shake from nerves.

Before stepping into the house, the matchmaker had walked around its perimeter to assess the financial condition of the household. From all appearances, the neighborhood talk of their stable situation could be confirmed. In the kitchen garden, ponytail radishes, grown fat and heavy from the early spring rain, were ready to be pulled from the brown earth. Pollack and squid strung neatly across a long clothesline dried in the lacy spring sun. Beside the outhouse, three black pigs were kept in a clean pen built from local stone and mortar. The matchmaker counted seven chickens and a rooster in the backyard. Their prosperity was more evident inside the house.

In the kitchen, stacks of rice and soup bowls rested on well-built shelves, and braids of white garlic and red chilies hung from the low kitchen rafters. In the corner, near the washbasin, there was an enormous woven basket heaped with freshly dug potatoes. The comforting aroma of barley and millet steaming in the black rice pot wafted through the small house.

Satisfied with the boardinghouse's comfortable situation in a country growing steadily poorer, the matchmaker was certain that even Hoonie could have a healthy bride, so she plowed ahead.

The girl was from the other side of the island, beyond the dense woods. Her father, a tenant farmer, was one of the many who'd lost his lease as a result of the colonial government's recent land surveys. The widower, cursed with four girls and no sons, had nothing to eat except for what was gathered from the woods, fish he couldn't sell, or the occasional charity from equally impoverished neighbors. The decent father had begged the

matchmaker to find grooms for his unmarried daughters, since it was better for virgins to marry anyone than to scrounge for food when men and women were hungry, and virtue was expensive. The girl, Yangjin, was the last of the four girls and the easiest to unload because she was too young to complain, and she'd had the least to eat.

Yangjin was fifteen and mild and tender as a newborn calf, the matchmaker said. "No dowry, of course, and surely, the father could not expect much in the way of gifts. Perhaps a few laying hens, cotton cloth for Yangjin's sisters, six or seven sacks of millet to get them through the winter." Hearing no protest at the tally of gifts, the matchmaker grew bolder, "Maybe a goat. Or a small pig. The family has so little, and bride prices have come down so much. The girl wouldn't need any jewelry." The matchmaker laughed a little.

With a flick of her thick wrist, Hoonie's mother showered the radish with sea salt. The matchmaker could not have known how hard Hoonie's mother was concentrating and thinking about what the woman wanted. The mother would have given up anything to raise the bride price demanded; Hoonie's mother found herself surprised at the imaginings and hopes rising within her breast, but her face remained collected and private; nevertheless, the matchmaker was no fool.

"What I wouldn't give to have a grandson of my own one day," the matchmaker said, making her closing gambit while peering hard at the boardinghouse keeper's creased, brown face. "I have a granddaughter but no grandsons, and the girl cries too much."

The matchmaker continued. "I remember holding my first son when he was a baby. How happy I was! He was as white as a basket of fresh rice cakes on New Year's—soft and juicy as warm dough. Tasty enough to take a bite. Well, now he's just a big dolt," feeling the need to add a complaint to her bragging.

Hoonie's mother smiled, finally, because the image was almost too vivid for her. What old woman didn't yearn to hold her grandson when such a thought had been inconceivable before this visit? She clenched her teeth to calm herself and picked up the mixing bowl. She shook it to even out the salt.

"The girl has a nice face. No pockmarks. She's well mannered and obeys her father and sisters. And not too dark. She's a little thing, but she has strong hands and arms. She'll need to gain some weight, but you understand that. It's been a difficult time for the family." The matchmaker smiled at the basket of potatoes in the corner as if to suggest that here, the girl would be able to eat as much as she wanted.

Hoonie's mother rested the bowl on the counter and turned to her guest.

"I'll speak to my husband and son. There's no money for a goat or a pig. We may be able to send some cotton wool with the other things for the winter. I'll have to ask."

The bride and groom met on their wedding day, and Yangjin had not been scared by his face. Three people in her village had been born that way. She'd seen cattle and pigs with the same thing. A girl who lived near her had a strawberry-like growth between her nose and split lip, and the other children called her Strawberry, a name the girl did not mind. When Yangjin's father had told her that her husband would be like Strawberry but also with a crooked leg, she had not cried. He told her that she was a good girl.

Hoonie and Yangjin were married so quietly that if the family had not sent out mugwort cakes to the neighbors, they would have been accused of stinginess. Even the boarders were astonished when the bride appeared to serve the morning meal the day following the wedding.

When Yangjin became pregnant, she worried that her child would have Hoonie's deformities. Her first child was born with a cleft palate but had good legs. Hoonie and his parents were not upset when the midwife showed him to them. "Do you mind it?" Hoonie asked her, and she said no, because she did not. When Yangjin was alone with her firstborn, she traced her index finger around the infant's mouth and kissed it; she had never loved anyone as much as her baby. At seven weeks, he died of a fever. Her second baby had a perfect face and good legs, but he, too, died before his *baek-il* celebration from diarrhea and fever. Her sisters, still unmarried, blamed her weak milk flow and advised her to see a shaman.

Hoonie and his parents did not approve of the shaman, but she went without telling them when she was pregnant for the third time. Yet in the midst of her third pregnancy, she felt odd, and Yangjin resigned herself to the possibility that this one, too, may die. She lost her third to smallpox.

Her mother-in-law went to the herbalist and brewed her healing teas. Yangjin drank every brown drop in the cup and apologized for the great expense. After each birth, Hoonie went to the market to buy his wife choice seaweed for soup to heal her womb; after each death, he brought her sweet rice cakes still warm from the market and gave them to her: "You have to eat. You must get your strength."

Three years after the marriage, Hoonie's father died, then months after, his wife followed. Yangjin's in-laws had never denied her meals or clothing. No one had hit her or criticized her even as she failed to give them a surviving heir.

At last, Yangjin gave birth to Sunja, her fourth child and the only girl, and the child thrived; after she turned three, the parents were able to sleep through the night without checking the pallet repeatedly to see if the small form lying beside them was still breathing. Hoonie made his daughter dollies out of corn husks and forsook his tobacco to buy her sweets; the three ate each meal together even though the lodgers wanted Hoonie to eat with them. He loved his child the way his parents had loved him, but he found that he could not deny her anything. Sunja was a normal-looking girl with a quick laugh and bright, but to her father, she was a beauty, and he marveled at her perfection. Few fathers in the world treasured their daughters as much as Hoonie, who seemed to live to make his child smile.

In the winter when Sunja was thirteen years old, Hoonie died quietly from tuberculosis. At his burial, Yangjin and her daughter were inconsolable. The next morning, the young widow rose from her pallet and returned to work.

2

November 1932

The winter following Japan's invasion of Manchuria was a difficult one. Biting winds sheared through the small boardinghouse, and the women stuffed cotton in between the fabric layers of their garments. This thing called the Depression was found everywhere in the world, the lodgers said frequently during meals, repeating what they'd overheard from the men at the market who could read newspapers. Poor Americans were as hungry as the poor Russians and the poor Chinese. In the name of the Emperor, even ordinary Japanese went without. No doubt, the canny and the hardy survived that winter, but the shameful reports—of children going to bed and not waking up, girls selling their innocence for a bowl of wheat noodles, and the elderly stealing away quietly to die so the young could eat—were far too plentiful.

That said, the boarders expected their meals regularly, and an old house needed repairs. The rent had to be paid each month to the landlord's agent, who was persistent. In time, Yangjin had learned how to handle money, deal with her suppliers, and say no to terms she did not want. She hired two orphaned sisters and became an employer. She was a thirty-seven-year-old widow who ran a boardinghouse and no longer the shoeless teenager who'd arrived on its doorstep clutching a set of clean undergarments wrapped in a square bit of fabric.

Yangjin had to take care of Sunja and earn money; they were fortunate to have this business even though they didn't own the house. On the first

of every month, each lodger paid twenty-three yen for room and board, and increasingly, this was not enough to buy grain at the market or coal for heat. The lodging fees couldn't go up, because the men were not making any more money, but she still had to feed them the same amount. So from shinbones, she made thick, milky broths and seasoned the garden vegetables for tasty side dishes; she stretched meals from millet and barley and the meager things they had in the larder when there was little money left at the end of the month. When there wasn't much in the grain sack, she made savory pancakes from bean flour and water. The lodgers brought her fish they couldn't sell in the market, so when there was an extra pail of crabs or mackerel, she preserved them with spices to supplement the scantier meals that were sure to come.

For the previous two seasons, six guests took turns sleeping in the one guest room: The three Chung brothers from Jeollado fished at night and slept during the day shift, and two young fellows from Daegu and a widower from Busan worked at the seaside fish market and went to sleep in the early evening. In the small room, the men slept beside each other, but none complained, because this boardinghouse was better than what they were used to back at their respective homes. The bedding was clean, and the food was filling. The girls laundered their clothing well, and the boardinghouse keeper patched up the lodgers' worn work clothes with scraps to make them last another season. None of these men could afford a wife, so for them, this setup was not half bad. A wife could have given some physical comfort to a workingman, but a marriage could beget children who would need food, clothing, and a home; a poor man's wife was prone to nagging and crying, and these men understood their limits.

The rise in prices accompanied by the shortage of money was distressing, but the lodgers were almost never late with the rent. The men who worked at the market were occasionally paid in unsold goods, and Yangjin would take a jar of cooking oil in place of a few yen on rent day. Her mother-in-law had explained that you had to be very good to the lodgers: There were always other places for workingmen to stay. She explained, "Men have choices that women don't." At the end of each season, if there were any coins left over, Yangjin dropped them into a dark earthenware

crock and stowed it behind a panel in the closet where her husband had put away the two gold rings that had belonged to his mother.

At meals, Yangjin and her daughter served the food noiselessly while the lodgers talked brashly about politics. The Chung brothers were illiterate, but they followed the news carefully at the docks and liked to analyze the fate of the country at the boardinghouse dining table.

It was the middle of November, and the fishing had been better than expected for the month. The Chung brothers had just woken up. The evening-shift lodgers would soon be heading home to sleep. The fishermen brothers would eat their main meal before going out to sea. Well rested and feisty, the brothers were convinced that Japan couldn't conquer China.

"Yes, the bastards can take a nibble, but China will not be eaten whole. Impossible!" exclaimed the middle Chung brother.

"Those dwarves can't take over such a great kingdom. China is our elder brother! Japan is just a bad seed," Fatso, the youngest brother, cried, slapping down his cup of warm tea. "China will get those sons of bitches! You watch!"

The poor men mocked their powerful colonizer within the shabby walls of the boardinghouse, feeling secure from the colonial police, who wouldn't bother with fishermen with grandiose ideas. The brothers boasted of China's strengths—their hearts yearning for another nation to be strong since their own rulers had failed them. Korea had been colonized for twenty-two years already. The younger two had never lived in a Korea that wasn't ruled by Japan.

"*Ajumoni*," Fatso shouted genially. "*Ajumoni*."

"Yes?" Yangjin knew he wanted more to eat. He was a puny young man who ate more than both his brothers combined.

"Another bowl of your delicious soup?"

"Yes, yes, of course."

Yangjin retrieved it from the kitchen. Fatso slurped it down, and the men left the house for work.

The evening-shift lodgers came home soon after, washed up, and ate their suppers quickly. They smoked their pipes, then went to sleep. The

women cleared the tables and ate their simple dinner quietly because the men were sleeping. The servant girls and Sunja tidied the kitchen and cleaned the dirty washbasins. Yangjin checked the coal before she prepared for bed. The brothers' talk of China lingered in her mind. Hoonie used to listen carefully to all the men who brought him news, and he would nod, exhale resolutely, and then get up to take care of the chores. "No matter," he would say, "no matter." Whether China capitulated or avenged itself, the weeds would have to be pulled from the vegetable garden, rope sandals would need to be woven if they were to have shoes, and the thieves who tried often to steal their few chickens had to be kept away.

The dampened hem of Baek Isak's woolen coat had frozen stiff, but at last Isak found the boardinghouse. The long trip from Pyongyang had exhausted him. In contrast to the snowy North, the cold in Busan was deceptive. Winter in the South appeared milder, but the frosty wind from the sea seeped into his weakened lungs and chilled him to the marrow. When he'd left home, Isak had been feeling strong enough to make the train journey, but now he felt depleted again, and he knew he had to rest. From the train station in Busan, he had found his way to the small boat that ferried him across to Yeongdo, and once off the boat, the coal man from the area had brought him to the door of the boardinghouse. Isak exhaled and knocked, ready to collapse, believing that if he could sleep well for the night, he would be better in the morning.

Yangjin had just settled onto her cotton-covered pallet when the younger servant girl tapped on the doorframe of the alcove room where all the women slept together.

"*Ajumoni*, there's a gentleman here. He wants to speak to the master of the house. Something about his brother who was here years ago. The gentleman wants to stay. Tonight," the servant girl said, breathless.

Yangjin frowned. Who would ask for Hoonie? she wondered. Next month would mark three years since his death.

On the heated floor, her daughter, Sunja, was asleep already, snoring lightly, her loose hair crimped by the braids she'd worn during the day and spread across her pillow like a shimmering rectangle of black silk. Be-

side her remained just enough space for the maids to turn in when they finished their work for the evening.

"Didn't you tell him that the master passed away?"

"Yes. He seemed surprised. The gentleman said his brother had written to the master but hadn't heard back."

Yangjin sat up and reached for the muslin *hanbok* that she'd just removed, which was folded in a neat pile by her pillow. She put on the quilted vest over her skirt and jacket. With a few deft movements, Yangjin put her hair into a bun.

At the sight of him, it made sense that the maid hadn't turned him away. He was formed like a young pine, straight and elegant, and he was unusually handsome: slender smiling eyes, a strong nose, and long neck. The man had a pale, unlined brow, and he looked nothing like the grizzled lodgers who yelled for their food or teased the maids for being unmarried. The young man wore a Western-style suit and a thick winter coat. The imported leather shoes, leather suitcase, and trilby were all out of place in the small entryway. From the looks of him, the man had enough money for a room downtown in a larger inn for merchants or tradespeople. Nearly all the inns of Busan where Koreans could stay were full, but for good money, it was possible to get something. He could have passed for a rich Japanese in the way he dressed. The maid stared at the gentleman with her mouth slightly agape, hoping he would be allowed to stay.

Yangjin bowed, not knowing what to say to him. No doubt, the brother had sent a letter, but she did not know how to read. Once every few months, she asked the schoolmaster in town to read her mail, but she hadn't done so this winter for lack of time.

"*Ajumoni*"—he bowed—"I hope I didn't wake you. It was dark when I got off the ferry. I didn't know about your husband until today. I am sorry to hear the sad news. I am Baek Isak. I come from Pyongyang. My brother Baek Yoseb stayed here many years ago."

His northern accent was mild, and his speech was learned.

"I'd hoped to stay here for a few weeks before going to Osaka."

Yangjin looked down at her bare feet. The guestroom was already full, and a man like this would expect his own sleeping quarters. At this time of

night, to find a boatman to take him back to the mainland would be hard.

Isak withdrew a white handkerchief from his trousers and covered his mouth to cough.

"My brother was here almost ten years ago. I wonder if you remember him. He had admired your husband very much."

Yangjin nodded. The older Baek stood out in her memory because he wasn't a fisherman or someone who worked in the market. His first name was Yoseb; he'd been named after a person in the Bible. His parents were Christians and founders of a church up north.

"But your brother—that gentleman didn't look like you very much. He was short, with round metal spectacles. He was headed to Japan; he stayed for several weeks before going."

"Yes, yes." Isak's face brightened. He hadn't seen Yoseb in over a decade. "He lives in Osaka with his wife. He's the one who wrote to your husband. He insisted that I stay here. He wrote about your stewed codfish. 'Better than home,' he said."

Yangjin smiled. How could she not?

"Brother said your husband worked very hard." Isak didn't bring up the club foot or the cleft palate, though of course, Yoseb had mentioned these things in his letters. Isak had been curious to meet this man who'd overcome such difficulties.

"Have you had dinner?" Yangjin asked.

"I'm all right. Thank you."

"We could get you something to eat."

"Do you think I could rest here? I realize you were not expecting me, but I've been traveling now for two days."

"We don't have an empty room, sir. This is not a big place, you see...."

Isak sighed, then smiled at the widow. This was his burden, not hers, and he did not want her to feel bad. He looked about for his suitcase. It was near the door.

"Of course. Then I should return to Busan to find a place to stay. Before I head back, would you know of a boardinghouse around here that might have a spare room for me?" He straightened his posture, not wanting to appear discouraged.

"There's nothing around here, and we don't have an empty room," Yangjin said. If she put him with the others, he might be upset about the smell of the men. No amount of washing could remove the fish odors from their clothes.

Isak closed his eyes and nodded. He turned to leave.

"There's some extra space where all the lodgers sleep. There's only one room, you see. Three guests sleep during the day and three at night, depending on their work schedule. There's just enough space for an extra man, but it wouldn't be comfortable. You could look in if you like."

"It will be fine," Isak said, relieved. "I would be very grateful to you. I can pay you for the month."

"It might be more crowded than you are used to. There weren't as many men here when your brother stayed with us. It was not so busy then. I don't know if—"

"No, no. I would just like a corner to lie down."

"It's late, and the wind is very strong tonight." Yangjin felt embarrassed suddenly by the condition of her boardinghouse, when she had never felt this way before. If he wanted to leave the next morning, she would give him back his money, she thought.

She told him the monthly rate that had to be paid up front. If he left before the end of the month, she'd return the remainder. She charged him twenty-three yen, the same as a fisherman. Isak counted out the yen and handed them to her with both hands.

The maid put down his bag in front of the room and went to fetch a clean bedroll from the storage cabinet. He would need hot water from the kitchen to wash. The servant girl lowered her eyes but she was curious about him.

Yangjin went with the servant girl to make up the pallet, and Isak watched them quietly. Afterward, the maid brought him a water basin filled with warm water and a clean towel. The boys from Daegu slept side by side neatly, and the widower slept with his arms raised over his head. Isak's pallet was parallel to the widower's.

In the morning, the men would fuss a little about having to share the space with another lodger, but it wasn't as if Yangjin could have turned him out.

3

At dawn, the Chung brothers returned from their boat. Right away, Fatso noticed the new lodger, who remained asleep in the room.

He grinned at Yangjin. "I'm glad to see that a hardworking lady like you is so successful. The news of your great cooking has reached the rich. Next, you'll be taking in Japanese guests! I hope you charged him triple what we poor fellows pay."

Sunja shook her head at him, but he didn't notice. Fatso fingered the necktie hanging by Isak's suit.

"So is this what *yangban* wear around their necks to look important? Looks like a noose. I've never seen such a thing up close! *Waaaah*—smooth!" The youngest brother rubbed the tie against his whiskers. "Maybe this is silk. A real silk noose!" He laughed out loud, but Isak did not stir.

"Fatso-ya, don't touch that," said Gombo sternly. The eldest brother's face was covered in pockmarks, and when he was angry, his pitted skin turned red. Ever since their father had died, he had watched over his two brothers by himself.

Fatso let go of the tie and looked sheepish. He hated upsetting Gombo. The brothers bathed, ate, then all three fell asleep. The new guest continued to sleep beside them, his slumber punctuated now and then by a muffled cough.

Yangjin went to the kitchen to tell the maids to look out for the new

lodger in case he woke up. They were to have a hot meal ready for him. Sunja was crouched in the corner scrubbing sweet potatoes, not looking up when her mother entered the room or when she left it. For the past week, they had been speaking only when necessary. The servant girls couldn't figure out what had happened to make Sunja so quiet.

In the late afternoon, the Chung brothers woke up, ate again, and went to the village to buy tobacco before getting on the boat. The evening lodgers had not yet returned from work, so the house was still for a couple of hours. The sea wind seeped through the porous walls and around the window edges, causing a considerable draft in the short hallway connecting the rooms.

Yangjin was seated cross-legged nearby one of the hot spots on the heated floor of the alcove room where the women slept. She was mending a pair of trousers, one of the half dozen in the pile of the guests' well-worn garments. The men's clothes were not washed often enough, since the men owned so little and didn't like to bother.

"They'll only get dirty again," Fatso would complain, though his older brothers preferred them clean. After laundering, Yangjin patched up whatever she could, and at least once a year, she'd change the collars of shirts and jackets that could no longer be repaired or cleaned. Every time the new lodger coughed, her head bobbed up. She tried to focus on her neat stitches rather than on her daughter, who was cleaning the floors of the house. Twice a day, the yellow wax-papered floors were swept with a short broom, then mopped by hand with a clean rag.

The front door of the house opened slowly, and both mother and daughter looked up from their work. Jun, the coal man, had come for his money.

Yangjin rose from the floor to meet him. Sunja bowed perfunctorily, then returned to her work.

"How is your wife?" Yangjin asked. The coal man's wife had a nervous stomach and was occasionally bedridden.

"She got up early this morning and went to the market. Can't stop that woman from making money. You know how she is," Jun said with pride.

"You're a fortunate man." Yangjin pulled out her purse to pay him for the week's coal.

"*Ajumoni*, if all my customers were like you, I'd never go hungry. You always pay when the bill is due!" He chuckled with pleasure.

Yangjin smiled at him. Every week, he complained that no one paid on time, but most people went with less food to pay him, since it was too cold this winter not to have coal. The coal man was also a portly gentleman who took a cup of tea and accepted a snack at every house on his route; he would never starve even in such lean years. His wife was the best seaweed hawker in the market and made a tidy sum of her own.

"Down the street, that dirty dog Lee-seki won't cough up what he owes—"

"Things are not easy. Everyone's having troubles."

"No, things are not easy at all, but your house is full of paying guests because you are the best cook in Kyungsangdo. The minister is staying with you now? Did you find him a bed? I told him your sea bream is the finest in Busan." Jun sniffed the air, wondering if he could grab a bite of something before his next house, but he didn't smell anything savory.

Yangjin glanced at her daughter, and Sunja stopped cleaning the floor to go to the kitchen to fix the coal man something to eat.

"But did you know, the young man had already heard of your cooking from his brother who stayed ten years ago? Ah, the belly has a better memory than the heart!"

"The minister?" Yangjin looked puzzled.

"The young fellow from the North. I met him last night, wandering around the streets looking for your house. Baek Isak. Sort of a fancy-looking fellow. I showed him your place and would have stopped in, but I had a late delivery for Cho-seki, who finally found the money to pay me after a month of dodging—"

"Oh—"

"Anyway, I told the minister about my wife's stomach troubles and how hard she works at the stall, and you know, he said he would pray for her right then and there. He just dropped his head and closed his eyes! I don't know if I believe in that mumbling that people do, but I can't see how it can hurt anyone. Very nice-looking young man, don't you think? Has he left for the day? I should say hello."

Sunja brought him a wooden tray holding a cup of hot barley tea, a teapot, and a bowl of steamed sweet potatoes and set it before him. The coal man plopped down on the floor cushion and devoured the hot potatoes. He chewed carefully, then started to speak again.

"So this morning, I asked the wife how she felt, and she said things were not so bad and went to work! Maybe there's something to that praying after all. Ha!—"

"Is he a Cath-o-lic?" Yangjin didn't mean to interrupt him so frequently, but there was no other way to speak with Jun, who could have talked for hours. For a man, her husband used to say, Jun had too many words. "A priest?"

"No, no. He's not a priest. Those fellows are different. Baek is a Protes-tant. The kind that marries. He's going to Osaka, where his brother lives. I don't remember meeting him." He continued to chew quietly and took small sips from his teacup.

Before Yangjin had a chance to say anything, Jun said, "That Hirohito-seki took over our country, stole the best land, rice, fish, and now our young people." He sighed and ate another bite of potato. "Well, I don't blame the young people for going to Japan. There's no money to be made here. It's too late for me, but if I had a son"—Jun paused, for he had no children, and it made him sad to think of it—"I'd send him to Hawaii. My wife has a smart nephew who works on a sugar plantation there. The work is hard, but so what? He doesn't work for these bastards. The other day when I went to the docks, the sons of bitches tried to tell me that I couldn't—"

Yangjin frowned at him for cursing. The house being so small, the girls in the kitchen and Sunja, who was now mopping the alcove room, could hear everything, and they were no doubt paying attention.

"May I get you more tea?"

Jun smiled and pushed his empty cup toward her with both hands.

"It's our own damn fault for losing the country. I know that," he continued. "Those goddamn aristocrat sons of bitches sold us out. Not a single *yangban* bastard has a full set of balls."

Both Yangjin and Sunja knew the girls in the kitchen were giggling at the coal man's tirade, which didn't vary from week to week.

"I may be a peasant, but I'm an honest workingman, and I wouldn't have let some Japanese take over." He pulled out a clean, white handkerchief from his coal dust–covered coat and wiped his runny nose. "Bastards. I better get on with my next delivery."

The widow asked him to wait while she went to the kitchen. At the front door, Yangjin handed Jun a fabric-tied bundle of freshly dug potatoes. One slipped out of the bundle and rolled onto the floor. He pounced on it and dropped it into his deep coat pockets. "Never lose what's valuable."

"For your wife," Yangjin said. "Please say hello."

"Thank you." Jun slipped on his shoes in haste and left the house.

Yangjin remained by the door watching him walk away, not going back inside until he stepped into the house next door.

The house felt emptier without the blustering man's lofty speeches. Sunja was crawling on her knees finishing up the hallway connecting the front room with the rest of the house. The girl had a firm body like a pale block of wood—much in the shape of her mother—with great strength in her dexterous hands, well-muscled arms, and powerful legs. Her short, wide frame was thick, built for hard work, with little delicacy in her face or limbs, but she was quite appealing physically—more handsome than pretty. In any setting, Sunja was noticed right away for her quick energy and bright manner. The lodgers never ceased trying to woo Sunja, but none had succeeded. Her dark eyes glittered like shiny river stones set in a polished white surface, and when she laughed, you couldn't help but join her. Her father, Hoonie, had doted on her from birth, and even as a small child, Sunja had seen it as her first duty to make him happy. As soon as she learned to walk, she'd tagged behind him like a loyal pet, and though she admired her mother, when her father died, Sunja changed from a joyful girl to a thoughtful young woman.

None of the Chung brothers could afford to marry, but Gombo, the eldest, had said on more than one occasion that a girl like Sunja would have made a fine wife for a man who wanted to go up in the world. Fatso admired her, but prepared himself to adore her as an elder sister-in-law,

though she was only sixteen years old, the same age as he. If any of the brothers could marry, Gombo, the firstborn, would take a wife before the others. None of this mattered anymore, since recently Sunja had lost all of her prospects. She was pregnant, and the baby's father was unable to marry her. A week ago, Sunja had confessed this to her mother, but, of course, no one else knew.

"*Ajumoni, ajumoni!*" the older servant girl shrieked from the front of the house, where the lodgers slept, and Yangjin rushed to the room. Sunja dropped her rag to follow her.

"There's blood! On the pillow! And he's soaked with sweat!"

Bokhee, the older sister of the two servant girls, breathed deeply to calm herself. It wasn't like her to raise her voice, and she hadn't meant to frighten the others, but she didn't know if the lodger was dead or dying, and she was too afraid to approach him.

No one spoke for a moment, then Yangjin told the maid to leave the room and wait by the front door.

"It's tuberculosis, I think," Sunja said.

Yangjin nodded. The lodger's appearance reminded her of Hoonie's last few weeks.

"Get the pharmacist," Yangjin told Bokhee, then changed her mind. "No, no, wait. I might need you."

Isak lay asleep on the pillow, perspiring and flushed, unaware of the women staring down at him. Dokhee, the younger girl, had just come from the kitchen, and she gasped loudly, only to be hushed by her sister. When the lodger had arrived the night before, his ashen pallor was noticeable, but in the light of day, his handsome face was gray—the color of dirty rainwater collecting in a jar. His pillow was wet with numerous red pindots where he had coughed.

"*Uh-muh*—" Yangjin uttered, startled and anxious. "We have to move him immediately. The others could get sick. Dokhee-ya, take everything out of the storage room now. Hurry." She would put him in the storage room, where her husband had slept when he was ill, but it would have been far easier if he could have walked to the back part of the house rather than her attempting to move him by herself.

Yangjin pulled on the corner of the pallet in an attempt to jostle him awake.

"Pastor Baek, sir, sir!" Yangjin touched his upper arm. "Sir!"

Finally, Isak opened his eyes. He couldn't remember where he was. In his dream, he had been home, resting near the apple orchard; the trees were a riot of white blooms. When he came to, he recognized the boardinghouse keeper.

"Is everything all right?"

"Do you have tuberculosis?" Yangjin asked him. Surely, he must have known.

He shook his head.

"No, I had it two years ago. I've been well since." Isak touched his brow and felt the sweat along his hairline. He raised his head and found it heavy.

"Oh, I see," he said, seeing the red stains on the pillow. "I'm so sorry. I would not have come here if I had known that I could harm you. I should leave. I don't want to endanger you." Isak closed his eyes because he felt so tired. Throughout his life, Isak had been sickly, his most recent tuberculosis infection being just one of the many illnesses he'd suffered. His parents and his doctors had not wanted him to go to Osaka; only his brother Yoseb had felt it would be better for him, since Osaka was warmer than Pyongyang and because Yoseb knew how much Isak didn't want to be seen as an invalid, the way he had been treated for most of his life.

"I should return home," Isak said, his eyes still closed.

"You'll die on the train. You'll get worse before getting better. Can you sit up?" Yangjin asked him.

Isak pulled himself up and leaned against the cold wall. He had felt tired on the journey, but now it felt as if a bear was pushing against him. He caught his breath and turned to the wall to cough. Blood spots marked the wall.

"You will stay here. Until you get well," Yangjin said.

She and Sunja looked at each other. They had not gotten sick when Hoonie had this, but the girls, who weren't there then, and the lodgers would have to be protected somehow.

Yangjin looked at his face. "Can you walk a little to the back room? We would have to separate you from the others."

Isak tried to get up but couldn't. Yangjin nodded. She told Dokhee to fetch the pharmacist and Bokhee to return to the kitchen to get the supper ready for the lodgers.

Yangjin made him lie down on his bedroll, and she dragged the pallet slowly, sliding it toward the storage room, the same way she had moved her husband three years before.

Isak mumbled, "I didn't mean to bring you harm."

The young man cursed himself privately for his wish to see the world outside of his birthplace and for lying to himself that he was well enough to go to Osaka when he had sensed that he could never be cured of being so sickly. If he infected any of the people he had come into contact with, their death would be on his head. If he was supposed to die, he hoped to die swiftly to spare the innocent.

4

June 1932

At the very beginning of summer, less than six months before the young pastor arrived at the boardinghouse and fell ill, Sunja met the new fish broker, Koh Hansu.

There was a cool edge to the marine air on the morning Sunja went to the market to shop for the boardinghouse. Ever since she was an infant strapped to her mother's back, she had gone to the open-air market in Nampo-dong; then later, as a little girl, she'd held her father's hand as he shuffled there, taking almost an hour each way because of his crooked foot. The errand was more enjoyable with him than with her mother, because everyone in the village greeted her father along the way so warmly. Hoonie's misshapen mouth and awkward steps seemingly vanished in the presence of the neighbors' kind inquiries about the family, the boarding-house, and the lodgers. Hoonie never said much, but it was obvious to his daughter, even then, that many sought his quiet approval—the thoughtful gaze from his honest eyes.

After Hoonie died, Sunja was put in charge of shopping for the boardinghouse. Her shopping route didn't vary from what she had been taught by her mother and father: first, the fresh produce, next, the soup bones from the butcher, then a few items from the market *ajumma*s squatting beside spice-filled basins, deep rows of glittering cutlass fish, or plump sea bream caught hours earlier—their wares arrayed attractively on turquoise and red waxed cloths spread on the ground. The vast market

for seafood—one of the largest of its kind in Korea—stretched across the rocky beach carpeted with pebbles and broken bits of stone, and the *ajumma*s hawked as loudly as they could, each from her square patch of tarp.

Sunja was buying seaweed from the coal man's wife, who sold the best quality. The *ajumma* noticed that the new fish broker was staring at the boardinghouse girl.

"Shameless man. How he stares! He's almost old enough to be your father!" The seaweed *ajumma* rolled her eyes. "Just because a man's rich doesn't give him the right to be so brazen with a nice girl from a good family."

Sunja looked up and saw the new man in the light-colored Western suit and white leather shoes. He was standing by the corrugated-tin and wood offices with all the other seafood brokers. Wearing an off-white Panama hat like the actors in the movie posters, Koh Hansu stood out like an elegant bird with milky-white plumage among the other men, who were wearing dark clothes. He was looking hard at her, barely paying attention to the men speaking around him. The brokers at the market controlled the wholesale purchases of all the fish that went through there. Not only did they have the power to set the prices, they could punish any boat captain or fisherman by refusing to buy his catch; they also dealt with the Japanese officials who controlled the docks. Everyone deferred to the brokers, and few felt comfortable around them. The brokers rarely mixed socially outside their group. The lodgers at the boardinghouse spoke of them as arrogant interlopers who made all the profits from fishing but kept the fish smell off their smooth white hands. Regardless, the fishermen had to stay on good terms with these men who had ready cash for purchases and the needed advance when the catch wasn't any good.

"A girl like you is bound to be noticed by some fancy man, but this one seems too sharp. He's a Jeju native but lives in Osaka. I hear he can speak perfect Japanese. My husband said he was smarter than all of them put together, but crafty. *Uh-muh*! He's still looking at you!" The seaweed *ajumma* flushed red straight down to her collarbone.

Sunja shook her head, not wanting to check. When the lodgers flirted

with her, she ignored them and did her work, and she would behave no differently now. The *ajumma*s at the market tended to exaggerate, anyway.

"May I have the seaweed that my mother likes?" Sunja feigned interest in the oblong piles of dried seaweed, folded like fabric, separated in rows of varying quality and price.

Remembering herself, the *ajumma* blinked, then wrapped a large portion of seaweed for Sunja. The girl counted out the coins, then accepted the parcel with two hands.

"Your mother is taking care of how many lodgers now?"

"Six." From the corner of her eye, Sunja could see that the man was now talking to another broker, but still looking in her direction. "She's very busy."

"Of course she is! Sunja-ya, a woman's life is endless work and suffering. There is suffering and then more suffering. It's better to expect it, you know. You're becoming a woman now, so you should be told this. For a woman, the man you marry will determine the quality of your life completely. A good man is a decent life, and a bad man is a cursed life—but no matter what, always expect suffering, and just keep working hard. No one will take care of a poor woman—just ourselves."

Mrs. Jun patted her perpetually bloated stomach and turned to the new customer, allowing Sunja to return home.

At dinner, the Chung brothers mentioned Koh Hansu, who had just bought their entire catch.

"For a broker, he's okay," Gombo said. "I prefer a smart one like him who doesn't suffer fools. Koh doesn't haggle. It's one price, and he's fair enough. I don't think he's trying to screw you like the others, but you can't refuse him."

Fatso then added that the ice broker had told him that the fish broker from Jeju was supposed to be unimaginably rich. He came into Busan only three nights a week and lived in Osaka and Seoul. Everyone called him Boss.

Koh Hansu seemed to be everywhere. Whenever she was in the market, he would turn up, not concealing his interest. Although she tried to over-

look his stares and go about her errands, her face felt hot in his presence.

A week later, he spoke to her. Sunja had just finished her shopping and was walking alone on the road toward the ferry.

"Young miss, what are you cooking for dinner at the boardinghouse tonight?"

They were alone, but not far from the bustle of the market.

She looked up, then walked away briskly without answering. Her heart was pounding in fear, and she hoped he wasn't following her. On the ferry ride, she tried to recall what his voice had sounded like; it was the voice of a strong person who was trying to sound gentle. There was also the slightest Jeju lilt to his speech, a lengthening of certain vowels; it was different from how Busan people talked. He pronounced the word "dinner" in a funny way, and it had taken her a moment to figure out what he was saying.

The next day, Hansu caught up with her as she headed home.

"Why aren't you married? You're old enough."

Sunja quickened her steps and left him again. He did not follow.

Though she had not replied, Hansu didn't stop trying to talk to her. It was one question always, never more than that and never repeated, but when he saw her, and if Sunja was within hearing distance, he'd say something, and she'd hurry away without saying a word.

Hansu wasn't put off by her lack of replies; if she had tried to keep up a banter, he would have thought her common. He liked the look of her—glossy braided hair, a full bosom bound beneath her white, starched blouse, its long sash tied neatly, and her quick, sure-footed steps. Her young hands showed work; they were not the soft, knowing hands of a teahouse girl or the thin, pale hands of a highborn one. Her pleasant body was compact and rounded—her upper arms sheathed in her long white sleeves appeared pillowy and comforting. The hidden privacy of her body stirred him; he craved to see her skin. Neither a rich man's daughter nor a poor man's, the girl had something distinct in her bearing, a kind of purposefulness. Hansu had learned who she was and where she lived. Her shopping habits were the same each day. In the morning, she came to the market and left immediately afterward without dawdling. He knew that in time, they would meet.

It was the second week of June. Sunja had finished her shopping for the day and was going home carrying a loaded basket on the crook of each arm. Three Japanese high school students with their uniform jackets unbuttoned were heading to the harbor to go fishing. Too hot to sit still, the boys were skipping school. When they noticed Sunja, who was going in the direction of the Yeongdo ferry, the giggling boys surrounded her, and a skinny, pale student, the tallest of the three, plucked one of the long yellow melons out of her basket. He tossed it over Sunja's head to his friends.

"Give that back," Sunja said in Korean calmly, hoping they weren't getting on the ferry. These sorts of incidents happened often on the mainland, but there were fewer Japanese in Yeongdo. Sunja knew that it was important to get away from trouble quickly. Japanese students teased Korean kids, and occasionally, vice versa. Small Korean children were warned never to walk alone, but Sunja was sixteen and a strong girl. She assumed that the Japanese boys must have mistaken her for someone younger, and she tried to sound more authoritative.

"What? What did she say?" they snickered in Japanese. "We don't understand you, you smelly slut."

Sunja looked around, but no one seemed to be watching them. The boatman by the ferry was busy talking to two other men, and the *ajummas* near the outer perimeter of the market were occupied with work.

"Give it back now," she said in a steady voice, and stretched out her right hand. Her basket was lodged in the crook of her elbow, and it was getting harder to keep her balance. She looked directly at the skinny boy, who stood a head taller than her.

They laughed and continued to mutter in Japanese, and Sunja couldn't understand them. Two of the boys tossed the yellow melon back and forth while the third rummaged through the basket on her left arm, which she was now afraid to put down.

The boys were about her age or younger, but they were fit and full of unpredictable energy.

The third boy, the shortest, pulled out the oxtails from the bottom of the basket.

"*Yobos* eat dogs and now they're stealing the food of dogs! Do girls like you eat bones? You stupid bitch."

Sunja swiped at the air, trying to get the soup bones back. The only word she understood for certain was *yobo*, which normally meant "dear" but was also a derogatory epithet used by the Japanese to describe Koreans.

The short boy held up a bone, then sniffed it. He made a face.

"Disgusting! How do these *yobos* eat this shit?"

"Hey, that's expensive! Put that back!" Sunja shouted, unable to keep from crying.

"What? I don't understand you, you stupid Korean. Why can't you speak Japanese? All of the Emperor's loyal subjects are supposed to know how to speak Japanese! Aren't you a loyal subject?"

The tall one ignored the others. He was gauging the size of Sunja's breasts.

"The *yobo* has really big tits. Japanese girls are delicate, not like these breeders."

Afraid, Sunja decided to forget the groceries and start walking, but the boys crowded her and wouldn't let her pass.

"Let's squeeze her melons." The tall one grabbed her left breast with his right hand. "Very nice and full of juice. You want a bite?" He opened his mouth wide close to her breasts.

The short one held on to her light basket firmly so she couldn't move, then twisted her right nipple using his index finger and thumb.

The third boy suggested, "Let's take her somewhere and see what's beneath this long skirt. Forget fishing! She can be our catch."

The tall one thrust his pelvis in her direction. "How much do you want to have a taste of my eel?"

"Let me go. I'm going to scream," she said, but it felt like her throat was closing up. Then she saw the man standing behind the tallest boy.

Hansu grabbed the short hairs on the back of the boy's head with one hand and clamped the boy's mouth with his free hand. "Come closer," he hissed at the others, and to their credit, they did not abandon their friend, whose eyes were wide open in terror.

"You sons of bitches should die," he said in perfect Japanese slang. "If you ever bother this lady again or ever show your ugly faces near this area, I will have you killed. I will have you and your families murdered by the finest Japanese killers I know, and no one will ever know how you died. Your parents were losers in Japan, and that's why you had to settle here. Don't get any dumb ideas about how much better you are than these people." Hansu was smiling as he was saying this. "I can kill you now, and no one would do a thing, but that's too easy. When I decide, I can have you caught, tortured, then killed. Today, I am giving you a warning because I'm gracious, and we are in front of a young lady."

The two boys remained silent, watching their friend's eyes bulge. The man in the ivory-colored suit and white leather shoes pulled the boy's hair harder and harder. The boy didn't even try to scream, because he could feel the terrifying power of the man's unyielding force.

The man spoke exactly like a Japanese, but the boys figured that he had to be Korean from his actions. They didn't know who he was, but they didn't doubt his threats.

"Apologize, you pieces of shit," Hansu said to the boys.

"We're very sorry." They bowed formally to her.

She stared at them, not knowing what to do.

They bowed again, and Hansu released his grip on the boy's hair just slightly.

Hansu turned to Sunja and smiled.

"They said they are sorry. In Japanese, of course. Would you like them to apologize also in Korean? I can have them do that. I can have them write you a letter if you like."

Sunja shook her head. The tall boy was now crying.

"Would you like me to throw them into the sea?"

He was joking, but she couldn't smile. Sunja managed to shake her head again. The boys could have dragged her somewhere, and no one would have seen them go. Why wasn't Koh Hansu afraid of the boys' parents? A Japanese student could get a grown Korean man in trouble for certain, she thought. Why wasn't he worried? Sunja started to cry.

"It's all right," Hansu said to her in a low voice and let the tall boy go.

The boys put the melon and the bones back in the baskets.

"We are very sorry," they said, bowing deeply.

"Never ever come around here again. Do you understand, you shit-for-brains?" Hansu said in Japanese, smiling genially to make sure that Sunja did not understand his meaning.

The boys bowed again. The tall one had peed a little in his uniform. They walked in the direction of the town.

Sunja put the baskets down on the ground and sobbed. Her forearms felt like they were going to fall off. Hansu patted her shoulder gently.

"You live in Yeongdo."

She nodded.

"Your mother owns the boardinghouse."

"Yes, sir."

"I'm going to take you home."

She shook her head.

"I've troubled you enough. I can go home by myself." Sunja couldn't raise her head.

"Listen, you have to be careful not to travel alone or ever be out at night. If you go to the market by yourself, you must stay on the main paths. Always in public view. They are looking for girls now."

She didn't understand.

"The colonial government. To take to China for the soldiers. Don't follow anyone. It will likely be some Korean person, a woman or a man, who'll tell you there's a good job in China or Japan. It may be someone you know. Be careful, and I don't mean just those stupid boys. They're just bad kids. But even those boys could hurt you if you are not cautious. Do you understand?"

Sunja wasn't looking for a job, and she didn't understand why he was telling her any of this. No one had ever approached her about working away from home. She would never leave her mother, anyway, but he was right. It was always possible for a woman to be disgraced. Noblewomen supposedly hid silver knives in their blouses to protect themselves or to commit suicide if they were dishonored.

Hansu gave her a handkerchief, and she wiped her face.

"You should go home. Your mother will worry."

Hansu walked her to the ferry. Sunja rested her baskets on the floor of the ferryboat and sat down. There were only two other passengers.

Sunja bowed. Koh Hansu was watching her again, but this time his face was different from before; he looked concerned. As the boat moved away from the dock, she realized that she had not thanked him.

5

As Koh Hansu was putting her on the ferry, Sunja had the opportunity to observe him up close without distractions. She could even smell the mentholated pomade in his neatly combed black hair. Hansu had the broad shoulders and the thick, strong torso of a larger man; his legs were not very long, but he was not short, either. Hansu was perhaps the same age as her mother, who was thirty-six. His tawny brow was creased lightly, and faded brown spots and freckles had settled on his sharp cheekbones. His nose—narrow, with a bump below a high bridge—made him look somewhat Japanese, and small, broken capillaries lay beneath the skin around his nostrils. More black than brown, his dark eyes absorbed light like a long tunnel, and when he looked at her, she felt an uncomfortable sensation in her stomach. Hansu's Western-style suit was elegant and well cared for; unlike the lodgers, he didn't give off an odor from his labors or the sea.

On the following market day, she spotted him standing in front of the brokers' offices with a crowd of businessmen and waited until he could see her. She bowed to him. Hansu nodded ever so slightly, then returned to his work. Sunja went to finish her shopping, and as she walked to the ferry, he caught up with her.

"Do you have some time?" he asked.

She widened her eyes. What did he mean?

"To talk."

Sunja had been around men all her life. She had never been afraid of them or awkward in their presence, but around him, she didn't have the words she needed. It was difficult for her to stand near him even. Sunja swallowed and decided that she would speak to him no differently than to the lodgers; she was sixteen years old, not a scared child.

"Thank you for your help the other day."

"It's nothing."

"I should have said this earlier. Thank you."

"I want to talk to you. Not here."

"Where?" She should have asked why, she realized.

"I'll come to the beach behind your house. Near the large black rocks where the tide is low. You do the wash there by the cove." He wanted her to know that he knew a little about her life. "Can you come alone?"

Sunja looked down at her shopping baskets. She didn't know what to tell him, but she wanted to speak with him some more. Her mother would never allow it, however.

"Can you get away tomorrow morning? Around this time?"

"I don't know."

"Is afternoon better?"

"After the men leave for the day, I think," she found herself saying, her voice trailing off.

He was waiting for her by the black rocks, reading a newspaper. The sea was bluer than she had remembered, and the long, thin clouds seemed paler—everything seemed more vibrant with him here. The corners of his newspaper fluttered with the breeze, and he grasped them firmly, but when he saw her approaching, he folded the paper and put it under his arm. He didn't move toward her, but let her come to him. She continued to walk steadily, a large wrapped bundle of dirty clothes balanced on her head.

"Sir," she said, trying not to sound afraid. She couldn't bow, so she put her hands around the bundle to remove it, but Hansu quickly reached over to lift the load from her head, and she straightened her back as he laid the wash on the dry rocks.

"Sir, thank you."

"You should call me *Oppa*. You don't have a brother, and I don't have a sister. You can be mine."

Sunja said nothing.

"This is nice." Hansu's eyes searched the cluster of low waves in the middle of the sea and settled on the horizon. "It's not as beautiful as Jeju, but it has a similar feeling. You and I are from islands. One day, you'll understand that people from islands are different. We have more freedom."

She liked his voice—it was a masculine, knowing voice with a trace of melancholy.

"You'll probably spend your entire life here."

"Yes," she said. "This is my home."

"Home," he said thoughtfully. "My father was an orange farmer in Jeju. My father and I moved to Osaka when I was twelve; I don't think of Jeju as my home. My mother died when I was very young." He didn't tell her then that she looked like someone on his mother's side of the family. It was the eyes and the open brow.

"That's a great deal of laundry. I used to do laundry for my father and me. I hated it. One of the greatest things about being rich is having someone else wash your clothes and cook your meals."

Sunja had washed clothes almost since she could walk. She didn't mind doing laundry at all. Ironing was more difficult.

"What do you think about when you do the laundry?"

Hansu already knew what there was to know about the girl, but that was different from knowing her thoughts. It was his way to ask many questions when he wanted to know someone's mind. Most people told you their thoughts in words and later confirmed them in actions. There were more people who told the truth than those who lied. Very few people lied well. What was most disappointing to him was when a person turned out to be no different than the next. He preferred clever women over dumb ones and hardworking women over lazy ones who knew only how to lie on their backs.

"When I was a boy, my father and I each owned only one suit of clothes, so when I washed our things, we would try to have them dry

overnight and wore them still damp in the morning. Once—I think I was ten or eleven—I put the wet clothes near the stove to speed up the drying, and I went to cook our supper. We were having barley gruel, and I had to stir it in this cheap pot, otherwise the bottom would burn right away, and as I was stirring, I smelled something awful, and it turned out that I had burned a large hole in my father's jacket sleeve. I was scolded for that severely." Hansu laughed at the memory of the thrashing he got from his father. "A head like an empty gourd! A worthless idiot for a son!" His father, who had drunk all his earnings, had never blamed himself for being unable to support them and had been hard on his son, who was keeping them alive through foraging, hunting, and petty theft.

Sunja had not imagined that a person like Koh Hansu could do his own laundry. His clothes were so fine and beautifully tailored. She had already seen him wear several different white suits and white shoes. No one dressed like he did.

She had something to say.

"When I wash clothes, I think about doing it well. It's one of the chores I like because I can make something better than it was. It isn't like a broken pot that you have to throw away."

He smiled at her. "I have wanted to be with you for a long time."

Again, she wanted to ask why, but it didn't matter in a way.

"You have a good face," he said. "You look honest."

The market women had told her this before. Sunja could not haggle well and didn't try. However, this morning she hadn't told her mother that she was meeting Koh Hansu. She had not even told her about the Japanese students picking on her. The night before, she told Dokhee, who did the laundry with her, that she'd do the wash herself, and Dokhee had been overjoyed to get out of the task.

"Do you have a sweetheart?" he asked.

Her cheeks flushed. "No."

Hansu smiled. "You are almost seventeen. I'm thirty-four. I am exactly twice your age. I am going to be your elder brother and your friend. Hansu-oppa. Would you like that?"

Sunja stared at his black eyes, thinking that she had never wanted any-

thing more except for the time she'd wanted her father to recover from his illness. There wasn't a day when she didn't think of her father or hear his voice in her head.

"When do you do your wash?"

"Every third day."

"This time?"

She nodded. Sunja breathed deeply, her lungs and heart filling with anticipation and wonder. She had always loved this beach—the unending expanse of pale green and blue water, the tiny white pebbles framing the black rocks between the water and the rocky soil. The silence here made her safe and content. Almost no one ever came here, but now she would never see this place the same way again.

Hansu picked up a smooth, flat stone by her foot—black with thin gray striations. From his pocket, he took out a piece of white chalk that he used to mark the wholesale containers of fish, and he made an X on the bottom of the stone. He crouched and felt about the enormous rocks that surrounded them and found a dry crevice in a medium-sized rock, the height of a bench.

"If I come here and you're not here yet, but I have to go back to work, I'll leave this stone in the hollow of this rock so you'll know that I came. If you're here and I'm not, I want you to leave this stone in the same spot, so I can know that you came to see me."

He patted her arm and smiled at her.

"Sunja-ya, I better go now. Let's see each other later, okay?"

She watched him walk away, and as soon as he was gone, she squatted and opened the bundle to begin the wash. She took a dirty shirt and soaked it in the cool water. Everything had changed.

Three days later, she saw him. It took nothing to convince the sisters to let her do the wash by herself. Again, he was waiting by the rocks, reading the paper. He wore a light-colored hat with a black hatband. He looked elegant. He acted as if meeting her by the rocks was normal, though Sunja was terrified that they might be discovered. She felt guilty that she had not told her mother, or Bokhee and Dokhee, about him. Seated on the black

rocks, Hansu and Sunja spoke for half an hour or so, and he asked her odd questions: "What do you think about when it's quiet and you're not doing much?"

There was never a time when she wasn't doing anything. The boardinghouse required so much work; Sunja could hardly remember her mother ever being idle. After she told him she was always busy, she realized she was wrong. There were times when she was working when it felt like the work was nothing at all, because it was something she knew how to do without paying much attention. She could peel potatoes or wipe down the floors without thinking, and when she had this quiet in her mind, lately, she had been thinking of him, but how could she say this? Right before he had to go, he asked her what she thought a good friend was, and she answered he was, because he had helped her when she was in trouble. He had smiled at that answer and stroked her hair. Every few days, they saw each other at the cove, and Sunja grew more efficient with the wash and housework, so that no one at home noticed how she spent her time at the beach or at the market.

Before Sunja crossed the threshold of the kitchen door to leave the house for the market or the beach, she would check her reflection on the polished metal pot lid, primping the tight braid she'd made that morning. Sunja had no idea how to make herself lovely or appealing to any man, and certainly not a man as important as Koh Hansu, so she endeavored to be clean and tidy at the least.

The more she saw him, the more vivid he grew in her mind. His stories filled her head with people and places she had never imagined before. He lived in Osaka—a large port city in Japan where he said you could get anything you wanted if you had money and where almost every house had electric lights and plug-in heaters to keep you warm in the winter. He said Tokyo was far busier than Seoul—with more people, shops, restaurants, and theaters. He had been to Manchuria and Pyongyang. He described each place to her and told her that one day she would go with him to these places, but she couldn't understand how that would ever happen. She didn't protest, because she liked the idea of traveling with him, the idea of being with him longer than the few minutes they had at the cove. From his

travels, he brought her beautifully colored candies and sweet biscuits. He would unwrap the candies and put one in her mouth like a mother feeding a child. She had never tasted such lovely and delicious treats—pink hard candies imported from America, butter biscuits from England. Sunja was careful to throw away the wrappers outside the house, because she didn't want her mother to know about them.

She was enraptured by his talk and his experiences, which were far more unique than the adventures of fishermen or workers who had come from far-flung places, but there was something even more new and powerful in her relationship with Hansu that she had never expected. Until she met him, Sunja had never had someone to tell about her life—the funny habits of the lodgers, her exchanges with the sisters who worked for her mother, memories of her father, and her private questions. She had someone to ask about how things worked outside of Yeongdo and Busan. Hansu was eager to hear about what went on in her day; he wanted to know what she dreamed about even. Occasionally, when she didn't know how to handle something or someone, he told her what she could do; he had excellent ideas on how to solve problems. They never spoke of Sunja's mother.

At the market, it was strange to see him doing business, for he was this other person when he was with her—he was her friend, her elder brother, the one who'd lift the bundle of laundry from her head when she came to him. "How gracefully you do that," he would remark, admiring how straight and strong her neck was. Once, he touched the nape of her neck lightly with both his thick, square hands, and she sprang from his touch, shocked by the sensation she felt.

She wanted to see him all the time. Who else did he talk to or ask questions of? What did he do in the evening when she was at home serving the lodgers, polishing the low dining tables, or sleeping beside her mother? It felt impossible to ask him, so she kept those questions to herself.

For three months, they met in the same way, growing easier in each other's company. When fall arrived, it was brisk and cold by the sea, but Sunja hardly felt the chilly air.

Early September, it rained for five days straight, and when it finally

cleared, Yangjin asked Sunja to gather mushrooms at Taejongdae Forest the following morning. Sunja liked mushroom picking, and as she was about to meet Hansu at the beach, she felt giddy that she could tell him she was going to do something different from her regular chores. He traveled and saw new things often; this was the first time she was doing something out of her normal routine.

In her excitement, she blurted out her plans to pick mushrooms right after breakfast the next day, and Hansu said nothing for a few moments and stared at her pensively.

"Your Hansu-*oppa* is good at finding mushrooms and wild roots. I know a lot about the ones you can eat and the ones you can't. When I was a boy, I spent hours searching for roots and mushrooms. In the spring, I'd look for fernbrake and dry them. I used to catch rabbits for our dinner with a slingshot. Once, I caught a pair of pheasants before dusk—it was the first time we had meat in a long time. My father was so delighted!" His face softened.

"We can go together. How much time do you have to get the mushrooms?" he asked.

"You want to go?"

It was one thing to talk to him twice a week for half an hour, but she couldn't imagine spending a day with him. What would happen if someone saw them together? Sunja's face felt hot. What was she supposed to do? She had told him, and she couldn't keep him from going.

"I'll meet you here. I better go back to the market." Hansu smiled at her differently this time, like he was a boy, excitement beaming from his face. "We'll find a huge bundle of mushrooms. I know it."

They walked along the outer perimeter of the island, where no one would see them together. The coastline seemed more glorious than it had ever been. As they approached the forest located on the opposite side of the island, the enormous pines, maples, and firs seemed to greet them, decked in golds and reds as if they were wearing their holiday clothes. Hansu told her about living in Osaka. The Japanese were not to be vilified, he said. At this moment in time, they were beating the Koreans, and of course,

no one liked losing. He believed that if the Koreans could stop quarreling with each other, they could probably take over Japan and do much worse things to the Japanese instead.

"People are rotten everywhere you go. They're no good. You want to see a very bad man? Make an ordinary man successful beyond his imagination. Let's see how good he is when he can do whatever he wants."

Sunja nodded as he spoke, trying to remember his every word, to hold on to his every image, and to grasp whatever he was trying to tell her. She treasured his stories like the beach glass and rose-colored stones she used to collect as a girl—his words astonished her because he was taking her by the hand and showing her new, unforgettable things.

Of course, there were many subjects and ideas she didn't understand, and sometimes just trying to learn it all without experiencing it was difficult. Yet she crammed her mind the way she might have overfilled a pig intestine with blood sausage stuffing. She tried hard to figure things out because she didn't want him to think she was ignorant. Sunja didn't know her letters in either Korean or Japanese. Her father had taught her some addition and subtraction so she could count money, but that was all. Both she and her mother could not even write their names.

Hansu had brought a large kerchief so he could gather mushrooms as well. His obvious delight at their excursion made her feel better, but Sunja was still worried that someone would see them. No one knew they were friends. Men and women were not supposed to be that, and they were not sweethearts, either. He had never mentioned marriage, and if he wanted to marry her, he would have to speak to her mother, but he had not. In fact, after he asked her if she had a sweetheart three months before, he'd never raised the subject again. She tried not to think about what his life was like with women. It would not have been difficult for him to find a girl to be with, and his interest in her did not always make sense.

The long walk to the forest felt brief, and when they entered the woods, it felt even more isolated than the cove, but unlike the openness of the low rocks and the expanse of blue-green water, immense trees stood high above them, and it was like entering the dark, leafy house of a giant. She could hear birds, and she looked up and about to see what

kind they were. She noticed Hansu's face: There were tears in his eyes.

"*Oppa*, are you all right?"

He nodded. He had talked for the entire length of the walk about traveling and work, yet at the sight of the colored leaves and bumpy tree trunks, Hansu fell silent. He placed his right hand on her back and touched the end of her hair braid. He stroked her back, then removed his hand carefully.

Hansu had not been in a forest since he was a boy—that time before he became a tough teenager who could hustle and steal with the wisest street kids of Osaka. Before he moved to Japan, the wooded mountains of Jeju had been his sanctuary; he had known every tree on the volcano Halla-san. He recalled the small deer with their slender legs and mincing, flirtatious steps. The heavy scent of orange blossoms came back to him, though there were no such things in the woods of Yeongdo.

"Let's go," he said, walking ahead, and Sunja followed him. Less than a dozen paces in, he stopped to pluck a mushroom gently from the ground. "That's our first," he said, no longer crying.

He had not lied to her. Hansu was an expert at finding mushrooms, and he found numerous edible weeds for her, even explaining how to cook them.

"When you're hungry, you'll learn what you can eat and what you cannot." He laughed. "I don't like being hungry. So, where's your spot? Which way?"

"A few minutes from here—it's where my mother used to pick them after a heavy rain when she was a girl. She's from this side of the island."

"Your basket is not large enough. You could have brought two and had plenty to dry for the winter! You might have to return tomorrow."

Sunja smiled at him. "But, *Oppa*, you haven't even seen the spot!"

When they reached her mother's mushroom spot, it was carpeted with the brown mushrooms that her father had adored.

He laughed, as pleased as he could be. "Didn't I tell you? We should have brought something to make supper with. Next time, let's plan to have lunch here. This is too easy!" Immediately, he began to gather mushrooms by the handful and threw them into the basket on the ground

between them. When it grew full, he put more into his handkerchief, and when that was heaping, she untied the apron around her waist and gathered more.

"I don't know how I will carry them all," she said. "I'm being greedy."

"You are not greedy enough."

Hansu moved toward her. She could smell his soap and the wintergreen of his hair wax. He was cleanly shaven and handsome. She loved how white his clothes were. Why did such a thing matter? The men at the boardinghouse could not help being filthy. Their work dirtied all their things, and no amount of scrubbing would get the fish smell off their shirts and pants. Her father had taught her not to judge people on such shallow points: What a man wore or owned had nothing to do with his heart and character. She inhaled deeply, his scent mingled with the cleansing air of the forest.

Hansu slid his hands beneath her short traditional blouse, and she did not stop him. He untied the long sash that held her blouse together and opened it. Sunja started to cry quietly, and he pulled her toward him and held her, making low, soothing sounds, and she allowed him to comfort her as he did what he wanted. He lowered her on the ground tenderly.

"*Oppa* is here. It's all right. It's all right."

He had his hands firmly under her buttocks the entire time, and though he had tried to shield her from the twigs and leaves, bits of the forest had made red welts on the backs of her legs. When they separated, he used his handkerchief to clean the blood.

"Your body is pretty. Full of juice like a ripened fruit."

Sunja couldn't say anything. She had suckled him like an infant. While he was moving inside her, doing this thing that she had witnessed pigs and horses doing, she was stunned by how sharp and bright the pain was and was grateful that the ache subsided.

When they rose from the carpet of yellow and red leaves, he helped to straighten her undergarments, and he dressed her.

"You are my dear girl."

This was what he told her when they did this again.

6

Hansu had gone to Japan for business. He promised there would be a surprise for her when he returned. Sunja thought it would only be a matter of time before he would speak to her of marriage. She belonged to him, and she wanted to be his wife. She didn't want to leave her mother, but if she had to move to Osaka to be with him, she would go. Throughout the day, she wondered what he was doing at that moment. When she imagined his life away from her, she felt like she was part of something else, something outside of Yeongdo, outside of Busan, and now outside of Korea even. How was it possible that she had lived without knowing anything else beyond her father and mother? Yet that was all she had known. It was right for a girl to marry and bear children, and when she didn't menstruate, Sunja was pleased that she would give him a child.

She counted the days until his return, and if there had been a clock in the house, she would have measured the hours and minutes. On the morning of his return, Sunja hurried to the market. She walked by the brokers' offices until he spotted her, and in his discreet way, he set a meeting time at the cove for the following morning.

As soon as the lodgers left for work, Sunja gathered the laundry and ran to the beach, unable to wait any longer. When she saw her sweetheart waiting beside the rocks, wearing a handsome overcoat over his suit, she felt proud that a man like this had chosen her.

Unlike the other times, when she would approach him in careful, lady-

like steps, today she rushed to him impatiently with the bundle of laundry clutched in her arms.

"*Oppa!* You're back!"

"I told you—I always return." He embraced her tightly.

"I'm so happy to see you."

"How is my girl?"

She beamed in his presence.

"I hope you won't go away again too soon."

"Close your eyes," he said, and she obeyed him.

He opened her right hand and placed a thick disc in her palm. The metal felt cool in her hand.

"It's just like yours," she said, opening her eyes. Hansu had a heavy gold pocket watch from England. Similarly sized, hers was made of silver with a gold wash, he said. A while back, he'd taught her the difference between the long hand and the short and how to tell time. His watch hung from a solid gold chain with a T-bar that went through his vest buttonhole.

"You press this." Hansu pushed the crown and the pocket watch opened to reveal an elegant white face with curved numerals.

"This is the most beautiful thing I have ever seen. *Oppa,* thank you. Thank you so much. Where did you get it?" She could not imagine a store where they'd sell such things.

"If you have money, there's nothing you can't have. I had it ordered for you from London. Now we can know exactly when we will meet."

She couldn't imagine being happier than she was at that moment.

Hansu stroked her face and pulled her toward him.

"I want to see you."

She lowered her gaze and opened her blouse. The night before, she had bathed in hot water, scrubbing every pore of her body until her skin was red.

He took the watch from her hand and looped the thin sash of her slip through its hook.

"I'll order a proper chain and pin the next time I am in Osaka."

He pushed down her inner slip to expose her breasts and put his mouth over her. He opened her long skirt.

Her shock at the urgency of his needs had diminished somewhat since the first time they made love. They had been together many times, and by now, the pain was not as great as it had been for her initially. What Sunja liked about lovemaking was the gentle touching as well as the powerful desires of his body. She liked how his face changed from grave to innocent in those moments.

When it ended, she closed her blouse. In a few moments, he would have to return to work and she would wash the boardinghouse linens.

"I am carrying your child."

He opened his eyes and paused.

"Are you certain?"

"Yes, I think so."

"Well." He smiled.

She smiled in return, feeling proud of what they had done together.

"Sunja—"

"*Oppa?*" She studied his serious face.

"I have a wife and three children. In Osaka."

Sunja opened her mouth, then closed it. She could not imagine him being with someone else.

"I will take good care of you, but I cannot marry you. My marriage is already registered in Japan. There are work implications," he said, frowning. "I will do whatever I can to make sure we are together. I had been planning on finding a good house for you."

"A house?"

"Near your mother. Or if you want, it can be in Busan. It'll be winter soon, and we can't keep meeting outside." He laughed. He rubbed her upper arms, and she flinched.

"Is that why you went to Osaka? To see your—"

"I have been married since I was a boy nearly. I have three daughters," Hansu said. His girls were neither terribly clever nor interested in much of anything, but they were sweet and simple. One was pretty enough to marry, and the others were too skinny like their nervous mother, who looked fragile and perpetually bothered.

"Maybe it's a son you're carrying!" He couldn't help but smile at the

thought. "How do you feel? Is there anything you feel like eating?" He pulled out his wallet and withdrew a stack of yen bills. "You should buy whatever you want to eat. Also, you'll need more fabric for clothing for yourself and for the child."

She stared at the money but didn't reach for it. Her hands hung by her side. He sounded increasingly excited.

"Do you feel different?" He put his hands on her stomach and laughed with delight.

Hansu's wife, who was two years older than he was, hadn't been pregnant in years; they rarely made love. As recently as a year ago, when he had a string of mistresses, none had even missed a period, so he hadn't given much thought to Sunja having a child. Hansu had planned on getting Sunja a small house before winter, but now he'd find something much larger. The girl was young and obviously fertile, so he realized they could have more children. He felt happy at the prospect of having a woman and children in Korea. He was no longer a young man, but his desires for lovemaking had not declined with age. While he'd been away, he'd masturbated thinking about her. Hansu did not believe that man was designed to have sex with only one woman; marriage was unnatural to him, but he would never abandon a woman who had borne him children. He thought a man may need a number of women, but he found that he preferred this one girl. He loved the sturdiness of Sunja's body, the fullness of her bosom and hips. Her soft face comforted him, and he had come to depend on her innocence and adoration. After being with her, Hansu felt like there was little he couldn't do. It was true after all: Being with a young girl made a man feel like a boy again. He pressed the money into Sunja's hand, but she let the bills drop and scatter on the beach. Hansu bent down to pick them up.

"What are you doing?" He raised his voice a little.

Sunja looked away from him. He was saying something, but she couldn't hear what it was. It was as if her mind would no longer interpret his words with meaning. His talk was just sounds, beats of noise. Nothing made sense. He had a wife and three daughters in Japan? Since she had met him, he had been straightforward, she supposed. Every promise he'd

ever made had been kept. He said there would be a surprise, and he had brought a watch for her, but the surprise she had for him, she no longer wanted him to know. Nothing about him had ever made her suspect that he was a *jebi*—a kind of man who could flit from one woman to another. Did he make love to his wife, too? What did she know about men, anyway?

What was the wife like? Sunja wanted to know. Was she beautiful? Was she kind? Sunja could not look at his face anymore. She glanced at her white muslin skirt, its tattered hem remaining gray no matter how much she tried to clean it.

"Sunja, when can I go to speak to your mother? Should we go speak to her now? Does she know about the baby?"

It felt like a slap when he mentioned her mother.

"My mother?"

"Yes, have you told her?"

"No. No, I have not told her." Sunja tried not to think of her mother.

"I will buy that boardinghouse for you, and your mother and you won't have to keep lodgers anymore. You could just take care of the child. We could have more children. You could get a much bigger house if you like."

The bundle of laundry by her foot seemed to glow in the sun. There was work to do for the day. She was a foolish peasant girl who'd let a man take her on the grounds of a forest. When he had wanted her in the open air of the beach, she had let him have her body as much as he liked. But she had believed that he loved her as she loved him. If he did not marry her, she was a common slut who would be disgraced forever. The child would be another no-name bastard. Her mother's boardinghouse would be contaminated by her shame. There was a baby inside her belly, and this child would not have a real father like the one she'd had.

"I will never see you again," she said.

"What?" Hansu smiled in disbelief. He put his arms on her shoulders, and she shrugged him off.

"If you ever come near me again, I will kill myself. I may have behaved like a whore—" Sunja couldn't speak anymore. She could see her father so clearly: his beautiful eyes, broken lip, his hunched and delayed gait.

When he finished his long day's work, he would carve her dolls out of dried corncobs and branches. If there was a brass coin left in his pocket, he'd buy her a piece of taffy. It was better that he was dead so he would not see what a filthy creature she had become. He had taught her to respect herself, and she had not. She had betrayed her mother and father, who had done nothing but work hard and take care of her like a jewel.

"Sunja, my dear child. What is upsetting you? Nothing has changed." Hansu was confused. "I will take excellent care of you and the baby. There is money and time for another family. I will honor my obligations. My love for you is very strong; it is stronger than I had ever expected. I don't say this lightly, but if I could, I would marry you. You are someone I would marry. You and I, we are alike. Our child will be deeply loved, but I cannot forget my wife and three girls—"

"You never told me about them. You made me think—"

Hansu shook his head. The girl had never opposed him before; he had never heard a contrary word from her lips.

"I will not see you again," she said

He tried to hold her, and Sunja shouted, "Get away from me, you son of a bitch! I want to have nothing to do with you."

Hansu stopped and looked at her, needing to reevaluate the girl standing in front of him. The fire in her body had never been expressed in words, and now he knew she could be different.

"You don't care about me. Not really." Sunja felt clear suddenly. She expected him to treat her the way her own parents had treated her. She felt certain her father and mother would have preferred her to have any honest job than to be a rich man's mistress. "And what will you do if the child is a girl? Or what if she is born like my father? With a mangled foot and no upper lip?"

"Is that why you have not married?" Hansu furrowed his brow.

Sunja's mother had never pushed the idea of marriage when many girls in her village had married well before her. No one had come to her mother with proposals, and the lodgers who flirted with her were not serious prospects. Perhaps this was why, Sunja wondered. Now that she was pregnant, it dawned on her that she could give birth to a child who had

her father's deformities. Every year, she cleaned the graves of her siblings; her mother had told her that several had been born with cleft palates. He was expecting a healthy son, but how about if she couldn't produce one? Would he discard them?

"Were you trying to get me to marry you? Because you couldn't marry a normal fellow?"

Even Hansu realized the cruelty of his own words.

Sunja grabbed her bundle and ran home.

7

Pharmacist Chu had grown fond of the pastor from Pyongyang and was pleased to see his recovery. He visited Isak only once a week now, and the young man seemed completely well.

"You're too healthy to be in bed," the pharmacist said. "But don't get up just yet." Chu was seated beside Isak, who was lying flat on a bedroll in the storage closet. The draft from the gaps around the windowsill lifted Chu's white forelocks slightly. He placed the thick quilt over Isak's shoulders. "You're warm enough?"

"Yes. I'm indebted to you and *ajumoni.*"

"You still look too thin." Chu frowned. "I want to see you stout. There's no curve to your face. Don't you like the food here?"

The boardinghouse keeper looked as if she'd been scolded.

"The meals have been wonderful," Isak protested. "I'm eating far more than what I pay in board. The food here is better than at home." Isak smiled at Yangjin and Sunja, who were standing in the hallway.

Chu leaned in to Isak's chest, where he had placed the bell of his stethoscope. The breathing sounded strong and even, similar to the week before. The pastor seemed very fit.

"Make a coughing sound."

Chu listened thoughtfully to the timbre of the pastor's chest. "You've improved for certain, but you've been ill most of your life. And you had tuberculosis before. We need to be vigilant."

"Yes, but I feel strong now. Sir, I'd like to write to my church in Osaka to let them know my travel dates. That is, if you think I can travel. My brother made me promise that I'd get your permission first." Isak closed his eyes as if in prayer.

"Before you left Pyongyang, did your doctor think you could travel all the way to Osaka by yourself?"

"I was told that I could travel, but the doctor and my mother didn't encourage my leaving home. But I was the strongest I'd ever been when I left. But of course, since being here like this—no doubt, I should've listened to them. It's just that the church in Osaka wanted me to come."

"Your doctor told you not to go, but you went anyway." Chu laughed. "Young men can't be locked up, I suppose. So now you want to head out again, and this time you want my permission. How would it look if something happened to you on the way, or if you got sick when you got there?" Chu shook his head and sighed. "What can I say? I cannot stop you, but I think you should wait."

"How long?"

"At least two more weeks. Maybe three."

Isak glanced up at Yangjin and Sunja. He was embarrassed.

"I feel terrible that I've burdened you and put you at risk. Thank God no one has gotten sick. I'm so sorry. For everything."

Yangjin shook her head. The pastor had been a model guest; if anything, the other lodgers had improved their behavior in the proximity of such a well-mannered person. He had paid his bills on time. She was relieved that his health had improved so dramatically.

Chu put away his stethoscope.

"I'm in no rush for you to return home, however. The weather here is better for your lungs compared to the North, and the weather in Osaka will be similar to the weather here. The winters are not as severe in Japan," Chu said.

Isak nodded. The climate had been a major consideration for his parents' consent for Isak to go to Osaka.

"Then, may I write the church in Osaka? And my brother?"

"You'll take the boat to Shimonoseki and then the train?" Chu asked,

making a face. The journey would take a day, two at the most with delays.

Isak nodded, relieved that the pharmacist was signaling that he could leave.

"Have you been going out?"

"Not beyond the yard. You'd said that it wasn't a good idea."

"Well, you can now. You should take a good walk or two every day—each one longer than the one before it. You need to strengthen your legs. You're young, but you've been in bed and in the house for almost three months." The pharmacist turned to Yangjin. "See if he can make it as far as the market. He shouldn't go alone obviously. He could fall." Chu patted Isak on the shoulder before going and promised to return the following week.

The next morning, Isak finished his Bible study and prayers, then ate his breakfast in the front room by himself. The lodgers had already gone out for the day. He felt strong enough to go to Osaka, and he wanted to make preparations to leave. Before heading out to Japan, he had wanted to visit the pastor of a church in Busan, but there had been no chance for that. He hadn't contacted him for fear that he'd stop by and get sick. Isak's legs felt okay, not wobbly as before. In his room, he had been doing light calisthenics that his eldest brother, Samoel, had taught him when he was a boy. Having spent most of his life indoors, he'd had to learn how to keep fit in less obvious ways.

Yangjin came to clear his breakfast tray. She brought him barley tea, and he thanked her.

"I think I'd like to take a walk. I can go by myself," he said, smiling. "It wouldn't be for long. I feel very well this morning. I won't go far."

Yangjin couldn't keep her face blank. She couldn't keep him cooped up like a prized rooster in her henhouse, but what would happen if he fell? The area near her house was desolate. If he walked by the beach and had an accident, no one would see him.

"I don't think you should go by yourself, sir." The lodgers were at work or in town doing things she didn't want to know about. There was no one to ask to accompany him at the moment.

Isak bit his lip. If he didn't strengthen his legs, the journey would be delayed.

"It would be a big imposition." He paused. "You have a great deal of work, but perhaps you can take me for just a short while." It was outrageous to ask a woman to walk with him on the beach, but Isak felt he'd go insane if he didn't walk outside today. "If you cannot go, I understand. I will take a very short walk near the water. For a few minutes."

As a boy, he had lived the life of a privileged invalid. Tutors and servants had been his primary companions. When it was good weather and he wasn't well enough to walk, the servants or his elder brothers used to carry him on their backs. If the doctor wanted him to get air, the blade-thin gardener would put Isak in an A-frame and stroll through the orchard, letting the child pull off the apples from the lower branches. Isak could almost smell the heady perfume of the apples, feel the weight of the red fruit in his hands and taste the sweet crunch of the first bite, its pale juice running down his wrist. He missed home, and he felt like a sick child again, stuck in his room, begging for permission to see the sunlight.

Yangjin was seated on her knees with her small, coarse hands folded in her lap, not knowing what to say. It was not appropriate for a woman to walk with a man who wasn't a member of her family. She was older than he was, so she didn't fear any gossip, but Yangjin had never walked alongside a man who wasn't her father or husband.

He peered into her troubled face. He felt awful for making another imposition.

"You've already done so much, and I'm asking for more."

Yangjin straightened her back. She'd never gone on a leisurely walk on the beach with her husband. Hoonie's legs and back had given him profound pain throughout his brief life—he had not complained of it, but he would conserve his energies for the work he had to get done. How much he must have wanted to run as a normal boy, swallow lungfuls of salty air and chase the seagulls—things nearly every child in Yeongdo had done growing up.

"There is something very selfish in me," he said. "I'm sorry." Isak decided to wait until one of the lodgers could take him out.

Yangjin got up. "You'll need your coat," she said. "I'll get it."

The heavy scent of seaweed, the foamy lather of the waves along the rocky beach, and the emptiness of the blue-and-gray landscape but for the white circling birds above them—the sensations were almost too much to bear after being in that tiny room for so long. The morning sun warmed Isak's uncovered head. He had never been drunk on wine, but he imagined that this was how the farmers must have felt dancing during *Chuseok* after too many cups.

On the beach, Isak carried his leather shoes in his hands. He walked steadily, not feeling any trace of illness within his tall, gaunt frame. He didn't feel strong, but he felt better than he'd been.

"Thank you," he said, without looking in her direction. His pale face shone in the morning light. He closed his eyes and inhaled deeply.

Yangjin glanced at the smiling young man. He possessed an innocence, she supposed, a kind of childlike wholeness that couldn't be hidden. She wanted to protect him.

"You have been so kind."

She dismissed this with a wave, not knowing what to do with his gratitude. Yangjin was miserable. She had no time for this walk, and being outside made the dull weight in her heart take a definable shape; it pressed against her from the inside.

"May I ask you something?"

"Hmm?"

"Is your daughter all right?"

Yangjin didn't answer. As they were walking toward the other end of the beach, she'd been feeling as if she were somewhere else, though she couldn't say where exactly. This place didn't feel like the beach behind her house, just a few paces from her backyard. Being with the young pastor was disorienting, yet his unexpected question broke the gauzy spell. What had he noticed for him to ask about Sunja? Soon, her rising belly would be obvious, but she didn't look very different now. What would the pastor think of this? Did it matter?

"She's pregnant." She said this, and she knew it would be okay to tell him.

"It must be difficult for her with her husband being away."

"She doesn't have a husband."

It wouldn't have been unusual for him to think that the child's father worked in Japan in a mine or a factory.

"Is the man...?"

"She won't say anything." Sunja had told her that the man was already married and had children. Yangjin didn't know anything else. She couldn't tell the pastor, however; it was too shameful.

The woman looked hopeless. The lodgers brought Isak newspapers to read aloud for them, and lately, every story was a sad one. He felt an overwhelming sense of brokenness in the people. The country had been under the colonial government for over two decades, and no one could see an end in sight. It felt like everyone had given up.

"These things happen in all families."

"I don't know what will happen to her. Her life is ruined. It would have been difficult for her to marry before, but now..."

He didn't understand.

"My husband's condition. People don't want that in the bloodline."

"I see."

"It's a difficult thing to be an unmarried woman, but to bear a child without a husband— The neighbors will never approve. And what will happen to this baby who has no name? He cannot be registered under our family name." She had never talked so freely to a stranger. Yangjin continued to walk, but her pace slowed.

Since learning the news, she had tried to think of any possible way to make this easier, but could not come up with anything. Her unmarried sisters couldn't help her, and their father had died long ago. She had no brothers.

Isak was surprised, but not so much. He had seen this before at his home church. You saw all sorts of things in a church where forgiveness was expected.

"The father of the child—he's nowhere to be found?"

"I don't know. She won't speak of him. I haven't told anyone except for you. I know it's your job to counsel people, but we aren't Christians. I'm sorry."

"You saved my life. I would have died if you had not taken me in and nursed me. You've gone far beyond what an innkeeper does for his guest."

"My husband died of this thing. You're a young man. You should live a long life."

They continued to walk, and Yangjin did not seem interested in turning around. She stared at the light green–colored water. She felt like sitting down; she was so tired suddenly.

"Can she know that I know? May I speak with her?"

"You're not shocked?"

"Of course not. Sunja seems like a very responsible young woman; there must be some reason for this. *Ajumoni*, this must feel very terrible now, but a child is a gift from God."

There was no change in Yangjin's sad expression.

"*Ajumoni*, do you believe in God?"

She shook her head no. "My husband said Christians were not bad people. Some were patriots who fought for independence. Right?"

"Yes, my teachers at the seminary in Pyongyang fought for independence. My oldest brother died in 1919."

"Are you political, too?" She looked concerned; Hoonie had told her that they should avoid housing activists because it would be dangerous. "Like your brother?"

"My brother Samoel was a pastor. He led me to Christ. My brother was a brilliant man. Fearless and kind."

Yangjin nodded. Hoonie had wanted independence for Korea, but he believed that a man had to care for his family first.

"My husband didn't want us to follow anyone—not Jesus, not Buddha, not an emperor or even a Korean leader."

"I understand. I do."

"So many terrible things are happening here."

"God controls all things, but we don't understand his reasons. Sometimes, I don't like his actions, either. It's frustrating."

Yangjin shrugged.

"And we know that God causes all things to work together for good to those who love God, to those who are called according to his purpose," Isak said, reciting a favorite verse, but he could see that Yangjin was unmoved, and it occurred to him that she and her daughter could not love God if they did not know him.

"I am sorry that you are suffering. I'm not a parent, but I think parents hurt with their children."

The boardinghouse keeper was lost in her sadness.

"I'm glad you had a chance to walk a little today," she said.

"If you don't believe, I understand," he said.

"Does your family observe *jesa*?"

"No." Isak smiled. No one in his family observed the rituals for the dead. The Protestants he knew didn't, either.

"My husband thought it was unnecessary. He told me so, but I still make his favorite foods and prepare a shrine for him. I do it for his parents and my own. His parents thought it was important. They were very good to me. I clean their graves and the ones for all my dead babies. I talk to the dead although I don't believe in ghosts. But it makes me feel good to speak with them. Maybe that is what God is. A good God wouldn't have let my babies die. I can't believe in that. My babies did nothing wrong."

"I agree. They did nothing wrong." He looked at her thoughtfully. "But a God that did everything we thought was right and good wouldn't be the creator of the universe. He would be our puppet. He wouldn't be God. There's more to everything than we can know."

Yangjin said nothing but felt strangely calmer.

"If Sunja will talk to you, perhaps it can help. I don't know how, but maybe it might."

"I will ask her to walk with me tomorrow."

Yangjin turned back, and Isak walked beside her.

8

After Isak finished the letter to his brother, he rose from the low table and opened the narrow window in the front room. Isak pulled the crisp air deep into his lungs. His chest didn't hurt. Throughout his life, everyone around him had talked about his early death as a certainty. He had been sick as an infant and throughout his youth with serious ailments in his chest, heart, and stomach. Consequently, little had been expected of his future. When Isak graduated from seminary, even he had been surprised that he was alive to see such a day. Oddly enough, all the talk of his inevitable death hadn't discouraged him. He had become almost inured to death; his frailty had reinforced his conviction that he must do something of consequence while he had the time.

His brother Samoel, the eldest son, was never ill, but he had died young. He had been beaten badly by the colonial police after a protest and did not survive the arrest. Isak decided then that he would live a braver life. He had spent his youth indoors with his family and tutors, and the healthiest he had ever been was when he attended seminary while working as a lay pastor for his church back home. While alive, Samoel had been a shining light at the seminary and their home church, and Isak believed that his deceased brother was carrying him now, no different than how he had done so physically when Isak was a boy.

The middle Baek brother, Yoseb, wasn't religious like Samoel or Isak. He had never liked school, and at the first opportunity, he had struck out

for Japan in search of a different life. He had taught himself to be a machinist and now worked as a foreman of a factory in Osaka. He had sent for Kyunghee, the beloved daughter of a family friend, and they were married in Japan. They didn't have any children. It had been Yoseb's idea for Isak to come to Osaka, and he had found him the job at the church. Isak felt certain that Yoseb would understand his decision to ask Sunja to marry him. Yoseb was an open-minded person with a generous nature. Isak addressed the envelope and put on his coat.

He picked up his tea tray and brought it to the threshold of the kitchen. He had been reminded numerous times that there was no need for him to bring his tray to the kitchen, where men were not supposed to enter, but Isak wanted to do something for the women, who were always working. Near the stove, Sunja was peeling radishes. She was wearing her white muslin *hanbok* beneath a dark quilted vest. She looked even younger than her age, and he thought she looked lovely as she focused on her task. He couldn't tell if she was pregnant in her full-bodied *chima*. It was hard to imagine a woman's body changing. He had never been with a woman.

Sunja rushed to get his tray.

"Here, please let me take that."

He handed the tray to her and opened his mouth to say something but wasn't sure how.

She looked at him. "Do you need something, sir?"

"I was hoping to go into town today. To see someone."

Sunja nodded like she understood.

"Mr. Jun, the coal man, is down the street and will be headed to town. Do you want me to ask him to take you?"

Isak smiled. He had been planning on asking her to accompany him, but he lost his courage suddenly. "Yes. If Mr. Jun's schedule permits it. Thank you."

Sunja rushed outside to get him.

The church building had been repurposed from an abandoned wood-frame schoolhouse. It was located behind the post office. The coal man pointed it out to him and promised to take him back to the boardinghouse later.

"I have to run some errands. And I'll mail your letter."

"Do you know Pastor Shin? Would you like to meet him?"

Jun laughed. "I've been to a church once. That was plenty."

Jun didn't like going to places that asked for money. He didn't like monks who collected alms, either. As far as he was concerned, the whole religion thing was a racket for overeducated men who didn't want to do real work. The young pastor from Pyongyang didn't seem lazy, and he had never asked Jun for anything, so he was fine enough. That said, Jun liked the idea of having someone pray for him.

"Thank you for bringing me here."

"It's nothing. Don't be mad because I don't want to be a Christian. You see, Pastor Baek, I'm not a good man, but I'm not a bad one, either."

"Mr. Jun, you're a very good man. It was you who led me to the boardinghouse on the night when I was lost. I was so dizzy that evening, I could barely say my own name. You've done nothing but help me."

The coal man grinned. He wasn't used to being complimented.

"Well, if you say so." He laughed again. "When you're done, I'll be waiting for you across the street at the dumpling stand by the post office. I'll meet you over there after I finish with my errands."

The servant of the church was wearing a patched men's overcoat that was far too large for her tiny body. She was a deaf-mute, and she swayed gently while sweeping the chapel floor. At the vibration of Isak's step, she stopped what she was doing with a jolt and turned. Her worn-down broom grazed her stocking feet, and she clutched on to its handle in surprise. She said something, but Isak couldn't make out what she was saying.

"Hello, I'm here to see Pastor Shin." He smiled at her.

The servant scampered to the rear of the church, and Pastor Shin came out of his office at once. He was in his early fifties. Thick glasses covered his deep-set brown eyes. His hair was still black and he kept it short. His white shirt and gray trousers were well pressed. Everything about him seemed controlled and restrained.

"Welcome." Pastor Shin smiled at the nice-looking young man in the Western-style suit. "What may I do for you?"

"My name is Baek Isak. My teachers at the seminary have written to you, I think."

"Pastor Baek! You're finally here! I thought you'd be here months ago. I'm so pleased to see you. Come, my study is in the back. It's a bit warmer there." He asked the servant to bring them tea.

"How long have you been in Busan? We've been wondering when you'd stop by. You're headed to our sister church in Osaka?"

There was hardly any chance to reply to all his questions. The elder pastor spoke rapidly without pausing to hear Isak's reply. Pastor Shin had attended the seminary in Pyongyang near the time of its founding, and he was delighted to see a recent graduate. Friends who had been at the seminary with him had been Isak's professors.

"Do you have a place to stay? We could fix a room for you here. Where are your things?" Shin felt gleeful. It had been a long time since they'd had a new pastor stop by. Many of the Western missionaries had left the country due to the colonial government's crackdown, and fewer young men were joining the ministry. Lately, Shin had been feeling lonesome. "I hope you will stay awhile."

Isak smiled.

"I apologize for not calling on you sooner. I'd intended to come by, but I was very ill, and I've been recuperating at a boardinghouse in Yeongdo. The widow of Kim Hoonie and her daughter have been taking care of me. The boardinghouse is closer to the beach than the ferry. Do you know them?"

Pastor Shin cocked his head.

"No, I don't know many people on Yeongdo Island. I shall come see you there soon. You look well. A bit thin, but everyone is not eating enough lately, it seems. Have you eaten? We have food to share."

"I've eaten already, sir. Thank you."

When the tea was brought in, the men held hands and prayed, giving thanks for Isak's safe arrival.

"You're preparing to go to Osaka soon?"

"Yes."

"Good, good."

The elder pastor spoke at length about the troubles the churches had been facing. More people were afraid to attend services here and in Japan because the government didn't approve. The Canadian missionaries had already left.

Although Isak knew of these sad developments, he felt ready to face the trials. His professors had discussed the government's opposition with him. Isak grew quiet.

"Are you all right?" Shin asked.

"Sir, I was wondering if we could talk. Talk about the Book of Hosea."

"Oh? Of course." Pastor Shin looked puzzled.

"God makes the prophet Hosea marry a harlot and raise children he didn't father. I suppose the Lord does this to teach the prophet what it feels like to be wedded to a people who continually betray him. Isn't that right?" Isak asked.

"Well, yes, among other things. And the prophet Hosea obeys the Lord's request," Pastor Shin said in his sonorous voice. This was a story he had preached on before.

"The Lord continues to be committed to us even when we sin. He continues to love us. In some ways, the nature of his love for us resembles an enduring marriage, or how a father or mother may love a misbegotten child. Hosea was being called to be like God when he had to love a person who would have been difficult to love. We are difficult to love when we sin; a sin is always a transgression against the Lord." Shin looked carefully at Isak's face to see if he had reached him.

Isak nodded gravely. "Do you think it's important for us to feel what God feels?"

"Yes, of course. If you love anyone, you cannot help but share his suffering. If we love our Lord, not just admire him or fear him or want things from him, we must recognize his feelings; he must be in anguish over our sins. We must understand this anguish. The Lord suffers with us. He suffers like us. It is a consolation to know this. To know that we are not in fact alone in our suffering."

"Sir, the boardinghouse widow and her daughter saved my life. I reached their doorstep with tuberculosis, and they cared for me for three months."

Pastor Shin nodded with recognition.

"That is a wonderful thing they did. A noble and kind work."

"Sir, the daughter is pregnant, and she has been abandoned by the father of the child. She is unmarried and the child will not have a name."

Shin looked concerned.

"I think I should ask her to marry me, and if she says yes, I will take her to Japan as my wife. If she says yes, I would ask you to marry us before we go. I would be honored if—"

Pastor Shin covered his own mouth with his right hand. Christians did such things—sacrificed possessions and their own lives even—but such choices had to be made for good reason and soberly. St. Paul and St. John had said, "Test everything."

"Have you written to your parents about this?"

"No. But I think they would understand. I've refused to marry before, and they had not expected me to do so. Perhaps they will be pleased."

"Why have you refused to marry before?"

"I've been an invalid since I was born. I have been improving the past few years, but I got sick again on the journey here. No one in my family expected me to live past twenty-five. I am twenty-six now." Isak smiled. "If I'd married and had children, I would have made a woman a young widow and perhaps left orphans behind me."

"Yes, I see."

"I should have been dead by now, but I am alive, sir."

"I'm very glad of it. Praise God." Shin smiled at the young man, not knowing how to protect him from his wish to make such a grand sacrifice. More than anything, he was incredulous. If it hadn't been for the warm letters from his friends in Pyongyang attesting to Isak's intelligence and competence, Shin would have thought that Isak was a religious lunatic.

"What does the young woman think of this idea?"

"I don't know. I have yet to speak with her. The widow told me about her daughter only yesterday. And last night before my evening prayers, it occurred to me that this is what I can do for them: Give the woman and child my name. What is my name to me? It's only a matter of grace that I was born a male who could enter my descendants in a family registry.

If the young woman was abandoned by a scoundrel, it's hardly her fault, and certainly, even if the man is not a bad person, the unborn child is innocent. Why should he suffer so? He would be ostracized."

Shin was unable to disagree.

"If the Lord allows me to live, I shall try to be a good husband to Sunja and a good father to this child."

"Sunja?"

"Yes. She's the boardinghouse keeper's daughter."

"Your faith is good, son, and your intentions are right, but—"

"Every child should be wanted; the women and men in the Bible prayed patiently for children. To be barren was to be an outcast, isn't that right? If I do not marry and have children, I would be a kind of barren man." Isak had never articulated this thought before, and this surge of wanting a wife and family felt strange and good to him.

Shin smiled weakly at the young minister. After losing four of his children and his wife to cholera five years ago, Shin found that he could not speak much about loss. Everything a person said sounded glib and foolish. He had never understood suffering in this way, not really, until he had lost them. What he had learned about God and theology had become more graphic and personal after his family had died so gruesomely. His faith had not wavered, but his temperament had altered seemingly forever. It was as if a warm room had gotten cooler, but it was still the same room. Shin admired this idealist seated before him, his young eyes shining with faith, but as his elder, he wanted Isak to take care.

"Yesterday morning, I had begun the study of Hosea, and then a few hours later, the boardinghouse *ajumoni* told me about her pregnant daughter. By evening, I knew. The Lord was speaking to me. This has never happened to me before. I've never felt that kind of clarity." Isak felt it was safe to admit this here. "Has that ever happened to you?" He checked for doubt in the elder pastor's eyes.

"Yes, it has happened to me, but not always so vividly. I hear the voice of God when I read the Bible, so yes, I suppose I understand what you felt, but there are coincidences, too. We have to be open to that. It's dangerous to think that everything is a sign from God. Perhaps God is always

talking to us, but we don't know how to listen," Shin stated. It felt awkward to confess this uncertainty, but he thought it was important.

"When I was growing up, I can remember at least three unmarried girls who were abandoned after becoming pregnant. One was a maid in our house. Two of the girls killed themselves. The maid in our house returned to her family in Wonsan and told everyone that her husband had died. My mother, a woman who never lies, had told her to say this," Isak said.

"This sort of thing happens with greater frequency these days," Shin said. "Especially in difficult times."

"The boardinghouse *ajumoni* saved my life. Maybe my life can matter to this family. I had always wanted to do something important before I died. Like my brother Samoel."

Shin nodded. He had heard from his seminary friends that Samoel Baek had been a leader in the independence movement.

"Maybe my life can be significant—not on a grand scale like my brother, but to a few people. Maybe I can help this young woman and her child. And they will be helping me, because I will have a family of my own—a great blessing no matter how you look at it."

The young pastor was beyond dissuading. Shin took a breath.

"Before you do anything, I would like to meet her. And her mother."

"I'll ask them to come. That is if Sunja agrees to marry me. She doesn't know me really."

"That hardly matters." Shin shrugged. "I didn't see my wife until the wedding day. I understand your impulse to help, but marriage is a serious covenant made before God. You know that. Please bring them when you can."

The elder pastor put his hands on Isak's shoulders and prayed over him before he left.

When Isak returned to the boardinghouse, the Chung brothers were sprawled out on the heated floor. They had eaten their supper, and the women were clearing away the last of the dishes.

"Ah, has the pastor been walking around town? You must be well enough now to have a drink with us?" Gombo, the eldest brother, winked.

Getting Isak to have a drink with them was a joke the brothers had kept up for months.

"How was the catch?" Isak asked.

"No mermaids," Fatso, the youngest brother, answered with disappointment.

"That's a shame," Isak said.

"Pastor, would you like your dinner now?" Yangjin asked.

"Yes, thank you." Being outdoors had made him hungry, and it felt wonderful to want food in his stomach again.

The Chung brothers had no intention of sitting up properly, but they made room for him. Gombo patted Isak on the back like an old friend.

Around the lodgers, especially the good-natured Chung brothers, Isak felt more like a man, not a sickly student who'd spent most of his life indoors with books.

Sunja carried in a low dinner table for him, its small surface covered with side dishes, a piping hotpot brimming with stew, and a generously rounded portion of steamed millet and barley rice.

Isak bowed his head in prayer, and everyone else remained silent, feeling awkward, until he raised his head again.

"So, the good-looking pastor gets far more rice than I do," complained Fatso. "Why should I be surprised?" He tried to make an angry face at Sunja, but she didn't pay him any mind.

"Have you eaten?" Isak lifted his bowl to Fatso. "There's plenty here—"

The middle Chung brother, the sensible one, pulled back the pastor's outstretched arm.

"Fatso ate three bowls of millet and two bowls of soup. This one has never missed a meal. If we don't make sure that he's well fed, he'd chew off my arm! He's a pig."

Fatso poked his brother in the ribs.

"A strong man has a strong appetite. You're just jealous because mermaids prefer me to you. One day, I'm going to marry a beautiful market girl and have her work for me the rest of my days. You can repair the fishing nets by yourself."

Gombo and the middle brother laughed, but Fatso ignored them.

"Maybe I should have another bowl of rice. Is there any left in the kitchen?" he asked Sunja.

"Don't you want to leave some for the women?" Gombo interjected.

"Is there enough food for the women?" Isak put down his spoon.

"Yes, yes, there's plenty of food for us. Please don't worry. If Fatso wants more food, we can bring him some," Yangjin assured him.

Fatso looked sheepish.

"I'm not hungry. We should smoke a pipe." He rooted in his pockets for his tobacco.

"So, Pastor Isak, will you be leaving us soon for Osaka? Or will you join us on the boat and look for mermaids? You look strong enough to pull in the nets now," Fatso said. He lit the pipe and handed it to his eldest brother before smoking it himself. "Why would you leave this beautiful island for a cold city?"

Isak laughed. "I'm waiting for a reply from my brother. And as soon as I feel well enough to travel, I'll go to my church in Osaka."

"Think of the mermaids of Yeongdo." Fatso waved at Sunja, who was heading to the kitchen. "They will not be the same in Japan."

"Your offer is tempting. Perhaps I should find a mermaid to go with me to Osaka."

Isak raised his eyebrows.

"Is the pastor making a joke?" Fatso slapped the floor with delight.

Isak took a sip of his tea.

"It might be better if I had a wife for my new life in Osaka."

"Put down your tea. Let's pour this groom a real drink!" Gombo shouted.

The brothers laughed out loud and the pastor laughed, too.

In the small house, the women overheard everything the men said. At the thought of the pastor marrying, Dokhee's neck flushed scarlet with desire, and her sister shot her a look like she was crazy. In the kitchen, Sunja unloaded the dinner trays; she crouched down before the large brass basin and began to wash the dishes.

9

After she finished cleaning up in the kitchen, Sunja said good night to her mother and retreated to the makeshift bedroom they shared with the servant girls. Normally, Sunja went to bed at the same time as the others, but in the past month, she'd been more tired than she'd ever been; it was no longer possible to wait for them to finish their work. Waking up was no less difficult; in the morning, strong hands seemed to clamp down on her shoulders to keep her from rising. Sunja undressed quickly in the cold room and slipped under the thick quilt. The floor was warm; Sunja rested her heavy head on the lozenge-shaped pillow. Her first thought was of him.

Hansu was no longer in Busan. The morning after she'd left him at the beach, she'd asked her mother to go to the market in her place, claiming that she was nauseous and couldn't be far from the outhouse. For a week, she didn't go to the market. When Sunja finally returned to her usual routine of food shopping for the house, Hansu was no longer there. Each morning that she went to the market, she had looked for him, but he was not there.

The heat from the *ondol* floor warmed the pallet beneath her; all day she had been feeling chilled. Her eyes finally closed, Sunja rested her hands over the slight swell of her stomach. She could not yet feel the child, but her body was changing. Her keener sense of smell was the most noticeable change and hard to bear: Walking through the fish stalls made

her feel sick; the worst was the smell of crabs and shrimp. Her limbs felt puffier, almost spongy. She knew nothing about having a baby. What she was growing inside her was a secret—mysterious even to herself. What would the child be like? she wondered. Sunja wanted to talk about these things with him.

Since Sunja's confession to her mother, neither of them talked again about the pregnancy. Anguish had deepened the lines along her mother's mouth like a frown setting in for good. During the day, Sunja went about her work faithfully, but at night, before she went to bed, she wondered if he thought about her and their child.

If she had agreed to remain his mistress and waited for him to visit her, she would have been able to keep him. He could've gone to see his wife and daughters in Japan whenever he wanted. Yet this arrangement had felt impossible to her, and even in her present weakness, it felt untenable. She missed him, but she couldn't imagine sharing him with another woman he also loved.

Sunja had been foolish. Why had she supposed that a man of his age and position wouldn't have a wife and children? That he could want to marry some ignorant peasant girl was absurd indeed. Wealthy men had wives and mistresses, sometimes even in the same household. She couldn't be his mistress, however. Her crippled father had loved her mother, who had grown up even poorer than most; he had treasured her. When he was alive, after the boardinghouse guests were served their meals, the three would eat together as a family at the same low dinner table. Her father could've eaten before the women, but he'd never wanted that. At the table, he'd make sure that her mother had as much meat and fish on her plate as he did. In the summer, after finishing a long day, he'd tend to the watermelon patch because it was his wife's favorite fruit. Each winter, he'd procure fresh cotton wool to pad their jackets, and if there wasn't enough, he'd claim his own jacket didn't need new filling.

"You have the kindest father in the land," her mother would often remark, and Sunja had been proud of his love for them, the way a child from a rich family might have been proud of her father's numerous bags of rice and piles of gold rings.

Nevertheless, she couldn't stop thinking of Hansu. Whenever she'd met him at the cove, the cloudless sky and jade-colored water would recede from her sight, leaving only the images of him, and she used to wonder how their time together could vanish so quickly. What amusing story would he tell her? What could she do to make him stay even a few minutes longer?

So when he would tuck her in between two sheltering boulders and untie the long sash of her blouse, she let him do what he wanted even though the cold air cut her. She'd dissolve herself into his warm mouth and skin. When he slid his hands below her long skirt and lifted her bottom to him, she understood that this was what a man wanted from his woman. Lovemaking would make her feel alert; her body seemed to want this touch; and her lower parts accommodated the pressure of him. Sunja had believed that he would do what was good for her.

Sometimes, she imagined that if she carried the load of wash on her head and walked to the beach, he'd be waiting for her on that steep rock by the clear water, his open newspaper flapping noisily in the breeze. He'd lift the bundle from her head, tug at her braid gently, and say, "My girl, where were you? Do you know I would have waited for you until the morning." Last week, she'd felt the call of him so strongly that she made an excuse one afternoon and ran to the cove, and of course, it had been in vain. The chalk-marked rock they used to leave behind like a message was no longer in its crevice, and she was bereft because she would have liked to have drawn an X and left it in the hollow of the rocks to show him that she had come back and waited for him.

He had cared for her; those feelings were true. He had not been lying, she thought, but it was little consolation. Sunja opened her eyes suddenly when she heard the servant girls laughing in the kitchen, then quieting down. There was no sound of her mother. Sunja shifted her body away from the door to face the interior wall and placed her hand on her cheek to imitate his caress. Whenever he saw her, he would touch her constantly, like he could not help from doing so; after making love, his finger traced the curve of her face from her small, round chin to the bend of her ears

to the expanse of her pale brow. Why had she never touched him that way? She'd never touched him first; it was he who'd reached for her. She wanted to touch his face now—to memorize the continuous line of his bones.

In the morning, Isak put on his navy woolen sweater over his warmest undershirt and dress shirt and sat on the floor of the front room using a low dining table as his desk. The lodgers had left already, and the house was quiet except for the sounds of the women working. Isak's Bible lay open on the table; Isak had not begun his morning studies, because he couldn't concentrate. In the small foyer by the front room, Yangjin tended to the brazier filled with hot coals. He wanted to speak to her, yet feeling shy, Isak waited. Yangjin stirred the coals using a crude poker, observing the glowing embers.

"Are you warm enough? I'll put this by you." Yangjin got on her knees and pushed the brazier to where he was seated.

"Let me help you," Isak said, getting up.

"No, stay where you are. You just slide it." This was how her husband, Hoonie, used to move the brazier.

As she moved closer, he looked around to see if the others could hear.

"*Ajumoni*," Isak whispered, "do you think she would have me as a husband? If I asked her?"

Yangjin's crinkled eyes widened, and she dropped the poker, making a clanging sound. She picked up the metal stick quickly and laid it down with care as if to correct her earlier movement. She slumped beside him, closer than she'd ever sat next to another man except for her husband and father.

"Are you all right?" he asked.

"Why? Why would you do this?"

"If I had a wife, my life would be better in Osaka, I think. I've written my brother already. I know he and his wife would welcome her."

"And your parents?"

"They've wanted me to marry for years. I've always said no."

"Why?"

"Because I've always been ill. I feel well now, but it's not possible to know how and when I might die. Sunja knows this already. None of this would be a surprise."

"But, you know that she is—"

"Yes. And it is also likely that I'll make her a young widow. And you know that's not easy, but I would be the father. Until I die."

Yangjin said nothing; she was a young widow herself. Her husband was an honest man who had made the best of a difficult birth. When he died, she knew that he had been a very special man. She wished he were here to tell her what to do.

"I didn't mean to trouble you," Isak said, seeing the shock in her face. "I thought it might be something she could want. For the child's future. Do you think she'd agree? Perhaps she intends to stay here with you. Would that be better for her and the child?"

"No, no. Of course it would be far better for them if she went away," Yangjin replied, knowing the hard truth. "The child would have a terrible life here. You'd be saving my daughter's life as well. If you would take care of my daughter, I'd gladly pay you with my life, sir. I'd pay twice if I could." She bowed low, her head almost touching the yellow floor, and wiped her eyes.

"No, you mustn't say that. You and your daughter have been angels."

"I'll speak to her right away, sir. She'll be grateful."

Isak got quiet. He wanted to know how to say this next thing properly.

"I don't want that," he said, feeling embarrassed. "I'd like to ask her, to ask her about her heart. I'd like to know if she could love me one day." Isak felt embarrassed, because it had occurred to him that, like an ordinary man, he wanted a wife who'd love him, not just feel indebted to him.

"What do you think?"

"You should speak to her." How could Sunja not care for a man like this?

Isak whispered, "She's not getting a good bargain. I may fall ill again soon. But I'd try to be a decent husband. And I would love the child. He would be mine, too." Isak felt happy thinking of living long enough to raise a child.

"Please walk with her tomorrow. You can speak to her about all these things."

Her mother told her Baek Isak's intentions, and Sunja prepared herself to be his wife. If Baek Isak married her, a painful sentence would be lifted from her mother, the boardinghouse, herself, and the child. An honorable man from a good family would give the child his name. Sunja couldn't comprehend his reasons. Her mother had tried to explain, but neither thought what they'd done for him was so unusual. They would have done it for any lodger, and he had even paid his fees on time. "No normal man would want to raise another man's child unless he was an angel or a fool," her mother said.

He didn't seem like a fool. Perhaps he needed a housekeeper, yet that didn't seem like him. As soon as the pastor had been feeling better, and even when he wasn't entirely well, he'd carried his finished meal trays to the threshold of the kitchen. In the mornings, he shook out his own bedding and put away the pallet. He did more to care for himself than any of the lodgers. She'd never imagined an educated man from an upper-class family who'd grown up in a household with servants would ever do these things.

Sunja put on her thick coat. She wore straw sandals over two pairs of white cotton socks and waited by the door outside. The air was frigid and misty. In a month or so, it would be spring, but it felt like deep winter still. Her mother had asked the pastor to meet her outside, not wanting the servants to see the two together.

Isak came out momentarily, holding his felt hat.

"Are you well?" Isak stood parallel to her, not knowing where they should go. He'd never been out with a young woman before—not in this way, and never with the intention of asking her to marry him. He tried to pretend that he was counseling a female parishioner—something he had done many times back home.

"Would you like to go into town? We could take the ferry." The suggestion came to him spontaneously.

Sunja nodded and draped her head with a thick muslin scarf to cover her exposed ears. She resembled the women selling fish in the market.

They walked quietly toward the Yeongdo ferry, not knowing what the others who saw them together might think. The boatman accepted their fares.

The wooden boat was mostly empty, so they sat together for the duration of the short trip.

"Your mother spoke to you," Isak said, trying to keep his voice level.

"Yes."

He tried to read her feelings in her young, pretty face. She looked terrified.

"Thank you," she said.

"What do you think of it?"

"I'm very grateful. It's a heavy burden that you've taken off our shoulders. We don't know how to thank you."

"My life is nothing. It wouldn't have any meaning without putting it to good use. Don't you think?"

Sunja played with the side edge of her *chima*.

"I have a question," Isak said.

Sunja kept her eyes lowered.

"Do you think you can love God?" He inhaled. "If you could love God, then I know everything will be all right. It's a lot, I think, to ask of you. It might not make sense now. It will take time. I do understand that."

This morning, it had occurred to Sunja that he'd ask her something like this, and she'd given thought to this God that the pastor believed in. Spirits existed in the world—she believed this even though her father had not. After he died, she felt that he was with her. When they went to his grave for the *jesa*, it was easy to feel his comforting presence. If there were many gods and dead spirits, then she felt that she could love his god, especially if his god could encourage Baek Isak to be such a kind and thoughtful person.

"Yes," she said. "I can."

The boat docked, and Isak helped her off. The mainland was very cold, and Sunja tucked her hands into her jacket sleeves to warm them.

The sharp winds cut through their bodies. She worried that the bitter weather would be bad for the pastor.

Neither knew where they should go next, so she pointed to the main shopping street not far from the ferry. It was the only place she'd ever gone with her parents on the mainland. She walked in that direction, not wanting to take the lead, but he did not seem to care about that. He followed her steps.

"I'm glad you'll try—try to love God. It means a great deal. I think we can have a good marriage if we share this faith."

She nodded again, not entirely understanding what he meant, but she trusted that he had a sound reason for his request.

"Our lives will be strange at first, but we'll ask God for his blessing—on us and the child."

Sunja imagined that his prayer would act like a thick cloak to shield them.

Gulls hovered, shrieking loudly, then flew away. She realized that the marriage had a condition, but it was easy to accept it; there was no way for him to test her devotion. How do you prove that you love God? How do you prove that you love your husband? She would never betray him; she would work hard to care for him—this she could do.

Isak paused in front of a tidy Japanese restaurant that served noodles.

"Have you ever had udon?" He raised his eyebrows.

She shook her head no.

He led her inside. The customers there were Japanese, and she was the only female. The owner, a Japanese man in a spotless apron, greeted them in Japanese. The couple bowed.

Isak asked for a table for two in Japanese, and the owner relaxed upon hearing his language spoken so well. They chatted amiably, and the owner offered them seats at the edge of the communal table near the door with no one beside them. Isak and Sunja sat opposite each other, making it impossible to avoid each other's faces.

Sunja couldn't read the hand-painted menus on the plywood walls but recognized some of the Japanese numbers. Office workers and shopkeepers sat on three long tables covered in wax cloths and slurped from their

steaming bowls of soupy noodles. A Japanese boy with a shaved head went around pouring brown tea from a heavy brass kettle. He tipped his head to her slightly.

"I've never been to a restaurant before," she found herself saying, more out of surprise than from a wish to talk.

"I haven't been to many myself. This place looks clean, though. My father said that's important when you eat outside your home." Isak smiled, wanting Sunja to feel more comfortable. The warmth of being inside had brought color to her face. "Are you hungry?"

Sunja nodded. She hadn't eaten anything that morning.

Isak ordered two bowls of udon for them.

"It's like *kalguksu*, but the broth is different. I thought maybe you might like it. I'm sure it's sold everywhere in Osaka. Everything there will be new for us." More and more, Isak liked the idea of having her go with him.

Sunja had heard many stories about Japan from Hansu already, but she couldn't tell Isak this. Hansu had said that Osaka was an enormous place where you'd hardly ever see the same person twice.

As he talked, Isak observed her. Sunja was a private person. Even at the house, she did not talk much to the girls who worked there or even to her mother. Was she always this way? he wondered. It was hard to imagine that she'd had a lover.

Isak spoke to her quietly, not wishing to be heard by the others.

"Sunja, do you think you could care for me? As your husband?" Isak clasped his hands as if in prayer.

"Yes." The answer came quickly because this felt true to her. She cared for him now, and she didn't want him to think otherwise.

Isak felt light and clean inside, as if his diseased lungs had been scoured back to health. He took a breath.

"I expect it will be difficult, but would you try to forget him?" There, he said it. They would not have secret thoughts.

Sunja winced, not having expected him to speak of this.

"I'm not different from other men. I have my pride, which I know is probably wrong." He frowned. "But I'll love this child, and I will love you and honor you."

"I'll do my best to be a good wife."

"Thank you," he said. He hoped he and Sunja would be close, the way his parents were.

When the noodles arrived, he bowed to say grace, and Sunja laced her fingers together, copying his movements.

IO

A week later, Yangjin, Sunja, and Isak took the morning ferry to Busan. The women wore freshly laundered *hanbok* made of white hemp beneath padded winter jackets; Isak's suit and coat had been brushed clean and his shoes polished bright. Pastor Shin was expecting them after breakfast.

Upon their arrival, the church servant recognized Isak and led them to Pastor Shin's office.

"You're here," the elder pastor said, rising from his seat on the floor. He spoke with a northern accent. "Come in, come in." Yangjin and Sunja bowed deeply. They'd never been inside a church before. Pastor Shin was a thin man whose clothes were too big for him. The sleeve hems on his aging black suit were frayed, but the white collar at his throat was clean and well starched. His unwrinkled dark clothes appeared to flatten the bent C-curve of his shoulders.

The servant girl brought three floor cushions for the guests and laid them near the brazier in the center of the poorly heated room.

The three guests stood awkwardly until Pastor Shin took his seat. Isak was seated beside Pastor Shin, and Yangjin and Sunja opposite the elder minister.

Once they were seated, no one spoke, waiting for Pastor Shin to lead the meeting with a prayer. After he finished, the elder pastor took his time to assess the young woman whom Isak planned to marry. He'd been thinking a great deal about her since the young pastor's last visit. In preparation

for the interview, Shin had even reread the Book of Hosea. The elegant young man in his charcoal woolen suit contrasted dramatically with the stocky girl—Sunja's face was round and plain, and her eyes were lowered either in modesty or shame. Nothing in her prosaic appearance conjured up the harlot the prophet Hosea had been forced to marry. She was, in fact, unremarkable in her manner. Pastor Shin didn't believe in reading faces to determine a person's fate as his own father had, but if he were to filter her destiny through his father's eyes, it didn't look as if her life would be easy, but neither was it cursed. He glanced at her stomach, but he couldn't tell her condition under the full *chima* and her coat.

"How do you feel about going to Japan with Isak?" the elder pastor asked Sunja.

Sunja looked up, then looked down. She wasn't sure what it was that ministers did exactly or how they exercised their powers. Pastor Shin and Pastor Isak weren't likely to fall into spells like male shamans or chant like monks.

"I'd like to hear what you think," Shin said, his body leaning in toward her. "Please say something. I wouldn't want you to leave my office without my having heard your voice."

Isak smiled at the women, not knowing what to make of the elder pastor's stern tone of voice. He wanted to assure them that the pastor was well-meaning.

Yangjin placed her hand gently on her daughter's knee. She'd expected some sort of questioning but she hadn't realized until now that Pastor Shin thought badly of them.

"Sunja-ya, tell Pastor Shin what you think about marrying Baek Isak," Yangjin said.

Sunja opened her mouth, then closed it. She opened it again, her voice tremulous.

"I'm very grateful. To Pastor Baek for his painful sacrifice. I will work very hard to serve him. I will do whatever I can to make his life in Japan better."

Isak frowned; he could see why she'd say this, but all the same, Sunja's sentiment saddened him.

"Yes." The elder pastor clasped his hands together. "This is indeed a painful sacrifice. Isak is a fine young man from a good family, and it cannot be easy for him to undertake this marriage, given your situation."

Isak lifted his right hand slightly in a weak protest, but he kept quiet in deference to his elder. If Pastor Shin refused to marry them, his parents and teachers would be troubled.

Pastor Shin said to Sunja, "You've brought this condition upon yourself; is this not true?"

Isak couldn't bear to look at her hurt expression and wanted to take the women back to the boardinghouse.

"I made a serious mistake. I'm very sorry for what I have done to my mother and for the burden I made for the good pastor." Tears filled Sunja's dark eyes. She looked even younger than she normally did.

Yangjin took her daughter's hand and held it, not knowing if it was right or wrong; she broke into sobs herself.

"Pastor Shin, she is suffering so much already," Isak blurted out.

"She must recognize her sin and wish to be forgiven. If she asks, our Lord will forgive her." Shin said each word thoughtfully.

"I suppose she would want that." Isak had not wanted Sunja to turn to God in this way. Love for God, he'd thought, should come naturally and not out of fear of punishment.

Pastor Shin looked hard at Sunja.

"Do you, Sunja? Do you want to be forgiven for your sin?" Pastor Shin didn't know if the girl knew what sin was. In the young man's exuberance to be a kind of martyr or prophet, had Isak explained any of this to her? How could he marry a sinful woman who would not turn from sin? And yet this was precisely what God had asked the prophet Hosea to do. Did Isak understand this?

"To have been with a man without marrying is a sin in the eyes of God. Where is this man? Why must Isak pay for your sin?" Shin asked.

Sunja tried to mop up the tears on her flushed cheeks using her jacket sleeve.

In the corner, the deaf servant girl could make out some of what was being said by reading their lips. She withdrew a clean cloth from her over-

coat pocket and gave it to Sunja. She gestured to Sunja to wipe her face, and Sunja smiled at her.

Pastor Shin sighed. Although he didn't want to upset the girl any further, he felt compelled to protect the earnest young minister.

"Where is the father of your child, Sunja?" Pastor Shin asked.

"She does not know, Pastor Shin," Yangjin replied, though she was curious to know the answer herself. "She's very sorry for this." Yangjin turned to her daughter: "Tell the pastor—tell him that you want forgiveness from the Lord."

Neither Yangjin nor Sunja knew what that would mean. Would there be a ritual like when you gave the shaman a sow and money to make the crops grow? Baek Isak had never once mentioned this thing about forgiveness.

"Could you? Could you forgive me?" Sunja asked the older minister.

Pastor Shin felt pity for the child.

"Sunja, it's not up to me to forgive you," he replied.

"I don't understand," she said, finally looking directly at Pastor Shin's face, unable to keep her eyes lowered. Her nose was running.

"Sunja, all you have to do is ask the Lord to forgive you. Jesus has paid our debts, but you still have to ask for forgiveness. Promise that you'll turn from sin. Repent, child, and sin no more." Pastor Shin could sense that she wanted to learn. He felt something inside, and he was reminded of the infant within her who had done nothing wrong. Then Shin recalled Gomer, Hosea's harlot wife, who remained unrepentant and later cheated on him again. He frowned.

"I'm very sorry," Sunja repeated. "I won't do it again. I will never be with another man."

"It makes sense that you'd want to marry this young man. Yes, he wants to marry you and to take care of the child, but I don't know if this is prudent. I worry that he is perhaps too idealistic. His family isn't here, and I need to make sure that he will be all right."

Sunja nodded in agreement, her sobs subsiding.

Yangjin gulped, having feared this ever since Baek Isak had mentioned that they'd need to speak with Pastor Shin.

"Pastor Shin, I believe Sunja will be a good wife," Isak pleaded. "Please

marry us, sir. I'd like your blessing. You speak from deep and wise concern, but I believe this is the Lord's wish. I believe this marriage will benefit me as much as it will benefit Sunja and the child."

Pastor Shin exhaled.

"Do you know how difficult it is to be a pastor's wife?" he asked Sunja.

Sunja shook her head no. Her breathing was more normal now.

"Have you told her?" he asked Isak.

"I'll be the associate pastor. I don't expect that much will be expected of her. The congregation isn't large. Sunja is a hard worker and learns quickly," Isak said. He had not thought much about this, however. The pastor's wife at his home church in Pyongyang had been a great lady, a tireless woman who'd borne eight children, worked alongside her husband to care for orphans and to serve the poor. When she died, the parishioners had wailed as if they'd lost their own mother.

Isak, Sunja, and Yangjin sat quietly, not knowing what else to do.

"You must swear that you'll be faithful to this man. If you're not, you'll bring far greater shame on your mother and your dead father than what you've already done. You must ask the Lord for forgiveness, child, and ask Him for faith and courage as you make your new home in Japan. Be perfect, child. Every Korean must be on his best behavior over there. They think so little of us already. You cannot give them any room to think worse of us. One bad Korean ruins it for thousands of others. And one bad Christian hurts tens of thousands of Christians everywhere, especially in a nation of unbelievers. Do you understand my meaning?"

"I want to," she said. "And I want to be forgiven, sir."

Pastor Shin got on bended knees and placed his right hand on her shoulder. He prayed at length for her and Isak. When he finished, he got up and made the couple rise and married them. The ceremony was over in minutes.

While Pastor Shin went with Isak and Sunja to the municipal offices and the local police station to register their marriage, Yangjin made her way to the shopping street, her steps rapid and deliberate. She felt like running. At the wedding ceremony, there were many words she had not

understood. It was preposterous and ungrateful for her to have wished for a better outcome under the circumstances, but Yangjin, no matter how practical her nature, had hoped for something nicer for her only child. Although it made sense to marry at once, she hadn't known that the wedding would take place today. Her own perfunctory wedding had taken minutes, also. Perhaps it didn't matter, she told herself.

When Yangjin reached the sliding door of the rice shop, she knocked on the wide frame of the entrance prior to entering. The store was empty of customers. A striped cat was slinking about the rice seller's straw shoes and purring happily.

"*Ajumoni*, it's been a long time," Cho greeted her. The rice seller smiled at Hoonie's widow. There was more gray in her bun than he remembered.

"*Ajeossi*, hello. I hope your wife and girls are well."

He nodded.

"Could you sell me some white rice?"

"*Waaaaah*, you must have an important guest staying with you. I'm sorry, but I don't have any to sell. You know where it all goes," he said.

"I have money to pay," she said, putting down the drawstring purse on the counter between them. It was Sunja who had embroidered the yellow butterflies on the blue canvas fabric of the purse—a birthday present from two years back. The blue purse was half full, and Yangjin hoped it was enough.

Cho grimaced. He didn't want to sell her the rice, because he had no choice but to charge her the same price he would charge a Japanese.

"I have so little stock, and when the Japanese customers come in and there isn't any, I get into very hot water. You understand. Believe me, it's not that I don't want to sell it to you."

"*Ajeossi*, my daughter married today," Yangjin said, trying not to cry.

"Sunja? Who? Who did she marry?" He could picture the little girl holding her crippled father's hand. "I didn't know she was betrothed! Today?"

"The guest from the North."

"The one with tuberculosis? That's crazy! Why would you let your

daughter marry a man who has such a thing. He's going to drop dead any minute."

"He'll take her to Osaka. Her life will be less difficult for her than living at a boardinghouse with so many men," she said, hoping this would be the end of it.

She wasn't telling him the truth, and Cho knew it. The girl must have been sixteen or seventeen. Sunja was a few years younger than his second daughter; it was a good time for a girl to marry, but why would he marry her? Jun, the coal man, had said he was a fancy sort from a rich family. She also had diseases in her blood. Who wanted that? Though there weren't as many girls in Osaka, he supposed.

"Did he make a good offer?" Cho asked, frowning at the little purse. Kim Yangjin couldn't have given a man like that any kind of decent dowry; the boardinghouse woman would barely have a few brass coins left after she fed those hungry fishermen and the two poor sisters she shouldn't have taken in.

His own daughters had married years ago. Last year, the younger one's husband had run away to Manchuria because the police were after him for organizing demonstrations, so now Cho fed this great patriot's children by selling his finest inventory to rich Japanese customers whom his son-in-law had been so passionate about expelling from the nation. If his Japanese customers refused to patronize him, Cho's shop would shut down tomorrow and his family would starve.

"Do you need enough rice for a wedding party?" he asked, unable to fathom how the woman would pay for such a thing.

"No. Just enough for the two of them."

Cho nodded at the small, tired woman standing in front of him who wouldn't meet his eyes.

"I don't have much to sell," he repeated.

"I want only enough for the bride and groom's dinner—for them to taste white rice again before they leave home." Yangjin's eyes welled up in tears, and the rice seller looked away. Cho hated seeing women cry. His grandmother, mother, wife, and daughters—all of them cried endlessly. Women cried too much, he thought.

His older daughter lived on the other side of town with a man who worked as a printer, and his younger one and her three children lived at home with him and his wife. As much as the rice seller complained about the expense of upkeep of his daughter and grandchildren, he worked hard and did the bidding of any Japanese customer who'd pay the top price because he could not imagine not providing for his family; he could not imagine having his girls live far away—in a nation where Koreans were treated no better than barn animals. He couldn't imagine losing his flesh and blood to the sons of bitches.

Yangjin counted out the yen notes and placed them on the wooden tray on the counter beside the abacus.

"A small bag if you have it. I want them to eat their fill. Whatever's left over, I'll make them some sweet cake."

Yangjin pushed the tray of money toward him. If he still said no, then she would march into every rice shop in Busan so her daughter could have white rice for her wedding dinner.

"Cakes?" Cho crossed his arms and laughed out loud; how long had it been since he heard women talking of cakes made of white rice? Such days felt so distant. "I suppose you'll bring me a piece."

She wiped her eyes as the rice seller went to the storeroom to find the bit he'd squirreled away for occasions such as these.

11

At last, the lodgers had relented and allowed their work clothes to be washed. The smell was no longer bearable even to themselves. Carrying four enormous bundles, Bokhee, Dokhee, and Sunja went to the cove. Their long skirts gathered up and tied, the women crouched by the stream and set up their washboards. The icy water froze their small hands, the skin on them thickened and rough from years of work. With all her might, Bokhee scrubbed the wet shirts on the ridged wooden board while her younger sister, Dokhee, sorted the remainder of the filthy clothing beside her. Sunja was tackling a pair of dark trousers belonging to one of the Chung brothers, stained with fish blood and guts.

"Do you feel different being married?" Dokhee asked. The girls had been the first to be told the news immediately after the marriage was registered. They'd been even more astonished than the lodgers. "Has he called you *yobo*?"

Bokhee looked up from her work for Sunja's reaction. She would've chided her sister's impertinence, but she was curious herself.

"Not yet," Sunja said. The marriage had taken place three days ago, but for lack of space, Sunja still slept in the same room with her mother and the servant girls.

"I'd like to be married," Dokhee said.

Bokhee laughed. "Who'd marry girls like us?"

"I would like to marry a man like Pastor Isak," Dokhee said without

blinking. "He's so handsome and nice. He looks at you with such kindness when he talks to you. Even the lodgers respect him, even though he doesn't know anything about the sea. Have you noticed that?"

This was true. Routinely, the lodgers made fun of upper-class people who went to schools, but they liked Isak. It was still difficult for Sunja to think of him as her husband.

Bokhee slapped her sister's forearm. "You're crazy. A man like that would never marry you. Get these stupid ideas out of your head."

"But he married Sunja—"

"She's different. You and I are servants," Bokhee said.

Dokhee rolled her eyes.

"What does he call you, then?"

"He calls me Sunja," she said, feeling freer to talk. Before Hansu, Sunja had chatted more often with the sisters.

"Are you excited about going to Japan?" Bokhee asked. She was more interested in living in a city than being married, which seemed like a horrible thing. Her grandmother and mother had been more or less worked to death. She had never once heard her mother laugh.

"The men said that Osaka is a busier place than Busan or Seoul. Where will you live?" Bokhee asked.

"I don't know. At Pastor Isak's brother's house, I guess." Sunja was still thinking about Hansu and how he might be nearby. More than anything, she was afraid of running into him. Yet it would be worse, she thought, never to see him at all.

Bokhee peered into Sunja's face.

"Are you afraid of going? You mustn't be. I think you're going to have a wonderful life there. The men said there are electric lights everywhere— on trains, cars, streets, and in all the houses. They said Osaka has all the things you could possibly want to buy in stores. Maybe you'll become rich and you can send for us. We can keep a boardinghouse there!" Bokhee was amazed at such a prospect that she had just invented for them. "They must need boardinghouses, too. Your mother can cook, and we can clean and wash—"

"You think I have crazy thoughts in my head?" Dokhee slapped her sister's shoulder, leaving a wet handprint on her sister's jacket sleeve.

Sunja had difficulty wringing out the wet trousers because they were so heavy.

"Can a minister's wife be rich?" Sunja asked.

"Maybe the minister will make lots of money!" Dokhee said. "And his parents are rich, right?"

"How do you know that?" Sunja asked. Her mother had said that Isak's parents owned some land, but many of the landowners had been selling off their plots to the Japanese to pay the new taxes. "I don't know if we'll have much money. It doesn't matter."

"His clothes are so nice, and he's educated," Dokhee said, not clear as to how people had money.

Sunja started to wash another pair of trousers.

Dokhee glanced at her sister. "Can we give it to her now?"

Bokhee nodded, wanting to take Sunja's mind off leaving. The girl looked anxious and sad, nothing like a happy bride.

"You're like a little sister to us, but you've always felt older because you're smart and patient," Bokhee said, smiling.

"When you're gone, who'll defend me when I get a scolding from your mother? You know my sister won't do anything," Dokhee added.

Sunja laid aside the pants she was washing by the rocks. The sisters had been with her ever since her father had died; she couldn't imagine not living with them.

"We wanted to give you something." Dokhee held out a pair of ducks carved out of acacia wood hanging from a red silk cord. They were the size of a baby's hand.

"The *ajeossi* at the market said ducks mate for life," Bokhee said. "Maybe you can come back home in a few years and bring home your children to show us. I'm good at taking care of babies. I raised Dokhee almost by myself. Although she can be naughty."

Dokhee pushed up her nostrils with her index finger to make a piggy face.

"Lately, you've been looking so unhappy. We know why," Dokhee said.

Sunja was holding the ducks in her hand, and she looked up.

"You miss your father," Bokhee said. The sisters had lost their parents as little girls.

Bokhee's broad face broke into a sad smile. Her tiny, gracious eyes, which resembled tadpoles, pulled downward to meet her knobby cheekbones. The sisters had almost identical faces; the younger one was shorter and slightly plump.

Sunja wept and Dokhee folded her into her strong arms.

"*Abuji*, my *abuji*," Sunja said quietly.

"It's all right, it's all right," Bokhee said, patting Sunja on the back. "You have a kind husband now."

Yangjin packed her daughter's things herself. Every article of clothing was folded with care, then stacked in a broad square of fabric to form a manageable bundle. The fabric corners were tied neatly into a loop handle. In the days before the couple left, Yangjin kept thinking that she'd forgotten something, forcing her to unpack one of the four bundles and repeat the process. She wanted to send more pantry items like dried jujubes, chili flakes, chili paste, large dried anchovies, and fermented soybean paste to give to Isak's sister-in-law, but Isak told her that they could not carry too much on the ferry. "We can purchase things there," he assured her.

Bokhee and Dokhee remained at the house on the morning Yangjin, Sunja, and Isak went to the Busan ferry terminal. The good-byes with the sisters were difficult; Dokhee cried inconsolably, afraid that Yangjin might leave for Osaka and abandon the sisters in Yeongdo.

The Busan ferry terminal was a utilitarian brick and wooden structure that had been built hastily. Passengers, family members who'd come to see them off, and hawkers milled around noisily in the crowded terminal. Immense lines of passengers waited to show their papers to the police and immigration officials before embarking on the Busan ferry to Shimonoseki. While Isak stood in line to speak to the police, the women sat on a bench nearby, ready to spring up in case he needed anything. The large ferry was already docked and waiting for the passengers' inspections to be completed. The algae scent of the sea mingled with the fuel smells

of the ferry; Sunja had been queasy since morning, and she looked sallow and exhausted. She had vomited earlier and had nothing left in her stomach.

Yangjin held the smallest bundle close to her chest. When would she see her daughter again? she wondered. The whole world felt broken. What was better for Sunja and the child no longer seemed to matter. Why did they have to go? Yangjin would not be able to hold her grandchild. Why couldn't she go with them? There must be work for her in Osaka, she reasoned. But Yangjin knew she had to stay. It was her responsibility to care for her in-laws' graves and her husband's. She couldn't leave Hoonie. Besides, where would she stay in Osaka?

Sunja doubled over slightly, emitting a little cry of pain.

"Are you okay?"

Sunja nodded.

"I saw the gold watch," Yangjin said.

Sunja folded her arms and hugged herself.

"Was it from that man?"

"Yes," Sunja said, not looking at her mother.

"What kind of man can afford something like that?"

Sunja didn't reply. There were only a few men left in front of Isak in the line.

"Where is the man who gave you the watch?"

"He lives in Osaka."

"What? Is that where he's from?"

"He's from Jeju, but he lives in Osaka. I don't know if that's where he is now."

"Are you planning on seeing him?"

"No."

"You cannot see this man, Sunja. He abandoned you. He's not good."

"He's married."

Yangjin took a breath.

Sunja could hear herself talking to her mother, yet it felt like she was another person.

"I didn't know he was married. He didn't tell me."

Yangjin sat still with her mouth opened slightly.

"At the market, some Japanese boys were bothering me, and he told them off. Then we became friends."

It felt natural to speak of him finally; she was always thinking of him but there had been no one to talk about him with.

"He wanted to take care of me and the baby, but he couldn't marry me. He said he had a wife and three children in Japan."

Yangjin took her daughter's hand.

"You cannot see him. That man"—Yangjin pointed at Isak—"that man saved your life. He saved your child. You're a member of his family. I've no right to ever see you again. Do you know what that's like for a mother? Soon, you'll be a mother. I hope that you'll have a son who won't have to leave you when he marries."

Sunja nodded.

"The watch. What will you do with it?"

"I'll sell it when I get to Osaka."

Yangjin was satisfied with this answer.

"Save it for an emergency. If your husband asks where you got it, tell him that I gave it to you."

Yangjin fumbled with the purse tucked beneath her blouse.

"This belonged to your father's mother." Yangjin gave her the two gold rings her mother-in-law had given her before she died.

"Try not to sell these unless you have to. You should have something in case you need money. You're a thrifty girl, but raising a child requires money. There will be things you can't expect, like doctor's visits. If it's a boy, you'll need fees for school. If the pastor doesn't give you money for the household, earn something and put aside savings for emergencies. Spend what you need but just throw even a few coins into a tin and forget that you have it. A woman should always have something put by. Take good care of your husband. Otherwise, another woman will. Treat your husband's family with reverence. Obey them. If you make mistakes, they'll curse our family. Think of your kind father, who always did his best for us." Yangjin tried to think of anything else she was supposed to tell her. It was hard to focus.

Sunja slipped the rings into the fabric bag beneath her blouse where she kept her watch and money.

"*Omoni*, I'm sorry."

"I know, I know." Yangjin closed her mouth and stroked Sunja's hair. "You're all I have. Now, I have nothing."

"I will ask Pastor Isak to write to you when we arrive."

"Yes, yes. And if you need anything, ask Isak to write me a letter in plain Korean, and I'll ask someone in town to read it for me." Yangjin sighed. "I wish we knew our letters."

"We know our numbers, and we can do sums. Father taught us."

Yangjin smiled. "Yes. Your father taught us.

"Your home is with your husband," Yangjin said. This was what her father had told her when she married Hoonie. "Never come home again," he'd said to her, but Yangjin couldn't say this to her own child. "Make a good home for him and your child. That's your job. They must not suffer."

Isak returned, looking calm. Dozens of people had been turned away for lack of papers or fees, but Sunja and he were fine. Every item required had been satisfied. The officers could not trouble him. He and his wife could go.

12

Osaka, April 1933

When Yoseb Baek tired of shifting his weight from one foot to the other, he paced about the Osaka train station like a man in a cell. If he'd come with a friend, he would've been able to keep still just by shooting the breeze, but he was alone. Yoseb was an easy talker by nature, and though his Japanese was better than proficient, his accent never failed to give him away. From appearances alone, he could approach any Japanese and receive a polite smile, but he'd lose the welcome as soon as he said anything. He was a Korean, after all, and no matter how appealing his personality, unfortunately he belonged to a cunning and wily tribe. There were many Japanese who were fair-minded and principled, but around foreigners they tended to be guarded. *The smart ones, especially, you have to watch out for those—Koreans are natural troublemakers.* After living in Japan for over a decade, Yoseb had heard it all. He didn't dwell on these things; that seemed pathetic to him. The sentry patrolling Osaka Station had noticed Yoseb's restlessness, but waiting anxiously for a train to arrive was not a crime.

The police didn't know he was a Korean, because Yoseb's manner and dress wouldn't have given him away. Most Japanese claimed they could distinguish between a Japanese and a Korean, but every Korean knew that was rubbish. You could ape anyone. Yoseb wore the street clothes of a modest workingman in Osaka—plain trousers, a Western-style dress shirt, and a heavy woolen coat that didn't show its wear. Long ago, he'd

put aside the finery that he'd brought from Pyongyang—expensive suits his parents had ordered from a tailor who made clothes for the Canadian missionaries and their families. For the past six years, Yoseb had been working as the foreman at a biscuit factory, overseeing thirty girls and two men. For his employment, he needed to be neat—that was all. He didn't need to dress better than his boss, Shimamura-san, who'd made it plain that he could replace Yoseb by morning. Every day, trains from Shimonoseki and boats from Jeju brought more hungry Koreans to Osaka, and Shimamura-san could have the pick of the litter.

Yoseb was grateful that his younger brother was arriving on a Sunday, his only day off. Back home, Kyunghee was preparing a feast. Otherwise, she'd have tagged along. They were both terribly curious about the girl Isak had married. Her circumstances were shocking, but what Isak had decided to do was not at all surprising. No one in the family would have ever been taken aback by Isak's acts of selflessness. As a child, he'd been the kind who'd have sacrificed all his meals and possessions to the poor if allowed. The boy had spent his childhood in his sickbed reading. His abundant meals were sent to his room on a lacquered jujube tray. Yet he remained as slender as a chopstick, though every grain of rice would have been picked off its metal bowl when his tray was returned to the kitchen. Naturally, the servants had never gone without a sizable portion of his meals, which Isak had given away deliberately. Your rice and fish were one thing, Yoseb thought, but this marriage seemed excessive. To agree to father another man's child! His wife, Kyunghee, had made him promise to reserve judgment until they had a chance to get to know her. She, much like Isak, was tenderhearted to a fault.

When the Shimonoseki train arrived at the station, the awaiting crowd dispersed with a kind of organized precision. Porters dashed to help first-class passengers; everyone else seemed to know where to go. A head taller than the others, Isak stood out from the mob. A gray trilby was cocked on his beautiful head, and his tortoiseshell glasses were set low on his straight nose. Isak scanned the crowd and, spotting Yoseb, he waved his bony right hand high in the air.

Yoseb rushed to him. The boy had become an adult. Isak was even thinner than he last remembered; his pale skin was more olive, and radial

lines had surfaced around his gentle, smiling eyes. Isak had their brother Samoel's face; it was uncanny. The Western suit, handmade by the family tailor, hung slack on his drawn frame. The shy, sickly boy Yoseb had left eleven years ago had grown into a tall gentleman, his gaunt body depleted further by his recent illness. How could his parents have let him come to Osaka? Why had Yoseb insisted?

Yoseb wrapped his arms around his brother and pulled him close. Here, the only other person Yoseb ever touched was his wife, and it was gratifying to have his kin so near—to be able to feel the stubble of his brother's face brush against his own ears. His little brother had facial hair, Yoseb marveled.

"You grew a lot!"

They both laughed because it was true and because it had been far too long since they had last seen each other.

"Brother," Isak said. "My brother."

"Isak, you're here. I'm so glad."

Isak beamed, his eyes fixed to his elder brother's face.

"But you've grown much bigger than me. That's disrespectful!"

Isak bowed waist-deep in mock apology.

Sunja stood there holding her bundles. She was comforted by the brothers' ease and warmth. Isak's brother Yoseb was funny. His joking reminded her a little of Fatso, the boardinghouse guest. When Fatso first learned that she'd married Isak, he had pretended to faint, making a *splat* sound on the floor of the front room. Moments later, he took out his wallet and gave her two yen—over two days of a workman's wages—telling her to buy something tasty to eat with her husband when she got to Osaka. "When you're munching on sweet rice cakes in Japan, remember me, lonely and sad in Yeongdo, missing you; imagine Fatso's heart torn out like the mouth of a sea bass hooked too young." He had pretended to cry, rubbing his meaty fists into his eyes and making loud *boo-hoo* noises. His brothers had told him to shut up, and each of them had also given her two yen as a wedding present.

"And you're married!" Yoseb said, looking carefully at the small girl beside Isak.

Sunja bowed to her brother-in-law.

"It's good to meet you again," Yoseb said. "You were just a little thing, though; you used to follow your father around. Maybe you were five or six? I don't think you can remember me."

Sunja shook her head because she had tried but couldn't.

"I remember your father very well. I was sorry to hear about his death; he was a very wise man. I enjoyed talking with him. He didn't have extra words, but everything he said was well considered. And your mother made the most outstanding meals."

Sunja lowered her eyes.

"Thank you for letting me come here, Elder Brother. My mother sends her deepest thanks for your generosity."

"You and your mother saved Isak's life. I'm grateful to you, Sunja. Our family is grateful to your family."

Yoseb took the heavy suitcases from Isak, and Isak took Sunja's lighter bundles. Yoseb noticed that her stomach protruded, but her pregnancy was not entirely obvious. He looked away in the direction of the station exits. The girl didn't look or talk like some village harlot. She seemed so modest and plain that Yoseb wondered if she could have been raped by someone she knew. That sort of thing happened, and the girl might have been blamed for having misled a fellow.

"Where's Sister?" Isak asked, looking around for Kyunghee.

"At home, cooking your dinner. You better be hungry. The neighbors must be dying of jealousy from the smells coming from the kitchen!"

Isak smiled; he adored his sister-in-law.

Sunja pulled her jacket closer to her body, aware of the passersby staring at her traditional dress. No one else in the station was wearing a *hanbok*.

"My sister-in-law's a wonderful cook," Isak said to Sunja, happy at the thought of seeing Kyunghee again.

Yoseb noticed the people staring at the girl. She'd need clothes, he realized.

"Let's go home!" Yoseb guided them out of the station in no time.

The road opposite the Osaka station was teeming with streetcars;

hordes of pedestrians streamed in and out of the main entrances. Sunja walked behind the brothers, who darted carefully through the crowd. As they walked toward the trolley, she turned back for a moment and caught sight of the train station. The Western-style building was like nothing she had ever seen before—a stone and concrete behemoth. The Shimonoseki station, which she'd thought was big, was puny compared to this immense structure.

The men walked quickly, and she tried to keep up. The trolley car was approaching. In her mind, she had been to Osaka before. In her mind, she had ridden the Shimonoseki ferry, the Osaka train, and even the trolley that could outpace a boy running or cycling. As cars drove past them, she marveled that they did look like metal bulls on wheels, which was what Hansu had called them. She was a country girl, but she had heard of all these things. Yet she could not let on that she knew of uniformed ticket collectors, immigration officers, porters, and of trolleys, electric lamps, kerosene stoves, and telephones, so at the trolley stop, Sunja remained quiet and still like a seedling sprouting from new soil, upright and open to collect the light. She would have uprooted herself to have seen the world with him, and now she was seeing it without him.

Yoseb directed Sunja to the only empty seat at the back of the trolley and deposited her there. She took back the bundles from Isak and held them in her lap. The brothers stood close to each other and caught each other up on family news. Sunja didn't pay any mind to the men's conversation. As before, she held her bundles close to her heart and belly to inhale the lingering scent of home on the fabric covering their possessions.

The wide streets of downtown Osaka were lined with rows of low brick buildings and smart-looking shops. The Japanese who had settled in Busan resembled the ones here, but there were many more kinds of them. At the station, there were young men in fancy Western suits that made Isak's clothing look dated and fusty, and beautiful women wearing glorious kimonos that would have made Dokhee swoon with pleasure at their exceptional colors and embroidery. There were also very poor-looking people who must have been Japanese—that was something she had never

seen in Busan. Men spat in the streets casually. The trolley ride felt brief to her.

They got off at Ikaino, the ghetto where the Koreans lived. When they reached Yoseb's home, it looked vastly different from the nice houses she'd passed by on the trolley ride from the station. The animal stench was stronger than the smell of food cooking or even the odors of the outhouses. Sunja wanted to cover her nose and mouth, but kept from doing so.

Ikaino was a misbegotten village of sorts, comprised of mismatched, shabby houses. The shacks were uniform in their poorly built manner and flimsy materials. Here and there, a stoop had been washed or a pair of windows polished, but the majority of the facades were in disrepair. Matted newspapers and tar paper covered the windows from inside, and wooden shims were used to seal up the cracks. The metal used on the roof was often rusted through. The houses appeared to have been put up by the residents themselves using cheap or found materials—not much sturdier than huts or tents. Smoke vented from makeshift steel chimneys. It was warm for a spring evening; children, half-dressed in rags, played tag, ignoring the drunken man asleep in the alley. A small boy defecated by a stoop not far from Yoseb's house.

Yoseb and Kyunghee lived in a boxlike shack with a slightly pitched roof. Its wooden frame was covered with corrugated steel. A plywood panel with a metal covering served as the front door.

"This place is fit for only pigs and Koreans," Yoseb said, laughing. "It's not quite like home, is it?"

"No, but it'll do very well for us," Isak said, smiling. "I'm sorry for the inconvenience we'll be causing."

Sunja couldn't believe how poorly Yoseb and his wife lived. It could not be possible that a foreman of a factory could live in such impoverished quarters.

"The Japanese won't rent decent properties to us. We bought this house eight years ago. I think we're the only Koreans who own a house on this row, but no one can know that."

"Why?" Isak asked.

"It's not good to let on that you're an owner. The landlords here are bastards; that's all everyone complains about. I bought this with the money Father gave me when I moved out here. I couldn't afford to buy it now."

Pig squeals came from the house next door with the tar-papered windows.

"Yes, our neighbor raises pigs. They live with her and her children."

"How many children?"

"Four children and three pigs."

"All in there?" Isak whispered.

Yoseb nodded, raising his eyebrows.

"It can't be that expensive to live here," Isak said. He had planned on renting a house for Sunja, himself, and the baby.

"Tenants pay more than half their earnings on rent. The food prices are much higher than back home."

Hansu owned many properties in Osaka. How did he do that? she wondered.

The side door that led to the kitchen opened, and Kyunghee looked out. She put down the pail she was carrying by the doorstep.

"What! What are you doing standing outside? Come in, come in! *Uh-muh!*" Kyunghee cried out loud. She rushed over to Isak and held his face in her hands. "*Uh-muh*, I'm so happy. You're here! Praise God!"

"Amen," Isak said, letting himself be petted over by Kyunghee, who'd known him since he was an infant.

"The last time I saw you was right before I left home! Go inside the house now!" she ordered Isak playfully, then turned to Sunja.

"You don't know how long I've wanted a sister. I've been so lonely here wanting to talk to a girl!" Kyunghee said. "I was worried that you didn't make your train. How are you? Are you tired? You must be hungry."

Kyunghee took Sunja's hand in hers, and the men followed the women.

Sunja hadn't expected this warmth. Kyunghee had a remarkably pretty face—eyes shaped and colored like persimmon seeds and a beautiful mouth. She had the complexion of white peonies. She appeared far more appealing and vibrant than Sunja, who was more than a dozen years

younger. Her dark, smooth hair was rolled up with a wooden hairpin, and Kyunghee wore a cotton apron over her plain blue Western-style dress. She looked like a wispy schoolgirl more than a thirty-one-year-old housewife.

Kyunghee reached for the brass teakettle resting above the kerosene heater. "Did you get them something to drink or eat at the station?" she asked her husband. She poured tea into four terra-cotta cups.

He laughed. "You said to come home as fast as possible!"

"What a brother you are! Never mind. I'm too happy to nag. You brought them home." Kyunghee stood close by Sunja and stroked her hair.

The girl had an ordinary, flat face and thin eyes. Her features were small. Sunja was not ugly, but not attractive in any obvious way. Her face and neck were puffy and her ankles heavily swollen. Sunja looked nervous, and Kyunghee felt sorry for her and wanted her to know that she needn't be anxious. Two long braids hanging down Sunja's back were bound with thin strips of ordinary hemp. Her stomach was high; and Kyunghee guessed that the child might be a boy.

Kyunghee passed her the tea, and Sunja bowed as she accepted the cup with two shaky hands.

"Are you cold? You're not wearing much." Kyunghee put down a floor cushion near the low dining table and made the girl sit there. She wrapped a quilt the color of green apples over Sunja's lap. Sunja sipped her hot barley tea.

The exterior of the house belied its comfortable interior. Kyunghee, who'd grown up in a household with many servants, had taught herself to keep a clean and inviting house for her and her husband. They owned a six-mat house with three rooms for just the two of them, which was unheard-of in this crowded Korean enclave where ten could sleep in a two-mat room; nevertheless, compared to the grand houses where she and her husband had grown up, their house was absurdly small, not fit for an aging servant. The couple had bought the house from a very poor Japanese widow who had moved to Seoul with her son when Kyunghee arrived to join Yoseb in Osaka. There were many different kinds of Koreans

who lived in Ikaino, and they had learned to be wary of the deceitfulness and criminality among them.

"Never lend anyone money," Yoseb said, looking straight at Isak, who appeared puzzled by this order.

"Can't we discuss these things after they've eaten? They just got here," Kyunghee pleaded.

"If you have extra money or valuables, let me know. We'll put it aside. I have a bank account. Everyone who lives here needs money, clothes, rent, and food; there's very little you can do to fix all of their problems. We'll give to the church—no different than how we were raised—but the church has to hand things out. You don't understand what it's like here. Try to avoid talking to the neighbors, and never ever let anyone in the house," Yoseb said soberly to Isak and Sunja.

"I expect you to respect these rules, Isak. You're a generous person, but it can be dangerous for us. If people think we have extra, our house will be robbed. We don't have a lot, Isak. We have to be very careful, too. Once you start giving, it will never stop. Some people here drink and gamble; the mothers are desperate when the money runs out. I don't blame them, but we must take care of our parents and Kyunghee's parents first."

"He's saying all this because I got us in trouble," Kyunghee said.

"What do you mean?" Isak asked.

"I gave food to the neighbors when I first got here, and soon they were asking us every day, and I was giving away our dinners, and they didn't understand when I had to keep back some food for your brother's lunch the next day; then one day, they broke into our house and took our last bag of potatoes. They said it wasn't them, someone they knew—"

"They were hungry," Isak said, trying to understand.

Yoseb looked angry.

"We're all hungry. They were stealing. You have to be careful. Just because they're Korean doesn't mean they're our friends. Be extra careful around other Koreans; the bad ones know that the police won't listen to our complaints. Our house has been broken into twice. Kyunghee has lost her jewelry." Yoseb stared at Isak again with warning in his eyes.

"And the women are home all day. I never keep money or other valuable things in the house."

Kyunghee said nothing else. It had never occurred to her that giving up a few meals would lead to her wedding ring and her mother's jade hairpin and bracelets being stolen. After the house was broken into the second time, Yoseb was angry with her for days.

"I'll fry the fish now. Why don't we talk as we eat?" she said, smiling, heading to the tiny kitchen by the back door.

"Sister, may I please help you?" Sunja asked.

Kyunghee nodded and patted her back.

She whispered, "Don't be afraid of the neighbors. They're good people. My husband—I mean, your brother-in-law—is right to be cautious. He knows more about these things. He doesn't want us to mingle with the people who live here, so I don't. I've been so alone. I'm so glad you're here. And there will be a baby!" Kyunghee's eyes lit up. "There will be a child in this house, and I'll be an aunt. What a blessing this is."

The heartbreak in Kyunghee's beautiful face was obvious, but her suffering and privation had made her finer in a way. In all these years, there had been no child for them, and Isak had told Sunja that this was all Kyunghee and Yoseb had ever wanted.

The kitchen was no more than a stove, a pair of washtubs, and a workbench that doubled as a cutting board—the space was a fraction of the size of the kitchen in Yeongdo. There was just enough room for the two of them to stand side by side, but they could not move about much. Sunja rolled up her sleeves and washed her hands with the hose in the makeshift sink by the floor. The boiled vegetables had to be dressed, and the fish had to be fried.

"Sunja-ya—" Kyunghee touched her forearm lightly. "We'll always be sisters."

The young woman nodded gratefully, devotion already taking root in her heart. The sight of the prepared dishes made her hungry for the first time in days.

Kyunghee picked up a pot lid—white rice.

"Just for today. For your first night. This is your home now."

13

After dinner, the two couples walked to the public bathhouse, where the men and women bathed separately. The bathers were Japanese mostly, and they refused to acknowledge Kyunghee and Sunja. This had been expected. After scrubbing away the dirt of the long journey and having a long soak, Sunja felt elated. They put on clean undergarments beneath their street clothes and walked home, clean and ready to sleep. Yoseb sounded hopeful—yes, life in Osaka would be difficult, but things would change for the better. They'd make a tasty broth from stones and bitterness. The Japanese could think what they wanted about them, but none of it would matter if they survived and succeeded. There were four of them now, Kyunghee said, and soon five—they were stronger because they were together. "Right?" she said.

Kyunghee linked arms with Sunja. They walked closely behind the men.

Yoseb warned his brother: "Don't get mixed up in the politics, labor organizing, or any such nonsense. Keep your head down and work. Don't pick up or accept any of the independence-movement or socialist tracts. If the police find that stuff on you, you'll get picked up and put in jail. I've seen it all."

Isak had been too young and ill to participate in the March 1 Independence Movement, but many of its founding fathers had been graduates of his seminary in Pyongyang. Many of the seminary teachers had marched in 1919.

"Are there many activists here?" Isak whispered, though no one on the road was nearby.

"Yeah, I think so. More in Tokyo and some hiding out in Manchuria. Anyway, when those guys get caught, they die. If you're lucky, you get deported, but that's rare. You better not do any of that stuff under my roof. That's not why I invited you to Osaka. You have a job at the church."

Isak stared at Yoseb, who was raising his voice.

"You won't give the activists a minute. Right?" Yoseb said sternly. "It's not just you now. You have to think of your wife and child."

Back home in Pyongyang, when Isak had been feeling strong enough to make the journey to Osaka, he had considered reaching out to the patriots fighting against colonization. Things were getting worse at home; even his parents had been selling parcels of their property to pay taxes from the new land surveys. Yoseb was sending them money now. Isak believed that it was Christlike to resist oppression. But in a few months, everything had changed for Isak. These ideals seemed secondary to his job and Sunja. He had to think of the safety of others.

Isak's silence worried Yoseb.

"The military police will harass you until you give up or die," Yoseb said. "And your health, Isak. You have to be careful not to get sick again. I've seen men arrested here. It's not like back home. The judges here are Japanese. The police are Japanese. The laws aren't clear. And you can't always trust the Koreans in these independence groups. There are spies who work both sides. The poetry discussion groups have spies, and there are spies in churches, too. Eventually, each activist is picked off like ripe fruit from the same stupid tree. They'll force you to sign a confession. Do you understand?" Yoseb slowed down his walking.

From behind, Kyunghee touched her husband's sleeve.

"*Yobo*, you worry too much. Isak's not going to get mixed up in such things. Let's not spoil their first night."

Yoseb nodded, but the anxiety in his body felt out of control, and warning his brother—even if it meant sounding hysterical—felt necessary to dissipate some of that worry. Yoseb remembered how good it was before the Japanese came—he was ten years old when the country was colonized;

and yet he couldn't do what their elder brother, Samoel, had done so bravely—fight and end up as a martyr. Protesting was for young men without families.

"Mother and Father will kill me if you get sick again or get into trouble. That will be on your conscience. You want me dead?"

Isak swung his left arm around his elder brother's shoulder and embraced him.

"I think you've gotten shorter," Isak said, smiling.

"Are you listening to me?" Yoseb said quietly.

"I promise to be good. I promise to listen to you. You mustn't worry so much. Your hair will gray, or you will lose what's left of it."

Yoseb laughed. This was what he had needed—to have his younger brother near him. It was good to have someone who knew him this way and to be teased even. His wife was a treasure, but it was different to have this person who'd known you almost from birth. The thought of losing Isak to the murky world of politics had scared him into lecturing his younger brother on his first night in Osaka.

"A real Japanese bath. It's wonderful," Isak said. "It's a great thing about this country. Isn't it?"

Yoseb nodded, praying inside that Isak would never come to any harm. His unqualified pleasure at his brother's arrival was short-lived; he hadn't realized what it would mean to worry about another person in this way.

On their walk home, Kyunghee told Isak and Sunja about the famous noodle shops near the train station and promised to take them. Once they returned to the house, Kyunghee turned on the lights, and Sunja remembered that this was now where she lived. The street outside was quiet and dark, and the tiny shack was lit with a clean, bright warmth. Isak and Sunja went to their room, and Kyunghee said good night, closing the panel door behind them.

Their windowless room was just big enough for a futon and a steamer trunk converted into a dresser. Fresh paper covered the low walls; the tatami mats had been brushed and wiped down by hand; and Kyunghee had plumped up the quilts with new cotton padding. The room had its own kerosene heater, a midpriced model that was nicer than the one in

the main room, where Kyunghee and Yoseb slept, and it emitted a steady, calming hum.

Isak and Sunja would sleep on the same pallet. Before Sunja left home, her mother had spoken to her about sex as if everything was new to her; she explained what a husband expected; and she said that relations were allowed when pregnant. *Do what you can to please your husband. Men need to have sex.*

A single electric bulb hung from the ceiling and cast a pale glow about the room. Sunja glanced at it, and Isak looked up, too.

"You must be tired," he said.

"I'm fine."

Sunja crouched down to open up the folded pallet and quilt on the floor. What would it be like to sleep beside Isak, who was now her husband? The bed was made up quickly, but they were still wearing street clothes. Sunja pulled out her nightclothes from her clothing bundle—a white muslin nightgown her mother had fashioned from two old slips. How would she change? She knelt by the pallet, the gown in her hands.

"Would you like me to turn out the light?" he asked.

"Yes."

Isak pulled the chain cord, and the switch made a loud clicking sound. The room was still suffused with the dim glow from the adjoining room, separated by a paper screen door. On the other side of the thin wall was the street; pedestrians talked loudly; the pigs next door squealed now and then. It felt like the street was inside rather than out. Isak removed his clothes, keeping on his underwear to sleep in—intimate garments Sunja had already seen, since she'd been doing his wash for months. She had already seen him vomit, have diarrhea, and cough up blood—aspects of illness that no young wife should have had to witness so early on in a relationship. In a way, they'd been living together longer and more intimately than most people who got married, and each had seen the other in deeply compromised situations. They shouldn't feel nervous around the other, he told himself. And yet Isak was uncomfortable. He had never slept next to a woman, and though he knew what should happen, he was not entirely sure of how it should begin.

Sunja removed her day clothes. At the bathhouse under the electric lights, she had been alarmed by the darkening vertical stripe reaching from her pubis to the base of her round, sloping breasts. She put on her nightgown.

Like children fresh from their baths, Isak and Sunja slipped quickly beneath the blue-and-white quilt, carrying with them the scent of soap.

Sunja wanted to say something to him, but she didn't know what. They'd started off with him being ill, her having done something shameful, and him saving her. Perhaps here in their new home, they could each begin again. Lying in this room that Kyunghee had made for them, Sunja felt hopeful. It occurred to her that she'd been trying to bring Hansu back by remembering him, but that didn't make sense. She wanted to devote herself to Isak and her child. To do that, she would have to forget Hansu.

"Your family is very kind."

"I wish you could meet my parents, too. Father is like my brother—good-natured and honest. My mother is wise; she seems reserved, but she'd protect you with her life. She thinks Kyunghee is right about everything and always takes her side." He laughed quietly.

Sunja nodded, wondering how her mother was.

Isak leaned his head closer to her pillow, and she held her breath.

Could he have desire for her? she wondered. How was that possible?

Isak noticed that when Sunja worried, she furrowed her brow like she was trying to see better. He liked being with her; she was capable and level-headed. She was not helpless, and that was appealing because, although he wasn't helpless himself, Isak knew that he was not always sensible. Her competence would be good for what his father had once termed Isak's "impractical nature." Their journey from Busan would have been difficult for anyone, let alone a pregnant woman, but she hadn't whimpered a complaint or spoken a cross word. Whenever he forgot to eat or drink, or to put on his coat, she reminded him with no trace of rebuke. Isak knew how to talk with people, to ask questions, and to hear the concerns in a person's voice; she seemed to understand how to survive, and this was something he did not always know how to do. He needed her; a man needed a wife.

"I feel well today. My chest doesn't have that pulling feeling," he said.

"Maybe it was the bath. And that good dinner. I don't remember having eaten so well. We had white rice twice this month. I feel like a rich person."

Isak laughed. "I wish I could get white rice for you every day." In the service of the Lord, Isak wasn't supposed to care about what to eat, where to sleep, or what to wear, but now that he was married, he thought he ought to care about her needs.

"No, no. I didn't mean that. I was just surprised by it. It's not necessary for us to eat such luxurious things." Sunja berated herself privately, not wanting him to think that she was spoiled.

"I like white rice, too," he said, though he rarely gave much thought to what he ate. He wanted to touch her shoulder to comfort her and wouldn't have hesitated if they were dressed, but lying so close and wearing so little, he kept his hands by his sides.

She wanted to keep talking. It felt easier to whisper to him in the dark; it had felt awkward to talk on the ferry or train when all they had was time for longer conversations.

"Your brother is very interesting; my mother had mentioned that he told funny stories and made Father laugh—"

"I shouldn't have favorites, but he's always been my closer sibling. When we were growing up, he was scolded a lot because he hated going to school. Brother had trouble with reading and writing, but he's good with people and has a remarkable memory. He never forgets anything he hears and can pick up most languages after just a little while of hearing it. He knows some Chinese, English, and Russian, too. He's always been good at fixing machines. Everyone in our town loved him, and no one wanted him to go to Japan. My father wanted him to be a doctor, but of course that wasn't possible if he wasn't good at sitting still and studying. The schoolmasters chastised him all the time for not trying hard enough. He used to wish that he was the one who was sick and had to stay home. Schoolmasters came to the house to teach me my lessons, and sometimes he'd get me to do his work for him when he'd skip school to go fishing or swimming with his buddies. I think he left for Osaka to avoid fighting with Father. He wanted to make a fortune, and he knew he'd never be a

doctor. He couldn't see how he'd ever make any money in Korea when honest Koreans were losing property every day."

Neither of them spoke, and they listened to the street noises—a woman yelling at her children to come inside, a group of tipsy men singing off-key, "*Arirang, arirang, arariyo*—" Soon, they could hear Yoseb's snoring and Kyunghee's light, steady breathing as if they were lying beside them.

Isak put his right hand on her belly but felt no movement. She never spoke about the baby, but Isak often wondered what must be happening to the growing child.

"A child is a gift from the Lord," he said.

"It must be, I think."

"Your stomach feels warm," he said.

The skin on the palms of her hands was rough with calluses, but the skin on her belly was smooth and taut like fine fabric. He was with his wife, and he should have been more sure of himself, but he wasn't. Between his legs, his cock had grown to its full measure—this thing that had happened to him each morning since he was a boy felt different now that he was lying beside a woman. Of course, he had imagined what this might be like, but what he hadn't anticipated was the warmth, the nearness of her breath, and the fear that she might dislike him. His hand covered her breast—its shape plush and heavy. Her breath changed.

Sunja tried to relax; Hansu had never touched her like this with such care and gentleness. When she'd met him at the cove, sex was initiated in haste, with her not knowing what it was supposed to mean—the awkward thrusting, his face changing with relief and gratitude, then the need to wash her legs in cold seawater. He used to stroke her jawline and neck with his hands. He had liked to touch her hair. Once, he wanted her to take her hair out of her braids and she did so, but it had made her late in returning home. Within her body, his child was resting and growing, and he could not feel this because he was gone.

Sunja opened her eyes; Isak's eyes were open, too, and he was smiling at her, his hand rubbing her nipple; she quickened at his touch.

"*Yobo*," he said.

He was her husband, and she would love him.

14

Early next morning, using the map his brother Yoseb had drawn for him on a scrap of butcher paper, Isak found the Hanguk Presbyterian Church—a slanted wooden frame house in the back streets of Ikaino, a few steps away from the main *shotengai*—its only distinguishing mark a humble white cross painted on its brown wooden door.

Sexton Hu, a young Chinese man raised by Pastor Yoo, led Isak to the church office. Pastor Yoo was counseling a brother and sister. Hu and Isak waited by the office door. The young woman was speaking in low tones, and Yoo nodded sympathetically.

"Should I return later?" Isak asked Hu quietly.

"No, sir."

Hu, a matter-of-fact sort of person, examined the new minister carefully: Pastor Baek Isak did not look very strong. Hu was impressed by the man's obvious handsomeness, but Hu believed that a man in the prime of his life should have greater physical stature. Pastor Yoo was once a much larger man, able to run long distances and play soccer skillfully. He was older now and diminished in size; he suffered from cataracts and glaucoma.

"Each morning, Pastor Yoo has been asking for any word from you. We didn't know when you'd come. If we'd known that you were arriving yesterday, I would've come to pick you up at the station." Hu was no older than twenty; he spoke Japanese and Korean very well and had the mannerisms of a much older man. Hu wore a shabby white dress shirt with a

blown-out collar, tucked into a pair of brown woolen trousers. His dark blue sweater was knit from heavy wool and patched in places. He was wearing the winter remnants of Canadian missionaries who hadn't had much themselves.

Isak turned away to cough.

"My child, who is that with you?" Yoo turned his head to the voices by the door and pushed up his heavy horn-rimmed eyeglasses closer to his face, though doing so hardly helped to sharpen his vision. Behind the milky gray cast clouding his eyes, his expression remained calm and certain. His hearing was acute. He could not make out the shapes by the door, but he knew that one of them was Hu, the Manchurian orphan who'd been left at the church by a Japanese officer, and that the man he was speaking with had an unfamiliar voice.

"It's Pastor Baek," Hu said.

The siblings seated on the floor by the pastor turned around and bowed.

Yoo felt impatient to end the meeting with the brother and sister, who were no closer to a resolution.

"Come to me, Isak. It's not so easy for me to reach you."

Isak obeyed.

"You have come at last. Hallelujah." Yoo put his right hand lightly over Isak's head.

"The Lord bless you, my dear child."

"I'm sorry to have kept you waiting. I arrived in Osaka last night," Isak said. The elder pastor's unfocused pupils were ringed with silver. He wasn't blind, but the condition was severe. Despite his nearly lost vision, the minister appeared vigorous; his seated posture was straight and firm.

"My son, come closer."

Isak drew near, and the older man clasped Isak's hands at first, then cradled his face between his thick palms.

The brother and sister looked on without saying anything. By the transom of the door, Hu sat on bended knees, waiting for Yoo's next instruction.

"You were sent to me, you know," Yoo said.

"Thank you for allowing me to come."

"I'm pleased that you're here at last. Did you bring your wife? Hu read me your letter."

"She's at home today. She will be here on Sunday."

"Yes, yes." The older man nodded. "The congregation will be so pleased to have you here. Ah, you should meet this family!"

The siblings bowed again to Isak. They'd noticed that the pastor looked happier than they'd ever seen him.

"They've come to see us about a family matter," Yoo said to Isak, then turned to the siblings.

The sister did little to hide her irritation. The brother and sister were from a rural village in Jeju, and they were far less formal than young people from cities. The dark-skinned girl with the thick black hair was wholesome looking; she was remarkably pretty while appearing very innocent. She wore a long-sleeved white shirt buttoned to the collar and a pair of indigo-colored *mompei*.

"This is the new associate pastor, Baek Isak. Should we ask for his counsel, too?" From the tone of Yoo's voice, there was no possibility of the siblings' dissent.

Isak smiled at them. The sister was twenty or so; the brother was younger.

The matter was complicated but not out of the ordinary. The brother and sister had been arguing about money. The sister had been accepting gifts of money from a Japanese manager at the textile factory where she worked. Older than their father, the manager was married with five children. He took the sister to restaurants and gave her trinkets and cash. The girl sent the entire sum to their parents living with an indigent uncle back home. The brother felt it was wrong to take anything beyond her salary; the sister disagreed.

"What does he want from her?" the brother asked Isak bluntly. "She should be made to stop. This is a sin."

Yoo craned his head lower, feeling exhausted by their intransigence.

The sister was furious that she had to be here at all, having to listen to her younger brother's accusations. "The Japanese took our uncle's farm.

We can't work at home because there are no jobs; if a Japanese man wants to give me some pocket money to have dinner with him, I don't see the harm," the sister said. "I'd take double what he gives me if I could. He doesn't give that much."

"He expects something, and he's cheap," said the brother, looking disgusted.

"I'd never let Yoshikawa-san touch me. I sit, smile, and listen to him talk about his family and his work." She didn't mention that she poured his drinks and wore the rouge that he bought for her, which she scrubbed off before coming home.

"He pays you to flirt with him. This is how a whore behaves." The brother was shouting now. "Good women don't go to restaurants with married men! While we work in Japan, Father said I'm in charge and must watch out for my sister. What does it matter that she's older? She's a girl and I'm a man; I can't let this continue. I won't allow it!"

The brother was four years younger than his nineteen-year-old sister. They were living with a distant cousin in an overcrowded house in Ikaino. The cousin, an elderly woman, never bothered them as long as they paid their share of the rent; she didn't come to church, so Pastor Yoo didn't know her.

"Father and Mother are starving back home. Uncle can't feed his own wife and children. At this point, I'd sell my hands if I could. God wants me to honor my parents. It's a sin not to care for them. If I have to be disgraced—" The girl started to cry. "Isn't it possible that the Lord is providing Yoshikawa-san as our answer?" She looked at Pastor Yoo, who took the girl's hands into his and bent his head as if in prayer.

It wasn't uncommon to hear rationalizations of this sort—the longing to transform bad deeds into good ones. No one ever wanted to hear that God didn't work that way; the Lord would never want a young woman to trade her body to follow a commandment. Sins couldn't be laundered by good results.

"*Aigoo*," Yoo sighed. "How difficult it must be to bear the weight of this world on your small shoulders. Do your parents know where you're getting this money?"

"They think it's from my wages, but that barely covers our rent and expenses. My brother has to go to school; Mother told me that it's my responsibility for him to finish. He's threatening to quit his studies so he can work, but that's a foolish decision in the long run. Then we'll always be working these terrible jobs. Without knowing how to read and write Japanese."

Isak was astonished by her clarity; she had thought this through. He was half a dozen years older than she was, and he had not thought of such things. He'd never given his parents one sen of his wages, since he'd never earned money before. When he served briefly as a lay pastor at his church back home, he had gone without a salary because the church had so little for the senior clergy and the congregation had such great needs. He wasn't certain what he would earn here. When he received the call to work at this church, the terms hadn't been discussed; he'd assumed that his compensation would be enough to support him—and now, his family. With money always in his pocket and more readily available when he asked his parents or brother, Isak hadn't bothered to figure out his earnings or his expenses. In the presence of these young people, Isak felt like a selfish fool.

"Pastor Yoo, we want you to decide. She won't listen to me. I cannot control where she goes after work. If she keeps meeting with that goat, he'll do something terrible, and no one will care what happens to her. She'll listen to you," the brother said quietly. "She has to."

The sister kept her head down. She did not want Pastor Yoo to think badly of her. Sunday mornings were very special to her; church was the only place she felt good. She wasn't doing anything wrong with Yoshikawa-san, but she was certain that his wife didn't know about these meetings, and often he wanted to hold her hand, and though it didn't seem harmful, it didn't seem innocent, either. Not long ago, he'd mentioned that she should accompany him to a marvelous *onsen* in Kyoto, but she had demurred, saying she had to take care of her brother's meals.

"We must support our family, this is true," Yoo prefaced, and the sister appeared visibly relieved, "but we have to be careful of your virtue—it is more valuable than money. Your body is a sacred temple where the Holy

Spirit dwells. Your brother's concern is legitimate. Apart from our faith and speaking practically, if you are to marry, your purity and reputation are important, too. The world judges girls harshly for improprieties—and even accidents. It's wrong, but it is the way this sinful world works," Yoo said.

"But he can't quit school, sir. I promised Mother—" the sister said.

"He's young. He can go to school at a later time," Yoo countered, though he knew this was not likely.

At this, the brother perked up; he hadn't expected this suggestion. He hated school—the Japanese teachers thought he was stupid and the kids taunted him daily for his clothes and accent; the brother planned on making as much money as possible so his sister could quit or work elsewhere and so he could send money to Jeju.

The young woman sobbed.

Yoo swallowed and said calmly, "You're right, it'd be better if your brother could go to school. Even for a year or two so he could know how to read and write. There's no better choice than education, of course; our country needs a new generation of educated people to lead us."

The sister quieted down, thinking the pastor might take her side. It wasn't that she wanted to continue seeing Yoshikawa, a silly old man who smelled of camphor, but she believed that her being here in Osaka had a noble purpose, that there was a respectable future for them if she worked and her brother went to school.

Isak listened to Yoo in admiration, observing that the senior pastor was an exceptional counselor, at once sympathetic and powerful.

"Yoshikawa-san doesn't want anything but your company for now, but he may wish for other things later, and you'll find yourself in his debt. You'll feel the obligation. You may fear the loss of your job. Then it may be too late. You may think you're using him, but is that who we are? Shall we exploit because we have been exploited, my dear child?"

Isak nodded in agreement, gratified by the pastor's compassion and wisdom. He wouldn't have known what to say.

"Isak, would you bless these children?" Yoo asked, and Isak began to pray for them.

The brother and sister left without argument and, no doubt, would return on Sunday morning to worship.

The sexton, who had disappeared, returned, bringing three large bowls of wheat noodles in a black bean sauce. The three men prayed before eating. They sat on the floor, their legs crossed, their hot lunches on top of the low dining table that Hu had made from abandoned crates. The room was chilly, and it didn't help that there were no floor cushions. Isak was surprised at himself for noticing this; he'd always believed that he was not the kind of person who cared about such niceties, but it was uncomfortable sitting on a concrete floor.

"Eat, son. Hu is a fine cook. I'd go hungry without him," Yoo said, and started to eat.

"Will the sister stop seeing him, do you think?" Hu asked Pastor Yoo.

"If the girl gets pregnant, Yoshikawa will throw her away, and then there would be no school for the brother anyway. The manager is just one of those romantic old fools who wants to be with a young girl and to feel like he's in love. Soon he will need to lie with her, then eventually he will lose interest. Men and women are not very difficult to understand," Yoo said. "She must stop seeing the manager, and the brother must get a job. She should change her workplace immediately. Together they will make enough money to live and to send to their parents."

Isak was surprised by the pastor's change in tone; he sounded cold, almost haughty.

Hu nodded and ate his noodles quietly as if he were ruminating deeply about this.

Yoo turned in Isak's direction. "I've seen this many times. Girls think they'll have the upper hand because these kinds of men seem so pliable, when in fact, the girls are the ones who end up paying bitterly for their mistakes. The Lord forgives, but the world does not forgive."

"Yes," Isak murmured.

"How's your wife settling in? There's enough space at your brother's for you two?"

"Yes. My brother has room. My wife is expecting a baby."

"So fast! How wonderful," Yoo said with pleasure.

"That's wonderful," Hu said excitedly, sounding young for the first time. Seeing all the small children running about in the back of the sanctuary was Hu's favorite part of attending services. Before coming to Japan, he'd lived in a large orphanage, and he liked hearing children's voices.

"Where does your brother live?"

"Only a few minutes from here. I understand that good housing is difficult to find."

Yoo laughed. "No one will rent to the Koreans. As pastor, you'll get a chance to see how the Koreans live here. You can't imagine: a dozen in a room that should be for two, men and families sleeping in shifts. Pigs and chickens inside homes. No running water. No heat. The Japanese think Koreans are filthy, but they have no choice but to live in squalor. I've seen aristocrats from Seoul reduced to nothing, with no money for bathhouses, wearing rags for clothing, shoeless, and unable to get work as porters in the markets. There's nowhere for them to go. Even the ones with work and money can't find a place to live. Some are squatting illegally."

"The men who were brought here by Japanese companies—wouldn't they provide housing?"

"There are camps attached to mines or larger factories in places like Hokkaido, but the camps aren't for families. The camps are no better; the conditions are deplorable," Yoo said without emotion. Again, Yoo's tone sounded unfeeling, and it surprised Isak. When the siblings had been there, Yoo had seemed concerned about their hardship.

"Where do you live?" Isak asked.

"I sleep in the office. In that corner." Yoo pointed to the area beside the stove. "And Hu sleeps in that corner."

"There are no pallets or bedding—"

"They're in the cupboard. Hu makes the beds each night and clears them up in the morning. We could make room for you and your family if you need to stay here. That would be part of your compensation."

"Thank you, sir. But I think we are all right for now."

Hu nodded, though he would've liked to have had a baby living with them; the church building was too drafty for a child.

"And your meals?"

"Hu fixes our meals on the stove at the back of the house. There's a sink with running water; the outhouse is by the back. The missionaries put those in, thankfully."

"You don't have a family?" Isak asked Yoo.

"My wife passed away two years after we arrived. That was fifteen years ago. We never had children." Yoo added, "But Hu is a son to me. He is my blessing, and now you've arrived to bless us both."

Hu blushed, pleased by this mention.

"How are you with money?" Yoo asked.

"I meant to speak with you," Isak said, wondering if he should discuss this in front of Hu, but realizing that Hu had to be present to function as the pastor's eyes.

Yoo lifted his head and spoke firmly, like a hard-nosed merchant:

"Your wages will be fifteen yen per month. It isn't enough for one man to live on. Hu and I don't take a salary. Just living expenses. Also, I can't guarantee fifteen yen per month, either. The Canadian churches send us some support, but it's not steady, and our congregation doesn't give much. Will you be all right?"

Isak didn't know what to say. He'd no idea what his contribution was to be for living at his brother's. He couldn't imagine asking his brother to support him and his wife and child.

"Can your family help?" It had been part of Yoo's calculation in hiring Isak. The boy's family owned land in Pyongyang; his references there had mentioned that the family had money, so Isak's salary would likely not be so important. They told him that he hadn't even asked for a salary when he served as a lay pastor. Isak was sickly and not a strong hire. Yoo had been counting on Isak's family's financial support for the church.

"I ... I cannot ask my brother for help, sir."

"Oh? Is that so?"

"And my parents cannot help at this time."

"I see."

Hu felt sorry for the young pastor, who looked both stunned and ashamed.

"Our parents have been selling their land in large parcels to pay taxes, and things are precarious now. My brother has been sending them money so they could get by. I think he may also be supporting my sister-in-law's family."

Yoo nodded. This had not been expected, though it made sense, of course. Isak's family was no different from the others who had been assessed egregiously by the colonial government. He'd been counting on Isak's being able to sustain himself. With his vision so heavily impaired, Yoo needed a bilingual pastor to help him to write sermons as well as to deal with administrative matters with the local officials.

"There isn't enough from the offerings, I suppose..." Isak said.

"No." Yoo shook his head vigorously. There were seventy-five to eighty regular attendees on Sunday mornings, but it was really five or six of the better-off congregants who made up the lion's share of the giving. The rest could hardly afford two shabby meals a day.

Hu picked up the empty bowls from the table.

"The Lord has always provided for us, sir," Hu said.

"Yes, my son, you've spoken well." Yoo smiled at the young man, wishing he could've provided him with an education. The boy had such natural intelligence and tremendous aptitude; he would have made a fine scholar, even a pastor.

"We will find a way," Yoo said. "This must be very disappointing to you." His tone of voice sounded the way he had spoken to the sister earlier.

"I'm grateful for this job, sir. I'll speak with my family about the salary. Hu is right, of course; the Lord will provide," Isak said.

"All I have needed Thy hand hath provided; Great is Thy faithfulness, Lord, unto me!" Pastor Yoo sang in his rich tenor voice. "The Lord provided you for our church. Surely, He will care for all of our material needs."

15

The summer had come fast. The Osaka sun felt hotter than the sun back home, and the brutal humidity slowed down Sunja's heavy movements. However, her workdays were easy, and until the baby came, she and Kyunghee had to care only for themselves and their husbands, who didn't come home until late in the evening. Isak spent long days and nights at the church serving the needs of a growing congregation, and Yoseb managed the biscuit factory during the day and repaired machines in factories in Ikaino in the evenings for extra money. The daily tasks of cooking, laundry, and cleaning for four were considerably less onerous than caring for a boardinghouse. Sunja's life felt luxurious in contrast to her old life in Busan.

She loved spending the day with Kyunghee, whom she called Sister. After two brief months, they found themselves enjoying a close friendship—an unexpected gift for two women who'd neither expected nor asked for much happiness. Kyunghee was no longer alone in the house all day, and Yoseb was grateful that Isak had brought the boardinghouse daughter as his wife.

In the minds of Yoseb and Kyunghee, the cause of Sunja's pregnancy had long been settled with a rationalization of their making: The girl had been harmed through no fault of her own, and Isak had rescued her because it was his nature to make sacrifices. No one asked her the particulars, and Sunja did not speak of the matter.

Kyunghee and Yoseb hadn't been able to have children, but Kyunghee was undeterred. Sarah in the Bible had a child in old age, and Kyunghee didn't believe that God had forgotten her. A devout woman, she spent her time helping the poor mothers at the church. She was also a thrifty housewife, able to save every extra sen that her husband entrusted to her. It had been Kyunghee's idea to buy the Ikaino house with the money Yoseb's father had given him combined with her dowry, even when Yoseb had had his doubts. "Why would we pay rent to the landlord and have nothing left when the month is over?" she'd said. Because Kyunghee stuck to a careful budget, they'd been able to send money to Yoseb's parents and her own—both families having lost all of their arable land.

Kyunghee's dream was to own her own business selling kimchi and pickles at the covered market near Tsuruhashi Station, and when Sunja moved in, she finally had a person who'd listen to her plans. Yoseb disapproved of her working for money. He liked coming home to a rested and pretty housewife who had his supper ready—an ideal reason for a man to work hard, he believed. Each day, Kyunghee and Sunja made three meals: a hot, traditional breakfast with soup; a packed lunch for the men to take to work; and a hot dinner. Without refrigeration or the cold Pyongyang climate, Kyunghee had to cook often to avoid waste.

It was unusually warm for the beginning of summer, and the thought of making soup on the stone stove at the back of the house would have been unappealing to any normal housewife, but Kyunghee didn't mind. She enjoyed going to the market and thinking about what to fix for their meals. Unlike most of the Korean women in Ikaino, she spoke decent Japanese and was able to negotiate with the merchants for what she wanted.

When Kyunghee and Sunja entered the butcher shop, Tanaka-san, the tall young proprietor, snapped to attention and shouted *"Irasshai!"* to welcome them.

The butcher and his helper, Koji, were delighted to see the pretty Korean and her pregnant sister-in-law. They weren't big customers; in fact, they spent very little money, but they were steady, and as Tanaka's father and grandfather had taught him—the eighth generation of sons to run the shop—the daily, cumulative payments were more valuable than the

infrequent, outsize purchases. Housewives were the backbone of the business, and the Korean women couldn't fuss like the local women, which made them preferable customers. It was also rumored that one of his great-grandfathers may have been Korean or *burakumin*, so the young butcher had been raised by his father and mother to be fair to all the customers. Times might have changed, to be sure, but butchery, which required touching dead animals, was still a shameful occupation—the chief reason given as to why the matchmaker had such difficulty arranging an *omiai* for him—and Tanaka couldn't help but feel a kind of kinship with foreigners.

The men ogled Kyunghee, altogether ignoring Sunja, who had by now grown used to this invisibility whenever the two went anywhere. Kyunghee, who looked smart in her midi skirts and crisp white blouses, easily passing for a schoolteacher or a merchant's modest wife with her fine features, was welcomed in most places. Everyone thought she was Japanese until she spoke; even then, the local men were pleasant to her. For the first time in her life, Sunja felt aware of her unacceptable plainness and inappropriate attire. She felt homely in Osaka. Her well-worn, traditional clothes were an inevitable badge of difference, and though there were enough older and poorer Koreans in the neighborhood who wore them still, she had never been looked upon with scorn with such regularity, when she had never meant to call attention to herself. Within the settled boundaries of Ikaino, one would not be stared at for wearing a white *hanbok*, but outside the neighborhood and farther out from the train station, the chill against identifiable Koreans was obvious. Sunja would have preferred to wear Western clothes or *mompei*, but it would make no sense to spend money on fabric to sew new things now. Kyunghee promised to make her new clothes after the baby was delivered.

Kyunghee bowed politely to the men, and Sunja retreated into the corner of the shop.

"How can we help you today, Boku-san?" Tanaka-san asked.

Even after two months, it still surprised Sunja to hear her husband's family name pronounced in its Japanese form. Due to the colonial gov-

ernment's requirements, it was normal for Koreans to have at least two or three names, but back home she'd had little use for the Japanese *tsumei*—Junko Kaneda—written on her identity papers, because Sunja didn't go to school and had nothing to do with official business. Sunja was born a Kim, yet in Japan, where women went by their husband's family name, she was Sunja Baek, which was translated into Sunja Boku, and on her identity papers, her *tsumei* was now Junko Bando. When the Koreans had to choose a Japanese surname, Isak's father had chosen Bando because it had sounded like the Korean word *ban-deh*, meaning objection, making their compulsory Japanese name a kind of joke. Kyunghee had assured her that all these names would become normal soon enough.

"What will you be cooking today, Boku-san?" the young owner asked.

"May I please have shinbones and a bit of meat? I'm making soup," Kyunghee said in her radio announcer–style Japanese; she regularly listened to Japanese programs to improve her accent.

"Right away." Tanaka grabbed three large hunks of shinbone from the stock of beef bones and oxtails he kept in the ice chest for Korean customers; Japanese did not have any use for bones. He wrapped up a handful of stew meat. "Will that be all?"

She nodded.

"Thirty-six sen, please."

Kyunghee opened her coin purse. Two yen and sixty sen had to last her for eight more days until Yoseb gave her his pay envelope.

"*Sumimasen desu*, how much would it be for just the bones?"

"Ten sen."

"Please pardon my error. Today, I'll take only the bones. Meat another time, I promise."

"Of course." Tanaka returned the meat to the case. It wasn't the first time a customer didn't have enough money to pay for food, but unlike his other customers, the Koreans didn't ask him for credit, not that he would have agreed to it.

"You're making a broth?" Tanaka wondered what it might be like to have such an elegant wife worrying about his meals and being thrifty with

her pin money. He was the first son, and although he was eager to be married, he lived with his mother as a bachelor. "What kind?"

"*Seolleongtang.*" She looked at him quizzically, wondering if he knew what that was.

"And how do you make this soup?" Tanaka folded his arms leisurely and leaned into the counter, looking carefully into Kyunghee's lovely face. She had beautiful, even teeth, he thought.

"First, you wash the bones very carefully in cold water. Then you boil the bones and throw that first batch of water out because it will have all the blood and dirt that you don't want in your broth. Then you boil it again with clean, cold water, then simmer it for a long, long time until the broth is white like tofu, then you add daikon, chopped scallions, and salt. It's delicious and very good for your health."

"It would be better to have some meat with it, I would imagine."

"And white rice and noodles! Why not?" Kyunghee laughed, her hand raised reflexively to cover her teeth.

Both men laughed with pleasure, understanding her joke, since rice was costly even for them.

"And do you eat kimchi with that?" Tanaka asked, never having had such a long conversation with Kyunghee. It felt safe for him to talk with her with his assistant and her sister-in-law present. "Kimchi is a bit spicy for me, yet I think it's nice with grilled chicken or grilled pork."

"Kimchi is delicious with every meal. I will bring you some from our house next time."

Tanaka reopened the paper packet of bones and put back half of the meat he'd just returned to the case.

"It's not much. Just enough for the baby." Tanaka smiled at Sunja, who was surprised that the butcher had noticed her. "A mother must eat well if she's to raise a strong worker for the Emperor."

"I couldn't take anything for free," Kyunghee said, perplexed. She didn't know what he was doing exactly, but she really couldn't afford the meat today.

Sunja was confused by their conversation. They were saying something about kimchi.

"This is the first sale of the day. Sharing will bring me luck," Tanaka said, feeling puffed up like any man who could give something worthwhile to an attractive woman whenever he pleased.

Kyunghee placed the ten sen on the spotless money dish resting on the counter, smiled, and bowed to both men before she left.

Outside the shop, Sunja asked what happened.

"He didn't charge us for the meat. I didn't know how to make him take it back."

"He likes you. It was a present." Sunja giggled, feeling like Dokhee, the younger servant girl back home, who'd joke about men whenever she had the chance. Though she thought of her mother often, it had been a while since she'd thought about the sisters back home. "I'll call Tanaka-san your boyfriend from now on."

Kyunghee swatted playfully at Sunja, shaking her head.

"He said it's for your baby, so he can grow up to be a good worker for the country." Kyunghee made a face. "And Tanaka-san knows I'm Korean."

"Since when do men care about such things? Mrs. Kim next door told me about the quiet lady who lives at the end of the road who's Japanese and married to the Korean who brews alcohol in his house. Their kids are half Japanese!" This had shocked Sunja when she'd first heard of it, though everything Mrs. Kim, the lady who raised pigs, told her was shocking. Yoseb didn't want Kyunghee and Sunja to speak with Mrs. Kim, who also didn't go to church on Sundays. They weren't allowed to speak to the Japanese wife, either, because her husband was routinely sent to jail for his bootlegging.

"If you run away with the nice butcher, I'll miss you," Sunja said.

"Even if I weren't married, I would not choose that man. He smiles too much." Kyunghee winked at her. "I like my cranky husband who's always telling me what to do and worries about everything.

"Come on, we have to buy vegetables now. That's why I didn't buy the meat. We should try to find some potatoes to roast. Wouldn't that be good for our lunch?"

"Sister—"

"Yes?" Kyunghee said.

"We're not contributing to the house. The groceries, fuel, *sento* fees— I've never seen such prices in my life. Back home, we had a garden, and we never paid for vegetables. And the price of fish! My mother would never eat it again if she knew the cost. Back home, we scrimped, but I didn't realize how easy we had it—we got free fish from the guests, and here, an apple costs more than beef ribs in Busan. Mother was careful with money, the way you are, but even she couldn't have made the kinds of delicious things you make on a budget. Isak and I think you should take the money he makes to help with the food budget at least."

The fact that Sister and Brother wouldn't allow Isak and her to pay for a single thing was difficult to accept, and it wasn't as if they could afford to rent a place separately. Besides, even if they could have afforded to do so, it would have hurt Sister's feelings deeply for Isak and Sunja to move out.

"I'm sure you ate much better and more filling things back home," Kyunghee said, appearing sad.

"No, no. That's not what I meant. We just feel terrible that you won't let us contribute to the enormous expenses."

"Yoseb and I won't allow it. You should be saving money for the baby. We'll have to get clothes for him and diapers, and one day he'll go to school and become a gentleman. Won't that be something? I hope he'll like school like his father and not dodge books like his uncle!" The thought of a baby living with them made Kyunghee smile. This child felt like an answer to her prayers.

"Mother sent me three yen in her last letter. And we have money we brought and Isak's recent earnings to help. You shouldn't have to worry about expenses so much or selling kimchi to support two extra mouths— and soon, three," Sunja said.

"Sunja-ya, you're being disrespectful. I'm your elder. We can manage just fine. Also, if I can't talk about my wish to earn money without you jumping in about wanting to contribute, then I can't talk about my pipe dreams of becoming the kimchi *ajumma* of Tsuruhashi Station."

Kyunghee laughed. "Be a good little sister and let me dream out loud about my business where I'll make so much money that I can buy us a castle and send your son to medical school in Tokyo."

"Do you think housewives would buy another woman's kimchi?"

"Why not! Don't you think I make good kimchi? My family cook made the finest pickles in Pyongyang." Kyunghee lifted her chin, then broke down laughing. She had a joyous laugh. "I'd make a great kimchi *ajumma*. My pickled cabbage would be clean and delicious."

"Why can't you start now? I have enough money to buy cabbage and radish. I can help you make it. If we sell a lot, it would be better for me than working in a factory, because I can watch the baby at home when he's born."

"Yes, we would be really good at it, but Yoseb would kill me. He said he'd never have his wife work. Never. And he wouldn't want you to work, either."

"But I grew up working with my mother and father. He knows that. My mother served the guests and did all the cooking, and I cleaned and washed—"

"Yoseb is old-fashioned." Kyunghee sighed. "I married a very good man. It's my fault. If I had children, I wouldn't feel so restless. I just don't want to be so idle. This isn't Yoseb's fault. No one works harder than he does. Back in the olden days, a man in his situation could've thrown me out for not having a son." Kyunghee nodded to herself, recalling the numerous stories of barren women that she'd heard as a child, never having considered that such a thing could happen to her. "I'll listen to my husband. He has always taken such good care of me."

Sunja could neither agree nor disagree, so she let the statement hang in the air. Her brother-in-law, Yoseb, was in actuality saying that a *yangban* woman like Kyunghee couldn't work outside the house; Sunja was an ordinary peasant's daughter, so working in a market was fine for her. The distinction didn't trouble Sunja, since she agreed that Kyunghee was a superior person in so many ways. Nevertheless, living with Kyunghee and speaking so truthfully with her about everything, Sunja also knew that her sister-in-law was heartbroken about what she

could not have and might have been far happier trying her luck as a kimchi *ajumma*.

Regardless, it wasn't her place to say. All this was what her brother-in-law would call "foolish women's talk." For Kyunghee's sake, Sunja brightened up and linked arms with her sister-in-law, who seemed to drag a little. Arm in arm, they went to buy cabbage and daikon.

16

Kyunghee didn't recognize the two men at her door, but they knew her name.

The taller one with the pointy face smiled more frequently, but the shorter one had the kinder expression. They were dressed similarly in workmen's clothing—dark slacks and short-sleeved shirts—but both wore expensive-looking leather shoes. The taller one spoke with a distinct Jeju accent; he dug out a folded sheet of paper from the back pocket of his pants.

"Your husband signed this," he said, flashing her the formal-looking document. Part of it was written in Korean but much of it was in Japanese and Chinese characters. On the upper right-hand corner, Kyunghee recognized Yoseb's name and *hanko*. "He's late on his payments."

"I don't know anything about this. My husband's at work now."

Kyunghee thought she might cry and put her hand on the door, hoping the men would leave. "Please come by later when he's home."

Sunja stood close by her, her hands resting on her abdomen. The men didn't look dangerous to Sunja. Physically, they resembled the lodgers back home, but her sister-in-law appeared flustered.

"He'll be home late tonight. Come back then," Sunja repeated, but much more loudly than Kyunghee had.

"You're the sister-in-law, right?" the shorter one said to her. He had dimples when he smiled.

Sunja said nothing, trying not to appear surprised by the fact that he knew who she was.

The taller one continued grinning at Kyunghee. His teeth were large and square and rooted in pale pink gums.

"We've already spoken to your husband, but he hasn't been responsive so we thought we'd drop by and visit with you." He paused and said her name slowly: "Baek Kyunghee—I had a cousin named Kyunghee. Your *tsumei* is Bando Kimiko, *nee*?" The man placed his wide hand on the door and pressed it in slightly toward her. He glanced at Sunja. "The fact that we're meeting your sister-in-law just doubles our pleasure. Right?" The men laughed heartily together.

Again, Kyunghee attempted to scan the document held before her. "I don't understand it," she said finally.

"This is the important part: Baek Yoseb owes my boss a hundred twenty yen." He pointed to the number 120 written in kanji in the second paragraph. "Your husband has missed the last two payments. We're hoping that you'll get him to make them today."

"How much are the payments?" Kyunghee asked.

"Eight yen plus interest per week," the shorter man said; he had a strong accent from the Kyungsangdo region. "Maybe you keep some money at home and can pay us?" he asked. "It comes out to about twenty yen."

Yoseb had just given her the food money for the next two weeks. She had six yen in her purse. If she gave that to him, they'd have no money for food.

"Is a hundred twenty yen the whole amount?" Sunja asked. The paper didn't make any sense to her, either.

The short man looked a little worried and shook his head.

"By now, it's almost double if you include the interest. Why? Do you have the money?"

"As of today, the total would be two hundred thirteen yen," the taller man said. He'd always been good at doing sums in his head.

"*Uh-muh*," Kyunghee exclaimed. She closed her eyes and leaned her body against the doorframe.

Sunja stepped forward and said calmly, "We'll get you the money." She spoke to them the same way she would've spoken to Fatso, the lodger, as to when he could expect his wash to be ready. She didn't even glance in their direction. "Just come back in three hours. Before it gets dark."

"We'll see you later," the taller one said.

The sisters-in-law walked briskly toward the shopping street near Tsuruhashi Station. They didn't linger in front of the fabric shop window or pause at the *senbei* stall; they didn't greet the friendly vegetable sellers. Rather, their bodies moved in unison toward their destination.

"I don't want you to do this," Kyunghee said.

"Father told me about people like this. If the entire debt isn't paid off immediately, the interest gets higher and higher, and you'll never be able to pay it all back. Father said that you always end up owing a great deal more than you borrow. Think about it—how did a hundred twenty yen become two hundred thirteen?"

Hoonie Kim had witnessed his neighbors lose everything after borrowing a small amount of money to buy seedlings or equipment; when the moneylenders were through with them, his neighbors would end up giving them all their crops on top of their initial loans. Sunja's father had loathed moneylenders and had warned her often about the dangers of debt.

"If I'd known, I would've stopped sending money to our parents," Kyunghee mumbled to herself.

Sunja looked straight ahead, avoiding eye contact with anyone on the busy street who glanced in their direction. She was trying to figure out what she'd say to the broker.

"Sister, you saw his sign in Korean, right?" Sunja said. "That would make him Korean, right?"

"I'm not sure. I don't know anyone who's ever been there."

Following the Korean signs posted on the facade of the low brick building, the women climbed up the wide stairs to the second floor. The pawnbroker's office door had a curtained window, and Sunja opened it gingerly.

It was a warm, breezeless day in June, but the older man behind the desk wore a green silk ascot tucked into his white dress shirt and a brown woolen vest. The three square windows facing the street were open, and two electric fans whirred quietly in the opposite corners of the office. Two younger men with similar chubby faces played cards by the middle window. They glanced up and smiled at the two women.

"Welcome. How can I be of service?" the pawnbroker asked them in Korean. His hometown accent was hard to place. "Would you like to sit down?" He motioned to the chairs, and Sunja told him she'd prefer to stand. Kyunghee stood next to Sunja and refused to look at the men.

Sunja opened the palm of her hand to show him the pocket watch.

"*Ajeossi*, how much could you give us for this?"

The man raised his gray-black eyebrows and pulled out a loupe from his desk drawer.

"Where did you get this?"

"My mother gave it to me. It's solid silver and washed in gold," Sunja said.

"She knows you're selling it?"

"She gave it to me to sell. For the baby."

"Wouldn't you prefer a loan for the watch? Maybe you don't want to let go of it," he asked. Loans were rarely repaid, and he'd be able to keep the collateral.

Sunja spoke slowly: "I want to sell it. If you don't wish to buy it, I won't trouble you any longer."

The broker smiled, wondering if the pregnant girl had already been to his competitors. There were three pawnbrokers just a few streets away. None of the others were Korean, but if she spoke any Japanese, it would have been easy to sell the watch. The pretty woman who accompanied the pregnant one before him looked a little Japanese in the way she dressed; it was hard to tell. It was possible that the pretty one had brought the pregnant girl along to negotiate with him and that the watch belonged to her.

"If you have a need to sell it," the broker said, "I always take pleasure helping a person from home."

Sunja said nothing. In the market, say very little, her father had taught her.

Kyunghee marveled at her sister-in-law appearing calmer than she'd ever seen her.

The pawnbroker examined the watch with care, opening its silver casing to study the mechanical workings visible through its open crystal back. It was an extraordinary pocket watch, and impossible to believe that this pregnant woman's mother could have owned such a thing. The watch was maybe a year old if that and without a scratch. He turned it faceup again and laid it on the green leather blotter on his desk.

"Young men prefer wristwatches these days. I'm not even sure if I can sell this."

Sunja noticed that the broker had blinked hard after saying this, but he hadn't blinked once when he was talking to her before.

"Thank you for looking at it," Sunja said, and turned around. Kyunghee was trying not to appear worried. Sunja picked up the watch and gathered the tail end of her long *chima*, preparing to walk out of the office. "We appreciate your time. Thank you."

"I'd like to help you," the broker said, raising his voice slightly.

Sunja turned around.

"If you need the money right away, perhaps it would be easier for you to sell it here than walking around in this hot day in your condition. I can help you. It looks like you'll have the child soon. I hope it's a boy who'll take good care of his mother," he said.

"Fifty yen," he said.

"Two hundred," she said. "It's worth at least three hundred. It's made in Switzerland and brand-new."

The two men by the window put down their cards and got up from their seats. They'd never seen a girl talk like this.

"If you think it's worth so much, then why don't you sell it for a higher price elsewhere," the broker snapped, irritated by her insolence. He couldn't stand women who talked back.

Sunja bit her inner lower lip. If she sold it to a Japanese pawnbroker, Sunja feared that the broker may alert the police about the watch. Hansu

had told her that the police were involved in nearly all the businesses here.

"Thank you. I won't waste any more of your time," Sunja said.

The pawnbroker chuckled.

Kyunghee suddenly felt confident of her sister-in-law, who had been so helpless upon her arrival in Osaka that she had to carry her name and address written in Japanese on a card in case she got lost.

"What did your mother do back home?" the pawnbroker asked. "You sound like you're from Busan."

Sunja paused, wondering if she had to answer the question.

"Did she work in the markets there?"

"She's a boardinghouse keeper."

"She must be a clever businesswoman," he said. The broker had figured that her mother must have been a whore or a merchant of some sort who collaborated with the Japanese government. The watch could also have been stolen. From her speech and dress, the pregnant girl was not from a wealthy family. "Young lady, you're sure that your mother gave this to you to sell. You are aware that I will need your name and address in case there's any trouble."

Sunja nodded.

"Okay, then. A hundred twenty-five yen."

"Two hundred." Sunja didn't know if she'd get this amount, but she felt certain that the broker was greedy, and if he was willing to go to 125 from fifty, then surely the Japanese brokers would think it was valuable, too.

The broker burst out laughing. The young men were now standing by the desk, and they laughed as well. The younger one said, "You should work here."

The broker folded his arms close to his chest. He wanted the watch; he knew exactly who would buy it.

"Father, you should give the little mother her price. If only because she's so persistent!" the young one said, knowing his father didn't like to lose a bargain and would need some coaxing. He felt sorry for the girl with the puffy face. She wasn't the usual kind of girl who came up here to sell gold rings whenever she was in trouble.

"Does your husband know you're here?" the pawnbroker's younger son asked.

"Yes," Sunja replied.

"Is he a drinker or a gambler?" The son had seen desperate women before, and the stories were always the same.

"Neither," she said in a stern voice, as if to warn him not to ask any more questions.

"A hundred seventy-five yen," the broker said.

"Two hundred." Sunja could feel the warm, smooth metal in her palm; Hansu would have held firm to his price.

The broker protested, "How do I know that I can sell it?"

"Father," the older son said, smiling. "You'd be helping a little mother from home."

The broker's desk was made of an unfamiliar wood—a rich dark brown color with teardrop-shaped whorls the size of a child's hand. She counted three teardrop whorls on the surface. When she'd gone to collect mushrooms with Hansu, there had been innumerable types of trees. The musty smell of wet leaves on the forest carpet, the baskets filled to bursting with mushrooms, the sharp pain of lying with him—these memories would not leave her. She had to be rid of him, to stop this endless recollection of the one person she wished to forget.

Sunja took a deep breath. Kyunghee was wringing her hands.

"We understand if you don't wish to buy this," Sunja said quietly, and turned to leave.

The pawnbroker held up his hand, signaling her to wait, and went to the back room, where he kept his cashbox.

When the two men returned to the house for the payments, the women stood by the door and didn't invite them inside.

"If I pay you the money, how do I know that the debt is totally gone?" Sunja asked the taller one.

"We'll get the boss to sign the promissory note to say it's canceled," he said. "How do I know that you have the money?"

"Can your boss come here?" Sunja asked.

"You must be crazy," the taller one said, in shock at her request.

Sunja sensed that she shouldn't give these men the money. She tried to close the door a little so she could speak with Kyunghee, but the man pushed it back with his foot.

"Listen, if you really have the money, you can come with us. We'll take you right now."

"Where?" Kyunghee spoke up, her voice tremulous.

"By the sake shop. It's not far."

The boss was an earnest-looking young Korean, not much older than Kyunghee. He looked like a doctor or a teacher—well-worn suit, gold-wire spectacles, combed-back black hair, and a thoughtful expression. No one would have thought he was a moneylender. His office was about the size of the pawnbroker's, and on the wall opposite the front door, a shelf was lined with books in Japanese and Korean. Electric lamps were lit next to comfortable-looking chairs. A boy brought the women hot *genmaicha* in pottery cups. Kyunghee understood why her husband would borrow money from a man like this.

When Kyunghee handed him all the money, the moneylender said thank you and canceled the note, placing his red seal on the paper.

"If there's anything else I can ever do for you, please let me be of service," he said, looking at Kyunghee. "We must support each other while we're far from home. I am your servant."

"When, when did my husband borrow this money?" Kyunghee asked the moneylender.

"He asked me in February. We're friends, so of course, I obliged."

The women nodded, understanding. Yoseb had borrowed the money for Isak and Sunja's passage.

"Thank you, sir. We shall not bother you again," Kyunghee said.

"Your husband will be very pleased to have the matter settled," he said, wondering how the women had raised the money so quickly.

The women said nothing and returned home to make dinner.

17

W here did you get the money?" Yoseb shouted, clutching the canceled promissory note.

"Sunja sold the watch her mother gave her," Kyunghee replied.

Invariably, each night on their street, someone was yelling or a child was crying, but loud noises had never come from their house. Yoseb, who didn't anger easily, was enraged. Sunja stood wedged in the back corner of the front room, her head lowered—mute as a rock. Tears streamed down her reddened cheeks. Isak wasn't home yet from church.

"You had a pocket watch worth over two hundred yen? Does Isak know about this?" he shouted at Sunja.

Kyunghee raised her hands and put herself between him and Sunja.

"Her mother gave her the watch. To sell for the baby."

Sunja slid down the wall, no longer able to stand. Sharp pains pierced her pelvis and back. She shut her eyes and covered her head with her forearms.

"Where did you sell this watch?"

"At the pawnbroker by the vegetable stand," Kyunghee said.

"Are you out of your mind? What kind of women go to pawnbrokers?" Yoseb stared hard at Sunja. "How can a woman do such a thing?"

From the floor, Sunja looked up at him and pleaded, "It's not Sister's fault—"

"And did you ask your husband if you could go to a pawnbroker?"

"Why are you getting so upset? She was just trying to help us. She's pregnant. Leave her alone." Kyunghee averted her eyes, trying to keep from talking back to him. He knew full well that Sunja hadn't spoken to Isak. Why did Yoseb have to pay for everything? Why did he control all the money? The last time they'd argued was when she'd wanted to get a factory job.

"Sunja was worried about us. I'm sorry that she had to sell that beautiful watch. Try to understand, *yobo*." Kyunghee laid her hand gently on his forearm.

"Stupid women! Every time I walk down the street, how am I supposed to face these men again, knowing that some foolish women paid my debts? My nuts are shriveling."

Yoseb had never spoken in such a vulgar way before, and Kyunghee understood that he was insulting Sunja. He was calling Sunja stupid, Sunja foolish; Kyunghee was also being blamed because she'd allowed it to happen. But it was smarter for them to pay off this debt; if she'd been allowed to get a job before, they would've had savings.

Sunja couldn't stop crying. The agonizing pains around her lower abdomen had returned with greater force, and she didn't know what to say. It wasn't clear what was happening to her body.

"*Yobo*, please, please understand," Kyunghee said.

Yoseb said nothing. Sunja's legs were splayed out like a drunk on the street with her swollen hands holding up her enormous belly. He wondered if he should've let her into his house. How could a gold pocket watch have come from her mother? It had been years, but he'd met both her mother and her father. Hoonie Kim was the crippled son of two peasants who'd operated a boardinghouse on a minuscule rented plot. Where would his wife have gotten such a valuable thing? Their lodgers were mainly fishermen or men who worked at the fish market. He could've accepted that the girl had been given a few gold rings worth thirty or forty yen by her mother. Perhaps a jade ring worth ten. Had she stolen the watch? he wondered. Could Isak have married a thief or a whore? He couldn't bring himself to say these things, so Yoseb opened the corrugated metal door and left.

* * *

When he came home, Isak was alarmed at the sight of the sobbing women. He tried to calm them so they could speak more coherently. He listened to their broken explanations.

"So where did he go?" Isak asked.

"I don't know. He doesn't go out normally. I didn't realize he'd be this—" Kyunghee stopped, not wanting to upset Sunja any further.

"He'll be all right," Isak said, and turned to Sunja.

"I didn't know you had such a valuable thing from home. It's from your mother?" Isak asked tentatively.

Sunja was still crying, and Kyunghee nodded in her place.

"Oh?" Isak looked again at Sunja.

"Where did your mother get this, Sunja?" Isak asked.

"I didn't ask. Perhaps someone owed her money."

"I see." Isak nodded, not sure what to make of this.

Kyunghee stroked Sunja's feverish head. "Will you explain this to Yoseb?" she asked her brother-in-law. "You understand why we did this, right?"

"Yes, of course. Brother borrowed the money to help me. Sunja sold the watch to pay that debt, so in fact she sold it to help us get here. The passage here was expensive, and how was he to raise all that money so quickly? I should've thought it through. I was naïve and childish, as usual, and Brother was just taking care of me. It's unfortunate that Sunja had to sell the watch, but it's right for us to pay our debts. I'll say all this to him, Sister. Please don't worry," he said to the women.

Kyunghee nodded, feeling a little better finally.

A spasm flared through Sunja's side, knocking her back almost. "*Uh-muh. Uh-muh!*"

"Is it? Is it—?"

Warm water rushed down Sunja's leg.

"Should I get the midwife?" Isak asked.

"Sister Okja—three houses down on our side of the street," Kyunghee said, and Isak ran out of the house.

"It's okay, it's okay," Kyunghee cooed, holding Sunja's hand. "You're

doing mother's work. Women suffer, don't they? Oh, my dear Sunja. I'm so sorry you're in pain." Kyunghee prayed over her, "Lord, dear Lord, please have mercy—"

Sunja took a fistful of her skirt material and put it in her mouth to keep from screaming. It felt as if she was being stabbed repeatedly. She bit down hard on the coarse fabric. "*Umma, umma,*" she cried out.

Sister Okja, the midwife, was a fifty-year-old Korean from Jeju who'd delivered most of the children in the ghetto. Well trained by her aunt, Okja had kept her own children housed and fed through midwifery, nursing, and babysitting. Her husband, the father of their six children, was as good as dead to her, though he was alive and living in her house several days a week in a drunken stupor. When she wasn't delivering babies, Okja minded the children of the neighborhood women who worked in the factories and markets.

This delivery was no trouble at all. The boy was long and well shaped, and the labor, as terrifying as it might have been for the new mother, was brief, and thankfully for the midwife, the baby didn't arrive in the middle of the night but only in time to interrupt her making dinner. Sister Okja hoped her daughter-in-law, who lived with them, hadn't burned the barley rice again.

"Hush, hush. You did well," Okja said to the girl who was still crying for her mother. "The boy's very strong and nice looking. Look at all that black hair! You should rest a little now. The child will need to feed soon," she said, before getting up to leave.

"Damn these knees." Okja rubbed her kneecaps and shins and got up leisurely, making sure that the family had enough time to find her some money.

Kyunghee got her purse and gave Sister Okja three yen.

Okja was unimpressed. "If you have any questions, just get me."

Kyunghee thanked her; she felt like a mother herself. The child was beautiful. Her heart ached at the sight of his small face—the shock of jet hair and his blue-black eyes. She was reminded of the Bible character Samson.

After Kyunghee bathed the child in the dinged-up basin normally used to salt cabbage, she handed the baby, wrapped in a clean towel, to Isak.

"You're a father," Kyunghee said, smiling. "He's handsome, isn't he?"

Isak nodded, feeling more pleased than he'd imagined he'd be.

"*Uh-muh*, I have to make soup for Sunja. She has to have soup right away." Kyunghee went to check on Sunja, who was already fast asleep, leaving Isak with the child in the front room. In the kitchen, as Kyunghee soaked the dried seaweed in cold water, she prayed that her husband would come home soon.

In the morning, the house felt different. Kyunghee hadn't slept. Yoseb hadn't come home the night before. Isak had tried to stay awake, too, but she'd made him go to sleep, because he had to give a sermon the next morning and work at church the whole Sunday. Sunja slept so soundly that she snored and had only gotten up to feed; the child latched on her breast well and fussed very little. Kyunghee had cleaned the kitchen, prepared breakfast, and sewed shirts for the baby while waiting for Yoseb. Every few minutes, she glanced at the window.

While Isak was finishing his breakfast, Yoseb came in the house smelling of cigarettes. His eyeglasses were smudged and his face stubbly. As soon as Kyunghee saw him, she went to the kitchen to get his breakfast.

"Brother." Isak got up. "Are you all right?"

Yoseb nodded.

"The baby was born. It's a boy," Isak said, smiling.

Yoseb sat down on the floor by the low acacia dining table—one of the few things he'd brought from home. He touched the wood and thought of his parents.

Kyunghee placed his food tray in front of him.

"I know you're upset with me, but you should eat something and rest," she said, patting his back.

Isak said, "Brother, I'm sorry about what happened. Sunja's very young, and she was worried for us. The debt's really mine, and—"

"I can take care of this family," Yoseb said.

"That's true, but I put a burden on you that you hadn't anticipated.

I put you in that position. The fault is mine. Sunja thought she was helping."

Yoseb folded his hands. He couldn't disagree with Isak or be upset with him. It was hard to see his brother's sad face. Isak needed to be protected like a fine piece of porcelain. All night, Yoseb had nursed a bottle of *doburoku* at a bar that Koreans frequented not far from the train station, wondering all the while if he should've brought the frail Isak to Osaka. How long would Isak live? What would happen to Isak if Sunja was not a good woman after all? Kyunghee was already so attached to the girl, and once the baby came, Yoseb was responsible for one more. His parents and in-laws were counting on him. At the crowded bar, men were drinking and making jokes, but there hadn't been a soul in that squalid room—smelling of burnt dried squid and alcohol—who wasn't worried about money and facing the terror of how he was supposed to take care of his family in this strange and difficult land.

Yoseb covered his face with his hands.

"Brother, you're a very good man," Isak said. "I know how hard you work."

Yoseb wept.

"Will you forgive Sunja? For not going to you first? Will you forgive me for making you take on a debt? Can you forgive us?"

Yoseb said nothing. The moneylender would see him like all the other men who sponged off their wives toiling in factories or working as domestics. His wife and pregnant sister-in-law had paid his debt with what was likely a stolen watch. What could he do?

"You have to go to work, don't you?" Yoseb asked. "It's Sunday."

"Yes, Sister said she'd stay here with Sunja and the baby."

"Let's go," Yoseb said.

He would forgive. It was too late for anything else.

When the men stepped outside the house, Yoseb held his brother's hand.

"So you're a father now."

"Yes." Isak smiled.

"Good," Yoseb said.

"I want you to name him," Isak said. "It takes a lot of time for us to write to Father and to wait. You're the head of our house here—"

"It shouldn't be me."

"It must be you."

Yoseb took a breath and faced the empty street, and it came to him. "Noa."

"Noa," Isak repeated, smiling. "Yes. That's wonderful."

"Noa—because he obeyed and did what the Lord asked. Noa—because he believed when it was impossible to do so."

"Maybe you should give the sermon today," Isak said, patting his brother on the back.

The brothers walked briskly toward the church, their bodies close, one tall, frail, and purposeful, and the other short, powerful, and quick.

Motherland

1939–1962

I thought that no matter how many hills and brooks you crossed, the whole world was Korea and everyone in it was Korean.

—Park Wan-suh

I

Osaka, 1939

Yoseb inhaled deeply and planted his feet squarely on the threshold—ready to be tackled by a six-year-old boy who had been waiting all week for his bag of taffy. He slid open the front door, steeling himself for what would come.

But nothing.

There was no one in the front room. Yoseb smiled. Noa must be hiding.

"*Yobo*. I've arrived," he shouted in the direction of the kitchen.

Yoseb closed the door behind him.

Pulling out the packet of candy from his coat pocket, Yoseb said dramatically, "Huh, I wonder where Noa could be. I suppose if he isn't home, then I can eat his share of the candy. Or I can put it aside for his brother. Maybe today would be a good day for baby Mozasu to have his first taste of candy. One can never be too young for a treat! He's already a month old. Before you know it, Mozasu and I'll be wrestling, too, just like Noa and me! He'll need some pumpkin taffy to make him stronger." Not hearing a sound, Yoseb unfolded the crinkly paper with a flourish and pretended to put a chunk of taffy in his mouth.

"*Wah*, this is the best batch of pumpkin taffy that Piggy *ajumma* has ever made! *Yobo*," he shouted, "come out here, you must have some of this! Really tasty!" he said, making chewing noises while checking behind the clothing chest and the screen door—Noa's usual hiding spots.

The mere mention of Noa's infant brother, Mozasu, should have made the boy bolt out from hiding. Normally a well-behaved child, Noa had been in trouble at home lately for pinching his brother, given the chance.

Yoseb checked the kitchen, but there was no one there. The stove was cool to the touch, and the side dishes had been put out on the small table by the door; the rice pot was empty. Dinner was always made by the time he came home. The soup kettle was half-filled with water, cut-up potatoes, and onions, waiting to be put on the fire. Saturday evening meals were Yoseb's favorite, because there was no work on Sundays, and yet nothing had been prepared. After a leisurely Saturday dinner, the family would go to the bathhouse together. He opened the kitchen back door and stuck his head out, only to face the filthy gutters. Next door, Piggy *ajumma*'s oldest girl was fixing supper for her family and didn't even look out from her open window.

They could have gone to the market, he supposed. Yoseb sat down on a floor cushion in the front room and opened up one of his many newspapers. Printed columns of words about the war floated in front of his eyes—Japan would save China by bringing technological advancements to a rural economy; Japan would end poverty in Asia and make it prosper; Japan would protect Asia from the pernicious hands of Western imperialism; and only Germany, Japan's true and fearless ally, was fighting the evils of the West. Yoseb didn't believe any of it, but propaganda was inescapable. Each day, Yoseb read three or four papers to glean some truth from the gaps and overlaps. Tonight, all the papers repeated virtually the same things; the censors must've been working especially hard the night before.

In the quiet of the house, Yoseb felt impatient and wanted his dinner. If Kyunghee had gone to pick up something at the market, there was still no reason why Sunja, Noa, and the baby would've gone, too. No doubt, Isak was busy at church. Yoseb put on his shoes.

On the street, no one knew where his wife was, and when he reached the church, his brother wasn't there. The office in the back was empty, except for the usual group of women seated on the floor, their heads bowed, mumbling their prayers.

He waited for a long time until the women raised their heads.

"I'm sorry to bother you, but have you seen Pastor Baek or Pastor Yoo?"

The women, middle-aged *ajummas* who came to church nearly every evening to pray, recognized him as Pastor Baek's older brother.

"They've taken him," the eldest one cried, "and Pastor Yoo and the Chinese boy Hu. You have to help them—"

"What?"

"The police arrested them this morning—when everyone went to the Shinto shrine to bow, one of the village leaders noticed Hu mouthing the words of the Lord's Prayer when they were supposed to be pledging allegiance to the Emperor. The police officer who was supervising questioned Hu, and Hu told him that this ceremony was idol worshipping and he wouldn't do it anymore. Pastor Yoo tried to tell the police that the boy was misinformed, and that he didn't mean anything by it, but Hu refused to agree with Pastor Yoo. Pastor Baek tried to explain, too, but Hu said he was willing to walk into the furnace. Just like Shadrach, Meshach, and Abednego! Do you know that story?"

"Yes, yes," Yoseb said, annoyed by their religious excitement. "Are they at the station now?"

The women nodded.

Yoseb ran outside.

Noa was sitting on the steps of the police station, holding his baby brother, who was asleep.

"Uncle," Noa whispered, smiling with relief. "Mo is very heavy."

"You're a very good brother, Noa," Yoseb said. "Where's your aunt?"

"In there." He tilted his head toward the station, unable to use his hands. "Uncle, can you hold Mozasu? My arms hurt."

"Can you wait here just a little longer? I'll be right back, or I'll send your mother outside."

"*Umma* said she'd give me a treat if I didn't pinch Mozasu and kept him still. They won't let babies inside," Noa said soberly. "But I'm hungry now. I've been here forever and ever."

"Uncle will give you a treat, too, Noa. Uncle will be right back," Yoseb said.

"But, Uncle—Mo's—"

"Yes, Noa, but you're very strong."

Noa straightened his shoulders and sat up. He didn't want to disappoint his uncle, who was his favorite person.

Yoseb was about to open the door of the station, but he turned at the sound of Noa's voice.

"Uncle, what do I do if Mozasu cries?"

"You should sing him a song while you walk back and forth. The way I did when you were his age. Maybe you remember?"

"No, I don't remember," he said, looking tearful.

"Uncle will be right out."

The police wouldn't let them see Isak. The women had been waiting inside the station, with Sunja going outside to check on Noa and Mozasu every few minutes. Children weren't allowed in the station, so Kyunghee had remained near the front desk, since she was the one who spoke Japanese. When Yoseb entered the waiting area, Kyunghee gasped, then exhaled. Seated beside her, Sunja was doubled over, weeping.

"Do they have Isak?" Yoseb asked.

Kyunghee nodded.

"You have to talk quietly," she said, continuing to pat Sunja on the back. "I don't know who's listening."

Yoseb whispered, "The ladies at the church told me what happened. Why did that boy make such a fuss about the bowing?" Back home, the colonial government had been rounding up Christians and making them bow at the shrines each morning. Here, the volunteer community leaders made you do this only once or twice a week. "Is there a fine we can pay?"

"I don't think so," Kyunghee said. "The officer told us to go home, but we waited in case they'd let him out—"

"Isak can't be inside a jail," Yoseb said. "He can't."

At the front desk, Yoseb lowered his shoulders and bowed deeply from the waist.

"My brother's in poor health, sir; he has been this way since he was a

boy, and it would be difficult for him to be in jail. He just recovered from tuberculosis. Is there any way he can go home and come back to the station tomorrow so he can be questioned?" Yoseb asked, using honorific Japanese.

The officer shook his head politely, indifferent to these appeals. The cells were full of Koreans and Chinese, and according to their family members, nearly all of them had some sort of serious health problem that should preclude them from jail time. Although the officer felt bad for the man pleading for his truant brother, there was nothing he could do. The minister would be held for a very long time—these religious activists always were. In times of war, there had to be crackdowns against troublemakers for the sake of national security. It was pointless to say any of this, however. Koreans caused trouble, then made excuses.

"You and the women should go home. The minister is being questioned, and you will not be able to see him. You're wasting your time."

"You see, sir, my brother isn't against the Emperor or the government in any way. He's never been involved in anything against the government," Yoseb said. "My brother is not interested in politics, and I'm sure he—"

"He's not allowed to have visitors. If he's cleared of all charges, you can be assured that he'll be released and sent home." The officer smiled politely. "No one wants to keep an innocent man here." The officer believed this—the Japanese government was a fair and reasonable one.

"Is there anything I can do?" Yoseb said in a lowered voice, patting his pockets for his wallet.

"There's nothing you or I can do," the officer said, peeved. "And I hope you're not suggesting a bribe. Making such an attempt would only exacerbate your brother's crime. He and his colleagues refused to acknowledge loyalty to the Emperor. This is a serious offense."

"I didn't mean any harm. I beg your pardon for my foolish words— I would never insult your honor, sir." Yoseb would have crawled on his belly across the floor of the station if that would have made Isak free. Their eldest brother, Samoel, had been the brave one, the one who would've confronted the officers with audacity and grace, but Yoseb knew he was no hero. He would have borrowed more money and sold their

shack if the police would take a bribe in exchange for Isak; Yoseb didn't see the point of anyone dying for his country or for some greater ideal. He understood survival and family.

The officer adjusted his spectacles and looked past Yoseb's shoulder, though no one else was standing there.

"Perhaps you can take your women home? They have no place here. The boy and the baby are outside. You people are always letting your kids play in the streets even in the evening. They should be at home. If you don't take care of your children, they'll end up in jail one day," the officer said, appearing exhausted. "Your brother will be staying here tonight. Do you understand?"

"Yes, sir. Thank you, sir. I'm sorry to bother you. May I bring him his things tonight?"

The officer replied patiently. "In the morning. You can bring him clothes and food. Religious books are not allowed, however. Also, all reading material must be in Japanese." The officer's tone of voice was calm and thoughtful. "Unfortunately, he cannot have visitors. I'm very sorry about that."

Yoseb wanted to believe that this uniformed man was not all bad—he was just another man who was doing a job he didn't like, and he was tired because it was the end of the week. Perhaps he, too, wanted his dinner and his bath. Yoseb saw himself as a rational person, and it was too simplistic to believe that all Japanese police officers were evil. Also, Yoseb needed to believe that there were decent people watching over his brother; the alternative was unbearable.

"We shall bring his things tomorrow morning, then," Yoseb said, peering into the guarded eyes of the officer. "Thank you, sir."

"Of course."

The man tipped his head slightly.

Noa was allowed to eat all the taffy and to play outside, and while Sunja fixed dinner in the kitchen, Yoseb fielded Kyunghee's questions. She was standing with Mozasu tied to her back with a narrow blanket.

"Can you contact someone?" she asked quietly.

"Who?"

"The Canadian missionaries," she suggested. "We met them a few years ago. Remember? They were so nice, and Isak said they send money regularly to support the church. Maybe they can explain to the police that the pastors weren't doing anything wrong." Kyunghee paced in small circles, and Mozasu burbled contentedly.

"How would I reach them?"

"By letter?"

"Can I write them in Korean? How long would it take for them to get the letter and to reply? How long can Isak survive in—?"

Sunja entered the room and untied Mozasu from Kyunghee's back and took him to the kitchen to nurse. The scent of steaming barley rice filled the small house.

"I don't think the missionaries spoke Korean. Can you get someone to help you write a proper letter in Japanese?" Kyunghee asked.

Yoseb said nothing. He would write a letter to them somehow, but he didn't see why the police would care what a Canadian missionary had to say when there was a war going on. A letter would take at least a month.

Sunja returned with Mozasu.

"I put together some things for him. Can I take them tomorrow morning?" she asked.

"I'll take them," Yoseb said. "Before work."

"Can you ask your boss to help? Maybe they'll listen to a Japanese?" Kyunghee said.

"Shimamura-san would never help anyone in jail. He thinks that Christians are rebels. The people who were in charge of the March 1 *demo* were Christians. All the Japanese know that. I don't even tell him that I go to church. I don't tell him anything. He'd just fire me if he thought I was mixed up in any kind of protest activity. Then where would we be? There are no jobs for people like me."

No one said anything after that. Sunja called Noa in from the street. It was time for him to eat.

2

Each morning, Sunja walked to the police station and handed over three *onigin* made with barley and millet. If there was money in the budget for a chicken egg, she'd hard-boil it, soak the peeled egg in vinegary shoyu to supplement Isak's modest bento. No one could be sure if the food ever reached him, but she couldn't prove that it didn't. Everyone in the neighborhood knew someone who'd gone to jail, and the wildly varying reports were at best troubling and at worst terrifying. Yoseb wouldn't speak about Isak, but Isak's arrest had altered him considerably. Patches of gray smudged his once jet-black hair, and he suffered from intense stomach cramps. He stopped writing to his parents, who couldn't be told about Isak, so Kyunghee wrote to them instead, making excuses. At meals, Yoseb put aside much of his food for Noa, who sat beside him quietly. Yoseb and Noa shared a kind of unspeakable grief over Isak's absence.

Despite numerous personal appeals, no one had been allowed to see Isak, but the family believed he was alive, because the police had not told them otherwise. The elder minister and the sexton remained in jail as well, and the family hoped that the three of them sustained each other somehow, though no one knew how the prisoners were being housed. A day after the arrest, the police had come to the house to confiscate Isak's few books and papers. The family's comings and goings were monitored; a detective visited them every few weeks to ask questions. The police padlocked the church, yet the congregation continued to meet secretly in

small groups led by the church elders. Kyunghee, Sunja, and Yoseb never met the parishioners for fear of putting them in danger. By now, most of the foreign missionaries back home and here had returned to their native countries. It was rare to see a white person in Osaka. Yoseb had written the Canadian missionaries about Isak but there'd been no reply.

Under considerable duress, the decision-making authority of the Presbyterian Church had deemed that the mandatory Shinto shrine ceremony was a civic duty rather than a religious one even though the Emperor, the head of the state religion, was viewed as a living deity. Pastor Yoo, a faithful and pragmatic minister, had believed that the shrine ceremony, where the townspeople were required to gather and perform rites, was in fact a pagan ritual drummed up to rouse national feeling. Bowing to idols was naturally offensive to the Lord. Nevertheless, Pastor Yoo had encouraged Isak, Hu, and his congregation to observe the Shinto bowing for the greater good. He didn't want his parishioners, many of them new to the faith, to be sacrificed to the government's predictable response to disobedience—prison and death. Pastor Yoo found support for such ideas in the letters of the apostle Paul. So whenever these gatherings at the nearest shrine took place, their frequency varying from town to town, the elder pastor, Isak, and Hu had attended when necessary along with whoever else was in the church building at the time. However, with his weakened vision, the elder pastor had not known that at every Shinto ceremony, the sexton Hu had been mouthing Our Father like an unbroken loop even as he bowed, sprinkled water, and clapped his hands like all the others. Isak had noticed Hu doing this, of course, but had said nothing. If anything, Isak had admired Hu's faith and gesture of resistance.

For Sunja, Isak's arrest had forced her to consider what would happen if the unthinkable occurred. Would Yoseb ask her and her children to leave? Where would she go, and how would she get there? How would she take care of her children? Kyunghee would not ask her to leave, but even so— she was only a wife. Sunja had to have a plan and money in case she had to return home to her mother with her sons.

So Sunja had to find work. She would become a peddler. It was one

thing for a woman like her mother to take in boarders and to work along-side her husband to earn money, but something altogether different for a young woman to stand in an open market and sell food to strangers, shout-ing until she was hoarse. Yoseb tried to forbid her from getting a job, but she could not listen to him. With tears streaming down her face, she told her brother-in-law that Isak would want her to earn money for the boys' schooling. To this, Yoseb yielded. Nevertheless, he prohibited Kyunghee from working outdoors, and his wife obeyed. Kyunghee was allowed to put up the pickles with Sunja, but she couldn't sell them. Yoseb couldn't protest too much, because the household was desperate for cash. In a way, the two women tried to obey Yoseb in their disobedience—they did not want to hurt Yoseb by defying him, but the financial burdens had become impossible for one man to bear alone.

Her first day of selling took place one week after Isak was jailed. After Sunja dropped off Isak's food at the jail, she wheeled a wooden cart hold-ing a large clay jar of kimchi to the market. The open-air market in Ikaino was a patchwork of modest retail shops selling housewares, cloth, tatami mats, and electric goods, and it hosted a collection of hawkers like her who peddled homemade scallion pancakes, rolled sushi, and soybean paste.

Kyunghee watched Mozasu at home. Nearby the peddlers selling *gochujang* and *doenjang*, Sunja noticed two young Korean women selling fried wheat crackers. Sunja pushed her cart toward them, hoping to wedge herself between the cracker stall and the soybean-paste lady.

"You can't stink up our area," the older of the two cracker sellers said. "Go to the other side." She pointed to the fish section.

When Sunja moved closer to the women selling dried anchovies and seaweed, the older Korean women there were even less welcoming.

"If you don't move your shitty-looking cart, I'll have my sons piss in your pot. Do you understand, country girl?" said a tall woman wearing a white kerchief on her head.

Sunja couldn't come up with a reply, because she was so surprised. None of them were even selling kimchi, and *doenjang* could smell just as pungently.

She kept walking until she couldn't see any more *ajumma*s and ended up near the train station entrance where the live chickens were sold. The intense funk of animal carcasses overwhelmed her. There was a space big enough for her cart between the pig butcher and the chickens.

Wielding an enormous knife, a Japanese butcher was cutting up a hog the size of a child. A large bucket filled with its blood rested by his feet. Two hogs' heads lay on the front table. The butcher was an older gentleman with ropy, muscular arms and thick veins. He was sweating profusely, and he smiled at her.

Sunja parked her cart in the empty lot by his stall. Whenever a train stopped, she could feel its deceleration beneath her sandals. Passengers would disembark, and many of them came into the market from the entrance nearby, but none stopped in front of her cart. Sunja tried not to cry. Her breasts were heavy with milk, and she missed being at home with Kyunghee and Mozasu. She wiped her face with her sleeves, trying to remember what the best market *ajumma*s would do back home.

"Kimchi! Delicious kimchi! Try this delicious kimchi, and never make it at home again!" she shouted. Passersby turned to look at her, and Sunja, mortified, looked away from them. No one bought anything. After the butcher finished with his hog, he washed his hands and gave her twenty-five sen, and Sunja filled a container for him. He didn't seem to mind that she didn't speak Japanese. He put down the kimchi container by the hogs' heads, then reached behind his stall to take out his bento. The butcher placed a piece of kimchi neatly on top of his white rice with his chopsticks and ate a bite of rice and kimchi in front of her.

"*Oishi! Oishi nee! Honto oishi*," he said, smiling.

She bowed to him.

At lunchtime, Kyunghee brought Mozasu for her to nurse, and Sunja remembered that she had no choice but to recoup the cost of the cabbage, radish, and spices. At the end of the day, she had to show more money than they had spent.

Kyunghee watched the cart while Sunja nursed the baby with her body turned toward the wall.

"I'd be afraid," Kyunghee said. "You know how I'd said that I wanted

to be a kimchi *ajumma*? I don't think I realized what it would feel like to stand here. You're so brave."

"What choice do we have?" Sunja said, looking down at her beautiful baby.

"Do you want me to stay here? And wait with you?"

"You'll get in trouble," Sunja said. "You should be home when Noa gets back from school, and you have to make dinner. I'm sorry I can't help you, Sister."

"What I have to do is easy," Kyunghee said.

It was almost two o'clock in the afternoon, and the air felt cooler as the sun turned away from them.

"I'm not going to come home until I sell the whole jar."

"Really?"

Sunja nodded. Her baby, Mozasu, resembled Isak. He looked nothing like Noa, who was olive-skinned with thick, glossy hair. Noa's bright eyes noticed everything. Except for his mouth, Noa looked almost identical to a young Hansu. At school, Noa sat still during lessons, waited for his turn, and he was praised as an excellent student. Noa had been an easy baby, and Mozasu was a happy baby, too, delighted to be put into a stranger's arms. When she thought about how much she loved her boys, she recalled her parents. Sunja felt so far away from her mother and father. Now she was standing outside a rumbling train station, trying to sell kimchi. There was no shame in her work, but it couldn't be what they'd wanted for her. Nevertheless, she felt her parents would have wanted her to make money, especially now.

When Sunja finished nursing, Kyunghee put down two sugared rolls and a bottle filled with reconstituted powdered milk on the cart.

"You have to eat, Sunja. You're nursing, and that's not easy, right? You have to drink lots of water and milk."

Kyunghee turned around so Sunja could tuck Mozasu into the sling on Kyunghee's back. Kyunghee secured the baby tightly around her torso.

"I'll go home and wait for Noa and make dinner. You come home soon, okay? We're a good team."

Mozasu's small head rested between Kyunghee's thin shoulder blades,

and Sunja watched them walk away. When they were out of earshot, Sunja cried out, "Kimchi! Delicious Kimchi! Kimchi! Delicious kimchi! *Oishi desu! Oishi* kimchi!"

This sound, the sound of her own voice, felt familiar, not because it was her own voice but because it reminded her of all the times she'd gone to the market as a girl—first with her father, later by herself as a young woman, then as a lover yearning for the gaze of her beloved. The chorus of women hawking had always been with her, and now she'd joined them. "Kimchi! Kimchi! Homemade kimchi! The most delicious kimchi in Ikaino! More tasty than your grandmother's! *Oishi desu, oishi!*" She tried to sound cheerful, because back home, she had always frequented the nicest *ajummas*. When the passersby glanced in her direction, she bowed and smiled at them. *"Oishi! Oishi!"*

The pig butcher looked up from his counter and smiled at her proudly.

That evening, Sunja did not go home until she could see the bottom of the kimchi jar.

Sunja could sell whatever kimchi she and Kyunghee were able to make now, and this ability to sell had given her a kind of strength. If they could've made more kimchi, she felt sure that she could've sold that, too, but fermenting took time, and it wasn't always possible to find the right ingredients. Even when they made a decent profit, the price of cabbages could spike the following week, or worse, they might not be available at all. When there were no cabbages at the market, the women pickled radishes, cucumbers, garlic, or chives, and sometimes Kyunghee pickled carrots or eggplant without garlic or chili paste, because the Japanese preferred those kinds of pickles. Sunja thought about land all the time. The little kitchen garden her mother had kept behind the house had nourished them even when the boardinghouse guests ate double what they paid. The price of fresh food kept rising, and working people couldn't afford the most basic things. Recently, some customers would ask to buy a cup of kimchi because they couldn't afford a jar of it.

If Sunja had no kimchi or pickles to sell, she sold other things. Sunja roasted sweet potatoes and chestnuts; she boiled ears of corn. She had

two carts now, and she hooked them together like the cars of a train—one cart with a makeshift coal stove and another just for pickles. The carts took up the better part of the kitchen because they had to keep them inside the house for fear of them getting stolen. She split the profits equally with Kyunghee, and Sunja put aside every sen she could for the boys' schooling and for their passage back home in case they had to leave.

When Mozasu turned five months old, Sunja also started selling candy at the market. Produce had been getting increasingly scarce, and by chance, Kyunghee had obtained two wholesale bags of black sugar from a Korean grocer whose Japanese brother-in-law worked in the military.

At her usual spot by the pork butcher's stall, Sunja stoked the fire beneath the metal bowl used to melt sugar. The steel box that functioned as a stove had been giving her trouble; as soon as she could afford it, Sunja planned on having a proper stove made up for her cart. She rolled up her sleeves and moved the live coals around to circulate the air and raise the heat.

"*Agasshi*, do you have kimchi today?"

It was a man's voice, and Sunja looked up. About Isak's age, he dressed like her brother-in-law—tidy without drawing much attention to himself. His face was cleanly shaven, and his fingernails were neat. The lenses of his eyeglasses were very thick and the heavy frames detracted from his good features.

"No, sir. No kimchi today. Just candy. It's not ready, though."

"Oh. When will you have kimchi again?"

"Hard to say. There isn't much cabbage to buy, and the last batch of kimchi we put up isn't ready yet," Sunja said, and returned to the coals.

"A day or two? A week?"

Sunja looked up again, surprised by his insistence.

"The kimchi might be ready in three days or so. If the weather continues to get warmer, then it might be two, sir. But I don't think that soon," Sunja said flatly, hoping he would let her start with the candy making. Sometimes, she sold a few bags to the young women getting off the train at about this time.

"How much kimchi will you have when it's ready?"

"I'll have plenty to sell you. Do you know how much you want? Most of my customers like to bring their own containers. How much do you think you need?" Her customers were Korean women who worked in factories and didn't have time to make their own *banchan*. When she sold sweets, her customers were children and young women. "Just stop by in three days, and if you bring your own container—"

The young man laughed.

"Well, I was thinking that maybe you can sell me everything you make." He adjusted his eyeglasses.

"You can't eat that much kimchi! And how would you keep the rest of it fresh?" Sunja replied, shaking her head at his foolishness. "It's going to be summer in a couple of months, and it's hot here already."

"I'm sorry. I should have explained. My name is Kim Changho, and I manage the *yakiniku* restaurant right by Tsuruhashi Station. News of your excellent kimchi has spread far."

Sunja wiped her hands on the apron that she wore over her padded cotton vest, keeping a close eye on the hot coals.

"It's my sister-in-law who knows what she's doing in the kitchen. I just sell it and help her make it."

"Yes, yes, I'd heard that, too. Well, I'm looking for some women to make all the kimchi and *banchan* for the restaurant. I can get you cabbage and—"

"Where, sir? Where do you get cabbage? We looked everywhere. My sister-in-law goes to the market early in the morning and still—"

"I can get it," he said, smiling.

Sunja didn't know what to say. The candy-making metal bowl was hot already, and it was time to put in the sugar and water, but she didn't want to start now. If this person was serious, then it was important to hear him out. She heard the train arrive. She had missed her first batch of customers already.

"Where's your restaurant again?"

"It's the big restaurant on the side street behind the train station. On the same street as the pharmacy—you know, the one owned by the skinny

Japanese pharmacist, Okada-san? He wears black glasses like mine?" He pushed his glasses up on his nose again and smiled like a boy.

"Oh, I know where the pharmacy is."

This was the shop where all the Koreans went when they were really sick and were willing to pay for good medicine. Okada was not a friendly man, but he was honest; he was reputed to be able to cure many ailments.

The young man didn't seem like anyone who was trying to take advantage of her, but she couldn't be sure. In the few short months working as a vendor, she'd given credit to a few customers and had not been repaid. People were willing to lie about small things and to disregard your interests.

Kim Changho gave her a business card. "Here's the address. Can you bring your kimchi when it's done? Bring all of it. I'll pay you in cash, and I'll get you more cabbage."

Sunja nodded, not saying anything. If she had only one customer for the kimchi, then she'd have more time to make other things to sell. The hardest part had been procuring the cabbage, so if this man could do that, then the work would be much easier. Kyunghee had been scouring the market with Mozasu on her back to track down these scarce ingredients and often returned home with a light market basket. Sunja promised to bring him what she had.

The restaurant was the largest storefront on the short side street parallel to the train station. Unlike the other businesses nearby, its sign was lettered handsomely by a professional sign maker. The two women admired the large black letters carved and painted into a vast wooden plaque. They wondered what the words meant. It was obviously a Korean *galbi* house— the scent of grilled meat could be detected from two blocks away—but the sign had difficult Japanese lettering that neither of them could read. Sunja grasped the handlebar of the carts loaded with all the kimchi they'd put up in the past few weeks and took a deep breath. If the kimchi sales to the restaurant were steady, they'd have a regular income. She could buy eggs more often for Isak's and Noa's meals and get heavy wool cloth for Kyunghee, who wanted to sew new coats for Yoseb and Noa.

Yoseb had been staying away from home, complaining of the sight and smell of all the kimchi ingredients spilling out from the kitchen. He didn't want to live in a kimchi factory. His dissatisfaction was the primary reason why the women preferred to sell candy, but sugar was far more difficult to find than cabbage or sweet potatoes. Although Noa didn't complain of it, the kimchi odor affected him the most. Like all the other Korean children at the local school, Noa was taunted and pushed around, but now that his clean-looking clothes smelled immutably of onions, chili, garlic, and shrimp paste, the teacher himself made Noa sit in the back of the classroom next to the group of Korean children whose mothers raised pigs in their homes. Everyone at school called the children who lived with pigs *buta*. Noa, whose *tsumei* was Nobuo, sat with the *buta* children and was called garlic turd.

At home, Noa asked his aunt for snacks and meals that didn't contain garlic, hoping this would keep the children from saying bad things to him. When she asked him why, Noa told his aunt the truth. Even though it cost more, Kyunghee bought Noa large milk rolls from the bakery for his breakfast and made him potato *korokke* or *yakisoba* for his school bento.

The children were merciless, but Noa didn't fight them; rather, he worked harder on his studies, and to the surprise of his teachers, he was the first or second in academic rank in his second grade class. At school, Noa didn't have any friends, and when the Korean children played in the streets, he didn't join them. The only person he looked forward to seeing was his uncle, but these days, when Yoseb was home, he was not himself.

In the street, Kyunghee and Sunja stood quietly in front of the restaurant, unable to enter. The door was ajar, but it was not open for business. Despite Kyunghee's initial excitement at the prospect of selling more kimchi, she'd been reasonably skeptical of the offer and had refused to let Sunja go to an unknown place by herself. She'd insisted on coming along, toting Mozasu on her back. They didn't tell Yoseb about coming here, but they planned on telling him everything after the first meeting.

"I'll stay out here with the cart and wait," Kyunghee said, patting Mozasu rhythmically with her right hand. The baby was resting calmly in the sling on Kyunghee's back.

"Shouldn't I bring the kimchi in?" Sunja said.

"Why don't you ask him to come outside?"

"We can both go in."

"I'll wait outside. But if you don't come outside soon, then I'll come in, all right?"

"But how will you push the cart and—"

"I can push the cart. Mozasu is fine." The baby was now laying his head drowsily on her back, and she kept up a reliable rocking motion.

"Go on inside, and I'll wait. Just ask Kim Changho to come out here. Don't keep talking to him inside, all right?"

"But I thought we'd talk to him together."

Sunja stared at her sister-in-law, not knowing what she should do, and then it occurred to her that her sister-in-law was afraid of going into the restaurant. If her husband asked her what had happened, she could say honestly that she was outside the whole time.

3

April 1940

It was the second restaurant she'd ever entered in her life. The main dining room was nearly five times the size of the udon shop in Busan that she'd gone to with Isak. The lingering smells of burnt meat and stale cigarettes from the previous night scraped against her throat. There were two rows of dining tables on a raised tatami-covered platform. Below the platform was a space for the guests' shoes. In the open kitchen, a teenage boy wearing a white undershirt washed beer glasses two at a time. With the water running and the clinking of the glasses, he didn't hear Sunja coming into the restaurant; she stared at his sharp profile as he concentrated on his work, hoping he'd notice her.

The man from the market had never specified the time of day for her to show up with the kimchi, and it had never occurred to her to ask whether to come by in the morning or afternoon. Kim Changho was nowhere to be seen. What if he was out today, or only came to work in the afternoons or evenings? If she went outside without speaking to anyone, Kyunghee wouldn't know what to do, either. Her sister-in-law was susceptible to endless worrying, and Sunja didn't want to trouble her.

The water in the sink stopped running, and the boy, exhausted from the night-to-morning shift, stretched his neck from side to side. The sight of the young woman surprised him. She wore Japanese trousers and a blue padded jacket that had faded from wear.

"*Agasshi*, we're not open right now," he said in Korean. She wasn't a customer, but she wasn't a beggar, either.

"Excuse me. I'm sorry to bother you, but do you know where Kim Changho is? He asked me to come by with the kimchi. I wasn't sure when I—"

"Oh! Is that you?" The boy grinned in relief. "He's just down the street. Boss told me to get him if you came by today. Why don't you sit down and wait. Did you bring the kimchi? The customers have been complaining about the side dishes for weeks. Are you going to work here, too? Hey, how old are you anyway?" The boy wiped his hands and opened the kitchen door in the back. The new girl was sweet looking, he thought. The last kimchi *ajumma* had been a toothless granny who'd yell at him for nothing. She'd been fired for drinking too much, but this one looked younger than he was.

Sunja was confused. "Wait, Kim Changho isn't here?"

"Have a seat. I'll be right back!"

The boy dashed out the door.

Sunja looked around, and, realizing that she was alone, she went outside.

Kyunghee whispered, "The baby's sleeping now."

She was sitting on the stubby market stool that normally hung on the side of the cart. In the bright sun, a slight breeze blew against the puffy tufts of Mozasu's hair and his smooth brow. It was early in the morning, and there were hardly any passersby on the street. The pharmacy hadn't even opened yet.

"Sister, the manager's on his way. Do you still want to wait outside?" Sunja asked.

"I'll be fine here. You go in and wait by the window so I can see you. But come out when he gets here, okay?"

Back inside the restaurant, Sunja was afraid to sit down, so she stood a foot away from the door. She knew they could have sold this kimchi today at the market. She was here because the man said he could get her cabbage—that alone was enough to make her stay and wait for him. Without the cabbage, they didn't have a business.

"How nice to see you!" Changho shouted, entering from the kitchen door. "Did you bring the kimchi?"

"My sister-in-law is watching the cart outside. We brought a lot."

"I hope you can make more."

"You haven't even tried it," she said quietly, confused by his enthusiasm.

"I'm not worried. I did my homework. I heard it's the most delicious kimchi in Osaka," he said, walking briskly toward her. "Let's go outside then."

Kyunghee bowed as soon as she saw him, but she didn't speak.

"Hello, my name is Kim Changho," he said to Kyunghee, a little startled by the woman's beauty. He couldn't tell how old she was, but the baby strapped to her back was not more than six months.

Kyunghee said nothing. She looked like a lovely, nervous mute.

"Is this your baby?" he asked.

Kyunghee shook her head, glancing at Sunja. This wasn't like talking to Japanese merchants—something she had to do to buy groceries or things needed for the house. Yoseb had told her on numerous occasions that money and business were men's issues, and suddenly she felt incapable of saying anything. Before getting here, it had been her plan to help Sunja with the negotiations, but now she felt like if she said anything at all, it would be unhelpful or wrong.

Sunja asked, "Do you know how much kimchi you'd like? On a regular basis, I mean. Do you want to wait to make an order after you try this batch?"

"I'll take all that you can make. I'd prefer it if you could make the kimchi here. We have refrigerators and a very cold basement that might be good for your purposes."

"In the kitchen? You want me to pickle the cabbages in there?" Sunja pointed to the restaurant door.

"Yes." He smiled. "In the mornings, you two can come here and make the kimchi and the side dishes. I have cooks who come in the afternoon to cut up the meat and fix the marinades, but they can't handle the kimchi and *banchan*. That sort of thing requires more skills. The customers want

more home-style dishes for the pickles. Any fool can make a marinade and grill meat, but the customer needs a fine array of *banchan* to make him feel like he's dining like a king, wouldn't you say?"

He could see that they were still uncomfortable with the idea of working in a restaurant kitchen.

"Besides, you wouldn't want me to deliver boxes and boxes of cabbages and vegetables to your house, would you? That can't be very comfortable."

Kyunghee whispered to Sunja, "We can't work in a restaurant. We should make the kimchi at home, and we can bring it here. Or maybe they can send the boy to pick it up if we can't carry it all."

"You don't understand. I need you to make much, much more than whatever you were making before. I manage two more restaurants that require kimchi and *banchan*—this one is the central location and has the largest kitchen, though. I'd provide all your ingredients; you just tell me what you want. You'd be paid a good salary."

Kyunghee and Sunja looked at him, not understanding his meaning.

"Thirty-five yen a week. Each of you would get the same amount, so it's seventy yen in total."

Sunja opened her mouth in surprise. Yoseb earned forty yen per week.

"And every now and then, you could take some meat home," Kim said, smiling. "We'd have to see what we can do to make you enjoy working here. Maybe even some grains. If you need a lot of things for your personal use, I'd charge you what we pay for them. We can figure that out later."

After paying for the ingredients, Sunja and Kyunghee netted approximately ten to twelve yen a week from peddling. If they could earn seventy yen a week, they wouldn't worry about money. No one at home had eaten any chicken or fish in the past six months because of the cost; buying beef or pork had been impossible. Each week, they still bought soup bones and splurged on the occasional egg for the men, but Sunja wanted the boys, Isak, and Yoseb to eat other things besides potatoes and millet. With so much money, it would be possible to send more money to their parents, who were suffering far more than they let on.

"And I could be home when my older son, Noa, gets home?" Sunja blurted out without meaning to.

"Yes, of course," Kim said, as if he'd thought this through. "You could leave when you're done with your work. You could be finished before lunchtime even, I suppose."

"And my baby?" Sunja pointed to Mozasu, who slept on Kyunghee's back. "Can I bring him? He could stay in the kitchen with us," Sunja said, unable to imagine leaving him with one of the overwhelmed grannies in the neighborhood who watched the workingwomen's children. When there was no one to watch them at home, or if they couldn't afford to pay the grannies, a few women at the market tethered their very small children to their carts with ropes; the children with ropes crisscrossed around their torsos seemed happy to wander about or to sit by their mothers playing with cheap toys.

"The baby's not much trouble at all," Sunja said.

"Why not? As long as the work gets done, I don't care. There are no customers here at the time you're working, so they won't be in the way," he said. "If you need to stay late and your older son wants to come here from school, that's fine, too. There are no customers here until dinner-time."

Sunja nodded. She wouldn't have to spend another cold winter standing outside, waiting for customers, all the while worrying about Noa and Mozasu.

Seeing that Kyunghee looked more agitated than pleased at this job offer, which would change everything, Sunja said, "We have to ask. For permission—"

After the dinner table was cleared, Kyunghee brought her husband a cup of barley tea and his ashtray so he could have a smoke. Seated cross-legged near his uncle, Noa played with the brightly painted top that Yoseb had bought for him, and the child was mesmerized by how fast it could go. The wooden toy made a pleasant whirring sound against the floor. Sunja, who held Mozasu in her arms, watched Noa playing, wondering how Isak was. Ever since Isak's arrest, Sunja barely spoke at home for fear of up-

setting her brother-in-law, whose temperament had altered greatly. When he got angry, he'd walk out of the house; sometimes, he wouldn't even bother coming home until very late. The women knew that Yoseb would be against their working at the restaurant.

After Yoseb lit his cigarette, Kyunghee told him about the jobs. They needed the work, she said, using the word "work" rather than "money."

"Have you lost your mind? First, you make food to sell under a bridge by a train station, and now both of you want to work in a restaurant where men drink and gamble? Do you know what kind of women go into such places? What, next you'll be pouring drinks for—?" Yoseb's unsmoked cigarette shook between his trembling fingers. He was not a violent man, but he'd had enough.

"Did you actually go into the restaurant?" he asked, not quite believing this conversation.

"No," Kyunghee replied. "I stayed outside with the baby, but it was a big, clean place. I saw it through the window. I went to the meeting with Sunja in case the place wasn't nice, because Sunja shouldn't go there by herself. The manager, Kim Changho, was a well-spoken young man, and you should meet him. We wouldn't go there if you didn't give us permission. *Yobo*—" Kyunghee could see how upset he was, and she felt terrible about it. She respected no one more than Yoseb. Women complained about their men, but there were no bad words to say about her husband; Yoseb was a truthful person who kept his word. He tried all he could; he was honorable. He did his best to care for them.

Yoseb put out his cigarette. Noa stopped spinning his top, and the boy looked frightened.

"Maybe if you met him . . ." Kyunghee knew they had to take this job, but she knew her husband would be humiliated by it. In their marriage, he had denied her nothing except for her ability to earn money. He believed that a hardworking man should be able to take care of his family by himself, and that a woman should remain at home.

"He could pay you instead of us; we'd just save the money for Isak's boys and send more to your parents. We could buy Isak better food and send him clothes. We don't know when he's—" Kyunghee stopped her-

self. Noa had sidled up closer to his uncle as if to protect him. He patted his uncle's leg the same way his uncle would pat his back when Noa fell down or got discouraged by something at school.

Although his head was full of arguments, Yoseb couldn't speak. He was working two full-time jobs—managing two factories for Shimamura-san, who paid him half the salary of one Japanese foreman. Lately, he repaired broken metal presses for a Korean factory owner after hours, but he couldn't count on that for a steady income. He hadn't mentioned this recent job to his wife, because he preferred for her to think of him working as a manager rather than as a mechanic. Before he got home, he'd scrub his hands ruthlessly with a bristle brush, using diluted lye to get out the machine oil stains from beneath his fingernails. No matter how hard he worked, there was never enough money—the yen notes and coins dropped out of his pockets as if they had gaping holes.

Japan was in trouble; the government knew it but would never admit defeat. The war in China pressed on without letting up. His boss's sons fought for Japan. The older one, who'd been sent to Manchuria, had lost a leg last year, then died of gangrene, and the younger one had been sent to Nanjing to take his place. In passing, Shimamura-san had mentioned that Japan was in China in order to stabilize the region and to spread peace, but the way he'd said all this hadn't given Yoseb the impression that Shimamura-san believed any of it. The Japanese were going deeper into the war in Asia, and there were rumors that Japan would soon be allied with Germany in the war in Europe.

Did any of this matter to Yoseb? He'd nodded at the right times and grunted affirmatively when his Japanese boss was talking about the war, because you were supposed to nod when the boss told you his stories. Nevertheless, to every Korean he knew, Japan's expanding war in Asia seemed senseless. China was not Korea; China was not Taiwan; China could lose a million people and still keep on. Pockets of it may fall, but it was an unfathomably vast nation; it would endure by sheer number and resolve. Did Koreans want Japan to win? Hell no, but what would happen to them if Japan's enemies won? Could the Koreans save themselves? Apparently not. So save your own ass—this was what Koreans believed

privately. Save your family. Feed your belly. Pay attention, and be skeptical of the people in charge. If the Korean nationalists couldn't get their country back, then let your kids learn Japanese and try to get ahead. Adapt. Wasn't it as simple as that? For every patriot fighting for a free Korea, or for any unlucky Korean bastard fighting on behalf of Japan, there were ten thousand compatriots on the ground and elsewhere who were just trying to eat. In the end, your belly was your emperor.

Every minute of every day, Yoseb was worried about money. If he dropped dead, what would happen? What kind of man let his wife work in a restaurant? He knew this *galbi* place—who didn't? There were three of them, and the main one was by the train station. The gangsters ate there late at night. The owners set the prices high to keep out the regular people and the Japanese. When Yoseb had needed to borrow money for Isak and Sunja's passage to Japan, he'd gone there. Which was worse—his wife working for moneylenders or him owing money to them? For a Korean man, the choices were always shit.

4

May 1942

Noa Baek was not like the other eight-year-olds in the neighborhood. Each morning before he went to school, he'd scrub his face until his cheeks were pink, smooth three drops of oil on his black hair, then comb it away from his forehead as his mother had taught him to do. After a breakfast of barley porridge and miso soup, he'd rinse his mouth and check his white teeth in the small round hand mirror by the sink. No matter how tired his mother was, she made certain that Noa's shirts were ironed the night before. In his clean, pressed clothes, Noa looked like a middle-class Japanese child from a wealthier part of town, bearing no resemblance to the unwashed ghetto children outside his door.

At school, Noa was strong in both arithmetic and writing, and he surprised the gym teacher with his adept hand-eye coordination and running speed. After classes ended, he tidied the shelves and swept the classroom floors without being asked and walked home alone, trying not to draw any undue attention to himself. The boy managed to look unafraid of the tougher children while setting himself apart with a perimeter of quiet privacy that could not be disturbed. When he got home, Noa went directly into the house to do his schoolwork without lingering on the street with the neighborhood children who played until dinnertime.

When his mother and aunt moved the kimchi-making business to the restaurant, the house no longer smelled relentlessly of fermenting cabbage and pickles. Noa hoped he'd no longer be called garlic turd. If anything,

lately, their house smelled less of cooking than the others in the neighborhood, because his mother and aunt brought home cooked food from the restaurant for their family meals. Once a week, Noa got to eat tidbits of grilled meat and white rice from the restaurant.

Like all children, Noa kept secrets, but his were not ordinary ones. At school, he went by his Japanese name, Nobuo Boku, rather than Noa Baek; and though everyone in his class knew he was Korean from his Japanized surname, if he met anyone who didn't know this fact, Noa wasn't forthcoming about this detail. He spoke and wrote better Japanese than most native children. In class, he dreaded the mention of the peninsula where his parents were born and would look down at his papers if the teacher mentioned anything about the colony of Korea. Noa's other secret: His father, a Protestant minister, was in jail and had not been home in over two years.

The boy tried to remember his father's face, but couldn't. When asked to tell family stories for class assignments, Noa would say that his father worked as a foreman at a biscuit factory, and if some children inferred that Uncle Yoseb was his father, Noa didn't correct them. The big secret that he kept from his mother, aunt, and even his beloved uncle was that Noa did not believe in God anymore. God had allowed his gentle, kindhearted father to go to jail even though he had done nothing wrong. For two years, God had not answered Noa's prayers, though his father had promised him that God listens very carefully to the prayers of children. Above all the other secrets that Noa could not speak of, the boy wanted to be Japanese; it was his dream to leave Ikaino and never to return.

It was a late spring afternoon; Noa returned home from school and found his snack, left out by his mother before she went to work, waiting for him on the low table where the family ate their meals and where Noa did his homework. Thirsty, he went to the kitchen to get some water, and when he returned to the front room, he screamed. Near the door, there was a gaunt and filthy man collapsed on the floor.

Unable to rise, the man leaned the weight of his torso on the crook of his left elbow and tried to push up to sitting, but couldn't manage it.

Should he scream again? Noa wondered. Who would help him? His mother, aunt, and uncle were at work, and no one had heard him the first time. The beggar didn't seem dangerous; he looked ill and dirty, but he could've been a thief, too. Uncle had warned Noa about burglars and thieves who could break into the house looking for food or valuables. He had fifty sen in his trouser pocket; he'd been saving it for an illustrated book on archery.

The man was sobbing now, and Noa felt bad for him. There were many poor people on his street, but no one looked as bad as this man. The beggar's face was covered with sores and black scabs. Noa reached into his pocket and pulled out the coin. Afraid that the man might grab his leg, Noa stepped just close enough to place the coin on the floor near the man's hand. Noa planned to walk backward to the kitchen and run out the back door to get help, but the man's crying made him pause.

The boy looked carefully at the man's gray-bearded face. His clothes were torn and grimy but the shape of them resembled the dark suits that his principal at school wore.

"It's *appa*," the man said.

Noa gasped and shook his head no.

"Where's your mother, child?"

It was his voice. Noa took a step forward.

"*Umma*'s at the restaurant," Noa replied.

"Where?"

Isak was confused.

"I'll go now. I'll get *umma*. Are you okay?" The boy didn't know what to do exactly. He was still a bit afraid, though it was certainly his father. The gentle eyes beneath the jutting cheekbones and scaly skin were the same. Perhaps his father was hungry. His shoulder bones and elbows looked like sharp tree branches beneath his clothing. "Do you want to eat something, *appa*?"

Noa pointed to the snack his mother had left for him: two rice balls made from barley and millet.

Isak shook his head, smiling at the boy's concern.

"*Aga*—can you get me some water?"

When Noa returned with the cup of cold water from the kitchen, he found his father slumped to the ground with his eyes closed.

"*Appa*! *Appa*! Wake up! I have your water! Drink your water, *appa*," Noa cried.

Isak's eyes fluttered open; he smiled at the sight of the boy.

"*Appa* is tired, Noa. *Appa* is going to sleep."

"*Appa*, drink your water." The boy held out the cup.

Isak raised his head and took a long drink, then closed his eyes again.

Noa bent over, close to his father's mouth, to check his breathing. He retrieved his own pillow and tucked it beneath Isak's bushy gray head. He covered him with the heavy quilt and closed the front door behind him quietly. Noa ran to the restaurant as fast as he could.

He burst into the dining room, but no one in the front area noticed him. None of the grown men working there minded the well-mannered boy who never said much beyond yes and no. The toddler, Mozasu, was sleeping in the storage room; when awake, the two-year-old tore through the dining room, but asleep, he looked like a statue of an angel. The manager, Kim, never complained about Sunja's children. He bought toys and comic books for the boys and occasionally watched Mozasu while he worked in the back office.

"*Uh-muh*." Kyunghee looked up from her work, alarmed at the sight of Noa, breathless and pale, in the kitchen. "You're sweating. Are you okay? We'll be done soon. Are you hungry?" She got up from her crouching position to fix him something to eat, thinking he'd come by because he was lonesome.

"*Appa* came home. He looks sick. He's sleeping on the floor at home."

Sunja, who'd been quiet, waiting for Noa to speak up, wiped her wet hands on her apron. "Can I go? Can we leave now?" She'd never left early before.

"I'll stay here and finish. You go. Hurry. I'll be right there after I'm done."

Sunja reached for Noa's hand.

*   *   *

Halfway down the street, Sunja shouted, "Mozasu!" and Noa looked up at her.

"*Umma*, Aunt will bring him home," he said calmly.

She clutched his hand tighter and walked briskly toward the house.

"You ease my mind, Noa. You ease my mind."

Without the others around, it was possible to be kind to her son. Parents weren't supposed to praise their children, she knew this—it would only invite disaster. But her father had always told her when she had done something well; out of habit, he would touch the crown of her head or pat her back, even when she did nothing at all. Any other parent might've been chided by the neighbors for spoiling a daughter, but no one said anything to her crippled father, who marveled at his child's symmetrical features and normal limbs. He took pleasure in just watching her walk, talk, and do simple sums in her head. Now that he was gone, Sunja held on to her father's warmth and kind words like polished gems. No one should expect praise, and certainly not a woman, but as a little girl, she'd been treasured, nothing less. She'd been her father's delight. She wanted Noa to know what that was like, and she thanked God with every bit of her being for her boys. On the days when it felt impossible to live another day in her husband's brother's house—to work through the whole day and night, then to wake up again before the sun to start again, to go to the jail and hand over a meal for her husband—Sunja thought of her father, who had never said a cross word to her. He had taught her that children were a delight, that her boys were her delight.

"Did *appa* look very ill?" Sunja asked.

"I didn't know it was him. *Appa* was usually so clean and nicely dressed, *nee?*"

Sunja nodded, having told herself long ago to expect the worst. The elders in her church had warned her that the Korean prisoners were usually sent home just as they were about to die, so that they would not die in jail. The prisoners were beaten, starved, and made to go without clothing to weaken them. Just that morning, Sunja had gone to the jail to drop off his meal and this week's clean set of undershirts. Brother had been right then; her husband must not have received any of these things. As she and

Noa walked down the busy street, oblivious to the crowds, it occurred to her that she'd never thought to prepare her son for Isak's return. If anything, she had been so busy preparing for his death by working and saving money that she had not thought about what the boy might think of his father's return, or worse, his death. She felt so sorry for not having told him what to expect. It must have been a terrible shock for Noa.

"Did you eat your snack today?" she asked him, not knowing what else to say.

"I left it for *appa*."

They passed a small throng of uniformed students streaming out of a confectionery, eating their treats happily. Noa looked down, but didn't let go of his mother's hand. He knew the children, but none were his friends.

"Do you have homework?"

"Yes, but I'll do it when I get home, *umma*."

"You never give me any trouble," she said, feeling his five perfect fingers in hers, and she felt grateful for his sturdiness.

Sunja opened the door slowly. Isak was on the floor, sleeping. She knelt by his head. Dark, mottled skin stretched across his eye sockets and high cheekbones. His hair and beard were nearly white; he looked years older than his brother, Yoseb. He was no longer the beautiful young man who had rescued her from disgrace. Sunja removed his shoes and peeled off his holey socks. Dried crusts of blood covered his cracked, raw soles. The last toe on his left foot had turned black.

"*Umma*," Noa said.

"Yes." She turned to him.

"Should I get Uncle?"

"Yes." She nodded, trying not to cry. "Shimamura-san may not let him leave early, Noa. If Uncle can't leave, tell him that I'm with him. We don't want Uncle to get in trouble at work. Okay?"

Noa ran out of the house, not bothering to slide the door fully shut, and the incoming breeze woke Isak; he opened his eyes to see his wife sitting next to him.

"*Yobo*," he said.

Sunja nodded. "You're home. We're so glad you're home."

He smiled. The once-straight white teeth were either black or missing—the lower set cracked off entirely.

"You've suffered so much."

"The sexton and the pastor died yesterday. I should've died a long time ago."

Sunja shook her head, unable to speak.

"I'm home. Every day, I imagined this. Every minute. Maybe that's why I am here. How hard it must have been for you," he said, looking at her kindly.

Sunja shook her head no, wiping her face with her sleeve.

The Korean and Chinese girls who worked at the factory smiled at the sight of Noa. The delicious scent of freshly baked wheat biscuits greeted him. A girl packing biscuit boxes near the door whispered in Korean how tall he was getting. She pointed to his uncle's back. He was crouched over the motor of the biscuit machine. The factory floor was long and narrow, designed like a wide tunnel for the easy inspection of workers; the owner had set up the imposing biscuit machine by his office with the conveyor belts moving toward the workers, who stood in parallel rows. Yoseb wore safety goggles and was poking about inside the service panel with a pair of pliers. He was the foreman and the factory mechanic.

The din of the heavy machine blocked out normal speaking voices. The girls weren't supposed to talk on the factory floor, but it was nearly impossible to catch them if they whispered and made minimal facial gestures. Forty unmarried girls, hired for their nimble fingers and general tidiness, packed twenty thin wheat biscuits into wooden boxes that would be shipped to army officers stationed in China. For every two broken biscuits, a girl was fined a sen from her wages, forcing her to work carefully as well as swiftly. If she ate even a broken corner of a biscuit, she'd be terminated immediately. At the end of the day, the youngest girl gathered the broken biscuits into a fabric-lined basket, packed them into small bags, and was sent out to the market to sell

them at a discount. If they didn't sell, Shimamura sold the biscuits for a nominal amount to the girls who packed the most boxes without error. Yoseb never took broken biscuits home, because the girls made so little money, and even the biscuit crumbs meant so much to them.

Shimamura, the owner, was sitting in his glassed-in office, the size of a utility closet. The plate glass window allowed him to check the girls' work. If he found anything amiss, he'd call Yoseb in and tell him to give the girl a warning. On the second warning, the girl was sent home without pay even if she'd worked for six days. Shimamura kept a blue, cloth-bound ledger with warnings listed next to the names of the girls, written in his beautiful hand-lettering. His foreman, Yoseb, disliked punishing the girls, and Shimamura viewed this as yet another example of Korean weakness. The factory owner believed that if all Asian countries were run with a kind of Japanese efficiency, attention to detail, and high level of organization, Asia as a whole would prosper and rise—able to defeat the unscrupulous West. Shimamura believed he was a fair person with perhaps a too-soft heart, which explained why he hired foreigners when many of his friends wouldn't. When they pointed to the slovenly nature of foreigners, he argued how could the foreigners ever learn unless the Japanese taught them to loathe incompetence and sloth. Shimamura felt that standards must be maintained for posterity's sake.

Noa had been inside the factory only once, and Shimamura had not been pleased then. About a year ago, Kyunghee was sick with a high fever and had fainted in the market, and Noa was sent to fetch Yoseb. Shimamura had reluctantly allowed Yoseb to attend to his wife. The next morning, he explained to Yoseb that there would be no repeat of this incident. How could he, Shimamura asked, run two machine-based factories without the presence of a competent mechanic? If Yoseb's wife were to get sick again, she would have to rely on a neighbor or family member; Yoseb could not just leave the factory in the middle of the day. The biscuits were war orders, and they had to be met promptly. Men were risking their lives fighting for their country; each family must make sacrifices.

So when Shimamura spotted the boy again, only a year after that un-

comfortable speech that he had not wanted to make, he was furious. He snapped open his newspaper, pretending not to see the boy tapping his uncle's lower back.

Yoseb, startled by Noa's light touch, turned around.

"*Uh-muh*, Noa, what are you doing here?"

"*Appa*'s home."

"Really?"

"Can you come home now?" Noa asked. His mouth made a small red O.

Yoseb removed his goggles and sighed.

Noa closed his mouth and looked down. His uncle would have to get permission, the way his mother had to ask Aunt Kyunghee or Mr. Kim—the same way he had to ask his teacher to go to the bathroom. Sometimes, when it was sunny outside, Noa dreamed of not telling anyone and going to Osaka Bay. He'd been there once with his father on a Saturday afternoon when he was very small, and he always thought it would be nice to go back.

"Is he all right?" Yoseb studied Noa's expression.

"*Appa*'s hair turned gray. He's very dirty. *Umma*'s with him. She said if you can't come, it's okay, but she wanted you to know. To know that *appa* is home now."

"Yes, that's right. I'm glad to know."

Yoseb glanced at Shimamura, who was holding up his newspaper, pretending to read, but was no doubt watching him very carefully. His boss would never allow him to go home now. Also, unlike when Kyunghee fainted, Shimamura knew Isak had gone to jail because the sexton had refused to observe the Shinto ceremony. Periodically, the police came by to question Yoseb as well as to speak with Shimamura, who defended Yoseb as a model Korean. If he left, Yoseb would lose his job, and if the police picked him up for questioning, he would lose his character reference.

"Listen, Noa, work will be done in less than three hours, and then afterwards, I'll hurry home. It's irresponsible for me to leave now without finishing my work. As soon as I'm done, I'll run home faster than you can run. Tell your *umma* that I'll come home right away. And if your *appa* asks, tell him that Brother will be there very soon."

Noa nodded, not understanding why Uncle was crying.

"I have to finish, Noa, so you run home. Okay?" Yoseb put on his safety goggles and turned around.

Noa moved quickly toward the entrance. The sweet scent of biscuits wafted out the door. The boy had never eaten one of those biscuits, never having asked for one.

5

Noa burst through the doors of the house, his head and heart pounding from the breathless run. Gulping in deep lungfuls of air, he told his mother, "Uncle can't leave work."

Sunja nodded, having expected this. She was bathing Isak with a wet towel.

Isak's eyes were closed but his chest rose and fell slightly, punctuated now and then by a series of painful coughs. A light blanket covered his long legs. Ridges of scar tissue furrowed diagonally across Isak's shoulders and discolored torso, making haphazard diamond-shaped intersections. Every time Isak coughed, his neck flushed red.

Noa approached his father quietly.

"No, no. Move back," Sunja said sternly. "*Appa* is very sick. He has a bad cold."

She pulled the blanket up to Isak's shoulders, though she wasn't nearly finished with cleaning him. In spite of the strong soap and several changes of basin water, his body emitted a sour stench; nits clung to his hair and beard.

Isak had been alert for a few moments, his violent coughs waking him, but now when he opened his eyes, he didn't say anything, and when he looked at her, he didn't seem to recognize her.

Sunja changed the compress on Isak's feverish head. The nearest hospital was a long trolley ride away, and even if she could move him by

herself, an all-night wait wouldn't ensure that a doctor would see him. If she could tuck him into the kimchi cart and wheel him to the trolley stop, she could possibly get him into the car, but then what would she do with the cart itself? It wouldn't pass through the trolley door. Noa might be able to push it back home, but then how would she get Isak from the stop to the hospital without the cart? And what if the driver wouldn't let them board? More than once, she'd witnessed the trolley driver asking a sick woman or man to get off.

Noa sat by his father's legs to keep away from his coughing. He felt an urge to pat his father's sharp knee bone—to touch him, to make sure he was real. The boy pulled out his notebook from his satchel to do his homework, keeping close watch on Isak's breathing.

"Noa, you have to put your shoes back on. Go to the drugstore and ask Pharmacist Kong to come. Can you tell him that it's important—that *umma* will pay him double?" Sunja decided that if the Korean pharmacist wouldn't come, she'd ask Kyunghee to plead with the Japanese pharmacist to come by the house, though that was unlikely.

The boy got up and left without a murmur. She could hear him running down the street in his even, rapid steps.

Sunja wrung out the hand towel she was using to bathe Isak above the brass basin. Fresh welts from recent beatings and a number of older scars covered his wide, bony back. She felt sick as she washed his dark and bruised frame. There was no one as good as Isak. He'd tried to understand her, to respect her feelings; he'd never once brought up her shame. He'd comforted her patiently when she'd lost the pregnancies between Noa and Mozasu. Finally, when she gave birth to their son, he'd been overjoyed, but she'd been too worried about how they'd survive with so little money to feel his happiness. Now that he was back home to die, what did money matter, anyway? She should've done more for him; she should've tried to know him the way he had tried to know her; and now it was over. Even with his gashed and emaciated frame, his beauty was remarkable. He was the opposite of her, really; where she was thick and short, he was slender and long-limbed—even his torn-up feet were well shaped. If her eyes were small and anxious, his were large and full of ac-

ceptance. The basin water was now gray, and Sunja got up to change it again.

Isak woke up. He saw Sunja wearing farmer pants and walking away from him. He called out to her, "*Yobo*," but she didn't turn around. He felt like he didn't know how to raise his voice. It was as if his voice was dying while his mind was alive.

"*Yobo*," Isak mumbled, and he reached for her, but she was almost in the kitchen already. He was in Yoseb's house in Osaka. This had to be true because he was, in fact, waking from a dream where he was a boy. In the dream, Isak had been sitting on a low bough of the chestnut tree in his childhood garden; the scent of the chestnut blossoms still lingered in his nose. It was like many of the dreams he'd had in prison where, while he dreamed, he was aware that the dream itself wasn't real. In real life, he'd never been on a tree. When he was young, the family gardener would prop him below that very tree to get some fresh air, but he'd never been strong enough to climb it the way Yoseb could. The gardener used to call Yoseb "Monkey." In the dream, Isak was hugging the thick branches tightly, unable to break from the embrace of the dark green foliage, the clusters of white blossoms with their dark pink hearts. From the house, cheerful voices of the women called to him. He wanted to see his old nursemaid and his sister, though they had died years ago; in the dream, they were laughing like girls.

"*Yobo*—"

"*Uh-muh.*" She put down the washbasin at the threshold of the kitchen and rushed back to him. "Are you all right? Can I get you something?"

"My wife," he said slowly. "How have you been?" Isak felt drowsy and uncertain, but relieved. Sunja's face was different than he remembered—a little older, more weary. "How must've struggled here. I am so sorry."

"Shhh—you must rest," she said.

"Noa." He said the boy's name like he remembered something good. "Where is he? He was here before."

"He went to fetch the pharmacist."

"He looks so healthy. And bright." It was hard to get the words out, but his mind felt clear suddenly, and he wanted to tell her the things he'd been saving up for her.

"You're working at a restaurant now? Are you cooking there?" Isak began to cough and couldn't stop. Pindots of blood splattered on her blouse, and she wiped his mouth with a towel.

When he tried to sit up, she placed her left hand beneath his head and her right over his chest to calm him, fearful that he might hurt himself. The coughs wracked his body. His skin felt hot even through the blankets.

"Please rest. Later. We can talk later."

He shook his head.

"No, no. I—I want to tell you something."

Sunja rested her hands on her lap.

"My life wasn't important," he said, trying to read her eyes, so full of anguish and exhaustion. He needed her to understand that he was thankful to her—for waiting for him, for taking care of the family. It humbled him to think of her laboring and earning money for their family when he wasn't able to support them. Money must've been very hard with him gone and with inflation from the war. The prison guards had complained incessantly of the prices of things—no one had enough to eat, they said. *Quit complaining about the bugs in the gruel.* Isak had prayed constantly for his family's provision. "I brought you here and made your life more difficult."

She smiled at him, not knowing how to say—*you saved me.* Instead, she said, "You must get well." Sunja covered him with a thicker blanket; his body was burning hot, but he shivered. "For the boys, please get well." *How can I raise them without you?*

"Mozasu—where is he?"

"At the restaurant with Sister. Our boss lets him stay there while we work."

Isak looked alert and attentive, as if all his pain had vanished; he wanted to know more about his boys.

"Mozasu," Isak said, smiling. "Mozasu. He saved his people from slavery—" Isak's head throbbed so intensely that he had to close his eyes again. He wanted to see his two sons grow up, finish school, and get married. Isak had never wanted to live so much, and now, just when he wanted to live until he was very old, he'd been sent home to die. "I have

two sons," he said. "I have two sons. Noa and Mozasu. May the Lord bless my sons."

Sunja watched him carefully. His face looked strange, yet peaceful. Not knowing what else to do, she kept talking.

"Mozasu is becoming a big boy—always happy and friendly. He has a wonderful laugh. He runs everywhere. So fast!" She pumped her arms to imitate the toddler's running, and she found herself laughing, and he laughed, too. It occurred to her then that there was only one other person in the world who'd want to hear about Mozasu growing up so well, and until now, she'd forgotten that she could express a prideful joy in her boys. Even when her brother- and sister-in-law were pleased with the children, she couldn't ignore their sadness at their lack; sometimes, she wanted to hide her delight from them for fear that it could be seen as a kind of boasting. Back home, having two healthy and good sons was tantamount to having vast riches. She had no home, no money, but she had Noa and Mozasu.

Isak's eyes opened, and he looked at the ceiling. "I can't go until I see them, Lord. Until I see my children to bless them. Lord, let me not go—"

Sunja bowed her head, and she prayed, too.

Isak closed his eyes again, his shoulders twitching in pain.

Sunja placed her right hand on his chest to check his faint breathing.

The door opened, and as expected, Noa had returned home alone. The pharmacist couldn't come now but promised to come later tonight. The boy returned to his spot by Isak's feet and did his sums while his father slept. Noa wanted to show Isak his schoolwork; even Hoshii-sensei, the hardest teacher in his grade, told Noa that he was good at writing his letters and that he should work hard to improve his illiterate race: "One industrious Korean can inspire ten thousand to reject their lazy nature!"

Isak continued to sleep, and Noa concentrated on his work.

Later, when Kyunghee arrived home with Mozasu, the house felt lively for the first time since Isak's arrest. Isak woke briefly to see Mozasu, who didn't cry at the sight of the skeletal man. Mozasu called him "Papa" and patted his face with both hands, the way he did when he liked someone. With his white, chubby hands, Mozasu made little pats on Isak's sunken

cheeks. The toddler sat still in front of him briefly, but as soon as Isak closed his eyes, Kyunghee removed him, not wanting the baby to get sick.

When Yoseb returned home, the house grew somber again, because Yoseb wouldn't ignore the obvious.

"How could they?" Yoseb said, staring hard at Isak's body.

"My boy, couldn't you just tell them what they wanted to hear? Couldn't you just say you worshipped the Emperor even if it isn't true? Don't you know that the most important thing is to stay alive?"

Isak opened his eyes but said nothing and closed his eyes again. His eyelids felt so heavy that it was painful to keep them open. He wanted to speak with Yoseb, but the words would not come out.

Kyunghee brought her husband a pair of scissors, a long razor blade, a cup of oil, and a basin of vinegar.

"The nits and lice won't die. He should be shaved. It must be so itchy for him," she said, her eyes wet.

Grateful to his wife for giving him something to do, Yoseb rolled up his sleeves, then poured the cup of oil over Isak's head, massaging it into his scalp.

"Isak-ah, don't move," Yoseb said, trying to keep his voice normal. "I'm going to get rid of all these itchy bastards."

Yoseb made clean strokes across Isak's head and threw the cut hair into the metal basin.

"*Yah*—Isak-ah." Yoseb smiled at the memory. "You remember how the gardener used to cut our hair when we were kids? I used to holler like a crazy animal but you never did. You sat there like a baby monk, calm and peaceful, and you never once complained." Yoseb grew quiet, wanting what he saw in front of him not to be true. "Isak-ah, why did I bring you to this hell? I was so lonesome for you. I was wrong, you know, to bring you here, and now I'm punished for my selfishness." Yoseb rested his blade in the basin.

"I will not be all right if you die. Do you understand? You cannot die, my boy. Isak-ah, please don't die. How can I go on? What will I tell our parents?"

Isak continued to sleep, oblivious to his family encircling his pallet.

Yoseb wiped his eyes and shut his mouth, clamping down on his jaws. He picked up the blade again, working steadily to take off the bits of gray hair remaining on his head. When Isak's head was smooth, Yoseb poured oil over his brother's beard.

For the remainder of the evening, Yoseb, Kyunghee, and Sunja rid him of nits and lice, dropping the bugs into jars of kerosene, only stopping to put the boys to bed. Later, the pharmacist came to tell them what they already knew. There was nothing a hospital or a doctor could do for Isak now.

At dawn, Yoseb returned to work. Sunja remained with Isak, and Kyunghee went to the restaurant. Yoseb didn't bother complaining about Kyunghee going to work alone. He was too tired to argue, and the wages were badly needed. Outside the house, the street was filled with the morning bustling of men and women heading to work and children running to school. Isak slept in the front room, his breathing fast and shallow. He was clean and smooth like an infant—all the hair from his body shaved.

After Noa finished breakfast, he laid down his chopsticks neatly and looked up at his mother.

"*Umma*, may I stay home?" he asked, never having dared to ask for such a thing, even when things were awful at school.

Sunja looked up from her sewing, surprised.

"Are you feeling ill?"

He shook his head.

Isak, who was half-awake, had heard the boy's request.

"Noa—"

"Yes, *appa*."

"*Umma* told me that you're becoming a fine scholar."

The child beamed but, out of habit, looked down at his feet.

When Noa received high marks in school, he thought first of his father.

Yoseb had told the boy several times that his father had been a prodigy, having taught himself Korean, Classical Chinese, and Japanese from books with scant tutoring. By the time he went to seminary, Isak had already read the Bible several times.

When school felt difficult, knowing that his father was a learned man had strengthened the boy's resolve to learn.

"Noa."

"Yes, *appa*?"

"You must go to school today. When I was a boy, I wanted to go to school with the other children very much."

The boy nodded, having heard this detail about his father before.

"What else can we do but persevere, my child? We're meant to increase our talents. The thing that would make your *appa* happy is if you do as well as you've been doing. Wherever you go, you represent our family, and you must be an excellent person—at school, in town, and in the world. No matter what anyone says. Or does," Isak said, then paused to cough. He knew it must be taxing for the child to go to a Japanese school.

"You must be a diligent person with a humble heart. Have compassion for everyone. Even your enemies. Do you understand that, Noa? Men may be unfair, but the Lord is fair. You'll see. You will," Isak said, his exhausted voice tapering off.

"Yes, *appa*." Hoshii-sensei had told him that he had a duty to Koreans, too; one day, he would serve his community and make Koreans good children of the benevolent Emperor. The boy stared at his father's newly shaved head. His bald pate was so white in contrast to his dark, sunken cheeks. He looked both new and ancient.

Sunja felt bad for the child; he'd never had a day with both his parents and no one else. When she was growing up, even when there were others around, it had been just the three of them—her father, mother, and her— an invisible triangle. When she thought back to her life at home, this closeness was what she missed. Isak was right about school, but it wouldn't be much longer. Soon, Isak would be gone. She would have given anything to see her father again, but how could she go against Isak's wishes? Sunja picked up Noa's satchel and handed it to the boy, who was crestfallen.

"After school, come home straight away, Noa. We'll be here," Isak said.

Noa remained fixed to his spot on the floor, unable to take his eyes off his father for fear that he'd disappear. The child hadn't realized how much

he'd missed his father until he returned. The ache of missing him had surfaced in his small, concave chest, and he felt anxious about the pain that was sure to return. If he remained home, Noa felt certain that his father would be okay. They wouldn't even have to talk. Why couldn't he study at home the way his father had? Noa wanted to ask this, but it was not in his nature to argue.

Isak, however, didn't want Noa to see him like this anymore. The boy was already afraid, and there was no need to make him suffer any more than he already had. There were many things he hadn't told the child yet about life, about learning, about how to talk to God.

"Is it very hard at school?" Isak asked.

Sunja turned to look at the boy's face; she'd never thought to ask him this.

Noa shrugged. The work was okay, not impossible. The good students, who were all Japanese, the ones he admired, wouldn't speak to him. They wouldn't even look at him. He believed that he could enjoy going to school if he were a regular person and not a Korean. He couldn't say this to his father or to anyone else, because it was certain he'd never be a regular Japanese. One day, Uncle Yoseb said, they would return to Korea; Noa imagined that life would be better there.

Carrying his book bag and bento, Noa lingered by the front door, memorizing his father's kindly face.

"Child, come here," Isak said.

Noa approached him and sat on bended knees. *Please God, please. Please make my father well. I'll ask this just once more. Please.* Noa shut his eyes tightly.

Isak took Noa's hand and held it.

"You are very brave, Noa. Much, much braver than me. Living every day in the presence of those who refuse to acknowledge your humanity takes great courage."

Noa chewed on his lower lip and didn't say anything. He wiped his nose with his hand.

"My child," he said, and Isak let go of his son's hand. "My dear boy. My blessing."

6

December 1944

Like most shops in Osaka with nothing to sell, the restaurant was shuttered frequently, but its three remaining workers showed up six days a week. Food had virtually disappeared from the markets, and even when the rations arrived and the shops opened for half a day to long lines, the offerings were unacceptably sparse and undesirable. You could wait six hours for fish and come home with a scant handful of dried anchovies, or worse, nothing at all. If you had high-level military connections, it was possible to obtain some of what you needed; of course, if you had a great deal of money, there was always the black market. City children were sent alone to the country by train to buy an egg or a potato in exchange for a grandmother's kimono. At the restaurant, Kim Changho, who was in charge of procuring food, kept two storage bins: one, which could be safely inspected by the neighborhood association leaders, who liked to make surprise visits to restaurant kitchens, and another, behind a false wall in the basement, for food bought from the black market. Sometimes, customers—usually wealthy businessmen from Osaka and travelers from abroad—brought their own meat and alcohol to the restaurant. The men who used to cook in the evening were gone now; Kim made up the whole of the evening staff; it was up to him to cook the meats and wash the dishes for the occasional customer.

It was the twelfth month of the year—a mild, wintry morning. When Sunja and Kyunghee arrived for work, Kim asked the women to have a seat at

the square table pushed up against the wall outside the kitchen. This was where they usually took their meals and breaks. He'd already placed a pot of tea on the table. Once seated, Kyunghee poured each of them a cup.

"The restaurant will be closed tomorrow," Kim said.

"For how long?" Sunja asked.

"Till the war is over. This morning, I gave up the last of the metal things. The kitchen's almost empty now. All the steel rice bowls, basins, cooking pots, utensils, steel chopsticks were requisitioned. Even if I could find new ones and remain open, the police will know that we've kept things back and confiscate them. The government doesn't pay us for what they take. We can't keep replacing—" Kim took a sip of his tea. "Well, so it has to be."

Sunja nodded, feeling bad for Kim, who looked upset. He glanced briefly at Kyunghee.

"And what will you do?" Kyunghee asked him.

Kim, younger than Isak, addressed her as Sister. Lately, he depended on her to accompany him to the market to support his civilian status when stopped. Suspicious of military service dodgers, the police and neighborhood association leaders routinely questioned any male not in uniform. To put them off, he'd taken to wearing the dark glasses of a blind man on the streets.

"Can you find another job?" Kyunghee asked.

"Don't worry about me. At least I don't have to fight"—he laughed, touching his eyeglasses; his poor vision had kept him from fighting and from working in the mines when other Koreans had been conscripted— "which is good, since I'm a coward."

Kyunghee shook her head.

Kim stood up.

"We have some customers coming this evening from Hokkaido. I kept back two cooking pans and a few bowls for the meal; we can use those. Sister, I wonder if you can come with me to the market," he said, then he turned to Sunja. "Will you stay here and wait for the liquor man to come? He's supposed to bring a package by. Oh, the customer has asked for your bellflower *muchim* for tonight. I left a packet of dried

bellflowers in the downstairs cupboard. You'll find the other ingredients there."

Sunja nodded, wondering how he'd found dried bellflowers and sesame oil.

Kyunghee got up and put on her old blue coat over her sweater and worker pants. She was still a lovely woman, clear skinned and slender, but now, fine crinkles around her eyes and marionette lines by her mouth appeared when she smiled. Heavy kitchen work had ruined her once-supple white hands, but she did not mind. Yoseb, who held her small right hand when they slept, didn't seem to notice the red scaly patches on her palms resulting from day after day of pickling. After Isak died, Yoseb had become a different man—sullen, brooding, and uninterested in anything but work. His change had transformed their household and their marriage. Kyunghee tried to cheer up her husband, but she could do little to dispel his gloom and silence. At home, no one seemed to talk except for the boys. Yoseb was almost unrecognizable from the boy she had loved from girlhood. He had become this cynical, broken man—something she could never have predicted. So it was only at the restaurant that Kyunghee behaved like herself. Here, she teased Kim like a younger brother and giggled with Sunja while they cooked. Now, even this place would be gone.

After Kim and her sister-in-law left for the market, Sunja shut the door behind them. As she turned toward the kitchen, she heard the knock.

"Did you forget something?" Sunja asked, opening the door.

Hansu stood before her, wearing a black coat over a gray wool suit. His hair was still dark and his face more or less the same, with a slight thickening along his jawline. Reflexively, Sunja checked to see if he was wearing the white leather shoes he used to wear long ago. He wore black leather lace-up shoes.

"It's been a long time," Hansu said calmly, entering the restaurant. Sunja stepped several paces away from him.

"What are you doing here?"

"This is my restaurant. Kim Changho works for me."

Her head felt foggy, and Sunja slumped down on the nearest seat cushion.

*   *   *

Hansu had located her eleven years ago when she'd pawned the silver pocket watch he'd given her. The pawnbroker had tried to sell him that watch, and the rest had been simple detective work. Since then, Hansu had been tracking her daily. After Isak went to prison, he knew she needed money and created this job for her. Sunja learned that the moneylender who'd loaned Yoseb the money worked for him as well. In fact, Hansu's wife was the eldest daughter of a powerful Japanese moneylender in Kansai, and Hansu had been legally adopted by his father-in-law, Morimoto, because the man did not have a son. Koh Hansu, whose legal name was Haru Morimoto, lived in an enormous house outside of Osaka with his wife and three daughters.

Hansu led her back to the table where she'd sat only a few moments ago with Kim and Kyunghee.

"Let's have some tea. You stay here, and I'll get a cup. You seem troubled by my appearance."

Familiar with where everything was, Hansu returned from the kitchen right away with a teacup.

Sunja stared at him, still unable to speak.

"Noa is a very smart boy," he said proudly. "He's a handsome child and an excellent runner."

She tried not to look afraid. How did he know these things? She now recalled every conversation she'd ever had with Kim about her sons. There had been numerous occasions when Noa and Mozasu had been with her at the restaurant when there'd been no school for Noa.

"What do you want?" she asked finally, trying to appear calmer than she felt.

"You have to leave Osaka immediately. Convince your sister and your brother-in-law to go. For the safety of the children. However, if they don't want to go, there's little you can do. I have a place for you and the boys."

"Why?"

"Because the real bombing will start soon here."

"What are you talking about?"

"The Americans are going to bomb Osaka in a matter of days. The

B-29s have been in China. Now they found more bases on the islands. The Japanese are losing the war. The government knows it can never win but won't admit it. The Americans know that the Japanese military has to be stopped. The Japanese military would kill every Japanese boy rather than admit its error. Fortunately, the war will end before Noa is recruited."

"But everyone says Japan is doing better."

"You mustn't believe what you hear from the neighbors or what the newspapers say. They don't know."

"Shhh—" Sunja looked around instinctively at the plate glass window and the front door. If anyone was caught saying such treacherous things, he could be sent to jail. She had repeatedly told her boys to never, ever say anything negative about Japan or the war. "You shouldn't talk like this. You could get in trouble—"

"No one can hear us."

She bit her lower lip and stared, still unable to believe the sight of him. It had been twelve years. Yet here was the same face—the one she had loved so much. She had loved his face the way she had loved the brightness of the moon and the cold blue water of the sea. Hansu was sitting across from her, and he returned her gaze, looking kindly at her. However, he remained composed, certain of every measured word he uttered. There had never been any hesitation in him. He was unlike her father, Isak, her brother-in-law, or Kim. He was unlike any other man she had ever known.

"Sunja-ya, you have to leave Osaka. There's no time to think about it. I came here to tell you this, because the bombs will destroy this city."

Why had he not come sooner? Why had he kept back like a watchful shadow over her life? How many times had he seen her when she had not seen him?

The anger she felt toward him surprised her. "They won't leave, and I can't just—"

"You mean your brother-in-law. He might be a fool, but that's not your problem. The sister-in-law will go if you tell her. This city is made of wood and paper. It'll take no more than a match for it to incinerate. Imagine what will happen with an American bomb." He paused. "Your sons will be killed. Is that what you want? I've already sent my daughters away

a long time ago. A parent must be decisive; a child cannot protect himself."

She understood then. Hansu was worried about Noa. He had a Japanese wife and three daughters. He had no son.

"How do you know? How do you know what will happen?"

"How did I know that you needed work? How did I know where Noa goes to school, that his math teacher is a Korean who pretends to be Japanese, that your husband died because he didn't get out of prison in time, and that you're alone in this world. How did I know how to keep my family safe? It's my job to know what others don't. How did you know to make kimchi and sell it on a street corner to earn money? You knew because you wanted to live. I want to live, too, and if I want to live, I have to know things others don't. Now, I'm telling you something valuable. I'm telling you something so you can save your sons' lives. Don't waste this information. The world can go to hell, but you need to protect your sons."

"My brother-in-law will not abandon his house."

He laughed. "The house will be a pile of ashes. The Japanese will not give him a sen for his pain when it's gone."

"The neighbors said that the war will end soon."

"The war will end soon, but not the way they think. The wealthy Japanese have already sent their families to the country. They've already converted their cash into gold. The rich do not care about politics; they will say anything to save their skin. You're not rich, but you're smart, and I'm telling you that you have to leave today."

"How?"

"Kim will take you, your brother-in-law and sister-in-law, and the boys to a farm outside Osaka prefecture. A sweet-potato farmer owes me a favor. He has a big place, and there'll be plenty of food there. All of you will have to work for him until the war's over, but you'll have a place to sleep and more than enough to eat. Tamaguchi-san has no children; he won't harm you."

"Why did you come?" Sunja began to cry.

"It's not the time to discuss this. Please don't be a foolish woman. You're smarter than that. It's time to take action. The restaurant will be

destroyed no different than your house will be," he said, speaking quickly. "This building is made of wood and a few bricks. Your brother-in-law should sell his house immediately to the next idiot and get out. Or at the very least, he should take his ownership papers with him. Soon, people will be fleeing here like rats, so you have to leave now before it's too late. The Americans will finish this stupid war. Maybe tonight, maybe in a few weeks, but they're not going to put up with this nonsense war for very long. The Germans are losing, too."

Sunja folded her hands together. The war had been going on for so long. Everyone was sick of it. Without the restaurant, the family would have starved even though everyone was working and earning money. Their clothes were threadbare and holey. Cloth, thread, and needles were unavailable. How were Hansu's shoes so shiny when no one had any shoe polish? She and Kyunghee loathed the neighborhood association's endless meetings, yet if they didn't go, the leaders would take it out on their rations. The latest military drills had become ludicrous—on Sunday mornings, grandmothers and little children were required to practice spearing the enemy with sharpened bamboo spears. They said American soldiers raped women and girls and that it would be better to kill yourself than to surrender to such barbarians. Back in the restaurant office, there was a cache of bamboo spears for the workers and the customers in case the Americans landed. Kim kept two hunting knives in his desk drawer.

"Can I go back home? To Busan?"

"There's nothing to eat there, and it isn't safe for you. Women are being taken away from smaller villages in greater numbers."

Sunja looked puzzled.

"I've told you this before: Never listen to anyone who tells you there's good factory work in China or any of the other colonies. Those jobs don't exist. Do you understand me?" His expression grew severe.

"Is my mother all right?"

"She's not young so they won't take her. I'll try to find out."

"Thank you," she said quietly.

Worried about her boys, Sunja hadn't paid enough attention to her mother's welfare. In Yangjin's sparse letters, written for her by a harried

schoolteacher, she'd say that she was fine, expressing more concern for Sunja and the boys than for herself. Sunja hadn't seen her mother in as many years as she had not seen Hansu.

"Can you be ready to go tonight?"

"Why would my brother-in-law listen to me? How can I possibly explain—"

"Tell him that Kim told you that you must leave today. He's talking to your sister-in-law now. Tell him that he learned this privileged information from his boss. I can send Kim to speak to him at your house."

Sunja said nothing. She didn't believe that anyone could convince Yoseb to leave.

"There should be no hesitation. The boys have to be protected."

"But Sister will—"

"So what about her? Listen to me. Choose your sons over everyone else. Don't you know this by now?"

She nodded.

"Bring everyone here at dusk. Kim will keep the restaurant open. No one should know where you're going. You want to get out of here before everyone else tries to as well." Hansu got up and looked at her soberly. "Leave the others if you have to."

7

1945

On the day that Hansu told her to take the boys to the country, Yoseb got a job offer. Earlier that afternoon, a friend of a friend had stopped by Yoseb's biscuit factory and told him of the position: A steel factory in Nagasaki needed a foreman to manage its Korean workers. There would be a housing camp for men, including room and board, but Yoseb couldn't bring his family. The pay was almost triple his current salary. The family would be separated for a while. When Yoseb came home, excited about the offer, Kyunghee and Sunja had news of their own. Hansu's hand was in everything, but what could Sunja say?

At dusk, Kim moved the women and boys to Tamaguchi's farm. The next morning, Yoseb quit his job at the factory, packed one bag, and locked up the house. That afternoon, Yoseb headed to Nagasaki, recalling the time he left Pyongyang for Osaka—the last time he'd left on a journey by himself.

Short months passed before the bombings started, but once they began, the bombing continued through the summer. Hansu was wrong about the timing, but he was right that the neighborhood would turn to ashes.

Tamaguchi, a fifty-eight-year-old sweet-potato farmer, did not mind having the extra pairs of hands. His regular workers and seasonal ones had been conscripted years ago, and there were no able-bodied men to replace them. Several of his former workers had already died in Manchuria,

with two badly disabled in battle, and there had been scant news of the others sent to Singapore and the Philippines. Each morning, as Tamaguchi rose from his futon, he suffered from the routine aches that accompanied aging; however, he was relieved to be old, since he would not have to fight the stupid war. The shortage of men impaired his ambitions for his farm, especially at a time when there was a growing demand for potatoes. Tamaguchi could command any illegal price he wanted, it seemed, and now that he had tasted wealth, so much so that he'd been forced to hide troves of treasure in various parts of the farm, he was willing to do whatever it took to squeeze every golden drop from this national calamity.

Night and day, Tamaguchi cultivated potato slips, turned the earth, and planted. Without men, it was nearly impossible to complete the endless chores of the farm, and without men, there was no one to marry his wife's two sisters, whom he'd been forced to take in—worthless city girls not built for any kind of work. With their chatter and made-up ailments, the sisters distracted his wife from her labors, and he hoped he wouldn't be saddled with them for much longer. Thankfully, his wife's parents were dead. For seasonal work, Tamaguchi had been hiring the elderly men and women in the village, but they were given to endless whining about the difficult nature of planting in the warm weather and harvesting in the cold.

It would never have occurred to Tamaguchi to hire city Koreans or to board them on his farm when he'd turned away many city Japanese who'd sought refuge, but Koh Hansu he could not refuse.

Upon the receipt of Hansu's telegram, the farmer and his overworked wife, Kyoko, configured the barn to make it habitable for the Korean family from Osaka. Only days after their arrival, however, Tamaguchi learned that it was he who'd gotten the better end of the bargain. Hansu had furnished him with two strong women who could cook, clean, and plow; a young man who couldn't see well but could dig and lift; and two clever boys who took instruction perfectly. The Koreans ate plenty, but they earned their keep and bothered no one. They didn't ever complain.

From the first day, Tamaguchi put Noa and Mozasu in charge of feeding the three cows, eight pigs, and thirty chickens; milking the cows;

collecting the eggs; and cleaning the henhouse. The boys spoke Japanese like natives, so he was able to take them to the market to help sell; the older one was excellent with calculations, and his letters were neat enough for the ledger. The two Korean women, sisters-in-law, were fine housekeepers and hardy outdoor workers. The skinny married one was not young but very pretty, and her Japanese was good enough that Kyoko tasked her with the cooking, washing, and mending. The shorter one, the quiet widow, tended the kitchen garden ably and worked in the fields alongside the young man. The two labored like a pair of oxen. For the first time in years, Tamaguchi felt relaxed; even his wife was less irritable, scolding him and her sisters less than usual.

Four months after their arrival, Hansu's truck drove up to the farm at dusk. Hansu stepped out of the truck, and he had with him an older Korean woman. Tamaguchi rushed to meet him. Normally, Hansu's men came by in the evenings to pick up the produce for sale in the city, but it was rarely the boss himself.

"Tamaguchi-san." Hansu bowed. The old woman bowed to Tamaguchi from the waist. She wore a traditional dress and in each hand she clutched fabric parcels.

"Koh-san." Tamaguchi bowed, smiling at the older woman. As he drew closer, Tamaguchi could see that the woman was not very old; in fact, she might have been younger than he was. Her brown face was drawn and malnourished.

"This is Sunja's mother. Kim Yangjin *desu*," Hansu said. "She arrived from Busan earlier today."

"Kim-u Yangjin-san." The farmer said each syllable slowly, realizing that he had a new guest. He scanned her face, searching for any resemblance to the young widow, mother to the two boys. There was some similarity around the mouth and jaw. The woman's brown hands were strong like a man's, with large knobbed fingers. She would make a good worker, he thought. "Sunja's mother? Is that so? Welcome, welcome," he said, smiling.

Yangjin, her eyes downcast, appeared afraid. She was also exhausted.

Hansu cleared his throat.

"And how are the boys? I hope they're not giving you any trouble."

"No, no. Not at all. They're excellent workers! Wonderful boys." Tamaguchi meant this. He had not expected the boys to be so capable. With no children of his own, he had expected city children to be spoiled and lazy like his sisters-in-law. In his village, prosperous farmers complained about their foolish sons, so the childless Tamaguchi and his wife had not envied parents very much. Also, Tamaguchi hadn't had any idea of what Koreans would be like. He was not a bigoted man, but the only Korean he knew personally was Koh Hansu, and their relationship had begun with the war and was not an ordinary one. An open secret, several of the larger farms sold their produce on the city's black markets through Koh Hansu and his distribution network, but no one discussed this. Foreigners and yakuza controlled the black market, and there were serious repercussions for selling produce to them. It was an honor to help Koh Hansu; favors created obligations, and the farmer was determined to do anything he could for him.

"Koh-san, please come inside the house for tea. You must be thirsty. It is very hot today." Tamaguchi walked into the house, and even before taking off his own shoes, the farmer offered house slippers to his guests.

Shaded by ancient, sturdy poplars, the interior of the large farmhouse was pleasantly cool. The fresh grass smell of new tatami mats greeted the guests. In the main room, paneled in cedar, Tamaguchi's wife, Kyoko, sat on a blue silk floor cushion, sewing her husband's shirt; her two sisters, lying on their stomachs with their ankles crossed, flipped through an old movie magazine they'd read so many times before that they'd memorized its text. The three women, exceptionally well dressed for no one in particular, looked out of place in the farmhouse. Despite the rationing of cloth, the farmer's wife and her sisters had not suffered any privation. Kyoko wore an elegant cotton kimono, more suited for a Tokyo merchant's wife, and the sisters wore smart navy skirts and cotton blouses, looking like college co-eds from American films.

When the sisters lifted their chins to see who'd walked into the house, their pale, pretty faces emerged from the long bangs of their stylishly bobbed haircuts. The war had brought priceless treasures to the

Tamaguchi home—valuable calligraphy scrolls, bolts of fabric, more kimonos than the women could ever wear, lacquered cupboards, jewels, and dishes—possessions of city dwellers who'd been willing to trade heirlooms for a sack of potatoes and a chicken. However, the sisters yearned for the city itself—new films, Kansai shops, the unblinking electric lights. They were sick of the war, the endless green fields, and farm life in general. Bellies full and well housed, they had only contempt for the smell of lamp oil, loud animals, and their hick brother-in-law, who was always talking about the prices of things. The American bombs had burned down the cinemas, department stores, and their beloved confectioneries, but glittering images of such urban pleasures called to them still, feeding their growing discontent. They complained daily to their elder sister—the plain and sacrificial one—whom they had once mocked for marrying their distant country cousin, who now prepared gold and kimonos for their dowries.

When Tamaguchi cleared his throat, the girls sat up and tried to look busy. They nodded at Hansu and stared at the filthy hem of the Korean woman's long skirt, unable to keep from making a face.

Yangjin bowed deeply to the three women and remained by the door, not expecting to be invited in, and she was not. From where she stood, Yangjin could see a portion of the bent back of a woman working in the kitchen, but it didn't look like Sunja.

Hansu spotted the woman in the kitchen as well and asked Tamaguchi's wife, "Is that Sunja-san in the kitchen?"

Kyoko bowed to him again. The Korean seemed too confident for her taste, but she recognized that her husband needed the fellow more than ever.

"Koh-san, welcome. It's so nice to see you," Kyoko said, rising from her seat; she gave her sisters a reproving look, which stirred them sufficiently to stand up and bow to the guest. "The woman in the kitchen is Kyunghee-san. Sunja-san is planting in the fields. Please, sit down. We shall get you something cool to drink." She turned to Ume-chan, the younger of the two sisters, and Ume trudged to the kitchen to fetch cold oolong-*cha*.

Hansu nodded, trying not to show his irritation. He'd expected Sunja to work, but it hadn't occurred to him that she'd be doing outdoor labor.

Kyoko sensed the man's displeasure. "Surely, you must want to see your daughter, ma'am. Tako-chan, please accompany our guest to her daughter."

Tako, the middle of the three sisters, complied because she had no choice; it was pointless to defy Kyoko, who could hold a grudge for days in punitive silence. Hansu told Yangjin in Korean to follow the girl who'd take her to Sunja. As Tako put on her shoes in the stone-paved foyer, she caught a whiff of the old woman's sour, peculiar odor, only aggravated by two days of travel. Filthy, she thought. Tako walked briskly ahead of her, keeping as many paces between them as she could.

After Kyoko poured the tea that Ume had brought from the kitchen, the women disappeared, leaving the men to speak alone in the living room.

The farmer asked Hansu for news of the war.

"It can't last much longer. The Germans are being crushed, and the Americans are just getting started. Japan will lose this war. It's a matter of when." Hansu said this without a trace of regret or joy. "It's better to stop this madness sooner than later than to have more nice boys get killed, is it not?"

"Yes, yes. That is so, isn't it?" Tamaguchi replied in a whisper, dispirited. Of course, he wanted Japan to win, and no doubt Hansu knew the realities, but even if Japan would not win, the farmer had no wish for the war to end just yet. There had been talk of fermenting sweet potatoes into airplane fuel; if that happened, and even if the government paid only a little—if anything at all—the farmer expected prices to rise even higher on the black market, because the cities were desperate for food and alcohol. With just one or two more harvests, Tamaguchi would have enough gold to buy the two vast tracts of land beside his. The owner of the plots was only getting older and less interested in working. To own the entire south side of the region in one unbroken lot had been his grandfather's dearest wish.

Hansu interrupted the farmer's reverie.

"So, how is it? Having them here?"

Tamaguchi nodded favorably. "They help a great deal. I wish they didn't have to work so much, but, as you know, I'm short on men—"

"They'd expected to work." Hansu nodded reassuringly, fully cognizant that the farmer was getting back his room and board and making a large profit, but this was okay with him as long as Sunja and her family weren't being mistreated.

"Will you stay with us tonight?" Tamaguchi asked. "It's too late to travel, and you must have dinner with us. Kyunghee-san is an exceptional cook."

Tako didn't have to walk the old woman far. When Yangjin spotted her daughter bent over in the vast, dark field, she grabbed the tail end of her long skirt and wound it around her body to free her legs. She ran as fast as she could in the direction of her daughter.

Sunja, who heard the rushed footfalls, looked up from her planting. A tiny woman in an off-white-colored *hanbok* was running toward her, and Sunja dropped her hoe. The small shoulders, the gray bun gathered at the base of the neck, the bow of the short blouse knotted neatly in a soft rectangle: *Umma*. How was that possible? Sunja trampled the potato slips in her path to get to her.

"Oh, my child. My child. Oh, my child."

Sunja held her mother close, able to feel the sharpness of Yangjin's collarbone beneath the blouse fabric. Her mother had shrunk.

Hansu ate his dinner quickly, then went to the barn to speak with the others. He wanted merely to sit with them, not to have them fuss over him. He would have preferred to eat with Sunja and her family, but he didn't want to offend Tamaguchi. During the meal, he had thought only of her and the boy. They had never shared a meal. It was hard to explain, even to himself, his yearning to be with them. In the barn, he realized that Kyunghee had made two dinners in the Tamaguchi kitchen—a Japanese one for the Tamaguchi family and a Korean for the others. In the barn, the Koreans ate their meals on a low, oilcloth-covered table that Kim had built

for them with leftover beams. Sunja had just cleared the dinner dishes. Everyone looked up when he walked in.

The animals were quieter in the evening, but they were not silent. The smells were stronger than Hansu remembered, but he knew the odor would be less noticeable soon enough. The Koreans were housed in the back part of the barn, and the animals were nearer the front, with haystacks between them. Kim had built a wooden partition, and he and the boys slept on one side with the women on the other.

Yangjin, who'd been sitting on the ground between her grandsons, got up and bowed to him. On the way to the farm, she'd thanked him numerous times, and now, reunited with her family, she kept repeating thank you, thank you, clutching on to her grandsons, who looked embarrassed. She bawled like an old Korean woman.

Kyunghee was still in the farmhouse kitchen, washing the dinner dishes. When she finished with that, she would prepare the guest room for Hansu. Kim was in the shed behind the barn that was used for bathing, busy heating water for everyone's bath. Kyunghee and Kim had taken over Sunja's evening chores to allow her to remain with her mother. None of them suspected the reasons why Hansu had gone through the trouble of getting Yangjin from Korea. As Yangjin sobbed, Sunja observed Hansu, unable to make sense of this man who had never left her life.

Hansu sat down on the thick pile of hay, opposite the boys.

"Did you eat enough dinner?" Hansu asked them in plain Korean.

The boys looked up, surprised that Hansu spoke Korean so well. They'd thought that the man who'd brought their grandmother might be Japanese, because he was so well dressed and since Tamaguchi-san had treated him with such deference.

"You are Noa," Hansu said, considering the boy's face carefully. "You are twelve years old."

"Yes, sir," Noa replied. The man wore very fine clothes and beautiful leather shoes. He looked like a judge or an important person in a movie poster.

"How do you like being on the farm?"

"It is good, sir."

"I'm almost six years old," Mozasu interrupted, something he did out of habit whenever his older brother spoke. "We eat a lot of rice here. I can eat bowls and bowls of rice. Tamaguchi-san said that I need to eat well to grow. He told me not to eat potatoes but to eat rice! Do you like rice, sir?" the boy asked Hansu. "Noa and I will have baths tonight. In Osaka, we couldn't take baths often because there was no fuel for hot water. I like the baths on the farm better because the tub is smaller than the one at the *sento*. Do you like baths? The water is so hot, but you get used it, *nee*, and the tips of my fingers get wrinkled like an old man when I don't come out of the water." Mozasu opened his eyes wide. "My face doesn't wrinkle, though, because I am young."

Hansu laughed. The younger child had none of Noa's formality. He seemed so free.

"I'm glad you're eating well here. That's good to know. Tamaguchi-san said that you boys are excellent workers."

"Thank you, sir," Mozasu said, wanting to ask the man more questions but stopping himself when the man addressed his brother.

"What are your chores, Noa?"

"We clean the stalls here, feed the animals, and take care of the chickens. I also keep records for Tamaguchi-san when we go to the market."

"Do you miss school?"

Noa did not reply. He missed doing math problems and writing Japanese. He missed the quiet of doing his work—how no one bothered him when he was doing his homework. There was never any time to read at the farm, and he had no books of his own.

"I was told that you're a very good student."

"Last year, there wasn't much school."

Back home, school had been canceled often. Unlike the other boys, Noa had disliked the bayonet practices and pointless air raid drills. Although he had not wanted to be separated from Uncle Yoseb, the farm was better than being in the city, because he felt safe here. At the farm, he never heard any planes, and there were far fewer bomb shelter drills. Meals were abundant and delicious. They ate eggs every day and drank fresh milk. He slept deeply and woke up feeling well.

"When the war ends, you will return to school, I suppose. Would you like that?" Hansu asked.

Noa nodded.

Sunja wondered how they would manage then. After the war, she had planned on going back to Yeongdo, but her mother said there was nothing left. The government had assessed taxes on the boardinghouse owner, and the owner had sold the building to a Japanese family. The servant girls had taken factory jobs in Manchuria, and there had been no news of them. When Hansu had located Yangjin, she had been working as a housekeeper for a Japanese merchant in Busan, sleeping in the storeroom.

Hansu pulled out two comic books from his jacket pocket.

"Here."

Noa accepted them with both hands, the way his mother had taught him. The writing was in Korean.

"Thank you, sir."

"Do you read Korean?"

"No, sir."

"You can learn," Hansu said.

"Aunt Kyunghee can help us read this," Mozasu said. "Uncle Yoseb isn't here, but when we see him next time, we can surprise him."

"You boys should know how to read Korean. One day, you may return," Hansu said.

"Yes, sir," Noa said. He imagined that Korea would be a peaceful place where he would be normal. His father had told him that Pyongyang, where he'd grown up, was a beautiful city, and Yeongdo, his mother's hometown, was a serene island with abundant fish in blue-green waters.

"Where are you from, sir?" Noa asked.

"Jeju. It isn't far from Busan, where your mother is from. It's a volcanic island. They have oranges there. The people from Jeju are descendants of gods." He winked. "I will take you there one day."

"I don't want to live in Korea," Mozasu cried. "I want to stay here at the farm."

Sunja patted Mozasu's back.

"*Umma*, we should live on the farm forever. Uncle Yoseb will come here soon, right?" Mozasu asked.

Kyunghee walked in then, having finished her work. Mozasu ran to her with the comic books.

"Can you read this for me?"

Mozasu led her to the pile of folded futons, which they used as chairs. Kyunghee nodded.

"Noa, come. I'll read these to you boys."

Noa bowed quickly to Hansu and joined Kyunghee and Mozasu. Yangjin followed Noa, leaving Sunja at the table. When Sunja started to get up, Hansu gestured for her to sit down.

"Stay." Hansu looked serious. "Stay for a little while. I want to know how you are."

"I'm well. Thank you." Her voice was shaky. "Thank you for bringing my mother here," Sunja said. There was more she needed to say, but it was hard.

"You asked for news of her, and I thought it would be better for her to come here. It's very bad in Japan, but it's worse in Korea right now. When the war ends, it may get better, but it'll be worse before it stabilizes."

"What do you mean?"

"When the Americans win, we don't know what the Japanese will do. They'll pull out of Korea, but who'll be in charge of Korea? What will happen to all those Koreans who supported the Japanese? There will be confusion. There will be more bloodshed. You don't want to be around it. You don't want your sons around it."

"What will you do?" she asked.

He looked directly at her.

"I'll take care of myself and my people. You think I'd trust my life to a bunch of politicians? The people in charge don't know anything. And the ones who do don't care."

Sunja thought about this. Perhaps that was right, but why should she trust him? She pushed herself off the ground with her hands, but Hansu shook his head.

"Is it so difficult to talk with me? Please sit."

Sunja sat down.

"I have to take care of my sons. You should understand that."

The boys were staring intently at the comic book pages. Kyunghee was reading the lines with feeling, and even Yangjin, who was unable to read, found herself laughing with the children at the silly things the characters were saying. They were absorbed in the comic book, and their faces seemed softer somehow, like they were calm.

"I'll help you," Hansu said. "You don't have to worry about money or—"

"You're helping us now because I have no choice. When the war ends, I'll work to take care of them. I'm working now to earn our keep—"

"When the war ends, I can find you a home and give you money to take care of the boys. The boys should be going to school, not pushing cow dung around. Your mother and sister-in-law can stay, too. I can get your brother-in-law a good job."

"I can't explain you to my family," Sunja said. She felt like she was lying all the time. What was he thinking? she wondered. Surely, he could not desire her anymore. She was a twenty-nine-year-old widow with two young children to feed and educate. Sunja was not old, but she could not imagine that any man would want her now. If she had never been beautiful before, she was not even appealing now. She was a plain woman with a country face, her skin spotted and wrinkled by the sun. Her body was strong and stout, larger than when she had been a girl. In her life, she'd been desired by two men; it was difficult to imagine having that again. Sometimes, she felt like a serviceable farm animal who'd one day be useless. Before that day arrived, it was important to make sure her boys would be okay when she was gone.

"You have children, don't you?"

"Three daughters."

"And what would your daughters say about me? About us?" she whispered.

"My family has nothing to do with you."

"I understand." Sunja swallowed, her mouth dry. "I'm grateful for this opportunity—to work and to be safe. But when the war ends, I'll get an-

other job and support the boys and my mother. I'll work until I cannot work anymore."

Sunja got up from the floor and brushed the hay off her work pants.

Unable to breathe normally, she turned from him and stared at the oxen—their enormous dark eyes, full of eternal suffering. Had the others noticed them talking? They seemed to be focused on the comic book. Sunja covered her left hand with her right; despite her washing, her cuticles were still brown from the dirt.

8

Again, Hansu was not wrong. The war did end, faster than he had predicted, but even he could not have imagined the final bombs. A bunker had shielded Yoseb from the worst, but when he finally climbed out to the street, a burning wall from a nearby wooden shed struck his right side, engulfing him in orange-and-blue flames. Someone he knew from the factory floor put out the fire, and Hansu's men found him at a pathetic hospital in Nagasaki at last.

It was a starry evening, breathlessly quiet after an extended season of cicadas, when Hansu brought Yoseb to Tamaguchi's farm on an American military truck. Mozasu was the first to spot the truck, and the small and quick boy darted to the pig stalls to retrieve the bamboo spears. The family stood by the half-open barn door, observing the truck as it came closer.

"Here," Mozasu said, handing out the rattling, hollow spears to his mother, grandmother, brother, and aunt, keeping back two. Kim Changho was having his bath. He whispered to his brother, "You have to get *ajeossi* from the bath. Give him his weapon." The child gave Noa a spear for Kim and kept one for himself. Mozasu clutched his spear tightly, preparing for attack. Noa's holey hand-me-down sweater hung loosely over Mozasu's flour-sack work pants. He was tall for a six-year-old.

"The war's over," Noa reminded Mozasu firmly. "It's probably Hansu *ajeossi*'s men. Put that thing down before you hurt yourself."

The truck stopped, and two Koreans working for Hansu brought out a stretcher carrying Yoseb, who was bandaged and deeply sedated.

Kyunghee let go of the spear, letting it fall on the soft earth, and she put her hand on Mozasu's shoulder to steady herself.

Hansu stepped out of the cab of the truck while the driver, a ginger-haired American GI, stayed behind. Mozasu snuck glances at the soldier. The driver had light, freckled skin and pale, yellow-reddish hair like fire; he didn't look mean, and Hansu *ajeossi* didn't look afraid. Back in Osaka, Haru-san, the leader of the neighborhood association, who was most often in charge of rations, had warned the neighborhood children that Americans kill indiscriminately so everyone must flee at the sight of any American soldiers. Death at your own hands was preferable to capture. When the driver noticed Mozasu looking at him, he waved, showing his straight, white teeth.

Kyunghee approached the stretcher slowly. At the sight of his burns, she clasped her mouth with both her hands. Despite the terrifying news reports about the bombings, she had believed that Yoseb was alive, that he would not die without letting her know. She had prayed for him continually, and now he was home. She dropped to her knees and bowed her head. Everyone was silent until she rose. Even Kim was crying.

Hansu nodded at the slight, pretty woman who was weeping and gave her a large parcel wrapped in paper and a military-sized tub of burn liniment from America.

"You'll find some medicine in there. Mix a very small spoon of the powder with water or milk and give it to him at night so he can sleep. When it runs out, there's no more, so you have to wean him off it little by little. He'll beg you for more, but you have to tell him that you're trying to make it last."

"What is it?" she asked. Sunja stood by her sister-in-law and said nothing.

"He needs it. For the pain, but it's not good to keep taking it, because it's addictive. Anyway, keep changing the bandages. They must be sterile. Boil the fabric before you use it. There's more in there. He'll need the liniment because his skin is getting tighter. Can you do this?"

Kyunghee nodded, still staring at Yoseb. His mouth and cheek were half gone, as if he had been consumed by an animal. He was a man who had done everything he could for his family—this had happened to him because he had gone to work.

"Thank you, sir. Thank you for all that you've done for us," Kyunghee said to Hansu, who shook his head and said nothing. He left them to speak to the farmer. Kim, who had returned by then, having finished his bath, followed Hansu as he walked to the farmer's house.

The women and the boys led the men carrying the stretcher inside the barn and made a place for him in an empty horse stall. Kyunghee moved her pallet there.

A short while later, Hansu and the men drove off without saying good-bye.

The farmer didn't complain about having one more Korean on his property, because the other Koreans did Yoseb's share of the work as well as their own; harvest season was approaching, and he would need them. Though none of them had mentioned it, Tamaguchi sensed that soon enough, they'd ask him for money to leave, and the farmer was determined to get as much work as he could out of them before they left for home. He had told them they were welcome to stay for as long as they liked, and the farmer meant this. Tamaguchi had been hiring returning veterans for small jobs, but they grumbled about the dirtier tasks and openly refused to work alongside foreigners. Even if he could replace all the Koreans with Japanese veterans, Tamaguchi needed Hansu to transport his sweet potatoes to the markets. All the Koreans could stay.

The transport truck returned regularly, but Hansu didn't come back for weeks. Yoseb suffered. He had lost the hearing in his right ear. He was either shouting in anger or crying in agony. The medicine powder was now gone, and Yoseb wasn't much better. In the evenings, he cried like a child, and there was little anyone could do. During the day, he tried to help out on the farm, repairing tools or attempting to sort the potatoes, but the pain was too great for him to work. Now and then, Tamaguchi, who abhorred alcohol, gave him some holiday sake out of pity. However,

when Kyunghee started to beg him each day for more, he told her that he couldn't spare any, not because he was a stingy man, because Tamaguchi wasn't, but because he had no intention of having a drunk on his property.

A month later, Hansu returned. The afternoon sun had dimmed only a little, and the workers had just returned to the fields after their midday meal to begin their second shift. In the cold barn, Yoseb was alone, lying down on his straw-filled pallet.

Hearing the footfalls, Yoseb lifted his head, then laid it back down again on the straw pillow.

Hansu placed two enormous crates in front of him, then sat down on the thick slab of wood by the pallet, which was being used as a bench. Despite his well-tailored suit and highly polished leather brogues, Hansu appeared at ease in the barn, indifferent to the harsh smells of the animals and the cold drafts.

Yoseb said, "You're the father of the boy, aren't you?"

Hansu studied the man's scarred face, the ragged edges of a once-sloping jawline. Yoseb's right ear was now a tight bud of a flower, folding into itself.

"That's why you do all this," Yoseb said.

"Noa is my son," Hansu said.

"We owe you a debt—something we may never be able to repay."

Hansu raised his eyebrows but said nothing. It was always better to say less.

"But you have no business being around him. My brother gave the child a name. He should never know anything else."

"I can give him a name, too."

"He has a name. It's wrong to do this to the boy."

Yoseb frowned; the smallest movement hurt. Noa had his younger brother's mannerisms—from the way he spoke in Isak's measured cadences to the way he ate his meals in modest bites, chewing neatly. He behaved exactly like Isak. Whenever Noa had any time to spare, he would take his old exercise books from school and practice writing, though no one told him to do so. Yoseb would never have believed that this yakuza was Noa's biological father except that the upper half of Noa's face was

virtually a mirror image of Hansu's. In time, Noa would see this. He had not mentioned it to Kyunghee, but even if she had guessed at the truth herself, she would have kept her suspicions from Yoseb to protect Sunja, who was closer to her than a sister.

"You don't have a son," Yoseb said, taking another guess.

"Your brother was kind to help Sunja, but I would've taken care of her and my son."

"She must not have wanted that."

"I'd offered to take care of her, but she didn't want to be my wife in Korea. Because I have a Japanese wife in Osaka."

Lying on his back, Yoseb stared at the barn roof. Jagged slats of light broke through the beams. Column slivers of dust floated upward in diagonal lines. Before the fire, he had never noticed such small things; also, he had never hated anyone. Though he shouldn't, Yoseb hated this man—his expensive clothes, flashy shoes, his unchecked confidence, reeking of a devilish invulnerability. He hated him for not being in pain. He had no right to claim his brother's child.

Hansu could see Yoseb's anger.

"She wanted me to go, so I left at first, planning to come back. When I returned, she was gone. Already married. To your brother."

Yoseb didn't know what to believe. He had learned almost nothing about Sunja from Isak, who had seemed to believe that Noa's origins were best forgotten.

"You should leave Noa alone. He has a family. After the war, we'll do everything possible to repay you."

Hansu folded his arms close to his chest and smiled before speaking.

"You son of a bitch, I paid. I paid for your life. I paid for everyone's life. Everyone would be dead without me."

Yoseb shifted to his side a little and winced from the pain. Sometimes he felt like he was still on fire.

"Did Sunja tell you?" Hansu asked.

"Just look at the child's face. It doesn't make sense for anyone to go through all this trouble, and I know you're not some sort of saint. I know what you are—"

Hansu laughed out loud. It was almost out of respect for Yoseb's directness.

"We're going back home," Yoseb said, and closed his eyes.

"Pyongyang's controlled by the Russians, and the Americans are in charge of Busan. You want to go back to that?"

"It's not going to be like that forever," Yoseb said.

"You'll starve there."

"I'm done with Japan."

"And how will you go back to Pyongyang or Busan? You can't even walk down the length of this farm."

"The company owes me my wages. When I'm well enough, I'll go back to Nagasaki to collect my pay."

"When's the last time you read a newspaper?" Hansu pulled out a sheaf of Korean and Japanese newspapers he'd brought for Kim from the crates. He put the stack beside Yoseb's pallet.

Yoseb glanced at the papers but refused to pick them up.

"There's no money for you." Hansu spoke to him slowly as if Yoseb were a child. "The company will never pay you. Never. There are no records for your work, and you can't prove it. The government wants nothing more than for every poor Korean to go back, but it won't give you the fare or a sen for your troubles. Ha."

"What do you mean? How do you know?" Yoseb asked.

"I know. I know Japan," Hansu said, looking privately disappointed. He had lived among the Japanese for all of his adult life. His father-in-law was unquestionably the most powerful Japanese moneylender in Kansai. Hansu could say with confidence that the Japanese were pathologically intractable when they wanted to be. In this, they were exactly like the Koreans except their stubbornness was quieter, harder to detect.

"Do you know how hard it is to get money out of the Japanese? If they don't want to pay you, they will never ever pay you. You're wasting your time."

Yoseb's body felt itchy and warm.

"Every day, for every one boat that heads out to Korea filled with idiots wanting to go home, two boats filled with refugees come back because

there's nothing to eat there. The guys who come straight from Korea are even more desperate than you. They'll work for week-old bread. Women will whore after two days of hunger, or one if they have children to feed. You're living for a dream of a home that no longer exists."

"My parents are there."

"No. No, they're not."

Yoseb turned to look at Hansu's eyes.

"Why do you think I brought back only Sunja's mother. Do you really think I couldn't find your parents and your in-laws?"

"You don't know what happened to them," Yoseb said. Neither he nor Kyunghee had heard from them in over a year.

"They were shot. All landowners who were foolish enough to stick around were shot. Communists see people only in simple categories."

Yoseb wept and covered his eyes.

The lie had to be told, and Hansu did not mind telling it. If the parents weren't dead already, Yoseb's and Kyunghee's parents would starve to death or die of old age inevitably. They could have very well been shot. The conditions in the communist-occupied North were awful. There were numerous landowners who'd been rounded up, killed, and shoved into mass graves. No, he didn't know for certain if Yoseb's parents were alive or not, and yes, he could have learned the truth if he didn't mind risking some of his men to find them, but he didn't see the point of it. He didn't see how their lives could be useful for his purposes. It had been easy to find Sunja's mother—barely two days of his man's time. In the scheme of things, it was preferable for Yoseb and Kyunghee to lose their parents, because Sunja would have followed them blindly out of some preposterous sense of duty. Yoseb and Kyunghee would be better off in Japan for now, anyway. Hansu would never allow his son to go to Pyongyang.

Hansu opened one of the parcels and withdrew a large bottle of soju. He opened it and passed it to Yoseb, then left the barn to see Tamaguchi about a payment.

After finishing her work, Sunja finally returned to the barn, and she found Hansu waiting for her. He was sitting by himself by the feed bins at the

far end of the barn, a good distance away from the boys, who were read-ing. Yoseb was sleeping soundly. Kyunghee and Yangjin were in the house cooking dinner while Kim loaded the sacks of potatoes in the cold shed. Hansu said hello to her first and waved her toward him openly, no longer feeling the need to be discreet.

Sunja stood by the bench opposite Hansu.

"Sit, sit," he insisted, but she refused.

"Tamaguchi tells me that he wants to adopt your sons," Hansu said quietly, smiling.

"What?"

"I told him you'd never let them go. He offered to take just one of them even. The poor man. Don't worry. He can't take them."

"Soon, we'll go to Pyongyang," she said.

"No. That's not going to happen."

"What do you mean?"

"Everyone there is dead. Kyunghee's parents. Your in-laws. All shot for owning property. These things happen when governments change. You have to get rid of your enemies. Landlords are enemies of the workers," Hansu said.

"*Uh-muh.*" Sunja sat down at last.

"Yes, it's sad, but nothing can be done."

Sunja was a pragmatic woman, but even she thought Hansu was un-usually cruel. The more she got to know this man, the more she realized that the man she'd loved as a girl was an idea she'd had of him—feelings without any verification.

"You should be thinking about Noa's education. I brought him some books to study for his college entrance examinations."

"But—"

"You cannot return home. You're going to have to wait until things are more stable."

"It's not your decision to make. My boys have no future here. If we can't go back home now, we'll go back when it's safer."

Her voice had trembled, but she'd said what she'd needed to say.

Hansu remained silent for a moment.

"Whatever you decide to do later is one thing, but in the meantime, Noa should be studying for university. He's twelve."

Sunja had been thinking of Noa's schooling but hadn't known how to help him. Also, how would she pay for school? They didn't even have enough money for the passage home. Out of Yoseb's hearing, the three women talked about this all the time. They had to get back to Osaka to figure out a way to make money again.

"Noa should study while he's in this country. Korea will be in chaos for a long time. Besides, he's already a good Japanese student. When he goes back, he'll have a degree from a good Japanese university. That's what all the rich Koreans are doing, anyway—sending their kids abroad. If Noa gets into a university, I'll pay for it. I'll pay for Mozasu as well. I could get them some tutors when they return—"

"No," she said loudly. "No."

He decided not to fight her, because she was stubborn. He had learned this. Hansu pointed to the crates by Yoseb's pallet.

"I brought meat and dried fish. There's also canned fruit and chocolate bars from America. I brought the same things for Tamaguchi's family, too, so you don't have to give them any of yours. There's fabric in the bottom crate; all of you need clothing, I think. There's scissors, thread, and needles," he added, proud of himself for having brought these things. "I'll bring wool next time."

Sunja didn't know what she was supposed to do anymore. It wasn't that she was ungrateful. Mostly, she felt ashamed of her life, her powerlessness. With her sun-browned hands and dirty fingernails, she touched her uncombed hair. She didn't want him to see her this way. It occurred to her that she would never be lovely again.

"I brought some newspapers. Have someone read them to you. The stories are the same—you can't go back now. It would be terrible for the boys."

Sunja faced him.

"That's how you got me to come here, and now that's how you're trying to get me to stay in Japan. You'd said it would be better for the boys so I brought them to the farm."

"I wasn't wrong."

227

"I don't trust you."

"You are trying to hurt me, Sunja. That makes no sense." He shook his head. "Remember, your husband would have wanted the boys to go to school. I also want what's best for the boys and for you, Sunja. You and I—we're good friends," he said calmly. "We will always be good friends. We will always have Noa."

He waited to see if she would say anything, but it was as if her face had closed like a door. "And your brother-in-law knows. About Noa. I didn't tell him. He figured it out."

Sunja covered her mouth with her hand.

"You needn't worry. Everything will be fine. If you want to move back to Osaka, Kim will make the arrangements. Refusing my help would be selfish. You should give your sons every advantage. I can give both your sons many advantages."

Before she could speak, Kim had returned to the barn. He walked past the boys, who were still absorbed in their books.

"Boss," Kim said. "It's good to see you. Can I get you something to drink?"

Hansu said no.

Sunja realized she'd failed to offer him anything.

"So, are you ready to return to Osaka?" Hansu asked Kim.

"Yes, sir," Kim said, smiling. Sunja appeared distressed, but he said nothing to her for now.

"Boys," Hansu shouted across the length of the barn, "how are the books?"

Kim waved at them to come closer, and the boys ran to him.

"Noa, do you want to go back to school?" Hansu asked.

"Yes, sir. But—"

"If you want to go back to school, you need to go back to Osaka right away."

"How about the farm? And Korea?" Noa asked, straightening his back.

"You can't go back to Korea for a while, but in the meantime, you can't let your head become empty," Hansu said, smiling. "What do you think of those exam books I brought you? Are they difficult?"

"Yes, sir, but I want to learn them. I need a dictionary, I think."

"We'll get you one," Hansu said proudly. "You study, and I will send you to school. A boy shouldn't have to worry about school fees. It's important that older Koreans support young Koreans in their studies. How else will we have a great nation unless we support our children?"

Noa beamed, and Sunja could not say anything.

"But I want to stay at the farm," Mozasu interrupted. "That's not fair. I don't want to go back to school. I hate school."

Hansu and Kim laughed.

Noa pulled Mozasu toward him and bowed. They headed to the other side of the barn.

When they were far enough away from the grown-ups, Mozasu said to Noa, "Tamaguchi-san said we could live here forever. He said we were like his sons."

"Mozasu, we can't keep living in this barn."

"I like the chickens. I didn't get pecked even once this morning when I got the eggs. The barn is nice to sleep in, especially since Aunt Kyunghee made us those hay blankets."

"Well, you'll feel differently when you get older," Noa said, cradling the thick volumes of the examination books in his arms. "*Appa* would've wanted us to go to university and become educated people."

"I hate books," Mozasu said, scowling.

"I love them. I could read books all day and do nothing else. *Appa* loved to read, too."

Mozasu plowed into Noa in an attempt to wrestle him, and Noa laughed.

"Brother, what was *appa* like?" Mozasu sat up and looked at his brother soberly.

"He was tall. And he had light-colored skin like you. He wore glasses like me. He was very good at school and good at teaching himself things from books. He loved learning. He was happy when he was reading; he told me so."

Noa smiled.

"Like you," Mozasu said. "Not like me. Well, I like manga."

"That's not real reading."

Mozasu shrugged.

"He was always nice to *umma* and me. He used to tease Uncle Yoseb and make him laugh. *Appa* taught me how to write my letters and remember the multiplication tables. I was the first one in school to know them by heart."

"Was he rich?"

"No. Ministers can't be rich."

"I want to be rich," Mozasu said. "I want to have a big truck and a driver."

"I thought you wanted to live in a barn," Noa said, smiling, "and collect chicken eggs every morning."

"I'd rather have a truck like Hansu *ajeossi*."

"I'd rather be an educated man like *appa*."

"Not me," Mozasu said. "I want to make a lot of money, then *umma* and Aunt Kyunghee wouldn't have to work anymore."

9

Osaka, 1949

After the family returned to Osaka, Hansu gave Kim the job of collecting fees from the store owners at Tsuruhashi market. In exchange for these fees, Hansu's company gave the owners protection and support. Naturally, no one wanted to pay these not-insignificant sums, but there was little choice in the matter. On the rare instances when someone cried poor or foolishly refused to pay, Hansu sent his other men, not Kim, to address the situation. For a store owner, such fee payments were a long-established practice—just one more cost of doing business.

Any agent who worked for Hansu had to look the part of the larger organization, and the men who worked for Hansu, both Japanese and Korean, took special pains to keep a low profile, avoiding any unnecessary negative attention. Except for his nearsightedness, corrected with his thick eyeglasses, Kim was a pleasant-looking man—humble, diligent, and well-spoken. Hansu preferred Kim to do the collection because Kim was effective and unfailingly polite; he was the clean wrapper for a filthy deed.

It was Saturday evening, and Kim had just collected the week's payments—over sixty packets of cash, each covered in fresh paper and labeled with the name of the business. No one had missed a payment. When he reached Hansu's parked sedan, Kim bowed to his boss, who was just stepping out of the car. His driver would pick them up later.

"Let's have a drink," Hansu said, patting Kim on the back. They walked in the direction of the market. Along the road, men continuously

bowed to Hansu, and he acknowledged them with nods. He stopped for no one, however.

"I'm going to take you to a new place. Pretty girls there. You must want one after living in a barn for so long."

Kim laughed out of surprise. His boss didn't normally discuss such things.

"You like the married one," Hansu said. "I know."

Kim kept walking, unable to reply.

"Sunja's sister-in-law," Hansu said, looking straight ahead as they walked down the narrow market street. "She's still good-looking. Her husband can't do it anymore. He's drinking more, *nee?*"

Kim removed his glasses and cleaned the lenses with his handkerchief. He liked Yoseb and felt bad for not saying something. Yoseb drank a lot, but he was not a bad man. It was clear that the men in the neighborhood still admired him. At home, when Yoseb felt well enough, he helped the boys with schoolwork and taught them Korean. On occasion, he fixed machines for some factory owners he knew, but in his condition, he couldn't work regularly.

"How's the house?" Hansu asked.

"I've never lived so well."

Kim was telling the truth. "The meals are delicious. The house is very clean."

"The women need a workingman to watch over them. But I worry that you're too attached to the married one."

"Boss, I've been thinking more about going back home. Not to Daegu, but to the North."

"This again? No. End of discussion. I don't care if you go to those socialist meetings, but don't start believing that horseshit about returning to the motherland. The heads of *Mindan* are no better. Besides, they'll kill you in the North, and they'll starve you in the South. They all hate Koreans who've been living in Japan. I know. If you go, I will never support it. Never."

"The leader Kim Il Sung fought against Japanese imperialism—"

"I know his guys. Some of them might actually believe the message, but

most of them are just trying to collect a pay envelope each week. The ones in charge who live here are never going back. You watch."

"But don't you think we must do something for our country? These foreigners are cutting up the nation into—"

Hansu put both his hands on Kim's shoulders and faced him squarely.

"You haven't had a girl in such a long time that you can't think straight." Hansu smiled, then looked serious again. "Listen, I know the heads of both the Association and *Mindan*"—he snorted—"I know them very, very well—"

"But *Mindan*'s a mere puppet of the American—"

Hansu smiled at Kim, amused by the young man's sincerity.

"How long have you worked for me?"

"I must've been twelve or thirteen when you gave me a job."

"How many times have I really talked politics with you?"

Kim tried to remember.

"Never. Not really. I'm a businessman. And I want you to be a businessman. And whenever you go to these meetings, I want you to think for yourself, and I want you to think about promoting your own interests no matter what. All these people—both the Japanese and the Koreans— are fucked because they keep thinking about the group. But here's the truth: There's no such thing as a benevolent leader. I protect you because you work for me. If you act like a fool and go against my interests, then I can't protect you. As for these Korean groups, you have to remember that no matter what, the men who are in charge are just men—so they're not much smarter than pigs. And we eat pigs. You lived with that farmer Tamaguchi who sold sweet potatoes for obscene prices to starving Japanese during a time of war. He violated wartime regulations, and I helped him, because he wanted money and I do, too. He probably thinks he's a decent, respectable Japanese, or some kind of proud nationalist—don't they all? He's a terrible Japanese, but a smart businessman. I'm not a good Korean, and I'm not a Japanese. I'm very good at making money. This country would fall apart if everyone believed in some samurai crap. The Emperor does not give a fuck about anyone, either. So I'm not going to tell you not to go to any meetings or not to join any group. But know this:

Those communists don't care about you. They don't care about anybody. You're crazy if you think they care about Korea."

"Sometimes, I'd like to see my home again," Kim said quietly.

"For people like us, home doesn't exist." Hansu took out a cigarette, and Kim rushed to light it.

Kim had not been back home in over twenty years. His mother had died when he was a toddler, and his tenant farmer father died not much later; his older sister did what she could for him but eventually married, then disappeared, leaving him to beg. Kim wanted to go to the North to help with the reunification efforts, but he also wanted to go to Daegu to clean his parents' graves and do a proper *jesa* now that he could afford it.

Hansu took a long drag of his cigarette.

"You think I like it here? No, I don't like it here. But here, I know what to expect. You don't want to be poor. Changho-ya, you've worked for me, you've had enough food and money, so you've started to think about ideas—that's normal. Patriotism is just an idea, so is capitalism or communism. But ideas can make men forget their own interests. And the guys in charge will exploit men who believe in ideas too much. You can't fix Korea. Not even a hundred of you or a hundred of me can fix Korea. The Japs are out and now Russia, China, and America are fighting over our shitty little country. You think you can fight them? Forget Korea. Focus on something you can have. You want that married one? Fine. Then either get rid of the husband or wait until he's dead. This is something you can fix."

"She's not going to leave him."

"He's a loser."

"No, no, he's not," Kim said gravely. "And she's not the kind of woman who'd just—" He couldn't talk about this anymore. He could wait until Yoseb died, but it was wrong to want a man to die. He believed in many ideas, including the idea that a wife must be loyal to her husband. If Kyunghee left a broken man, she would be less worthy of his devotion.

At the end of the street, Hansu stopped walking and tilted his head toward a plain-looking bar.

"You want a girl now, or do you want to go back to the house and want someone else's wife?"

Kim stared at the handle of the door, then pulled it open, letting his boss enter first before following him inside.

The new house in Osaka was two tatami mats larger than the old one and sturdier—built out of tile, solid wood, and brick. As Hansu had predicted, the bombings had razed the original house. Kyunghee had sewn their legal documents in the lining of her good coat, and when it came time, Hansu's lawyer made the municipal government recognize Yoseb's property rights. With the gift money Tamaguchi had given them when they left the farm, Yoseb and Kyunghee bought the vacant lot adjacent to their original house. They rebuilt their home with the help of Hansu's construction company. Again, Yoseb told none of their neighbors that he was the owner of the house—it always being wiser to appear poorer than you are. The exterior of the house was nearly identical to the other dwellings on their street in Ikaino. The family had agreed that Kim should live with them, and when Yoseb asked him, he did not refuse. The women papered the walls with good-quality paper and bought strong, thick glass for their little windows. They spent a little extra for better fabric to make warm quilts and floor cushions and bought a low Korean dining table for meals and for the boys to do their homework.

Though from the facade the house didn't look like much more than a roomy shack, inside was an exceptionally clean and well-organized house with a proper kitchen that had enough space to store their food carts overnight. It had an attached outhouse, which could be entered from the kitchen door. Yangjin, Sunja, and the boys slept in the middle room, which during the day served as the main room; Yoseb and Kyunghee slept in the large storage room by the kitchen, and Kim slept in the tiny front room, its two walls made up of paper screen doors. All seven of them—three generations and one family friend—lived in the house in Ikaino. Considering the neighborhood, their accommodations were almost luxurious.

Late in the evening, when Kim finally returned home from the bar, everyone was asleep. Hansu had paid for a Korean girl, an exceptionally attractive one, and Kim went to the back room with her. Afterward, he'd wanted to go to a bathhouse, but the ones near the house were closed for the night. He

washed up as well as he could in the sink by the outhouse, but he still had the waxy flavor of the girl's frosty pink lipstick in his mouth.

The girl had been young, twenty if that, and when she wasn't in the back rooms, she worked as a waitress. The war and the American occupation had toughened her, like the other girls who worked at the bar, and because she was so pretty, she had been with many men. She went by the name Jinah.

In one of the back rooms reserved for paying customers, Jinah shut the door and took off her floral-print dress right away. She wore no underwear. Her body was long and thin, with the round, high breasts of a young girl who didn't need a brassiere and the skinny legs of a hungry peasant. She sat on his lap, making a soft grinding gesture, and made him hard, then gingerly led him to an oxblood-colored pallet on the floor. She undressed him, wiped him expertly with a warm, wet towel, then put a prophylactic on him with her painted mouth. It had been a long time since he had been with a girl. He'd only been with whores, but this one had the loveliest face and figure, and he could understand why she cost so much even though he wasn't paying this time. Jinah called him *Oppa*, and asked if he wanted to enter her now, and he had nodded, astonished by her skillfulness—at once charming and professional. She pushed him down gently and clambered on his hips and pulled him inside her in a single thrust. She kissed his forehead and hair, letting him bury his head between her breasts as they fucked. He didn't know if she was pretending, but she seemed to like what she was doing, unlike the other whores, who'd pretended to be virginal. There was no false protest, and Kim found himself deeply excited by her and came almost right away. She lay in his arms for a little while, then got up to get a towel for him. As she cleaned him, she called him her handsome brother and asked him to return to see her soon, because Jinah would be thinking about his eel. Kim almost wanted to stay the night to try to have her again, but Hansu was waiting for him at the bar, so Kim promised to return.

In his room, someone had already unfolded his pallet to make his bed. Kim lay down on his clean, starched cotton pallet, imagining Kyunghee's slender fingers smoothing down the blankets on which he rested, and as

usual, he imagined making love to her. A married woman could not be surprised by sex, he thought, but he wondered if she could enjoy it the way Jinah seemed to. What would he think of her if she did? In the barn, he'd always fallen asleep before the women, and he was grateful for this schedule, because he could not bear the idea of Yoseb being on top of her. Fortunately, he never heard any noises, and in this house, he did not hear them, either. He felt sure that Yoseb no longer slept with his wife, and this knowledge gave him permission to love her and to not hate him. This way, she was his, too. Hansu had detected his feelings, because he was obvious about them; he could not resist watching her soft face, her graceful quiet movements. He thought if he could be with her, he would die. What would it be like to be with her each night? When they'd worked beside each other at the restaurant, and when he was alone with her at the farm, it had been almost maddening to keep from clasping her body to his. What kept him from doing so was the knowledge that she would never respond to him; she loved her husband, and she loved *Yesu Kuristo*, her god, whom Kim could not believe in and who did not allow his followers to have sex outside of marriage.

Kim closed his eyes, wanting her to open the thin paper door to his room. She could slip off her dress the way the whore had done and put her mouth over him. He would pull her up to him and tuck her into his body. He would make love to her and wish for his death, because his life would have been perfect at that moment. Kim could envision her small breasts, pale stomach and legs, the shadow of her pubis. He grew hard again and laughed quietly, thinking that he was like a boy tonight, because he felt he could do it again and again and never have enough. Hansu was wrong to think that a pretty whore would take his mind off Kyunghee; in fact, he wanted her more now, far more than he ever had. He had tasted something sweet and cool tonight, and now he wanted an immense tubful of it—enough to bathe deeply in its refreshment.

Kim rubbed himself and fell asleep with his glasses on.

In the morning, Kim rose before the others and went to work without having breakfast. That evening, as he walked home, he noticed a pair of slight

shoulders pushing a confection cart down the street. He ran to catch up with her.

"Let me."

"Oh, hello." Kyunghee smiled in relief. "We were worried about you this morning when you were gone. We didn't see you last night. Did you eat today?"

"I'm all right. You don't need to worry about me."

He noticed that the stack of bags used to pack up the candies were all gone. "You're out of bags. You did well today?"

She nodded, smiling again. "I sold everything, but the price of black sugar has gone up again. Maybe I can make jellies. They require less sugar. I need to find some new recipes." Kyunghee stopped walking to wipe her brow with the back of her hand.

Kim took the cart from her to push it.

"Is Sunja at home already?" he asked.

Kyunghee nodded, looking worried.

"What's the matter, Sister?"

"I'm hoping there won't be a fight tonight. My husband's being too hard on everyone lately. Also, he's—" She didn't want to say any more. Yoseb's health was declining precipitously, but he was unfortunately well enough to feel the horrible discomfort of his burns and injuries. Every little thing upset him, and when he was angry, he never held back anymore. His poor hearing made him shout, a thing he had never done before the war.

"It's about the boys' school. You know."

Kim nodded. Yoseb had been telling Sunja that the boys had to go to a Korean school in the neighborhood because the family had to be ready to go back. The boys had to learn Korean. Hansu was telling Sunja the opposite. Sunja couldn't say anything, but everyone knew it was a terrible time to return.

The road to their house was empty. As the sun set, the dusk gave off a muted gray-and-pink light.

"It's nice when it's quiet," she said.

"Yes." Kim grasped the cart handle a little tighter.

Strands of her bun had come loose, and Kyunghee smoothed her hair behind her ears. Even at the end of a long workday, there was still something so clean and bright in her expression; it could not be defiled.

"Last night, he yelled at her again about the schools. My husband means well. He's also in a lot of pain. Noa wants to go to Japanese school. He wants to go to Waseda University. Can you imagine? Such a big school like that!" She smiled, feeling proud of his grand dream. "And, well, Mozasu never wants to go to school at all." She laughed. "Of course, it isn't clear when we can return now, but the boys need to learn how to read and write. Don't you think?" Kyunghee found herself crying, but couldn't explain why.

From his coat pocket, Kim dug out a handkerchief that he used to clean his glasses and gave it to her.

"There are so many things we can't control," he said.

She nodded.

"Do you want to go home?"

Without looking at his face, she said, "I can't believe my parents are dead. In my dreams, they seem alive. I'd like to see them again."

"But you can't go back now. It's dangerous. When things get better—"

"Do you think that will be soon?"

"Well, you know how we are."

"What do you mean?" she asked.

"Koreans. We argue. Every man thinks he's smarter than the next. I suppose whoever is in charge will fight very hard to keep his power." He repeated only what Hansu had told him, because Hansu was right, especially when it came to seeing the worst in people—in this, he was always right.

"So you're not a communist, then?" she asked.

"What?"

"You go to those political meetings. I thought if you went to them, then perhaps they're not so bad. And they're against the Japanese government, and they want to reunify the country, right? I mean, aren't the Americans trying to break up the country? I hear things at the market from the others, but it's hard to know what to believe. My husband said that the commu-

nists are a bad lot; they're the ones who shot our parents. You know, my father smiled at everyone. He always did good things."

Kyunghee could not understand why her parents were killed. Her father had been the third son, so his plot had been very small. Had the communists killed all the landowners? Even the insignificant ones? She was curious as to what Kim thought, too, because he was a good man and knew a lot about the world.

Kim leaned in to the cart, and he looked at her carefully, wanting to comfort her. He knew she was looking to him for advice, and it made him feel important. With a woman like this by him, he wondered if he would even care about politics anymore.

"Are there different kinds of communists?" she asked.

"I think so. I don't know if I'm a communist. I am against the Japanese taking over Korea again, and I don't want the Russians and the Chinese to control Korea, either. Or the Americans. I wonder why Korea can't be left alone."

"But you just said, we quarrel. I suppose it's like when two grannies have a dispute, and the villagers constantly whisper in their ears about the wickedness of the other one. If the grannies want to have any peace, they have to forget everyone else and remember that they used to be friends."

"I think we should put you in charge," he said, pushing the cart toward the house. Even if it was just this brief walk, he felt happy to be with her, but of course, it made him want more. He'd gone to those meetings to get out of the house, because sometimes being near her was too much. He lived in that house because he needed to see her every day. He loved her. This would never change, he thought. His situation was impossible.

Only a few paces from home, the two walked slowly, murmuring this and that about their day, content and only a little less shy. He would continue to suffer with love.

10

Osaka, January 1953

Worried about money, Sunja had woken up in the middle of the night to make candies to sell. When Yangjin noticed that her daughter wasn't in bed, she went to the kitchen.

"You don't sleep anymore," Yangjin said. "You'll get sick if you don't sleep."

"*Umma*, I'm fine. You should go back to bed."

"I'm old. I don't need to sleep so much," Yangjin said, putting on her apron.

Sunja was trying to make extra money for Noa's tutoring fees. He had failed his first attempt at the Waseda exams by a few points, and he felt certain that he'd be able to pass on his next try if he could be tutored in mathematics. The fees for the tutors were exorbitant. The women had been trying to earn more so Noa could leave his job as a bookkeeper to study full time, but it was difficult enough to manage their household costs and Yoseb's medical bills on his salary and their earnings from selling food. Each week, Kim gave them money for his room and board. He had tried to add to Noa's tutoring fund, but Yoseb forbade the women from taking any more than what was a reasonable sum. Yoseb would not allow Sunja to accept any money from Hansu for Noa's schooling.

"Did you sleep at all last night?" Yangjin asked.

Sunja nodded, laying a clean cloth over the large chunks of black sugar to muffle the sound of the mortar and pestle.

Yangjin was exhausted herself. In three years, she'd turn sixty. When she was a girl, she'd believed that she could work harder than anyone under any circumstances, but she no longer felt that way. Lately, Yangjin felt tired and impatient; small things bothered her. Aging was supposed to make you more patient, but in her case, she felt angrier. Sometimes, when a customer complained about the small size of the portions, she wanted to tell him off. Lately, what upset her most was her daughter's impossible silence. Yangjin wanted to shake her.

The kitchen was the warmest room in the house, and the electric lights emitted a steady light. Against the papered walls, the two bare lightbulbs attached to the ceiling by their electric cords made stark shadows, resembling two lonely gourds hanging from leafless vines.

"I still think about our girls," Yangjin said.

"Dokhee and Bokhee? Didn't they find work in China?"

"I shouldn't have let them go with that smooth-talking woman from Seoul. But the girls were so excited about traveling to Manchuria and earning money. They promised to return when they made enough to buy the boardinghouse. They were good girls."

Sunja nodded, recalling their sweetness. She didn't know people like that anymore. It seemed as if the occupation and the war had changed everyone, and now the war in Korea was making things worse. Once-tenderhearted people seemed wary and tough. There was innocence left only in the smallest children.

"At the market, I hear that the girls who went to work in factories were taken somewhere else, and they had to do terrible, terrible things with Japanese soldiers." Yangjin paused, still confounded. "Do you think this can be true?"

Sunja had heard the same stories, and Hansu had warned her on more than one occasion of the Korean recruiters, working for the Japanese army, falsely promising good jobs, but she didn't want her mother to worry any more. Sunja ground the sugar as finely as she could.

"What if the girls were taken? For that?" Yangjin asked.

"*Umma*, we don't know," Sunja whispered. She lit the fire in the stove and poured sugar and water into the pan.

"That's what happened. I just feel it." Yangjin nodded to herself. "Your *appa*—it would make him so sad that we lost our boardinghouse—*aigoo*. And now this fighting in Korea. We can't go back yet because the army would take Noa and Mozasu. Isn't that right?"

Sunja nodded. She could not let her sons become soldiers.

Yangjin shivered. The draft seeping through the kitchen window stung her dry, brown skin, and she tucked a towel around the sill. Yangjin pulled her shabby cotton vest tightly over her nightclothes. She started to crush sugar for the next batch while Sunja watched the bubbling pot on the low flame.

Sunja stirred the pot as the sugar caramelized. Busan seemed like another life compared to Osaka; Yeongdo, their little rocky island, stayed impossibly fresh and sunny in her memory, though she hadn't been back in twenty years. When Isak had tried to explain heaven, she had imagined her hometown as paradise—a clear, shimmering beauty. Even the memory of the moon and stars in Korea seemed different than the cold moon here; no matter how much people complained about how bad things were back home, it was difficult for Sunja to imagine anything but the bright, sturdy house that her father had taken care of so well by the green, glassy sea, the bountiful garden that had given them watermelons, lettuces, and squash, and the open-air market that never ran out of anything delicious. When she was there, she had not loved it enough.

The news reports from back home were so horrific—cholera, starvation, and soldiers who kidnapped your sons, even little boys—that their meager life in Osaka and their pathetic attempts to scrounge up enough money to send Noa to college seemed luxurious in contrast. At least they were together. At least they could work toward something better. The war in Korea roused commerce in Japan, and there were more jobs to be had by all. At least here, the Americans were still in charge, so the women were able to find sugar and wheat. Although Yoseb prohibited Sunja from taking money from Hansu, when Kim found any of the scarce ingredients the women needed through his connections, the women knew enough not to ask too many questions or to talk about it with Yoseb.

As soon as the taffy cooled on the metal pan, the women worked quickly to cut the candy into neat squares.

"Dokhee used to tease me about the sloppy way I cut onions," Sunja said, smiling. "And she couldn't bear how slowly I washed the rice pots. And every morning when I would clean the floors, she would say without fail, 'Always use two rags to clean the floors. First, sweep, then wipe with a clean rag, and then wipe it again with a fresh one!' Dokhee was the cleanest person I have ever met." As she spoke the words, Sunja could recall Dokhee's round and simple face growing somber while giving instructions. Her expressions, mannerisms, and voice were equally vivid, and Sunja, who did not pray often, prayed to God in her heart for the girls. She prayed that they were not taken for the soldiers. Isak used to say that we could not know why some suffered more than others; he said we should never hasten to judgment when others endured agony. Why was she spared and not them? she wondered. Why was she in this kitchen with her mother when so many were starving back home? Isak used to say that God had a plan, and Sunja believed this could be so, but it gave her little consolation now, thinking of the girls. Those girls had been more innocent than her sons when they were very little.

When Sunja looked up from her task, her mother was weeping.

"Those girls lost their mother, then their father. I should've done more for them. Tried to help them get married, but we had no money. A woman's lot is to suffer. We must suffer."

Sunja sensed that her mother was right that the girls had been tricked. They were likely dead now. She put her hand on her mother's shoulder. Her mother's hair was nearly all gray, and during the day, she wore the old-fashioned bun at the base of her neck. It was night, and her mother's gray, scant braid hung down her back. The years of outdoor work had creased her brown oval face with deep grooves on her forehead and around her mouth. For as long as she could remember, her mother had been the first to rise and the last to go to bed; even when the girls had worked with them, her mother had worked as hard as the younger one. Never one to talk much, as she'd gotten older her mother had a lot more to say, but Sunja never seemed to know what to say to her.

"*Umma*, remember digging up the potatoes with *appa*? *Appa*'s beauti-

ful potatoes. They were fat and white and so good when you baked them in the ashes. I haven't had a good potato like that since—"

Yangjin smiled. There had been happier times. Her daughter had not forgotten Hoonie, who had been a wonderful father to her. So many of their babies had died, but they'd had Sunja. She had her still.

"At least the boys are safe. Maybe that's why we're here. Yes." Yangjin paused. "Maybe that's why we're here." Her face brightened. "You know, your Mozasu is such a funny one. Yesterday, he said he wants to live in America and wear a suit and hat like in the movies. He said he wants to have five sons!"

Sunja laughed, because that sounded like Mozasu.

"America? What did you say?"

"I told him it's okay as long as he visited me with his five sons!"

The kitchen smelled of caramel, and the women worked nimbly until sunlight filled the house.

School was a misery. Mozasu was thirteen and tall for his age. With broad shoulders and well-muscled arms, he appeared more manly than some of his teachers. Because he could not read or write at grade level—despite Noa's prodigious efforts to teach him kanji—Mozasu had been placed in a class full of ten-year-olds. Mozasu spoke Japanese just as well as his peers; if anything, he had tremendous verbal facility, which served him well in his regular battles with the older children. In arithmetic, he could keep up with the class, but writing and reading Japanese lamed him brutally. His teachers called him a Korean fool, and Mozasu was biding his time so he could be done with this hell. In spite of the war and all their academic privations, Noa had finished high school, and whenever he wasn't working, he was studying for his college entrance examinations. He never left the house without an exam study book and one of his old English-language novels, which he bought from the bookseller.

Six days a week, Noa worked for Hoji-san, the cheerful Japanese who owned most of the houses in their neighborhood. It was rumored that Hoji-san was in fact part *burakumin* or Korean, but no one said too much about his shameful blood, since he was everyone's landlord. It was possi-

ble that the vicious rumor that he was not pure Japanese could have been started by an unhappy tenant, but Hoji-san did not seem to care. As his bookkeeper and secretary, Noa kept Hoji-san's ledgers in excellent order and wrote letters to the municipal offices in beautiful Japanese on his behalf. Despite his smiles and jokes, Hoji-san was ruthless when it came to getting his rent money. He paid Noa very little, but Noa did not complain. He could've made more money working for Koreans in the pachinko business or in *yakiniku* restaurants, but Noa didn't want that. He wanted to work in a Japanese office and have a desk job. Like nearly all Japanese business owners, Hoji-san would not normally hire Koreans, but Hoji-san's nephew was Noa's high school teacher, and Hoji-san, a man who knew how to find bargains, hired his nephew's most brilliant pupil.

In the evening, Noa helped Mozasu with his schoolwork, but they both knew it was pointless, since Mozasu had no interest in memorizing kanji. As his long-suffering tutor, Noa focused on teaching his brother sums and basic writing. With remarkable patience, Noa never got upset when Mozasu did poorly on his examinations. He knew how it was for most Koreans at school; most of them dropped out, and he didn't want this to happen to Mozasu, so he did not focus on exam grades. He even asked Uncle Yoseb and his mother to refrain from getting upset with Mozasu's report cards. He told them that the goal was to make sure that Mozasu had better-than-average skills as a worker. If Noa hadn't tried so hard and taught him with such care, Mozasu would've done what nearly all the other Korean boys in the neighborhood did rather than go to school— collect scrap metal for money, search for rotting food for the pigs their mothers bred and raised in their homes, or worse, get in trouble with the police for petty crimes.

Ever the student, after Noa helped Mozasu, he studied English with a dictionary and a grammar book. In the only academic reversal, Mozasu, who was more interested in English than Japanese or Korean, would help his older brother learn new vocabulary words by drilling Noa on English words and phrases.

At the dreadful local school, Mozasu hung back and kept to himself during lunch and recess. There were four other Koreans in the class, but

they all went by their Japanese pass names and refused to discuss their background, especially in the presence of other Koreans. Mozasu knew with certainty who they were, because they lived on his street and he knew their families. All of them were only ten years old, so the Koreans in his grade were smaller than he was, and Mozasu stayed away from them, feeling both contempt and pity.

Most Koreans in Japan had at least three names. Mozasu went by Mozasu Boku, the Japanization of Moses Baek, and rarely used his Japanese surname, Bando, the *tsumei* listed on his school documents and residency papers. With a first name from a Western religion, an obvious Korean surname, and his ghetto address, everyone knew what he was— there was no point in denying it. The Japanese kids would have nothing to do with him, but Mozasu no longer gave a shit. When he was younger, getting picked on used to bother him, though far less than it had bothered Noa, who had compensated by outperforming his classmates academically and athletically. Every day, before school began and after school ended, the bigger boys told Mozasu, "Go back to Korea, you smelly bastard." If there was a crowd of them, Mozasu would keep walking; however, if there were only one or two assholes, he would hit them as hard as he could until he saw blood.

Mozasu knew he was becoming one of the bad Koreans. Police officers often arrested Koreans for stealing or home brewing. Every week, someone on his street got in trouble with the police. Noa would say that because some Koreans broke the law, everyone got blamed. On every block in Ikaino, there was a man who beat his wife, and there were girls who worked in bars who were said to take money for favors. Noa said that Koreans had to raise themselves up by working harder and being better. Mozasu just wanted to hit everyone who said mean things. In Ikaino, there were homely old women who cussed and men who were so drunk that they slept outside their houses. The Japanese didn't want Koreans to live near them, because they weren't clean, they lived with pigs, and the children had lice. Also, Koreans were said to be even lower than *burakumin* because at least *burakumin* had Japanese blood. Noa told Mozasu that his former teachers had told him he was a good Korean, and Mozasu understood that with his own poor grades

and bad manners, those same teachers would think Mozasu was a bad one.

So the fuck what? If the other ten-year-olds thought he was stupid, that was okay. If they thought he was violent, that was okay. If necessary, Mozasu was not afraid to clean out all the teeth right from their mouths. You think I'm an animal, Mozasu thought, then I can be an animal and hurt you. Mozasu did not intend to be a good Korean. What was the point in that?

Before spring, a few months before the war in Korea ended, a new boy from Kyoto joined his class. He was eleven, going on twelve. Haruki To-toyama was obviously a poor kid, evident from his shabby uniform and pathetic shoes. He was also wiry and nearsighted. The boy had a small, triangular face, and he might have been acceptable to the others, but unfortunately, someone let it out that he lived on the border street between the Korean ghetto and the Japanese poor. Quickly, rumors spread that Haruki was a *burakumin*, though he wasn't. Then it was discovered that Haruki had a younger brother with a head shaped like a dented summer melon. Even as a Japanese, it had been difficult for Haruki's mother to find a better place for them to live, because many of the Japanese landlords thought the family was cursed. Haruki did not have a father; this would have been understandable if his father had died in the war as a soldier, but the truth was that at Haruki's brother's birth, the father had taken one look at the child and left.

Unlike Mozasu, Haruki cared deeply about fitting in and tried very hard, but even the kids with the lowest social status wouldn't give him a chance. He was treated like a diseased animal. The teachers, who followed the cues of the student leaders, kept their distance from Haruki. The new boy had been hoping that this school might be different from his old one in Kyoto, but he saw that he didn't have a chance here, either.

At lunchtime, Haruki sat at the end of the long table with two seat gaps around him like an invisible parenthesis while the other boys in their dark woolen uniforms stuck together like a tight row of black corn kernels. Not far from this table, Mozasu, who always sat alone, watched the new boy trying to say something now and then to the group of boys, though, of course, Haruki never got a reply.

After a month of this, Mozasu finally said something to him in the boys' washroom.

"Why do you try to make those kids like you?" Mozasu asked.

"What choice do I have?" Haruki replied.

"You can tell them to fuck off and get a life of your own."

"And what kind of life do you have?" Haruki asked. He didn't mean to be rude; he just wanted to know if there was an alternative.

"Listen, if people don't like you, it's not always your fault. My brother told me that."

"You have a brother?"

"Yeah. He works for Hoji-san, you know, the landlord."

"Is your brother the young guy in the glasses?" Haruki asked. Hoji-san was their landlord, too.

Mozasu nodded, smiling. He was proud of Noa, who cut an impressive figure in the neighborhood. Everyone respected him.

"I better go back to class," Haruki said. "I'll get in trouble if I'm late."

"You're a pussy," Mozasu said. "Do you really give two shits if the teacher yells at you? Kara-sensei is an even bigger pussy than you are."

Haruki gulped.

"If you want, I'll let you sit with me during recess," Mozasu said. He had never made such an offer before, but he didn't think he could bear it if Haruki tried to talk to those assholes one more time and was rejected. In a strange way, just watching his efforts was painful and embarrassing.

"Truly?" Haruki said, smiling.

Mozasu nodded, and even when they were men, neither one ever forgot how they became friends.

II

October 1955

Mozasu kept a photograph of the wrestler Rikidozan taped to the inside lid of his trunk, where he kept his special things like his favorite comics, old coins, and his father's eyeglasses. Unlike the Korean wrestler, Mozasu did not like to get too close to his opponent and tussle for too long. Rikidozan was known for his famous karate chop, and similarly, Mozasu had deadly aim with his strikes.

Over the years, he had hit many different kinds of boys: He had hit them when they called him names; when they picked on his friend Haruki; and when they hassled his mother or grandmother at their confectionery stall at Tsuruhashi Station. By this time, Sunja had gotten used to the notes and visits from teachers, counselors, and angry parents. There was little she could do to stop her son from fighting, and she was terrified that he would get into serious trouble or argue with the wrong boy. After each incident, Yoseb and Noa would speak to him, and the fighting would stop for a while. Nevertheless, once incited, Mozasu would pound anyone who deserved it.

When Sunja asked him what happened, she could always expect two things from him: a sincere apology to her and his family for bringing them shame, and the defense that he didn't start it. Sunja believed him. By nature, her boy, who was sixteen, was not violent. He avoided fights when he could and for as long as he could, but when things got bad, he would put a stop to the harassment with a quick, effective punch to the instiga-

tor's face. Mozasu had broken the noses of several boys and blackened as many eyes. By now, only a stubborn fool or a new bully at school would bother Mozasu. Even the teachers respected the boy's physical authority, and everyone knew that he did not abuse his power and preferred to be left alone.

To keep him out of trouble, Mozasu was required to go to the confectionery stand after school. Kyunghee stayed at home with Yoseb, and Noa wanted Mozasu to help their mother and grandmother. When the family had enough money to buy a store, it was hoped that Mozasu would help his mother and grandmother run it. Mozasu did not want to do this. Working in the market was women's work, and though the boy respected the women, he did not want to make candy or sell *taiyaki* for the rest of his life.

For now, he did not mind helping his mother and grandmother by fetching more coal for the box stove beneath the *taiyaki* griddle and candy burner. At the end of the day, Sunja and Yangjin were relieved to have a strong boy to push the carts home, since they had been working since dawn. However, between the hours of four and seven, there wasn't enough for Mozasu to do, because Sunja and Yangjin were able to cook the sweets and handle the customers without him. It was never that busy then.

It was a late fall afternoon, when business was exceedingly slow and the market women were busy talking with each other since there were so few customers; Mozasu made excuses about getting some *gimbap* on the other side of the market, and no one seemed to mind. Mozasu went to see Chiyaki, the girl who sold socks.

She was an eighteen-year-old Japanese orphan whose parents had died in the war. She lived and worked with her elderly grandparents, who owned the large sock store. Petite and curvy, Chiyaki was a flirt. She didn't like other girls very much and preferred the company of the boys who worked in the market. Chiyaki teased Mozasu because she was two years older than he was, but of all the boys she liked, she thought he was the most handsome. It was a pity, she thought, that he was Korean, because her grandparents would disown her if she dated him. They both knew this, but there was no harm in talking.

When Chiyaki's grandparents went home in the afternoon and left her alone to manage and close the shop, Mozasu or other boys came by to keep her company. Chiyaki had quit school years before because she hated all the stuck-up girls who ruled the school. Besides, her grandparents couldn't see the point in her finishing. They were arranging her marriage to the tatami maker's second son, who Chiyaki thought was boring. Chiyaki liked sharp dressers who talked a good game. Despite her interest in boys, she was very innocent and had never done anything with a boy. She would inherit her grandparents' store, and she was pretty enough to get a guy to take her to a café if she wanted. Her value was obvious, and what she liked best was to make a man give her his devotion.

When Mozasu knocked on the doorframe of the stall and handed her his grandmother's famous *taiyaki*, still warm from the griddle, Chiyaki smiled and licked her lips. She smelled it appreciatively at first, then took a little bite.

"*Oishi*! *Oishi*! Mo-san, thank you so much," she said. "A handsome young man who can make sweets. You are perfect, *nee*?"

Mozasu smiled. She was adorable; there was no one like her. She had a reputation for talking to a lot of guys, but he still enjoyed being in her company. Also, he'd never seen her with another guy, so he didn't know if the rumors were true. She had a cute figure and wore a berry-colored lipstick, which made her small mouth look delicious.

"How's business?" he asked.

"Not bad. I don't care. I know we made enough for the week, because Grandfather said so."

"The sandal lady is looking at us," Mozasu said. Watanabe-san owned the store opposite Chiyaki's, and she was best friends with Chiyaki's grandmother.

"That old bat. I hate her. She's going to tell Grandmother about me again, but I don't care."

"Are you going to get in trouble for talking to me?"

"No. I'll only get in trouble if I keep letting you give me sweets," she said.

"Well, I'll stop then."

"*Iyada!*" Chiyaki took another bite of her cake and shook her head like a willful little girl.

They both looked up when a young man dressed like an office worker stopped in front of the shop. Chiyaki gestured to the empty stool in the corner of the shop, and Mozasu sat down and busied himself with the newspaper.

"May I help you, sir?" Chiyaki asked the man. He had been by earlier when her grandparents were there, but had returned. "Did you want to see those black socks again?"

"You remember me?" the man said excitedly.

"Sure. You were here this morning."

"A pretty girl like you remembered me. I like that. I'm glad I came back for you."

Mozasu looked up from the paper, then looked down again.

"How many would you like?"

"How many do you have?"

"At least twenty pairs your size," she said. Sometimes a person would buy ten pairs. Once, a mother bought two boxes for her son who was at university.

"I'll take two, but I'll take more if you put them on me."

Mozasu folded the paper and glanced at the man, who didn't seem to notice his irritation.

"I'll wrap up these two, then," Chiyaki said.

"What's your name?" he asked.

"Chiyaki."

"I have a cousin with that name. Gosh, you are very beautiful. You got a boyfriend?"

Chiyaki got quiet.

"No? I think you should be my girlfriend then." The man put money in her hand and held it.

Chiyaki smiled at him. She had dealt with this sort of fellow before, and she knew what he was implying. She pretended not to understand. Mozasu was jealous, but she didn't mind. She stuck out her chest a little.

In the bathhouse, the older women always stared at her high, round breasts and told her she was lucky.

The man stared exactly where Chiyaki wanted him to and said, "Nice. When can I pick you up tonight? I'll buy you some yakitori."

"You can't," she said, putting the money away in the cashbox. "You're too old for me."

"You little tease."

"You're not my type," Chiyaki said, unafraid.

"You're too young to have a type. I make good money, and I know how to fuck." The man pulled her to him and put his hands on her behind and squeezed her. "Nice and full back there. Good tits, too. Close the shop. Let's go."

Mozasu got up from his chair quietly and walked over to the man. He hit him square in the mouth as hard as he could. The man fell over and blood poured down his lip. From the pain in his knuckles, Mozasu knew that he had loosened some of the man's teeth.

"You should take the socks and go home now," he said.

The man stared at the blood on his blue shirt and trousers as if the blood belonged to someone else.

"I'm calling the police," he said.

"Go ahead, call the police," Chiyaki said to the man. She waved frantically to the sandal lady, who was now rushing over.

"Mo-san, go now," she said. "Hurry, get out. Go. I'll deal with this."

Mozasu walked briskly toward the confection stand.

The police found him in no time. Only a few minutes before, Mozasu had come back to the stall with blood on his hand and told his mother and grandmother what had happened with Chiyaki.

The police officer confirmed the story.

"Your son hit a gentleman who was buying some socks. This sort of behavior warrants an explanation. The young lady said that that man was trying to molest her and your son was protecting her, but the customer denies it," the officer said.

Goro-san, the pachinko parlor owner, who was heading to the stand

for his afternoon snack, rushed toward them when he saw the police-man.

"Hello, officer." He winked at Sunja. "Is everything okay?" Goro asked.

Mozasu sat on the old wooden stool by the cart, looking guilty for troubling his mother and grandmother.

"Mozasu was defending a young lady who works at the sock store from a man who grabbed her. Mozasu hit him in the face," Sunja said calmly. She kept her head high and refused to apologize for fear of admitting guilt on his behalf. Her heart was pounding so hard that she thought they could hear it. "He was only trying to help."

Yangjin nodded firmly and patted Mozasu's back.

"*Maji?*" Goro said, laughing. "Is that right, officer?"

"Well, that's what the young lady said in the shop, and Watanabe-san agreed with her version of the events. The man who was hit denies it, but I've heard from some other store owners that he is a creep who often bothers the younger girls who work here." The police officer shrugged. "Nevertheless, the man thinks his jaw is broken. His two lower teeth are loose. I wanted to warn the young man that he can't just hit people even if they're wrong. He should have called the police."

At this, Mozasu nodded. He had been in trouble before, but no one had ever called the police. All his life, he had known about his father, who had been wrongfully imprisoned. Lately, Noa was warning him that since the Koreans in Japan were no longer citizens, if you got in trouble, you could be deported. Noa had told him that no matter what, Mozasu had to respect the police and be very deferential even if they were rude or wrong. Only a month ago, Noa had said a Korean had to be extra good. Once again, Mozasu felt bad for messing up and dreaded the look of disappointment that would surely appear on Noa's face.

Goro considered the boy and Sunja, one of his favorite *ajumma*s in the market.

"Officer, I know this family. They're very hardworking, and Mozasu is a good kid. He won't get in trouble again. Right, Mozasu?" Goro stared directly at Mozasu.

"*Hai*," Mozasu replied.

The officer repeated his speech about how citizens should never take the law into their own hands, and Mozasu, Sunja, and Goro nodded as if the officer were the Emperor himself. After he left, Goro lightly smacked Mozasu in the back of head with his felt hat. Mozasu winced, but of course it hadn't hurt.

"What are you going to do with this boy?" Goro asked the women, both exasperated and amused.

Sunja looked at her hands. She had tried everything she could, and now she had to ask a stranger. Yoseb and Noa would be angry with her, but she had to try something else besides what they were doing now.

"Could you help him?" Sunja asked. "Could he work for you? You wouldn't have to pay him very much—"

Goro waved her away and shook his head and turned his attention to Mozasu. That was all he needed to hear.

"Listen, you're going to quit school tomorrow morning and start working for me. Your mother doesn't need this shit. After you tell the school that you're done, you're going to head to my shop, and you're going to work very hard. I'm going to pay you what you deserve. I don't steal from my employees. You work, you get paid. You got it? And stay away from the sock girl. She's trouble."

"Does your parlor need a boy?" Sunja asked.

"Sure, but no fighting. That's not the only way to be a man," he said, feeling sorry for the kid who didn't have a father. "Being a man means you know how to control your temper. You have to take care of your family. A good man does that. Okay?"

"Sir, you are gracious to give him a chance. I know he'll work—"

"I can see that," Goro said to Sunja, smiling. "We'll make him a pachinko boy and keep him off the streets."

Mozasu got up from his stool and bowed to his new boss.

12

March 1956

Goro was a fat and glamorous Korean, notably popular with beautiful women. His mother had been an abalone diver in Jeju Island, and in the neighborhood of Ikaino where Goro lived in a modest stand-alone house by himself, there was talk of Goro having once been an agile and powerful swimmer. That said, it was rather difficult to imagine him doing much beyond telling funny stories and eating the tasty snacks he liked to fix for himself in his kitchen. There was something plush and sensual about his thickly rounded arms and swollen belly; it might have been the smoothness of his clear, tawny skin, or the way he fit into a well-made suit, resembling a self-satisfied seal gliding across a city street. He was a good talker—the sort of man who could sell lumber to a woodcutter. Though he made plenty of money from his three pachinko parlors, he lived simply and preferred to avoid expensive habits. He was known for being generous with women.

For six months, Mozasu had been working for Goro in his main pachinko parlor, doing whatever was needed. In that time, the sixteen-year-old had learned more about the world than in all his years of school. Making money was ten times easier and more pleasant than trying to stuff the kanji he had no use for into his head. It was a tremendous relief to forget the dry books and exams. At work, nearly everyone was Korean, so nothing stupid was said about his background. At school, Mozasu hadn't thought that the taunts had bothered him much, but when the mean re-

marks had utterly disappeared from his daily life, he realized how peaceful he could feel. He hadn't had a single fight since he'd started working for Goro.

Each Saturday evening, Mozasu handed his pay envelope to his mother who, in turn, gave him an allowance. She used what she needed for the household expenses, but she was saving as much as she could, because Mozasu wanted to be his own boss one day. Each morning, Mozasu rushed to work and stayed as late as he could keep his eyes open; he was happy just to sweep up the cigarette butts or to wash the dirty teacups when Kayoko, the kitchen girl, was busy.

It was a mild morning in March, only a couple of hours after dawn. Mozasu ducked into the back door of the shop and found Goro setting up the pins on his chosen machine. Each day, before the store opened, Goro would gently tap a few straight pins on the vertical pachinko machines with his tiny rubber-coated hammer. He was tapping the pins very, very slightly to alter the course of the metal balls to affect the machine's payout. You never knew which machine Goro would choose, or which direction Goro would direct the pins. There were other pachinko parlors in the area that had decent businesses, but Goro was the most successful, because he had a kind of touch—a true feel for the pins. The minuscule adjustments he made were sufficiently frustrating to the regular customers who'd studied the machines before closing hours for better payouts in the morning, yet there was just enough predictability to produce attractive windfalls, drawing the customers back to try their luck again and again. Goro was teaching Mozasu how to tap the pins, and for the first time in his life, Mozasu had been told that he was a good student.

"Good morning, Goro-san," Mozasu said, running into the shop.

"Early again, Mozasu. Good for you. Kayoko has made some chicken rice; you should eat some breakfast. You're a big kid, but you need to fill out some more. Women like to have something to grab on to!" Goro laughed heartily, raising his eyebrows. "Isn't that so?"

Mozasu smiled, not minding the teasing. Goro-san talked to him as if Mozasu, too, had many women when in fact, he'd never once been with a girl.

"My mother made soup this morning, so I already ate. Thank you." Mozasu sat down beside his boss.

"How is your mother?"

"Good, good."

Despite Noa's strict disapproval of Mozasu working in a pachinko parlor, Sunja had relented in the end. She had allowed him to work with Goro, a widely respected man in Ikaino. Mozasu had fought against the other schoolboys so often that she'd feared for his safety and let him leave school for good. Mozasu would never finish school, but Noa was still trying to get into Waseda, and this was the family consolation—at least one of the boys would be educated like their father.

"How's her business? Sugar is an addictive substance. Good for making money, *nee*?" He laughed while tapping gently at one pin then another.

Mozasu nodded. He was proud of the confectionery stall his mother, aunt, and grandmother ran in the open market by the train station. They wanted to have a proper shop of their own, but they'd have to wait until they had the money to buy the building, because no one would rent good locations to Koreans. Mozasu wanted to make enough money to pay for Noa's tutoring and to buy his mother a beautiful shop.

Goro handed Mozasu the hammer.

"Try it."

Mozasu tapped the pins while Goro watched him.

"So, last night, I met my lady friend Miyuki, and we drank too much. Mozasu, don't be like me and spend all your free time with fast girls," Goro said, smiling. "Well, unless they are very pretty. Ha."

"Miyuki-san is pretty," Mozasu said.

"*Soo nee.* Beautiful tits and a stomach like a mermaid. Women are so tasty. Like candy! I don't know how I'll ever settle down," Goro said. "Then again, I don't see why I should. You see, Mozasu, I don't have a mother or a father anymore, and though this makes me sad, no one cares enough for me to get married and is willing to arrange it." He nodded, not looking at all troubled by this.

"And who were you out with last night?" Goro asked.

Mozasu smiled.

"You know I was here until the closing. Then I went home."

"So you didn't even chase Kayoko around the kitchen?"

"No." Mozasu laughed.

"Ah, yes, I suppose that was me. Poor girl. She is so very ticklish. Not bad looking and will one day have a fine figure, but for now, she is too young. One day, someone will buy her some rouge and powder, and she will leave us. And so this is the way of women."

Mozasu couldn't understand why his boss would be interested in the kitchen girl when he regularly escorted actresses and dancers.

"Kayoko is perfectly suitable for tickling, however. She has a cute laugh." Goro knocked against Mozasu's knee with his own. "You know, Mozasu, I like having you kids here. It makes this place feel more jolly." Goro kept Mozasu at the main shop because he had a wonderful energy about him. Goro could now afford to hire enough employees in all his shops. It wasn't that long ago that, as a new owner, he did the same work Mozasu did. Goro looked up and down at the boy and frowned.

Mozasu looked at his boss, puzzled.

"You wear the same white shirt and black trousers each day. You look clean, but you look like a janitor. You have two shirts and two pairs of trousers. Isn't that so?" Goro said this kindly.

"Yes, sir." Mozasu glanced down. His mother had ironed his shirt the night before. He didn't look bad, but Goro-san was right—he didn't look important. There was no extra money for clothing. After food, tutoring, and transportation, Uncle Yoseb's doctor's bills ate up all their spare cash. He'd been getting worse and remained in bed most of the day.

"You need some more clothes. Let's go." Goro shouted, "Kayo-chan, I'm going to go out with Mozasu for a few minutes. Don't let anyone in. Okay?"

"Yes, sir," Kayoko shouted from the kitchen.

"But I need to put the trays of balls out and sweep the front. The machines need to be cleaned, and I wanted to help Kayoko with the hand towels—" Mozasu listed his morning duties, but his boss was already at the door.

"Mozasu, come on! I don't have all day. You can't look like that any-

more!" he shouted, while smiling, not the least bit ruffled by the boy's confusion.

The woman who answered the small wooden door was surprised to see the tall boy standing by her customer, Goro-san.

Mozasu recognized Haruki's mother immediately. He'd never been to his friend's house before but had met her on the street several times, and Haruki had introduced her to him.

"Totoyama-san! Hello." Mozasu bowed deep from the waist.

"Mozasu-san, hello. Welcome. I'd heard that you were working for Goro-san."

Goro smiled. "He is a good boy. I'm sorry to come so early, Totoyama-san, but Mozasu needs a few things."

As Mozasu entered, he was surprised by the smallness of the living quarters. The space was a third the size of his house. It was basically one small room divided by a wall-to-wall screen—the front part held the sewing machine, dressmakers' dummies, work table, and fabrics. Some sort of sandalwood incense covered the shoyu and mirin smells from cooking. The room was meticulously clean. It was hard to believe that Haruki lived somewhere so cramped with his mother and brother. Seeing this made him miss his friend more. Mozasu had not seen Haruki since he left school and started work.

"Mozasu is going to be my new morning foreman. My youngest one yet."

"*Ehh?*" Mozasu said out loud.

"But a foreman cannot look like the boy who cleans the machines and passes out hand towels and cups of tea," Goro said. "Totoyama-san, please make him two proper jackets and matching trousers."

Totoyama nodded gravely, unspooling her measuring tape to gauge the size of his shoulders and arms. With a stubby pencil, she took notes on a pad made out of used wrapping paper.

"Mama! Mama! Can I come out now?"

It was the voice of a larger male but with the pleading tone of a small boy.

"Excuse me. My son is curious. We don't usually have customers so early in the morning."

Goro-san waved her away, letting her check on her son.

When she left the room, Goro made a sad face. "The boy is—"

Mozasu nodded, because he knew about Haruki's younger brother. It had been almost six months since he had last seen Haruki, who was still in school. Haruki wanted to become a police officer. Neither had realized that school had made their relationship possible until one of them left; there'd been no chance to see him since Mozasu worked all the time.

The sliding walls between the rooms were made of paper and thin slats of wood, and Goro and Mozasu could hear everything.

"Daisuke-chan, Mama will be right back, *nee*? I'm in the next room. You can hear me, *nee*?"

"Mama, is brother back home from school?"

"No, no, Daisuke-chan. Haruki left only an hour ago. We must wait for him patiently. He will not be home until much later. Mama has to make some jackets for Haruki's good friend. Can you stay here and do your puzzle?"

"Is this Mozasu-san?"

Startled at hearing his name, Mozasu glanced at the closed screen door.

"I want to meet him, Mama. This is the Korean boy. Can I meet him, please? Brother said Mozasu curses. I want to hear that!" Daisuke burst out laughing.

Goro patted Mozasu's back as if he was trying to assure him somehow. Mozasu could feel Goro's sympathy and kindness.

"Oh, Mama! Mama! I want to meet the Korean friend. Oh, Mama, please?"

Suddenly, it got quiet, and Totoyama's voice lowered to a low murmur like a bird cooing. "Daisuke-chan, Daisuke-chan, Daisuke-chan," she chanted. Haruki's mother repeated his name until the boy quieted.

"You should stay here and do your puzzle and help Mama. Okay? You are my good child. Haruki will be home in a few hours. He will want to see your progress on your puzzles."

"Yes, Mama, yes. I will play with my top first. Then I will do my puz-

zles. Can we have rice today, do you think? If we have customers, can we have rice? Sometimes you buy rice when we have customers. I want a big rice ball, Mama."

"Later, Daisuke-chan. We will talk later. Daisuke-chan, Daisuke-chan, Daisuke-chan," she murmured.

Totoyama returned to the room and apologized. Goro said it was nothing. For the first time, Mozasu saw that Goro could look troubled. He smiled a lot at Totoyama, but his downward-sloping eyes showed his anguish at the sight of her stoic yet gentle face.

"Maybe you should make the boy two jackets, two sets of trousers, and a proper winter coat. He is always wearing some shabby thing. I want my customers to see that the employees of my shops are neat and well dressed."

Goro-san handed her some bills, and Mozasu turned away. He looked for signs of his friend in the tiny room, but there were no photographs, books, or images. There was a portrait-sized mirror on the wall beside the curtained dressing area.

"I will send Kayoko later today so you can make her something that matches Mozasu's uniform. I think they should wear a striped tie or some striped thing that matches each other. I saw that in a Tokyo parlor last month. She should wear a neat dress with an apron. Maybe the apron could be striped. What do you think? Well, I leave that to you. She should have two or three uniforms made. They should be sturdy." Goro peeled off some more bills and put them in her hands.

Totoyama bowed and bowed again. "It is too much," she said, looking at the money.

Goro gestured to Mozasu. "We should go back now. The customers will be itchy to touch their machines!"

"Goro-san, I shall have the jackets and trousers ready by the end of the week. I will work on the coat last. Mozasu-san will come again to try on the jacket, please. Can you come by in three days?"

Mozasu glanced at Goro-san, who nodded firmly.

"Come along, Mozasu. We mustn't keep the customers waiting."

Mozasu followed his boss out the door, unable to find out anything

about his friend, who would be suffering through morning classes about now.

Totoyama bowed when they left and remained at the threshold until they turned the corner and could no longer see her. She shut the door tight and locked the door behind her. There would be money for rent and food that month. Totoyama sat down in front of her door and cried from relief.

13

1957

There has to be a way to raise that money," Kyunghee said.

"We have whatever's left from the savings for the shop," Yangjin said.

"It's mostly gone," Sunja whispered. Trying to save money while paying medical bills was like pouring oil into a broken jar.

The women were speaking in low voices in the kitchen for fear of waking Yoseb. His latest skin infection made him itch terribly and kept him from resting. He had only just gone to bed after taking a large draft of Chinese medicine. The herbalist had given him a very strong dose this time, and it had worked. After all these years, the women were used to paying a lot for the medications, but this concoction had been shockingly expensive. Regular medicines no longer worked for his ailments, and he continued to suffer a great deal. Mozasu, who gave his full pay envelope each week to his mother, said that whatever they had left after living expenses should go toward the best possible care for Uncle Yoseb. Noa felt the same way. Despite the family's thrift and diligence, the savings seemed to vanish with each visit to the pharmacy. How would they pay for Waseda?

At last, Noa had passed the entrance exam. This should have been a good day, perhaps the greatest day in the family's life, but they didn't know how to pay even a portion of his first tuition bill. Also, the school was in Tokyo, and he would need room and board in the most expensive city in the country.

Noa intended to continue working for Hoji-san up until almost the first day of school, then get a job in Tokyo while going to university. Sunja didn't know how that could be possible. Koreans didn't get jobs so easily, and they knew no one in Tokyo. Noa's boss, Hoji-san, was furious that his best bookkeeper was going to quit working to study something as useless as English literature. Hoji-san would never help Noa get a job in Tokyo.

Kyunghee thought they should buy another cart and set up in another part of town to try to double their earnings, but Yoseb could not be left alone. He could no longer walk, and the muscles in his legs had atrophied so much that what had once been thick, powerful calves were now bony stalks sheathed with scabs.

He was not asleep, and he could hear them. The women were in the kitchen worrying about Noa's tuition. They were worried when he was studying for his exams, and now that he had finally passed, they were worried about how they would pay. Somehow, they had to live without Noa's salary, come up with the cost of the boy's education, and pay for his medicines. It would have been better if he were dead. Everyone knew it. As a young man, the only thing Yoseb had wanted to do was to take care of his family, and now that he was helpless to do so, he could not even die to help them. The worst thing had happened: He was eating up his family's future. Back home, in the olden days, he could have asked someone to carry him off to the mountains to die, perhaps to be eaten by tigers. He lived in Osaka, and there were no wild animals here—only expensive herbalists and doctors who could not help him get well, but rather keep him from just enough agony to fear death more while hating himself.

What surprised him was that as he felt closer to death, he felt the terror of death, its very finality. There were so many things he had failed to do. There were even more things he should never have done. He thought of his parents, whom he should never have left; his brother, whom he should never have brought to Osaka; and he thought of the job in Nagasaki he should never have taken. He had no children of his own. Why did God bring him this far? He was suffering, and in a way, he could manage that;

but he had caused others to suffer, and he did not know why he had to live now and recall the series of terrible choices that had not looked so terrible at the time. Was that how it was for most people? Since the fire, in the few moments when he felt clear and grateful to breathe without pain, Yoseb wanted to see the good in his life, but he couldn't. He lay on his well-laundered pallet, dwelling on the mistakes that seemed so obvious in hindsight. He was no longer angry at Korea or Japan; most of all, he was angry about his own foolishness. He prayed that God would forgive him for being an ungrateful old man.

Softly, he called out "*Yobo*." He didn't want to wake the boys, who were sleeping in the back room, and Changho, who slept in the room by the front door. Yoseb tapped the floor gently in case Kyunghee could not hear him.

When he saw her at the threshold, he asked her to bring Sunja and Yangjin.

The three women sat on the floor by his pallet.

"You can sell my tools first," he said. "They're worth something. Maybe they'll pay for his books and his moving fees. You should sell all the jewelry you have. That will help, too."

The women nodded. Among the three of them, they had two gold rings left.

"Mozasu should ask his boss, Goro-san, for an advance against his salary equal to Noa's tuition, room, and board. And the three of you and he can work down the debt. During the school breaks, Noa can find whatever temporary jobs he can get and save. The boy has to go to Waseda. He deserves to go. Even if no one hires Koreans here, with his degree he can go back to Korea and work for a better salary. Or move to the United States. He'll know how to speak English. We have to think of his education as an investment."

He wanted to say more. He wanted to apologize for not providing for them and for the expense he caused them, but he couldn't say these things now.

"The Lord will provide," Kyunghee said. "He's always taken care of our every need. When the Lord saved your life, he saved our lives."

"Send Mozasu to me when he comes home. I'll tell him that he must ask for an advance from Goro-san so he can pay for the tuition."

Sunja shook her head slightly.

"Noa won't allow his younger brother to pay for his tuition," she said. "He's already told me so." She didn't look at him while speaking. "Koh Hansu has said that he would pay for the tuition and board. Even if Mozasu got an advance—"

"No. That's the foolish talk of an unthinking woman! You can't take that bastard's money! It's filthy."

"Shhh," Kyunghee said gently. "Please don't get upset." She didn't want Kim Changho to hear them talking about his boss. "Noa said that he'll get a job in Tokyo, and it's true, he did say that Mozasu cannot pay for the tuition. That he'll manage. You know Noa won't go if Mozasu pays."

"I should be dead," Yoseb said. "I'd rather be dead than listen to this. How can that boy work and go to a school like Waseda? Impossible. A boy who studied hard like this must go. I'll ask Goro-san myself if Noa can borrow the money. I'll tell Noa that he has to take it from him."

"But we don't know if Goro-san will lend it. And asking him could hurt Mozasu's job. I don't want to let Koh Hansu pay for the fees, either, but how else? We can make it a loan, and we can pay it back in increments so that Noa doesn't owe him anything," Sunja said.

"Borrowing from Goro-san and hurting Mozasu's future in pachinko is far better than taking money from Koh Hansu," Yoseb said firmly. "That Koh Hansu is bad. Take money from him for Noa, and there will be no end to him. He wants to control the boy. You know that. For Goro-san, it's just money."

"But why is Goro's pachinko money cleaner than Koh Hansu's money? Koh Hansu owns construction companies and restaurants. There's nothing wrong with those things," Kyunghee said.

"Shut up."

Kyunghee pursed her lips. The Bible said that a wise person must rein in his tongue. Not everything you wanted to say should be said.

Sunja said nothing as well. She had never wanted anything from Hansu before, but she reasoned that it would be preferable to ask a man who

had already offered the money than bother a total stranger. Goro had already been so gracious to Mozasu, and Mozasu was very happy in his job. She didn't want to bring shame to Mozasu, who had only just started out. The boy had been talking of opening his own parlor one day. Besides, she knew Noa wouldn't allow Mozasu to borrow that money. Yoseb could insist all he wanted, but Noa would not listen to this.

"How about Kim Changho? Can he help?" Yangjin asked.

"That man works for Koh Hansu. Changho doesn't have that kind of money, and if he got it, he would have gotten it from his boss. These debts are not easy, but Goro-san is the best option. He won't charge some exorbitant rate, or hurt Noa. Mozasu will be fine," Yoseb replied. "I'm going to rest now."

The women left the room and closed the door.

The next day, Hansu asked Noa to come by his office in Osaka with his mother. That same evening, without telling the family, the mother and son went to see Hansu. The office had two receptionists, dressed in matching black suits and crisp white shirts, and one of them brought them tea in thin blue porcelain cups on a lacquer tray lined in white gold foil. The waiting area was filled with beautiful floral arrangements. As soon as Hansu's call ended, the older one ushered them into Hansu's immense, wood-paneled office. Hansu sat on a tufted black-leather chair behind a mahogany partners desk from England.

"Congratulations!" Hansu said, getting up from his big chair. "I'm so glad you could come. We should go have sushi! Can you go now?"

"No, no, thank you. We have to get home," Sunja replied.

Noa glanced at his mother, wondering why she wouldn't go to dinner. They didn't have any plans. After the meeting, they would likely just go back home and eat something simple that Aunt Kyunghee made.

"I asked you to come today because I want Noa to know that he has achieved something great. Not just for himself or his family but for all Koreans. You are going to university! And to Waseda, an excellent Japanese university! You are doing everything a great man can do in his time—you are pursuing your education. So many Koreans could not go

to school, but you kept studying and studying. And even when the exams were not good, you persevered. You deserve a great reward! How wonderful! I'm so proud. So proud." Hansu beamed.

Noa smiled shyly. No one had fussed nearly this much. Everyone at home had been happy, but mostly they had been anxious about the cost. Noa had been concerned, too, about the money, but he felt that somehow, everything would be okay. He had worked since high school, and he would keep working even at Waseda. After getting into Waseda, he felt like he could do anything. He didn't mind working in any kind of job as long as he could go to classes and study.

"I am sorry to ask this, but a while ago, you had said that you may be able to help Noa with the fees," Sunja said. "Do you think you could help us?"

"*Umma*, no." Noa flushed. "I can get a job. That's not why we're here. Kim-san said that Koh-san wanted us to come by to congratulate me. *Nee*?" Noa was surprised by his mother's request. She didn't like to ask for anything. She didn't even like taking free samples at the bakery.

"Noa, I'm asking for a loan. We would pay everything back. With interest," Sunja said. She hadn't wanted to ask now, but it was better this way, she thought. Now he would know the terms from the beginning. There was no way to do this perfectly, so she had to just say it. "The tuition is due now, and if you could help us, then we can write up a loan paper, and I will stamp it with my *hanko*. I brought it." Sunja nodded for emphasis. For a second, she wondered: What would she do if he said no?

Hansu laughed and shook his head dismissively.

"That's not necessary, and Noa need never worry about tuition, board, and fees. I've already taken care of it. As soon as I heard the great news from Kim Changho, I sent the money to the school. I called my friend in Tokyo and found a good room near the school, which I will take you to see next week. Then I asked Kim Changho to ask you and Noa to come by so I could invite you to dinner. So, now, let's go eat sushi. The boy deserves a magnificent meal!"

Hansu looked at Sunja's face with pleading in his eyes. He wanted so much to celebrate his son's great accomplishment.

"You sent the money? And found a room in Tokyo? Without my permission? It's supposed to be a loan," she said, feeling more anxious.

"Sir, it's far too generous. My mother is right. We should return the money to you. I will get a job in Tokyo. Perhaps you can help me with that rather than pay the fees. I'd like to earn it myself. I feel like I can do that."

"No. You have to study. You had to take that exam again and again, not because you are not smart. You are very smart. You didn't have the time to study like a normal student. You took much longer than you needed because you didn't have schooling and you had to work full time to support your family. You didn't have all the proper tutoring that the average Japanese middle-class child would have had. And during the war, you were in that farm without any lessons. No. I will no longer watch idly while you and your mother pretend that the rules of human performance do not apply to you. A hardworking scholar should not have to worry about money. I should have forced my way earlier. Why should it take many more years for you to graduate from school? Do you want to be an old man by the time you finish Waseda? You study and learn as much as you can. I will pay," Hansu said, laughing. "Do it my way. Be smart, Noa. This is what I can do for the next generation as a responsible Korean elder."

Noa bowed.

"Sir, you have been very kind to our family. I am very grateful."

Noa looked at his mother, who remained seated quietly by his side. Her hands twisted the handle of her homemade canvas bag, stitched from Mozasu's leftover coat material. He felt sorry for her, because she was a proud woman, and this was humiliating for her. He knew she wanted to pay for his tuition.

"Noa, can you go outside and ask Mieko-san to call the restaurant for us?" Hansu asked.

Noa looked again at his mother, who seemed lost in her heavily upholstered chair.

"*Umma?*"

Sunja glanced up at her son, who was already standing by the door. She could see that he wanted to go to dinner with Hansu. The boy looked so handsome and pleased. She couldn't imagine what this must have meant

to him. Noa had not refused Hansu. He had already accepted the money, because the boy wanted so much to go to this university. In her mind, she could hear Yoseb yelling at her—to stop this now, that she was a foolish woman who had not thought this through. But the boy, her first child, was happy. He had done this tremendous, near impossible thing, and she could not imagine unmaking it to the thing it was yesterday, before he had passed—this glittering, brilliant object that could be taken away at a moment's notice through lack of money. She nodded, and her son understood that they would dine with Hansu.

When the door closed, and Hansu and Sunja were alone in his office, she tried again:

"I want this to be a loan. And I want papers so I can show Noa that I paid for his school."

"No, Sunja. This, this I get to do. He's my son. If you don't let me do this, I will tell him."

"Are you crazy?"

"No. Paying for his school is nothing to me financially, but it is everything to me as his father."

"You're not his father."

"You don't know what you're saying," Hansu said. "He is my child. He has my ambition. He has my abilities. I will not let my own blood rot in the gutters of Ikaino."

Sunja gathered her bag and got up. Yoseb was not wrong, and she could not take this back.

"Let us go then. The boy is waiting outside. He must be hungry," he said.

Hansu opened the door and let her out first.

14

December 1959

On a Saturday morning when the others would be at work, Kyunghee wanted to go to church. Missionaries from America who spoke Japanese but not Korean were visiting their church, and the minister had asked her to help him greet them since her Japanese was so good. Normally, she couldn't get out of the house because she wouldn't leave Yoseb by himself, but Changho offered to watch Yoseb. It wouldn't be for very long, and Changho wanted to do one last thing for her.

Changho sat cross-legged on the warm floor near Yoseb's bedding to help him do some of the stretches the doctor had recommended.

"You've made up your mind, then?" Yoseb asked.

"Brother, I should go. It's time I went home."

"Really, tomorrow?"

"In the morning, I'll take the train to Tokyo, then head to Niigata from there. The ship leaves next week."

Yoseb said nothing. His face contorted a little in pain as he lifted his right leg toward the ceiling. Changho kept his right hand beneath Yoseb's thigh to steady him down slowly. They switched to the left leg.

Yoseb exhaled audibly after doing two more sets.

"If you wait until I die, then you can take my ashes and bury me there. That would be a good thing, I suppose. Though I think it doesn't much matter in the end. You know, I still believe in heaven. I believe in Jesus, even after all this. I suppose being married to Kyunghee will do that. Her

faith brought me closer to the Lord. I am not a good man, but I believe that I am saved. My father once said that when you die and go to heaven, you get your body back. I can finally get rid of this one. That will be good. And I feel ready to go home, too."

Changho put his right arm beneath Yoseb's head, and Yoseb raised his arms above his head slowly, then lowered them. His arms were much stronger than his legs.

"Brother, you can't talk that way. It's not time. You're still here, and I can still feel the power in your body."

Changho grasped Yoseb's good hand, which was unmarred by burns. He could feel the man's delicate bones. How had he survived for so long?

"And...if you wait...if you wait until I die, then you can marry her," Yoseb said. "But you can't take her there. I ask that. I ask that of you."

"What?" Changho shook his head.

"I don't trust the communists. I wouldn't want her to go back home when they're in charge. And this can't last forever. Japan will be a rich country again soon, and Korea won't always be divided. You still have your health. You can make money here and take care of my..." Yoseb couldn't say her name then.

"I've made her suffer so much. She loved me when I was just a boy. I always knew that we'd be together, even when we were kids. She was the most beautiful girl I had ever seen. You know, I've never wanted to be with another woman. Ever. Not just because she's so lovely, but because she's so good. Never, not once, did she complain about me. And I have not been a husband to her for such a long time." He sighed. His mouth felt dry. "I know you care for her. I trust you. I wish you didn't work for that thug, but there aren't that many jobs here. I understand. Why don't you just wait until I die?" The more he said these things, the more Yoseb felt that it was right. "Stay here. I'll die soon. I feel it. You're needed here, too. You can't fix that country. No one can."

"Brother, you're not going to die."

"No, I must. We must try to build a nation again. We can't only think of our own comfort." Even as Yoseb said this, Changho felt the possibility of being with her again, something he had given up.

*   *   *

As Kyunghee walked home from church, she saw Changho sitting on the bench in front of the convenience store, a block from the house. He was reading a newspaper and drinking juice from a glass bottle. Changho was friendly with the owner, and he liked this quiet spot beneath the tarpaulin awning on the busy intersection.

"Hello," she said. Kyunghee was happy to see him. "Is he okay? It's not easy being cooped up, is it? Thank you so much for watching him. I better go back. You stay."

"He's fine. I just stepped out. Before he went to sleep, he asked me to get him some papers for when he wakes up. He wanted me to get some air."

Kyunghee nodded and turned from him to rush home.

"Sister, I was hoping I'd get a chance to speak with you."

"Oh? Let's go back home. I better start dinner. He'll be hungry."

"Wait. Can you sit with me? Can I get you a juice from the store?"

"No, no. I'm all right." She smiled at him and sat down, her hands folded over her lap. She was wearing her winter Sunday coat over her navy wool dress with her nice leather shoes.

Without delay, Changho told her what her husband said, almost word for word. He was nervous, but he knew he had to do it now.

"You could come with me. The first ship leaves next week, but we can go later. Korea needs more people who have the energy to rebuild a nation. We're supposed to get our own apartment with all the latest appliances, and we'll be in our own country. White rice three times a day. We can take his ashes there, and we can visit your parents' graves. Do a proper *jesa*. We can go home. You can be my wife."

Stunned, Kyunghee said nothing. She could not imagine that Yoseb would have offered her to him, but she could not imagine that Changho would lie to her. The only thing that made sense was that Yoseb was worried enough about her to suggest such a plan. After the meeting at the church broke up, she had asked the minister to pray for Changho's journey and well-being in Pyongyang. Changho didn't believe in God or Christianity, but Kyunghee had wanted to pray for him, because she

didn't know what else she could do for him. If the Lord watched over him, then she would not worry.

He had told her that he was leaving only a week ago, and it was difficult to think of him being gone, but it was the right thing. He was a young man who believed in building a great country for others. She admired him, because he didn't even have to go there. He had a good job and friends. Pyongyang wasn't even his home—Changho was from Kyungsangdo. It was she who was from the North.

"Is it possible?" he asked.

"But you said—that you wanted to go. I thought you'd marry someone back home."

"But you know that—that I've cared. That I do—"

Kyunghee looked around. The shopkeeper of the convenience store was seated in the back and couldn't hear them over the noise of his radio program. On the road, a few cars and bicycles passed by, but not many, because it was Saturday morning. The red-and-white pinwheels attached to the store awning spun slowly in the light winter breeze.

"If you said it is possible—"

"You can't talk that way," she said softly. She didn't want to hurt him. All these years, his adoration and kindness had nourished her but had also caused her anguish, because she could not care for him in that way. It was wrong to do so. "Changho, you have a future. You must find a young woman and have children. There isn't a day when I don't feel heartbroken that my husband and I couldn't have them. I know it was the Lord's plan for me, but I think you might have some. You'd make a wonderful husband and father. I couldn't ask you to wait. It would be sinful."

"It's because you don't want me to wait. Because I would if you told me to."

Kyunghee bit her lip. She felt cold suddenly and put on her blue wool mittens.

"I have to make dinner."

"I leave tomorrow. Your husband said I should wait. Isn't that what you wanted? For him to give you permission? Wouldn't that make it okay in the eyes of your god?"

"It isn't up to Yoseb to change God's laws. My husband is alive, and I wouldn't want to hasten his death. I care for you very much, Changho. You have been the dearest friend to me. I'm not sure if I can bear it when you go, but I know we're not supposed to be man and wife. To even talk about it while he is alive cannot be right. I pray that you'll understand."

"No. I don't understand. I will never understand. How could your faith allow such suffering?"

"It isn't just suffering. It isn't. I pray that you will forgive me. That you will—"

Changho laid down the juice bottle carefully on the bench and got up.

"I'm not like you," he said. "I'm just a man. I don't want to be holy. I'm a minor patriot." He left, walking away from the direction of the house and didn't return until late in the evening when everyone was asleep.

Early in the morning, when Kyunghee went to the kitchen to get water for Yoseb, she saw that Changho's room door was open. She looked in, and he was gone. The bedding had been folded neatly. Changho had never had many possessions, but the room looked even more empty without his pile of books, his extra pair of glasses resting on top of them. The family was supposed to have accompanied him to Osaka Station to see him off, but he had taken an earlier train.

Kyunghee stood by his door crying, when Sunja touched her arm. She was wearing her work apron over her nightclothes.

"He left in the middle of the night. He told me to tell everyone goodbye. I only saw him because I got up to make candy."

"Why didn't he wait? Until we could go with him to the train station?"

"He said he didn't want to make a fuss. He said he had to go. I tried to make him breakfast, but he said he'd buy something later. That he couldn't eat."

"He wanted to marry me. After Yoseb died. Yoseb had told him that it was okay."

"*Uh-muh*," Sunja gasped.

"But that's not right, is it? He should be with someone young. He has

a right to have children. I couldn't give him any. I don't even have blood anymore."

"Maybe you're more important than children."

"No. I could not disappoint two men," she said. "He is a good man."

Sunja held her sister-in-law's hand.

"You told him no?" Her sister-in-law's face was wet with tears, and Sunja wiped it with a corner of her apron.

"I have to get water for Yoseb," Kyunghee said, remembering suddenly why she'd gotten out of bed.

"Sister, he would not have cared about children. He would have been happy to have just been with you. You are like an angel in this world."

"No. I'm selfish. Yoseb isn't."

Sunja didn't understand.

"It was selfish to keep him here, but I did because he meant so much to me. I prayed every day for the courage to let him go, and I know the Lord wanted me to let him go. It cannot be right to have two men care for you that way and to allow it."

Sunja nodded, but it didn't make sense. Were you supposed to have only one person in your life? Her mother had her father and no one else. Was her person Hansu or Isak? Did Hansu love her or had he just wanted to use her? If love required sacrifice, then Isak had really loved her. Kyunghee had served her husband faithfully without complaint. There was no one as kindhearted and lovely as her sister-in-law—why couldn't she have more than one man love her? Why did men get to leave when they didn't get what they wanted? Or had Changho suffered enough waiting? Sunja wanted her sister-in-law to make Changho wait, but it wouldn't have been Kyunghee if she had made him do so. Changho had loved someone who would not betray her husband, and perhaps that was why he had loved her. She could not violate who she was.

Kyunghee moved toward the kitchen, and Sunja followed, a few steps behind. Morning sunlight broke through the kitchen window, and it was hard to see straight ahead, but the light cast a glowing outline around her sister-in-law's slight frame.

Celebrating 115 Years of Service to Our Customers!

PLEASE NOTE - CHANGE IN OUR HOURS

MAIN LIBRARY is OPEN Tuesday, Wednesday, Thursday 9:30am-6:30pm / Monday & Friday 9:30am-5pm. Saturday 9 AM to 5 PM RICHMOND BRANCH is OPEN Tuesday, Wednesday, and Thursday from 12-5pm.

Atlantic City Free Public Library - Richmond Branch

Checked out to 23352008222133

02/06/2019 12:45 PM

....

Checked Out

Pachinko
Barcode: 33352004421729
Date due: 02 27/2019 11:59 PM

Time and again
Barcode: 33352001794326
Date due: 02 27/2019 11:59 PM

Overdues

15

Tokyo, 1960

It took some time, but after two years at Waseda, Noa finally felt comfortable about his place there. Always an excellent student with good habits, after a few hiccups and several thoughtful attempts, Noa learned how to write English literature papers and take university-level exams. University life was glorious in contrast to secondary school, where he had learned and memorized many things he no longer valued. None of his requirements even seemed like work; Waseda was pure joy to him. He read as much as he could without straining his eyes, and there was time to read and write and think. His professors at Waseda cared deeply about the subjects they taught, and Noa could not understand how anyone could ever complain.

Hansu had procured for him a well-appointed apartment and gave him a generous allowance, so Noa did not have to worry about housing, money, or food. He lived simply and managed to send some money home each month. "Just study," Hansu had said. "Learn everything. Fill your mind with knowledge—it's the only kind of power no one can take away from you." Hansu never told him to study, but rather to learn, and it occurred to Noa that there was a marked difference. Learning was like playing, not labor.

Noa was able to buy every book he needed for his classes, and when he couldn't find one at the bookstore, all he had to do was go to the immense university library, which was deeply underutilized by his peers. He didn't

understand the Japanese students around him, because they seemed so much more interested in things outside of school rather than learning. He knew well enough from schools past that the Japanese didn't want much to do with Koreans, so Noa kept to himself, no different than when he was a boy. There were some Koreans at Waseda, but he avoided them, too, because they seemed too political. During one of their monthly lunches, Hansu had said that the leftists were "a bunch of whiners" and the rightists were "plain stupid." Noa was alone mostly, but he didn't feel lonely. Even after two years, he was still in thrall with just being at Waseda, with just having a quiet room to read in. Like a man starved, Noa filled his mind, ravenous for good books. He read through Dickens, Thackeray, Hardy, Austen, and Trollope, then moved on to the Continent to read through much of Balzac, Zola, and Flaubert, then fell in love with Tolstoy. His favorite was Goethe; he must have read *The Sorrows of Young Werther* at least half a dozen times.

If he had an embarrassing wish, it was this: He would be a European from a long time ago. He didn't want to be a king or a general—he was too old for such simple wishes. If anything, he wanted a very simple life filled with nature, books, and perhaps a few children. He knew that later in life, he also wanted to be let alone to read and to be quiet. In his new life in Tokyo, he had discovered jazz music, and he liked going to bars by himself and listening to records that the owners would select from bins. Listening to live music was too expensive, but he hoped that one day, when he had a job again, he would be able to go to a jazz club. At the bar, he would have one drink that he'd barely touch to pay for his seat, then he'd go back to his room, read some more, write letters to his family, then go to sleep.

Every few weeks, he saved some of his allowance and took an inexpensive train ride home and visited his family. At the beginning of each month, Hansu took him for a sushi lunch to remind Noa of his mission in the world for some higher purpose that neither could articulate fully. His life felt ideal, and Noa was grateful.

That morning, as he walked across campus to his George Eliot seminar, he heard someone calling his name.

"Bando-san, Bando-san," a woman shouted. It was the radical beauty on campus, Akiko Fumeki.

Noa stopped and waited. She had never spoken to him before. He was, in fact, a little afraid of her. She was always saying contrary things to Professor Kuroda, a soft-spoken woman who had grown up and studied in England. Though the professor was polite, Noa could tell that she didn't like Akiko much; the other students, especially the females, could barely tolerate her. Noa knew it was safer to keep his distance from the students that the professors disliked. In the seminar room, Noa sat one seat away from the professor, while Akiko sat in the very back of the room below the high windows.

"Ah, Bando-san, how are you?" Akiko asked, flushed and out of breath. She spoke to him casually, as if they had talked many times before.

"Well, thank you. How are you?"

"So what do you think of Eliot's final masterpiece?" she asked.

"It's excellent. Everything by George Eliot is perfect."

"Nonsense. *Adam Bede* is a bore. I almost died reading that thing. *Silas Marner* is barely tolerable."

"Well, *Adam Bede* was not as exciting or developed as *Middlemarch*, but it remains a wonderful depiction of a brave woman and an honest man—"

"Oh, please." Akiko rolled her eyes, and she laughed at him.

Noa laughed, too. He knew she was a Sociology major, because everyone had had to introduce himself or herself on the first day of class.

"You have read everything by George Eliot? That's impressive," he said, never having met anyone else who had done so.

"You're the one who's read absolutely everything. It's sickening, and I'm almost irritated at you for doing so. But I admire it, too. Although, if you like everything you read, I can't take you that seriously. Perhaps you didn't think about these books long enough." She said this with a serious face, not in the least bit concerned about offending him.

"*Soo nee.*" Noa smiled. It had not occurred to him that any book that a professor would choose and admire could be inferior even in relation to that author's own works. Their professor had loved *Adam Bede* and *Silas Marner*.

"You sit so close to the professor. I think she's in love with you."

In shock, Noa halted.

"Kuroda-san is sixty years old. Maybe seventy." Noa moved toward the building door and opened it for her.

"You think women want to stop having sex just because they're sixty? You're absurd. She's probably the most romantic woman in Waseda. She's read far too many novels. You're perfect for her. She'd marry you tomorrow. Oh, the scandal! Your George Eliot married a young man, too, you know. Although her groom did try to kill himself on their honeymoon!" Akiko laughed out loud, and the students who were walking up the staircase to their classroom stared at her. Everyone seemed puzzled by their interaction, since Noa was almost as famous as the campus beauty, but for being aloof.

Once in their classroom, she sat at her old seat in the back, and Noa returned to his seat by the professor. He opened his notebook and retrieved his fountain pen, then looked down at the sheet of white paper lined in pale blue ink. He was thinking about Akiko; she was even prettier up close.

Kuroda-san sat down to give her lecture. She wore a pea-green sweater over her Peter Pan–collar white blouse and a brown tweed skirt. Her tiny feet were shod with a childish pair of Mary Janes. She was so small and thin that she gave the impression that she could almost fly away like a sheet of paper or a dry leaf.

Kuroda-san's lecture was primarily an extensive psychological portrait of the heroine in *Daniel Deronda*, the self-centered Gwendolen Harleth, who changes as a result of her suffering and the goodness of Daniel. The professor put great emphasis on a woman's lot being determined by her economic position and marriage prospects. Unsurprisingly, the professor compared Gwendolen to the vain and greedy Rosamond Vincy of *Middlemarch*, but argued that in contrast, Gwendolen achieves the Aristotelian anagnorisis and peripeteia. Kuroda-san spent most of the lecture on Gwendolen, then right before the period ended, she spoke a little about Mirah and Daniel, the Jews of the book. Kuroda-san gave some background on Zionism and the role of Jews in Victorian novels.

"Jewish men are often seen as exceptionally brilliant, and the women are often beautiful and tragic. Here we have a situation where a man does not know his own identity as an outsider. He is like Moses, the infant in Genesis who learns that he is Jewish and not Egyptian—" As Kuroda-san was saying this, she glanced at Noa, but he was not aware of it, because he was taking notes.

"However, when Daniel learns that he is indeed a Jew, Daniel is free to love the virtuous Mirah, another talented singer like his Jewish mother, and they will go east to Israel." Kuroda-san sighed quietly, as if she was pleased by Eliot's ending.

"So are you saying that it is better for people to only love within their race, that people like the Jews need to live apart in their own country?" Akiko asked, without raising her hand. She did not seem to believe in that formality.

"Well, I think George Eliot is arguing that there is great nobility in being Jewish and wanting to be part of a Jewish state. Eliot recognizes that these people were often persecuted unfairly. They have every right to a Jewish state. The war has taught us that bad things happened to them, and that can't happen again. The Jews have done no wrong, but the Europeans—" Kuroda-san spoke more quietly than usual, as if she was afraid that someone might overhear her and she would get in trouble. "It's complicated, but Eliot was far ahead of her contemporaries to think about the issue of discrimination based on religion. *Nee?*"

There were nine students in the class, and everyone nodded, including Noa, but Akiko looked irritated nonetheless.

"Japan was an ally of Germany," Akiko said.

"That is not part of this discussion, Akiko-san."

The professor opened her book nervously, wanting to change the subject.

"Eliot is wrong," Akiko said, undeterred. "Maybe the Jews have a right to have their own state, but I see no need for Mirah and Daniel to have to leave England. I think this nobility argument or a greater nation for a persecuted people is a pretext to eject all the unwanted foreigners."

Noa did not look up. He found himself writing down everything Akiko

said, because it upset him to think that this could be true. He had admired Daniel's courage and goodness throughout the book, and he had not thought much about Eliot's political design. Was it possible that Eliot was suggesting that foreigners, no matter how much she admired them, should leave England? At this point in the course, everyone in the room despised Akiko, but suddenly he admired her courage to think so differently and to suggest such a difficult truth. He felt lucky to be at a university and not in most other settings, where the person in charge was always right. Nevertheless, until he really listened to Akiko disagree with the professor, he had not thought for himself fully, and it had never occurred to him to disagree in public.

After class, he walked home alone, deep in thoughts of her, and he knew that he wanted to be with her, even if it would not be easy. The following Tuesday, before the seminar began, Noa went early to class to claim the chair next to hers. The professor tried not to show that she was hurt by this defection, but of course, she was.

16

Osaka, April 1960

At some point in the past four years, Mozasu had worked as a foreman at all six of Goro's pachinko parlors. Goro had opened new parlors in rapid succession, and Mozasu had helped him to start each new one. Mozasu was twenty years old, and he did little else but mind the shops and fix whatever needed fixing while Goro scouted for new locations and came up with inspired ideas for his growing empire, which oddly seemed to work out. In business, Goro could not miss, it seemed, and he credited some of his good fortune to Mozasu's willingness to labor without ceasing.

It was April and early in the morning when Mozasu arrived at the manager's office at Paradaisu Six—the newest pachinko parlor.

"*Ohayo*. The car is waiting. I'm taking you to Totoyama-san's for new clothes. Let's go," Goro said.

"*Maji?* Why? I have enough suits for this year and next. I'm the best-dressed foreman in Osaka," Mozasu said, laughing. Unlike his brother, Noa, Mozasu had never cared for nice clothing. He wore the well-tailored clothes Goro wanted him to wear only because his boss was fastidious about how his staff should look. Goro's employees were an extension of himself, he believed, and Goro was strict about their personal hygiene as well.

Mozasu had too much to do, and he didn't feel like going down to Totoyama-san's place. He was eager to phone the newspapers to put out

ads for more workers. Paradaisu Six needed men to work the floor on the late shift, and since the interiors of Paradaisu Seven would be finished in a month, he had to start thinking about hiring for Seven as well.

"You have the right clothes for a foreman, but you'll need new suits to be the manager of Seven."

"*Ehh*? I can't be manager of Seven!" Mozasu replied, startled. "That's Okada-san's job."

"He's gone."

"What? Why? He was looking forward to being manager."

"Stealing."

"What? I don't believe it."

"*Honto desu*," Goro said, nodding. "I caught him. I had suspected it, and it was confirmed."

"That's terrible." Mozasu couldn't fathom anyone stealing from Goro. It would be like stealing from your father. "Why did he do that?"

"Gambling. He owed some goons money. He said he was going to pay me back, but the losses got bigger. You know. Anyway, his mistress came by this morning to apologize for him. She's pregnant. He finally gets her pregnant and then he loses his job. Moron."

"Oh, shit." Mozasu recalled all the times Okada had spoken of wanting a son. Even a daughter would do, he'd said. Okada was crazy about kids and pachinko. Even with all his experience, no pachinko parlor in Osaka would hire him if Goro had gotten rid of him for stealing. No one stole from Goro. "Did he say he was sorry?"

"Of course. Cried like a child. I told him to get out of Osaka. I don't want to see his face anymore."

"*Soo nee*," Mozasu said, feeling bad for Okada, who had always been nice to him. He had a Korean mother and a Japanese father, but he always said he felt like a full Korean because he was such a passionate man. "Is his wife okay?" Mozasu knew Goro got along with both women.

"Yeah. His wife and mistress are fine," Goro replied. "But I told the mistress that he shouldn't show up around here. I wouldn't be so nice next time."

Mozasu nodded.

"Let's go to Totoyama-san's. I'm tired of feeling sad. Seeing To-toyama's girls will cheer me up," Goro said.

Mozasu followed his boss to the car. He knew enough not to ask about his new salary; Goro didn't like to talk about money, strangely enough. The manager's salary would be better than that of a foreman. Mozasu had been saving carefully for his mother's confection shop, and they were pretty close to having enough to buy a small store near the train station. With Uncle Yoseb's health worsening, Aunt Kyunghee couldn't make candy to sell when she was home. With only his mother and grandmother working in the stall and with Noa in his third year at Waseda in Tokyo, any extra money would be good for the family, he figured. Each Satur-day evening, Mozasu felt proud handing his mother his fat pay envelope; she'd tried to increase his allowance, but he had refused except for his bus fare. He didn't need much, since he ate his meals at the employee cafete-ria and Goro bought him his work clothes. Mozasu worked seven days a week and slept at home; if it was very late, he slept in one of the spare em-ployee dorm rooms at the parlors.

The shop door shut behind them after they exited.

"Boss, I don't know. Do you think the guys will listen to me? Like the way they do Okada?" Mozasu asked. It wasn't that Mozasu wasn't ambi-tious; it was that he enjoyed being the morning or evening foreman at the shops; he was very good at it. Being a manager was more serious; everyone looked up to the manager. He would be in charge whenever Goro wasn't there. Okada was almost thirty-five and tall like a baseball player.

"I'm flattered and grateful, but you know, I think some of the other managers might—"

"Shut up, kid. I know what I'm doing. You're smarter than the other managers, and you know how to solve problems by yourself. This is the most important shop. If I'm running around checking the others, I need you to be sharp."

"But Seven is going to need almost fifty employees. How am I sup-posed to find fifty men?"

"Actually, you're going to need at least sixty men and twenty pretty girls for the prize counters."

"Really?" Mozasu was always game for Goro's outlandish plans, but this seemed a bit much, even for him. "How will I find—"

"You will. You always do. And you can hire any kind of girl you want for the prize counters—Okinawans, *burakumin*, Koreans, Japanese, I don't care. They just have to be cute and pretty, but not so slutty they'll scare the men. The girls are always important. Ha."

"I didn't realize that the dorm could accommodate so many—"

"You worry a lot. That's why you'll be perfect." Goro smiled widely.

Mozasu thought about that and had to agree. No one worried about the shops nearly as much as he did.

In the car ride to Totoyama's workshop, the driver and Goro talked about wrestling, while Mozasu sat quietly. In his mind, he was making lists of all the things that had to be done for Seven. As he pondered over which of the men he would shuffle around from the other shops, he realized that maybe he was ready after all to become a manager of a shop, and it made him smile a little. Goro was never wrong; maybe he wasn't wrong about him, either. Mozasu wasn't smart like his brother, who was now studying English literature at Waseda in Tokyo and who could read thick novels in English without a dictionary. Noa wanted to work for a real Japanese company; he wouldn't have wanted to work in a pachinko parlor. Noa thought that after the family bought the confectionery, Mozasu should work with the family. Like most Japanese, Noa thought pachinko parlors were not respectable.

The car stopped in front of a squat redbrick building that had been used as a textile factory before the war. A large persimmon tree shaded the gray metal door. As Goro's exclusive uniform maker, Totoyama had earned and saved enough to move her shop here from her home-cum-workshop near Ikaino. She and her sons, Haruki and Daisuke, now lived in three of the back rooms, and she used the rest of the building as the workroom. She employed half a dozen assistants who worked six days a week filling orders for uniforms. By word of mouth, she had picked up work from other Korean business owners in Osaka and now made uniforms for *yakiniku* restaurants and other pachinko parlors in the Kansai

region, but Goro's work always came first, because it was he who had told the others to hire her.

When Goro rang the bell, Totoyama answered the door herself. A hired girl, another apprentice, brought them hot fragrant tea and imported wheat biscuits on a lacquered tray. Totoyama led Mozasu to the mirror so she could take his measurements. With pins in her mouth, she measured the width of his long arms.

"You are getting thinner, Mozasu-san," Totoyama said.

"*Soo nee,*" he answered. "Goro-san tells me I need to eat more."

Goro nodded as he munched on the biscuits and drank a second cup of *genmaicha*. He was seated on a cedar bench covered with indigo fabric–covered cushions. He felt peaceful, watching Totoyama work. He always felt better when he solved problems. Okada had turned out to be a crook, so he got rid of him. Now he was going to promote Mozasu.

The large and airy workroom had been whitewashed recently, but the wood floors were shabby and old. The floors were cleaned each day, but the morning's bits of fabric and thread littered the areas around the work-tables. In the slant of light from the skylight, a pale column of dust motes pierced the room. The long workroom was lined with six sewing machines, and a girl sat behind each one. They tried not to look at the men, but couldn't help being drawn to the young one who came by the shop at least once a year. Mozasu had grown noticeably more attractive. He had his father's purposeful gaze and welcoming smile. He liked to laugh, and this was one of the reasons why Goro liked the boy so much. Mozasu was enthusiastic, not prone to moodiness. He was wearing a foreman's uniform that had been made in this workshop, and the girls who had worked on his clothing felt connected to him in this way but could hardly admit this. They knew he didn't have a girlfriend.

"There's a new face here," Goro said, folding his arms over his chest. He scanned the girls carefully and smiled. He got up from his seat and walked toward them. He bowed deeply, and this was funny because he was such an important person. The girls rose up simultaneously and bowed. Goro shook his head and made a silly face, scrunching up his nose to make them laugh.

"Sit, sit," he said.

He had a kind of comic facility combined with a physical smoothness. To make women laugh, he could walk while wiggling his shoulders. He was a stout little man with funny movements who liked flirting with all kinds of women. You remembered him. You wanted him to like you. Because he could be silly, it was possible to forget that he was a powerful businessman and wealthy enough to own seven pachinko parlors. With a word, he could make grown men leave Osaka for good.

"Eriko-san, Reiko-san, Midori-san, Hanako-san, and Motoko-san, *nee*?" Goro recited their names perfectly, then stopped in front of the new girl.

"Goro *desu*," he said, presenting himself to the new girl. "You have lovely hands."

"Yumi *desu*," the young woman replied, slightly annoyed at him for distracting her from her sewing.

Totoyama looked up from her measurements and frowned at the new girl. Yumi's sewing was neater than the others', but she was often too purposely aloof, taking lunch alone or reading during her breaks rather than talking. Her skills and personal nature were secondary to the fact that she had to respect Goro-san, to humor him even. To Totoyama, Goro-san was a great man who was truly good. Though he joked with girls, he was never inappropriate. Goro had never asked any of the girls out or done any of the bad things her other male customers had tried to do. Yumi had been working for her for two months. From her papers, Totoyama knew she was Korean, but Yumi went by her pass name and never brought up her background. Totoyama didn't care about a person's background as long as the employee did her job. Yumi was an elegant girl with good skin and a high bosom. She did not have a good figure for a kimono but had the sort of curves that men liked. It was natural that Goro-san would have noticed her.

"Goro-san, so Mozasu-san is the new manager of Seven?" Totoyama asked. "How wonderful for such a young man."

Mozasu looked down, avoiding the looks of curiosity and wonder in the eyes of the seamstresses, except for Yumi, who continued her sewing.

"Yes. Mozasu-san will need three dark suits. Use a good fabric, please. He will need some nice neckties. Something different from the others. Something elegant, older looking."

Mozasu stood in front of the three-way mirror and noticed Yumi, who was working diligently. She was lovely. Her shoulders were thin and wide and her neck long, reminding him of an illustration of a swan on a box of detergent.

When Totoyama finished taking Mozasu's measurements, the men returned to the car.

"Yumi-san, the new girl, is very pretty. A terrific ass," Goro said.

Mozasu nodded.

Goro laughed. "Finally, some interest from the hardworking boy! She'd be a good one for you."

The following week, when he returned alone for another fitting, Totoyama was finishing up with a customer and asked Yumi to get him his suit.

Yumi handed him the partially finished suit and pointed to the dressing room behind the indigo fabric curtain.

"Thank you," he said in Japanese.

She said nothing at all, but stood there coolly, waiting to be discharged from her duties by Totoyama.

When Mozasu came out, Yumi was standing in front of the mirror holding a scarlet wool pincushion. Totoyama was still occupied with another customer on the other side of the room.

Yumi looked at his neckline and cocked her head. The lapel needed some work, she noticed.

"I'm Mozasu Boku. It's a pleasure to meet you."

Yumi frowned at the lapel and pulled out a pin from the cushion to mark the place.

"You're not going to poke me, are you?" he said, laughing.

Yumi walked behind him to check the yoke.

"You're not going to speak to me? Really?"

"I'm not here to speak with you. I'm here to check your fit."

"If I buy you dinner, maybe you can find a few words for me," Mozasu said, repeating a line he'd heard Goro use on women. Mozasu had never asked a girl out. He was a manager now at Paradaisu Seven. A girl might find that impressive, he thought.

"No dinner. No thank you."

"You have to eat." This was another one of Goro's stock phrases. "You finish work around seven thirty. I know because I've been here before to pick up uniforms."

"I go to school after work. I don't have time for nonsense."

"I'm nonsense?"

"Yes."

Mozasu smiled at her. She didn't talk like anyone he knew.

"What are you studying anyway?"

"English."

"I know English. I can help you."

"You don't know English."

"Hello, Miss Yumi. My name is Moses Park. How are you?" He repeated the lines he'd practiced with Noa from his English books. "What kind of weather are you having in Tulsa, Oklahoma?" he asked. "Is it rainy or dry? I like hamburgers. Do you like hamburgers? I work at a place called Paradise."

"Where did you learn that? You didn't even finish high school," Yumi said.

"How do you know that?" He smiled.

"Never mind," she said, seeing Totoyama approaching them.

"Miss Yumi, do you like the fascinating novels of Mr. Charles Dickens? He is my brother's favorite author. I think his books are very long. There are no pictures in his books."

Yumi smiled a little, then bowed to her boss before pointing out the areas that needed work. She bowed again before leaving them to return to her sewing machine.

"I'm so sorry to keep you waiting, Mozasu-san. How are you? How is Goro-san?"

Mozasu answered her politely, and when she was nearly done with the

pins, he turned and sneezed dramatically, curving his back as if to bend forward and ripping the carefully basted seams.

"Oh, I'm a fool. I'm so sorry," he said, glancing at Yumi, who was trying not to laugh. "Should I come back tomorrow or the next day? I may be able to come by before you close."

"Oh, yes, please," Totoyama said, assessing the torn seams, oblivious to the two young people studying each other. "We'll have it ready for you by tomorrow night."

17

October 1961

Mozasu leaned against the maple tree opposite Totoyama-san's workshop, his profile only slightly obscured by its trunk. This was their arranged meeting place. Three nights a week, Mozasu met Yumi after work. For over a year, he'd been accompanying her to the English class at the church, then heading back to her rented room where she'd fix them a simple dinner. Often, they would make love before Mozasu returned to Paradaisu Seven, where he worked until closing before falling asleep in his quarters at the employee dormitory.

It was already October, and though the early evening breezes had yet to lose the supple warmth of summer, the leaves on the trees were beginning to turn gold and shiny. The tall tree above him formed a burnished metallic lace against the blurry evening sky. Laborers and other men in uniform were returning home from work, and small children popped out of their homes to greet their fathers. In the past year, the road where Totoyama had her new workshop had improved, with families moving into the abandoned houses near the river. A local vegetable seller had done so well in his once-desolate spot that he was now able to rent the adjacent lot for his brother-in-law to sell dry goods. The new bakery selling Portuguese-style sponge cakes, which perfumed the street invitingly, had achieved sufficient fame in Osaka to command long lines each morning.

The seamstresses at Totoyama-san's were working later than usual, so Mozasu studied his crumpled list of homework words. He'd never

thought much of his memory when he was at school, but he found that he was able to remember English words and phrases very well. His recall was useful for impressing Yumi. Unlike most girls, who cared about gifts of cash, dresses, or trinkets, Mozasu's girlfriend cared only about learning. Yumi seemed happiest with him when he gave the right answers when their teacher, the Reverend John Maryman, called on him. Yumi, who wanted to live in America, believed that she had to learn English well if she was to live there one day.

There was only a little natural light left to read by, but when a man's shadow passed over him, he couldn't make out the words on the page. Noticing the solemn pair of men's work shoes a few paces from him, Mozasu glanced up.

"Is it possible that you are studying, Mo-san? *Honto*?"

"Hey, Haruki!" Mozasu shouted. "Is that you? I haven't seen you since I don't know when!" He clasped his friend's hand heartily and shook it. "I'm always asking your mother about you. She's real proud of you. Not like she's bragging, but you know, in her quiet, polite Totoyama-san way. And look at you! Haruki, the—police officer!" Mozasu whistled at Haruki's academy uniform. "You look really serious. Makes me want to commit a crime. You're not going to tell on me, right?"

Haruki smiled and hit Mozasu on the shoulder lightly with his fist, feeling shy around his old school friend. It had been difficult to keep away from Mozasu, but Haruki had done so because his feelings for him had been too strong. There had been other infatuations over the years and encounters with strangers. Recently, there was a fellow at the academy, Koji, another tough and funny guy. As he had done with Mozasu, Haruki did his best to keep away from Koji, because he knew well enough to draw a thick line between what was public and what was private.

"What the hell are you doing around here? Don't you live near the academy?"

Haruki nodded. "I have the week off."

"So? When do you become a cop? I mean detective." Mozasu chuckled, pretending to bow formally.

"Two years."

Upon seeing Mozasu by the maple tree, Haruki had been afraid to cross the street. The mere image of him had been overwhelming. As a boy, Haruki had worshipped Mozasu, who had saved him from the anguish of school. When Mozasu had dropped out to work for Goro-san and then disappeared into his job, Haruki had felt the loss like a deadly punch to the chest. After Mozasu left to work at the pachinko parlors, the sheep, witches, and ghouls of their high school emerged to the fore, forcing Haruki to retreat to any available sanctuary. During his free periods, he had filled his burgeoning sketchbooks with pencil drawings in the safety of a kindhearted art teacher's classroom. Home was always the same: His younger brother would never grow up, and his mother could never quit working until her eyes failed. His art teacher, whose husband and brothers were police detectives, had given Haruki the suggestion to go to the police academy. Interestingly, the teacher had not been wrong. Haruki loved the academy with its rules and hierarchy. He did what he was told to do, and he did it very well. Also, it was easier just to start again in a new place where no one knew you.

"Why are you standing out here?" Haruki asked. The sun was very low, and its orange-red color moved him.

"I'm waiting for Yumi. She works for your mother. No one's supposed to know about us, though. Of course, I don't think your mother would care. I'm not such a terrible guy."

"I won't say anything," Haruki said, thinking that Mozasu had become more appealing. He had always admired Mozasu's smooth brow, the strong nose, and neat white teeth, but in his manager suit he looked like a grown man in charge of his life. Haruki wanted to follow him.

The workshop windows were still brightly lit, and the girls labored with their dark heads bowed at their worktables. Mozasu could imagine Yumi's thin fingers flying across the fabric. When she focused on her work, Yumi could not be distracted. She was like that about everything and could be left alone working for hours. Mozasu couldn't imagine being so quiet all the time; he would miss the bustle of the pachinko parlor. He loved all the moving pieces of his large, noisy business. His Presbyterian minister father had believed in a divine design, and Mozasu believed that

life was like this game where the player could adjust the dials yet also expect the uncertainty of factors he couldn't control. He understood why his customers wanted to play something that looked fixed but which also left room for randomness and hope.

"Do you see her?" Mozasu pointed with pride. "There! She's the fourth desk from the—"

"Yumi-san. Yes, I've met her. She's a good seamstress. A very elegant person. You're lucky," Haruki said. "And how's your work? Have you made your fortune?"

"You should come by. I'm at the Paradaisu Seven now. Come tomorrow. I'm there all day and night nearly, except for when I meet Yumi and take her to the English class."

"I don't know. I have to see my brother while I'm home."

"I hear he's been a little down."

"That's why I came home. Mother said he's getting a little strange. Not giving her trouble or anything, but she says that he talks less and less. The doctors don't know what to do. They want him to go live in an institution. They say he might be happier living with other people like himself, but I doubt that. Those places can be—" Haruki sucked wind between his clenched teeth. "Of course, Mother would never allow it. Daisuke is a very good child." Haruki said this quietly, having known for as long as he could remember that Daisuke would be his responsibility after his mother could no longer care for him. Who Haruki married would be determined by her willingness to be good to Daisuke and his aging mother.

"Yumi says that it might be good for him in America. Then again, she thinks everyone is better off in America. She said it's not like it is here in Japan, where a person can't be different."

Mozasu thought his girlfriend was irrationally biased in favor of America and anything from America. Like his brother, Noa, Yumi thought English was the most important language and America was the best country.

"Yumi said there are better doctors in America." Mozasu shrugged.

"That's probably true."

Haruki smiled, having often wished that he could live somewhere else, where he didn't know anyone.

As Yumi walked toward the meeting spot, she recognized her employer's older son. It would have been awkward to turn around so she stayed her course.

"You know Haruki-san," Mozasu said to Yumi, smiling. "He was my only friend in high school. And now he will be fighting crime!"

Yumi nodded, smiling uncomfortably.

"Yumi-san. It's good to see you again. I'm grateful to you that I got to see my friend again after so many, many years."

"You are home from the academy, Haruki-san?" Yumi kept her posture both formal and demure.

Haruki nodded, then made excuses about Daisuke waiting for him at home. Before leaving them, however, Haruki promised to visit Mozasu at the pachinko parlor the following morning.

Their English class met in the large conference room in the offices of the new Korean church, built recently with large donations from some wealthy *yakiniku* families. Despite his European name, the teacher, John Maryman, was a Korean who had been adopted as an infant by American missionaries. English was his first language. As a result of his superior diet, rich in both protein and calcium, John was significantly taller than the Koreans and Japanese. At nearly six feet, he caused a commotion wherever he went, as if a giant had descended from heaven. Though he spoke Japanese and Korean proficiently, he spoke both languages with an American accent. In addition to his size, his mannerisms were distinctly foreign. John liked to tease people he didn't know well, and if something was funny, he laughed louder than most. If it hadn't been for his patient Korean wife, who possessed masterful *noonchi* and was able to explain to others tactfully that John just didn't know any better, he would have gotten into trouble far more often for his many cultural missteps. For a Presbyterian pastor, John seemed far too jovial. He was a good man whose faith and intelligence were irreproachable. His mother, Cynthia Maryman, an automobile tire heiress, had sent him to Princeton and Yale

Divinity School, and to his parents' delight, he had returned to Asia to spread the gospel. His lovely coloring was more olive than golden and his fringed, ink-black eyes, constantly bemused, invited women to linger in his presence.

A girl normally hard to win over, Yumi admired her teacher, whom all the students called Pastor John. To her, John represented a Korean being from a better world where Koreans weren't whores, drunks, or thieves. Yumi's mother, a prostitute and alcoholic, had slept with men for money or drinks, and her father, a pimp and a violent drunk, had been imprisoned often for his criminality. Yumi felt that her three elder half sisters were as sexually indiscriminate and common as barn animals. Her younger brother had died as a child, and soon after, at fourteen years old, Yumi ran away from home with her younger sister and somehow supported them with small jobs in textile factories until the younger sister died. Over the years, Yumi had become an excellent seamstress. She refused to acknowledge her family, who lived in the worst sections of Osaka. If she spotted a woman who had even a passing resemblance to her mother on any street, Yumi would cross to the other side or turn around to walk away. From watching American movies, she had decided that one day she would live in California and planned on becoming a seamstress in Hollywood. She knew Koreans who had returned to North Korea and many more who had gone back to the South, yet she could not muster any affection for either nation. To her, being Korean was just another horrible encumbrance, much like being poor or having a shameful family you could not cast off. Why would she ever live there? But she could not imagine clinging to Japan, which was like a beloved stepmother who refused to love you, so Yumi dreamed of Los Angeles. Until Mozasu, with his swagger and enormous dreams, Yumi had never let a man into her bed, and now that she had attached herself to him, she wanted both of them to go to America to make another life where they wouldn't be despised or ignored. She could not imagine raising a child here.

The English class had fifteen pupils who attended three nights a week. Until Mozasu showed up, Yumi had been Pastor John's best student. Mozasu had an enormous advantage over her since he had been uninten-

tionally studying with his brother, Noa, for years by being his at-home English quiz partner, but Yumi did not mind. She was relieved that he was better than she was at this, that he made more money than she did, and that he was relentlessly kind to her.

Each class began with Pastor John going around the room asking each person a series of questions.

"Moses," Pastor John said in his teaching voice, "how is the pachinko parlor? Did you make a lot of money today?"

Mozasu laughed. "Yes, Pastor John. Today, I earned lot money. Tomorrow, I make more! Do you need money?"

"No, thank you, Moses. But please remember to help the poor, Moses. There are many among us."

"The pachinko money isn't mine, Pastor John. My boss is rich, but I am not a rich man yet. One day, I will rich."

"You will *be* rich."

"Yes, I will *be* rich man, Pastor John. A man must have money."

John smiled at Moses kindly, wanting to disabuse him of such idolatrous notions, but he turned to Yumi.

"Yumi, how many uniforms did you make today?"

Yumi smiled and color rushed to her face.

"Today, I made two vests, Pastor John."

John moved on to the others, encouraging the reserved students to talk to each other as well as to the class. He wanted the Koreans to speak well; he wanted no one ever to look down on them. He had left his beautifully comfortable life in Princeton, New Jersey, because he felt sorry for the impoverished Koreans in Japan. In his wonderful childhood, filled with the warmth of his loving parents, he had always felt bad for the Koreans who had lost their nation for good. People like Moses and Yumi had never been to Korea. There was always talk of Koreans going back home, but in a way, all of them had lost the home in their minds for good. His parents had adopted him alone, and he had no known siblings. Because John had always felt so happy with his parents, he'd felt guilty that many others hadn't been chosen the way he was. Why was that? He wanted to know. There were unhappy adoptions, to be sure, but John knew his lot was bet-

ter than almost anyone's. "Chosen" was always the word his mother had used with him.

"We chose you, our darling John. You had the loveliest smile, even as a small baby. The ladies at the orphanage loved holding you, because you were such an affectionate child."

Teaching English class wasn't part of his job as a pastor. He didn't proselytize his students, most of whom were not parishioners. John loved the sound of English words, the sounds of Americans talking. He wanted to give this to the poor Koreans in Osaka. He wanted them to have another language that wasn't Japanese.

Like his students, John was born in Japan to Korean parents. His biological parents had left him with their landlord. John didn't know how old he was exactly. His parents had given him the birthday of Martin Luther, November 10. The only fact he knew about his birth parents was that they had left their rented room in the early hours of the morning without paying the rent and had left him behind. His adoptive mother said this must have been because the landlord had money and shelter, and wherever his biological parents were going, they may not have been able to give these things to him. Their sacrifice of leaving him was an act of love, his mother had said every time John had asked about them. Nevertheless, whenever John saw an older Korean woman or man who could be the age of his parents, he wondered. He could not help it. He wished he could give them money now, for John was a very wealthy man, and he wished he could meet his biological parents and give them a house to keep them warm and food to eat when they were hungry.

As Pastor John teased the two sisters in the back about their fondness for sweets, Mozasu knocked his knee gently against Yumi's. Mozasu had long thighs, and he had to move his thigh only a little to graze the skirt fabric covering Yumi's pretty legs. She tapped him back in slight annoyance, though she did not mind.

Pastor John had asked the younger sister about what she did when it rained, and instead of listening to the girl stumble in English, casting about for the word "umbrella," Mozasu found himself staring at Yumi. He loved to look at her soft profile, the way her dark, sad eyes met her high cheekbones.

"Moses, how can you learn English if you are just staring at Yumi?" John asked, laughing.

Yumi blushed again. "Behave," she whispered to Mozasu in Japanese.

"I cannot stop, Pastor John. I love her," Mozasu declared, and John clapped in delight.

Yumi looked down at her notes.

"Will you two marry?" Pastor John asked.

Yumi appeared stunned at this question, though she shouldn't have been. Pastor John was liable to say anything.

"She will marry me," Mozasu said. "I am confident."

"What?" Yumi cried.

The women in the back were near tears laughing. Two men in the middle of the class pounded on their desks, cheering loudly.

"This is fun," John said. "I think we are witnessing a proposal. 'Proposal' means an invitation to marry."

"Of course, you will marry me, Yumi-chan. You love me, and I love you very much. We will marry. You see," Mozasu said calmly in English, "I have plan."

Yumi rolled her eyes. He knew she wanted to go to America, but he wanted to stay in Osaka and open his own pachinko parlor in a few years. He intended to buy his mother, aunt, uncle, and grandmother a huge house when he was rich. He said that if they wanted to move back to Korea, he would make so much money that he would build them castles. He couldn't make this kind of money in Los Angeles, he'd explained. He couldn't leave his family, and Yumi knew this.

"You and I love each other. *Soo nee*, Yumi-chan?" Mozasu smiled at her and took her hand.

The pupils clapped loudly and stamped their feet as if watching a baseball game.

Yumi bent her head down, mortified by his behavior, but she couldn't be angry at him. She could never be angry with him. He was the only friend she'd ever had.

"We'll have to plan a wedding then," John said.

18

Tokyo, March 1962

Is he married?" Akiko asked. Her eyes brightened with anticipation.

"Yes. He's married, and his wife is expecting in a few months," Noa answered, almost flattening his voice.

"I want to know more about your family. C'mon," she pleaded.

Noa got up to get dressed.

She couldn't help it. Akiko was training to be a sociologist. She collected pieces of data, and her lover was her favorite puzzle. Yet the more she inquired, the more reticent he grew. When he answered her in his pithy manner, she had a habit of saying, "*Sooo?*" as if the facts of his life were something marvelous to behold. Everything about him was fascinating to her, but Noa didn't want to be fascinating. He wanted just to be with her. He didn't mind when she turned her headlights on strangers; it was far more interesting to hear her attempts at demystifying others.

He was Akiko's first Korean lover. In bed, she wanted him to speak Korean.

"How do you say 'pretty'?" she'd asked just a few hours before.

"*Yeh-puh-dah.*" Such a simple word felt strange in his mouth when he'd said it to her. Akiko was stunning; "pretty" wouldn't suffice in describing her beauty. "*Ah-reum-dop-da,*" he should have said, but Noa didn't. She was an excellent social scientist not to have asked for the Korean word for love, because he would have no doubt revealed his hesitation in the translation.

Not wishing to be a specimen under her glass, Noa didn't talk about his mother, who had peddled kimchi and, later, confections so he could go to school, or his father, who'd died from harsh imprisonment during the colonial era. These aspects of his biography had happened a long time ago as far as he was concerned. He wasn't ashamed of his past; it wasn't that. He resented her curiosity. Akiko was a Japanese girl from an upper-class family who had grown up in Minami-Azabu; her father owned a trading company and her mother played tennis with expatriates in a private club. Akiko adored rough sex, foreign books, and talking. She had pursued him, and Noa, who had never had a serious girlfriend before, did not know what to make of her.

"Come back to me," she said flirtatiously, fingering her white cotton top.

Noa retreated to the futon.

After making love between classes, they had been lolling in Noa's rented room—an exceptionally large living space for a university student, with two square windows that let in the morning light and immense floor space for a double futon and a furry beige rug. Thick piles of novels covered his large pine desk—Dickens, Tolstoy, Balzac, and Hugo. The fancy electric lamp with a green glass shade was off. Noa couldn't have conceived of anything as nice as this room and could not believe his luck at the incredibly low rent. Hansu's friend was the landlord, and it had come furnished with new, elegant things—ideal for a student studying literature and English. Noa had had to bring only his clothes packed in his father's old suitcase.

Akiko claimed that none of the other students lived in a place as nice, even if they lived at home in Tokyo. She lived in a beautiful apartment with her family in Minami-Azabu, but in a room half the size of his; she spent all her free time between classes at his place. Her things were on his desk, in his bathroom, and in his closet. The commonplace idea that girls were neater than boys was not true in her case.

Despite Akiko's best efforts, Noa couldn't do it again so soon. Embarrassed, he finished dressing. She, too, rose to fix herself a cup of tea.

There was no kitchen here, but Noa had an electric kettle that Hansu

had bought for him. All Noa had to do was study, Hansu had said. "Learn everything you can. Learn for all the Koreans, for every Korean who couldn't go to a school like Waseda." Hansu paid the tuition in full before the start of each term. Freed from worrying about money, Noa studied more fervently than he ever had. He reread books and studied as many critical essays as he could find. His only relief from work was this lovely girl whom he had fallen for. She was brilliant, sensual, and creative.

"What is he like?" Akiko asked, sprinkling tea leaves into the iron teapot.

"Who?"

"Koh Hansu, your benefactor. You're leaving me in ten minutes to meet him. You do this on the first of the month."

Noa hadn't told her, but of course, she had guessed. Akiko wanted to meet Hansu. She had asked numerous times if she could tag along, but Noa did not think it was appropriate.

"He's a good friend of the family. I told you. My mother and grandmother knew him before they came to Japan. He's from Jeju, which is not very far from Busan. He owns a construction company."

"Is he good-looking?"

"What?"

"Like you. Korean men are really good-looking."

Noa smiled. What could he say to this? Of course, not all Korean men were good-looking, and not all Korean men were bad-looking, either. They were just men. Akiko liked to make positive generalizations about Koreans and other foreigners. She reserved her harshest words for well-off Japanese.

Akiko put down her teacup and pushed him down on the futon playfully, and Noa fell on his back. She straddled him and removed her shirt. She wore a white cotton bra and panties. She looked so beautiful, he thought. Her black hair fell like glossy, iridescent feathers around her face.

"Is he like you?" She rubbed against him.

"No, no. We're very different." Noa exhaled and removed her gently from his hips, puzzled himself by his answer. "I mean, I don't know. He's a generous man. I told you before: He doesn't have a son, and his daugh-

ters don't want to go to university, so he has been supporting me. I intend to pay him back. He's helped my family in difficult times. He's my benefactor; that's all."

"Why do you have to pay him back? Isn't he loaded?"

"I don't know." Noa went to get his socks from the dresser. "It doesn't matter. It's a debt. I will pay him back."

"Don't you want to stay with me?" Akiko removed her brassiere to reveal her champagne glass–sized tits.

"You are tempting me, my beauty," he said. "But I must get going. I will see you tomorrow, *nee*?"

There was absolutely no time to have sex again, he told himself, even if he could get another erection, which he doubted.

"Can't I come and meet him, Noa-chan? When will I meet your family?"

"He's not my family, and I don't know. I haven't met yours, either."

"You don't want to meet Mother and Father. They are racists," she said. "*Honto desu.*"

"Oh," Noa said. "I will see you tomorrow. Lock up, please."

The *sushi-ya* was less than a mile away from his place. The interior was recently repaneled in fresh cedar, and the walls gave off the faint scent of clean, new wood. Hansu preferred to meet Noa here each month in the private room in the back. No one ever disturbed them except to bring them course after course of exceptional delicacies, brought in from various remote fishing villages in Japan.

Normally, the two men talked about his classes, because Hansu was curious about what it was like to attend such a wondrous and fabled university. He had never attended secondary school or university. Hansu had taught himself both how to read and write Korean and Japanese from books, and as soon as he could afford it, Hansu had hired tutors to learn the kanji and *hanja* necessary to read difficult Japanese and Korean newspapers. He knew many rich men, strong men, and brave men, yet he was most impressed with educated men who could write well. He sought friendships with great journalists, because he admired their well-

composed thoughts and points of view on the issues of the day. Hansu did not believe in nationalism, religion, or even love, but he trusted in education. Above all, he believed that a man must learn constantly. He loathed waste of any kind, and when all three of his daughters forsook school for baubles and gossip, he grew to despise his wife, who had allowed this to happen. The girls had good minds and unlimited resources, and she had let them throw these things away like garbage. The girls were lost to him, but he now had Noa. It thrilled him that Noa could read and write English so beautifully—a language he knew was essential in the world. Noa had recommended books to him, and Hansu had read them, because he wanted to know the things his son knew.

The young man's extraordinary scholarship was something Hansu knew he had to nurture. Hansu was not sure what he wanted Noa to do when he graduated; he was careful not to say too much, because it was clear that Noa had some of his own ideas. Hansu wanted to back him, the way he wanted to back good business plans.

The two sat cross-legged on the pristine tatami floor with a low acacia wood table between them.

"You should have more of the sea urchin. The chef had it brought for us from Hokkaido last night," Hansu said. He enjoyed watching Noa, a poor student, eat these rare things that he himself consumed regularly.

Noa nodded in appreciation and finished his portion. He didn't enjoy eating this way or even this kind of food. Noa knew how proper Japanese people behaved and could imitate their mannerisms faultlessly, so he ate whatever was put in front of him and was grateful. However, he preferred to eat a nourishing bowl of simple food quickly and be done with it. He ate the way most working Koreans did: Tasty food was merely necessary fuel, something to be eaten in a rush so you could return to your work. Well-off Japanese considered this sort of eating—high volume, strong flavors, and deliberate speed—nothing short of vulgar. In his benefactor's presence, Noa aped the ruling-class Japanese, not wishing to disappoint Hansu, yet Noa was simply not interested in food or sitting still very long for a meal. Akiko teased him about this

as well, but they did not go to luxurious restaurants, so it was of little consequence in their relationship.

Noa liked being with Hansu, but it was tedious watching another person drink while eating so little. Obviously, Hansu could drink a great deal and somehow manage a successful construction company, but Noa was suspicious of any form of drinking. As a little boy on his way to school, he used to have to step over grown men who were sleeping off their drunken binges from the night before. When he worked as a bookkeeper for the real estate company in Ikaino, he had seen many fathers unable to pay the rent, resulting in their families being thrown out of their homes—the trouble having started with a few harmless drinks on payday. And every winter, homeless alcoholic Koreans froze to death near the Sumida River, their bodies unaware of the deadly frost. Noa didn't drink. Hansu could drink bottles of sake or soju without any visible effect, so in accordance with Korean tradition, Noa poured his elder's drink, cup after cup, dragging the precious meal out even further.

As Noa was pouring the sake into the Oribe sake cup, the gentle knock on the paper screen door startled him.

"Enter," Hansu said.

"Excuse me, Koh-san," said the young waitress, who had no makeup on. She wore a simple indigo day kimono with a mushroom-colored obi.

"Yes?" Hansu said.

Noa smiled at the waitress, who looked and behaved like a well-mannered girl child.

"There is a lady who says she would like to say hello to you."

"Really?" Hansu said. "To me?"

"Yes." The waitress nodded.

"Very well," Hansu said. Few people knew that he ate at this restaurant. It was possible that one of his boss's secretaries was bringing a private message for him, but that was odd, because more commonly, young men from the company were sent on such errands. Hansu's driver and bodyguard were outside the restaurant standing guard; they would have prevented anyone dangerous from reaching him. They would have examined her for certain.

The waitress closed the door, and in a few moments knocked again.

This time, Noa rose to his feet and opened the door himself. It felt good to stretch his legs.

"Akiko," Noa said, his mouth momentarily agape.

"Hello," she said, standing by the waitress, waiting to be invited in.

"Is this your friend, Noa?" Hansu asked, smiling at this gorgeous thing who looked Japanese.

"Yes."

"Welcome. Please have a seat. You wanted to see me?"

"Noa thought I should stop by and say hello to his benefactor, so I came by at his insistence," Akiko said, smiling.

"Yes," Noa said, not sure why he was agreeing to this story but lacking an alternative narrative. "I should have mentioned that Akiko might be stopping by. I'm sorry if I took you by surprise."

"Not at all. I'm very happy to meet a friend of Noa. You must join us for lunch."

Hansu looked up at the waitress, who was still standing by the door.

"Please bring another setting and a sake cup for Noa's friend," Hansu said, feeling both curious and pleased that the boy would want him to meet his girlfriend. He wanted to welcome her.

Immediately, a place setting and a wine cup appeared before her. The chef himself brought them a dish of fried oysters sprinkled with transparent flakes of English salt. Noa poured Hansu a cup of wine, then Hansu poured a cup for Akiko.

"To new friends," Hansu said, raising his cup.

19

The young couple remained standing by the restaurant door as Hansu got into his car. Akiko and Noa bowed deep from the waist in the direction of the rear passenger seat, where Hansu was seated. The chauffeur closed the passenger door, bowed to the couple, then got behind the wheel to take Hansu to his next meeting.

"I don't see why you're so upset," Akiko said, still smiling like a proper Japanese schoolgirl, though Hansu was already gone. "Koh-san is wonderful. I'm glad I met him."

"You lied," Noa said, his voice trembling. He didn't want to speak for fear of saying something awful, but he couldn't help himself. "I . . . I didn't invite you to the lunch. Why did you say that to Koh-san? The lunch could have turned out badly. This man is important to our family. He's supporting my education. I owe him a great deal."

"Nothing happened. It was an ordinary lunch with relatives at a fancy *sushi-ya*. Big deal. I've been to dozens of them. I behaved perfectly. He liked me," Akiko said, puzzled by his irritation. She had always been confident of her ability to win grown-ups over.

"Are you ashamed of me?" Akiko asked, laughing, strangely delighted to be having a fight with Noa, who was normally so calm and silent that she didn't know what went through his mind. Besides, it was his fault: He was so difficult to understand, she'd felt compelled to go to this lunch without an invitation. She hadn't done it to upset him. He should have

been pleased that she cared enough about him to get to know his friends.

"You would never have let me. I was right to go." She touched his arm, and he moved away.

"Akiko, why, why do you always have to be right? Why do you always have to have the upper hand? Why can't I decide when and where you can meet someone personal to me? I would never do this to you. I would respect your privacy," Noa sputtered, and he put his hand over his mouth.

Akiko stared at him, not understanding. She was not used to a man saying no to her. His cheeks were flushed; he was having trouble getting the words out. This wasn't the same man who would explain difficult passages of her sociology texts to her or help her with her statistics homework. Her gentle and wise Noa was furious.

"What is it? Is it that you are embarrassed that you are Korean?"

"What?" Noa took a step back. He looked around to see if anyone could hear their argument. "What are you saying?" He looked at her as if she was deranged.

Akiko grew calm and she spoke slowly.

"I'm not embarrassed that you are Korean. I think it's great that you are Korean. It doesn't bother me at all. It might bother any ignorant person or even my racist parents, but I love that you are Korean. Koreans are smart and hardworking, and the men are so handsome," she said, smiling at him like she was flirting. "You are upset. Listen, if you want, I can arrange for you to meet my whole family. They'd be lucky to meet such an excellent Korean. It would change the way they—"

"No," he said, shaking his head. "No. No more of this."

Akiko moved closer to him. An older woman passed by and glanced at them, but Akiko didn't pay her any attention.

"Noa-chan, why are you so angry with me? You know that I think you're the best. Let's go home, and you can fuck me."

Noa stared at her. She would always believe that he was someone else, that he wasn't himself but some fanciful idea of a foreign person; she would always feel like she was someone special because she had condescended to be with someone everyone else hated. His presence would prove to the world that she was a good person, an educated person, a lib-

eral person. Noa didn't care about being Korean when he was with her; in fact, he didn't care about being Korean or Japanese with anyone. He wanted to be, to be just himself, whatever that meant; he wanted to forget himself sometimes. But that wasn't possible. It would never be possible with her.

"I will pack up your things and have them sent to your house by messenger. I don't want to see you anymore. Please never come see me again."

"Noa, what are you saying?" Akiko said, astonished. "Is this the Korean temper that I've never seen before?" She laughed.

"You and I. It cannot be."

"Why?"

"Because it cannot." There was nothing else he could think of, and he wanted to spare her the cruelty of what he had learned, because she would not believe that she was no different than her parents, that seeing him as only Korean—good or bad—was the same as seeing him only as a bad Korean. She could not see his humanity, and Noa realized that this was what he wanted most of all: to be seen as human.

"He's your father, isn't he?" Akiko said. "He looks exactly like you. You told me your father died, but he's not dead. You just didn't want him to meet me, because you didn't want me to meet your yakuza papa. And you didn't want me to know that he's a gangster. How else do you explain that ridiculous car and uniformed chauffeur? How else can he put you up in that enormous apartment? Even my father can't afford that apartment, and he owns a trading company! Come on, Noa, how can you get mad at me when all I wanted was to learn more about you? I don't care about what he does. It doesn't matter—I don't mind that you're Korean. Don't you see?"

Noa turned around and walked away. He walked until he couldn't hear her scream his name anymore. He walked rigidly and calmly, not believing that a person you loved—yes, he had loved her—could end up being someone you never knew. Perhaps he had known all along about her, but he couldn't see it. He just couldn't. When Noa reached the train station, he went down the stairs to the platform slowly. He felt like he might fall down. He would take the first train to Osaka.

* * *

It was early evening when he reached the house. His Aunt Kyunghee started when she answered the door. He was distraught and wanted to speak to his mother. Uncle Yoseb was sleeping in the back room, and his mother was in the front room sewing. He wouldn't take off his coat. When Sunja came to the door, Noa asked if they could go outside to talk.

"What? What's the matter?" Sunja asked, putting on her shoes.

Noa wouldn't answer. He went outside to wait for her.

Noa led her away from the shopping street to a spot where there were very few people.

"Is it true?" Noa asked his mother. "About Koh Hansu."

He couldn't say the words out loud exactly, but he had to know.

"Why he pays for my school, and why he's always been around. You were together—" he said. It was easier to say this than the other thing.

Sunja had been buttoning her faded woolen coat, and she stopped walking and stared at her son's face. She understood. Yoseb had been right all along. She shouldn't have allowed Hansu to pay for his education. But she hadn't been able to find another way. Noa had gone to work each day and saved every bit of his earnings and studied every night until his eyes were red-rimmed in the morning, and he had finally passed the entrance examination for Waseda.

How could she have said no? There were no loans for this. There was no one else who could help. She had always been afraid of Hansu's presence in Noa's life. Would that money keep Noa tied to Hansu? she had wondered. But not to take the money. Was that possible?

A child like Noa, a child who worked so hard, deserved to fulfill his wish to study and to become someone. Throughout his life, Noa's teachers had said that he was an ideal student, far smarter than anyone else; "A credit to your country," they'd said, and this had pleased her husband, Isak, so much, because he knew the Japanese thought Koreans were worth so little, fit only for the dirty, dangerous, and demeaning tasks. Isak had said that Noa would help the Korean people by his excellence of character and workmanship, and that no one would be able to look down on him. Isak had encouraged the boy to know everything as well as he could, and

Noa, a good son, had tried his best to be the very best. Isak had loved the boy so much. Sunja could not say anything, and her mouth was dry. All she could think of was how good Isak had been to give Noa a name and to give them his protection.

"How could this be?" Noa shook his head. "How could you betray him?"

Sunja knew he meant Isak, and she tried to explain.

"I met him before I met your father. I didn't know Koh Hansu was married. I was a girl, and I believed that he would marry me. But he couldn't, because he was already married. When I was pregnant with you, your father, Isak, stayed at our inn; he married me even when he knew. Baek Isak wanted you as his son. Blood doesn't matter. Can you understand that? When you are young, you can make serious mistakes. You can trust the wrong people, but I am so grateful to have you as my son and so grateful to your father for marrying me—"

"No." He looked at her with disdain. "This kind of mistake I cannot understand. Why didn't you tell me sooner? Who else knows?" His voice grew colder.

"I didn't think it was necessary to tell anyone. Listen to me, Noa, the man who chose to be your father is Baek—"

Noa acted like he didn't even hear her.

"Then Uncle Yoseb and Aunt Kyunghee—do they know?" His mind couldn't accept that no one had told him this.

"We've never discussed it."

"And Mozasu? He is Baek Isak's son? He doesn't look like me."

Sunja nodded. Noa called his father Baek Isak; he'd never done that before.

"My half brother then—"

"I met Koh Hansu before your father. I've always been faithful to Baek Isak—my only husband. Koh Hansu found us when your father was in prison. He was worried that we didn't have money."

A part of her had always feared Noa finding out, but even against such a possibility, she had trusted that Noa would understand, because he was so smart and had always been such an easy child—the one who never made

her worry. But the young man who stood in front of her was like cold metal, and he looked at her as if he could not remember who she was to him.

Noa stopped moving and took a deep breath, then exhaled, because he felt so dizzy.

"That's why he's always helping us—why he found that farm for us during the war. Why he brought us things."

"He was trying to make sure that you were okay. He wanted to help you. It had nothing to do with me. I was someone he knew a long time ago."

"You know that he's a yakuza? Is that right?"

"No. No, I do not know that. I do not know what he does. He used to be a wholesale fish broker who lived in Osaka when I knew him. He bought fish in Korea for Japanese companies. He was a businessman. He owns a construction company and restaurants, I think. I don't know what else he does. I hardly ever speak to him. You know that—"

"Yakuza are the filthiest people in Japan. They are thugs; they are common criminals. They frighten shopkeepers; they sell drugs; they control prostitution; and they hurt innocent people. All the worst Koreans are members of these gangs. I took money for my education from a yakuza, and you thought this was acceptable? I will never be able to wash this dirt from my name. You can't be very bright," he said. "How can you make something clean from something dirty? And now, you have made me dirty," Noa said quietly, as if he was learning this as he was saying it to her. "All my life, I have had Japanese telling me that my blood is Korean—that Koreans are angry, violent, cunning, and deceitful criminals. All my life, I had to endure this. I tried to be as honest and humble as Baek Isak was; I never raised my voice. But this blood, my blood is Korean, and now I learn that my blood is yakuza blood. I can never change this, no matter what I do. It would have been better if I were never born. How could you have ruined my life? How could you be so imprudent? A foolish mother and a criminal father. I am cursed."

Sunja looked at him with shock. If he had been a little boy, she might have told him to hush, to mind his manners, never to dishonor your par-

ents, but she couldn't say that now. How could she defend gangsters? There were organized criminals everywhere, she supposed, and she knew that they did bad things, but she knew that many of the Koreans had to work for the gangs because there were no other jobs for them. The government and good companies wouldn't hire Koreans, even educated ones. All these men had to work, and there were many of them who lived in their neighborhood who were far kinder and more respectful than the men who didn't work at all. She couldn't say this to her son, however, because Noa was someone who had studied, labored, and tried to lift himself out of their street, and he thought all the men who hadn't done so weren't very bright, either. He would not understand. Her son could not feel compassion for those who did not try.

"Noa," Sunja said, "forgive me. *Umma* is sorry. I just wanted you to go to school. I know how much you wanted that. I know how hard you—"

"You. You took my life away. I am no longer myself," he said, pointing his finger at her. He turned around and walked back to the train.

20

Osaka, April 1962

They didn't receive letters often, and when one arrived, the family gathered around Yoseb's bedside to hear it read. He was lying on his back, his head propped up by a buckwheat-filled pillow. Of course, Sunja recognized her son's handwriting on the envelope. Though illiterate, she was able to make out her name and signs in both Japanese and Korean. Normally, Kyunghee read the letters out loud, asking Yoseb for help when there were difficult characters she could not recognize. Yoseb's vision had worsened; he was unable to read his beloved newspapers, so Kyunghee read them to him. If Kyunghee described the image of the character, Yoseb could sometimes guess it from the context. Kyunghee read in her clear, mild-toned voice. Sunja's face was white with fear, and Yangjin stared at the thin sheet of paper, wondering what her grandson had to say. Yoseb's eyes were closed, but he was awake.

Umma,

I have withdrawn from Waseda. I have moved out of the apartment. I am in a new city and have found a job.

This may be very difficult for you to understand, but I ask that you not look for me. I have thought about this very deeply. This is the best way for me to live with myself and to maintain my integrity. I want to start a new life, and to do that there is no other way.

317

I have had to pay some bills in starting out, and as soon as I earn some more money, I will send you something as often as I can. I will not neglect my duties. Also, I will earn enough money to repay Koh Hansu. Please make sure that he never reaches me. I do not wish to know him.

I send regards to you, Uncle Yoseb, Aunt Kyunghee, Grandmother, and Mozasu. I am sorry I did not get a chance to say good-bye properly, but I will not be returning. Please do not worry about me. This cannot be helped.

Your son,
Noa

Noa had written his brief message in simple Japanese rather than Korean, a language he had never written well. When Kyunghee finished reading, no one said anything. Yangjin patted her daughter's knee, then got up to go to the kitchen to fix dinner, leaving Kyunghee to put her arm around her sister-in-law, who now sat wordless and pale.

Yoseb exhaled. Would anything bring the boy back? he wondered. He did not think so. This life had too much loss. When Isak died, Yoseb had thought of his brother's little boys and vowed to watch over them. Noa and Mozasu were not his own, but what did that matter? He had wanted to be a good man for them. Then after the war, after his accident, he had resigned himself to death and looked forward only to the boys' future. The stupid heart could not help but hope. Life had seemed almost bearable; though Yoseb was nearly cut off from the living, confined to his pallet, his family had persisted. Life continued. To Yoseb, Noa had seemed so much like Isak that it had been possible to forget that the boy's blood father was someone else—someone wholly different from his gentle Isak. But now, the poor boy had learned somehow that he had descended from another line. The boy had decided to leave them, and his departure was punishment. Yoseb could understand the boy's anger, but he wanted another chance to talk to him, to tell Noa that a man must learn to forgive—to know what is important, that to live without forgiveness was a

kind of death with breathing and movement. However, Yoseb did not have enough energy to rise from his pallet, let alone search for his dear nephew, a boy who was like his own flesh.

"Could he have gone to the North?" Kyunghee asked her husband. "He wouldn't do something like that, isn't that so?"

Sunja glanced at her brother-in-law.

"No, no." Yoseb's pillow made a gravelly noise as he moved his head from side to side.

Sunja covered her eyes with her hands. No one who went to the North came back. There was still hope as long as he had not gone there. Kim Changho had left in the last month of 1959, and in more than two years, they'd heard from him only twice. Kyunghee rarely spoke of him, but it made sense that her first thought was Pyongyang.

"And Mozasu? What do we tell him?" Kyunghee asked. Still holding Noa's letter, she patted Sunja's back with her free hand.

"Wait until he asks about him. The boy is so busy as it is. If he asks, just say you don't know. Then later, if you have to, tell him that his brother ran away," Yoseb said, his eyes still shut. "Tell him that school was too hard for Noa, so he left Tokyo and he was too ashamed to return home after all those attempts to get into school. For all we know, that could be the reason." It sickened Yoseb to say these words, so he said nothing else.

Sunja couldn't speak. Mozasu would never believe that, yet she couldn't tell him the truth, either, because he would go look for his brother. And she could not tell Mozasu about Hansu. Mozasu was hardly sleeping lately, because he had so many responsibilities at work, and Yumi had miscarried only a few weeks before. The boy did not need any more worries.

Since that evening when Noa had come home from school to speak to her, Sunja had thought daily of going to Tokyo to talk to him, but she could not do so. A month had passed and now this. What did he say to her? *You took my life away.* He had withdrawn from Waseda. Sunja felt unable to think, to breathe even. All she wanted was to see her son again. If that wasn't possible, it would be better to die.

Wiping her wet hands on her apron, Yangjin came out of the kitchen

and told them that dinner was ready. Yangjin and Kyunghee stared at Sunja.

"You should eat something," Kyunghee said.

Sunja shook her head. "I have to go. I have to find him."

Kyunghee clutched her arm, but Sunja broke free and got up.

"Let her go to him," Yangjin said.

It turned out that Hansu lived only thirty minutes away by train. His preposterously immense house stood out prominently on the quiet street. A pair of tall, carved mahogany doors, flanked by grand picture windows, centered the two-story limestone structure like a giant maw. The house had been the residence of an American diplomat after the war. Heavy drapery shaded the interiors, making it impossible to look inside. As a young girl, Sunja had imagined where he might live, but she could never have conceived of anything like this. He lived in a castle, it seemed to her. The taxi driver assured her that this was the address.

A young, short-haired servant girl wearing a shimmering white apron answered the door, opening it only halfway. The master of the house was not in, she said in Japanese.

"Who's that?" an older woman asked, emerging from the front parlor. She tapped the servant girl lightly, and she moved aside. The door opened fully to expose the grand entryway.

Sunja realized who this must be.

"Koh Hansu, please," she said in her best Japanese. "Please."

"Who are you?"

"My name is Boku Sunja."

Hansu's wife, Mieko, nodded. The beggar was no doubt a Korean who wanted money. The postwar Koreans were numerous and shameless, and they took advantage of her husband's soft nature toward his countrymen. She did not begrudge his generosity, but she disapproved of the beggars' boldness. It was evening, and this was no time for a woman of any age to beg.

Mieko turned to the servant girl, "Give her what she wants and send her away. There's food in the kitchen if she is hungry." This was what her

husband would do. Her father had also believed in hospitality toward the poor.

The servant bowed as the mistress walked away.

"No, no," Sunja said in Japanese. "No money, no food. Speak Koh Hansu, please. Please." She clasped her hands together as if in prayer.

Mieko returned, taking deliberate steps. Koreans could be insistent like unruly children. They could be loud and desperate, with none of the coolness and placidity of the Japanese. Her children were half of this blood, but fortunately, they did not raise their voices or have slovenly habits. Her father had loved Hansu, claiming that he was not like the others and that it would be good for her to marry him, because he was a real man and he would take care of her. Her father was not wrong; under her husband's direction, the organization had only grown stronger and wealthier. She and her daughters had enormous wealth in Switzerland as well as innumerable fat packets of yen hidden in the stone walls of this house. She lacked for nothing.

"How did you learn that he lives here? How do you know my husband?" Mieko asked Sunja.

Sunja shook her head, because she didn't understand exactly what the woman was asking. She understood the word "husband." His wife was clearly Japanese—early sixties with gray hair, cut short. She was very beautiful, with large dark eyes fringed with unusually long lashes. She wore a light green kimono over her elegant frame. The rouge on her lips was the color of *umeboshi*. She looked like a kimono model.

"Fetch the garden boy. He speaks Korean." Hansu's wife extended her left hand and gestured to Sunja to remain by the door. She noted the rough and worn cotton clothing and the tired hands, spotted from outdoor work. The Korean could not be very old; there was some prettiness in her eyes, but her youth was spent. Her waist was thick from childbearing. She was not attractive enough to be one of Hansu's whores. To her knowledge, all of Hansu's whores were Japanese hostesses, some younger than their daughters. They knew better than to grace her doorstep.

The garden boy came running to the front of the house from the backyard, where he'd been weeding.

"Yes, ma'am," he said, bowing to the mistress of the house.

"She's a Korean," Mieko said. "Ask her how she learned where the master lives."

The boy glanced at Sunja, who looked terrified. She wore a light gray coat over her cotton work clothes. She was younger than his mother.

"*Ajumoni*," he said to Sunja, trying not to alarm her. "How can I help you?"

Sunja smiled at the boy, then, seeing the concern in his eyes, she burst into tears. He had none of the hardness of the house servant and the wife. "I'm looking for my son, you see, and I think your master knows where he is. I need to speak"—she had to stop speaking to breathe through her tearful gulps—"to your master. Do you know where he is?"

"How does she know my husband lives here?" Hansu's wife asked again calmly.

In his wish to help the desperate woman, the boy had forgotten his mistress's request.

"The mistress wants to know how you know that the master lives here. *Ajumoni*, I have to give her an answer; do you understand?" The boy peered into Sunja's face.

"I worked for Kim Changho at a restaurant your master owned. Kim Changho gave me your master's address to me before he left for the North. Did you know Mr. Kim? He went to Pyongyang."

The boy nodded, recalling the tall man with the thick eyeglasses who always gave him pocket money for candy and played soccer with him in the backyard. Mr. Kim had offered to take the boy with him to the North on the Red Cross ship, but his master had forbidden it. The master never spoke about Mr. Kim and would get angry if anyone brought him up.

Sunja stared hard at the boy as if he could find Noa himself.

"You see, your master might know where my son is. I have to go find him. Do you think you can tell me where your master is? Is he here now? I know he would see me."

The boy looked down and shook his head, and at that moment, Sunja looked up and started to take in the interior of Hansu's house.

The magnificent, cavernous foyer behind the boy resembled the inte-

rior of an old train station with its high ceilings and pale white walls. She imagined Hansu descending the carved cherrywood staircase to ask what was the matter. This time, she would beg for his help in a way she had never done before. She would plead for his mercy, for all of his resources, and she would not leave his side until her son was found.

The boy turned to the mistress and translated everything Sunja had said.

Hansu's wife studied the weeping woman.

"Tell her that he is away. That he will be gone for a long time." Mieko turned around and while walking away said, "If she needs any train fare or food, send her to the back and give her what she needs; otherwise, send her away."

"*Ajumoni*, do you need any money or food?" he asked.

"No, no. I just need to speak to your master. Please, child. Please help me," Sunja said.

The boy shrugged, because he didn't know where Hansu was. The servant, her white apron glinting in the brilliant electric lights of the foyer, stood by the door like a maiden sentry and looked off into the distance as if to give these poor, messy people some privacy.

"*Ajumoni*, I'm sorry, but my mistress wants you to leave. Would you like to go to the kitchen? In the back of the house? I can get you something to eat. The mistress said—"

"No. No."

The maid closed the front door quietly, while the boy remained outside. He had never walked through the front door and never expected to do so.

Sunja turned to the darkened street. A half-moon was visible in the navy-colored sky. The mistress had returned to the parlor to study her flower magazines, and the servant resumed her work in the pantry. From the house, the boy watched Sunja walking toward the main road. He wanted to tell her that the master came home every now and then, but rarely slept at home when he returned. He traveled all over the country for his work. The master and the mistress were very polite to one another, but they did not seem like an ordinary husband and wife. Perhaps this was

the way of rich people, the boy thought. They were nothing like his own parents. His father had been a carpenter before he died from a bad liver. His mother, who never stopped working, had doted on him, though he'd never made any money. The gardener boy knew that the master stayed in a hotel in Osaka sometimes; the head servants and the cook talked about his mansion apartment in Tokyo, but none of them had been there except for the driver, Yasuda. The boy had never given it much thought. He had never been to Tokyo or anywhere else besides Osaka, where he was born, and Nagoya, where his family now lived. The only people who would ever know for certain where the master would be were Yasuda and his brawny guard Chiko, but it had never occurred to the boy to ask them the master's whereabouts. Sometimes, the master went to Korea or Hong Kong, they said.

The streets were empty except for the Korean woman's small figure walking slowly toward the train station, and the gardener boy ran quickly to catch up with her.

"*Ajumoni, ajumoni*, where, where do you live?"

Sunja stopped and turned to the boy, wondering if he might know something.

"In Ikaino. Do you know the shopping street?"

The boy nodded, hunched over and holding his knees to catch his breath. He stared at her round face.

"I live three blocks from the shopping street by the large bathhouse. My name is Baek Sunja or Sunja Boku. I live in the house with my mother, brother-in-law, and sister-in-law, Baek Yoseb and Choi Kyunghee. Just ask anyone where the lady who sells sweets lives. I also sell confections in the train station market with my mother. I'm always at the market. Will you come find me if you know where Koh Hansu is? And when you see him, will you tell him that I need to see him?" Sunja asked.

"Yes, I will try. We don't see him often." The boy stopped there, because it didn't seem right to tell her that Hansu was never home. He had not seen him in many months, maybe even a year. "But if I see my master, I'll tell him that you came by. I'm sure the mistress will tell him, too."

"Here." Sunja fished in her purse to find some money for the boy.

"No, no, thank you. I have everything I need. I'm all right." The boy looked at the worn rubber soles of her shoes; they looked identical to the ones his mother wore to the market.

"You're a good boy," she said, and Sunja started to cry again, because all her life, Noa had been her joy. He had been a steady source of strength for her when she had expected so little from this life.

"My *umma* works in a market in Nagoya; she helps another lady who sells vegetables," he found himself telling her. He had not seen his mother and sisters since New Year's. The only person he spoke to in Korean here was with the master himself.

"She must wish to see you, too."

Sunja smiled weakly at the boy, feeling sorry for him. She touched his shoulder, then walked to the train station.

BOOK III

Pachinko

1962–1989

I propose the following definition of the nation: it is an imagined political community—and imagined as both inherently limited and sovereign.

It is *imagined* because the members of even the smallest nation will never know most of their fellow-members, meet them, or even hear of them, yet in the minds of each lives the image of their communion...

The nation is imagined as *limited* because even the largest of them, encompassing perhaps a billion living human beings, has finite, if elastic, boundaries, beyond which lie other nations...

It is imagined as *sovereign* because the concept was born in an age in which Enlightenment and Revolution were destroying the legitimacy of the divinely-ordained, hierarchical dynastic realm...

Finally, it is imagined as a *community*, because, regardless of the actual inequality and exploitation that may prevail in each, the nation is always conceived as a deep, horizontal comradeship. Ultimately it is this fraternity that makes it possible, over the past two centuries, for so many millions of people, not so much to kill, as willingly die for such limited imaginings.

—Benedict Anderson

I

Nagano, April 1962

Noa hadn't meant to linger at the café by the Nagano train station, but it wasn't as if he knew where to go exactly. He hadn't made a plan, which was unlike him, but after he'd left Waseda, his days had made little sense to him. Reiko Tamura, a cheerful middle school teacher who had been kind to him, was from Nagano, and for some reason, he'd always considered her hometown as a place populated with gentle, benevolent Japanese. He recalled his teacher's childhood stories of the snowstorms that were so severe that when she walked outside her little house to go to school, she could hardly see the streetlights. Osaka had snow occasionally, but nothing resembling Tamura-san's storms. He had always wanted to visit his teacher's hometown—in his mind, it was always blanketed with fresh snow. This morning, when the man at the ticket counter had asked him where to, he'd replied, "Nagano, please." Finally, he was here. He felt safe. Tamura-san had also spoken of school trips to the famed Zenkoji temple, where she'd eat her modest bento outdoors with her classmates.

Seated alone at a small table not far from the counter, Noa drank his brown tea and took only a few bites of his omelet rice while considering a visit to the temple. He was raised as a Christian, but he felt respectful of Buddhists, especially those who had renounced the spoils of the world. The Lord was supposed to be everywhere, which was what Noa had learned at church, but would God keep away from temples or shrines?

Did such places offend God, or did He understand those who may wish to worship something, anything? As always, Noa wished he'd had more time with Isak. The thought of him saddened Noa, and the thought of Hansu, his biological father, shamed him. Koh Hansu didn't believe in anything but his own efforts—not God, not Jesus, not Buddha, and not the Emperor.

The heavyset waiter came by with a teapot.

"Is everything to your satisfaction, sir?" the waiter asked him while refilling Noa's cup. "Is the meal not to your liking? Too much scallion? I always tell the cook that he is too heavy with the—"

"The rice is very good, thank you," Noa replied, realizing that it had been some time since he had spoken to anyone at all. The waiter had a broad smile, thin, tadpole eyes, and uneven teeth. His ears were large and his lobes thick—physical features Buddhists admired. The waiter stared at Noa, though most Japanese would have looked away out of politeness.

"Are you visiting for a while?" The waiter glanced at Noa's suitcase, which was set by the empty chair.

"Hmm?" Noa was surprised by the waiter's personal question.

"I apologize for being so nosy. My mother always said I would get in trouble because I am far too curious. Forgive me, sir, I am just a chatty country boy," the waiter said, laughing. "I haven't seen you here before. Please forgive the café for being so quiet. Normally we have many more customers. Very interesting and respectable ones. I cannot help but have questions when I meet someone new, but I know I should not ask them."

"No, no. It's natural to want to know things. I understand. I am here to visit, and I heard such nice things about Nagano that I thought I would like to live here." Noa was surprised to hear himself say this. It felt easy to talk to this stranger. It had not occurred to him before to live in Nagano, but why not? Why not for a year at least? He would not return to Tokyo or Osaka—this much he had resolved.

"Move here? To live? *Honto?* How wonderful. Nagano is a very special place," the waiter said with pride. "My entire family is from here. We have always been from here. Eighteen generations, and I am the dumbest one in my family. This is my little café, which my mother bought for me to

keep me out of trouble!" The waiter laughed. "Everyone calls me Bingo. It is a game from America. I have played it once."

"Nobuo *desu*," Noa said, smiling. "Nobuo Ban *desu*."

"Ban-san, Ban-san," Bingo chirped happily. "I once loved a short girl from Tokyo named Chie Ban, but she did not love me. Of course! Lovely girls do not love me. My tall wife is not lovely, but she loves me nonetheless!" Again, he laughed. "You know, you are smart to wish to settle in Nagano. I have been to Tokyo only once, and that was enough for me. It's dirty, expensive, and full of fast—" The waiter stopped himself. "Wait, you're not from Tokyo, are you?"

"No. I'm from Kansai."

"Ah, I love Kansai. I have been to Kyoto twice, and though it is too expensive for a simple man like myself, I am fond of truly delicious udon, and I believe one can eat delicious udon there for a reasonable sum. I prefer the chewy kind of udon."

Noa smiled. It was pleasant to listen to him talk.

"So what will you do for work?" the waiter asked. "A man must have work. My mother always says this, too." Bingo clasped his right hand over his mouth, embarrassed at being so forward, but he was unable to keep from talking so much. The stranger seemed so attractive and humble, and Bingo admired quiet people. "Did you have a job you liked in Kansai?" he asked, his sparse eyebrows raised.

Noa looked down at his barely eaten meal.

"Well, I have worked as a bookkeeper. I can also read and write in English. Perhaps a small business may need a bookkeeper. Or maybe a trading company may wish to have documents translated—"

"A young man like you could work in lots of places. Let me think." Bingo's round face grew serious. He tapped his small chin with his index finger. "You seem very smart."

"I don't know about that, but that's kind of you to say." Noa smiled.

"Hmm." The waiter made a face. "Sir, I don't know if you're picky, but if you need work right away, the pachinko parlor hires people from out of town. Office jobs are not so common lately."

"Pachinko?" Noa tried not to look offended. Did the waiter think he was Korean? Most Japanese never assumed he was Korean until he told them his Korean surname, Boku. His identification card from Waseda stated his *tsumei* name, Nobuo Bando. Noa wasn't sure why he had dropped the "-do" from his surname when he'd introduced himself to Bingo, but now it was too late to change it back. "I don't know much about pachinko. I have never—"

"Oh, I didn't mean to offend you. They pay very well, I hear. Takano-san, the manager of the best parlor in Nagano, is a great gentleman. Maybe you wouldn't work in any ordinary pachinko parlor, but Cosmos Pachinko is a grand establishment run by an old family from the area. They change their machines very often! However, they do not hire foreigners."

"Eh?"

"They do not hire Koreans or Chinese, but that will not matter to you since you are Japanese." Bingo nodded several times.

"*Soo desu,*" Noa agreed.

"Takano-san is always looking for office workers who are smart. He pays handsomely. But he cannot hire foreigners." Bingo nodded again.

"Yes, yes," Noa said sympathetically, sounding as if he understood. Long ago, he had learned how to keep nodding even when he didn't agree, because he noticed that the motion alone kept people talking.

"Takano-san is a regular customer. He was here just this morning. Every day, he takes his coffee at the window table." Bingo pointed. "Black coffee and two sugar cubes. Never any milk. This morning, he tells me, 'Bingo-san, I have a headache that will not go away, because it is so hard to find good workers. The fools here have pumpkins for heads, and seeds are not brains.'" The waiter clasped his thick meaty fingers over his head in a comic imitation of the anguished Takano-san.

"Hey, why don't you go over there and tell Takano-san that I sent you," Bingo said, smiling. This was the sort of thing he loved to do best—help people and make introductions. He had already arranged three marriages for his high school friends.

Noa nodded and thanked him. Years later, Bingo would tell anyone that he was Ban-san's first friend in Nagano.

Takano-san's business office was located in another building, separate from the immense pachinko parlor, almost two city blocks away. From the conservative appearance of the brick building, it would have been impossible to know the purpose of this office. Noa might have missed it altogether if Bingo hadn't drawn a map for him on a sheet of notepaper. Except for its number, the building had no sign.

Hideo Takano, the parlor manager, was a sharp-looking Japanese in his late thirties. He wore a beautiful dark woolen suit with a striped purple necktie and a matching pocket handkerchief; each week, he paid a neighborhood boy to shine all his leather shoes to a mirror sheen. He dressed so well that he looked more like a clothing salesman than a man who worked in an office. Behind his desk were two black safes, the size of doors. His large office was adjacent to half a dozen modest-sized rooms, each filled with office workers wearing white shirts—mostly young men and plain-faced office ladies. Takano had a small bump on the bridge of his handsome nose and round black eyes that sloped downward, and when he spoke, his velvety eyes were expressive and direct.

"Sit down," Takano said. "My secretary said you are looking for a clerk position."

"My name is Nobuo Ban *desu*. Bingo-san from the café said that you were looking for workers. I recently arrived from Tokyo, sir."

"Ha! Bingo sent you? But I don't need anyone to pour my coffee here." From behind his large metal desk, Takano leaned forward in his chair. "So, Bingo is listening to my sad troubles after all. I thought I was mostly listening to his."

Noa smiled. The man seemed genial enough; he didn't seem like someone who hated Koreans. He was glad to have worn a clean shirt and a tie today; Koh Hansu had mentioned often that a man should look his best each day. For Koreans, this was especially important: Look clean and be well groomed. In every situation, even in ones when you have a right to be angry, a Korean must speak soberly and calmly, he'd said.

"So, friend of Bingo-san, what can you do?" Takano asked.

Noa sat up straighter. "I'm trained as a bookkeeper and have worked for a landlord in Kansai. I've collected rents and kept books for several years before I went to university—"

"Yeah? University? Really? Which one?"

"Waseda," Noa answered, "but I haven't finished my degree in literature. I was there for three years."

"Literature?" Takano shook his head. "I don't need an employee who will be reading books when he should be working. I need a bookkeeper who's smart, neat, and honest. He needs to show up to work each morning when he's supposed to, not hungover and not dealing with girl problems. I don't want any losers. I fire losers." Takano tilted his head after saying all this. Noa looked very respectable; he could see why Bingo would send him over.

"Yes, sir. Of course. I am a very precise bookkeeper, and I am very good at writing letters, sir."

"Modest."

Noa did not apologize. "I will do my best if you hire me, sir."

"What's your name again?"

"Nobuo Ban *desu*."

"You're not from here."

"No, sir. I'm from Kansai."

"Why did you leave school?"

"My mother died, and I didn't have enough money to finish my degree. I was hoping to earn money to return to school one day."

"And your father?"

"He is dead."

Takano never believed it when out-of-towners said their parents were dead, but he didn't care either way.

"So why should I train you so you can leave to continue your study of literature? I'm not interested in helping you finish your university education. I need a bookkeeper who will stick around. Can you do that? I won't pay you very well when you start, but you'll be able to get by. What the hell are you going to do with literature, anyway? There's no money in that. I

never finished high school, and I can hire you or fire you a hundred times. Your generation is foolish."

Noa didn't reply. His family thought he wanted to work in a company, but that wasn't entirely true. It had been a private dream of his to be a high school English teacher. He'd thought that if he graduated from Waseda then it might be possible to get a good job at a private school. Public schools didn't hire Koreans, but he thought the law may be changed one day. He had even considered becoming a Japanese citizen. He knew he could at least work as some sort of private tutor.

"Well, you don't have the money for university now, and you need a job, or else you wouldn't be here. So where are you living?"

"I arrived in Nagano today. I was going to find a boardinghouse."

"You can sleep in the dormitory behind the shop. You'll have to share a room at first. No smoking in the rooms, and you cannot bring girls. You are allowed three meals in the cafeteria. As much rice as you want. There's meat twice a week. As for girls, there are hotels for that sort of thing. I don't care what you do on your time off, but your first duty is to the company. I am a very generous manager, but if you mess up, you will be terminated instantly without any back pay."

Noa wondered if his younger brother spoke this way to employees. The fact that he was going to work for a pachinko business, no different than Mozasu, a kid who had flunked out of school essentially, was stunning to Noa.

"You can start today. Find Ikeda-san in the office next to mine. He has gray hair. Do whatever he tells you. He's my head accountant. I'll try you out for a month. If you do okay, I'll pay you a good enough salary. You have no overhead. You can save quite a bit."

"Thank you, sir."

"Where are your people from?"

"Kansai," Noa replied.

"Yeah, you said. Where in Kansai?"

"Kyoto," Noa replied.

"What do your parents do?"

"They're dead," Noa replied, hoping to end the questions.

"Yeah, you said. So what did they do?"

"My father worked in a udon shop."

"Yeah?" Takano looked puzzled. "So a noodle man sends his son to Waseda? Really?"

Noa said nothing, wishing he was a better liar.

"You're not a foreigner, right? You swear."

Noa tried to look surprised by such a question. "No, sir. I am Japanese."

"Good, good," Takano replied. "Get out of my office and see Ikeda-san."

The dormitory of the pachinko parlor slept sixty employees. On his first night, Noa slept in one of the smallest rooms, sharing it with an older worker who snored like a broken motor. Within a week, he established a routine. When he woke up, Noa washed his face quickly, having bathed the night before in the public bath, and he went down to the cafeteria where the cook served rice, mackerel, and tea. He worked methodically and won over Ikeda-san, who had never met such a smart bookkeeper. When the trial month passed, Noa was kept on. Years later, Noa learned that the Japanese owner had liked Noa from the start. After the first month, the owner told Takano to give Noa a raise and a better room at the year's end, but not before, because the others might fuss over any favoritism. The owner suspected that Nobuo Ban was a Korean, but he said nothing, because as long as no one else knew, it didn't matter.

2

Osaka, April 1965

In three years, Yumi had lost two pregnancies, and she found herself pregnant again. Against the advice of her husband, Mozasu, she'd worked through the previous pregnancies. In her quiet and deliberate way, Yumi's boss, Totoyama-san, insisted that she work from home for this pregnancy. Yumi refused.

"Yumi-chan, there isn't much work this season, and you need to rest," Totoyama-san would say, and only occasionally, Yumi went home before it got too dark.

It was a late spring afternoon. Yumi had just completed an order of bow ties for hotel uniforms when she felt sharp pains along her lower abdomen. This time, Totoyama-san refused to hear a word of protest from Yumi. She sent for Mozasu, who picked up his wife, and he took her to a famous Japanese baby doctor in downtown Osaka, whom Totoyama-san had learned of, rather than to Yumi's regular doctor in Ikaino.

"It's elementary, Boku-san. You have very high blood pressure. Women like you often fight pregnancy," the doctor said calmly.

He walked away from the examination table and returned to his desk. His office had been painted recently, and the faint smell of paint lingered. Except for a medical chart of a woman's reproductive organs, everything in the office was white or stainless steel.

Yumi said nothing and thought about what he said. Could it be true?

she wondered. Could she have somehow aborted her prior pregnancies by fighting them?

"I am less worried about the previous miscarriages. It is a sad thing, of course, but miscarriages reveal the wisdom of nature. It's for the best that you don't give birth when it isn't good for your health. A miscarriage indicates that the woman can conceive, so it is not necessarily a fertility matter. But, as for this pregnancy, I do not see much danger to the child; there is danger only to the mother; so for the remainder of the pregnancy, you must remain in bed."

"But I have to work," Yumi said, looking terrified.

The doctor shook his head.

"Yumi-chan," Mozasu said, "you have to listen to the doctor."

"I can work less. Go home early, the way Totoyama-san wants me to."

"Boku-san, it's possible for the mother to die of preeclampsia. As your physician, I cannot allow you to work. My patients must listen to me, or else we cannot work together."

The famous doctor looked away from her, pretending to glance at the few papers on his desk, confident that Yumi would remain his patient. She'd be a fool to choose otherwise. He jotted down some notes about her diet, advising her to avoid sweets or too much rice. She must not gain much weight, since she'd be retaining an enormous amount of water, and the baby would be too big to deliver vaginally.

"Please call me any time you do not feel comfortable. This is critical. If we have to deliver early, then we need to take precautions. Boku-san, there is no need to be stoic. That can come after you have the child. A woman has a right to be a little difficult before she has her first child." The doctor smiled at both of them. "Make a fuss about your food cravings, or if you want extra pillows at night."

Mozasu nodded, grateful for the doctor's humor and inflexible tone. Any good doctor would need to match his wife's stubbornness. Mozasu had never had reason to disagree with Yumi on anything important, but he wondered if he had not done so because he'd sensed that she would not have listened to him anyway.

When the couple returned home, Yumi lay down on the futon, her

dark hair mussed and spread out across the narrow pillow. Mozasu was seated on the bed, cross-legged by her side, not knowing what else to say to his wife, who did not want a glass of water or anything to eat. With her, he felt a little dumb, because she was so stalwart and clever. Her goals had always seemed absurdly fantastic. Sometimes, he wondered how she allowed herself to dream for so much. He had never seen her cry or complain about anything difficult. He knew Yumi did not want to be at home by herself, unable to work or go to her English classes.

"Would you like your English books?" he asked.

"No," she said, not looking at him. "You have to go back to work, *nee*? I'll be fine. You can go."

"Can't I get you something? Anything?"

"Why can't we go to America? We could have a good life there."

"You remember what the immigration lawyer said. It would be impossible almost."

"The minister Maryman-san may be able to sponsor us."

"Why would he do that? I'm not going to become a missionary and neither are you. You don't even believe in God. Besides, what could I do in America that would make as much money as I do here? I'm not going back to school. I'm not a college boy; I'm your oaf. I count on you to think for the two of us, and soon, for the three of us." He laughed, hoping she would smile.

"Yumi-chan, very soon I will open my own parlor in Yokohama, and if it is successful, I'll make more money than twenty college graduates. Can you imagine? Then I can buy you anything you want. If it's not successful, I can still work for Goro-san and make us a nice life."

"I know how to make money."

"Yes, I know. I know you are independent. But it would give me pleasure to buy something for you that you cannot get for yourself. And I promise you will like Yokohama; it's an international city. There are lots of Americans there. As soon as you have the baby, and the doctor says it is okay, I will take you to visit. We can stay in a beautiful hotel, and you can see what it's like. And it will be easier for you to study English there. We can find you a tutor, and you can go to school if you like," Mozasu

said. Although he tried not to think of Noa because it made him too sad, Mozasu could not help but think of his brother, who had quit Waseda and run away without explanation.

"The Japanese do not like us. How will our baby live here?" Yumi asked.

"Some Japanese like us very much. The baby will live here with us. She will live like us." From the very first pregnancy, Mozasu had determined that the baby was a girl—a child just like Yumi.

Mozasu stroked her forehead. His dark hand looked enormous on her small, pale brow. For a very young woman, his wife could appear ancient in her sternness, able to push herself through the most difficult tasks, but when sad, she had the face of a disappointed child, lost and bereft. He loved her face, how it showed every trace of feeling; she could be silent, but she was incapable of hiding herself from others.

"What else can we do?" Mozasu asked, looking to her for the answer. "Besides go to America?" He had never understood what she thought she'd find there. Sometimes, he wondered if Noa had gone to the States— this magical place so many Koreans in Japan idealized. "What else, Yumi-chan, what else would you like to do?"

She shrugged. "I don't want to stay in the house until the baby comes. I don't like to be lazy."

"You will never be lazy. It's impossible." He laughed. "When the baby comes, and it will be soon," he said, "you will be chasing after her. You and she will be the fastest moving females in Osaka—never ever bound by the house."

"Mozasu, I can feel her moving. I didn't lose the baby."

"Of course not. The doctor said the baby is fine. Baby-chan will look just like you. We'll give her a wonderful home. You're going to be a wonderful mother."

She smiled, not believing him but wanting him to be right.

"I called my mother. She'll come here tonight."

Yumi crinkled her eyes, worried.

"You like her, *nee?*"

"Yes," Yumi said. It was true; Yumi admired her mother-in-law, yet

they were strangers to one another. Sunja was not like most mothers of sons; she never said anything intrusive, and her reluctance to speak her mind had only increased after Noa disappeared. When Mozasu and Yumi had asked her and Mozasu's grandmother to move into their house, Sunja had declined, saying that it would be better for the young couple to live without old women bothering them.

"I thought she wanted to stay with her mother and Aunt Kyunghee."

"Yes, but she wants to help us. She will come by herself. It will not be permanent. Grandmother will stay with Aunt Kyunghee to help with the store. I'll hire some girls for them to replace my mother while she's here."

After two weeks of bed rest, Yumi felt like she was going out of her mind. Mozasu had bought her a television, but she had no interest in watching it, and heartburn kept her from reading. Her wrists and ankles were so swollen that if she pushed her thumb lightly onto her wrist, she could make a deep impression in her flesh. Only the baby's movements and occasional hiccups kept Yumi glued to her futon and from fleeing out of doors. Since her arrival, her mother-in-law remained by herself in the small room beside the kitchen—no matter how many times Mozasu insisted that she stay in the larger, unused room by the master bedroom. Sunja did all the cooking and cleaning. At whatever hour of the night Mozasu came home, she had his dinner ready.

It was morning when Sunja knocked on Yumi's door to bring her breakfast.

"Come in, *omoni*," Yumi said. Her own mother could not make a pot of rice or a cup of tea, in contrast to Mozasu's mother, who had supported her family on her cooking.

As usual, Sunja carried in a tray with an assortment of tempting dishes, all covered with a clean white cloth. She smiled at her daughter-in-law.

Yumi, who would normally have relished such good meals, felt bad, because all she could manage to keep down lately was rice porridge.

"I feel terrible that I'm lying in bed all day while you work so much,"

Yumi said, hoping that Sunja would stay and talk with her. "Have you eaten breakfast?"

"Yes, I ate. You work hard all the time. But now, you're supposed to be resting. A pregnancy is not an easy thing. My mother had six miscarriages before having me," she said. "She wanted to come and take care of you, but I told her to stay at home."

"Six miscarriages. I've only had two."

"Two is not easy, either," Sunja said. "You should have your breakfast. You and the baby need nourishment."

Yumi sat up a bit. "Mozasu left early today for Yokohama."

Sunja nodded. She'd fixed his breakfast before he got on the morning train.

"You saw him then." Yumi admired the tray. "This looks delicious."

Sunja hoped her daughter-in-law would eat. She was terrified that she would miscarry again, but didn't want to appear worried. She regretted having mentioned the number of her mother's miscarriages. The minister at the church had warned against the sins of the careless tongue; it was always better to speak less, Sunja thought.

"Thank you for taking such good care of us."

Sunja shook her head.

"This is nothing. You'll do this for your children," Sunja said.

Unlike the *ajumma*s in the open market with their tight, black, permanent-wave curls, Sunja hadn't colored her graying hair and wore it cut short like a man's. Her mature figure was solid, neither small nor large. She had worked out of doors for so many years that the sun had carved thin grooves into her round, dark face. Like a Buddhist nun, Sunja wore no makeup, not even moisturizer. It was as if she had decided some time ago that she would not care what she looked like beyond being clean, as if to pay penance for having once cared about such things, when in fact she had not.

"Did Mozasu tell you about my mother?" Yumi picked up the spoon.

"That she worked in a bar," Sunja said.

"She was a prostitute. My father was her pimp. They weren't married."

Sunja nodded and stared at the tray of uneaten food. When Mozasu

had told her about Yumi's family, Sunja had imagined as much. The occupation and the war had been difficult for everyone.

"I'm sure she was a good person. I'm sure she cared for you very much."

Sunja believed this. She had loved Hansu, and then she had loved Isak. However, what she felt for her boys, Noa and Mozasu, was more than the love she'd felt for the men; this love for her children felt like life and death. After Noa had gone, she felt half-dead. She could not imagine any mother feeling differently.

"My mother isn't a good person. She beat us. She cared more about drinking and getting money than anything else. After my brother died, if my sister and I hadn't run away, she would have put us to work. Doing what she did. Not once did she ever say a kind thing to me," Yumi said. She'd never told anyone this.

"Mozasu told me your sister passed away."

Yumi nodded. After she and her sister had left home, they'd found shelter in an abandoned clothing factory. In the winter, they both got sick with a high fever, but her sister had died in her sleep. Yumi had slept beside her sister's dead body for nearly a day, waiting to die herself.

Sunja shifted her seat and moved toward her.

"My child, you have suffered too much."

Yumi did not deliver a girl. Her baby Solomon was an enormous boy, over nine pounds, even larger than the famous doctor had expected. The birth took over thirty hours, and the doctor had to call in a colleague to help him through the night. The baby was strong and well. In a month's time, Yumi recovered fully and returned to work, bringing Solomon with her to the workshop. On his first birthday ceremony, Solomon clutched the crisp yen note over the ink brush, string, or cakes—signifying that he would have a rich life.

3

Yokohama, November 1968

W hen the floor manager came by to tell Mozasu that the police were waiting in his office to see him, he assumed that it was about the pachinko machine permits. It was that time of the year. Once he reached his office, he recognized the young men from the precinct and invited them to sit down, but they remained standing and bowed, not saying a word at first. The floor manager, who remained by the door, was unable to meet his glance; preoccupied earlier, Mozasu hadn't noticed that the floor manager's face was so solemn.

"Sir," the shorter of the two officers said, "your family is in the hospital at the moment, and we've come to take you there. The captain would have come himself, but—"

"What?" Mozasu left his side of the desk and went to the door.

"Your wife and son were hit by a taxi this morning. A block from your son's school. The driver was inebriated from the night before and had fallen asleep while driving."

"Are they all right?"

"Your son broke his ankle. Otherwise, he is well."

"And my wife?"

"She died in the ambulance before reaching the hospital."

Mozasu ran out of the office without his coat.

*   *   *

346

The funeral was held in Osaka, and Mozasu would always be able to recall some parts of it vividly and some not at all. During the service, he had held on to Solomon's small hand, fearing that if he let go, the boy might disappear. The three-and-a-half-year-old boy stood, leaning on his crutches, insisting on greeting each person who'd come to pay his respects to his mama. After an hour, he agreed to sit down but did not leave his father's side. Several witnesses had recounted that Yumi had pushed her son onto the sidewalk when the taxi lost control. At the funeral, Mozasu's childhood friend Haruki Totoyama had observed that Yumi must have had incredible hand-eye control in a moment of such intense pressure.

Several hundred guests came. They were people Mozasu knew from his business and many more from his father's church, where his grandmother and Aunt Kyunghee still worshipped. Mozasu did his best to greet them, but he could hardly speak; it was as if he had forgotten both Korean and Japanese. He didn't want to go on anymore without Yumi, but this was something he could not say. She was his lover, but more than anything, she was his wise friend. He could never replace her. And he felt he had done her a great injustice by not having told her this. He had expected to have a long life with her, not a few years. Who would he tell when a customer did something funny? Who would he tell that their son had made him so proud, standing on crutches and shaking the hands of grown-ups and being braver than any other person in the room? When the mourners wept at the sight of the little boy in the black suit, Solomon would say, "Don't cry." He calmed one hysterical woman by telling her, "Mama is in California." When the mourner looked puzzled, neither Solomon nor Mozasu explained what this meant.

He had never taken her there. They'd meant to go. With some difficulty, it was possible now for them to get the passports, but he hadn't bothered. Most Koreans in Japan couldn't travel. If you wanted a Japanese passport, which would allow you to reenter without hassles, you had to become a Japanese citizen—which was almost impossible, and no one he knew would do that anyway. Otherwise, if you wanted to travel, you could get a South Korean passport through *Mindan*, but few wanted to be affiliated with the Republic of Korea, either, since the

impoverished country was run by a dictator. The Koreans who were affiliated with North Korea couldn't go anywhere, though some were allowed to travel to North Korea. Although nearly everyone who had returned to the North was suffering, there were still far more Koreans in Japan whose citizenship was affiliated with the North than the South. At least the North Korean government still sent money for schools for them, everyone said. Nevertheless, Mozasu wouldn't leave the country where he was born. Where would he go, anyway? So Japan didn't want them, so fucking what?

Images of her filled his mind, and even as the mourners spoke to him, all he could hear was her practicing English phrases from her language books. No matter how many times Mozasu had said he would not emigrate to the United States, Yumi had not given up hope that one day they would live in California. Lately, she had been suggesting New York.

"Mozasu, don't you think it would be wonderful to live in New York City or San Francisco?" she'd ask him occasionally, and it was his job to say that he couldn't decide between the two coasts.

"There, no one would care that we are not Japanese," she'd say. *Hello, my name is Yumi Baek. This is my son, Solomon. He is three years old. How are you?* Once, when Solomon asked her what California was, she had replied, "Heaven."

After most of the funeral guests left, Mozasu and Solomon sat down at the back of the funeral hall. Mozasu patted the boy's back, and his son leaned into him, fitting into the crook of his father's right arm.

"You're a good son," Mozasu said to him in Japanese.

"You are a good papa."

"Do you want to get something to eat?"

Solomon shook his head and looked up when an older man approached them.

"Mozasu, are you okay?" the man asked him in Korean. He was a virile-looking gentleman in his late sixties or early seventies, wearing an expensive black suit with narrow lapels and a dark necktie.

The face was familiar, but Mozasu couldn't place it. He felt unable to answer him. Not wanting to be rude, Mozasu smiled, but he wanted to be

left alone. Perhaps it was a customer or a bank officer; Mozasu couldn't think right now.

"It's me. Koh Hansu. Have I aged that much?" Hansu smiled. "Your face is the same, of course, but you've become a man. And this is your boy?" Hansu touched Solomon's head. Throughout the day, nearly everyone had patted the boy's glossy chestnut-colored hair.

Mozasu shot up from his seat.

"*Uh-muh.* Of course, I know who you are. It's been so long. Mother had been looking for you for a while but couldn't get ahold of you. To see if you might know where Noa is. He's disappeared."

"It's been too long." Hansu shook his hand. "Have you heard from Noa?"

"Well, yes and no. He sends Mother money each month, but he won't give his whereabouts. He sends a lot of money actually, so he can't be too badly off. I just wish we knew where he—"

Hansu nodded. "He sent me money, too. To pay me back, he said. I wanted to return it, but there's no way. I thought I'd give it to your mother for her to keep for him."

"Are you still in Osaka?" Mozasu asked.

"No, no. I live in Tokyo now. I live near my daughters."

Mozasu nodded. He felt weak suddenly and wanted to sit again. When Hansu's driver appeared, Hansu promised to call on Mozasu another day.

"Sir, I am very sorry to bother you, but there is a small matter outside. The young woman said it was an emergency."

Hansu nodded and walked out of the building with his driver.

As he approached the car, Hansu's new girl, Noriko, beckoned him from within.

The long-haired beauty clapped when she saw him open the door. Her pink pearl nail polish glinted from her fingertips.

"Uncle is here!" she cried happily.

"What's the matter?" Hansu asked. "I was busy."

"Nothing. I was bored, and I missed my uncle," she replied. "Take me shopping, please. I have waited for so long and so patiently for you to

come back in this car. And the driver is no fun! My friends in Ginza told me cute bags from France came in this week!"

Hansu closed the car door. The bulletproof windows shut out all daylight. The interior lamps of the Mercedes sedan lit up Noriko's oval-shaped face.

"You called me in here because you wanted to go shopping, *nee*?"

"Yes, Uncle," she said sweetly, and extended her pretty small hand on his lap like a kitten's paw. Her rich clients loved her petulant-niece routine. Men wanted to buy girls nice things. If Uncle wanted to remove her white cotton panties, he'd have to buy her as many luxury items from France as she wanted for months and months. Koh Hansu was the most important patron of the hostess bar where Noriko worked; Noriko's mama-san had promised her that Koh Hansu liked spoiling his new girls. This was their second lunch date, and on their first, he had bought her a Christian Dior purse before lunch. Noriko, an eighteen-year-old former beauty contestant, was not used to being kept waiting in a car. She had worn her most expensive peach-colored georgette silk dress with matching heels and a real pearl necklace, borrowed from mama-san.

"Did you ever go to high school?" he asked.

"No, Uncle. I'm not a good schoolgirl," she said, smiling.

"No, of course not. You are stupid. I can't stand stupid."

Hansu hit the girl's face so hard that blood gushed from her pink mouth.

"Uncle, Uncle!" she cried. She swatted at his thick, clenched fist.

He hit her again and again, banging her head against the side lamp of the car until she stopped making any noise. Blood covered her face and the front of her peach-colored dress. The necklace was splattered with red spots. The driver sat motionless in the front until Hansu was finished.

"Take me to the office, then take her back to her mama-san. Tell the mama-san that I don't care how pretty a girl is, I cannot bear a girl who does not have any sense. I was at a funeral. I will not return to the bar until this ignorant thing is removed from my sight."

"I'm sorry, sir. She said it was an emergency. That she had to speak to you or else she would start to scream. I didn't know what to do."

"No hooker is ever to be given precedence over a funeral. If she was sick, then you should have taken her to hospital. Otherwise, she could have screamed her head off. What does it matter, you oaf?"

The girl was still alive. She sat crumpled and half-awake in the corner of the expansive backseat like a crushed butterfly.

The driver was terrified, because he could still be punished. He should never have listened to some bar girl and her stories. A lieutenant he knew in the organization had lost part of his ring finger for failing to line up the guests' shoes properly outside Koh Hansu's apartment when he was much younger and training through the ranks.

"I am sorry, sir. I am very sorry. Please forgive me, sir."

"Shut up. Go to the office." Hansu closed his eyes and leaned his head against the leather-covered rest.

After the driver dropped Hansu off, he took Noriko to the bar where she worked. The horrified mama-san took her to the hospital, and even after the surgeons did their work, the girl's nose would never look the same again. Noriko was ruined. The mama-san couldn't recover her expenses so she sent Noriko off to a *toruko* where she would have to bathe and serve men in the nude until she was too old to work that job. Her tits and ass would last half a dozen years at most in the hot water. Then she would have to find something else to do.

Six days a week, Sunja took her grandson to school and picked him up. Solomon attended an international preschool where only English was spoken. At school, he spoke English and at home, Japanese. Sunja spoke to him in Korean, and he answered in Japanese sprinkled with a few words in Korean. Solomon loved going to school, and Mozasu thought it was good to keep him occupied. He was a cheerful child who wanted to please his teachers and elders. Wherever he went, the news of his mother's death preceded him, wrapping the child in a kind of protective cloud; teachers and mothers of his friends were watchful on his behalf. Solomon was certain that he would see his mama in heaven; he believed that she could see him. She visited him in his dreams, he said, and told him that she missed holding him.

In the evenings, grandmother, father, and son ate dinner together even if Mozasu had to return to work immediately after his meal. Twice, Mozasu's friend Haruki Totoyama had come from Osaka to visit, and once, they'd gone to Osaka to see the family, since Uncle Yoseb was too frail to travel.

Another school day almost over, Sunja waited patiently outside the preschool alongside the sweet-natured Filipina nannies and the friendly Western mothers who were also waiting to collect their children. Sunja couldn't speak to them, but she smiled and nodded in their presence. As usual, Solomon was one of the first to run out. He shouted good-bye to his teachers, then bolted outside to hug his grandmother's torso before joining the other boys to race to the corner candy store. Sunja tried to keep up with his pace. She was oblivious to Hansu, who'd been watching her from his car.

Sunja was wearing a black wool coat, nothing expensive but not shabby, either. It looked store-bought. She had aged considerably, and Hansu felt sorry for her. Only a little over fifty, she looked much older than that. As a girl, she had been bright and taut, so very appealing. The memory of her fullness and vitality aroused him. The years in the sun had darkened her face and covered her hands lightly with pale brown spots. Shallow crags had settled in her once-smooth brow. In place of the maiden's dark, glossy braids, she now kept her hair short, and it was gray mostly. Her middle had thickened. Hansu remembered her large breasts and lovely pink nipples. They had never spent more than a few hours together, and it had always been a wish of his to make love to her more than once in the course of a day. He'd had many women and girls, yet her innocence and trust had excited him more than even the sexiest of whores who were willing to do anything.

Her pretty eyes were still the same—bright and hard like river stones—the light shimmered in them. He had loved her passionately, the way an older man could love a young girl who could restore his youth and vigor; he had loved her with a kind of gratitude. He knew that he'd loved her more than any other girl. She was not beautiful anymore, but he desired her still. The recollection of taking her in the forest often made him hard,

and if he had been alone in the car, he would have jerked off, happy for the rare erection.

Several times each day, Hansu thought of her. What was she doing at the moment? Was she all right? Did she think of him? His mind turned to her as often as it did toward his dead father. When Hansu learned that she was looking for him to find out where Noa was, he did not contact her, because he had no news. He could not imagine disappointing Sunja. He had used every resource to locate the boy but to no avail. Noa had disappeared so perfectly that if Hansu hadn't had the mortuary logs inspected regularly throughout Japan, he might have thought that the boy was dead. At the funeral, he learned that Noa still sent his mother money. That was a relief. The boy was alive, then, and living somewhere in Japan. It had been Hansu's plan to find Noa first, then to contact Sunja, but Yumi's funeral had reminded him that time was not always in his favor. Then last month, his doctor had diagnosed him with prostate cancer.

As Sunja walked past his car, Hansu rolled down the car window.

"Sunja, Sunja."

She gasped.

Hansu told his driver to stay and opened the car door himself to get out.

"Listen, I got to Yumi's funeral late. Mozasu said you'd left. You live with him now, right?"

Sunja stood on the pavement and stared at him. He didn't seem to age. Had it really been eleven years since she last saw him? It had been at his office with Noa, then that expensive dinner to celebrate Noa's admission to Waseda. Noa had been gone six years now. Sunja glanced in the direction of her grandson, who'd run into the store with the other boys to look over comics and debate over which candies to purchase. Without replying, Sunja walked in Solomon's direction. Mozasu had mentioned that Hansu had come to the funeral, that when asked about Noa, Hansu had said nothing.

"Can't you stop for a moment to speak with me? The little boy's fine. He's in the shop. You can see him through the glass." Solomon was in the cluster of boys standing by the rotating comic-book kiosk.

"I begged your wife to tell you that I was looking for you. The gardening boy. I'm sure he gave you my message even if she didn't. Since I've known you, I've done everything I could to never be a burden to you; I have asked you for nothing. Six years have passed since I went to your house. Six."

Hansu opened his mouth, but Sunja spoke again.

"Do you know where he is?"

"No."

Sunja walked toward the candy store.

Hansu touched her arm, and Sunja pushed him back hard with the palm of her hand, knocking him back a step. The chauffeur and bodyguard, who'd been standing near the car, ran toward him, but he waved them away.

"I'm fine," he mouthed to them.

"Go back to your car," she said. "Go back to your crooked life."

"Sunja—"

"Why do you bother me now? How can you not see that you've destroyed me? Why can't you let me alone? Noa is gone from me. There is nothing between us."

Her wet, shining eyes blinked, lit up like lanterns. Her young face shone through the old one.

"Can I drive you and Solomon home? Maybe we can go to a café? I need to speak to you."

Sunja looked down at the large squares of concrete below her feet, unable to stop the flow of tears.

"I want my son. What did you do to him?"

"How can you blame me for that? I just wanted to send him to school."

Sunja sobbed. "It's my fault that I let you know him. You're a selfish person who'd take whatever you want, no matter the consequences. I wish I'd never met you."

Passersby gaped until Hansu stared back at them, forcing them to look away. The boy was still in the shop.

"You're the worst kind of man, because you won't let go until you get your way."

"Sunja, I'm dying."

4

Cradling his copies of *Tetsuwan Atomu* and *Ultraman*, Solomon sat quietly between Sunja and Hansu in the backseat of the large sedan.

"How old are you?" Hansu asked.

Solomon held up three fingers.

"*Soo nee*. Are you going to read those now?" Hansu asked, pointing to the boy's new comics. "Can you read already?"

Solomon shook his head. "I'm going to wait until Toto comes tonight so he can read them to me." He opened up his red satchel and put the comics inside.

"Who is Toto?" Hansu asked.

"He's my papa's friend from when they were boys. He's a real Japanese policeman. He's caught murderers and robbers. I've known him since I was born."

"Is that so? All that time?" Hansu smiled.

The small boy nodded gravely.

"Grandma, what will you make Toto for dinner?" Solomon asked.

"Fish *jeon* and chicken *jorim*," Sunja replied. Mozasu's friend Haruki Totoyama would arrive this evening and stay for the weekend, and she'd already planned all the meals.

"But Toto likes *bulgogi*. It's his favorite meal."

"I can make that tomorrow night. He won't leave until Sunday afternoon."

Solomon looked worried.

Hansu, who'd been observing Solomon carefully, said, "I love chicken *jorim*. That's the kind of dish you can only get at a nice home. Anyone can have *bulgogi* at a restaurant, but only your grandmother can make—"

"Do you want to meet Toto? He's my best grown-up friend."

Sunja shook her head, but Hansu ignored her.

"I've known your father since he was a boy your age. I'd love to have dinner at your house. Thank you, Solomon."

In the front hall, Sunja removed her coat and helped Solomon with his. With his right forearm raised and his left tucked close to his body, the boy ran to the den to watch *Tetsuwan Atomu*. Hansu followed Sunja to the kitchen.

She poured shrimp chips into a small basket and retrieved a yogurt drink from the refrigerator and arranged them on the round Ultraman tray.

"Solomon," she called out.

The boy came to the kitchen to take the tray, and he carried it carefully back to the den to watch his programs.

Hansu sat down by the Western-style breakfast table.

"This is a good house."

Sunja didn't reply.

It was a brand-new three-bedroom in the Westerners' section of Yokohama. Of course, Hansu had driven past it before; he'd seen the exterior of every place she'd ever lived. With the exception of the farmhouse during the war, this was the first one he'd been inside. The furnishings resembled sets from American films—upholstered sofas, high wooden dining tables, crystal chandeliers, and leather armchairs. Hansu guessed that the family slept on beds rather than on the floor or on futons. There were no old things in the house—no traces of anything from Korea or Japan. The spacious, windowed kitchen looked out onto the neighbors' rock garden.

Sunja wasn't speaking to him, but she didn't seem angry, either. She was facing the stove with her back turned to him. Hansu could make out the outline of her body in her camel-colored sweater and brown woolen

trousers. The first time he'd spotted her, he'd noticed her large, full bosom beneath the traditional Korean blouse. He'd always preferred a girl with big breasts and a pillowy bottom. He had never seen her completely naked; they'd only made love outside, where she had always worn a *chima*. His famously beautiful wife had no chest, hips, or ass, and he had dreaded fucking her because she'd loathed being touched. Before bed, he had to bathe, and after lovemaking she had to have a long bath at no matter what hour. After she gave birth to three girls, he quit trying for a son; even his father-in-law, whom Hansu loved, had said nothing about the other women.

He believed that she'd been foolish for refusing to be his wife in Korea. What did it matter that he had a marriage in Japan? He would have taken excellent care of her and Noa. They would have had other children. She would never have had to work in an open market or in a restaurant kitchen. Nevertheless, he had to admire her for not taking his money the way any young girl did these days. In Tokyo, it was possible for a man to buy a girl for a bottle of French perfume or a pair of shoes from Italy.

If Hansu was comfortable reminiscing in her kitchen, Sunja was more than a little unsettled at the sight of him sitting at the breakfast table. From the moment she'd met him, she'd felt his presence all around her. He was an unwanted constant in her imagination. And after Noa vanished, it was as if she were continually haunted by both father and son. Hansu was now in her kitchen waiting patiently for her attention. He was staying for dinner. In all these years, they had never eaten a meal together. Why had he come? When would he go? It was his way to appear then disappear, and as she boiled water for their tea, she thought, I could turn around and he could be gone. Then what?

Sunja opened a blue tin of imported butter cookies and put some on a plate. She filled the teapot with hot water and floated a generous pinch of tea leaves. It was easy to recall a time when there was no money for tea and a time when there was none to buy.

"On the first of each month, Noa sends me cash with a brief note saying that he's well. The postmarks are always different," she said.

"I've looked for Noa. He doesn't want to be found. I'm looking for him still. Sunja, he's my son, too."

How can you blame me for that? Hansu had once said to her. She poured him a cup of tea and excused herself.

The reflection in the bathroom mirror disappointed her. She was fifty-two years old. Her sister-in-law, Kyunghee, who'd been diligent about wearing her hat and gloves to protect her from spots and lines, looked much younger than she did, though Kyunghee was fourteen years older. Sunja touched her short, graying hair. She had never been lovely, and certainly now, she didn't believe that any man would ever want her. That part of her life had ended with Mozasu's father. She was plain and wrinkled; her waist and thighs were thick. Her face and hands belonged to a poor, hard-working woman, and no matter how much money she had in her purse now, nothing would make her appealing. A long time ago, she had wanted Hansu more than her own life. Even when she broke with him, she had wanted him to return, to find her, to keep her.

Hansu was seventy, yet he had changed very little; if anything, his features had improved. He still trimmed his thick white hair carefully and tamed it with scented oil; in his fine wool suit and handmade shoes, Hansu looked like an elegant statesman—a handsome grandfather. No one would have pegged him for a yakuza boss. Sunja didn't want to leave the bathroom. Before she'd left the house, she hadn't even bothered to look in the mirror. She wasn't hideous or shameful to look at, but she had prematurely reached the stage in a woman's life when no one noticed her entering or leaving a room.

Sunja opened the cold-water spigot and washed her face. Despite everything, she wanted him to desire her a little—this knowledge was embarrassing. In her life, there had been two men; that was better than none, she supposed; so that had to be enough. Sunja dried her face on a hand towel and turned off the light.

In the kitchen, Hansu was eating a biscuit.

"Are you okay living here?"

She nodded.

"And the little boy. He's well behaved."

"Mozasu checks in on him all the time."

"When will he be home?"

"Soon. I better make dinner."

"Can I help you cook?" Hansu pretended to take off his suit jacket. Sunja laughed.

"At last. I thought you'd forgotten how to smile."

They both looked away.

"Are you dying?" she asked.

"It's prostate cancer. I have very good doctors. I don't think I'll die of this. Not very soon, anyway."

"You lied then."

"No, Sunja. We're all dying."

She felt angry with him for lying, but she felt grateful, too. She had loved him, and she could not bear the thought of him being gone from this life.

Solomon shrieked with happiness when the door opened. Rolling up his red sweater sleeves hastily, Solomon raised his left arm, bent into a sharp L, and his right hand bisected his left forearm to make an off-centered cross. The child made static sounds to announce the laser beams emitting from his left hand and held his fierce pose.

Haruki fell down onto the floor. He moaned, then made the sound of an explosion.

"Ah, the *kaiju* has been defeated!" Solomon shouted, and jumped on top of Haruki.

"It's very good to see you again," Mozasu said to Hansu. "This is my friend Haruki Totoyama."

"*Hajimemashite.* Totoyama *desu.*"

Solomon resumed his pose.

"Have mercy, Ultraman. *Kaiju* Toto must say hello to your grandmother."

"It's good to see you," Sunja said.

"Thank you for having me."

Solomon moved in between Sunja and Haruki.

"*Kaiju* Toto!"

"*Hai*!" Haruki bellowed.

"Papa bought me a new *Ultraman* yesterday."

"Lucky, lucky," Haruki said, sounding envious.

"I'll show you. C'mon!" Solomon pulled on Haruki, and the grown man hurtled dramatically toward Solomon's room.

Hansu kept a file on every person in Sunja's life. He knew all about Detective Haruki Totoyama, the elder son of a seamstress who owned a uniform manufacturer in Osaka. He had no father and a younger brother who was mentally disabled. Haruki was a homosexual who was engaged to an older woman who worked for his mother. In spite of his relative youth, Haruki was highly regarded in his precinct.

The dinner table talk was happy and relaxed.

"Why can't you move to Yokohama and live with us?" Solomon asked Haruki.

"Hmm. Tempting, *nee*? Then I can play Ultraman every day. *Soooo*. But, Soro-chan, my mother and brother live in Osaka. I think I'm supposed to live there, too."

"Oh," Solomon sighed. "I didn't know you had a brother. Is he older or younger?"

"Younger."

"I'd like to meet him," Solomon said. "We could be friends."

"*Soo nee*, but he's very shy."

Solomon nodded.

"Grandma is shy, too."

Sunja shook her head, and Mozasu smiled.

"I wish you could move here with your brother," Solomon said quietly.

Haruki nodded. Before Solomon was born, he had not been very interested in children. From a young age, having a handicapped brother had made him wary of the responsibilities of caring for another person.

"My girlfriend Ayame prefers Tokyo over Osaka. Perhaps she would be happier here, too," Haruki said.

"Maybe you can move here when you get married," Solomon said.

Mozasu laughed. "*Soo nee.*"

Hansu sat up straighter.

"The Yokohama chief of police is a friend. Please let me know if I can be of service if you'd like to transfer," Hansu said, making an offer he could realize. He took out his business card and handed it to the young officer, and Haruki received it with two hands and a small bow of the head.

Mozasu raised his eyebrows.

Sunja, who had been quiet, continued to observe Hansu. Naturally, she was suspicious of his help. Hansu was not an ordinary person, and he was capable of actions she could neither see nor understand.

5

Nagano, January 1969

A maze of filing cabinets and metal desks created a warren of office workers in the business offices of Cosmos Pachinko. In the thicket of furniture, Risa Iwamura, the head filing clerk, was not very noticeable. By any conventional measure, Risa was, in fact, appealing in her face and form. However, she possessed a distant manner, preventing ease or intimacy with those around her. It was as if the young woman were turning down her lights to minimize any possibility of attraction or notice. She dressed soberly in white blouses and inexpensive black poly skirts requiring little maintenance; she wore the black leather shoes of an old woman. In the winter, one of her two gray wool cardigans graced her thin shoulders like a cape—her only ornament, an inexpensive silvertone wristwatch, which she consulted often, though she never seemed to have anywhere to go. When she performed her tasks, Risa needed little guidance; she anticipated the needs of her employers faultlessly and executed the tasks without any reminders.

For nearly seven years, Noa had been living in Nagano, passing as a Japanese called Nobuo Ban. He had worked assiduously for the owner of Cosmos Pachinko and had settled into a small, invisible life. He was a valued employee, and the owner left him alone. The only thing that the owner brought up every January when he gave Noa his bonus and New Year's lecture was marriage: A man of his age and position should have his own home and children. Noa had been the head of the business offices ever since

Takano, the man who had hired him, had moved to Nagoya to run the multiple Cosmos businesses there. Nevertheless, Noa continued to live in the pachinko parlor dorms and took his meals regularly in the pachinko staff cafeteria. Although he had already paid Hansu back for the Waseda tuition and board, Noa still sent money to his mother each month. He spent almost nothing on himself beyond what was absolutely necessary.

After this year's New Year's lecture, Noa thought deeply about his boss's advice. He had been aware of Risa. Although she never spoke of it, everyone knew that she came from a middle-class family with a sad scandal.

When Risa was fourteen or so, her father, a beloved doctor at the local clinic, had dispensed improper medication to two patients during the flu season, resulting in their deaths. Shortly thereafter, the doctor took his own life, rendering his family both destitute and tainted. Risa was effectively unmarriageable, since a suicide in a family could indicate mental illness in her blood; even worse, her father was perceived to have done something so shameful that he felt that he needed to die. The relatives did not come to the funeral, and they no longer called on Risa and her mother. Risa's mother never recovered from the shock and no longer left the house even to run errands. After Risa completed secondary school, Takano, a former patient of Risa's father, hired her to do clerical work.

Noa had noticed her beautiful handwriting on the files even before he noticed her. It was possible that he was in love with the way she wrote the number two—her parallel lines expressing a kind of free movement inside the invisible box that contained the ideograph's strokes. If Risa wrote even an ordinary description on an invoice, Noa would pause to read it again, not because of what it said, but because he could detect that there was a kind of dancing spirit in the hand that wrote such elegant letters.

When Noa asked her to dinner one winter evening, she replied, in shock, "*Maji?*" Among the file clerks, Nobuo Ban was a fascinating topic of discussion, but after so many years, with so little change in his behavior, the interested girls had long since given up. It took two dinners, perhaps even less time than that, for Risa to fall in love with Noa, and the two intensely private young people married that winter.

On their wedding night, Risa was frightened.

"Will it hurt?"

"You can tell me to stop. I'd rather hurt myself than hurt you, my wife."

Neither had realized the loneliness each had lived with for such a long time until the loneliness was interrupted by genuine affection.

When Risa got pregnant, she quit her job and stayed home and raised her family with as much competence as she had run the file rooms of a successful pachinko business. First, she had twin girls; then a year later, Risa gave birth to a boy; then a year after that, another girl.

Every month, Noa traveled for work for two days, but otherwise he kept to a kind of reliable schedule that made it possible to work six days a week for Cosmos and raise his family attentively. Curiously, he did not drink or go out to clubs, even to entertain the police or to be entertained by pachinko machine salesmen. Noa was honest, precise, and could handle any level of business complication from taxes to machine licenses. Moreover, he was not greedy. The owner of Cosmos respected that Noa avoided *mizu shobai*. Naturally, Risa was grateful; it was easy to lose the affections of a husband to an ambitious bar hostess.

Like all Japanese mothers, Risa volunteered at the children's schools and did everything else she could to make sure that her four children were well and safe. Having so many little constituents kept her from having to involve herself with those outside her family. If her father's death had expelled her from the tribe of ordinary middle-class people, she had effectively reproduced her own tribe.

The marriage was a stable one, and eight years passed quickly. The couple did not quarrel. Noa did not love Risa in the way he had his college girl-friend, but that was a good thing, he thought. Never again, he swore, would he be that vulnerable to another person. Noa remained careful around his new family. Though he valued his wife and children as a kind of second chance, in no way did he see his current life as a rebirth. Noa carried the story of his life as a Korean like a dark, heavy rock within him. Not a day passed when he didn't fear being discovered. The only thing he continued to do from before was to read his English-language novels.

After marrying, he no longer ate at the employees' cafeteria. Now he allowed himself lunch at an inexpensive restaurant where he ate alone. Over lunch, for thirty minutes a day, he reread Dickens, Trollope, or Goethe, and he remembered who he was inside.

It was spring when the twin girls turned seven, and the family went to Matsumoto Castle for a Sunday picnic. Risa had planned the outing to cheer up her mother, who seemed to be retreating further into herself. The children were overjoyed, since they would get ice cream on the way home.

The doctor's widow, Iwamura-san, had never been a competent woman; in fact, she was often helpless. She had remained childishly pretty—soft, pale cheeks, naturally red lips, and dyed black hair. She wore simple beige smocks and cardigans, closed only on the top button. Her expression was perpetually one of a small child who had been disappointed by her birthday present. That said, she was hardly ignorant. She had been a doctor's wife, and though his death had destroyed her cherished social ambitions, she had not relinquished her wishes for her only child. It was bad enough that her daughter worked in pachinko, but now she had married a man who worked in the sordid business, cementing her caste in life. On her initial meeting with Nobuo Ban, she had guessed that there was something unusual about his past, since he had no family. No doubt, he was foreign. She felt suspicious of his character; however, there was also something so sad beneath his fine manners that reminded her of her dear husband, that the widow felt compelled to overlook his background as long as no one ever found out.

A sparse crowd was forming in front of Matsumoto-jo. A famous docent, popular with the locals, was about to lecture about Japan's oldest existing castle. The old man with wispy white eyebrows and a slight hunch had brought an easel with him and was setting up his poster-sized photographs and visual aids. Noa's third child, who had barely eaten anything except for half a rice ball, bolted from his seat and darted toward the guide. Risa was packing up the empty bento boxes and asked Noa to stand near Koichi, a tiny six-year-old boy with a remarkably well-shaped face

and head. He had no fear of strangers and would talk to anyone. Once, at the market, he told the greengrocer that his mother had burned the eggplant the week before. Adults enjoyed talking with Koichi.

"*Sumimasen, sumimasen!*" the boy shouted, pushing his little body through the group listening carefully to the guide's introduction to the castle's history.

The crowd parted to let the boy stand in the front. The guide smiled at Koichi and continued.

The boy's mouth was open a little, and he listened intently while his father stood in the back.

The guide turned to the next image on the easel. In the old black-and-white photograph, the castle leaned dramatically as if the edifice might collapse. The crowd gasped politely at the famous image. Tourists and children who had never seen it before looked at the image closely.

"When this magnificent castle started to list this much, everyone remembered Tada Kasuke's curse!" The guide widened his heavy-lidded eyes for emphasis.

The adults from the region nodded in recognition. There wasn't a soul in Nagano who didn't know about the seventeenth-century Matsumoto headman who'd led the Jokyo Uprising against unfair taxes and was executed with twenty-seven others, including his two young sons.

"What is a curse?" Koichi asked.

Noa frowned, because the child had been reminded repeatedly that he must not blurt out questions whenever he wished.

"A curse?" the guide said, then paused silently for dramatic effect.

"A curse is a terrible, terrible thing. And a curse with moral power is the worst! Tada Kasuke was unfairly persecuted when he was just trying to save all the good people of Nagano from the exploitation of those who lived in this castle! At his death, Tada Kasuke uttered a curse against the greedy Mizuno clan!" The guide grew visibly impassioned by his own speech.

Koichi wanted to ask another question, but his twin sisters, who were now standing by him, pinched the little bit of flesh around his right elbow. Koichi had to learn not to talk so much, they thought; policing him was a family effort.

"Almost two hundred years after Tada Kasuke's death, the ruling clan tried everything in their power to appease the spirit of the martyr to lift the curse. It must have worked, because the castle structure is straight again!" The guide raised both arms dramatically and gestured toward the building behind him. The crowd laughed.

Koichi stared at the poster-sized image of the listing castle. "How? How do you reverse a curse?" Koichi asked, unable to control himself.

His sister Ume stepped on his foot, but Koichi did not care.

"To appease the spirits, the ruling clan proclaimed that Tada Kasuke was a martyr and gave him an afterlife name. They had a statue built. Ultimately, the truth must be acknowledged!"

Koichi opened his mouth again, but this time Noa walked over and picked up his son gently and carried him back to his mother, who was seated with her mother on a bench. Even though he was in kindergarten, Koichi still loved to be picked up. The crowd smiled.

"Papa, that was so interesting, *nee*?"

"*Hai*," Noa replied. When he held the boy, he always recalled Mozasu, who would fall asleep easily in his arms, his round head resting on Noa's shoulder.

"Can I put a curse on someone?" Koichi asked.

"What? Who do you want to put a curse on?"

"Umeko. She stepped on my foot on purpose."

"That's not very nice, but it doesn't warrant a curse, *nee*?"

"But I can reverse a curse if I want."

"Oh, it isn't so easy to do so, Koichi-chan. And what would you do if someone put a curse on you?"

"*Soo nee.*" Koichi sobered at the thought of this, then broke into a smile when he saw his mother, whom he loved more than anyone. Risa was knitting a sweater as she chatted with her mother. The picnic bags rested at her feet.

The Ban family walked around the castle grounds, and when the children grew bored, Noa took them to eat ice cream, as he had promised.

6

Yokohama, July 1974

Haruki Totoyama married Ayame, the foreman of his mother's uniform shop, because his mother had wanted him to do so. It turned out to be a wise decision. When his mother was diagnosed with stomach cancer and could no longer manage the shop or take care of Haruki's brother, Daisuke, Ayame knew exactly what to do. For two years, Ayame managed the business ably, nursed her ailing mother-in-law, and took good care of Daisuke. When Totoyama-san finally died after a great deal of suffering, Haruki asked his exhausted wife what he should do with his mother's shop, and Ayame's answer surprised him.

"We should sell it and move to Yokohama. I don't want to live in Osaka anymore. I never liked working at the shop. I did it because I could never disappoint your mother. We don't have to worry about money anymore. If there's any free time, I want to learn how to bake cakes. Daisuke likes cakes. I will stay home and take care of him."

Haruki didn't know what to make of this, but he couldn't refuse her.

With the money from the sale of the business and his inheritance, Haruki bought a three-bedroom mansion-style apartment near the old cemetery in Yokohama. The apartment had a double wall oven for Ayame. One phone call to Mozasu led to a call from the Yokohama police chief, who offered Haruki the same job he had in Osaka. Naturally, Mozasu and Solomon were happy that Haruki was finally moving to Yokohama. Nevertheless, upon Haruki's family's arrival, Solomon was not allowed to visit

Haruki's house or to meet Haruki's younger brother, who was terrified of children.

Daisuke was almost thirty years old, but he was not much older than five or six mentally. He could not go outside often, because noise, crowds, and bright lights upset him. His mother's illness and death had been catastrophic for him, but Ayame, a longtime employee of his mother, was able to keep Daisuke calm. She created a predictable routine for him at their new home, and because there were so many foreigners in Yokohama, Ayame was able to find an American special education teacher who was willing to come to the house and work with him five days a week. Daisuke would never be able to go to a normal school, get a job, or live alone, but Ayame believed that he could do more and that he should know more than what was expected of him, which was very little. Haruki was grateful for her thoughtfulness. He could not help but admire his wife's ability to solve problems and manage so many new things without ever complaining. She was five years older than he was, the eldest daughter raised in a deeply conservative Buddhist family, and he assumed that her strict upbringing had much to do with her ability to forbear and endure. His mother told him on more than one occasion that Ayame loved him, though he didn't deserve it.

Daisuke took a nap in the early afternoon, ate a late lunch, then had three hours of at-home school with lessons, games, and story time with his teacher, Miss Edith. During his lessons, Ayame went to the public bath, then did her food shopping. The July heat in Yokohama was milder than back home, and Ayame didn't mind walking around after her bath. Invariably, street dust and humidity would spoil that pure feeling that came from a bath, but Ayame felt happy to be alone. She had well over an hour before Miss Edith would leave, so she took the greener path cutting through the wooded park by the cemetery. It was not yet dusk, and there was still a bluish light left over from the day. Beneath the canopy of bright green leaves, Ayame felt clean and joyful. For dinner, she planned on picking up a few sticks of the yakitori that Daisuke was so fond of, which an elderly couple sold a few blocks from their apartment.

As she walked past a thicket of evergreens, she heard the light rustle of branches. From childhood, Ayame had loved birds, even the enormous black crows that most children feared, and she gingerly approached the dense cluster of trees. As she moved closer to the sounds, she could see a nice-looking man leaning against a wide tree trunk with his eyes closed. His trousers were pulled down to his knees and another man knelt in front of him, his head hovering over the standing man's pale hips. Ayame held her breath and retreated quietly to the main path. The men had not seen her. She was not in danger, but she walked faster, her heart beating as if it would pound itself out of her body. The dry grass poked her sandaled feet. Ayame ran until she reached the pavement border, where she could see pedestrians.

On the crowded street opposite the cemetery, no one noticed her. Ayame wiped the perspiration from her brow. When was the last time her husband had wanted her? It had been his mother's suggestion that they marry, and in their brief courtship, Haruki had been thoughtful and kind. She was not a virgin when she married, having had sex with two men who had refused to marry her. There had been one other man, a fabric distributor who pursued her for months, but when Ayame learned that he was married, she refused to go to the love motel with him, because she had only slept with the others as a way to get married, and with this one there was really no point. Unlike the other men, Haruki had never asked her to go with him to a motel. She reasoned that it may have been awkward for him since she worked with his mother. She could not help admiring his high-mindedness and good manners.

Their marriage was consummated. In the beginning, when she and Haruki were trying to have a baby, he made love to her regularly—quickly and cleanly, respecting her wishes when it was not the right time of the month. After they had been attempting to have a child for two years, the doctors determined that she was infertile, and it seemed that Daisuke would effectively become her son. They did not make love again. She had never been interested in being the sexy lady, and he did not approach her for such transactions.

Ayame kept to Daisuke's schedule and went to bed early, while Haruki

woke up late and went to bed late. Their varying sleep times prevented regular encounters in bed. She may not have been interested in sex, but she was not unaware that in general, men needed sex, and that it was a preferable situation to have a husband who had sex periodically with his own wife. If Haruki and she no longer made love, Ayame blamed herself. She was older. Her yellowing face was ordinary and round, and she was far too thin, with spindly legs and arms. Wanting to fill out, she ate as much as she could, especially sweetmeats, but it was impossible for her to gain weight. When she was growing up, her brothers had teased her that her chest was more even than the floor. If she'd wanted, she could have worn clothing for middle school girls. Out of practicality and habit, each day, Ayame wore one of the many dark-colored jumpers that she'd sewed for herself. She had midi-length jumpers in every fabric and color. In the summer, her jumpers were made of linen or seersucker.

When Ayame reached Daisuke's favorite yakitori stand, she fished out her purse from the string bag holding her bath things and asked the old woman for grilled chicken wings, gizzards, and pieces of white meat with scallion. As the woman behind the smoky stand filled the order, Ayame recalled the man leaning against the tree—his rapturous face. Did Haruki want her to kneel before him? Of course, she knew of many things that men and women did, but she had never seen anyone else make love. She'd read two D. H. Lawrence novels. At thirty-seven years old, Ayame wanted to know even more about the things she had never done. Would Haruki be embarrassed for her?

Ayame checked her slender wristwatch with its tiny face, a birthday present from Haruki's mother. There were still forty minutes left until she had to head home. Ayame turned around.

When she returned to the thicket of evergreens, the two men were gone, but now there were at least five other couples; women and men were lying together in the more secluded areas, and two men who were not wearing pants stroked each other while whispering. One couple was lying on thick sheets of brown butcher paper that made noise with their movements. When a tall woman spotted her looking, she didn't flinch; rather, she closed her eyes and made noises of pleasure as the

man beside her continued to massage her small breasts. It felt as if the tall woman wanted Ayame to study them, and Ayame felt emboldened to move closer. The sounds of quiet moaning from the lovers were like evening bird calls. She remembered Daisuke, who would want his dinner.

Three days later, after another long bath, Ayame went directly to the park behind the cemetery. She recognized a woman and man from before, and there were others who did not seem to mind her solitary presence. Everyone here belonged to each other's secret, and Ayame felt safe among them. As she was leaving, a lovely girl approached her.

"Why do you come so early? It's more wonderful in the evening."

Ayame didn't know what to say, but she felt it would be impolite not to reply.

"What do you mean?"

"There are more people later if you want to do things." The girl laughed. "Don't you like to do things?"

Ayame shook her head.

"I, I…No."

"If you have money, I can do things for you. I prefer to be do things with girls."

Ayame held her breath. The girl was plump in a very pretty way, with vivid color in her cheeks. She had beautiful white arms, full and smooth like those of a woman in an Italian painting. In her sheer georgette blouse in a *cha* color and navy print skirt, she looked like an attractive office lady. The girl took Ayame's left hand and slipped it in her blouse; Ayame could feel the smooth rise of the girl's large nipple.

"I like this bone between your neck and shoulders. You're very cute. Come see me. I'm here in the evenings. Today, I started early, because I have a meeting, but he's a little late. I'm usually near the shrubs over there." She giggled. "I love to put things in my mouth. *Nee?*" She wet her lips with her strawberry-colored tongue. "And I can bring you toys," she said, before returning to her spot.

Stunned, Ayame nodded and walked home. Her left hand felt like it

was burning, and with it, she stroked her collarbone, never having given it any thought.

For three months after, Ayame stuck to her old route to the *sento* and went straight from there to the market streets to do her shopping. She returned faithfully to her routines with Daisuke, and when she took her baths at the *sento*, she tried not to think of that girl. Ayame was not ignorant; even as a girl, she knew that others did many curious things. What puzzled her was that so late in her life, she wanted to know more but had no one to ask. Her husband never seemed to change: He was hardworking, polite, and rarely home. He was affectionate with Daisuke. When he had time off, he went to see his Korean friend Mozasu and his son, Solomon, or took his brother for walks in the park or to the *sento* to give her some time alone. Occasionally, the three of them went to the same *yakiniku* restaurant, where the owner gave them a private room in the back. Daisuke liked cooking his meals on the grill. After Daisuke fell asleep for the night, her evenings were quiet. She read recipe books and sewing magazines and crocheted lace.

Despite her strong efforts, it was no longer just at the *sento*. Ayame wondered about the girl all day—when she was baking a golden sponge cake or merely dusting the furniture. What confused her was that the girl in the green blouse had looked so wholesome and amused, nothing at all like what she'd seen in maudlin films about a fallen woman from a bad family. The girl was luscious like a costly melon sold in a department store.

It was a Saturday evening at the end of November, and Daisuke had fallen asleep earlier than usual. Haruki was at the office catching up on writing reports where it was quiet enough for him to work undisturbed. In the living room, Ayame was trying to read a book about English baking techniques, but she found her mind drifting. Closing the book, she decided to have another bath, though she'd had one earlier that day. Daisuke was snoring quietly when she left the house.

At the *sento*, she soaked in the hot bathwater, fearing that someone could see the desire in her face. She wondered if she could find the nerve

to ask her husband to make love to her. When the tips of her fingers were horribly wrinkled, she dressed and combed her hair. Outside, the streetlamps shone brightly, and the black pavement glistened in the night. Ayame walked toward the cemetery.

Even in the cold, there were too many lovers to count. Couples watched others make love and masturbate each other. Naked bodies humped beneath large trees. Men lined up in a row while others on their knees bobbed their heads against them. Watching the men's faces thrilled her. She wanted Haruki to take her into his arms and make violent love to her there. There was only a little light in the evening sky, only a small misshapen moon and the faintest spray of winter stars. Ayame walked through the arrangements of men and women. By an impressive oak, two men embraced in lovemaking, and the taller man, whose arms clasped the younger one, wore a gray suit much like the one she had made for her husband. Ayame looked closer and saw him, his eyes shut tightly as he held on to the young man in the white cotton undershirt who was gasping with excitement. She retreated to the other side of the foliage to hide herself. Ayame held her breath, and she watched her husband making love. It was. It was him.

When Haruki and the young man in the white shirt were done, they put on their clothes without talking and walked away from one another without a bow or a good-bye. She didn't see Haruki giving the young man any money, but that could have happened earlier; she couldn't be sure of how these things worked. Would it matter if the man had been paid? she wondered.

Ayame sat down on the roots of an old tree not far from a couple having breathless intercourse, and she stared at the pads of her fingers, which were smooth again. There was no choice but to wait until he was long gone, but if he reached the house before she did, she'd have to tell him that she was at the *sento*, which wasn't true.

"Hi."

The girl wore a white blouse this time, and it shimmered in the dark, making her look like an angel.

"Did you bring money?"

The girl crouched down to Ayame's level and heaved her bosom toward her face as if readying to nurse her. She opened her blouse and pulled out her breasts, propping them over the fabric cups of her underwire brassiere.

The girl was beautiful. Ayame wondered why she could not possess features as lovely and alluring on her withered body that could neither conceive nor be loved.

"You can pay me after if you want." The girl glanced at Ayame's string bag. "You've had your bath like a good baby, and you're clean. Come to Mama. Here, you can put your mouth on them. I like that. Then I can do it to you. *Aka-chan*, you look afraid, but why? This will feel so nice and sweet." The girl took Ayame's right hand and pushed it up her skirt, and Ayame felt another woman for the first time. It was soft and plush.

"*Daijoubu?*" On her knees, the girl moved closer and took Ayame's left hand and put her ring finger into her mouth as she climbed onto Ayame's lap. She sniffed Ayame's wet hair. "I can almost drink your shampoo. You smell so pretty. *Aka, aka*, you'll feel better as we make love. You'll be in paradise."

Ayame folded herself into the warmth of the girl's body.

As she opened her mouth, the girl pulled the string bag to her.

"Do you have money here? I need a lot. Mama has to buy many things to look pretty for her baby."

Ayame recoiled and heaved the girl off her body, making her fall on her back.

"You're disgusting. Disgusting." She got up.

"You skinny old cunt!" the girl shouted, and Ayame could hear her throaty laugh from a distance. "You have to pay for love, you bitch!"

Ayame ran back to the *sento*.

When she finally returned home, Haruki was fixing his brother a snack.

"*Tadaima*," she said quietly.

"Where were you, A-chan?" Daisuke asked, his face folded with worry. He had the lopsided face of a pale, gaunt man with the extraordinary eyes

of a very young child—unguarded and capable of expressing joy. He wore the yellow pajamas that she had ironed for him that morning.

Haruki nodded and smiled at her. He had never before found his brother alone. Daisuke had been crying on his bed mat, asking for his mother. He didn't want to tell Ayame this for fear of making her feel bad about being late.

"I was at the bath, Dai-chan. I'm very sorry I'm late. I thought you were sleeping, and it was cold so I went to have another bath."

"I was afraid. I was afraid," Daisuke said, his eyes beginning to well up again. "I want Mama."

She felt unable to look at Haruki's face. He had not yet removed his suit jacket.

Daisuke went to her, leaving Haruki by the kitchen counter to put away the box of *senbei*.

"A-chan is clean. She had a bath. A-chan is clean. She had a bath." He sang the line that he liked to repeat after she came home from the *sento*.

"Are you tired now?" she asked him.

"No."

"Would you like me to read to you?"

"*Hai.*"

Haruki left them in the living room with her reading a picture book about old trains, and she nodded to him when he said good night before going to bed.

7

Yokohama, March 1976

A retiring detective had failed to complete a report of a suicide, and eventually it landed on Haruki's desk. A twelve-year-old Korean boy had jumped off the roof of his apartment building. The mother was too hysterical to finish the interview at the time, but the parents were willing to meet Haruki tonight after they finished work.

The boy's parents lived not far from Chinatown. The father was a plumber's assistant, and the mother worked in a glove factory. Tetsuo Kimura, the jumper, was the oldest of three and had two sisters.

Even before the apartment door opened, the familiar smells of garlic, shoyu, and the stronger miso that Koreans favored greeted him in the damp hallway. All the tenants of the six-story building owned by a Korean were also Koreans. The boy's mother, her face downcast and meek, let him into the three-room apartment. Haruki slipped off his street shoes to put on the slippers she gave him. In the main room, the father, wearing a workman's clean overalls, was already seated cross-legged on a blue floor cushion. The mother set out a discount-store tray brimming with teacups and wrapped biscuits from the *conbini*. The father held a bound book in his lap.

After handing the father his business card with two hands, Haruki sat down on a floor cushion. The mother poured him a cup of tea and sat with her knees folded.

"You didn't get a chance to see this." The father handed the book to

Haruki. "You should know what happened. Those children should be punished."

The father, a long-waisted man with an olive complexion and a square jaw, didn't make eye contact when speaking.

The book was a middle school graduation album. Haruki opened the thick volume to the page marked with a slip of blank notepaper. There were rows and columns of black-and-white photographs of students, all of them wearing uniforms—a few smiling, some showing teeth, with little variation overall. Right away he spotted Tetsuo, who had his mother's long face and his father's small mouth—a mild-looking boy with thin shoulders. There were a few handwritten messages over the faces of the photographs.

"Tetsuo—good luck in high school. Hiroshi Noda."

"You draw well. Kayako Mitsuya."

Haruki must have looked confused, because he didn't notice anything unusual. Then the father prompted him to check the flyleaf.

"Die, you ugly Korean."

"Stop collecting welfare. Koreans are ruining this country."

"Poor people smell like farts."

"If you kill yourself, our high school next year will have one less filthy Korean."

"Nobody likes you."

"Koreans are troublemakers and pigs. Get the hell out. Why are you here anyway?"

"You smell like garlic and garbage!!!"

"If I could, I'd cut your head off myself, but I don't want to get my knife dirty!"

The handwriting was varied and inauthentic. Some letters slanted right or left; multiple authors had tried purposefully to shield their identities.

Haruki closed the book and laid it beside him on the clean floor. He took a sip of tea.

"Your son, he never mentioned that others were bothering him?"

"No," the mother answered quickly. "He never complained. Never. He said he was never discriminated against."

Haruki nodded.

"It was not because he was Korean. That sort of thing was from long ago. Things are better now. We know many kindhearted Japanese," the mother said.

Even with the cover closed, Haruki could see the words in his mind. The electric fan on the floor circulated a constant flow of warm air.

"Did you speak with his teachers?" the mother asked.

The retired detective had. The teachers had said that the boy was a strong student but too quiet.

"He had top marks. The children were jealous of him because he was smarter than they were. My son learned to read when he was three," the mother said.

The father sighed and laid his hand gently on his wife's forearm, and she said no more.

The boy's father said, "Last winter, Tetsuo asked if he could stop going to school and instead work in the vegetable store that his uncle owns. It's a small shop near the little park down the street. My brother-in-law was looking for a boy to break down boxes and work as a cashier. Tetsuo said he wanted to work for him, but we said no. Neither of us finished high school, and we didn't want him to quit. It didn't make any sense for him to work in a job like that and to give up school when he's such a good student. My brother-in-law is barely getting by himself, so my son would not have made much of a salary. My wife wanted him to get a good job in an electronics factory. If he had finished high school, then—"

The father covered his head with his large, rough hands, pressing down on his coarse hair. "Working in the basement of a grocery store. Counting inventory. That's not an easy life for anyone, you know," he said. "He was talented. He could remember any face and draw it perfectly. He could do many things we didn't know how to do."

The mother said calmly, "My son was hardworking and honest. He never hurt anyone. He helped his sisters do their homework—"

Her voice broke off.

Suddenly, the father turned to face Haruki.

"The boys who wrote that should be punished. I don't mean go to jail, but they shouldn't be allowed to write such things." He shook his head.

"He should've quit school. It would've been better if he'd worked in a basement of a grocery store or peeling bags of onions in a *yakiniku* restaurant. I'd rather have my son than no son. My wife and I are treated badly here, but it's because we're poor. There are rich Koreans who are better off. We thought it could be different for our children."

"You were born here?" Haruki asked. Their accent was no different than that of native Japanese speakers from Yokohama.

"Yes, of course. Our parents came from Ulsan."

Ulsan was in what was now South Korea, but Haruki guessed that the family was affiliated with the North Korean government, as were many of the ethnic Koreans. *Mindan* was much less popular. The Kimuras probably lacked the tuition for the North Korean schools and sent them to the local Japanese school.

"You're *Chosenjin*?"

"Yes, but what does that matter?" the father said.

"It doesn't. It shouldn't. Excuse me." Haruki glanced at the album. "Does the school know? About this? There was nothing in the report about any other kids."

"I took the afternoon off to show it to the principal. He said it was impossible to know who wrote those things," the father said.

"*Soo, soo*," Haruki said.

"Why can't the children who wrote this be punished? Why?" the mother asked.

"There were several people who witnessed him jump with no one else on the roof. Your son was not pushed. We cannot arrest everyone who says or writes something mean-spirited—"

"Why can't the police make the principal—" The father looked directly at him, then, seeing Haruki's defeated expression, the father stared at the door instead. "You people work together to make sure nothing ever changes. *Sho ga nai. Sho ga nai.* That's all I ever hear."

"I'm sorry. I am sorry," he said before leaving.

* * *

Paradaisu Yokohama was crowded at eight o'clock in the evening. The volcanic rush of tinny bells, the clanging of tiny hammers across miniature metal bowls, the beeping and flashing of colorful lights, and the throaty shouts of welcome from the obsequious staff felt like a reprieve from the painful silence in his head. Haruki didn't even mind the thick swirls of tobacco smoke that hung like a layer of gray mist above the heads of the players seated opposite the rows upon rows of vertical, animated machines. As soon as Haruki stepped into the parlor, the Japanese floor manager rushed to him and asked if he would like tea. Boku-san was in the office in a meeting with a machine salesman and promised to be down shortly. Haruki and Mozasu had a standing dinner arrangement every Thursday, and Haruki was here to pick him up.

It was fair to say that almost everyone at the parlor wanted to make some extra money by gambling. However, the players also came to escape the eerily quiet streets where few said hello, to keep away from the loveless homes where wives slept with children instead of husbands, and to avoid the overheated rush-hour train cars where it was okay to push but not okay to talk to strangers. When Haruki was a younger man, he had not been much of a pachinko player, but since moving to Yokohama, Haruki allowed himself to find some comfort here.

It took no time for him to lose several thousand yen, so he bought another tray of balls. Haruki wasn't reckless about his inheritance, but his mother had saved so much that he'd have enough even if he was fired, and even if he lost a fortune. When Haruki paid young men to sleep with him, he could afford to be generous. Of all the vices, pachinko seemed like a petty one.

The small metal balls zigzagged rhythmically across the rectangular face of the machine, and Haruki moved the dial steadily to keep the action going. *No*, he had wanted to tell Tetsuo's father, *how can I prove guilt for a crime that doesn't exist? I cannot punish and I cannot prevent.* No, he could not say such things. Not to anyone. So much he could never say. Since he was a child, Haruki had wanted to hang himself, and he thought of it still. Of all the crimes, Haruki understood murder-suicides the best;

if he could have, he would've killed Daisuke, then himself. But he could never kill Daisuke. And now he could not do such an unspeakable thing to Ayame. They were innocent.

The machine died suddenly. He looked up and saw Mozasu holding the plug to the extension cord. He wore a black suit with a red Paradaisu Yokohama pin on his jacket lapel.

"How much did you lose, dummy?"

"A lot. Half my pay?"

Mozasu pulled out his wallet and handed Haruki a sheaf of yen notes, but Haruki wouldn't take it.

"It's my own fault. Sometimes I win, right?"

"Not that often." Mozasu tucked the money into Haruki's coat pocket.

At the *izakaya*, Mozasu ordered beer and poured Haruki his first drink from the large bottle. They sat at the long counter on carved wooden stools. The owner laid out the dish of warm, salted soybeans, because they always started with those.

"What's the matter with you?" Mozasu asked. "You look like shit."

"A kid jumped off a building. Had to talk with his parents today."

"Ugh. How old?"

"Middle school. Korean."

"*Ehh?*"

"You should have seen what the rotten kids wrote on his yearbook."

"Probably the same shit kids wrote in mine."

"*Maji?*"

"Yeah, every year, a bunch of knuckleheads would tell me to go back to Korea or to die a slow death. Just mean kid stuff."

"Who? Anyone I know?"

"It was a long time ago. Besides, what are you going to do? Arrest them?" Mozasu laughed. "So, you're sad about that? About the kid?"

Haruki nodded.

"You have a weakness for Koreans," Mozasu said, smiling. "You idiot."

Haruki started to cry.

"What the hell? Hey, hey." Mozasu patted his back.

The owner behind the counter looked away and wiped down the counter space of a customer who'd just left.

Haruki clasped his head with his right hand and closed his wet eyes.

"The poor kid couldn't take any more."

"Listen, man, there's nothing you can do. This country isn't going to change. Koreans like me can't leave. Where we gonna go? But the Koreans back home aren't changing, either. In Seoul, people like me get called Japanese bastards, and in Japan, I'm just another dirty Korean no matter how much money I make or how nice I am. So what the fuck? All those people who went back to the North are starving to death or scared shitless."

Mozasu patted down his pockets for cigarettes.

"People are awful. Drink some beer."

Haruki took a sip and coughed, having swallowed wrong.

"When I was a boy, I wanted to die," Haruki said.

"Me too. Every fucking day, I thought it would be better if I died, but I couldn't do it to my mother. Then after I left school, I didn't feel that way anymore. But after Yumi died, I didn't know if I was going to make it. You know? But then I couldn't do it to Solomon. And my mother, well, you know, she changed after Noa disappeared. I can never let her down like that. My mother said that my brother left because he couldn't handle Waseda and was ashamed. I don't think that's true. Nothing in school was ever hard for him. He's living somewhere else, and he doesn't want us to find him. I think he just got tired of trying to be a good Korean and quit. I was never a good Korean."

Mozasu lit his cigarette.

"But things get better. Life is shitty, but not all the time. Etsuko's great. I didn't expect her to come along. You know, I'm going to help her open a restaurant."

"She's a nice lady. Maybe you'll get married again." Haruki liked Mozasu's new Japanese girlfriend.

"Etsuko doesn't want to get married again. Her kids hate her enough already. It'd be hell for her if she married a Korean pachinko guy." Mozasu snorted.

Haruki's sad expression remained.

"Man, life's going to keep pushing you around, but you have to keep playing."

Haruki nodded.

"I used to think if my father hadn't left, then I'd be okay," Haruki said.

"Forget him. Your mother was a great lady; my wife thought she was the best of the best. Tough and smart and always fair to everyone. She was better than having five fathers. Yumi said she was the only Japanese she'd ever work for."

"Yeah. Mama was a great lady."

The owner brought out the fried oysters and *shishito* peppers.

Haruki wiped his eyes with a cocktail napkin, and Mozasu poured him another glass of beer.

"I didn't know kids wrote that stuff on your yearbooks. You were always watching out for me. I didn't know."

"Forget it. I'm okay. I'm okay now."

8

Nagano, August 1978

Hansu's driver found her waiting at the north gate of Yokohama Station as instructed, and he led Sunja to the black sedan, where Hansu was sitting in the back.

Sunja arranged herself in the plush velvet backseat, pulling down her suit jacket to cover the swell of her *ajumma* abdomen. She wore an imported French designer dress and Italian leather shoes that Mozasu's girlfriend, Etsuko, had selected for her. At sixty-two years, Sunja looked like what she was—a mother of two grown men, a grandmother, and a woman who had spent most of her life working outdoors. Despite the clothes of a wealthy Tokyo matron, her wrinkled and spotted skin and short white hair couldn't help but make her look rumpled and ordinary.

"Where are we going?"

"Nagano," Hansu replied.

"Is that where he is?"

"Yes. He goes by Nobuo Ban. He's been there continuously for sixteen years. He's married to a Japanese woman and has four children."

"Solomon has four cousins! Why couldn't he tell us?"

"He is now Japanese. No one in Nagano knows he's Korean. His wife and children don't know. Everyone in his world thinks he is pure Japanese."

"Why?"

"Because he does not want anyone to know about his past."

"Is it so easy to do this?"

"It's easy enough, and in his world, no one cares enough to dig around."

"What do you mean?"

"He runs a pachinko parlor."

"Like Mozasu?" There were Koreans in every aspect of the pachinko business, from the parlors and the *keihin* to the machine manufacturers, but she would have never expected Noa to do the same thing as Mozasu.

"*Soo nee.* How is Mozasu?" Hansu asked.

"Good." She nodded, having a hard time concentrating.

"His business okay?"

"He bought another parlor in Yokohama."

"And Solomon? He must be very big now."

"He's doing well at school. Studying hard. I want to know more about Noa."

"He is well off." Hansu smiled.

"Does he know we're coming to see him?"

"No."

"But—"

"He doesn't want to see us. Well, he doesn't want to see me. He may want to see you, but if he had, surely he would've let you know sooner."

"Then—"

"We should not speak to him today, but I thought if you wanted to see him with your own eyes, you could. He is going to be at his main office."

"How do you know this?"

"I just do," Hansu said, closing his eyes and leaning against the white lace-covered headrest. He was taking several medications, and they made him feel foggy.

It was his plan to wait until Noa came out of his office as he usually did to have lunch at the *soba-ya* across the street. Each weekday, he ate a simple lunch at a different restaurant, and on Wednesdays he ate soba. Hansu's private investigators had detailed Noa's life in Nagano in a twenty-six-page report, and what was most notable was his unwavering need for routine. Noa did not drink alcohol, gamble, or fool around with

women. He had no apparent religion, and his wife and four children lived like a middle-class Japanese family in a modest house.

"Will he eat lunch by himself, do you think?"

"He always eats lunch by himself. Today is Wednesday so he will eat *zaru soba*, taking less than fifteen minutes. He will read a little of his English novel, then return to his office. This is why he is so successful, I think. He does not make mistakes. Noa has a plan." There was a kind of territorial pride in Hansu's voice.

"Do you think he'll see me?"

"It's hard to tell," he said. "You should wait in the car and get a glimpse of him, then the driver will take us back to Yokohama. We can return next week if you like. Maybe you can write to him first."

"What's the difference between today and next week?"

"Maybe if you see him and know that he is well, then you will not need to see him so much. He has chosen this life, Sunja, and maybe he wants us to respect that."

"He's my son."

"And mine."

"Noa and Mozasu. They're my life."

Hansu nodded. He had never felt this way about his children. Not really.

"I've lived only for them."

This was wrong to say. At church, the minister preached about how mothers cared too much about their children and that worshipping the family was a kind of idolatry. One must not love one's family over God, he'd said. The minister said that families could never give you what only God could give. But being a mother who loved her children too much had helped her to understand a little of what God went through. Noa had children of his own now; perhaps he could understand how much she'd lived for him.

"Look. He's coming out," Hansu said.

Her son's face had changed only a little. The graying hair along the temples surprised her, but Noa was forty-five years old and no longer the university student. He wore round, golden spectacles much like those

Isak used to wear, and his black suit hung simply on his lean frame. His face was a copy of Hansu's.

Sunja opened the car door and stepped out.

"Noa!" she cried, and rushed toward him.

He turned around and stared at his mother, who stood not ten paces from him.

"*Umma*," he murmured. Noa moved close to her and touched her arm. He had not seen his mother cry since Isak's funeral. She was not the sort to cry easily, and he felt bad for her. He had imagined that this day would come and had prepared for it, but now that she was here, he was surprised by his own sense of relief.

"There's no need to be upset. We should go inside my office," he said. "How did you get here?"

Sunja couldn't speak because she was heaving. She took a deep breath. "Koh Hansu brought me here. He found you, and he brought me here because I wanted to see you. He's in the car."

"I see," he said. "Well, he can stay there."

Upon his return to the office, his employees bowed, and Sunja followed behind. He offered her a seat in his office and closed the door.

"You look well, *umma*," Noa said.

"It has been such a long time, Noa. I've worried so much about you."

Seeing his hurt expression, she stopped herself. "But I'm glad you wrote to me. I have saved all the money you sent. It was very thoughtful of you to do that."

Noa nodded.

"Hansu told me that you're married and you have children."

Noa smiled. "I have one boy and three girls. They are very good kids. All of them study except for my son, who is a good baseball player. He is my wife's favorite. He looks like Mozasu and acts like him, too."

"I know Mozasu would like to see you. When can you come to see us?"

"I don't know. I don't know if I can."

"Haven't we wasted enough time? All these years. Noa, have mercy.

Have mercy, please. *Umma* was a girl when I met Hansu. I didn't know he was married, and when I found out, I refused to be his mistress. Then your father married me so you could have a proper name. All my life, I was faithful to your father, Baek Isak, who was a great man. Even after he died, I have been true to his—"

"I understand what you did. However, my blood father is Koh Hansu. That cannot change," Noa said flatly.

"Yes."

"I'm a Korean working in this filthy business. I suppose having yakuza in your blood is something that controls you. I can never be clean of him." He laughed. "This is my curse."

"But you're not a yakuza," she protested. "Are you? Mozasu owns pachinko parlors and he's very honest. He's always saying how it is possible to be a good employer and to avoid the bad people as long as you—"

Noa shook his head.

"*Umma*, I am honest, but there are people you cannot avoid in this business. I run a very large company, and I do what I have to do." He made a face like he'd tasted something sour.

"You're a good boy, Noa. I know you are—" she said, then felt foolish for having called him a child. "I mean, I'm sure you're a good businessman. And honest."

The two sat quietly. Noa covered his mouth with his right hand. His mother looked like an old exhausted woman.

"Do you want some tea?" he asked. Over the years, Noa had imagined his mother or brother coming to his house, discovering him there rather than in his white, sun-filled office. She'd made it easier for him by coming here instead. Would Hansu come to his office next? he wondered. It had taken longer for Hansu to find him than he'd expected.

"Would you like something to eat? I can order something—"

Sunja shook her head. "You should come home."

He laughed. "This is my home. I am not a boy."

"I'm not sorry to have had you. You are a treasure to me. I won't leave—"

"No one knows I'm Korean. Not one person."

"I won't tell anyone. I understand. I'll do whatever—"

"My wife doesn't know. Her mother would never tolerate it. My own children don't know, and I will not tell them. My boss would fire me. He doesn't employ foreigners. *Umma,* no one can know—"

"Is it so terrible to be Korean?"

"It is terrible to be me."

Sunja nodded and stared at her folded hands.

"I have prayed for you, Noa. I have prayed that God would protect you. It is all a mother can do. I'm glad you are well." Each morning, she went to the dawn service and prayed for her children and grandson. She had prayed for this moment.

"The children, what are their names?"

"What does it matter?"

"Noa, I'm so sorry. Your father brought us to Japan, and then, you know, we couldn't leave because of the war here and then the war there. There was no life for us back home, and now it's too late. Even for me."

"I went back," he said.

"What do you mean?"

"I'm a Japanese citizen now, and I can travel. I went to South Korea to visit. To see my supposed motherland."

"You're a Japanese citizen? How? Really?"

"It's possible. It is always possible."

"And did you go to Busan?"

"Yes, and I visited Yeongdo. It was tiny but beautiful," he said.

Sunja's eyes filled with tears.

"*Umma,* I have a meeting now. I'm sorry, but why don't we see each other next week? I'll come by. I want to see Mozasu again. I have to take care of some urgent things now."

"Really? You'll come?" Sunja smiled. "Oh, thank you, Noa. I'm so glad. You're such a good—"

"It's best if you leave now. I'll phone you later tonight when you get home."

Sunja got up quickly from her seat, and Noa walked her back to the spot where they met. He would not look into Hansu's car.

"We'll talk later," he said, and crossed the street toward his building.

*   *   *

Sunja watched her son enter his office building, then tapped the passenger door of Hansu's car. The driver came out and held the door open for her.

Hansu nodded.

Sunja smiled, feeling light and hopeful.

Hansu looked at her face carefully and frowned.

"You should not have seen him."

"It went well. He'll come to Yokohama next week. Mozasu will be so happy."

Hansu told the driver to go. He listened to her talk about their meeting.

That evening, when Noa did not call her, she realized that she had not given him her home number in Yokohama. In the morning, Hansu phoned her. Noa had shot himself a few minutes after she'd left his office.

9

Yokohama, 1979

Etsuko Nagatomi loved all three of her children, but she did not love them all the same. Being a mother had taught her that this kind of emotional injustice was perhaps inevitable.

By midmorning, Etsuko had finished everything she had to get done for Solomon's party and was sitting in her office in the back of the airy, birch-paneled restaurant. She was forty-two years old, a native of Hokkaido who'd moved to Yokohama following her divorce six years before. She had maintained a youthful prettiness that she felt was important to being a restaurant owner. Etsuko wore her jet-colored hair in a chignon style to set off her lively, egg-shaped face. From afar she could appear stern, but up close her face was animated, and her small, friendly eyes missed nothing. She applied her makeup expertly, having worn rouge and powder since middle school, and the red wool Saint Laurent suit that Mozasu had bought her flattered her reedy figure.

Though Etsuko would normally have been pleased with herself for being so ahead of schedule, today she was not. She continued to stare at the phone message from her high school–aged daughter, Hana, with an unfamiliar Tokyo number. How did Hana get there from Hokkaido? Calls with her daughter could take five minutes or an hour, depending, and Mozasu was coming to pick her up soon. Her boyfriend was a patient man about many things, but he liked her to be punctual. Etsuko dialed anyway, and Hana picked up on the first ring.

"I've been waiting."

"I'm sorry. I just got the message." Etsuko was afraid of her fifteen-year-old daughter, but she had been trying to sound more firm, the way she was with her staff.

"Where are you?"

"I'm four months pregnant."

"*Nani?*"

Etsuko could almost see her daughter's large, unblinking eyes. Hana resembled the girls in comic books with her cute lollipop head and small, girlish body. She dressed to get attention—short skirts, sheer blouses, and high-heeled boots—and accordingly, she received that attention from all kinds of men. This was her *unmei*, Etsuko thought; her ex-husband used to dismiss this idea of fate as a lazy explanation for the bad choices people made. Regardless, life had only confirmed her belief that there was indeed a pattern to it all. To Etsuko, this had to happen, because as a girl she had been no different. When she was seventeen, she had been pregnant with Tatsuo, Hana's oldest brother.

Etsuko and Hana remained silent on the line, but the poor phone reception crackled like a campfire.

"I'm in Tokyo at a friend's."

"Who?"

"It's just some friend's cousin who lives here. Listen, I want to come to your place right away."

"Why?"

"What do you think? You have to help me with this."

"Does your father know?"

"Are you stupid?"

"Hana—"

"I know how to get to you. I have the money. I'll call you when I arrive." Hana hung up.

Two years after the divorce, when Hana was eleven, she'd asked Etsuko if they could talk to each other like friends rather than mother and child, and Etsuko had agreed because she was grateful that her daughter contin-

ued to talk to her at all. Also, Etsuko agreed because when she'd been a girl, she had lied to her mother and father about everything. But Etsuko found that being detached as a mother had its own burdens. She wasn't allowed to ask any prying questions, and if she sounded too concerned (something Hana hated), her daughter hung up the phone and wouldn't call for weeks.

Etsuko had many regrets about her life in Hokkaido, but what she was most sorry about was what her reputation had done to her children. Her grown sons still refused to talk to her. And she had only worsened matters by continuing to see Mozasu. Her sister Mari and her mother urged her to end it. The pinball business was dirty, they said; pachinko gave off a strong odor of poverty and criminality. But she couldn't give him up. Mozasu had changed her life. He was the only man she had never cheated on—something Etsuko had never believed could be possible.

The spring before her thirty-sixth birthday, when she was still married and living in Hokkaido, Etsuko had seduced another one of her high school boyfriends. She had been having a series of affairs for almost three years with various men from her adolescence. What amazed her was how difficult it was the first time but how effortless it was to have all the others that followed. Married men wanted invitations from married women. It was no trouble to phone a man she had slept with twenty years ago and invite him to her house for lunch when her children were at school.

That spring, she began sleeping with a boyfriend from her freshman year in high school. He'd grown into a handsome, married playboy who still had the tendency to talk too much. One afternoon, in her tiny Hokkaido living room, as the playboy was getting dressed to return to his office, he bemoaned the fact that she wouldn't leave her husband, who preferred the company of his work colleagues to hers. He laid his head between her small breasts and said, "But I can leave my wife. Tell me to do it." To this, she said nothing. Etsuko had no intention of leaving Nori and the children. Her complaint about her husband was not that he was boring or that he wasn't home enough. Nori was not a bad person. It was just that she felt like she had no clear sense of him after nineteen years of marriage, and she doubted that she ever would. He didn't seem to need

her except to be a wife in name and a mother to his children. For Nori, this was enough.

There was no good excuse for her behavior. She knew that. But at night, when Nori sat at the kitchen table to eat the dinner that had gotten cold because he'd come home late once again from another company gathering, she waited for something to come, some insight, some feeling. As she watched him with his eyes locked to his rice bowl, she wanted to shake him, because in all her life she had never expected this kind of loneliness. Around that time, someone had handed her a cult pamphlet as she came out of the grocery store. On the flimsy cover, a middle-aged housewife was pictured as half skeleton and half flesh. On the bottom of the page it said, "Every day you are closer to your death. You are half-dead already. Where does your identity come from?" She tossed the pamphlet away almost as soon as she got it, but the picture stayed with her for a long while.

The last time she saw the playboy, he gave her a sheaf of poems that he had written for her. As he left through the kitchen door, he confessed that he loved only her. His eyes pooled with tears as he told her that she was his heart. For the rest of the day, she ignored the housework and read and reread the maudlin and erotic poems. She couldn't say if they were good or not, but she was pleased by them. Etsuko privately marveled at the effort they must have taken, and she reasoned that in his showy way, he did love her. Finally, this one affair had given her what she had wanted from all the others—an assurance that whatever she had handed out so freely in her youth had neither died nor disappeared.

That night, when her family was sleeping, Etsuko soaked in the wooden tub and glowed in what felt to her like a victory. After her bath, she dressed in her blue-and-white *yukata* and headed toward her bedroom, where her innocent husband was snoring gently. One sad thing seemed clear to her: If she needed all the men who had ever loved her to continue loving her, she would always be divided. She would always cheat, and she'd never be a good person. It dawned on her then that being a good person was something she had not given up on completely after all. Would she die living this way? In the morning, she told the playboy not

to call her anymore, and he didn't. He just moved on to the next pretty housewife in town.

But a few months later, Nori found the poems that she should have destroyed, and he beat her for the first time in their marriage. Her sons tried to stop him, and Hana, just nine years old then, screamed and screamed. That evening, Nori threw her out, and she made her way to her sister's house. Later, the lawyer said it would be pointless for her to try to get custody of the children since she had no job and no skills. He coughed in what seemed like politeness or discomfort and said it would also be pointless because of what she had done. Etsuko nodded and decided to give up her children, thinking that she would not trouble them anymore. Then, following a want ad for a restaurant hostess, Etsuko moved to Yokohama, where she knew no one.

Etsuko wanted to believe that being with Mozasu was changing her. That she was sexually faithful to him, she took as proof. She had once tried to explain this to her sister, and Mari had replied, "A snake that sheds its skin is still a snake." And her mother, on hearing that Mozasu wanted to marry her, said, "*Honto*? To a pachinko Korean? Haven't you done enough to your poor children? Why not just kill them?"

The penalties incurred for the mistakes you made had to be paid out in full to the members of your family. But she didn't believe that she could ever discharge these sums.

At noon, Mozasu came to get her. They were going to pick up Solomon at his school to take him to get his alien registration card. Koreans born in Japan after 1952 had to report to their local ward office on their fourteenth birthday to request permission to stay in Japan. Every three years, Solomon would have to do this again unless he left Japan for good.

As soon as she got in the car, Mozasu reminded her to put on her seat belt. Etsuko was still thinking about Hana. Before she'd left, she had phoned the doctor, and the procedure was scheduled for the end of the week.

Mozasu took her hand. Etsuko thought his face had strength to it; there was power in his straight neck. She hadn't known many Koreans before

him, but she imagined that his squared-off facial features were traditionally Korean—his wide jawbone, straight white teeth, thick black hair, and
the shallow-set, narrow, smiling eyes. He had a lean, slack body that reminded her of metal. When he made love to her, he was serious, almost
as if he was angry, and she found that this gave her intense pleasure.
His physical movements were deliberate and forceful, and she wanted
to surrender to them. Whenever she read about something or someone
Korean, she wondered what Korea was like. Mozasu's deceased father, a
Christian minister, was from the North, and his mother, who'd had a confection business, had come from the South. His plainspoken mother was
so humble in her manner and dress that she could be mistaken for a modest housekeeper rather than the mother of a millionaire pachinko parlor
owner.

Mozasu was holding a wrapped present, the size of a block of tofu. She
recognized the silver foil paper from his favorite jewelry store.

"Is that for Solomon?"

"No. It's for you."

"*Ehh*? Why?"

It was a gold-and-diamond watch nestled in a dark red velvet box.

"It's a mistress watch. I bought it last week, and I showed it to Kuboda-
san, the new night floor manager, and he said that these fancy watches are
what you give to your mistress because they cost the same as a diamond
ring but you can't give a ring to your mistress since you're already married."

He raised his eyebrows with amusement.

Etsuko checked to see if the glass partition separating them from the
driver was closed all the way; it was. Her skin flushed with heat.

"Make him stop the car."

"What's the matter?"

Etsuko pulled her hand away. She wanted to say that she wasn't his
mistress, but instead, she burst into tears.

"Why? Why are you crying? Every year for the past three years, I bring
you a diamond ring—each one bigger than the one before it—and you say
no to me. I go back to the jeweler, and he and I have to get drunk. Nothing

has changed for me." He sighed. "You are the one who says no. Refuses the pachinko yakuza."

"You're not yakuza."

"I am not yakuza. But everyone thinks Koreans are gangsters."

"None of that matters to me. It's my family."

Mozasu looked out the window, and when he spotted his son, Mozasu waved at him.

The car stopped, and Solomon got in the front passenger seat. The glass partition opened, and he stuck his head through to say hi. Etsuko reached over to straighten the rumpled collar of his white dress shirt.

"*Arigato* very much," he said. They often mixed up words in different languages as a joke. He dropped back into his seat and closed the glass partition so he could talk with the driver, Yamamoto-san, about the previous night's Tigers game. The Tigers had an American manager this year, and Solomon was hopeful for the season. Yamamoto was not so optimistic.

Mozasu picked up her left wrist gently and clasped the watch on it.

"You're a funny woman. I bought you a gift. Just say thanks. I never meant that you were a—"

The bridge of her nose hurt, and she thought she would start crying again.

"Hana called. She's coming to Yokohama. Today."

"Is she okay?" He looked surprised.

Etsuko went to Hokkaido twice yearly to see her children. Mozasu had never met them.

"Maybe she can go to Solomon's party. See the famous singer," Mozasu said.

"I don't know if she likes Hiromi-san," she replied. Etsuko had no idea if Hana liked pop music. As a child, she hadn't been the kind who sang or danced. Etsuko stared at the back of the driver's gray-streaked head. The driver nodded thoughtfully while Solomon talked to him, and their quiet gestures appeared intimate. She wished she had something like baseball that she could talk about with her daughter—a safe subject they could visit without subtext or aggression.

Etsuko told Mozasu that Hana had an appointment with a doctor in Yokohama. When he asked if she was sick, she shook her head no.

This was how life had turned out. Her oldest, Tatsuo, was twenty-five years old, and it was taking him eight years to graduate from a fourth-rate college. Her second son, Tari, a withdrawn nineteen-year-old, had failed his college entrance exams and was working as a ticket collector at a movie theater. She had no right to expect her children to hold the aspirations of other middle-class people—to graduate from Tokyo University, to get a desk job at the Industrial Bank of Japan, to marry into a nice family. She had made them into village outcasts, and there was no way for them to be acceptable anymore.

Etsuko unclasped the watch and put it back in the velvet case. She laid it down in the space between them on the white, starched doily covering the black leather seats. He handed it back to her.

"It's not a ring. Save me a trip to the jeweler."

Etsuko held the watch case in her hands and wondered how they'd stayed together with him not giving up and her not giving in.

The Yokohama ward office was a giant gray box with an obscure sign. The first clerk they saw was a tall man with a narrow face and a shock of black hair buzzed off at the sides. He stared at Etsuko shamelessly, his eyes darting across her breasts, hips, and jeweled fingers. She was over-dressed compared to Mozasu and Solomon, who wore white dress shirts, dark slacks, and black dress shoes. They looked like the gentle Mormon missionaries who used to glide through her village on their bicycles when she was a girl.

"Your name—" The clerk squinted his eyes at the form Solomon was filling out. "So-ro-mo-n. What kind of name is that?"

"It's from the Bible. He was a king. The son of King David. A man of great wisdom. My great-uncle named me." The boy smiled at the clerk as if he was sharing a secret. He was a polite boy, but because he had gone to school with Americans and other kinds of foreigners at his international schools, he sometimes said things that a Japanese person would never have said.

"So-ro-mo-n, a king. Great wisdom." The clerk smirked. "Koreans don't have kings anymore."

"What did you say?" Etsuko asked.

Quickly, Mozasu pulled her back.

She glanced at Mozasu. His temper was far worse than hers. Once, when a restaurant guest had tried to make her sit with him, Mozasu, who happened to be there that night, walked over, picked him up bodily, and threw him outside the restaurant, breaking the man's ribs. She was expecting no less of a reaction now, but Mozasu averted his eyes from the clerk and stared at Solomon's right hand.

Mozasu smiled.

"Excuse me, sir," he said with no trace of irritation or anger. "We're in a hurry to return home, because it's the boy's birthday. Is there anything else we should do?" Mozasu folded his hands behind him. "Thank you very much for understanding."

Confused, Solomon turned to Etsuko, and she flashed him a warning look.

The clerk pointed to the back of the room and told Mozasu and Etsuko to sit. Solomon remained standing opposite the clerk. In the long, rectangular room, shaped like a train car, with bank teller windows running parallel along opposite walls, half a dozen people sat on benches, reading their newspapers or manga. Etsuko wondered if they were Korean. From their seats, Etsuko and Mozasu could see Solomon talking to the clerk, but they couldn't hear anything.

Mozasu sat down, then got up again. He asked if she wanted a can of tea from the vending machine, and she nodded yes. She felt like slapping the clerk's face. In middle school, she had once slapped a bossy girl, and it had been satisfying.

When Mozasu returned with their tea, she thanked him.

"You must have known—" She paused. "You must have warned him. I mean, you told him that today would not be so easy?" She didn't mean to be critical, but after the words came from her mouth, they sounded harsh, and she was sorry.

"No. I didn't say anything to him." He opened and closed his fists

rhythmically. "I came here with my mother and brother, Noa, for my first registration papers. The clerk was normal. Nice even. So I asked you to come. I thought maybe having a woman by him might help." He exhaled through his nostrils. "It was stupid to wish for kindness."

"No. No. You couldn't have warned him. I shouldn't have said it like that."

"It is hopeless. I cannot change his fate. He is Korean. He has to get those papers, and he has to follow all the steps of the law perfectly. Once, at a ward office, a clerk told me that I was a guest in his country."

"You and Solomon were born here."

"Yes, my brother, Noa, was born here, too. And now he is dead." Mozasu covered his face with his hands.

Etsuko sighed.

"Anyway, the clerk was not wrong. And this is something Solomon must understand. We can be deported. We have no motherland. Life is full of things he cannot control so he must adapt. My boy has to survive."

Solomon returned to them. Next he had his photograph taken, and afterward, he had to go to another room to get fingerprinted. Then they could go home. The last clerk was a plump woman; her light green uniform flattened her large breasts and round shoulders. She took Solomon's left index finger and gently dipped it into the pot filled with thick black ink. Solomon depressed his finger onto a white card as if he were a child painting. Mozasu looked away and sighed audibly. The clerk smiled at the boy and told him to pick up the registration card in the next room.

"Let's get your dog tags," Mozasu said.

Solomon faced his father. "Hmm?"

"It's what we dogs must have."

The clerk looked furious suddenly.

"The fingerprints and registration cards are vitally important for government records. There's no need to feel insulted by this. It is an immigration regulation required for foreign—"

Etsuko stepped forward. "But you don't make your children get fingerprinted on their birthday, do you?"

The clerk's neck reddened.

"My son is dead."

Etsuko bit her lip. She didn't want to feel anything for the woman, but she knew what it was like to lose your children—it was like you were cursed and nothing would ever restore the desolation of your life.

"Koreans do lots of good for this country," Etsuko said. "They do the difficult jobs Japanese don't want to do; they pay taxes, obey laws, raise good families, and create jobs—"

The clerk nodded sympathetically.

"You Koreans always tell me that."

Solomon blurted out, "She's not Korean."

Etsuko touched his arm, and the three of them walked out of the airless room. She wanted to crawl out of the gray box and see the light of outdoors again. She longed for the white mountains of Hokkaido. And though she had never done so in her childhood, she wanted to walk in the cold, snowy forests beneath the flanks of dark, leafless trees. In life, there was so much insult and injury, and she had no choice but to collect what was hers. But now she wished to take Solomon's shame, too, and add it to her pile, though she was already overwhelmed.

10

One of her mother's waitresses had brought her a Coke, and Hana was sitting at a table near the bar, playing with the straw. No longer permed, her hair was straight and its natural color, a reddish black. It was cut in one even length and splayed across her small shoulders. She wore a neatly ironed, white cotton blouse and a dark pleated skirt coming to her knees, with gray wool stockings and flat schoolgirl shoes. She hadn't dressed like this since she was in primary school. Her stomach was flat, but her bud-like breasts looked fuller; otherwise, there was no way of knowing that she was pregnant.

Closed for a private event, the restaurant dining room was set up for the party. White linen cloths covered a dozen round tables, and in the middle of each sat an elegant floral arrangement and candlesticks. A busboy stood at the edge of the room, blowing up one red balloon after another with a helium tank. He let them all float up to the ceiling.

Etsuko and Solomon entered the restaurant quietly. He had insisted on coming by the restaurant to say hello to her daughter before heading home to change. At first, his mouth opened in surprise at the decorations and the dramatic transformation of the room. Then, seeing the girl at the empty table, he asked, "Is that her?"

"Yes."

Hana smiled shyly at them.

Solomon and Hana greeted each other formally. Their mutual curiosity

was obvious. Hana pointed to the balloons hiding the ceiling, and before Etsuko had a chance, Solomon replied quickly in Japanese, "It's my birthday. Why don't you come to the party? There's going be an American dinner here tonight, and then we're going to a real disco."

Hana answered, "If you wish. I might."

Etsuko frowned. She had to speak to the chef about the menu, but she was reluctant to leave them alone. A few minutes later, when she returned from the kitchen, they were whispering like a pair of young lovers. Etsuko checked her watch and urged Solomon to get home. At the door, he shouted, "Hey, I'll see you at the party," and Hana smiled like a courtesan as she waved good-bye.

"Why did you make him go? I was having fun."

"Because he has to get dressed."

"I looked in them." Hana glanced at the bags near the entrance. There were a hundred party bags in four long rows that had to be transported to the disco—each bag filled with tapes, a Sony Walkman cassette player, imported teen magazines, and boxed chocolates.

"I wish my dad was a yakuza."

"Hana, he's not—" Etsuko looked around to see if anyone could hear them.

"Your boyfriend's son doesn't seem like a brat."

"He doesn't have it easy."

"Not easy? American private schools, millions in the bank, and a chauffeur. Get some perspective, Mother."

"Today, he had to go to the ward office to request permission to stay in Japan for another three years. If he was denied, he could have been deported. He has to carry around an alien registration card and—"

"Oh, really? But he wasn't deported, right? Now he gets a fancy party that's nicer than most weddings."

"He was born in this country, and he had to be fingerprinted today on his birthday like he was a criminal. He's just a child. He didn't do anything wrong."

"We're all criminals. Liars, thieves, whores—that's who we are." The girl's carbon-colored eyes looked hard and ancient. "No one is innocent here."

"Why must you be so hard-hearted?"

"I'm the only one who still talks to you."

"I've said I'm sorry enough times." Etsuko tried to control her voice, but the waitresses heard everything, and suddenly it didn't matter anymore.

"I made the appointment."

Hana looked up.

"The day after tomorrow, we'll take care of your problem." Etsuko looked straight at her daughter's pale, angry face. "You shouldn't be a mother. You have no idea how hard it is to have children."

The steady line of Hana's lips crumpled, and she covered her manga-pretty face with her hands and began to cry.

Etsuko didn't know if she should say something. Instead, she put her hand on her daughter's head. Hana winced, but Etsuko didn't immediately pull her hand back. It had been so long since she had touched her daughter's satiny hair.

When Etsuko lived in the cramped, three-bedroom house in Hokkaido with its leaky roof and tiny kitchen, certain labors had sustained her. At this moment, with a kind of pinprick pain, Etsuko recalled watching her sons devour the shrimp that she had fried for dinner, piled high on paper-lined plates. Even in the middle of July, it had been worth it to stand in front of a hot tempura pan, dropping battered shrimp into bubbling peanut oil, because to her sons, Mama's shrimp was better than candy, they'd said. And it came to her like a tall and dark wave how much she'd loved combing Hana's freshly washed hair when her cheeks were still pink from the steamy bathwater.

"I know you didn't want us. My brothers told me, and I told them they were wrong even though I knew they weren't. I clung to you because I wasn't going to let you just leave what you started. How can you tell me how hard it is to have children? You haven't even tried to be a mother. What right do you have? What makes you a mother?"

Etsuko grew silent, utterly transfixed by the realization that how she saw herself was actually how her children saw her, too. They thought she was a monster.

"How can you think that I didn't want the three of you?" She recalled all the letters, gifts, and money she'd sent, which the boys had returned. And worse, the phone calls to the house to check on them when her husband wouldn't say anything beyond *moshi-moshi*, then would hand the phone to Hana because she was the only one who would take the receiver. Etsuko wanted to justify herself—her numerous and repeated attempts—to offer proof. Being a mother was what defined her more than any other thing—more than being a daughter, wife, divorced woman, girlfriend, or restaurant owner. She hadn't done it well, but it was who she was, and it was what had changed her inside forever. From the moment Tatsuo was born, she had been filled with grief and self-doubt because she was never good enough. Even though she had failed, being a mother was eternal; a part of her life wouldn't end with her death.

"But, but, I didn't marry Mozasu. I don't even live with him. So I wouldn't make things worse for you and your brothers."

Hana tilted her head back and laughed.

"Am I supposed to thank you for this great sacrifice? So you didn't marry a Korean gangster, and you want me to congratulate you for this? You didn't marry him because you didn't want to suffer. You're the most selfish person I know. If you want to sleep with him and take his money to set up a fancy place and not marry him, that's your self-serving choice. You didn't do it for me or my brothers." Hana dried her face with her shirt sleeve. "You don't want to be judged. That's why you haven't married him. That's why you left Hokkaido to hide out in the big city. You think you're such a victim, but you're not. You left because you're afraid, and you slept with all those men because you were afraid of getting old. You're weak and pathetic. Don't tell me about sacrifices, because I don't believe in such crap."

Hana started to cry again.

Etsuko slumped in her chair. If she married Mozasu, it would prove to everyone in Hokkaido that no decent Japanese man would touch a woman like her. She would be called a yakuza wife. If she married him, she'd no longer be considered the tasteful owner of a successful restaurant in the best part of Yokohama—an image she only half believed herself. Mozasu

must have thought that she was a better person than she actually was, but Hana wasn't fooled. Etsuko picked up Hana's travel bag next to her chair and nudged her daughter to stand up to go.

Etsuko's apartment was in a luxury building four blocks from the restaurant. On the way there, Hana said she didn't want to go to the party anymore. She wanted to be left alone so she could sleep until morning. Etsuko unlocked the front door to her apartment and led Hana to her bedroom. She would sleep on the sofa tonight.

Hana lay across the futon, and Etsuko pulled a light comforter over her thin young body and turned out the light. Hana curled into herself; her eyes were still open, and she said nothing. Etsuko didn't want to leave her. Despite everything, it struck her that what she was feeling was a kind of contentedness. They were together again. Hana had come to her for care. Etsuko sat down on the edge of the bed and stroked her daughter's hair.

"You have this scent," Hana said quietly, "I used to think it was your perfume. Joy, *nee*?"

"I still wear that."

"I know," Hana said, and Etsuko resisted the urge to sniff her own wrists.

"It's not just the perfume, though, it's all the other creams and things that you wear, and it makes up this smell. I used to walk around department stores wondering what it was. The smell of *mama*."

Etsuko wanted to say many things, but above all that she would try not to make any more mistakes. "Hanako—"

"I want to go to sleep now. Go to that boy's party. Leave me alone." Hana's voice was flat but more tender this time.

Etsuko offered to stay, but Hana waved her away. Etsuko mentioned then that her schedule was open the next day. Maybe they could go and buy a bed and a dresser. "Then you can always come back and visit me. I can make up a room for you," Etsuko said.

Hana sighed, but her expression was blank.

Etsuko couldn't tell what her daughter wanted. "I'm not saying you

have to go. Especially after—" Etsuko put her fingertips across her lips, then quickly removed them. "You can stay. Start school here even."

Hana shifted her head on her pillow and inhaled, still saying nothing.

"I can call your father. To ask."

Hana pulled the blanket up to her chin. "If you want."

Etsuko had to go back to the restaurant, but she settled on the sofa for a few minutes. When she had been a young mother there used to be only one time in her waking hours when she'd felt a kind of peace, and that was always after her children went to bed for the night. She longed to see her sons as they were back then: their legs chubby and white, their mushroom haircuts misshapen because they could never sit still at the barber. She wished she could take back the times she had scolded her children just because she was tired. There were so many errors. If life allowed revisions, she would let them stay in their bath a little longer, read them one more story before bed, and fix them another plate of shrimp.

II

The children invited to Solomon's party were the sons and daughters of diplomats, bankers, and wealthy expatriates from America and Europe. Everyone spoke English rather than Japanese. Mozasu had chosen the international school in Yokohama because he liked the idea of Westerners. He had specific ambitions for his son: Solomon should speak perfect English as well as perfect Japanese; he should grow up among worldly, upper-class people; and ultimately, he should work for an American company in Tokyo or New York—a city Mozasu had never been to but imagined as a place where everyone was given a fair shot. He wanted his son to be an international man of the world.

A line of black limousines snaked along the street. As the children left the restaurant, they thanked Mozasu and Etsuko for the fine dinner they'd eaten. Mozasu lined up the children in front of the restaurant and instructed, "Ladies first," a saying he had picked up from watching American movies. The girls trooped into the gleaming cars in sixes and drove away. Then the boys followed. Solomon rode in the last car with his best friends, Nigel, the son of an English banker, and Ajay, the son of an Indian shipping company executive.

The disco was dimly lit and glamorous. From the high ceiling, twenty or so mirrored balls hung at different heights, flooding the large room with tiny panes of light that flashed and swayed with the movements of the

balls. They had the effect of making anyone who walked across the floor shimmer like a fish underwater. After everyone arrived and sat down at the lounge tables, the manager, a handsome Filipino, got up on the elevated stage. He had a beautiful, round voice.

"Dear friends of Solomon Baek! Welcome to Ringo's!" He paused for the children's cheers. "For Solomon's birthday fiesta, Ringo's presents the hottest star in Japan—one day the world: Ken Hiromi and the Seven Gentlemen!"

The children didn't seem to believe him. The curtain rose to reveal the seven-piece rock band, and the singer emerged from the back. Hiromi looked utterly normal, almost disappointingly so. He dressed like a businessman who'd forgotten his necktie and wore thick-framed eyeglasses just like the ones on his album covers. His hair was impeccably combed. He couldn't have been more than thirty.

Solomon kept shaking his head, bewildered and delighted. The band was loud, and the kids rushed to the stage to dance wildly. When the long set ended, the emcee asked everyone to gather around the stage, and Ichiro, the cook, wheeled a spectacular ice cream cake shaped like a base-ball diamond toward Solomon. Tall thin candles lit the large surface of the cake. A girl shouted, "Don't forget to make a wish, baby!"

In one huff, Solomon blew out the candles, and everyone clapped and hollered.

Etsuko handed him the beribboned knife so he could cut the first slice. A spotlight shone on him as he poised the long, serrated blade over the cake.

"Do you need help?" she asked.

"I think I got it," he said, using both hands to make a straight cut.

"Oh," she uttered, seeing the ink under his nails. He'd washed off most of it, but a shadow of the stain remained on his fingertips.

Solomon looked up from what he was doing and smiled.

Etsuko guided his arm lightly to return him to his task. After the first slice, Solomon gave the knife back to her, and she cut the remaining pieces. Waiters passed out the cake, and Hiromi, who was sitting by him-self, accepted a piece. Mozasu gave Solomon a fat blue envelope filled

with yen notes and told him to give it to the singer. Ken Hiromi motioned to Solomon to sit down. In this light, Etsuko thought, no one else would notice the ink.

The band played another set, then a DJ played popular songs for the kids. As the party wound down, Etsuko felt pleasantly exhausted—the way she did after the restaurant closed. Mozasu was sitting in a booth drinking champagne by himself, and she sat down beside him. Mozasu refilled his glass and handed it to her, and she drank it in two gulps. She laughed. He said she did a good job for Solomon, and Etsuko shook her head. "*Iie.*"

Without thinking, she said, "I think she would have been pleased."

Mozasu looked confused. A moment later, he nodded. "Yes, she would have been so happy for him."

"What was she like?" Etsuko shifted her body to see his face. Little squares of light danced across his sharp features.

"I've told you before. She was a nice lady. Like you." It was difficult to say any more than that about Yumi.

"No, tell me something specific about her." Etsuko wanted to know how they were different, not how they were the same. "I want to know more."

"Why? She is dead." Mozasu looked hurt after saying this. He noticed that Solomon was now dancing with a tall Chinese girl with short hair. His forehead glistened with sweat as he followed the girl's elegant moves. Etsuko stared into her empty champagne glass.

"She wanted to name him Sejong," he said. "But it's tradition for the husband's father to name the grandson. My father's dead so my Uncle Yoseb named him Solomon." He paused. "Sejong was a king in Korea. He invented the Korean alphabet. Uncle Yoseb gave him the name of a king from the Bible instead. I think he did it because my father was a minister." He smiled.

"Why are you smiling?"

"Because Yumi"—Mozasu said her name out loud, and it surprised him to hear the sound of the two syllables—"was so proud of him. Her

son. She wanted to give him the life of a king. She was like my father and uncle, I think. Proud. She was proud of me and my work. It was nice. But now that I'm older, I wonder why." Mozasu sounded wistful. "What do we Koreans have to be so proud of?"

"It's good to be proud of your children." She smoothed down her skirt. When her children had been born, what she had felt was amazement at their physical perfection. She had marveled at their miniature human form and their good health. But not once did she consider a name taken from history—the name of a king. She had never been proud of her family or her country; if anything, she was ashamed.

"One of those girls came up to me today and said Solomon looked like his mother." He pointed to a cluster of girls in the corner of the room. They wore bandeau tops and jersey skirts clinging to their thin hips.

"How could she know that?"

"She meant you."

"Oh." Etsuko nodded. "I wish I was his mother."

"No. No, you don't." Mozasu said this calmly, and she felt like she deserved that.

"I'm no better than that woman clerk this afternoon, *nee*?"

Mozasu shook his head and placed his hand over hers.

Why did her family think pachinko was so terrible? Her father, a traveling salesman, had sold expensive life insurance policies to isolated housewives who couldn't afford them, and Mozasu created spaces where grown men and women could play pinball for money. Both men had made money from chance and fear and loneliness. Every morning, Mozasu and his men tinkered with the machines to fix the outcomes—there could only be a few winners and a lot of losers. And yet we played on, because we had hope that we might be the lucky ones. How could you get angry at the ones who wanted to be in the game? Etsuko had failed in this important way—she had not taught her children to hope, to believe in the perhaps-absurd possibility that they might win. Pachinko was a foolish game, but life was not.

Etsuko removed her new watch and put it in his hand. "It's not that I don't want a ring—"

Mozasu didn't look at her, but he put the watch in his pocket.

"It's late. Almost midnight," he said gently. "The children have to get home."

Etsuko rose from the table and went to hand out the party bags.

Not wanting the evening to end, Solomon claimed that he was hungry, so the three of them returned to her restaurant. The place was clean again and looked open for business.

"A little bit of everything," he said when she asked him what he wanted to eat. He looked so happy, and it pleased her to see him like this. She could count on him to be a happy person. Maybe that was what Solomon was for her and Mozasu.

At the very back of the dining room, Mozasu sat down at a table for four and opened his evening-edition newspaper. He looked like a middle-aged man waiting calmly for his train to arrive. Etsuko headed for the kitchen with Solomon trailing her.

She put down three white plates on the prep counter. From the refrigerator, she pulled out the tray of fried chicken and the bowl of potato salad—dishes that Ichiro had made following an American cookbook.

"Why didn't Hana come? Is she sick?"

"No." Etsuko didn't like to lie to a direct question.

"She's pretty, you know."

"Too pretty. That's her problem." Her own mother had once said this about her when a family friend had complimented Etsuko.

"Did you have fun tonight?" she asked.

"Yeah. I still can't believe it. Hiromi-san talked to me."

"What did he say?" She put two large pieces of chicken on Mozasu's and Solomon's plates and a small drumstick on hers. "Was he nice?"

"Very nice and cool. He said his best friends are Korean. He told me to be good to my parents."

Solomon hadn't denied her as his mother, and though this should have been a nice thing, it only made her feel more anxious.

"Your father told me tonight that your mother was proud of you. From the moment you were born."

Solomon said nothing.

She didn't think that he should need a mother anymore; he was already grown up, and he was doing better than most kids she knew who had mothers who were alive. He was almost a man.

"Come to the sink. Hold out your left hand."

"A present?"

She laughed and put his left hand over the sink basin and turned on the faucet. "There's still ink left."

"Can they make me leave? Really deport me?"

"Everything went well today," she replied, and softly scrubbed the pads of his fingers and nails with a dishwashing brush. "There's no need to worry, Solomon-chan."

He seemed satisfied with her answer.

"Hana told me she came to Yokohama to get rid of her little problem. Is she pregnant? Nigel got his girlfriend pregnant, and she had to get an abortion."

"Your friend Nigel?" She remembered the blond-haired boy who played Atari with him on the weekends. He was only a year older than Solomon.

He nodded. "Yup. Hana seems great."

"My children hate me."

Solomon picked at the ink beneath his fingernails. "Your kids hate you because you're gone." His face grew serious. "They can't help it. They miss you."

Etsuko bit the inside of her lower lip. She could feel the small muscles inside her mouth, and she stopped herself from drawing blood. She was afraid to look at his face, and though she had tried to restrain herself, she burst into tears.

"Why? Why are you crying?" he asked. "I'm sorry." Solomon's eyes welled up.

She inhaled to calm her breathing.

"When Hana was born, the nurses put her footprints on a card. They washed the ink off, but not very well, so when I went home I had to get it off. I don't think she could see anything really, because she was just born,

but I felt like she was looking at me like I was hurting her, and she just cried and cried—"

"Etsuko-chan, Hana will be okay. Nigel's girlfriend is fine. They might get married after college. That's what he said—"

"No, no. It's not that. I'm just so sorry that you might have thought that I didn't want to be your mother." She clutched her stomach, and she tried to regulate her breath. "I've hurt so many people. And you're such a good boy, Solomon. I wish I could take credit for you."

His dark, straight hair clung to the sides of his face, and he didn't brush it away. His eyes strained with worry.

"But I was born today, and isn't it funny how no one gets to remember that moment and who was there? It's all what's told to you. You're here now. You are a mother to me."

Etsuko covered her mouth with her open palm and let his words go through her. Somewhere after being sorry, there had to be another day, and even after a conviction, there could be good in the judgment. At last, Etsuko shut off the water and put down the swollen yellow sponge in the sink. The curved brass spout let go its last few drops, and the kitchen grew silent. Etsuko reached over to hold the child on his birthday.

12

Osaka, 1979

Sunja had left her son and grandson Solomon in Yokohama and returned to Osaka when she learned that her mother, Yangjin, had stomach
cancer. Through fall and winter, Sunja slept at the foot of her mother's
pallet to relieve her exhausted sister-in-law, Kyunghee, who had been
nursing Yangjin faithfully after her own husband, Yoseb, finally died.

Yangjin lived on her thick cotton pallet, more or less immobile, in the
front room, which had effectively become her bedroom. The largest room
in the house smelled of eucalyptus and tangerines. The floor had been
lined recently with fresh tatami mats, and a double row of greenery in ceramic pots flourished by the two sparkling windows. The large basket by
the pallet, filled to the brim with Kyushu tangerines—a costly gift from
fellow parishioners at the Korean church in Osaka—released a glorious
scent. The new Sony color television was on, its volume low, as the three
women waited to watch Yangjin's favorite program, *Other Lands.*

Sunja sat on the floor beside her mother, who was sitting up as well as
she could, and Kyunghee remained at her usual place on the other side of
the pallet by Yangjin's head. Both Sunja and Kyunghee were knitting sections of a navy woolen sweater for Solomon.

Strangely, as Yangjin's limbs and joints quit, one after the other, and as
her muscles softened into jelly, her mind felt clearer and more free. She
could imagine leaving her body to run swiftly like a deer. Yet in life, she
could hardly move at all; she could barely eat anything recognizable as

food. Nevertheless, the unexpected dividend of this illness was that for the first time in her life, perhaps since the moment she was able to walk and perform any chores, Yangjin felt no compulsion to labor. It was no longer possible to cook meals, wash dishes, sweep the floors, sew clothing, scrub toilets, tend to the children, do laundry, make food to sell, or do whatever else needed doing. Her job was to rest before dying. All she had to do was nothing at all. At best, she had a few days left.

Yangjin wasn't sure what happened after this was over—but she felt she would go home either to all those who had died before or to *Yesu Kuristo* and his kingdom. She wanted to see her husband, Hoonie, again; once, in church, she'd heard a sermon that said that in heaven, the lame could walk and the blind could see. Her husband had opposed the idea of God, but she hoped that if there was a God, He would understand that Hoonie was a good man who had endured enough with the restrictions of his body and deserved to be well. Whenever Yangjin tried to talk about dying, Kyunghee and Sunja would change the subject.

"So did you send the money to Solomon?" Yangjin asked. "I wanted you to send crisp, new bills from the bank."

"Yes, I sent it yesterday," Sunja replied, adjusting her mother's pillow so she could see the monitor better.

"When will he get it? I haven't heard from him."

"*Umma*, he'll get the card tonight or tomorrow."

Solomon hadn't phoned to speak to his great-grandmother this week, but that was understandable. He had just had a big birthday party, and Sunja was the one who would have reminded him to write a letter or to phone someone to say thank you or just to check in on them. "He's probably busy with school. I'll phone later."

"So is the singer really a famous talent?" Yangjin asked. Mozasu had furnished the house and provided for their upkeep ever since the women closed their confection business; it was still difficult for Yangjin to grasp that her grandson Mozasu could have so much money that he could hire pop stars for his son's birthday party.

"That must be so expensive! Is he really a celebrity?"

"Well, that's what Etsuko said." Sunja was also curious as to how

Solomon was faring; he would have had to get his identification card for the first time. She had been worried about that.

The show came on, and Kyunghee bolted up to adjust the antenna. The picture improved. The familiar Japanese folk music for the program drifted into the room.

"Where will Higuchi-san go today?" Yangjin smiled broadly.

In *Other Lands*, the interviewer Higuchi-san, a spry, ageless woman with dyed black hair, traveled all over the globe and interviewed Japanese people who had immigrated to other lands. The interviewer was no ordinary woman of her generation; she was unmarried, childless, and a skilled world-traveling journalist who could ask any intimate question. She was reputed to have Korean blood, and the rumor alone was enough for Yangjin and Kyunghee to find Higuchi-san's pluck and wanderlust relatable. They were devoted to her. When the women still ran their little confection shop, they'd rush straight home as soon as they closed to avoid missing even a minute of the program. Sunja had never been interested in the show, but now she sat through it for her mother's sake.

"Pillows!" Yangjin cried, and Sunja fixed them.

Kyunghee clapped her hands as the opening credits rolled. Despite all the restrictions, she had always hoped that Higuchi-san could somehow go to North Korea. Koh Hansu had told her husband that her parents and in-laws were dead, yet she still yearned to hear news of home. Also, she wanted to know if Kim Changho was safe. No matter how many sad stories she heard from the others whose family members had gone back, she could not imagine that the handsome young man with the thick eyeglasses had died.

As the opening music faded, a disembodied male voice announced that today, Higuchi-san was in Medellín to meet an impressive farming family who now owned the largest chicken farm in Colombia. Higuchi-san, wearing a light-colored raincoat and her famous green *boshi*, marveled how the Wakamura family had decided to migrate to Latin America at the end of the nineteenth century and how well they had raised their children to be good Japanese in the world. *"Minna nihongo hanase-masu!"* Higuchi-san's voice was full of wonder and admiration.

The camera zoomed in on Señora Wakamura, the surviving matriarch, a tiny, wrinkled woman who looked far older than her actual age of sixty-seven. Her large, sloping eyes, buried beneath layers of crepey, folded skin, appeared wise and thoughtful. Like her siblings, she was born in Medellín.

"Things were very difficult for my parents, of course. They didn't speak Spanish and didn't know anything about chickens. Father died of a heart attack when I was six, then Mother raised us by herself. My oldest brother stayed here with our mother, but our other two brothers went to study in Montreal, then returned. My sisters and I worked on the farm."

"That must have been difficult, difficult work," Higuchi-san exclaimed breathlessly.

"A woman's lot is to suffer," Señora Wakamura said.

"*Soo, soo.*"

The camera panned to show the interior of the cavernous farm, a moving sea of white feathers comprised of tens of thousands of fluffy chickens; brilliant red combs streaked the pale, fluttering mass.

At Higuchi-san's behest, Señora Wakamura listed the number of chores that she'd had since she was tall enough to sprinkle chicken feed and avoid getting pecked.

"How very hard all this must have been," Higuchi-san repeated, trying not to wince from the noxious odors.

Señora Wakamura shrugged. Her stoicism was undeniable as she showed all the moving parts of a working chicken farm, including lifting heavy machinery while trudging through muddy fields.

At the end of the thirty-minute program, Higuchi-san asked Señora Wakamura to say something to the viewers in Japanese.

The woman farmer with the ancient face turned to the camera shyly, then looked away like she was thinking.

"I have never been to Japan"—she frowned—"but I hope that wherever I am in life and whatever I do, I can be a good Japanese. I hope to never bring shame to my people."

Higuchi-san grew teary and signed off. As the closing credits rolled, the announcer said that Higuchi-san was now heading to the airport to reach

the next destination of *Other Lands*. "Till we countrymen meet again!" the announcer said brightly.

Sunja got up and turned off the television. She wanted to head to the kitchen to boil some water for tea.

"*Go-saeng*," Yangjin said out loud. "A woman's lot is to suffer."

"Yes, *go-saeng*," Kyunghee nodded, repeating the word for suffering.

All her life, Sunja had heard this sentiment from other women, that they must suffer—suffer as a girl, suffer as a wife, suffer as a mother— die suffering. *Go-saeng*—the word made her sick. What else was there be- sides this? She had suffered to create a better life for Noa, and yet it was not enough. Should she have taught her son to suffer the humiliation that she'd drunk like water? In the end, he had refused to suffer the conditions of his birth. Did mothers fail by not telling their sons that suffering would come?

"You're upset about Noa," Yangjin said, "I know. He's all that you ever think about. First it was Koh Hansu, and now it's Noa. You're suffering because you wanted that terrible man. A woman can't make a mistake like that."

"What else should I have done?" Sunja blurted out, then immediately regretted doing so.

Yangjin shrugged, almost in comic imitation of the woman farmer. "You brought shame on your child by having that man as his father. You caused your own suffering. Noa, that poor boy, came from a bad seed. You're fortunate that Isak married you. What a blessing that man was. Mozasu came from better blood. That's why he's so blessed in his work."

Sunja covered her mouth using both hands. It was said often that old women talked too much and said useless things, but it seemed like her mother had been storing these specific thoughts in reserve for her. This was like some sort of mean inheritance her mother had been planning to give her. Sunja couldn't fight her. What was the point?

Yangjin pursed her lips, then inhaled deeply through her nostrils.

"That man was bad."

"*Umma*, he brought you here. If he hadn't brought you—"

"That's true that he brought me here, but he was still awful. You can't change that. That poor boy didn't have a chance," Yangjin said.

"If Noa didn't have a chance, then why did I suffer? Why should I have even tried? If I'm so foolish, if I made such unforgivable mistakes, is that your fault?" Sunja asked. "I don't, I don't...I won't blame you."

Kyunghee looked at Yangjin imploringly, but the old woman seemed oblivious to her silent pleas.

"Sister," Kyunghee said gently. "May I get you something? To drink?"

"No." Yangjin turned to Sunja, pointing to Kyunghee. "She's been better to me than my own family. She cares more about me than you do. You just care about Noa and Mozasu. You only came back when you learned that I was going to die. You don't care about me. You don't care about anyone else except your children." Yangjin bawled.

Kyunghee touched Yangjin's arm gently.

"Sister, this is not what you mean. Sunja had to take care of Solomon. You know that. You said it yourself so many times. And Mozasu needed his mother's help after Yumi died," she said quietly. "Sunja has suffered so much. Especially after Noa—" Kyunghee could barely say Noa's name. "And you, you have had whatever you needed here, right?" She tried to sound as soothing as possible.

"Yes, yes, you have always done your best for me. I wish Kim Changho could have stayed in Japan. Then he could have married you after your husband died. I worry that after I die who will take care of you. Sunja-ya, you must take care of Kyunghee. She can't stay here by herself. *Aigoo*, if only Kim Changho hadn't rushed off to the North and probably gotten himself killed. *Aigoo*. The poor man probably died for nothing."

Kyunghee crumpled visibly.

"*Umma*, your medicine is making you say crazy things," Sunja said.

"Kim Changho only went to Korea because he couldn't marry our Kyunghee, and he couldn't suffer any more waiting," Yangjin said, having stopped crying. It was like watching a toddler whose tears could stop at will. "He was much nicer than Yoseb. After his accident, Yoseb was a drunk, but Kim Changho was a real man. He would've made our wonderful Kyunghee happy, but he's dead. Poor Kim Changho. Poor Kyunghee."

Seeing Kyunghee's shocked expression, Sunja said firmly, "*Umma,* you should go to sleep. We're going to leave you to rest. You must be tired. Come on, let's go to the back room and finish the knitting," Sunja said, helping Kyunghee up. At the door, Sunja turned out the light.

"I'm not tired! You're going to leave again, are you? When things get difficult, it's easy to leave. Fine. I'll die now, then you won't have to stay here, and you can rush back to your precious Mozasu! I never created a burden for you one single day of my life. Until I couldn't move, every minute I have been here, I have worked to support myself. I never took a yen above what I needed to eat and to put a roof over our heads. I always held up my share, you know. I raised you when your kindhearted father died—" At the mention of her husband, Yangjin began to cry again, and Kyunghee rushed to her, unable to watch her being so miserable.

Sunja watched Kyunghee pat her mother gently until she quieted down. Her mother was unrecognizable to her; it would have been easy to say that the illness had changed her, but it wasn't so simple, was it? Illness and dying had revealed her mother's truer thoughts, the ones her mother had been protecting her from. Sunja had made a mistake; however, she didn't believe that her son came from a bad seed. The Japanese said that Koreans had too much anger and heat in their blood. Seeds, blood. How could you fight such hopeless ideas? Noa had been a sensitive child who had believed that if he followed all the rules and was the best, then somehow the hostile world would change its mind. His death may have been her fault for having allowed him to believe in such cruel ideals.

Sunja knelt at her mother's pallet.

"I'm sorry, *umma.* I'm sorry. I'm sorry I was away. I'm sorry about everything."

The old woman looked weakly at her only child, hating herself suddenly. Yangjin wanted to say she was sorry, too, but strength passed from her body, forcing her to close her eyes.

13

"You're not a Christian, are you?" Hana asked Solomon. She was sitting next to him in the pew. The minister had just finished eulogizing his great-grandmother, and the organist began to play "What a Friend We Have in Jesus." The funeral service would end after the song and a closing prayer.

Solomon tried to shush Hana politely, but as ever, she was persistent.

"It's like a cult, *nee*? But you don't do anything interesting like get naked outdoors in a group or sacrifice babies? I read that people in America do things like that if they are serious Christians. But you don't seem like one of those. You probably have to give lots of your money away since you're rich, right?"

Hana was whispering to him in Japanese with her lips close to his ear, and Solomon made a serious face like he was trying to concentrate. He could smell her strawberry lip gloss.

He didn't know how to reply. Some Japanese did believe that Christianity was a cult. His friends at school who were foreigners didn't see it this way, but he didn't know many Japanese who were Christians.

Hana poked him in the ribs with her left pinkie finger while looking straight ahead at the choir.

The choir was singing his great-grandmother's favorite hymn. She used to hum it often.

Like everyone in his family, Solomon was a Christian. His paternal

grandfather, Baek Isak, had been one of the early Presbyterian ministers in Osaka. When Solomon was growing up, people at church referred to his grandfather as a martyr because he had been jailed for his faith and had died upon his release. Sunja, Mozasu, and Solomon went to service each Sunday.

"It's almost over, *nee?* I need a beer, Solomon. Let's go? I've been a good girl, and I sat through the whole thing."

"Hana, she was my great-grandmother," he said at last. Solomon remembered her as a gentle old woman who smelled like orange oil and biscuits. She didn't speak much Japanese but always had treats and coins for him in her dark blue vest pockets.

"We should be more respectful."

"Great-granny is now in heaven. Isn't that what Christians say?" Hana mimicked a peaceful face.

"Still, she's dead."

"Well, you don't seem very upset. Your grandmother Sunja doesn't seem very sad," she whispered. "Anyway, you're a Christian, right?"

"Yeah, I am a Christian. Why do you care so much?"

"I want to know what happens after you die. What happens to babies that die?"

Solomon didn't know what to say.

After her abortion, Hana had moved in with her mother. She'd refused to go back to Hokkaido and spent her days hanging out at Etsuko's restaurant, bored and irritated by everything. She couldn't handle the English at Solomon's school, and she hated kids her own age and refused to go to the local high school. Etsuko was trying to figure out what Hana should do, but in the meantime, Hana had decided that Solomon was her project and followed him around at every opportunity.

Like everyone else, Solomon thought that Hana was exceptionally pretty, but Etsuko warned him that her daughter was a troublemaker and that he should befriend girls from his school.

"Finally! The prayer is over. Come on, we can get out now before the exits clog up." Hana elbowed him gently, then pulled him out of his chair, and he let her lead him out of the building.

* * *

In the brightly lit alley behind the church, Hana leaned backward with one foot remaining on the ground and the other leg bent against the wall. She was smoking a cigarette. Again, she asked him why they couldn't get beers.

There were kids at his school who drank, but Solomon didn't like the taste much, and his friends invariably got in trouble when drunk. His father wouldn't have gotten mad at him for stuff like that, and in a way, Solomon felt free to say no to his friends at parties because it wasn't a big deal. But it was difficult to say no to Hana, because she was relentless when it came to what she wanted. Hana already thought he was too square.

Hana inhaled her cigarette deeply, making a lovely pout as she exhaled.

"No beer. Respects his great-grandmother's funeral. Never angry at his father. Oh, Solomon, maybe you can be a minister."

She clasped her hands in prayer and closed her eyes.

"I'm not going to be a minister. But what should I do when I grow up?" he asked.

An older boy at school had told a bunch of guys that all women are whores and all men are killers; girls cared about your future job because they wanted to marry rich guys.

"I don't know, Minister Pachinko." She laughed. "Hey, Christians aren't supposed to fuck before marriage, right?"

Solomon buttoned his suit jacket. It felt chilly outside, and his coat was still hanging in the hall closet upstairs.

"You're still a virgin," she said, smiling. "I know. That's okay. You're only fourteen. Do you want to?"

"What?"

"With me? I can, you know." She sucked on her cigarette again, even more suggestively. "I've done it. A lot. I know what you'll like." Hana held the necktie his father had tied for him that morning by the knot, then released her grasp slowly.

Solomon refused to look at her face.

The back door of the church opened slowly. Etsuko waved to them from the threshold.

"It's cold. Why don't you come inside? Solomon, you should be with your dad to greet the guests, right?"

Solomon could hear the anxiety in Etsuko's voice. Hana tossed her cigarette and followed him inside.

At the reception, Hana continued to trail after Solomon. She asked him to guess her bra size. Solomon had no idea, but he was now thinking of her breasts.

The guests, mostly old people, left them alone, so the two milled around the reception.

"Let's get beer at the 7-Eleven. We can go to my house to drink it. Or we can go to the park."

"I don't feel like beer."

"Maybe you feel like having some pussy."

"Hana!"

"Oh, shut up. You like me. I know you do."

"Why do you have to talk like that?"

"Because I'm not a nice girl, and you don't want to fuck a nice girl. Especially for your first time. Nobody does. I don't want to marry you, Solomon. I don't need your money."

"What are you talking about?"

"Fuck you," Hana said, and walked away from him.

Solomon caught up with her and grabbed her arm.

Hana gave him a chilly smile. It was as if she'd become someone else. She was wearing a dark blue wool dress with a white Peter Pan collar that made her look younger than him.

His grandmother Sunja appeared.

"*Halmoni*," Solomon said, relieved to see her. He felt excited around Hana, but she also made him nervous and afraid. In her presence, it felt safer to have an adult around. Just yesterday, he caught her stealing a packet of chocolate wafers at the *conbini*. When she left the shop, Solomon had lingered to give the clerk the money for the wafers, worried that the clerk might get in trouble. In his dad's business, if items were missing, clerks were fired immediately.

Sunja smiled at them. She touched Solomon's upper arm as if to calm him. He looked flustered.

"You look very handsome in your suit."

"This is Hana," Solomon said, and Hana bowed to her formally.

Sunja nodded. The girl was very beautiful, but she had a defiant chin.

Sunja was on her way to talk with Mozasu but felt funny leaving Solomon with the beautiful girl.

"I'll see you at home afterwards?" she asked.

Solomon nodded.

As soon as Sunja turned in the other direction, the girl led him outside the building.

Koh Hansu was walking with a cane. When he spotted Sunja walking diagonally across the reception room, he called out to her.

Sunja heard his voice; this was too much.

"Your mother was a tough woman. I always thought she was tougher than you."

Sunja stared at him. In the moments before her death, her mother had said that this man had ruined her life, but had he? He had given her Noa; unless she had been pregnant, she wouldn't have married Isak, and without Isak, she wouldn't have had Mozasu and now her grandson Solomon. She didn't want to hate him anymore. What did Joseph say to his brothers who had sold him into slavery when he saw them again? "You intended to harm me, but God intended it for good to accomplish what is now being done, the saving of many lives." This was something Isak had taught her when she'd asked him about the evil of this world.

"I came by to see if you were okay. If you needed anything."

"Thank you."

"My wife died."

"I'm sorry to hear that."

"I could never divorce her because her father was my boss. He had adopted me."

A while back, Mozasu had explained to her that after Hansu's father-

in-law retired, Hansu became the top man in the second most powerful yakuza family in all of Kansai.

"You don't have to explain anything to me. We don't have anything to talk about, you and I. Thank you for coming today."

"Why do you have to be so cold? I thought you'd marry me now."

"What? This is my mother's funeral. Why are you still alive and my Noa gone? I couldn't even go to my own child's—"

"He was my only—"

"No, no, no. He was my son. Mine."

Sunja marched to the kitchen, leaving him leaning on his cane. She could not stop sobbing, and when the women in the kitchen saw her, they embraced her. A woman she did not know rubbed her back gently. They thought she was grieving for her mother.

14

Yokohama, 1980

It was too exciting, and Solomon had never been with anyone. Hana knew a lot, so she taught him to think about other things, to close his eyes if he got too excited, because it was important for him to wait until she was done. Girls would not want to fuck again if he came in a minute, she said. Solomon did everything Hana told him to do, not just because he was in awe of her, but because he wanted to make her happy. He would have done almost anything to make her laugh, because even though she was smart, too lovely to bear almost, and thrilling, she was also sad and restless. She could not be still; she could not bear not to drink every day. It was also important for her to have sex, so for six months she made him her ideal lover, even though he was not yet fifteen. She was almost seventeen.

It started after Yangjin's funeral. Hana bought beer, and they went to Etsuko's apartment. She removed her dress and blouse, then she took off his clothes. She pulled him to her bed, put a rubber on his cock, and showed him what to do. He was amazed at her body, and she was amused by his happiness. Hana was not angry that he came right away—she had expected this—but after he did, she started her lessons.

Almost every day, they met at Etsuko's place and made love several times. Etsuko was never home, and Solomon told his grandmother that he was with friends. He went home for dinner, because his father expected him at the table, and usually she went to Etsuko's restaurant for her meal.

After being with her, Solomon felt different; he felt older and more serious about life. He was still a boy; he knew that, but he started to think about how he could be with her all the time, not just after school and during breaks. When he was at school, he did as much work as possible so he could see her without thinking about schoolwork. His father expected good grades, and Solomon was a strong student. When he wasn't with her, he wondered what she did when she went out. Often, he worried about losing her to an older boy, but she said there was nothing to worry about.

Etsuko and Mozasu did not know they were having sex, and Hana told Solomon that they must never know. She told him, "I'm your secret girl, and you are my secret boy, *nee?*"

One afternoon, about four months in, Solomon came over to the apartment and found Hana waiting for him wearing flesh-colored lingerie and high heels. She looked like a petite-sized centerfold in *Playboy*.

"Do you have any money, Solomon?" she asked.

"Yeah, sure. Why?"

"I want some. I have to buy things to turn you on. Like this. Pretty, *nee?*"

Solomon tried to embrace her, but she pushed her left hand out gently.

"Money, please."

Solomon pulled out his billfold and took out a thousand-yen note.

"What do you need it for?" he asked.

"I just do. Do you have any more?"

"Uh, sure." Solomon pulled out the emergency five-thousand-yen note that he kept folded in a square behind the wallet-sized photograph of his mother. His father told him he always had to have some money just in case something important came up.

"Give it to Hana-chan, please."

Solomon handed it to her, and Hana put it on the table with the thousand-yen note.

Hana walked slowly to the shelf where Etsuko kept a radio and fiddled with the channels until she found a pop song she liked. She bent over and started swaying her hips in time to the music, making sure that he was

watching her. Solomon went to her, and she turned around and unbuttoned his jeans. Without saying a word, she pushed him into the armchair near her and got on her knees. Solomon never knew what she was going to do.

Hana slid the straps of her lace-trimmed brassiere over her shoulders and pulled out her breasts over the small cups so he could see her nipples. He tried to touch them, but she swatted him away. With her hands cradling his bottom, she started to suck him.

When he was done, he saw that she was crying.

"Hana-chan, what's the matter?"

"Go home, Solomon."

"What?"

"You're finished."

"I came to see you. What's this all about?"

"Go home, Solomon! You're just this little boy who wants to fuck. I need money, and this isn't enough. What am I going to do?"

"What are you talking about?"

"Go home and do your homework. Go have dinner with your daddy and granny! You're all the same. I'm just a kid with divorced parents. You think I'm nothing. You think I'm a loser because my mother was the town whore."

"What are you talking about? Why are you mad at me? I don't think that, Hana. I could never think that. You can come over, too. I thought you were going to your mother's restaurant after I left."

Hana covered her breasts and went to the bathroom to get her robe. She returned, wearing a red *yukata*. She got really quiet, then told him to get more money and come back the next day.

"Hana, we are friends, *nee*? I love you. All the money I have, you can have. I have cash at home from my birthday presents, but my grandmother keeps it for me in her bureau. I can't take it out all at once. What do you need it for?"

"I have to go, Solomon. I can't stay here anymore. I have to be independent."

"Why? No. You can't go."

Every day and night, he had been thinking of what he could do for work so they could live together. They were too young to marry, but he thought that after he graduated from high school, he could get a job and he could take care of her. He would marry her. Once, she had said that if she married, she would never divorce, because she could never do that to her children. Her brothers and she had been treated worse than lepers after her mother left, she'd said. But Solomon's father wanted him to go to college in America. How could he leave her behind? He wondered if she would come with him. They could marry after he finished college.

"Solomon, I'm going to go to Tokyo and get a real life. I'm not going to stay in this apartment and wait for a fifteen-year-old to come and fuck me."

"What?"

"I have to do something with my life. Yokohama is stupid, and I'd rather be dead than return to Hokkaido."

"How about that school your mom found?"

"I can't go to school. I'm not smart like you. I want to be on television, like those girls in the dramas, but I don't know how to act. I can't sing, either. I have a terrible voice."

"Maybe you can learn how to act and sing. Aren't there schools for that? Can't we ask your mom to find you a school?"

Hana brightened for a moment, then looked disappointed again.

"She'd just think it's foolish. She wouldn't help me. Not for that. Besides, I can't read well, and you have to be able to read your lines and memorize them. I saw this really good actress interviewed on TV, and she said that she works really hard at reading and memorizing. I'm not good at anything—except sex. But what do I do when I'm not pretty anymore?"

"You'll always be beautiful, Hana."

She laughed.

"No, dummy. Women lose their looks fast. My mother is looking old. She better keep your dad. She's not going to do any better."

"Can you work for your mom?"

"No, I'd rather die. I hate the smell of shoyu and oil in my hair. It's

disgusting. I can't imagine bowing all day to lazy, fat customers who complain about nothing. She hates the customers, too. She's a hypocrite."

"Etsuko is not like that."

"That's because you don't know her."

Solomon stroked her hair, and Hana opened her robe and slipped off her panties.

"Can you do it now? Again?" she asked. "I need that thing inside me, you know? It's always better the second time, because it lasts longer."

Solomon touched her, and he could.

Every day, she asked for money, and every day he gave her some of his birthday money from the bureau until there was no more left. Whenever he came over, she wanted to try things, even when it hurt her a lot, because she told him that she needed to master this. Even if he didn't like a certain method, she made him practice it and play certain roles. She learned how to make sounds and to talk the way girls talked in sex movies. A week after the money ran out, Solomon found a note she had hidden in his pencil case: "One day, you will find a really good girl, not someone like me. I promise. But it was fun, *nee*? I am your dirty flower, Soro-chan." That afternoon, Solomon ran to Etsuko's apartment, and he learned that she was gone. He didn't see her again until three years later when she met him at a famous *unagiya* in Tokyo to give him a sweater before he went to college in New York.

15

New York, 1985

Where are you?" Solomon asked in Japanese. "Your mom doesn't know where you are. Everyone's worried."

"I don't want to talk about her," Hana replied. "So you have a girlfriend-o now?"

"Yes," Solomon answered without thinking. "Hana, are you okay?" No matter how many drinks she'd had, she tended to sound sober.

"Tell me about her. Is she Japanese?"

"No." Solomon wanted to keep her on the line. About five years before, after she moved out of Etsuko's apartment, she took a long string of hostessing jobs in Tokyo, refusing to tell anyone where she lived. Etsuko didn't know what to do anymore; she'd hired an investigator but had little luck tracking her down. "Hana, tell me where you are, and please call your mother—"

"Shut up, college boy. Or else I'll hang up."

"Oh, Hana. Why?" He had to smile, having missed even her petulance. "Why are you so difficult, Hana-chan?"

"And why are you so far away?"

Hana poured herself a smaller glass of wine, and Solomon heard the *glug* of the liquid hitting the glass. It was morning in Tokyo, and she was sitting on the bare floor of her tiny apartment in Roppongi, which she shared with three other hostesses. Two were sleeping off the whiskey tea from the night before, and the third hadn't returned home from a date.

"I miss you, Solomon. I miss my old friend. You were my only friend. You know that?"

"You're drinking. Are you okay?"

"I like to drink. Drinking makes me happy. I'm very good at drinking." She laughed and swallowed a thimbleful of wine. She wanted to make the bottle last. "I'm good at drinking and fucking. *Soo desu nee.*"

"Can you please tell me where you are?"

"I'm in Tokyo."

"Still working in a club in Roppongi?"

"Yes, but at another club. You don't know which one." She had been fired two nights ago, but she knew she could get another job. "I am an excellent hostess."

"I'm sure you would be excellent at whatever you decide to do."

"You do not approve of my work, but I do not care. I am not a prostitute. I pour drinks and make conversation with incredibly boring men and make them feel fascinating."

"I didn't say that I didn't approve."

"You lie."

"Hana-chan, why don't you go to school? I think you would like college. You're smarter than most of the kids here. Maybe you can study in America; learn English first, then apply to a college here. Your mom and my dad would pay for it. You know that."

"Why don't I finish high school first?" Hana replied tartly. "Hang on, is your girlfriend with you now?"

"No, but I have to meet her soon."

"No, you will not meet her, Solomon. You will talk to me. Because you are my old friend, and I want to talk to my old friend tonight. Can you cancel? And I will call you back."

"I'll call you. Yes, I'll cancel, then I'll call you back."

"I am not giving you my number. You cancel with girlfriend-o, and I will call you in five minutes."

"Are you okay, Hana?"

"Why don't you say you miss me, too, Solomon? You used to miss me desperately. Don't you remember?"

"Yes, I remember everything."

When they met for lunch after being apart for three years, she gave him a crimson-colored cashmere sweater from Burberry as a graduation present. "It's cold in Manhattan, *nee*? The sweater is bloodred and hot like our burning love." During the meal, however, she would not come close to him. She wouldn't even touch his arm. She had smelled wonderful, like jasmine and sandalwood.

"How could I forget you?" Solomon said quietly. Phoebe would be coming by in a few minutes. She had the key to his room.

"Ah, there. There is my Solomon. I can tell when you are hungry for me."

Solomon closed his eyes. She was right; this felt like hunger. It had been nothing short of physical pain when she had left him, and he'd had no words to describe her departure. He loved Phoebe, but it wasn't what he'd felt for Hana.

"Hana-chan. I have to go now, but may I please phone you later? May I please have your number?"

"No, Solomon. You may not have my number. I call you when I want to speak to you. You do not call me. Nobody calls me."

"And you get to leave when you want to leave," he said.

"Yes, I do get to leave, but Solomon, you will never tire of me, because I will never ask anything of you. Except for today. I want you to talk to me so I can go to sleep. I cannot sleep anymore, Solomon. I do not know why, but I cannot sleep anymore. Hana-chan is so tired."

"Why won't you let your mother help you? I'm in New York. You won't even tell me your number. How can I help—"

"I know, I know, you are studying and becoming an international businessman of the world! This is what your rich papa wants, and Solomon is a good boy and he will make his pachinko papa proud!"

"Hana, you have to be careful with the drinking, *nee*?" He tried to sound calm. She would disappear if he sounded cross.

The door opened, and it was Phoebe, looking happy at first, then puzzled because he was on the phone. Solomon smiled and gestured for her to sit down beside him. The dorm room had only a narrow bed and a ser-

viceable desk, but he was lucky to have a single. He put his finger to his lips, and Phoebe mouthed to ask if she should go. He paused, then shook his head no.

"Will you cancel with your girlfriend-o and help me sleep?" Hana asked. "If you were here, you'd fuck me, and I would sleep in your arms. We never got a chance to sleep in the same bed, because you were still a boy. Now you are twenty. I want to suck on your man cock."

"What do you want me to do, Hana? How can I help you?"

"So-lo-mon-Ul-tra-man. You should sing. You should sing to me. You know, the song about sunshine. I like that baby song about sunshine."

"I will sing if you will give me your phone number."

"You have to promise me that you will not give it to my mother."

"Okay. What is it?" Solomon wrote down the numbers on the backflap of his macroeconomics textbook. "I'm going to hang up, and then I will call you in a few seconds, okay?"

"Okay," she said weakly. She had finished the second bottle already. She felt awake but heavy, like her limbs were soaked through. "I'll hang up now. Call me. I want to hear you sing."

When he hung up, Phoebe asked, "Hey, what's going on?"

"One minute. Just one minute. I'll explain."

He dialed his father, and Mozasu picked up.

"Papa, this is Hana's number. I think she's really sick. Can you find out where she is just from this number? Can you ask Haruki or Etsuko's investigator? I better go. I have to call her back now. She sounds like she's drunk or drugged out."

Solomon dialed the number. It was for a Chinese restaurant in Roppongi.

Phoebe took off her overcoat and stripped down and got into bed. Her dark hair hung loosely around her pale collarbone.

"Who was that?"

"Hana. My stepmother's daughter."

"Which makes her your stepsister? The one who's working as a hooker."

"She's not a hooker. She's a hostess."

"They have sex for money, right?"

"No. Not always. Sometimes. Depends."

"Well, gosh, that's a major distinction. Once again, you've enlightened me on the finer points of Japanese culture. Thank you."

The phone rang, and Solomon rushed to pick up. It was Etsuko this time.

"Solomon. The number. It was for a Chinese restaurant."

"Yes, I'm sorry. But I did speak to her, Etsuko. She was very drunk. She said she's working at a different club now. Didn't her former mama-san say anything about where she is now?"

"We couldn't find anything. She'd been fired from two other places. Every time we get closer, she gets fired for drinking too much."

"If I hear anything, I'll let you know right away, okay?"

"It is night there, *nee?*"

"*Hai.* Hana said she couldn't sleep. I was worried she was taking speed while drinking. I heard girls do that at clubs."

"You should go to sleep, Solomon. Mozasu said you're doing well in school. We're proud of you," she said. "Night-night, Solomon-chan."

Phoebe smiled.

"So you lost your cherry to your hooker half sister, and now she's in trouble."

"Compassionate of you."

"Quite liberal and tolerant of me not to be upset that your ex is calling you drunk when she's a professional sex worker. Either I'm confident in my value, or I'm confident in our relationship, or I'm just ignorant of the fact that you're going to hurt my feelings when you return to a troubled young damsel whom I know you're interested in rescuing."

"I can't rescue her."

"You just tried and failed, because she does not want your help. She wants to die."

"What?"

"Yes, Solomon. This young woman wants to die." She pushed back his

forelocks and looked at him kindly. She kissed him on the mouth. "There are a lot of troubled young women in this world. We can't save them all."

Hana didn't phone him again. Months later, Etsuko learned that she was working in a Kabukicho *toruko-buro* where she bathed men for money. The investigator told her what time Hana would finish her shift, and Etsuko waited outside the building. Several girls came out, and Hana was the last to leave. Etsuko couldn't believe how much she'd aged. The investigator had explained that Etsuko might not recognize her because she would look much older. Hana's face was withered and dry. She wore no makeup, and her clothes didn't look clean.

"Hana," Etsuko said.

Hana saw her, then walked in the other direction.

"Leave me alone."

"Hana, oh, please, Hana."

"Go away."

"Hana, we can forget all this. Start again. I shouldn't have tried to make you go to school. I'm sorry."

"No."

"You don't have to work here. I have money."

"I don't want your money. I don't want the pachinko man's money. I can earn my own."

"Where do you live? Can we go to your place to talk?"

"No."

"I'm not going to go away."

"Yes, yes, you will. You're selfish."

Etsuko stood there, believing that if she could just listen and suffer, then maybe her daughter could be saved.

"I am terrible. *Soo desu.* Forgive me, Hana. Anything but this."

Hana dropped her large tote bag from her shoulder, and the two wine bottles wrapped in a towel made a muffled clinking sound on the pavement. She wept openly, her arms hanging by her side, and Etsuko knelt on the ground and held her daughter's knees, refusing to let her go.

16

Tokyo, 1989

Solomon was glad to be back home. The job at Travis Brothers was turning out better than expected. The pay was more than he deserved for a job a year out of college, and he enjoyed the numerous benefits of being hired as an expat rather than as a local. The HR people at Travis got him a fancy rental broker who found him a decent one-bedroom in Minami-Azabu, which Phoebe didn't think was too awful. As his corporate employer, Travis was named guarantor on the lease, since Solomon was legally a foreigner in Japan. Solomon, who had grown up in Yokohama in his father's house, had never rented an apartment before. For non-Japanese renters, requiring a guarantor was common practice, which, of course, incensed Phoebe.

After some cajoling, Phoebe had decided to follow him to Tokyo. They were thinking of getting married, and moving together to Japan was the first step. Now that she was here, he felt bad for her. Solomon was employed at the Japanese subsidiary of a British investment bank, so he worked alongside Brits, Americans, Aussies, Kiwis, and the occasional South African among the Western-educated locals, who were less parochial than the natives. As a Korean Japanese educated in the States, Solomon was both a local and a foreigner, with the useful knowledge of the native and the financial privileges of an expatriate. Phoebe, however, did not enjoy his status and privileges. Rather, she spent her days at home reading or wandering around Tokyo, not sure why she was here

at all since Solomon was rarely home. It was impossible for her to get a work visa, as they weren't married; she was thinking of teaching English, but she didn't know how to get a tutoring job. Now and then, when a Japanese person asked her an innocent question like if she was South Korean, Phoebe tended to overreact.

"In America, there is no such thing as a *Kankokujin* or *Chosenjin*. Why the hell would I be a South Korean or a North Korean? That makes no sense! I was born in Seattle, and my parents came to the States when there was only one Korea," she'd shout, relating one of the bigotry anecdotes of her day. "Why does Japan still distinguish the two countries for its Korean residents who've been here for four fucking generations? You were born here. You're not a foreigner! That's insane. Your father was born here. Why are you two carrying South Korean passports? It's bizarre."

She knew as well as he did that after the peninsula was divided, the Koreans in Japan ended up choosing sides, often more than once, affecting their residency status. It was still hard for a Korean to become a Japanese citizen, and there were many who considered such a thing shameful—for a Korean to try to become a citizen of its former oppressor. When she told her friends in New York about this curious historical anomaly and the pervasive ethnic bias, they were incredulous at the thought that the friendly, well-mannered Japanese they knew could ever think she was somehow criminal, lazy, filthy, or aggressive—the negative stereotypical traits of Koreans in Japan. "Well, everyone knows that the Koreans don't get along with the Japanese," her friends would say innocently, as if all things were equal. Soon, Phoebe stopped talking about it with her friends back home.

Solomon found it peculiar that Phoebe got so angry about the history of Koreans in Japan. After three months of living in Tokyo and reading a few history books, she'd concluded that the Japanese would never change. "The government still refuses to acknowledge its war crimes!" Strangely, in these conversations, Solomon found himself defending the Japanese.

They planned on visiting Seoul together for a week when the deal season ended and work slowed down. He hoped Seoul would be some sort

of neutral territory for them—a place to feel normal since they were both Korean immigrants of a kind. And it didn't hurt that Phoebe spoke very good Korean; his Korean was pathetic at best. He had visited South Korea with his father several times, and everyone there always treated them like they were Japanese. It was no homecoming; however, it was great to visit. After a while, it had been easier just to play along as Japanese tourists who had come to enjoy the good barbecue rather than to try to explain to the chest-beating, self-righteous Koreans why their first language was Japanese.

Solomon was in love with Phoebe. They had been together since sophomore year. He couldn't imagine life without her, and yet, seeing her discomfort here made him realize how different they were. They were both ethnically Korean and had grown up outside Korea, but they weren't the same. Back home, on the ground in Japan, their differences seemed that much more pronounced. They hadn't had sex in two weeks. Would it be that way when they married? Would it get worse? Solomon thought about these things as he headed to the game.

Tonight was his fourth poker night with the guys at work. Solomon and one other junior associate, Louis, a *hapa* M & A guy from Paris, had been asked to join; the rest of the players were managing directors and executive directors. The cast changed a little, but there were usually six or seven guys. Never any girls. Solomon was a brilliant poker player. In the first game, he had played it easy and come out neutral; in the second game, when he felt more comfortable, he came second, and after the third game, Solomon walked out with most of the 350,000-yen pot. The others were annoyed, but he thought it was worth making a point—when he wanted to win, he could.

This evening, he planned to pay up a little. The guys were a good bunch—no sore losers; Solomon hoped to keep playing with them. No doubt, they had invited him thinking he was more or less a fish; they didn't know that he was an econ major at Columbia who had double minored in poker and pool.

They played Anaconda, also called "Pass the Trash" because you could get rid of your bad cards to the guy on your left—first three cards,

then two cards, and then one more, betting all the while. A moron could have won the game, because there was so much luck involved, but what Solomon enjoyed was the betting. He liked watching others bet or go out.

The players met in the paneled basement of a no-name *izakaya* in Roppongi. The owner was a friend of Kazu-san, Solomon's boss and the most senior managing director at Travis, and he let them use the room once a month as long as they drank enough and ordered plenty of food. Each month, one guy hosted and picked up the tab. Initially, the managing directors thought it wasn't fair to make the associates pay, since they earned much less, but after Solomon won on the third game, enough of them said "The kid can buy dinner." Solomon was hosting this one.

Six guys were playing, and the pot was 300,000 yen. Three hands in, Solomon kept it safe: He won nothing and lost nothing.

"Hey, Solly," Kazu said, "what's going on? Did luck leave you, buddy?"

His boss, Kazu, was a Japanese national who was educated in California and Texas, and despite his bespoke suits and elegant Tokyo dialect, his English speech pattern was pure American frat boy. His family tree was filled with dukes and counts who had been stripped of their titles after the war, and his mother's side came from connected branches of shogun families. At Travis, Kazu made lots of rain. Five of the six most important banking deals last year took place because Kazu had made them happen. It was also Kazu who had brought Solomon into the game. The older guys grumbled about losing to the kid, but Kazu shut them up, saying that competition was good for everyone.

Solomon liked his boss; everyone did. He was lucky to be one of Kazu's boys and to be invited to the famous monthly poker games. There were guys in Kazu's team who had worked for Travis for ten years and had never been asked. Whenever Phoebe said Japanese people were racist, Solomon would bring up Etsuko and Kazu as personal evidence for his argument to the contrary. Etsuko was the obvious example of a Japanese person who was kindhearted and ethnically unbiased, but Phoebe barely understood her, since Etsuko's English was terrible. Kazu was Japanese, and he had been far kinder to Solomon than most Koreans in Japan, who

had occasionally eyed him with suspicion as a wealthy man's son or as competition at school. Yes, some Japanese thought Koreans were scum, but some Koreans were scum, he told Phoebe. Some Japanese were scum, too. There was no need to keep rehashing the past; he hoped Phoebe would get over it eventually.

It was time to discard, take new cards, and place bets. Solomon threw away a useless nine of diamonds and a two of hearts, then picked up the jack and a three he needed for a full house. Luck had never left him. Whenever Solomon played cards, he felt strong and smooth, like he couldn't lose; he wondered if he felt this way because he didn't care about the money. He liked being at the table; he liked the bullshit guy talk. With this hand, he had a solid chance at the current pot, which was easily over a hundred thousand yen. Solomon bet thirty thousand. Louis and Yamada-san, the Japanese Aussie, folded, leaving Solomon, Ono, Giancarlo, and Kazu. Ono's face was blank and Giancarlo scratched his ear.

Ono bet another twenty thousand, and immediately, Kazu and Giancarlo folded. Giancarlo said, laughing, "You two are assholes." He took a long sip of his whiskey. "Are there any more of those chicken things on sticks?"

"*Yakitori,*" Kazu said, "You live in Japan; dude, learn what to call chicken on a stick."

Giancarlo gave him the finger, smiling and revealing his short, even teeth.

Kazu signaled to the waiter and ordered for everyone.

It was time to show hands, and Ono only had two pairs. He'd been bluffing.

Solomon fanned out his cards.

"You son of a bitch," Ono said.

"Sorry, sir," Solomon said, sweeping the money toward him in an easy, practiced manner.

"Never apologize for winning, Solly," Kazu said.

"He can apologize a little for taking my money," Giancarlo retorted, and the others laughed.

"Man, I can't wait until I put you on one of my deals. You will be hang-

ing out with boxes of due diligence all fucking weekend, and I will make sure you only get ugly girls to work with," Ono said. He had a doctorate in economics from MIT and was on his fourth marriage. Each successive wife was even more gorgeous than the prior one. As a very senior electronics banker during the Japan boom, he had made obscene money and still worked without stopping. Ono said that the purpose of hard work was simple: Sex with pretty women was worth whatever it took.

"I will find the worst deal with the maximum diligence. Just for you, my little friend." Ono rubbed his hands together.

"He's taller than you," Giancarlo said.

"Status trumps size," Ono replied.

"*Gomen nasai*, Ono-san, *gomen nasai*." Solomon bowed theatrically.

"Don't worry about it, Solly," Kazu said. "Ono's got a heart of gold."

"Not true. I'm capable of holding a grudge and taking vengeance at the most opportune moment," Ono said.

Solomon raised his eyebrows and shivered. "I'm just a boy, sir," he pleaded. "Have mercy." He proceeded to make neat stacks of cash in front of him. "A rich boy who deserves some mercy."

"I heard you were filthy rich," Giancarlo said. "Your dad's a pachinko guy, right?"

Solomon nodded, not sure how he knew.

"I used to date a hot Japanese *hapa* who played a lot of pachinko. She was an expensive habit. Figures you know how to gamble. It must be that clever Korean blood," Giancarlo said. "Man, that girl used to go on and on about the tricky and smart Koreans who owned all the parlors and made fools out of the Japanese—but, man, she used to do this crazy thing with her tits when—"

"Impossible," Kazu said. "You never dated a hot girl."

"Yeah, you got me, *sensei*. I dated your wife, and she's not very hot. She's just a real—"

Kazu laughed. "Hey, how 'bout if we play poker?" He poured soda into his whiskey, lightening the color considerably. "Solly won fair and square."

"I'm not saying anything bad. It's a compliment. The Koreans here are

smart and rich. Just like our boy Solomon. It wasn't like I was calling him a yakuza! You're not going to get me killed, are you, Solly?" Giancarlo asked.

Solomon smiled tentatively. It wasn't the first time he'd heard these things, but it had been a very long while since anyone had mentioned his father's business. In America, no one even knew what pachinko was. It was his father who'd been confident that there would be less bigotry at the offices of a Western bank and had encouraged him to take this job. Giancarlo wasn't saying anything different from what other middle-class Japanese people thought or whispered; it was just strange to hear such a thing coming from a white Italian who had lived in Japan for twenty years.

Louis cut the cards, and Kazu shuffled and dealt the guys a fresh hand.

Solomon had three kings, but he discarded them one by one in three consecutive rounds, then folded, losing about ten thousand yen. At the end of the night, he paid the tab. Kazu said he wanted to talk to him, so they walked out to the street to hail a taxi.

17

Y ou lost on purpose. The three kings came from you," Kazu said to Solomon. They were standing outside the *izakaya* building. Kazu lit a Marlboro Light.

Solomon shrugged.

"That was dumb. Giancarlo is a social retard. He's one of those white guys who has to live in Asia because the white people back home don't want him. He's been in Japan for so long that he thinks when Japanese people suck up to him, it's because he's so special. What a fucking fantasy. That said, not a bad guy overall. Effective. Gets shit done. You gotta know this by now, that people here, even the non-Japanese, say the dumbest things about Koreans, but you gotta forget it. When I was in the States, people used to say stupid-ass crap about Asians, like we all spoke Chinese and ate sushi for breakfast. When it came to teaching US history, they'd forget the internment and Hiroshima. Whatever, right?"

"That stuff doesn't get to me," Solomon replied, scanning the dark streets for a taxi. The trains had stopped running half an hour before. "I'm good."

"Okay, tough guy," Kazu said. "Listen, there is a tax, you know, on success."

"Huh?"

"If you do well at anything, you gotta pay up to all the people who did

worse. On the other hand, if you do badly, life makes you pay a shit tax, too. Everybody pays something."

Kazu looked at him soberly.

"Of course, the worst one is the tax on the mediocre. Now, that one's a bitch." Kazu tossed his cigarette and crossed his arms. "Pay attention: The ones who pay the shit tax are mostly people who were born in the wrong place and the wrong time and are hanging on to the planet by their broken fingernails. They don't even know the fucking rules of the game. You can't even get mad at 'em when they lose. Life just fucks and fucks and fucks bastards like that." Kazu wrinkled his brow in resignation, like he was somewhat concerned about life's inequities but not very. He took a deep breath. "So, those losers have to climb Mount Everest to get out of hell, and maybe one or two in five hundred thousand break out, but the rest pay the shit tax all their lives, then they die. If God exists and if He's fair, then it makes sense that in the afterlife, those guys should get the better seats."

Solomon nodded, not understanding where this was going.

Kazu's stare remained unbroken. "But all those able-bodied middle-class people who are scared of their shadows, well, they pay the mediocre tax in regular quarterly installments with compounding interest. When you play it safe, that's what happens, my friend. So if I were you, I wouldn't throw any games. I'd use every fucking advantage. Beat anyone who fucks with you to a fucking pulp. Show no mercy to chumps, especially if they don't deserve it. Make the pussies cry."

"So then the success tax comes from envy, and the shit tax comes from exploitation. Okay." Solomon nodded like he was starting to get it. "Then what's the mediocre tax? How can it be wrong to—?"

"Good question, young Jedi. The tax for being mediocre comes from you and everyone else knowing that you are mediocre. It's a heavier tax than you'd think."

Solomon had never thought of such a thing before. It wasn't like he saw himself as terribly special, but he'd never seen himself as mediocre, either. Perhaps it was unspoken, even to himself, but he did want to be good at something.

"Jedi, understand this: There's nothing fucking worse than knowing that you're just like everybody else. What a messed-up, lousy existence. And in this great country of Japan—the birthplace of all my fancy ancestors—everyone, everyone wants to be like everyone else. That's why it is such a safe place to live, but it's also a dinosaur village. It's extinct, pal. Carve up your piece and invest your spoils elsewhere. You're a young man, and someone should tell you the real truth about this country. Japan is not fucked because it lost the war or did bad things. Japan is fucked because there is no more war, and in peacetime everyone actually wants to be mediocre and is terrified of being different. The other thing is that the elite Japanese want to be English and white. That's pathetic, delusional, and merits another discussion entirely."

Solomon thought some of this made sense. Everyone he knew who was really Japanese did think he was middle-class even when he wasn't. Rich kids at his high school whose fathers owned several country-club memberships worth millions and millions thought of themselves as middle-class. His uncle Noa, whom he'd never met, had apparently killed himself because he wanted to be Japanese and normal.

An empty taxi approached them, but Solomon didn't notice, and Kazu smiled.

"So, yeah, idiots are going to get on your case and notice that your dad owns pachinko parlors. And how do people know this?"

"I never talk about it."

"Everyone knows, Solomon. In Japan, you're either a rich Korean or a poor Korean, and if you are a rich Korean, there's a pachinko parlor in your background somewhere."

"My dad is a great guy. He's incredibly honest."

"I'm sure he is." Kazu faced him squarely, his arms still crossed against his chest.

Solomon hesitated but said it anyway: "He's not some gangster. He doesn't do bad things. He's an ordinary businessman. He pays all his taxes and does everything by the book. There are some shady guys in the business, but my dad is incredibly precise and moral. He owns three parlors. It's not like—"

Kazu nodded reassuringly.

"My father's never taken anything that wasn't his; he doesn't even care about money. He gives away so much of it—"

Etsuko had told him that Mozasu paid the nursing home bills for several of his employees.

"Solly, Solly. No, man, there's no need to explain. It's not like Koreans had a lot of choices in regular professions. I'm sure he chose pachinko because there wasn't much else. He's probably an excellent businessman. You think your poker skills came out of a vacuum? Maybe your dad could have worked for Fuji or Sony, but it wasn't like they were going to hire a Korean, right? I doubt they'd hire you now, Mr. Columbia University. Japan still doesn't hire Koreans to be teachers, cops, and nurses in lots of places. You couldn't even rent your own apartment in Tokyo, and you make good money. It's fucking 1989! Anyway, you can be polite about it, but that's fucked up. I'm Japanese but I'm not stupid. I lived in America and Europe for a long time; it's crazy what the Japanese have done to the Koreans and the Chinese who were born here. It's fucking bonkers; you people should have a revolution. You don't protest enough. You and your dad were born here, right?"

Solomon nodded, not understanding why Kazu was getting so worked up about this.

"Even if your dad was a hit man, I wouldn't give a shit. And I wouldn't turn him in."

"But he's not."

"No, kid, of course he's not," Kazu said, smiling. "Go home to your girlfriend. I heard she's a looker and smart. That's good. Because in the end, brains matter more than you think," he said, laughing.

Kazu hailed a taxi and told Solomon to take it before him. Everyone said that Kazu wasn't like regular bosses, and it was true.

A week later, he put Solomon on the new real estate deal, and Solomon was the youngest one on the team. This was the cool transaction that all the guys in the office wanted. One of Travis's heavyweight banking clients wanted to purchase land in Yokohama to build a world-class golf course.

Nearly all the details had been worked out; they needed to get three of the remaining landowners to sign on. Two were not impossible, just expensive, but the third was a headache—the old woman had no interest in money and could not be bought out. Her lot was where the eleventh hole would be. At the morning meeting, with the client present, two of the banking directors gave a strong presentation about the beneficial ways of structuring the mortgage, and Solomon took careful notes. Right before the meeting broke up, Kazu mentioned casually that the old woman was still holding up progress. The client smiled at Kazu and said, "No doubt, you will be able to handle the matter. We are confident."

Kazu smiled politely.

The client left quickly, and everyone else scattered out of the conference room shortly thereafter. Kazu stopped Solomon before he had a chance to return to his desk.

"What are you doing for lunch, Solly?"

"I was going to grab something from downstairs. Why? What's up?"

"Let's go for a drive."

The chauffeur took them to the old woman's lot in Yokohama. The gray concrete building was in decent condition, and the front yard was well maintained. No one seemed to be home. An ancient pine tree cast a triangular shade across the facade of the square structure, and a thin brook gurgled from the back of the house. It was a former fabric-dyeing factory and now the private residence of the woman. Her children were dead, and there were no obvious heirs.

"So how do you get a person to do what you want when she doesn't want to?" Kazu asked.

"I don't know," Solomon said. He'd figured that this was a kind of field trip for Kazu, and his boss wanted the company. Rarely did Kazu go anywhere alone.

The car was parked in the wide, dusty street opposite the old woman's lot. If she was home, she would have noticed the black town car idling not ten yards from her house. But no one came outside or stirred within.

Kazu stared at the house.

"So this is where Sonoko Matsuda lives. The client is confident that I can get Matsuda-san to sell."

"Can you?" Solomon asked.

"I think so, but I don't know how," Kazu said.

"This will sound stupid, but how can you get her to sign if you don't know how?" Solomon asked.

"I'm making a wish, Solly. I'm making a wish. Sometimes, that's how it starts."

Kazu asked the chauffeur to take them to an *unagi* restaurant not far from there.

18

Yokohama, 1989

On Sunday morning, after church services, Solomon and Phoebe took the train to Yokohama for lunch with his family.

As usual, the front door of the house was closed but unlocked, so they let themselves in. A designer friend of Etsuko's had recently renovated it, and the house was unrecognizable from the one of Solomon's childhood filled with dark American furniture. The designer had removed most of the original interior walls and knocked out the small back windows, replacing them with thick sheets of glass. Now it was possible to see the rock garden from the front of the house. Pale-colored furniture, white oak floors, and sculptural paper lamps filled the vast quadrant near the woodburning stove, leaving the large, square-shaped living room light and uncluttered. In the opposite corner of the room, tall branches of forsythia bloomed in an enormous celadon-colored ceramic jar on the floor. The house looked like a glamorous Buddhist temple.

Mozasu came out from the den to greet them.

"You're here!" he said to Phoebe in Korean. When she spent time with Solomon's family, the group spoke three languages. Phoebe spoke Korean with the elders and English with Solomon, while Solomon spoke mostly in Japanese to the elders and English to Phoebe; with everyone translating in bits, they made it work somehow.

Mozasu opened the shoe closet by the door and offered them house slippers.

"My mother and aunt have been cooking all week. I hope you're hungry."

"Something smells wonderful," she said. "Is everyone in the kitchen?" Phoebe smoothed her navy pleated skirt.

"Yes. I mean, sorry, no. Etsuko couldn't be here today. She's very sad to miss you. She asked me to apologize."

Phoebe nodded, glancing briefly at Solomon. It seemed impolite for her to ask where Etsuko was, but she couldn't understand why Solomon didn't ask his father where she was. Phoebe was curious about Etsuko. She was the only person Phoebe couldn't speak to directly, because neither woman spoke the other's language. Also, she wanted to meet Hana, who was never around.

Solomon grabbed Phoebe's hand and led her to the kitchen. Around his family, he felt younger than usual, almost giddy. The scents of all his favorite dishes filled the wide hallway connecting the front of the house with the kitchen.

"Solomon is here!" he shouted, no different than when he'd come home from school as a boy.

Kyunghee and Sunja stopped their work immediately and looked up, beaming. Mozasu smiled, seeing their happiness.

"Phoebe is here, too, Solomon!" Kyunghee said. She wiped her hands on her apron, then came out from behind the thick marble counter to embrace him.

Sunja followed her and put her arm around Phoebe's waist. Sunja was a head shorter than Phoebe.

"This is for both of you." Phoebe gave her a box of candy from the Tokyo branch of an exclusive French chocolate shop.

Sunja smiled. "Thank you."

Kyunghee untied the ribbon to take a peek. It was a large box of glazed fruits dipped in chocolate. Delighted, she said, "This looks expensive. You kids should be saving money at your age. But the candies look so delicious! Thank you."

She inhaled the chocolate aroma dramatically.

"It's so good to have you here," Sunja said in Korean, folding Phoebe's slender shoulders into her thick embrace.

Phoebe loved being with Solomon's family. It was much smaller than her own, but everyone seemed closer, as if each member were organically attached to one seamless body, whereas her enormous extended family felt like cheerfully mismatched Lego bricks in a large bucket. Phoebe's parents had at least five or six siblings each, and she had grown up with well over a dozen cousins just in California. There were relatives in New York, New Jersey, DC, Washington State, and Toronto. She had dated a couple of Korean American guys and had met their families, but Solomon's family was different. Solomon's family was warm but far more muted and intensely watchful. None of them seemed to miss anything.

"Is that for *pajeon*?" Phoebe asked. The mixing bowl was filled with creamy pancake batter flecked with thin slices of scallion and chunks of scallops.

"You like *pajeon*? So does Solomon! How does your *umma* make it?" Kyunghee asked; her tone was casual, though she held strong opinions about the ratio of scallions to shellfish.

"My mother doesn't cook," Phoebe said, looking only a little embarrassed.

"What?" Kyunghee gasped in horror and turned to Sunja, who raised her eyebrows, sharing her sister-in-law's surprise.

Phoebe laughed.

"I grew up eating pizza and hamburgers. And lots of Kentucky Fried Chicken. I love the KFC corn on the cob." She smiled. "Mom worked in my dad's medical office as his office manager and was never home before eight o'clock."

The women nodded, trying to understanding this.

"Mom was always working. She did all the medical paperwork at the dining table next to us kids while we did our homework. I don't think she ever went to bed until midnight—"

"But you didn't eat any Korean food?"

Kyunghee couldn't comprehend this.

"On the weekends we ate it. At a restaurant."

The women understood that the mother was busy and hardworking, but it seemed inconceivable to them that a Korean mother didn't cook for her family. What would Solomon eat if he married this girl? What would their children eat?

"She didn't have time. That makes sense, but does your mother know how to cook?" Kyunghee asked tentatively.

"She never learned. And none of her sisters cook Korean food, either."

Phoebe laughed, because the fact that none of them cooked Korean food was a point of pride. Her mother and her sisters tended to look down at women who cooked a lot and constantly tried to make you eat. The four of them were very thin. Like Phoebe, they were the kind of women who were constantly moving around and seemed uninterested in eating because they were so absorbed in their work. "My favorite aunt cooks only on the weekends and only for dinner parties. She usually makes Italian food. Our family always meets at restaurants."

Phoebe found it amusing to see their continuing shock and disbelief at such a mundane detail of her childhood. What was the big deal? Why did women have to cook, anyway? she wondered. Her mother was her favorite person in the world. "My brother and sisters don't even like kimchi. My mother won't even keep it in the refrigerator because of the smell."

"*Waaah*," Sunja sighed. "You really are American. Are your aunts married to Americans?"

"My aunts and uncles are married to non-Koreans. My brother and sisters married ethnically Korean people, but they're Americans like me. My older brother-in-law, the lawyer, speaks fluent Portuguese but no Korean; he grew up in Brazil. America is full of people like that."

"Really?" Kyunghee exclaimed.

"Who are your aunts married to?"

"I have aunts and uncles by marriage who are white, black, Dutch, Jewish, Filipino, Mexican, Chinese, Puerto Rican, and, let's see, there's one Korean American uncle and three Korean American aunts. I have a lot of cousins. Everyone's mixed," she added, smiling at the older women wearing spotless white aprons, who were paying such careful attention to what she was saying that it looked as if their minds were taking notes.

"When we get together, like on Thanksgiving and Christmas, it's really fun."

"I've met several of them," Solomon said, worried that his grand-mother and great-aunt wouldn't approve of her family, although he could tell they were more curious than reproachful. Neither of them had ever said that he had to marry a Korean person, but he knew his father's rela-tionship with Etsuko made them uncomfortable.

When the frying pan was hot enough, Sunja poured a scant cup of the scallion pancake batter into it. She checked the edges and lowered the heat. Phoebe was lively and good for the boy, she thought. Her mother used to say a woman's life was suffering, but that was the last thing she wanted for this sweet girl who had a quick, warm smile for everyone. If she didn't cook, then so what? If she took good care of Solomon, then noth-ing else should matter, though she hoped that Phoebe wanted children. Lately, Sunja wanted to hold babies. How wonderful it would be not to have to worry about a war or having enough food to eat, or finding shelter. Solomon and Phoebe wouldn't have to labor the way she and Kyunghee had, but could just enjoy their children.

"When are you going to marry Solomon?" Sunja asked, without shift-ing her focus from the frying pan. An older woman had a right to ask this sort of thing, though she was still a little afraid to do it.

"Yes, when are you two getting married? What are you waiting for? My sister and I have nothing to do—we'll move to Tokyo if you want help with the babies and the cooking!" Kyunghee giggled.

Solomon shook his head and smiled at the three women.

"And this is when I go to the den and talk man stuff with Dad."

"Thanks a lot, Solomon," Phoebe said. She didn't actually mind their questions, since she had been wondering about this, too.

Mozasu smiled, and the men left them in the kitchen.

Father and son sat down in the armchairs in the center of the large room. Baskets of fruits and bowls of nuts topped the glass and stainless-steel cof-fee table opposite the long low-back sofa. A stack of today's Korean and Japanese newspapers remained half-read.

Mozasu turned on the television and lowered the volume on the news; he was scanning the ticker running across the screen with stock prices. The two often talked with the television on.

"How's work?" Mozasu asked.

"Much easier than school. The boss is really great—a Japanese guy, but he went to college and business school in California."

"California? Your mother would've liked that," Mozasu said quietly. The boy resembled her so much, especially around the brow and nose.

"Where's Etsuko?" Solomon stared at the blue background of the news screen. The newscasters were talking about a flood in Bangkok. "Is it Hana? She okay?"

Mozasu sighed. "Etsuko will fill you in. Give her a call."

Solomon wanted to know more, but his father didn't know about what had happened between the two of them. Mozasu never liked to talk about Hana, because she upset Etsuko so much.

"Your grandmother and great-aunt like Phoebe. They want you to get married."

"Yes, I heard that. Five minutes ago."

Mozasu faced his son. "Does Phoebe want to live in Japan?"

"Not sure. She hates that she doesn't know Japanese."

"She can learn."

Solomon looked doubtful. "She wants to work. It's not easy to get your career going straight out of college in Japan. And she doesn't have the language skills. Staying home is not good for Phoebe."

Mozasu nodded. Solomon's mother had been the same way.

"You okay with money?"

"Yes, Dad," he replied, almost amused by his father's concern, "I have a good job now. Hey, Dad, do you know an older lady named Sonoko Matsuda? She owns an old textile factory in Yokohama. Not far from Goro-san's place."

"No." Mozasu shook his head. "Why?"

"Kazu, my boss, is trying to finalize this real estate transaction, and the lady, Matsuda-san, won't sell her property. It's holding up the deal.

I thought maybe you might know someone. You know a lot of people in Yokohama, I mean."

"I don't know her, but sure, I can find out. That's not hard," he said. "Your boss wants the lady to sell?"

"Yeah. Her lot is the last important piece for the golf course development."

"Huh, okay. That sort of thing does happen. I'll ask Goro-san or Haruki. One of them will know. Goro just sold his last pachinko parlor. Now he's only doing demolition, construction, and real estate. He wants me to go in with him, but I'm too busy. It's too late for me to start something new. I don't understand his business as well as pachinko."

"Why don't you sell the shops, too, Dad? Retire maybe. You're set, right? Pachinko is a lot of work."

"What? Quit the business? Pachinko put food on the table and sent you to school. I'm too young to retire!"

He shrugged.

"And what would happen if I sell my stores? They might fire my workers. And where would my older workers go? And we give work to the people who make the machines. Pachinko's a bigger business in Japan than car manufacturing."

Mozasu stopped talking and raised the volume on the news. The newscasters were now talking about the value of the yen.

Solomon nodded and stared at the screen, trying to pay attention to the currency news. His father didn't seem the least bit embarrassed by what he did for a living.

Mozasu caught a glimpse of his son's darkened expression.

"I'll call Goro tonight and ask about the lady. Your boss wants her to sell, right?"

"That would be great. Thanks, Dad."

On Monday afternoon, Mozasu called Solomon at the office. He had spoken to Goro-san. The old lady was Korean—an old-school Chongryon type whose children had returned to Pyongyang and died there; Matsuda was her *tsumei*. She didn't want to sell the property to the Japanese. Goro-

san thought the old lady was being stubborn; he said he could buy the property from the lady, because she said he'd sell it to her. Then he'd sell it to Kazu's client for the same price.

After Solomon got off the phone, he rushed to Kazu's office to tell him the good news.

Kazu listened carefully, then folded his hands together and smiled.

"Excellent work, Jedi. I can always spot a winner."

19

Tokyo, 1989

Even in her condition, Hana could not keep from flirting.

"You shouldn't have come," she said. "I look ugly. I wanted to be beautiful when you saw me again."

"I wanted to see you," Solomon replied. "And you are lovely, Hana. That will never change." He smiled, suppressing his shock at her altered appearance. Etsuko had warned him, but still, it was difficult to recognize her original features beneath the reddish scabs and sparse hair. The skeleton of her body made a distinct impression through the thin blue hospital sheet.

"Mama said you brought the girlfriend-o all the way to Tokyo," Hana said. Only her voice had not changed. It was difficult to know if she was teasing or not. "And I thought you were coming back to me. You will marry her, *nee*? Of course, I will try to forgive you because I know you loved me first."

With the curtain drawn, the ceiling lamp off, and only the light coming from the low-wattage electric bulb by her bedside, the room at the clinic was dark like night even though it was sunny outside.

"When are you going to get better?" he asked.

"Come here, Solomon." Hana raised her right arm, stick thin and chalky. She waved it like an elegant wand of death. "I have missed you so much. If I'd never left you that summer... Well, I would have made you marry me. I would have ruined you, though—I ruin everything. I ruin everything."

Solomon sat on the hard chair by her bed. None of the medications was working, Etsuko had told him. The doctors said there were only a few weeks or perhaps two months left at best. Dark lesions covered her neck and shoulders. Her left hand was unblemished, but her right was dry like her face. Her physical beauty had once been so extraordinary that it seemed to him that her current state was particularly cruel.

"Hana-chan, why can't you go to America to see the doctors there? There have been so many advances in the States. I know things are much better there for this—" He didn't want to play this stupid game where they wouldn't talk about what was real. Just hearing her voice and sitting in her room where she couldn't float away from him reminded him of everything magical and shining about her. He had been in her thrall, and oddly, even now, he felt so many things. He could not imagine her dying. He wanted to pick her up and spirit her away to New York. In America, everything seemed fixable, and in Japan, difficult problems were to be endured. *Sho ga nai, sho ga nai.* How many times had he heard these words? *It cannot be helped.* His mother had apparently hated that expression, and suddenly he understood her rage against this cultural resignation that violated her beliefs and wishes.

"Oh, Solomon. I don't want to go to America." Hana exhaled loudly. "I don't want to live. I'm ready to die. You know? Do you ever want to die, Solomon? I've wanted to die for so many years, but I was too cowardly to say it or to do anything to make my wish come true. Maybe you could have saved me, but you know, even wonderful you, even you, my Solomon, I don't think so. Everyone wants to die sometimes, *nee?*"

"That spring. When you left. I wanted to die." Solomon grew quiet, never having admitted this to anyone. Sometimes he'd forget about that time, but being with her made the memory sharp and mean.

Hana frowned and began to cry.

"If I had stayed, we would've loved each other too much, and I felt certain that I would hurt you. You see, I'm not a good person, and you are a good person. You shouldn't be with me. It's simple. Mama said you got tested in America for your life insurance and that you are okay. I'm grateful for this. You're the only person I have never ever wanted to hurt. And Mama told

me that your girlfriend-o is a nice girl and educated like you. I don't want to know if she is pretty. Tell me she's hideous but has a good soul. I do know that she is a Korean girl. *Tsugoi*, Solomon. How amazing. You should marry her. Maybe people should marry from the same background. Maybe life is easier then. I am going to imagine you having three or four beautiful Korean children—with lovely Korean skin and hair. You have such wonderful hair, Solomon. I would have liked to have met your mother. Name one of your little girls after me, *nee?* Because you see, I will not have any. Promise me you will love little Hana, and you will think of me."

"Shut up," he said quietly, knowing she'd never listen. "Please, please shut up."

"You know that you're the one I loved. *Hatsukoi* was such a stupid idea to me until I met you. I've been with so many men, Solomon, and they were disgusting. All the filthy things I let them do. I'm so sorry for all of it. You, I loved, because you are good."

"Hana, you are good."

She shook her head, but for a moment she looked peaceful.

"I did bad things with boys after Mama left. That's why I came to Tokyo. I was so angry when I met you, then when I was with you, I stopped being so upset. But I couldn't handle it so I left and started hostessing. I didn't want to love anybody. Then you went to America, and I was, I was—" Hana paused. "When I was drinking a lot, I thought you would look for me. Like in that American movie. I thought you would find where I lived, climb on a ladder up to the window, and carry me away. I used to tell all the girls that you would get me. All the girls wanted you to come for me."

Solomon stared at her mouth as she spoke. She had the prettiest mouth.

"It's disgusting, isn't it?"

"What?" He felt like someone had slapped him.

"This." She pointed to the lesions on her chin.

"No. I wasn't looking at that."

She didn't believe him. Her eyes fluttered lightly, and Hana leaned back into the pillow.

"I want to rest now, Solomon. Will you come back soon?"

"Yes, I'll come back," he said, rising from the chair.

When he returned to his desk, Solomon could not stop thinking about her. Why hadn't Etsuko helped her? Something inside him hurt, and the ache felt familiar. He could not read the documents in front of him. He was supposed to run through some projections for the golf club project, but it was as if he had forgotten how to use Excel. What would have happened if she had not left him that summer? Would he have been able to go to New York and stay away for so long?

Phoebe wanted to marry him now; he knew this, but she never brought it up because she was a proud person and wanted to be asked. When he heard Kazu's voice in the hallway, Solomon looked up to see his boss standing before him. Solomon's office mates were out; Kazu closed the door behind him, walked over to the credenza near Solomon's desk, and stood in the space between the credenza and the enormous window.

"She's dead," Kazu said.

"What? I just saw her."

"Who?"

"Hana. Did my father call you?"

"I don't know who that is, man, but Matsuda-san, the old lady, is dead, and it doesn't look good. When the client wanted the property, he didn't expect that the holdout seller would die a few days afterwards."

"What?" Solomon blinked. "The seller is dead?"

"Yes. She sold the property to your father's friend Goro-san, then our client bought the property from him. Our client is not in trouble, but it smells bad. Do you know what I mean?" Kazu said this in a flat, calm voice while staring at Solomon's face thoughtfully. He picked up the Hanshin Tigers baseball on the credenza, tossed it up and caught it.

"How did she die?"

"Not sure. It could have been a heart attack or a stroke. They don't know. There are two nieces apparently. I don't know if they're going to make a fuss or what the police might do."

"She could have died of natural causes. Wasn't she old?"

"Yes, I expect that could be true; however, our client has canceled this transaction for now because the news could affect their public offering next spring."

"What public offering?"

"Never mind that." Kazu sighed. "Listen, man, I have to let you go. I am sorry, Solomon. I really am."

"What? What did I do?"

"We have to do this. There's no other way. I think your father's friend responded a bit too enthusiastically about the land sale, *nee?*"

"But you have no proof, and you are accusing my father's friend of something impossible. Goro would never ever do anything to hurt—"

"I'm not accusing your father's friend of anything. But the facts remain that there is a dead woman who didn't want to sell her property. Everyone knew she wouldn't sell, and moments after she sold, she died."

"But Goro paid a lot of money for that property; it was fair market value; and he's Korean. She didn't mind selling it to a Korean. I thought that's how we were supposed to get around her refusal. He wouldn't have killed an old woman for something like this. All his life, he's helped all these poor people. What are you saying? Goro did this as a favor for my father and me—"

Kazu held the ball between his hands and looked down at the carpet.

"Solly, don't tell me anything more. Do you understand? The investigators are going to want to know what happened. They may not make a big deal of it, but the client is very spooked, dude. The client wanted to develop a country club; they weren't looking for a run-in with the yaks. Do you know what kind of hell they can raise in shareholder meetings?"

"Yaks? Goro is not yakuza."

Kazu nodded and tossed the ball again and caught it.

"The transaction is unfortunately contaminated, so it will be put on hold. This comes at a great financial cost to the client, and it looks poorly for us as a premiere banking company. My reputation—"

"But the client got the property."

"Yes, but no one was supposed to die. I didn't wish for that." Kazu made a face like he was tasting something sour.

Solomon shook his head. All he could think of were the innumerable times he had spent in Goro's presence listening to his hilarious stories about his many girlfriends and his constant encouragements for Solomon's future. Goro had this remarkable clarity about the world. A great man, his father always said about Goro—a noble man—a true *bushi* who understood sacrifice and leadership. It had been Goro alone who had built up Haruki Totoyama's mother's uniform business from nothing, and all because he'd felt bad for a single mother raising two boys. His father said that Goro was always doing good things for poor people quietly. It was absurd to consider that Goro could have been responsible for the lady's death. The woman would have sold the property to Goro because he was known as a good Korean businessman. Everyone knew this.

"Human Resources is waiting outside. Solomon, you don't know how it works, I don't think, because this is your first job at a bank, but when you're terminated from an investment bank, you have to leave the building immediately for internal security reasons. I'm sorry."

"But what did I do?"

"The transaction is postponed for now, and we will not need such a large team. I'm pleased to give you a reference. You can put me down for whatever you want. I would never mention this to your future employers."

Solomon leaned back in his chair and stared at Kazu's hardened jaw. He paused before speaking:

"You brought me in on purpose. Because you wanted me to get the Korean lady to sell. You knew—"

Kazu put down the baseball and moved to the door.

"Brother, I gave you a job, and you were fortunate to have it."

Solomon covered his mouth with his hands.

"You're a nice boy, Solomon, and you will have a future in finance, but not here. If you are trying to imply that you were being discriminated against, something that Koreans tend to believe, that would be incorrect and unfair to me. If anything, you have been preferred over the natives. I like working with Koreans. Everyone knows this about me. The whole department thought that you were my pet associate. I didn't want to fire you. I just don't agree with your father's tactics."

"My father? He had nothing to do with this."

"Yes, of course. It was this man, Goro," Kazu said. "I believe you. I do. Good luck, Solomon."

Kazu opened the office door and let the two women from Human Resources in before heading to his next meeting.

The speech from HR passed quickly, sounding like radio static in Solomon's head. They asked him for his identification card, and he gave it to them automatically. His mind kept returning to Hana, though he felt like he should call Phoebe to explain. He needed air. He threw things in the white banker's box but left the baseball on the credenza.

The HR women escorted him to the elevator and offered to send his box to his apartment by messenger, but Solomon refused. Through the glass-walled conference room, he saw the guys from the poker game but no Kazu. Giancarlo spotted him holding the white box against his chest, and he half smiled at him, then returned to what he was doing. On the street, Solomon got into a taxi and asked the driver to drive him all the way to Yokohama. He didn't think he could walk to the train station.

20

Yokohama, 1989

Empire Cafe was an old-style Japanese curry restaurant near China-town—a place Solomon used to go with his father on Saturday afternoons when he was a boy. Mozasu still ate there on Wednesdays with Goro and Totoyama. Empire served five different kinds of curries, only one kind of draft beer, and as much tea and pickles as you wanted. The cook, who was always in a bad mood, had a deft hand with the seasonings, and his curries were unrivaled in the city.

Late in the afternoon and long past lunch hour, the café was nearly empty except for the three old friends sitting at the corner table near the kitchen. Goro was telling one of his funny stories while making clown-ish faces and dramatic hand gestures. Mozasu and Totoyama took bites of their hot curry and sipped beer. All the while, they nodded and smiled at Goro, encouraging him to continue.

When Solomon pushed open the perpetually swollen front door, the cheap sleigh bells attached to the door jingled.

Scarcely bothering to turn from clearing the tables, the diminutive wait-ress bellowed, "*Irasshai!*"

Mozasu was surprised to see his son. Solomon bowed in the direction of the men.

"You skipping work?" Mozasu asked. The edge of his eyes crinkled deeply when he smiled.

"Good, good. Skip work," Goro interrupted. He was delighted to see

the boy. "I hear you go to the office on the weekends, too. That's no way to be for a handsome boy like you. You should be busy chasing skirt. If I had your height and your diploma, you'd feel sorry for all the women of Japan. I'd be breaking hearts at a rate that would shock a gentle boy like you."

Goro rubbed his hands together.

Totoyama said nothing; he was staring at the lower half of Solomon's face, which seemed fixed; the boy's lips made a thin, crumpled line above his chin. Totoyama's own face was flushed, since it took only half a small beer to redden his ears, nose, and cheeks.

"Solomon, sit down," Totoyama said. "You okay?"

He lifted his briefcase resting on the empty chair and set it down on the linoleum floor.

"I—" Solomon tried to speak, then gasped.

Mozasu asked his son, "You hungry? Did Etsuko tell you that you'd find us here gossiping like old women?"

He shook his head no.

Mozasu laid his hand on the boy's forearm. He'd bought the dark blue suit Solomon was wearing now from Brooks Brothers the time he'd visited Solomon in New York. It had been a nice feeling to be able to buy his son however many interview suits and whatever else he needed at such a nice American store. That was the whole point of money, wasn't it, to be able to get your kid whatever he needed?

"Have some curry," Mozasu said.

Solomon shook his head.

Goro frowned and waved the waitress over.

"Kyoko-chan, give the boy some tea, please."

Solomon looked up and stared at his father's former boss.

"I don't know what to say, Goro-san."

"Sure, you do. Just talk."

"My boss, Kazu, said that the lady, you know, the seller, she died. Is that right?"

"That's so. I went to the funeral," Goro said. "She was ancient. Died of a heart attack. She had two nieces who inherited all that money. Pleasant

girls. One married and one divorced. Beautiful skin. Nice, open brows. Real Korean faces. They reminded me of my mother and aunt."

The waitress brought his tea, and Solomon held the brown, squat mug between his hands. These were the same mugs that Empire had used ever since he could remember.

Totoyama patted the boy's shoulder gently as if to wake him.

"Who? Who died?"

"The lady. The Korean lady who sold the property to Goro-san. My boss's client wanted this property, and the lady wouldn't sell to a Japanese, so Goro-san bought it and sold it to the client, but the lady is dead now, and the boss's client won't touch the deal. Something about having a clean public offering and possible investigations."

Totoyama glanced at Mozasu, who looked equally puzzled.

"She died? Is that so?" Mozasu glanced at Goro, who nodded calmly.

"She was ninety-three years old, and she died a couple of days after she sold her property to me. What does that have to do with anything?" Goro shrugged. He winked at the waitress and tapped the edge of his mug for another beer. When he pointed to the empty beer mugs of Mozasu and Totoyama, the men shook their heads. Totoyama covered the top of his beer mug with his hand.

"What did you pay for the property?" Mozasu asked.

"A very good price, but not crazy. Then I sold it to that client for exactly what I paid for it. I sent Solomon's boss the copies of the contract. I didn't make a single yen. This was Solomon's first deal, and—"

Mozasu and Totoyama nodded. It was unthinkable that Goro would ever seek to profit from Solomon's career.

"The client bought it for less than what he would have if he'd bought it himself," Solomon said slowly, as if Kazu were in the room.

"The client got a piece of property that he would never have gotten because he's Japanese, and she had refused on several occasions to sell to him. He got it cheap." Goro grunted in disbelief. "So now the client is saying he won't build the country club? Bullshit."

"Kazu said the project will be on hold because they didn't want the bad news contaminating the public offering."

"What bad news? The old lady died in peace. Though it might take time to wash away that dirty Korean smell," Goro said. "I'm sick of this."

Totoyama frowned. "If there had been something questionable about her death, I would know. There's been no complaint."

"Listen, the deal's done. If this little prick wants to cheat you out of your cut, fine. I didn't expect him to give you a fair bonus, but remember this: That bastard will not profit from you again. I will watch that mother-fucker until the day I die." Goro inhaled, then calmly smiled at the boy.

"Now, Solomon, you should eat some curry and tell me about this American girl, Phoebe. I've always wanted to go to America to meet the women there. So beautiful, so beautiful." He smacked his lips. "I want a blonde American girlfriend with a big ass!"

The men smiled but they didn't laugh as they would have before. Solomon appeared unconsoled.

The waitress brought Goro a small beer and returned to the kitchen; Goro watched her walk away.

"Too skinny," he said, smoothing back his dyed black pompadour with his brown hands.

"I was fired," Solomon said.

"*Nani?*" the three men said at once. "For what?"

"Kazu said that the client is holding off on the deal. They don't need me anymore. He said that if there was an investigation because of—" Solomon stopped himself before saying the word "yakuza," because suddenly, he wasn't sure. His father wouldn't have associated with criminals. Should he be speaking like this in front of Totoyama? He was Japanese and a high-ranking detective with the Yokohama police; he wouldn't be friends with criminals. The suggestion alone would have hurt all the men deeply.

Goro studied Solomon's face and nodded almost imperceptibly, because he understood the boy's silence.

"Was she cremated?" Totoyama asked.

"Probably, but some Koreans get buried back home," Mozasu said.

"*Soo nee,*" Totoyama said.

"Solomon, the lady died of natural causes. The niece said it was the

heart. She was ninety-three years old. I had nothing to do with her death. Listen, your boss doesn't actually think I killed the old lady. If he did, he'd be too scared to fire you. What would keep me from killing him? This is crazy stuff from television. He used your connections, then he fired you by making up some excuse. The client just wanted the Korean shit to go away."

"You'll get a better job in finance. I'm sure of it," Mozasu said.

Goro was visibly irritated, however. "You should never work for a dirty bank again."

"*Iie.* Solomon majored in economics. He studied in America to work in an American bank."

"Travis is a British bank," Solomon said.

"Well, maybe that was the problem. Maybe you should work in an American bank. There are a lot of American investment banks, *nee?*" Mozasu said.

Solomon felt awful. The men at this table had raised him. He could see how upset they were.

"Don't worry about me. I'll get another job. I have savings, too. I better go now." Solomon stood up from his seat. "Papa, I left a box at your office. Can you send it to me in Tokyo? Nothing important."

Mozasu nodded.

"Here, why don't I take you home? We can take a drive to Tokyo."

"No, it's okay. I'll catch the train. It's faster. Phoebe is probably wondering about me."

When she didn't answer the phone, Solomon returned to the hospital. Hana was awake. Pop music played on the radio. The room was still dark, but the dance hit made the room feel lively, like a nightclub.

"You came back already? You must have really missed me, Solomon." He told her everything, and she listened without interrupting him.

"You should take over your father's business."

"Pachinko?"

"Yes, pachinko. Why not? All these idiots who say bad things about it are jealous. Your father is an honest person. He could be richer if he

was crooked, but he's rich enough. Goro is a good guy, too. He might be a yak, but who cares? I don't. And if he isn't, I'm sure he knows them all. It's a filthy world, Solomon. No one is clean. Living makes you dirty. I've met plenty of fancy people from IBJ and the BOJ who are from the best families, and they like to do some sick shit in bed. A lot of them do very bad things in business, but they don't get caught. Most of the ones I've fucked would steal if they had the chance. They're too scared to have any real ambition. Listen, Solomon, nothing will ever change here. Do you see that?"

"What do you mean?"

"You're a fool," she said, laughing, "but you are my fool."

Her teasing made him feel sad. He missed her already. Solomon couldn't remember ever feeling this lonesome before.

"Japan will never change. It will never ever integrate gaijin, and my darling, here you will always be a gaijin and never Japanese. *Nee?* The *zainichi* can't leave, *nee?* But it's not just you. Japan will never take people like my mother back into society again; it will never take back people like me. And we're Japanese! I'm diseased. I got this from some Japanese guy who owned an old trading company. He's dead now. But nobody cares. The doctors here, even, they just want me to go away. So listen, Solomon, you should stay here and not go back to the States, and you should take over your papa's business. Become so rich that you can do whatever you want. But, my beautiful Solomon, they're never going to think we're okay. Do you know what I mean?" Hana stared at him. "Do what I tell you to do."

"My own father doesn't want that. Even Goro-san sold his parlors and is doing real estate now. Papa wanted me to work in an American investment bank."

"What, so you can be like Kazu? I know a thousand Kazus. They're not fit to wipe your father's ass."

"There are good people in the banks, too."

"And there are good people in pachinko, too. Like your father."

"I didn't know you liked Papa."

"You know, after I got here, he visited me every Sunday when Mama needed a break. Sometimes, when I was pretending to be asleep, I'd catch

him praying for me in that chair. I don't believe in God, but I guess that doesn't matter. I never had someone pray for me before, Solomon."

Solomon closed his eyes and nodded.

"Your grandmother Sunja and great-aunt Kyunghee visit me on Saturdays. Did you know that? They pray for me, too. I don't understand the Jesus stuff, but it's something holy to have people touch you when you're sick. The nurses here are afraid to touch me. Your grandmother Sunja holds my hands, and your great-aunt Kyunghee puts cool towels on my head when I get too hot. They're kind to me, though I'm a bad person—"

"You're not bad. That's not true."

"I've done terrible things," she said drily. "Solomon, when I was a hostess, I sold drugs to one girl who ended up overdosing. I stole money from a lot of men. I've told so many lies."

Solomon said nothing.

"I deserve this."

"No. It's a virus. Everybody gets sick."

Solomon smoothed her brow and kissed it.

"That's okay, Solomon. I'm not doing bad things anymore. I've had time to think about my stupid life."

"Hana—"

"I know, Solomon. *Otomodachi, nee?*"

She pretended to bow formally as she was lying down, and she picked up the corner of her blanket as if she were holding a fold of her skirt to curtsey. The trace of flirtation remained in her still-lithe movements. He wanted to remember this little thing forever.

"Go home, Solomon."

"Okay," he said, and he did not see her again.

21

Tokyo, 1989

I never liked him," Phoebe said. "Too smooth."

"Well, I'm obviously an idiot, because I did," Solomon said. "Besides, how in the world did you get that impression of Kazu in the little time you had? You met him for about two minutes when we ran into him at Mitsukoshi. And you've never mentioned this before."

Slumped in the rented leather armchair, Solomon could barely face Phoebe. He wasn't sure what kind of reaction he'd expected from her, but he was surprised by how unruffled she was by the news. She seemed almost pleased. Phoebe sat on the bench near the window with her folded knees to her chest.

"I actually liked him," he said.

"Solomon, that guy screwed you."

Solomon glanced up at her placid profile, then dropped his head back again on the back of the armchair.

"He's a dick."

"I feel much better now."

"I'm on your team."

Phoebe didn't know if she should get up and sit by him. She didn't want him to think that she felt sorry for him. Her older sister used to say that men hated pity; rather, they wanted sympathy and admiration—not an easy combination.

"He was a phony. He talked to you like you were his little buddy. Like he's some big man on campus and you're one of his 'boys.' Does that system

still even exist? I hate that frat-boy brother shit." Phoebe rolled her eyes.

Solomon was dumbstruck. She had managed to encapsulate his entire relationship with Kazu from that brief, almost nonexistent encounter at the food court of the Mitsukoshi department store. How had she done this?

Phoebe hugged her knees, lacing her fingers together.

"You don't like him because he's Japanese."

"Don't get mad at me. It's not that I distrust the Japanese, but I don't know if I trust them entirely. You're going to say that I've been reading too much about the Pacific War. I know, I know, I sound a little bigoted."

"A little? The Japanese have suffered, too. Nagasaki? Hiroshima? And in America, the Japanese Americans were sent to internment camps, but the German Americans weren't. How do you explain that?"

"Solomon, I've been here long enough. Can we please go home? You can get a dozen terrific jobs back in New York. You're good at everything. No one interviews better than you."

"I don't have a visa to work in the States."

"There are other ways to get citizenship." She smiled.

Solomon's family had hinted on innumerable occasions that he wanted to marry her and that he should marry her; the only person who hadn't said so explicitly was the man himself.

Solomon's head lay immobile on the back of the armchair. Phoebe could see that he was staring at the ceiling. She got up from the bench and walked to the front hall closet. She opened the closet doors and pulled out both of her suitcases. The suitcase wheels rolled loudly across the wooden floor, and Solomon looked up.

"Hey, what are you doing?"

"I'm going home," she said.

"Don't be like that."

"Well, it occurs to me that I lost my life when I came here with you, and you're not worth it."

"Why are you being like this?"

Solomon rose from his chair and was now standing where she'd been only a moment ago. Phoebe dragged the suitcases behind her into the bedroom and shut the door quietly.

What could he say? He wouldn't marry her. He had known it almost as soon as they'd landed in Narita. Her confidence and self-possession had mesmerized him in college. Her equanimity, which had seemed so important in the States, seemed like aloofness and arrogance in Tokyo. She had lost her life here, this was true, but marrying her didn't seem like a solution.

Then the whole Japan-is-evil stuff. Sure, there were assholes in Japan, but there were assholes everywhere, *nee*? Ever since they got here, either she had changed or his feelings for her had changed. Hadn't he been leaning toward asking her to marry him? Yet now, when she put forward the idea of marrying for citizenship, he realized that he didn't want to become an American. It made sense for him to do so; it would have made his father happy. Was it better to be an American than a Japanese? He knew Koreans who had become naturalized Japanese, and it made sense to do so, but he didn't want to do that now, either. Maybe one day. She was right; it was weird that he was born in Japan and had a South Korean passport. He couldn't rule out getting naturalized. Maybe another Korean wouldn't understand that, but he didn't care anymore.

Kazu was a shit, but so what? He was one bad guy, and he was Japanese. Perhaps that was what going to school in America had taught him. Even if there were a hundred bad Japanese, if there was one good one, he refused to make a blanket statement. Etsuko was like a mother to him; his first love was Hana; and Totoyama was like an uncle, too. They were Japanese, and they were very good. She hadn't known them the way he had; how could he expect her to understand?

In a way, Solomon was Japanese, too, even if the Japanese didn't think so. Phoebe couldn't see this. There was more to being something than just blood. The space between Phoebe and him could not close, and if he was decent, he had to let her go home.

Solomon went to the kitchen and made coffee. He poured two cups and approached the bedroom door.

"Phoebe, may I come in?"

"The door's open."

The suitcases on the floor were brimming with clothes folded and

rolled like canisters. The closets were nearly empty. Solomon's five dark suits and half a dozen white dress shirts hung on the long rod with a yard of hanging space left. Her neat rows of shoes still took up most of the closet floor. Phoebe's shoes were black or brown leather; a pair of pink espadrilles, which had once given her terrible blisters, stood out from the others like a girlish mistake. During their junior year, they'd gone to a party, and she'd had to walk back to the dorm barefoot from 111th Street and Broadway because the pink espadrilles had been too narrow.

"Why do you still have those shoes?"

"Shut up, Solomon." Phoebe started to cry.

"What did I say?"

"I have never felt so stupid in my life. Why am I here?" She took a deep breath.

Solomon stared at her, not knowing how to comfort her. He was afraid of her; perhaps he had always been afraid of her—her joy, anger, sadness, excitement—she had so many extreme feelings. The nearly empty room with the solitary rented bed and floor lamp seemed to highlight her vividness. Back in New York, she had been spirited and wonderful. Here, Phoebe was almost too stark, awkward.

"I'm sorry," he said.

"No. You're not."

Solomon sat down on the carpeted floor cross-legged, leaning his long back against the narrow wall. The freshly painted walls were still bare. They hadn't hung anything on them because the landlord would have fined them for each nail hole.

"I'm sorry," he repeated.

Phoebe picked up her espadrilles and threw them into the overflowing waste basket.

"I think I'm going to work for my dad," he said.

"Pachinko?"

"Yeah." Solomon nodded to himself. It felt strange to say this out loud.

"He asked you?"

"No. I don't think he wants me to."

She shook her head.

"Maybe I can take over the business."

"You're kidding, right?"

"No."

Without saying a word, Phoebe continued to pack. She was willfully ignoring him, and he continued to look at her. She was more cute than pretty, more pretty than beautiful. He liked her long torso, slender neck, bobbed hair, and intelligent eyes. When she laughed at a joke, her laughter was whole. Nothing seemed to scare her—she thought anything was possible. Could he change her mind? Could he change his? Maybe the packing was just a dramatic gesture. What did he know about women? He'd known only two girls really.

She rolled up another sweater and dropped it on the growing pile.

"Pachinko. Well, that makes it easier then," she said finally. "I can't live here, Solomon. Even if you wanted to marry me, I can't live here. I can't breathe here."

"That first night we arrived, when you couldn't read the instructions on the aspirin bottle, and you started to cry. I should have known then."

Phoebe picked up another sweater and just stared at it like she didn't know what to do with it.

"You have to dump me," he said.

"Yes, I do."

She left in the morning. It was like Phoebe to make a clean exit. Solomon took her to the airport by train, and even though they were pleasant, she had changed literally overnight. She didn't seem sad or angry; she was cordial. If anything, she seemed stronger than before. She let him hug her good-bye, but they agreed not to talk for a long time.

"It would be better," she said, and Solomon felt powerless against her decision.

Solomon took the train to Yokohama.

His father's modest office was lined with gray metal shelves, and stacks of files rested on the credenzas along the walls. Three safes holding papers and the day's receipts were located below the high windows. Mozasu sat

behind the same battered oak table that he'd used as a desk for over thirty years. Noa had studied for his Waseda exams at this table, and when he moved to Tokyo, he'd left it for Mozasu.

"Papa."

"Solomon," Mozasu exclaimed. "Is everything okay?"

"Phoebe went back."

Saying it to his father made it real. Solomon sat down on the empty chair.

"What? Why? Because you lost your job?"

"No. I can't marry her. And I told her that I'd rather live in Japan. Work in pachinko."

"What? Pachinko? No, no." Mozasu shook his head. "You'll get another job in banking. That's why you went to Columbia, *nee*?"

Mozasu touched his brow, genuinely confused by this announcement.

"She's a nice girl. I thought you'd get married."

Mozasu walked around from his desk and handed his son a packet of tissues.

"Pachinko? *Honto*?"

"Yeah, why not?" Solomon blew his nose.

"You don't want to do this. You don't know what people say."

"None of that stuff is true. You're an honest business person. I know you pay your taxes and get all your licenses, and—"

"Yes, yes, I do. But people will always say things. They will always say terrible things, no matter what. It's normal for me. I'm nobody. There's no need for you to do this work. I wasn't smart at school like my brother. I was good at running around and fixing things. I was good at making money. I've always kept my business clean and stayed away from the bad things. Goro-san taught me that it's not worth it to get involved with the bad guys. But Solomon, this business is not easy, *nee*? It's not just tinkering with machines and ordering new ones and hiring people to work on the floor. There are so many things that can go wrong. We know lots of people who went belly-up, *nee*?"

"Why don't you want me to do this?"

"I sent you to those American schools so that no one would—" Mozasu paused. "No one is going to look down at my son."

"Papa, it doesn't matter. None of it matters, *nee*?" Solomon had never seen his father like this before.

"I worked and made money because I thought it would make me a man. I thought people would respect me if I was rich."

Solomon looked at him and nodded. His father rarely spent on himself, but he had paid for weddings and funerals for employees and sent tuition for their children.

Mozasu's face brightened suddenly.

"You can change your mind, Solomon. You can call Phoebe when she gets home and say you're sorry. Your mother was a lot like Phoebe—strong-willed and smart."

"I want to live here," Solomon said. "She will not."

"*Soo nee.*"

Solomon picked up the ledger from his father's table.

"Explain this to me, Papa."

Mozasu paused, then he opened the book.

It was the first of the month, and Sunja had woken up upset. She had dreamed of Hansu again. Lately, he had been appearing in her dreams, looking the way he did when she was a girl, wearing his white linen suit and white leather shoes. He always said the same thing: "You are my girl; you are my dear girl." Sunja would wake and feel ashamed. She should have forgotten him by now.

After breakfast, she would go the cemetery to clean Isak's grave. As usual, Kyunghee offered to come with her, but Sunja said it was okay.

Neither woman performed the *jesa*. As Christians, they weren't supposed to believe in ancestor worship. Nevertheless, both widows still wanted to talk to their husband and elders, appeal to them, seek their counsel. They missed their old rituals, so she went to the cemetery regularly. It was curious, but Sunja felt close to Isak in a way that she hadn't when he was alive. Then she had been in awe of him and his goodness. Dead, he seemed more approachable to her.

When the train from Yokohama reached Osaka Station, Sunja bought ivory-colored chrysanthemums from the old Korean woman's stall. She had

been there for years. The way Isak had explained it, when it was time to be with the Lord, your real body would be in heaven, so what happened to your remains didn't matter. It made no sense to bring a buried body favorite foods or incense or flowers. There was no need for bowing, since we were all equal in the eyes of the Lord, he'd said. And yet Sunja couldn't help wanting to bring something lovely to the grave. In life, he had asked for so little from her, and when she thought of him now, she remembered her husband as someone who had praised the beauty that God had made.

She was glad that Isak had not been cremated. She had wanted a place for the boys to visit their father. Mozasu visited the grave often, and before Noa disappeared, he had come with her, too. Had they talked to him, too? she wondered. It had never occurred to her to ask them this, and now it was too late.

Lately, every time she went to the cemetery, she wondered what Isak would have thought of Noa's death. Isak would have understood Noa's suffering. He would have known what to say to him. Noa had been cremated by his wife, so there was no grave to visit. Sunja talked to Noa when she was alone. Sometimes, something very simple like a delicious piece of pumpkin taffy would make her sorry that now that she had money, she couldn't buy him something that he had loved as a child. *Sorry, Noa, sorry.* It had been eleven years since he'd died; the pain didn't go away, but its sharp edge had dulled and softened like sea glass.

Sunja hadn't gone to Noa's funeral. He hadn't wanted his wife and children to know about her, and she had done enough already. If she hadn't visited him the way she had, maybe he might still be alive. Hansu had not gone to the funeral, either. Noa would've been fifty-six years old.

In her dream last night, Sunja had been happy that Hansu had come to see her again. They met at the beach near her old home in Yeongdo to talk, and recalling the dream was like watching another person's life. How was it possible that Isak and Noa were gone but Hansu was still alive? How was this fair? Hansu was living somewhere in Tokyo in a hospital bed under the watchful gaze of round-the-clock nurses and his daughters. She never saw him anymore and had no wish to. In her dreams, he was as vibrant as he had been when she was a girl. It was not Hansu that she missed, or even Isak. What she was seeing again in her dreams was her youth, her beginning, and

her wishes—so this was how she became a woman. Without Hansu and Isak and Noa, there wouldn't have been this pilgrimage to this land. Beyond the dailiness, there had been moments of shimmering beauty and some glory, too, even in this *ajumma*'s life. Even if no one knew, it was true.

There was consolation: The people you loved, they were always there with you, she had learned. Sometimes, she could be in front of a train kiosk or the window of a bookstore, and she could feel Noa's small hand when he was a boy, and she would close her eyes and think of his sweet, grassy smell and remember that he had always tried his best. At those moments, it was good to be alone to hold on to him.

She took the taxi from the train station to the cemetery, then walked the many rows to Isak's well-maintained grave. There was no need to clean anything, but she liked to wipe down the marble tombstone before she spoke to him. Sunja fell to her knees and cleaned the flat, square tombstone with the towels she'd brought for the purpose. Isak's name was carved in Japanese and Korean. 1907–1944. The white marble was clean now and warm from the sun.

He had been such an elegant and beautiful man. Sunja could recall how the servant girls back home had admired him; Bokhee and Dokhee had never seen such a handsome man before. Mozasu took after her more and had her plain face, but he had his father's straight carriage and steady stride.

"*Yobo*," she said, "Mozasu is well. Last week, he called me, because Solomon lost his job with that foreign bank, and now he wants to work with his father. Imagine that? I wonder what you'd make of this."

The silence encouraged her.

"I wonder how you are—" She stopped speaking when she saw Uchida-san, the groundskeeper. Sunja was sitting on the ground in her black woolen pants suit. She glanced at her handbag on the ground. It was an expensive designer bag that Etsuko had bought for her seventieth birthday.

The groundskeeper stopped before her and bowed, and she returned the bow.

Sunja smiled at the polite young man, who must have been about forty or forty-five. Uchida-san looked younger than Mozasu. How did she look to him? Her skin was deeply grooved from the years of sun, and her short

hair was bright white. No matter—seventy-three did not feel very old to her. Had the groundskeeper heard her mumbling in Korean? Ever since she'd stopped working at the confectionery, her limited Japanese had deteriorated further. It was not terrible, but lately she felt shy around native speakers. Uchida-san picked up his rake and walked away.

Sunja put both hands on the white marble, as if she could touch Isak from where she was.

"I wish you could tell me what will happen to us. I wish. I wish I knew that Noa was with you."

Several rows from her, the groundskeeper cleared wet leaves from stone markers. Now and then he would glance up at her, and Sunja felt embarrassed to be seen talking to a grave. She wanted to stay a little longer. Wanting to look like she was busy, Sunja opened her canvas bag to put away the dirty towels. In the bottom of her bag, she found her house keys on the key ring with thumbnail-sized photographs of Noa and Mozasu in a sealed acrylic frame.

Sunja started to weep, and she could not help her crying.

"Boku-san."

"*Hai?*" Sunja looked up at the groundskeeper.

"May I get you something to drink? I have a thermos of tea in the cottage. It is not very fine tea, but it is warm."

"No, no. Thank you. All time, you see people cry," she said in broken Japanese.

"No, actually, very few people come here, but your family visits regularly. You have two sons and a grandson, Solomon. Mozasu-sama visits every month or two. I haven't seen Noa-sama in eleven years, but he used to come on the last Thursday of each month. You could set a watch to him. How is Noa-sama? He was a very kind man."

"Noa come here? Come before 1978?"

"*Hai.*"

"From 1963 to 1978?" She mentioned the years he would have been in Nagano. She said the dates again, hoping that her Japanese was correct. Sunja pointed to Noa's photograph on the key ring. "He visit here?"

The groundskeeper nodded with conviction at the photograph, then looked up in the sky like he was trying to see some sort of calendar in his mind.

"*Hai, hai.* He came in those years and before, too. Noa-sama told me to go to school and even offered to send me if I wished."

"Really?"

"Yes, but I told him I have an empty gourd for a head, and that it would have been pointless to send me to school. Besides, I like it here. It's quiet. Everybody who comes to visit is very kind. He asked me never to mention his visits, but I have not seen him in over a decade, and I'd wondered if he moved away to England. He told me to read good books and brought me translations of the great British author Charles Dickens."

"Noa, my son, is dead."

The groundskeeper opened his mouth slightly.

"My son, my son," Sunja said quietly.

"I am very sad to hear that, Boku-san. Truly, I am," the groundskeeper said, looking forlorn. "I'd been hoping to tell him that after I finished all the books he'd brought me, I bought more of my own. I have read through all of Mr. Dickens's books in translations, but my favorite is the first one he gave me, *David Copperfield.* I admire David."

"Noa loved to read. The best. He loved to read."

"Have you read Mr. Dickens?"

"I don't know how," she said. "To read."

"*Maji?* If you are Noa's mother, you are very smart, too. Perhaps you can go to night school for adults. That is what Noa-sama told me to do."

Sunja smiled at the groundskeeper, who seemed hopeful about sending an old woman to school. She remembered Noa cajoling Mozasu to persevere with his studies.

The groundskeeper looked at his rake. He bowed deeply, then excused himself to return to his tasks.

When he was out of sight, Sunja dug a hole at the base of the tombstone about a foot deep with her hands and dropped the key ring photograph inside. She covered the hole with dirt and grass, then did what she could to clean her hands with her handkerchief, but dirt remained beneath her nails. Sunja tamped down the earth, then brushed the grass with her fingers.

She picked up her bags. Kyunghee would be waiting for her at home.

Acknowledgments

I got the idea for the story in 1989.

I was a junior in college, and I didn't know what I'd do after graduation. Rather than ponder my future, I sought distractions. One afternoon, I attended what was then called a Master's Tea, a guest lecture series at Yale. I'd never been to one before. An American missionary based in Japan was giving a talk about the *"Zainichi,"* a term used often to describe Korean Japanese people who were either migrants from the colonial era or their descendants. Some Koreans in Japan do not wish to be called *Zainichi* Korean because the term means literally "foreign resident staying in Japan," which makes no sense since there are often third, fourth, and fifth surviving generations of Koreans in Japan. There are many ethnic Koreans who are now Japanese citizens, although this option to naturalize is not an easy one. There are also many who have intermarried with the Japanese or who have partial Korean heritage. Sadly, there is a long and troubled history of legal and social discrimination against the Koreans in Japan and those who have partial ethnic Korean backgrounds. There are some who never disclose their Korean heritage, although their ethnic identity may be traced to their identification papers and government records.

The missionary talked about this history and relayed a story of a middle school boy who was bullied in his yearbook because of his Korean background. The boy jumped off a building and died. I would not forget this.

I graduated college in 1990 with a degree in history. I went to law school and practiced law for two years. After quitting the law, I decided to write as early as 1996 about the Koreans in Japan. I wrote many stories and novel drafts, which were never published. I was despondent. Then

in 2002, *The Missouri Review* published the story "Motherland," which is about a Korean Japanese boy who gets fingerprinted and receives a foreigner's identity card on his birthday, and later it won the Peden Prize. Also, I'd submitted a fictionalized account of the story I'd heard in college and received a New York Foundation for the Arts fellowship. With that grant money, I took classes and paid for a babysitter so I could write. This early recognition was critical, because it took me so long to publish anything at all. Moreover, the NYFA fellowship confirmed my stubborn belief that the stories of Koreans in Japan should be told somehow when so much of their lives had been despised, denied, and erased.

I wanted very much to get this story right; however, I felt that I didn't have all the knowledge or skills to do this properly. In my anxiety, I did an enormous amount of research and wrote a draft of a novel about the Korean Japanese community. Still, it did not feel right. Then in 2007, my husband got a job offer in Tokyo, and we moved there in August. On the ground, I had the chance to interview dozens of Koreans in Japan and learned that I'd gotten the story wrong. The Korean Japanese may have been historical victims, but when I met them in person, none of them were as simple as that. I was so humbled by the breadth and complexity of the people I met in Japan that I put aside my old draft and started to write the book again in 2008, and I continued to write it and revise it until its publication.

I have had this story with me for almost thirty years. Consequently, there are many people to thank.

Speer Morgan and Evelyn Somers of *The Missouri Review* believed in this story first. The NYFA gave me a fiction fellowship when I wanted to give up. Thank you.

When I lived in Tokyo, a great number of individuals agreed to sit with me and answer my many questions about the Koreans in Japan as well as about expatriate life, international finance, the yakuza, the history of colonial Christianity, police work, immigration, Kabukicho, poker, Osaka, Tokyo real estate deals, leadership in Wall Street, *mizu shobai*, and of course, the pachinko industry. When we could not meet in person, many spoke to me on the phone or answered my questions via e-mail. I am in debt to the following generous individuals: Susan Menadue Chun,

Jongmoon Chun, Ji Soo Chun, Haeng-ja Chung, Kangja Chung, the Reverend Yean Won Chung, Scott Callon, Emma Fujibayashi, Stephanie and Greg Guyett, Mary Hauet, Danny Hegglin, Gen Hidemori, Tim Hornyak, Linda Rhee Kim, Myeong Gu Kim, Alexander Kinmont, Tamie Matsunaga, Naoki Miyamoto, Rika Nakajima, Sohee Park, Alberto Tamura, Peter Tasker, Jane and Kevin Quinn, Hyang Yang, Paul Yang, Simon Yoo, and Chongran Yun.

I have to note here that this book could not have been written without the significant scholarship of the following authors: David Chapman, Haeng-ja Chung, Haruko Taya Cook, Theodore F. Cook, Erin Chung, George De Vos, Yasunori Fukuoka, Haeyoung Han, Hildi Kang, Sangjun Kang, Sarah Sakhae Kashani, Jackie J. Kim, Changsoo Lee, Soo im Lee, John Lie, Richard Lloyd Parry, Samuel Perry, Sonia Ryang, Tessa Morris-Suzuki, Stephen Murphy-Shigematsu, and Mary Kimoto Tomita. Although I relied heavily on their scholarship, any errors of fact are my own.

I want to thank my friends and family in Japan, South Korea, and the United States for their love, faith, and kindness. Without them, it would have been impossible to write, revise, and rewrite this book: the Reverend Harry Adams, Lynn Ahrens, Harold Augenbraum, Karen Grigsby Bates, Dionne Bennett, Stephana Bottom, Robert Boynton, Kitty Burke, Janel Anderberg Callon, Scott Callon, Lauren Cerand, Ken Chen, Andrea King Collier, Jay Cosgrove, Elizabeth Cuthrell, Junot Díaz, Charles Duffy, David L. Eng, Shelley Fisher Fishkin, Roxanne Fraser, Elizabeth Gillies, Rosita Grandison, Lois Perelson Gross, Susan Guerrero, Greg and Stephanie Guyett, Shinhee Han, Mary Fish Hardin, the Reverend Matthew Hardin, Robin Marantz Henig, Deva Hirsch, David Henry Hwang, Mihoko Iida, Matthew Jacobson, Masa and Michan Kabayama, Henry Kellerman, Robin F. Kelly, Clara Kim, Leslie Kim, Erika Kingetsu, Alex and Reiko Kinmont, Jean Hanff Korelitz, Kate Krader, Lauren Kunkler Tang, the Reverend Kate Latimer, Wendy Lamb, Hali Lee, Connie Mazella, Christopher W. Mansfield, Kathy Matsui, Jesper Koll, Nancy Miller, Geraldine Moriba Meadows, Tony and Suzanne O'Connor, Bob Ouimette, Asha Pai-Sethi, Kyoungsoo Paik, Jeff Pine, Cliff and Jennifer

Park, Sunny Park, Tim Piper, Sally Gifford Piper, Sharon Pomerantz, Gwen Robinson, Catherine Salisbury, Jeannette Watson Sanger, Linda Roberts Singh, Tai C. Terry, Henry Tricks, Erica Wagner, Abigail Walch, Nahoko Wada, Lindsay Whipp, Kamy Wicoff, Neil and Donna Wilcox, and Hanya Yanagihara.

My early readers Dionne Bennett, Benedict Cosgrove, Elizabeth Cuthrell, Junot Díaz, Christopher Duffy, Tom Jenks, Myung J. Lee, Sang J. Lee, and Erica Wagner gave me their invaluable time, keen insights, and the necessary courage to persevere. Thank you.

In 2006, I met my agent Suzanne Gluck, and I remain deeply grateful for her friendship, wisdom, and goodness. I want to thank Elizabeth Sheinkman, Cathryn Summerhayes, Raffaella De Angelis, and Alicia Gordon for their brilliant work and generous faith. I am thankful to Clio Seraphim for her thoughtful support.

Here I declare my profound gratitude to my amazing editor Deb Futter, whose clear-eyed vision, superb intelligence, and exceptional care shaped this book. Thank you, Deb. My brilliant publisher Jamie Raab has supported my writing from the very beginning, and I am thankful to call Jamie my friend. I want to acknowledge the very talented people at Grand Central Publishing and the Hachette Book Group: Matthew Ballast, Andrew Duncan, Jimmy Franco, Elizabeth Kulhanek, Brian McClendon, Mari Okuda, Michael Pietsch, Jordan Rubinstein, Karen Torres, and Anne Twomey. I am very grateful to Chris Murphy, Dave Epstein, Judy DeBerry, Roger Saginario, Lauren Roy, Tom McIntyre, and the excellent salespeople of HBG. Also, many thanks to my fantastic copy editor Rick Ball. As ever, many thanks to the wonderful Andy Dodds, whose passion and excellence inspire me. I thank the exquisite Lauren Cerand.

Here, I want very much to thank these tremendous individuals at my UK publishing house for their faith and support: Neil Belton, Madeleine O'Shea, and Suzanna Sangster. Thank you.

Mom, Dad, Myung, and Sang: thank you for your love. Christopher and Sam: You fill my life with wonder and grace. Thank you for being my family.

MJL

About the Author

Min Jin Lee is the national bestselling author of *Free Food for Millionaires*, and has received the New York Foundation for the Arts fellowship for Fiction, the Peden Prize for Best Story, and the Narrative Prize for New and Emerging Writer. She has written for the *New York Times*, *Condé Nast Traveler*, the London *Times*, *Vogue*, the *Wall Street Journal*, and *Food & Wine*, among others. For more information, please visit MinJinLee.com.

—— **About the Authors** ——

JOHN MCCAIN is a United States senator from Arizona. He retired from the Navy as a captain in 1981, and was first elected to Congress in 1982. He is currently serving his fifth term in the Senate. He and his wife, Cindy, live with their children in Phoenix, Arizona.

MARK SALTER worked on Senator McCain's staff for almost twenty years. He lives with his wife, Diane, and their two daughters in Alexandria, Virginia.

Tamarind and Date Chutney (*Imli Ki Chutney*) 56
Pear, Cherry, and Ginger Chutney (*Sukhe Phal Ki Chutney*) 57
Dried Cranberry Chutney 58
Mint Chutney (*Pudine Ki Chutney*) 59
Yogurt Mint Chutney (*Pudine Aur Dahi Ki Chutney*) 60
Walnut and Yogurt Chutney (*Akhrot Ki Chutney*) 61
Red Chile Chutney (*Lal Mirchi Ki Chutney*) 62
Green Chile Chutney (*Hari Mirch Ki Chutney*) 63
Coconut Chutney (*Naryal Ki Chutney*) 64
Chopped Salad of Cucumber, Tomato, and Red Onions (*Kachumber*) 65
Carrot and Cilantro Relish (*Gajjar Ka Kutra*) 66
Sweet and Sour Garbanzo Bean Relish (*Chatpatta Channas*) 67
Black-Eyed Pea Salad (*Lobia Kachumber*) 68
Sprouted Mung Bean Salad with Daikon and Green Mangoes
     (*Moongi Aur Mooli Ka Salat)*) 69
Composed Salad of Tomatoes, Red Onions, Cucumbers, and Beets (*Salat*) 70
Cucumber and Peanut Salad 71
California Tandoori Salad 72
Scallop and Paneer Salad 74

V. RICE AND BREAD   76

Plain Basmati Rice (*Chawal*) 78
Rice Pullao with Peas and Cumin (*Mattar Wale Chawal*) 79
Rice with Browned Onions (*Bhuga Chawal*) 80
Rice with Onions, Tomatoes, and Chiles (*Masala Chawal*) 81
Rice with Paneer and Peas (*Paneer Mattar Wale Chawal*) 82
Rice with Mixed Vegetables (*Sabzi Pullao*) 83
Rice with Chinese Long Beans (*Sem Pullao*) 84
Rice with Cauliflower (*Gobi Pullao*) 85
Chapatis 86
Oven-Baked Breads with Nigella Seeds (*Naans*) 88
Layered Indian Griddle Bread (*Parathas*) 90
Griddle Bread with Potato Stuffing (*Aloo Parathas*) 92
Griddle Bread with Ground Lamb Stuffing (*Keema Parathas*) 94
Griddle Bread with Daikon Stuffing (*Mooli Ki Roti*) 96
Griddle Bread with Cauliflower Stuffing (*Gobi Parathas*) 98
Griddle Bread with Cheese Stuffing (*Paneer Ki Roti*) 99
Griddle Bread with Onion, Chile, and Cumin (*Kokis*) 100
Puffed Whole Wheat Breads (*Puris*) 102

VI. LEGUMES (DAL)   104

Toor Lentils with Garlic and Tomatoes (*Tamatar Aur Lassoon Wali Toor Dal*) 106
Green Mung Beans with Browned Onions (*Hari Moong Dal*) 108
Mercin's Lemon Lentils (*Mercin Ki Khathi Dal*) 109
Brown Masoor Lentils with Tomatoes (*Masala Wale Saabat Masoor Ki Dal*) 110
Brown Masoor Lentils with Sambar Spices
    (*Saabat Masoor Aur Sambar Masala*) 111
South Indian Toor Dal (*Sambar*) 112
Yellow Mung Beans with Tomatoes and Cilantro (*Tamatar Wali Moongi Dal*) 114
Simple Yellow Mung Beans (*Saadi Moongi Dal*) 115
Yellow Mung Beans with Tomatoes and Onions (*Masala Wali Moongi Dal*) 116
Pink Masoor Lentils with Onions and Tomatoes (*Masala Masoor Dal*) 118
Pink Masoor Lentils with Browned Onions and Ginger
    (*Masala Dal Aur Bhunna Pyaaz*) 119
Pink Masoor Lentils with Tomatoes and Garlic (*Lassoon Wali Masoor Dal*) 120
Chickpeas with Opo Squash (*Ghia Channa Dal*) 122

VII. VEGETABLES   124

Asparagus with Tomatoes 126
Green Beans with Onions and Tomatoes (*Sem Sabzi*) 127
Bengali Green Beans and Potatoes with Panch Puran
    (*Bengali Sem Aur Aloos*) 128
South Indian Green Beans (*Dakshini Sem*) 129
Sautéed Mung Bean Sprouts with Marinated Onions 130
Cabbage with Garlic, Mustard Seeds, and Lemon (*Khatta Patta Gobi*) 131
Cauliflower with Ginger and Green Chiles (*Gobi Sabzi*) 132
Cauliflower and Peas (*Gobi Mattar Sabzi*) 133
Fresh Corn with Red Onions (*Makkai Aur Lal Pyaaz*) 134
Yogurt Curry with Daikon (*Dahi Aur Mooli Ki Kari*) 135
Sautéed Daikon with Cayenne and Mustard Seed (*Mooli Ki Sabzi*) 136
Smoked Eggplant Purée (*Bharta*) 137
Eggplant with Cilantro and Chickpea Flour Stuffing (*Bharele Baingan*) 138
Sweet and Sour Eggplant (*Khate Mithe Baingan*) 140
Sautéed Japanese Eggplant with Onions and Tomatoes (*Baingan Sabzi*) 142
Mushrooms and Green Peas (*Khumbi Mattar*) 143
Eggplant Layered with Tomato Conserve and Ginger Yogurt
    (*Baingan Deva*) 144

Spicy Mixed Greens in Mustard Oil (Sarson Ki Bhurji) 146
Spicy Mushrooms with Red Bell Peppers
    (Khumbi Aur Lal Simla Mirch Ki Sabzi) 147
Makhni Mushrooms and Paneer (Makhni Khumbi Aur Paneer) 148
Okra with Red Onions (Bhindi Sabzi) 149
Baby Okra with Green Chiles and Black Pepper (Bhindi Aur Kali Mirch) 150
Crisp Okra (Karari Bhindi) 151
Opo Squash with Tomatoes (Ghia Tamatar) 152
Opo Squash with Yogurt (Ghia Aur Dahi Ki Sabzi) 153
Scrambled Paneer with Peas (Paneer Mattar Ki Bhurji) 154
Sautéed Potatoes with Dried Mango Powder
    (Sukhe Aloo—Uttar Pradesh) 155
Potatoes with Mustard Seeds and Kari Leaves (Gujarati Sukhe Aloo) 156
Potatoes and Peas in Tomato Sauce (Rasedar Aloo Mattar) 157
Railway Station Potato Curry (Taridar Aloo) 158
Baby Red Potatoes in a Tomato-Yogurt Sauce (Dum Aloo) 160
Potatoes and Paneer in Tomato Sauce (Aloo Paneer Rasedar) 162
Potatoes and Green Peas with Cumin (Sukhe Aloo Mattar) 164
Fresh Spinach with Browned Garlic in Mustard Oil
    (Palak Sarson Ke Tel Mein) 165
Puréed Spinach with Homemade Indian Cheese (Palak Paneer) 166
Sugar Snap Peas with Cumin (Saabat Meethe Mattar) 167
Fresh Spinach with Homemade Indian Cheese (Kashmiri Palak Paneer) 168
Mixed Vegetable and Lentil Curry (Sindhi Curry) 170

VIII. FISH AND SEAFOOD   173

Petrale Sole Fillets with Dried Mango Powder (Sindhi Machchi) 174
Fish in Spinach Sauce (Palak Machchi) 175
Fish Wrapped in Banana Leaves (Patrel Nu Machchi) 176
Halibut with Onions and Tomatoes (Sel Machchi) 178
Tandoori Halibut (Tandoori Machchi) 179
Coconut Curry with Yellowtail (Goan Machchi Ki Curry) 180
Salmon Roll with Coconut Chutney and Cucumber Raita 182
Rice with Shrimp and Tomato (Jhinga Pullao) 185
Green Coconut Curry with Shrimp (Goan Jhinga Curry) 186
Aromatic Shrimp with Cilantro, Dill, and Tomatoes
    (Tamatar Aur Sua Jhinga) 188
Spicy Tiger Prawns in Fresh Tomato Sauce (Jhinga Tamatar) 189

IX. CHICKEN AND POULTRY 190

Chicken Curry (*Murghi Ki Curry*) 192
South Indian Chicken Curry with Fennel Seeds (*Saunf Murghi*) 194
Chicken Masala (*Murghi Masala*) 196
Chicken with Cardamom (*Illaichi Murghi*) 197
Grilled Marinated Chicken with Mint Chutney and Lime-Cilantro Onions
   (*Shaan-Eh-Murgh*) 198
Chicken Kabobs in Green Spices (*Mirch Masala Tikka*) 200
Pepper Chicken (*Kali Mirch Murghi*) 201
Stir-Fried Chicken with Tomatoes (*Karhai Murghi*) 202
Braised Chicken with Onions and Tomatoes (*Sindhi Sel Murghi*) 204
Chicken Kabobs in Tomato-Saffron Sauce (*Makhni Tikka*) 206
Rice with Chicken (*Murghi Pullao*) 208
Chicken and Spinach Curry (*Saag Murghi*) 210
Cornish Hens with Dried Mango Powder (*Sindhi Choosas*) 212

X. MEAT 215

Lamb Chops with Black Pepper and Vinegar (*Kali Mirch Ke Champa*) 216
Lamb Chops with Dried Mango Powder (*Sindhi Champa*) 217
Ground Lamb with Peas (*Keema Mattar*) 219
Browned Lamb with Onions, Tomatoes, and Spices (*Bhunna Meat*) 221
Lamb and Rice Casserole (*Shah Jahani Pullao*) 223
Rice with Ground Lamb, Green Beans, and Garbanzo Beans
   (*Keema Channa Pullao*) 226
Lamb with Puréed Spinach Curry (*Saag Gosht*) 228

XI. DESSERTS 230

Candied Ginger 231
Indian Cardamom Custard (*Phirni*) 232
Cardamom Custard with Mango and Ginger Brandy Coulis 233
Mango Sorbet 234
Lemon-Ginger Sorbet 236
Lime-Mint Sorbet 237
Ginger Ice Cream (*Adraki kulfi*) 238
Mango Ice Cream (*Mango kulfi*) 240
Yogurt-Saffron Pudding (*Shrikhand*) 241
Carrot Pudding (*Gajjar ka Halwa*) 242
Indian Rice Pudding (*Kheer*) 243

XII. DRINKS 244

Flavored Yogurt Drinks (*Lassi*) 245
Spiced Tea (*Masala Chai*) 247
Spiced Iced Tea 248
Sweetened Milk 248
Lemon-Ginger Fizz (*Adraki Nimbu Soda*) 249

GLOSSARY 250

MAIL-ORDER SOURCES 252

INDEX 253

Introduction

When I was growing up in Bombay, sometimes I would wander down to the kitchen, drawn by the fragrant aromas, to see what my mother's inspired cook, Chandan, had in store for us that day. He would lift a few lids to let me peek, give me a taste or two, and send me on my way happily looking forward to the next meal. There was always something mouth-watering to anticipate.

Chandan started every morning very early at the local market, choosing perfect, ripe vegetables for the evening meal. On the days he was serving meat or chicken, he carefully selected only the tenderest of cuts, the plumpest of birds at the butcher's. Perhaps he'd prepare my mother's favorite, Sindhi Chicken—poached in an aromatic stock and browned in ghee and fragrant spices. Or maybe it would be rich Lamb Chops with Black Pepper and Vinegar. On many nights, our meals would consist of a spectrum of delectable vegetarian dishes—perhaps Kashmiri Palak Paneer (spinach with fresh Indian cheese), Dum Aloos (baby potatoes in tomato yogurt sauce), or Bharta (smoked eggplant purée). As in every Indian household, the staples of every meal were rice and lentils; Chandan cooked these essentials so inventively—combining them with onions, garlic, other vegetables, and vibrant spices—that we never tired of them. Raitas (usually a vegetable and yogurt relish) and sweet and hot chutneys of amazing variety, on an array of platters and bowls, would surround these basics. Tirelessly, he browned individual chapatis (irresistible grilled flatbreads) or deep-fried airy puris (puffy breads with a crisp skin). Dessert might be a rice pudding with the flavor of cardamom or that day's most delectable fruit from the market.

It was impossible not to grow up loving food around Chandan. In many ways, I feel that he is the inspiration behind my Santa Monica restaurant, the Bombay Cafe. From him I learned the importance of first-rate ingredients—the best produce and meats, the freshest spices, toasted and ground by hand. I learned to pay attention to details—the thickness of a griddle bread, the proper browning of onions, the texture of homemade cheese.

Most important of all, these early experiences gave me the confidence to break the "rules" of Indian cooking I'd learned so carefully, in order to create a style that was all mine. That is what I have done both at the Bombay Cafe and in this cookbook. You'll find traditional favorites—but cooked with techniques that make them lighter and fresher-tasting than usual. You'll find the lively adaptations of my favorite "street foods" of India, based on originals I've bought throughout my travels from vendors with little carts. And you'll find many of my own inventions, thoroughly non-traditional but nevertheless completely Indian at heart.

One of the reasons Indian food allows me such freedoms is that it is less structured than Western food. For example, in India, visitors often drop by unexpectedly. My mother, like any other Indian hostess, always welcomed such guests to her dinner table. She and Chandan never panicked over the fact that he had prepared only a small amount of lamb, for example. Indian meals don't work that way. Perhaps Chandan would whip up an extra pea and potato curry, since no Indian kitchen is without a plentiful supply of potatoes. Perhaps he would merely provide larger servings of rice, dal and freshly baked bread, or naan. Guests would take small helpings of many dishes and no one would notice that a "main course" was being stretched.

The true joy of Indian food is the way the different textures, tastes, and temperatures of an entire meal work with each other. For this reason, the Indian approach to a meal is fundamentally different from a Westerner's. A Western meal might have a first course and a main course, usually a substantial portion of meat, poultry, or seafood, and small amounts of a vegetable and starch. In India, meats are much less affordable. The meat, poultry, or seafood dish might be considered the "main dish," in the sense that its ingredients are very costly, but it will be prepared as a sort of stew (like a curry), so that it goes further, and it will be eaten in small portions. The rest of the meal is made up of several seasonal vegetable or potato dishes, just as important in their own way as the meat dish, and served at the same time. And of course, many meals do not include meat at all, but focus on substantial vegetable or dairy dishes. Certain things, however, are essential: There is always one of the many varieties of dal, or lentils, and there is always rice or bread, and sometimes both, to absorb all the delicious sauces of the main dishes.

The basic planning of a meal is simple: I choose a "main dish" I want to serve—Sindhi Chicken, for example, a spicy, mahogany brown roast. Next I think of color—I'd want some vibrant ambers and greens, perhaps, like Baby Red Potatoes in a Tomato-Yogurt Sauce or Spicy Mixed Greens in Mustard Oil. Texture is important: Since Sindhi Chicken is a plain roast, I might choose to balance it with a saucelike dal, such as Mercin's Lemon Lentils. Then, depending on whether the chosen dishes are simple or complex, I'd choose a rice dish—in this case, rather than plain basmati rice, I'd like a colorful pea pullao (pilaf). The fun of Indian cooking is that one can—really must— use all the senses in meal planning and preparation (even hearing—some dishes are done only when the whole spices "pop," like popcorn).

Once one becomes accustomed to the flavors and methods, it's very easy to improvise, too. Here in California, I see so many wonderful non-Indian foods around me and I love to incorporate the best of them into my cooking. My salads are the perfect example. Even though salads don't really exist in India, my California Tandoori Salad is one of the favorites at the Bombay Cafe and at home; I think its Cilantro-Cumin Dressing is a great basic for any salad. Almost any meal can be given an Indian twist—and made all the better for it. One of my family's favorite dishes is one I made up after I was served a delicious French-style rolled, stuffed fillet of salmon at a dinner party. I couldn't wait to get home and try it my way—filled with leeks, green chiles and a lively cilantro-coconut chutney. It took me a few tries, but the results were so successful that I've served it at several parties and included the recipe here.

Yes, Chandan taught me to pay attention to detail. My advice to the beginning cook, and even to the seasoned one, is to read the first chapter, "Bombay Basics," before trying the recipes. Here, I pass along a few indispensable tips, basic guidelines, and master recipes that make all the difference between good Indian cooking and inspired Indian cooking.

Bombay Basics

■ Without a doubt, spices are the most important elements in Indian cooking. Although many Indian spices are available in ordinary grocery aisles, such as cinnamon, cardamom, and cumin, it is worth the effort to seek out authentic, imported versions. Sometimes there are noticeable differences in flavor (Indian cumin is quite distinct from Mexican cumin, for example), and the spices from a good importer are generally fresher than the bottled versions in supermarkets. (See page 252 for mail-order sources.) Note also that in Indian cooking there is no such thing as store-bought "curry powder." Every Indian cook I've worked with agrees that the word "curry" really refers to a method of cooking—a slow braising in spices—and not to a spice mixture itself. We do make our own freshly ground spice mixtures, called garam masalas, and they will vary according to their uses. These often contain cloves, cumin, cinnamon, cardamom, and others. Garam masalas are easy to make and keep, in small quantities, for whenever they are needed.

Important Note: Check the glossary (see pages 250 to 252) for more information about many other possibly unfamiliar spices and ingredients, as well as how to use them. Cooks following my recipes should refer to the glossary for full explanations of any ingredients or items marked with an asterisk (＊).

Basic Garam Masala

1 teaspoon black peppercorns

1/2 tablespoon whole cloves

6 pods black cardamom ✳

12 pods green cardamom ✳

2 (2-inch) pieces cinnamon stick or cassia ✳

1 tablespoon cumin seeds ✳

4 dried, whole red chiles

1. Grind all the ingredients in a spice grinder or clean coffee grinder until pulverized. It will keep for about a month or two in an airtight jar.

MAKES 1/3 CUP

GARAM MASALA I

To the basic recipe add 1/2 teaspoon of nutmeg and 1/2 teaspoon of mace.

GARAM MASALA II

To the basic recipe add 1 tablespoon coriander seed. Prior to grinding the mixture, roast all spices except for the dried red chile in a dry skillet. Allow to cool and grind as in basic recipe.

■ To make a proper Indian curry, one must begin with deeply browned onions, traditionally cooked slowly in a fair amount of oil. Especially in the meaty dishes of the northern Punjabi region, this can sometimes produce a heavy result. However, through trial and error, I have discovered an effective, lower-fat method for browning the onions without having them burn or stick to the pan. First, I chop the onions coarsely in a food processor, which makes the onions exude their juices. I heat a few tablespoons of vegetable oil in a heavy sauté pan. During the slow, caramelizing process, I watch the onions carefully and stir frequently as the onion juices gradually evaporate. I can then add small quantities of oil or water, if necessary, to complete the process.

■ Many of my favorite dishes include paneer, the homemade Indian cheese rather like firm farmer's cheese. It's easy to make and adds flavor as well as nutrition to many vegetarian dishes. Of course, it's best when made with whole milk, but it also works with low-fat milk and buttermilk. I leave that choice to you. The following recipe yields about 1 pound; you can make any quantity you want, following the basic proportions of 2 parts milk to 1 part buttermilk.

Paneer

> 1/2 gallon milk
> 1 quart buttermilk

1. Rinse a 4-quart saucepan and while it is still wet, pour the milk into it. (Using a wet pan helps prevent the formation of a skin on the pan during cooking.) Bring milk to the boil.

2. Remove from heat and pour in the buttermilk, stirring continuously. The solids will separate from the liquid, or whey.

3. Drape a colander with a fine, clean muslin cloth (not cheesecloth, because it is too porous) so that the ends hang over. Pour the mixture into the cloth, gather up the ends and twist them together firmly to force out excess whey.

   Place the tightly wrapped package on a slightly convex surface (such as an upside-down plate, bowl or pan) so that the remaining whey can drain away, and put a plate or flat pan on top. Weight the plate or pan with something heavy, such as a can, and let the paneer sit for about 30 minutes (unless directed otherwise by a specific recipe).

4. The resulting paneer will have a texture similar to firm farmer's cheese. It can be diced or sliced, as needed.

MAKES 3/4 POUND

■ Indian households always make fresh yogurt each night, Though you can substitute store-bought yogurt, this is so easy to make you may want to try it. Even though several types of yogurt makers are on the market, it is easy to make yogurt in a glass or ceramic bowl. I prefer to use whole milk for yogurt, but I find that low-fat milk can be substituted successfully. I don't recommend using nonfat milk.

Homemade Yogurt

> 3 cups milk
> 1 rounded teaspoon plain yogurt
> (store-bought or previously made)

1. Rinse a stainless steel pan with cold water and, without drying it, pour the milk into it. Bring the milk to a full boil. (This technique helps prevent the milk from burning on the bottom of the pan.)

2. Remove milk from heat and allow to cool to about 95 to 100 degrees, or until just warm to the touch.

3. Smear the yogurt starter around the bottom of a ceramic or glass bowl and pour the warm milk into the bowl. Cover and set in a dark, warm place overnight or at least 8 hours. When a thin film of whey, or clear liquid, rises to the top, you will know the yogurt has cultured. Refrigerate for a few hours before using so that the yogurt will set completely.

MAKES 3 CUPS

Note: Once you've made yogurt a few times, you'll see how easy it is. Watch out for a few common mistakes: Don't use too much starter or let the yogurt set too long, or it will be too tart. If the milk is allowed to cool too long before combining with the starter, or if you use too little starter, the yogurt will not set.

■ *Ghee,* or clarified butter, is traditionally used in Indian cooking for its rich, buttery flavor. I still use ghee in those dishes in which its flavor is essential, but in small quantities as a *tadka,* or finishing touch. Ghee is widely available, ready-made, in gourmet stores and Indian markets. It is sold in bottles and keeps indefinitely without refrigeration. For cooking, I use only unsaturated vegetable oils.

■ Some of the savories, or appetizers, in Indian cooking are deep-fried. It's important to cook with high heat in order to keep the foods from absorbing too much of the oil. The oil may be cooled, strained, and stored in a clean jar for reuse if the food you are frying is not too strong in flavor.

■ Meat dishes usually call for lean cuts that take well to slow cooking. All visible fat is removed before cooking. When a recipe calls for ground lamb, I recommend asking a butcher to trim a leg of lamb of excess fat and grind the meat to order. Prepackaged ground lamb is unacceptably fatty. The leanest ground beef can be substituted for ground lamb in any recipe. The yield, or portion size, in meat recipes may seem small, but again, that is traditionally Indian, since meat dishes are usually accompanied by vegetable and rice dishes as well as breads, raitas, and chutneys.

■ Chicken is always skinned before cooking, both in curries and in roasts, such as tandoori Chicken. This Indian classic is roasted in a special cone-shaped clay oven (called a tandoor) at high heat, which creates mouth-watering, tender chicken with a unique flavor. While a home oven cannot really recreate a tandoor, I have offered a tandoori-style marinade for use with grilled chicken that produces excellent results.

■ The combination of rice and lentils offers a complete protein, and for this reason, they form the backbone of every Indian meal in every region of the country. Lentils (or *dals*) come in many varieties and are cooked with a multitude of flavorings. They can be liquid, like a soup or sauce, or thick, like a stew. They can be served in small portions or as the basis of the meal, almost always served with either plain rice or elaborate rice

pullaos and sometimes bread, too. At the Bombay Cafe, I always offer a "Dal of the Day," some using different types of lentils and legumes, or unusual seasonings. Many of these favorite recipes appear in this book.

■ In this cookbook, I use the term *garbanzo bean* to refer to the kind commonly found in American markets. *Chickpea*, on the other hand, refers to the small split pea used to make *besan*, or chickpea flour, and is prevalent in Indian cooking. Both legumes appear in my recipes, but I do not recommend substituting one for the other.

■ As more than half of India is strictly vegetarian, there is a wide range of vegetable recipes and techniques to draw upon. I've included recipes for some vegetables that may be unfamiliar to Americans, but these are often available in Indian markets, or I have noted easily available substitutes. Vegetables are almost always cooked in a *karhai*, a special Indian pan shaped rather like a wok. Just as in Chinese stir-frying, the lidded karhai allows the vegetables to sauté rapidly in very little oil and then finish cooking in their own steam. Most meals, especially vegetarian ones, offer several vegetable dishes, including potatoes. Indians regard potatoes as an essential vegetable, rather than merely a starch, and often combine them with a second vegetable such as peas or green beans. For this reason, Indian meals often feature rice and bread as well as potatoes.

Breads are a central part of an Indian meal, where they usually serve in place of utensils to scoop up the various courses. You may not choose to employ them in this way, but I guarantee that you will enjoy eating them. I include simple *chapatis,* the daily bread of India, as well as layered and stuffed *parathas* and airy, deep-fried *puris.* I even came up with a wonderful version of *naan* designed for the home oven. Of course, these naans are not quite as sensational as the ones fresh from the Bombay Cafe's tandoor oven—but short of installing a charcoal-fired clay oven in your home, they're as good as you'll get.

Indians traditionally end their meals with fresh fruit. For more festive occasions, hosts offer rich sweets made from whole milk. I have come to prefer lighter, Western-style desserts—but with Indian flavors. I think my Mango Sorbet or Ginger Ice Cream provides the perfect punctuation point to an Indian meal—even if they are completely nontraditional. I also offer streamlined versions of my favorite traditional desserts, such as *Kheer,* or rice pudding.

Once you become accustomed to the flavors and methods of Indian cooking, it is very easy to improvise—even with nontraditional ingredients. For example, neither mushrooms nor red bell peppers are common in India, but I like them so much that I created a delicious, Indian-style sauté with cumin and chiles and serve it frequently with both Indian and Western meals. My Scallop and Paneer Salad is another example of nontraditional ingredients benefiting from an Indian sensibility. Feel free to experiment yourself, using my techniques and lively spices to create your own combinations.

The most important guideline is really an overall philosophy. For me, an Indian meal is an exercise in harmony. Each part of the meal should complement the others in color, texture, flavor, and aroma. The ingredients can be very basic, but they should be the best and freshest available. An Indian meal should be a welcoming experience too: There must always be enough food, even if it is simple, to share with guests. An Indian meal is meant to please— your eyes, your tastebuds, your soul, and your guests.

Over the years I have loved welcoming guests to the Bombay Cafe and sharing this vision of fresh, innovative Indian cuisine with them. As they come back time and again, I have learned a lot from them, too, about embracing some of the rich influences of other cuisines and traditions. Now, in this book, I am happy to share all these lessons with you. I know you'll find my approach to Indian food as much a delight to the senses as I do.

Savories

Indians look forward to teatime—usually about 4 o'clock—with great anticipation. For one thing, it's a long time until dinner—usually around 9 o'clock—so a between-meal snack is a matter of survival. But the main reason we can't wait for teatime is that the foods traditionally served then are among the most irresistible and delicious in all of Indian cuisine. We call them "savories."

Although the concept of "appetizers" doesn't really exist in Indian cooking, I frequently serve these delectable savories as just that. In my years at the Bombay Cafe—and as a caterer and hostess at home—I have found that many of these tidbits work beautifully as first courses for dinners served in a more Western style, or as buffet dishes and party fare. Among my favorite teatime snacks at home in India were delectable *pakoras* (vegetable, chicken or fish fritters, served with chutney) and *samosas* (fried pastries with a spicy pea and potato filling), which our cook, Chandan, would serve to us fresh from the stove. Both of these delicious goodies make fabulous first courses or finger foods, and you'll find recipes for them in this chapter.

Even though Indian meals are never broken down into separate courses, there are many traditional "main dish" recipes that need only minor adjustments to become first-rate starters or appetizers. For example, it's a simple matter to shape substantial Lamb Kabobs into smaller patties, making them perfect to pass at parties, along with a sweet chutney for dipping. The same is true with yummy *Uttapam* (Semolina Griddle Cakes with Coconut Chutney); although they are usually served whole and sliced at the table in India, I make them bite-sized, dollop a little Coconut Chutney on top and offer them as a memorable first course. In other cases, I have created my own unique dishes, sometimes inspired by other cuisines. The Shrimp with Garlic and Chiles came to me after I had scampi at an Italian restaurant and I couldn't wait to get home to experiment with an Indian version.

Any of the following recipes work beautifully as starters for dinner, as hors d'oeuvres to pass around during a cocktail party, or as part of a buffet. As this chapter illustrates, Indian food is very adaptable. You may have so much fun making and eating samosas, for example, that you will be inspired to make a whole meal out of them!

Shrimp with Garlic and Chiles
Lassoon Jhinga

The spicy marinade gives these simply prepared shrimp considerable zing.
To serve them as an hors d'oeuvre, choose small shrimp because they are easier
to eat; pass them with wooden picks. As a main dish for dinner, larger shrimp
work well. Buy fresh or flash-frozen shrimp, preferably in their shells,
since these always retain more flavor.

1 pound raw shrimp
(about 35 to 40 small shrimp,
thawed if frozen)

3 large cloves garlic, minced

2 green serrano chiles, minced

1/2 tablespoon fresh cilantro,
minced

1/2 teaspoon turmeric

1/4 to 1/2 teaspoon cayenne pepper

1 1/2 tablespoons ghee ✳

1 1/2 teaspoons mustard seeds ✳

1 1/2 teaspoons salt

Juice of 1 lemon

Mixed lettuce or greens,
optional, to line the platter

1. Shell and devein shrimp. Place in a mixing bowl with garlic, chiles, cilantro, turmeric, and cayenne. Toss to coat the shrimp with the spices and refrigerate for at least a 1/2 hour but not longer than 4 hours.

2. In a heavy nonstick skillet with a lid, heat the ghee over high heat. Tilt the pan so that the ghee forms a pool and carefully add mustard seeds to the ghee. Cover immediately, as they will sizzle and pop. After a few moments, when the popping has subsided, lift the lid and add the shrimp mixture to pan.

3. Stir and toss the shrimp until they turn pink, about 5 minutes. Sprinkle on the salt. Add the lemon juice. Stir to mix and remove from heat.

4. Line a small platter with greens and arrange shrimp in center. Pass with wooden picks.

SERVES 6 TO 8

Semolina Griddle Cakes with Coconut Chutney

Uttapams

Uttapams are delicious griddle cakes, fragrant with onions, cilantro, or whatever flavoring strikes your fancy. Their crowning glory is a dollop of rich and spicy Coconut Chutney. These easy pancakes can be made any size: Half-dollar rounds for appetizers, 6 inches in diameter for individual first courses, or platter-sized, to be sliced into wedges at the table. Uttapams are frequently served in homes in southern India as part of a brunch.

BATTER:

2 cups semolina flour
(available in Indian markets, or
substitute Cream of Wheat)

**10 ounces (1 1/4 cups)
plain yogurt,✳ store-bought
or homemade (see page 5)**

1 cup water

1 teaspoon salt

*BATTER TOPPINGS: 1/2 TO 1 CUP
ANY OR ALL OF THE FOLLOWING:*

Finely chopped onions

**Finely chopped green
serrano chiles**

Chopped fresh cilantro

Chopped tomatoes

1/2 cup corn oil

**1 cup Coconut Chutney
(see page 64)**

---

1. To make the batter, combine the semolina flour, yogurt, water, and salt, stirring until smooth. Cover the bowl with plastic wrap and set aside at room temperature for 2 hours. (The batter can be made a day in advance, but it should be refrigerated and then allowed to sit at room temperature for 2 hours before cooking.)

2. Heat a nonstick griddle or skillet until droplets of water dance, as for pancakes. Pour 1/4 cup of batter onto the hot griddle and spread it into a round about 1/4 inch thick. Quickly sprinkle the desired toppings onto the griddle cake, pressing them into the batter with the back of a spoon. Drizzle a teaspoon of oil around the edges of the pancake and cook 1 minute. Flip the cake over, drizzle a 1/2 teaspoon more oil and cook 1 to 2 minutes more, until lightly browned. Continue until all batter is used, keeping the uttapams under foil in a warm oven as they are made.

3. To serve, place on a warm platter with a tablespoon of chutney beside each uttapam.

MAKES 18 TO 20 MINI UTTAPAMS

Crisp Marinated Shrimp
Haldi Jhinga

With a crisp, melt-in-your-mouth texture similar to Japanese tempura, these incredible shrimp explode with lively Indian flavors. The marinade gives them punch, while the Cream of Rice in the batter gives them an especially light, crunchy coating. These disappear very fast whenever I serve them.

1½-inch piece ginger, peeled and coarsely chopped

2 to 3 green serrano chiles

½ cup fresh cilantro leaves

24 large shrimp, cleaned and deveined

2 teaspoons turmeric

1 scant teaspoon salt

1 cup Cream of Rice

Vegetable oil for frying

6 to 8 lemon wedges

1. Place the ginger, chiles and cilantro in the bowl of a food processor and process them until they are finely minced, scraping down the sides of the bowl as needed. Put the mixture in a small work bowl and add the shrimp, stirring and tossing to coat well.

2. Add the turmeric and again coat well. (Although you can use a spoon, coating works best if you use your fingers. However, the turmeric will stain them, so it is a good idea to wear food gloves, if you have them.) Allow to marinate in the refrigerator for at least 3 hours.

3. When ready to cook, remove the shrimp from the refrigerator. Sprinkle on the salt and allow to stand for 10 minutes. Meanwhile, put 1/4 cup of the Cream of Rice in a medium-sized plastic bag to have ready for the next step. (Do not use more than 1/4 cup at a time; otherwise, the marinade will make the Cream of Rice too moist to coat evenly.)

4. In a small, deep saucepan or karhai,* pour enough oil to completely cover the shrimp. Put 6 shrimp into the plastic bag, close it, and toss them to coat with the Cream of Rice. Place all the shrimp on a large slotted spoon and ease them into the hot oil. They will immediately sizzle. Turn over after 1 minute and fry for another minute, or until evenly golden. Remove and set aside on paper towels to absorb excess oil; repeat the process with another 6 shrimp. Using the rest of the Cream of Rice, repeat with the remaining shrimp, 6 at a time.

5. Serve garnished with lemon wedges.

MAKES 24

Lamb Kabobs with Sweet Tomato Chutney
Keema Kabobs

These gingery meatballs, dipped in tangy chutney, are addictive. It's important
to use lean lamb. If you cannot get your butcher to grind it to order for you, use
lean ground beef instead. Do not substitute fatty, prepackaged ground lamb. I
add chopped tomatoes to the meat mixture, which is not traditional, but
it keeps the lean meat moist and adds a bright flavor.

1 pound lean ground lamb,
preferably leg of lamb

1 small onion, (about $2/3$ cup)
finely chopped

$13/4$-inch piece ginger,
peeled and finely chopped

2 green serrano chiles,
finely chopped

1 medium tomato,
seeded and finely chopped

$11/2$ teaspoons Garam Masala I
(see page 3)

1 tablespoon fresh cilantro,
minced $11/2$ to $2/3$ teaspoon salt

1 cup Sweet Tomato Chutney
(see page 55)

1. Place all ingredients in a mixing
   bowl and knead with fingers until
   thoroughly mixed. Form into balls
   the size of a walnut and flatten
   slightly.

2. Use a large, nonstick skillet and place
   all the kabobs in it while the pan is
   still cold (this helps prevent sticking).
   Set pan over high heat. Cook the
   kabobs for 2 to 3 minutes on each
   side, until juices have evaporated and
   they are browned evenly and cooked
   through.

3. Place on platter with bowl of Sweet
   Tomato Chutney. Pass with wooden
   picks. Makes about 36 kabobs.

SERVES 6 TO 8

Chicken Kabobs with Saffron

Kesari Murgh Tikkas

The saffron gives these grilled chicken morsels a golden glow and distinctive, mellow flavor. Though the price of saffron has gone down a little because of increased production in Spain, it is still very expensive. My trick for getting the most flavor out of the least saffron is to dissolve the threads in warm milk before proceeding with the recipe.

1 tablespoon milk

1/8 teaspoon saffron threads

1 pound boneless, skinless chicken, either breasts or thighs, cut into bite-sized pieces

1-inch piece ginger, peeled and coarsely chopped

3 to 4 cloves garlic

1 teaspoon Garam Masala I (see page 3)

1/2 to 1 teaspoon cayenne pepper

1 teaspoon coriander powder *

1 tablespoon lemon juice

1/2 to 2/3 teaspoon salt

1 tablespoon vegetable oil

1. Warm milk briefly in the microwave and dissolve the saffron threads in it. Set aside for 5 to 10 minutes.

2. In a mixing bowl, combine chicken and saffron mixture. Stir to coat and set aside for 15 minutes.

3. Prepare marinade by puréeing all remaining ingredients except oil in a blender. Add a little water as necessary to make a smooth paste. Pour over chicken and saffron. Refrigerate for at least 1 hour but not more than 6. When ready to cook, stir the oil into the mixture.

4. For the most flavorful result, thread chicken pieces on skewers and grill for 3 to 4 minutes on each side over a medium charcoal fire. Alternatively, broil skewered chicken under medium heat, turning after 3 to 4 minutes, until done.

5. Garnish with lemon wedges.

SERVES 6

Mini Potato Pancakes
with Lemon and Cilantro
Aloo Ki Tikkis

These potato pancakes are a favorite street food all over India. There, they are pan-fried in the center of huge, outdoor concave griddles and pushed to the edges of the black steel pan to keep warm next to bowls of chopped onions, green chiles, and tamarind chutney. Just like at an American hot dog stand, customers can order the pancakes exactly to their liking. They are just as popular at the Bombay Cafe.

3/4 pound (3 to 4) medium
red rose potatoes

3 slices firm-textured white bread,
crusts removed

1 to 2 small green serrano chiles,
minced

1/2 tablespoon fresh cilantro,
minced

1/2 tablespoon lemon juice

1/2 teaspoon salt

Vegetable oil for frying

Sour cream and/or
chutney of choice (optional)

1. Boil unpeeled potatoes until easily pierced by a fork, about 20 to 25 minutes. Drain, but do not rinse in cold water (this prevents the potatoes from absorbing extra water and becoming damp or heavy). Let cool until easy to handle and remove the skins.

2. Dry out the bread slices in a low oven (250 degrees) for 10 minutes. Break the bread into the bowl of a food processor and process into crumbs.

3. In a large bowl, with a large fork or with your fingers, crumble and mash the potatoes. Do not use a masher or ricer, as the potatoes should retain some texture.

4. Add the chiles, cilantro, lemon juice, and salt and mix well. Taste for seasoning and adjust.

5. Form into balls the size of large walnuts and flatten into $\frac{1}{2}$-inch-thick patties.

6. In a deep, medium-sized skillet or Dutch oven, pour in oil to a depth of about $1\frac{1}{2}$ inches. Heat the oil over medium-high heat. Test the oil by dropping in a pinch of dough: If it rises quickly to the surface and sizzles, the oil is ready. Fry about 6 pancakes at a time, 2 to 3 minutes, or until golden brown. Set aside on absorbent paper while frying the remaining pancakes.

7. Serve plain, or with a dollop of sour cream, or with chutneys of your choice, such as Tamarind and Date-Chutney (see page 56) and Green Chile Chutney (see page 63).

MAKES ABOUT 18 POTATO PANCAKES

Note: If you are not serving the pancakes immediately, allow to cool completely before refrigerating. To reheat, place them on a cookie sheet in a 350 degree oven for about 5 minutes.

Paneer Puffs Stuffed with Spinach

Paneer aur Palak ke Kofte

The combination of delicious paneer (fresh Indian cheese) and spinach
is a favorite one in Indian cooking. Usually the mixture is served as a classic
vegetable dish, known as *Saag Paneer,* but I love the combination so much
that I created these toasty, cheesy appetizer puffs.

FOR SPINACH FILLING:

1 teaspoon vegetable oil

1/4 teaspoon mustard seeds ✳

1 large clove garlic, minced

1/2-inch piece ginger, peeled
and minced

1/2 pound fresh spinach, washed
thoroughly and stems removed

1/2 teaspoon cayenne pepper

1/2 teaspoon ground roasted
cumin ✳

1/4 teaspoon salt

FOR PANEER DOUGH:

3/4 pound paneer ✳ (see page 4,
but let paneer set for only 20 minutes,
so it does not become too firm)

2 teaspoons flour

1 1/2 tablespoons shallots, minced

1 small green serrano chile, minced

1 tablespoon fresh cilantro, minced

1/2 teaspoon salt

Nonstick cooking spray

1. In a small skillet with a lid, heat the oil over high heat. Tilt the pan to one side to form a pool and carefully add the mustard seeds. Cover at once to avoid splattering. After a few seconds, uncover and add the garlic and ginger. Sauté for one minute, until they are slightly browned.

2. Add the spinach leaves, stirring in a handful at a time.

3. Add cayenne, ground cumin, and salt. Cover and cook over low heat for 10 to 15 minutes, until spinach is cooked through and liquid has almost evaporated. Cool to room temperature before proceeding.

4. To make paneer puffs, place the paneer in a mixing bowl. Add flour and knead thoroughly, using fingers. Mix in remaining ingredients.

5. Preheat oven to 350 degrees. Spray two mini muffin pans with cooking spray.

6. Take a scant tablespoon of paneer mixture and form it into a ball. Place in a muffin cup and using thumb or knuckle, make an indentation in the middle. Place about $1/2$ to $2/3$ teaspoon spinach filling in the indentation. Cover the filling with about $1/2$ teaspoon of paneer mixture. Fill remaining muffin cups in the same manner. (The puffs can be made ahead and refrigerated, covered tightly with plastic wrap, up to 24 hours.)

7. Spray tops of paneer puffs lightly with cooking spray and bake for 10 to 12 minutes, until tops have puffed and browned lightly.

8. Loosen edges with a sharp knife. Remove from pans and serve immediately.

MAKES 24

Indian Crisp Crackers
Sev Puris

Probably one of the most popular savories at the restaurant, Sev Puris are one of my favorite of Indian street foods. Hand carts selling little tidbits of snack foods are seen all over India. Mostly vegetarian due to the lack of refrigeration, a large number of these foods are categorized as "chaat." Even though the making of the crisp puris and sev are a long, drawn-out procedure, I feel compelled to include this one and the recipe for Bhel Puri; the bases for them are readily available in Indian specialty markets.

18 to 24 crisp puris, store-bought

2 medium red potatoes, peeled, boiled, and diced small

1 medium onion, minced

1/4 cup Red Chile Chutney (see page 62)

1/4 cup Green Chile Chutney (see page 63)

1 cup Tamarind and Date Chutney (see page 56)

8 ounces crisp sev, store-bought

1/4 cup fresh cilantro, chopped

1. *To assemble:* Place 6 puris on a plate. Top each puri with a heaping teaspoon of the potatoes and a few minced onions.

2. Put a 1/4 teaspoon of the Red Chile Chutney and 1/4 teaspoon of the Green Chile Chutney on top of the potatoes and onions.

3. Put a heaping teaspoon of the Tamarind Chutney on top of the others.

4. Top everything with about 1 tablespoon of the crisp sev and garnish with the cilantro and serve. Repeat with the remaining, completing no more than 6 at a time.

SERVES 3 TO 4 PER PERSON FOR 6 PEOPLE

Note: The quantity of chutneys recommended are approximations as they can be adjusted to suit your palate. As the chile chutneys add heat and the Tamarind Chutney adds sweetness, you can certainly alter the amounts used to your taste. The puris and their trimmings can be presented in individual bowls for guests to assemble, or if you wish to prepare them yourself, don't do so all at once as they will become soggy and lose their crispness.

Bhel Puri

A tossed crisp melange of crackers, puffed rice, and crisp noodles

Along with the Sev Puri, Bhel Puri is my other favorite street food
from India. As with Sev Puris, preparing some of the key ingredients for
this recipe are long and complicated, so purchasing them makes it easy to put
together at the last minute. Like the Sev Puris, the quantity of chutneys
required are approximate and can be adjusted to individual palates.

2 cups kurmura (puffed rice),
store-bought

24 crisp puris, store-bought

1 cup crisp sev, store-bought

2 medium potatoes, boiled,
peeled, and diced small

1 small onion, minced

½ cup Tamarind and Date Chutney
(see page 56)

1 tablespoon Red Chile Chutney
(see page 62)

1 tablespoon Green Chile Chutney
(see page 63)

½ teaspoon ground cumin,✱
roasted

1 teaspoon black salt ✱

Juice of one lemon

Fresh cilantro, for garnish

1. Preheat oven to 350 degrees. Place the
   puffed rice kernels on a flat cookie
   sheet and toast in oven for 4 to 5
   minutes to re-crisp.

2. Place the kurmura in a large mixing
   bowl. Crush half the puris into the
   bowl. Add the sev, potatoes, and
   onions and toss well.

3. Add the chutneys according to taste,
   using more of the tamarind than the
   chile chutneys. Add the cumin and
   black salt and mix well. Season with
   the lemon juice.

4. Mound the mixture on 6 small plates.
   Garnish with cilantro and then prop
   two puris per plate into the mounded
   mixture. The puris work
   as spoons for the Bhel Puri.

SERVES 6

Vegetable Samosas

Samosas—small, fried, stuffed dumplings that are one of India's most popular snacks—are sold from carts all over the country. They vary in style from region to region: Some have thick, pastrylike wrappers, some are thin and crisp, with different styles of filling, too. Inspired by the way our cook, Chandan, made them at home, I like to serve samosas at the Bombay Cafe with thin, crisp wrappers plumped with a pea and potato stuffing. To make the process easier, the wrappers can easily be made ahead and refrigerated or frozen.

FOR THE SAMOSA "PATTIS" OR WRAPPERS:

2 1/2 cups flour

1 teaspoon salt

1/3 to 1 cup water

1/4 cup vegetable oil

FOR THE POTATO AND PEA FILLING:

3 tablespoons vegetable oil

1/2 teaspoon coriander seeds ✳

1 teaspoon cumin seeds ✳

1 medium onion minced

1-inch piece ginger, peeled and minced

1 green serrano chile, minced

1 tablespoon ground coriander ✳

1 teaspoon cayenne pepper

3 large potatoes, boiled and peeled

1/2 cup green peas, cooked

1 teaspoon salt

1 tablespoon fresh cilantro, chopped

TO ASSEMBLE:

1/4 cup flour

2 tablespoons water

Vegetable oil for deep-frying

1. *To make the wrappers:* sift the flour and salt together in mixing bowl. Add the water 1/3 of a cup at a time, mixing with your fingers, until a soft, pliable dough forms. Cover and set aside for about 15 minutes.

2. Divide dough into 6 equal parts. Roll each part into a ball, dredge it in flour and flatten into a 3-inch disk. Roll each disk into a 6-inch circle, dredging in flour as needed.

3. Place one disk on a work surface. Brush some oil on it and place the next disk on top of it. Brush oil on this one and continue until the last one is placed on top. Do not brush oil on to the top of the last disk. With the heel of your palm, flatten and press down the layer of disks. Then roll out the "pattis" to a 12- to 14-inch round, about 2/3 of an inch thick.

4. The cooking process is very rapid. Heat a large griddle, and carefully place the stack of wrappers on the griddle. Toast the bottom layer until lightly cooked, turning the disk rapidly in a circular manner with your hands (this ensures even cooking).

Flip the disk so that now the bottom is on top. The top layer will have begun to separate around the edges; gently peel this layer off and place it on a cool surface. Flip the disk again and peel the next layer. Flip again, and repeat the process until all 6 wrappers have been cooked. This process should take no more than 5 minutes.

5. Place the cooked wrappers on top of each other and cut into quarters. From each quarter, cut a half-oval shape, wasting as little of the wrapper as possible. You will have 24 half-ovals. (They can be refrigerated or frozen at this point, tightly wrapped in plastic wrap and foil. The leftover scraps can be deep-fried for wonderful samosa chips.)

6. *To make the filling:* Heat the oil in a medium-sized saucepan or skillet. Add the coriander and cumin seeds. When they stop sizzling, add the

onions and brown well for about 15 minutes. Stir frequently, and reduce the heat slightly if the onions begin to burn. When the onions are very well browned, add the ginger and chiles. Sauté for a minute and then stir in the ground coriander and cayenne. Cook for another minute or so, until all the spices are well blended. Remove from heat and allow to cool.

7. With your hands, crumble the boiled potatoes into a mixing bowl. Stir in the peas and the spice mixture. Add the salt and taste for seasoning. Add the cilantro and mix well. The filling should be lumpy.

8. *To assemble the samosas:* make a paste with the flour and water. (If using frozen wrappers, make sure they have been defrosted.) On a large heated griddle or skillet, warm the wrappers just lightly so they will be flexible enough to fold without cracking.

9. Take one wrapper at a time. Place on a clean work space with the straight edge facing you. Fold the right-hand corner two-thirds of the way toward the middle. Place your index finger just to the right of the point and fold the left-hand corner over it, so that a little flap overlaps.

Make sure the bottom point has been enclosed in this fold, to prevent the filling from leaking out. You should have a shape resembling an ice-cream cone.

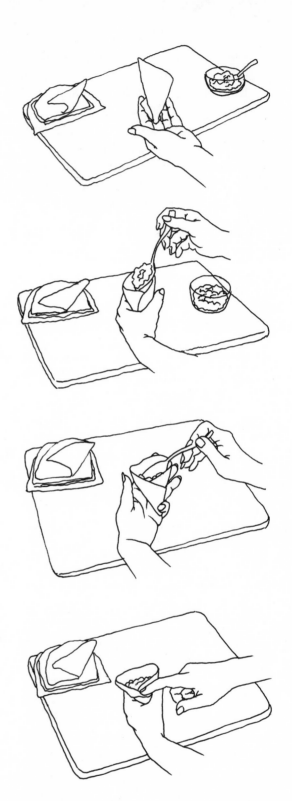

10. Holding the cone as you would an ice-cream cone, with the higher, rounded edge away from you, fill the cone with a heaping tablespoon of the potato-pea mixture.

Stuff it down towards the pointed end, but not so firmly that you force the point open.

Dip your index finger into the flour paste and run it along the side flap.

Press the side closed. With a little more paste, run your finger around the semicircular top edge and fold the edge over towards you.

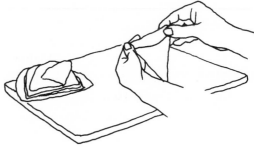

Seal it by pressing firmly.

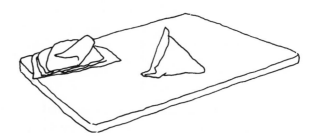

You should have a plump, triangular samosa. Repeat with the rest of the wrappers.

11. On a tray or plate, set the samosas aside, standing on edge. Allow them to dry completely. (You can refrigerate the dried samosas, uncovered, for up to 2 days.)

12. When ready to serve, fill a karhai,* or deep saucepan, with about 3 inches of oil. Heat over high heat until hot but not smoking. To test, drop a samosa-wrapper scrap into the oil; if it rises to the surface at once and sizzles, the oil is ready. Reduce to medium-high to maintain the temperature. Carefully drop 6 to 8 samosas into the oil and fry, turning once, for about 2 minutes. Serve with Tamarind and Date Chutney (see page 56) or any chutney of your choice.

MAKES 24

Vegetable Pakoras

Sabzi Pakoras

Crisp, crunchy, and addictive, these fritters are popular snacks in India and at the Bombay Cafe. Many different kinds of pakora can be found throughout India, but they are all made with a basic chick-pea batter. These are the simplest of pakoras— lightly battered pieces of vegetables, quickly fried, and served warm with chutney. The following recipe uses potatoes, cauliflower, mushrooms, spinach, and eggplant, but any vegetables can be substituted. I serve them with Sweet Tomato Chutney and Mint Chutney, but many other chutneys are delicious with these, too. This recipe makes enough for about 6 people, but I guarantee that they'll be clamoring for more.

FOR THE PAKORA BATTER:

1 cup besan ✳

Pinch baking soda

1/2 teaspoon cayenne pepper

1 teaspoon ground roasted cumin ✳

1/2 teaspoon salt

3/4 cup water

VEGETABLES:

2 medium red rose potatoes, peeled, thinly sliced, and set aside in warm salted water

16 to 18 medium cauliflower florets

16 to 18 small white mushrooms

18 to 20 medium, crisp spinach leaves, washed and completely dry

2 medium Japanese eggplants, cut into 1/2-inch thick, diagonal slices, and set aside in water

Vegetable oil for deep frying

Sweet Tomato Chutney (see page 55) and/or Mint Chutney (see page 59)

1. *To make the batter:* Sift besan into a mixing bowl and add baking soda, cayenne, cumin, and salt. With a whisk, slowly stir in the water to form a batter with the consistency of heavy cream. Set aside. (This recipe makes 1 cup batter. Any excess may be stored in the refrigerator for up to 1 week. The recipe may be halved.)

2. Fill a karhai,✳ or a large, deep sauce-pan, with about 2 to 3 inches of oil. Heat the oil over high heat until hot but not smoking. The correct temper-ature is important: If the oil is too hot, the batter will darken too fast, but if it is not hot enough, the pako-ras will absorb too much oil and remain greasy. Test the oil to see if it is ready by dropping in a little batter; if it rises immediately to the surface and sizzles, the temperature is cor-rect. Lower heat to medium high to maintain the temperature.

3. Dip 5 to 6 pieces of one vegetable into the batter, coating well. Drop them carefully into the hot oil. Turn the pieces once during cooking and fry them until they are golden brown. Potatoes and cauliflower usually take about 1½ minutes; mushrooms, spinach and eggplant about 1 minute.

4. Remove the vegetable from the oil and set on paper towels to drain. Once the pieces have been drained, place them on a platter and keep them warm in a low oven for no more than 15 minutes, or they will lose their crispness. Serve with chutney.

SERVES 6 TO 8

Chicken Pakoras
Murgh Pakoras

I don't believe in skimpy Chicken Pakoras made of measly bits of minced chicken. I make my chicken pakoras using big chunks of breast meat, marinated in seasonings and dipped in chick pea batter. The light frying keeps the chicken moist and tender and the spices give it incredible flavor. Sweet Tomato Chutney (see page 55) is my husband's favorite accompaniment. As you will see in the variation below, this method works perfectly with fish, too, producing delectable, crisp tidbits, as light as an ocean breeze.

15 large cloves garlic

3-inch piece ginger, peeled and coarsely chopped

1 tablespoon lemon juice

2 teaspoons paprika

1 teaspoon cayenne pepper

2 teaspoons ground roasted cumin ✳

2 teaspoons crushed anardana ✳

1/4 teaspoon mace

1/4 teaspoon nutmeg

1 teaspoon salt

12 chicken breast tenders, cut in half on the bias

4 to 5 tablespoons pakora batter (see page 26)

Vegetable oil for frying

1. In a blender, purée the garlic, ginger and lemon juice, using a small amount of water, if needed. (This works best in one of the small blender jars that are sold as accessories for some blenders.) Scrape the purée into a bowl and mix in all the dry spices.

2. Fill a karhai,* or large, deep saucepan, with about 2 to 3 inches of oil. Heat the oil over high heat until hot but not smoking. The correct temperature is important: If the oil is too hot, the batter will darken too fast, but if it is not hot enough, the pakoras will absorb too much oil and remain greasy. Test the oil to see if it is ready by dropping in a little batter; if it rises immediately to the surface and sizzles, the temperature is correct. Lower heat to medium-high to maintain the temperature.

3. Place 8 pieces of chicken at a time in a bowl. Add 1/3 of the masala mix and toss the chicken to coat. Then add 1/3 of the batter, tossing again to coat each piece. Carefully drop the chicken pieces into the oil and fry until golden reddish-brown, about 1 minute. Do not overcook. Remove and drain on paper towels. Once they have been drained, place them on a platter and keep them warm in a low oven for no more than 15 minutes, or they will lose their crispness. Serve with chutney.

SERVES 6 TO 8

Variation:

FISH PAKORAS
(MACHCHI PAKORAS)

Instead of chicken, substitute 1½ pounds of halibut or other firm, white fish, cut into 18 to 20 strips, about 1½ inches long and 1½ inches thick. Coat and fry them exactly as for Chicken Pakoras. Serve with lemon wedges instead of chutney.

South Indian Crepes Stuffed with Turmeric Potatoes

Masala Dosas

Dosas are to South India as tandoori meats are to the Punjab—the most characteristic, beloved food of the region. South Indians relish them at any meal, but absolutely insist on having them for Sunday lunch. Dosas are thin crepes made from a lightly fermented batter of rice flour and puréed lentils; the batter must be made at least one day in advance for proper flavor. In this recipe, the crepes are folded over a spicy mixture of potatoes and onions. They are delicious served with South Indian Toor Dal and Coconut Chutney (see pages 112 and 64).

FOR THE BATTER:

1 cup urad dal ✳

2 cups rice flour

3/4 cup water

1 teaspoon salt

FOR THE POTATOES:

3 tablespoons vegetable oil

1 teaspoon mustard seeds ✳

8 to 10 kari leaves ✳

1/2 teaspoon cumin seeds ✳

1 large onion, thinly sliced

2 green serrano chiles, minced

1 teaspoon turmeric

6 large red rose potatoes, peeled and boiled

1 1/2 teaspoons salt

1/4 cup vegetable oil

South Indian Toor Dal (see page 112)

Coconut Chutney (page 64)

1. *To make the batter:* Pick over, wash, and cover urad dal in cold water by at least 2 inches. Soak overnight.

2. In a large work bowl, mix the rice flour with 3/4 cups of water. Set aside.

3. Drain the soaked beans and place them in a blender. Purée on high with 1 1/2 cups of fresh water to form a thin, smooth paste. Pour the paste into the rice flour mixture. Mix well, add the salt, and set aside in a warm place for 2 hours to ferment. Refrigerate the batter for at least 3 hours, or until ready to prepare the dosas. The batter may be made ahead and refrigerated up to two days. Skim off any thin liquid that has risen to the top and stir well before using.

4. Heat oil on high in a medium saucepan with a lid, tilting to form a pool. Add the mustard seeds and the kari leaves and immediately cover to avoid splattering. When the splattering

subsides, after about 30 seconds, add the cumin seeds and let them sizzle for about 30 seconds more.

5. Add the onions and sauté until lightly browned, about 3 to 4 minutes.

6. Add the chiles, mix well, and reduce heat to low. Stir in the turmeric.

7. Add the potatoes, crushing and crumbling them with your hands to form small pieces. Add the salt, mix well, and cook, covered, for 10 minutes. Remove from heat and set aside. (The stuffing may be prepared a day ahead;

reheat it either in the microwave or over low heat in a skillet before proceeding.)

8. Heat a griddle or heavy skillet over high heat. Test it by sprinkling droplets of water on the surface, as for pancakes. When they sizzle and dance, the griddle is ready.

9. Baste the griddle with a little oil, let cook for 1 to 2 minutes to season the surface, and then wipe clean with a moist towel. The griddle should be wiped clean after preparing each dosa.

10. Using a ladle, spoon about 1/2 cup of batter onto the griddle. Using the base of the ladle, quickly spread the batter in a circular motion, starting from the center, to form an oblong crepe about 7 inches long and 4 to 5 inches wide.

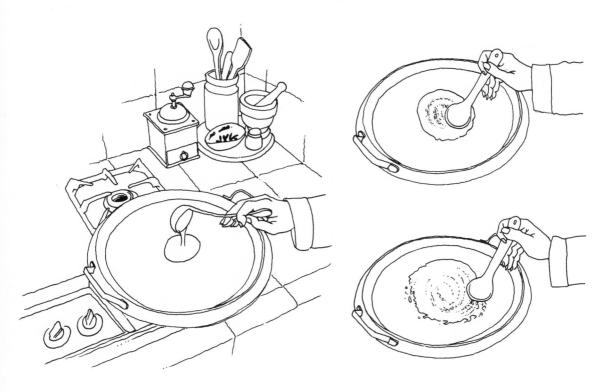

11. When the edges start to brown, after 1 or 2 minutes, sprinkle about 1 teaspoon of oil all around the edges and a few drops on the top of the dosa. Continue to cook for another 1 minute or so, until the whole dosa lifts off the griddle easily.

12. Using a thin metal spatula, lift the edges of the dosa to loosen.

Place 4 to 5 tablespoons of the potato masala lengthwise down the center.

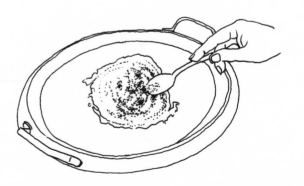

Fold over like a crepe and serve with a small bowl of South Indian Toor Dal and a tablespoon of Coconut Chutney. Repeat procedure to make additional dosas. These are best eaten as soon as possible after they are cooked. Keep warm.

MAKES 10 TO 12 DOSAS

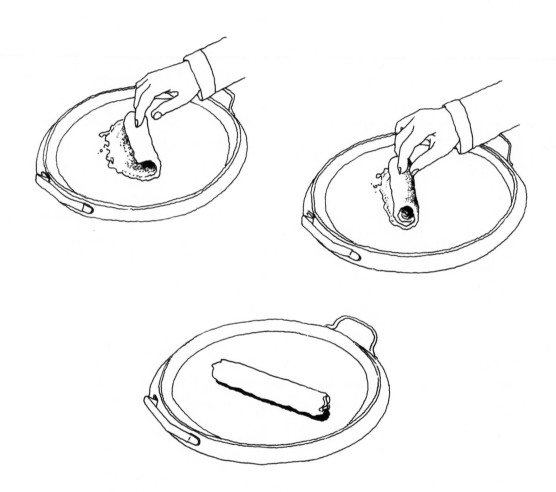

Frankies

Irresistible Frankies, one of Bombay's favorite fast foods, are sold from carts all over town. No one knows exactly how they came about, but they seem to be an Indian derivative of the ordinary frankfurter. You'd never guess its humble origins by tasting one of these delicious griddle breads ("rotis") wrapped around chunky, spicy fillings of Lamb Masala (see recipe right), Chicken Masala (see page 196) or Cauliflower Curry (see page 132), and topped with lively chutneys. This recipe seems complicated, but Frankies are quick to assemble, once you have the elements on hand. The griddle breads are easy and can be made in advance or frozen. The Lamb Masala filling is a devilishly spicy dish that also works as a main course, so you could make extra to use at another time. I love introducing people to the delights of India's "humble" street foods; clearly, my customers enjoy it too, because these Frankies have become one of the Bombay Cafe's most popular dishes.

1. *To make the rotis:* Sift 2 cups flour, sugar, and salt in a large mixing bowl. Make a well in the flour and add the yogurt. Mix with your fingers while adding milk, 1/4 cup at a time. Use only enough milk to form a soft pliable dough. Dust with a little of the remaining flour and set aside, covered, for about 15 to 20 minutes.

FOR THE ROTIS:

2 1/2 cups flour

1 teaspoon salt

1 teaspoon sugar

1/4 cup plain yogurt,✳ store-bought or homemade (see page 5)

1/2 to 3/4 cup milk

FOR THE LAMB MASALA:

6 cloves garlic

2-inch piece ginger, peeled

3 tablespoons oil

2 large onions, thinly sliced

1 1/2 pounds boneless lamb, preferably from the leg, cut into 1-inch cubes

1 tablespoon ground coriander ✳

1 teaspoon ground cumin ✳

1 1/2 teaspoons cayenne pepper

1/4 teaspoon turmeric

2 large tomatoes, halved and thinly sliced

3 green serrano chiles, halved, seeded, and sliced on the bias

1 teaspoon salt

FOR THE ASSEMBLY:

2 eggs

1/4 cup oil

1/2 cup Tamarind and Date Chutney (see page 56)

1/4 cup Green Chile Chutney (see page 63)

Lime-Cilantro Onions (see page 199)

2. Divide dough into 8 equal parts and roll each into a ball. Dredge in flour and flatten into disks 2½ to 3 inches in diameter. Roll them out into thin 8-inch rounds, using as much flour as needed.

3. Heat a griddle or large frying pan over medium-high heat and toast the rotis for about a minute on each side. Set aside to cool. (If freezing or refrigerating for later use, seal them tightly, first in plastic and then in aluminum foil, to ensure freshness.)

MAKES 8

4. *To make the lamb:* Purée the garlic and half the ginger in a blender using a little water as needed (This works best in one of the small blender jars that are sold as accessories for some blenders.) Set aside in a bowl. Slice the rest of the ginger into thin matchsticks and set aside.

5. Heat the oil in a large saucepan over high heat. Add the onion and sauté until it turns dark gold, about 5 to 6 minutes. Stir frequently so that they do not burn at the edges.

6. Add the garlic and ginger purée and the cubes of lamb, continuing to brown for another 5 to 6 minutes, until all the meat juices have almost dried up. Add the coriander, cumin, cayenne, and turmeric, combining well. Mix in the sliced tomatoes, chiles, sliced ginger, and salt. Reduce the heat to low, cover, and cook for about 1 hour and 15 minutes, or until the meat is tender enough to cut easily with a fork.

7. *To assemble Frankies:* Beat the eggs and set aside. Heat a large griddle or heavy skillet over high heat. Place a roti on it and turn after about 30 seconds. Brush on oil lightly and turn again. Oil the other side.

8. Pour about 1½ tablespoons beaten egg on top of a roti. When the egg starts to firm up, flip the roti to cook the egg into a light omeletlike coating on that side. This process should take no more than 2 minutes.

9. Remove to a plate, egg-side down. Place 3 tablespoons of warm Lamb Masala in the center lengthwise. Add some Lime-Cilantro Onions, 1 teaspoon Green Chile Chutney and 1 tablespoon Tamarind and Date Chutney. Fold the bottom end of the roti over about 1½ inches, and roll like a burrito. Serve immediately.

MAKES 8

Soups

Soup was never part of Indian cooking until the British brought their love of it to the country during their years of power and influence. Many Indian upper-class households adopted the British customs in numerous ways—clothing, manners, education, sports, and, of course, food. Therefore, soup became a familiar item on the table of many Indian families, mine included. (I remember frequently being served plain old cream of tomato soup both at home and at boarding school.)

Nevertheless, the Indian cook's repertoire of soups is small. The reasons for this are simple. As I have described, all the dishes in an Indian meal are served at once, and diners usually eat small amounts of many different dishes, all on one plate. This style of eating obviously does not work for soup. Another reason soups are not usually part of the cuisine is that many Indian dishes, especially dals, or lentil dishes, are very saucy—almost soupy—themselves, which makes soup a bit redundant.

However, some of these saucy dishes can be easily and deliciously adapted as soups. The following chapter includes four soups, two of which began as dals. And, in the Dals chapter, I have also noted some dishes which could be served as wonderful soups themselves. Any of these, served with chapatis or the toasted Indian crackers known as *poppadum*, make a lovely light lunch or first course when you're in the mood for a meal structured along Western lines.

Tomato–Lentil Soup

Rasam

Southern Indians might recognize this dish as a favorite regional dal, but I have transformed it into a deliciously simple soup. I often serve this as an uncomplicated lunch, accompanied by toasted lentil poppadums, or as a starter, followed by a simple meat dish such as Chicken Kabobs in Green Spices (see page 200) and some Potatoes with Mustard Seeds and Kari Leaves (see page 156).

2/3 cup dry toor dal ✳

1 teaspoon black peppercorns

1 teaspoon coriander seeds,✳ lightly
toasted in a dry pan

1/2 teaspoon cayenne pepper

1/4 teaspoon turmeric

1 1/4 teaspoons salt

2-inch piece tamarind pulp ✳

1 tablespoon vegetable oil

2 medium tomatoes, diced small

Fresh cilantro, chopped, to garnish

1. Pick over lentils and wash several times until water runs almost completely clear. Soak in hot water for 30 minutes.

2. Drain lentils and place in a large saucepan with 10 cups of water. Bring to a full boil, skimming off any foam that rises. Add peppercorns, coriander, cayenne, turmeric , and salt. Reduce heat to low and cook for one hour, partially covered. Skim foam occasionally from top and add water if it is absorbed too fast. The lentils should have a brothlike consistency.

3. Meanwhile, soak tamarind pulp in 2/3 cup hot water. After 15 minutes, mash pulp and force through a sieve, using fingers, to produce about 3 tablespoons of strained pulp.

4. When the lentils have cooked down completely, and are almost disintegrating, add the tamarind pulp. Strain the mixture through a fine sieve, discarding the whole spices and whatever solids remain. Return the strained lentil broth to the stove, over low heat.

5. Heat the oil over high heat in a skillet and sauté the tomatoes, stirring and pressing down on them with the back of a wooden spoon for about 2 to 3 minutes, until they resemble a coarse purée. Add the tomatoes to the lentils. Cook for another 10 minutes to blend the flavors. Garnish with cilantro.

SERVES 6

Cauliflower, Carrot, and Ginger Soup
Gobi Gajjar Ka Shorba

I developed this recipe as my contribution to a
potluck Thanksgiving dinner. Its rich, golden color is
in perfect harmony with that autumnal feast, but its
Indian flavors add a distinctly unexpected zing.

2-inch piece ginger, peeled

1 small cauliflower, about 1½ pounds

3 medium carrots

2 medium tomatoes, quartered

1 small potato, peeled and quartered

3 green serrano chiles, halved
lengthwise

1 small onion, peeled and quartered

1 teaspoon salt

2 tablespoons vegetable oil

1 teaspoon cumin seeds ✳

6 sprigs fresh cilantro, to garnish

6 lemon wedges

1. Slice half of the ginger into thin matchsticks and set aside for garnish. Chop the other half coarsely.

2. Discard the outer leaves of the cauliflower. Break into florets and select about 9 of the small, inner florets. Slice these in half and set aside these 18 florets for garnish. Chop the rest of the cauliflower, including stem and inner leaves, into large pieces.

3. Peel the carrots and slice one into thin matchsticks for garnish. Set aside. Chop the remaining carrots into large chunks.

4. Place the chopped ginger, cauliflower, carrots, tomatoes, potato, chiles, and onion in a 6-quart saucepan. Add 10 cups of water and the salt and bring to a boil. Reduce heat to low and cook, covered, for 1 hour. Strain the stock through a colander and carefully remove the potato, cauliflower, and half of the carrots, discarding the rest. Place these vegetables in a blender or food processor and purée. Return the purée to the soup. This can be done a day or two in advance. Refrigerate.

5. To serve, bring the soup to a full boil and reduce heat to a simmer while making the *tadka,** or finishing touch. Heat the oil over high heat in a small skillet and tilt the pan to form a pool. Add the cumin seeds to the oil and when they finish sizzling, add the reserved cauliflower florets. Let them brown briefly in the hot oil and add them to the hot soup. Cook for one minute.

6. Divide cut into matchsticks carrots and ginger among 6 soup bowls and ladle in the hot soup, being sure to include three cauliflower florets in each serving. Garnish each bowl with a sprig of cilantro and place a wedge of lemon on each plate. Serve immediately.

SERVES 6

Chicken Soup with Spinach, Tomatoes, and Rice

Murghi Shorba

I consider this recipe an Indian version of Mother's chicken soup and my customers agree: They frequently tell me it's good enough for whatever ails them. I created this soul-satisfying soup to make use of the large quantity of delicious stock produced when I make Cornish Hens with Dried Mango Powder (see page 212).

1 pound chicken backs, skinned

1 large onion, peeled and quartered

3 to 4 large cloves garlic

1½-inch piece ginger, peeled
and coarsely chopped

3 to 4 green serrano chiles, quartered
plus 2 for optional garnish

1 medium carrot, peeled and chopped

2 medium tomatoes, quartered, plus 1

2 to 3 black cardamom pods ✳

2 (1-inch) pieces cinnamon stick
or cassia ✳

5 to 6 cloves

8 to 10 whole black peppercorns

2 bay leaves

2 boneless, skinless chicken breasts
(about ½ pound)

1¼ teaspoons salt

1 cup cooked basmati rice ✳

12 large leaves fresh spinach, cut into
matchsticks

2 tablespoons fresh cilantro, chopped

Juice of 2 lemons

1. To prepare stock, place chicken backs in a large stockpot with 12 cups of water. Bring to a rapid boil, skimming off the foam. Add the onions, garlic, ginger, 3 or 4 quartered chiles, carrots, 2 quartered tomatoes, cardamom, cinnamon or cassia, cloves, peppercorns, and bay leaves. Bring to a boil again and then reduce heat to simmer for 1 hour.

2. Add the boneless chicken breasts and salt. Continue to cook over medium low heat for 20 minutes more.

3. Remove the chicken breasts and set aside. Strain the stock through a sieve, mashing down the vegetables to extract as much flavor as possible. The stock can be made a day ahead. Refrigerate the stock and the cooked breasts separately until ready to proceed.

4. When ready to serve, shred the chicken breasts and set aside. Cut the remaining tomato into a small dice. Mince the optional remaining chiles. Make sure these ingredients and the cup of cooked white rice are no cooler than room temperature.

5. Skim off and discard any congealed fat on the surface of the chilled stock. Place the pot over high heat and bring to a full boil. Meanwhile, divide the chicken, rice, tomato, spinach, and chiles among 6 large soup bowls. Ladle hot broth into each bowl. Sprinkle each serving with chopped cilantro and lemon juice. Serve hot.

SERVES 6

Lentil Soup with Lemon and Chiles

Gujerati Ossaman

In this recipe, versatile lentils get a tangy boost from lemons and ginger.
You can easily adjust the amount of chile according to individual taste. I adapted
this flavorful dish from a traditional dal served in Northwestern India,
and I like it even better served as a soup.

1 cup dry toor dal *

1 teaspoon salt

1 1/2 tablespoons melted ghee *

1/2 teaspoon mustard seeds *

1/2 teaspoon cumin seeds *

10 to 12 fresh kari leaves *

1/2-inch piece ginger,
peeled and minced

1 to 2 green serrano chiles, minced

Juice of 2 lemons

1. Pick over the lentils. Wash several times and soak for 30 minutes. Drain the lentils and place in a 6-quart saucepan with 10 cups of water. Bring to a full boil, skimming off any foam.

2. Add the salt and lower heat. Continue to cook, partially covered, over low heat, for 1 hour, skimming the foam from time to time and replacing water as needed. After 1 hour, the soup should be a thin broth, and the lentils will have disintegrated completely. The soup can be made up to this point a day or two in advance. Refrigerate until ready to proceed.

3. To serve, heat the soup to a full boil. In a small saucepan with a lid, heat the ghee over high heat and tilt the pan to form a pool. Combine mustard seeds, cumin seeds, kari leaves, ginger, and chiles, and add them all together to the hot ghee. Cover immediately until the sizzling subsides. Carefully add this mixture to the hot soup; avoid splattering. Stir in the lemon juice and serve hot.

SERVES 6 TO 8

Raitas, Chutneys, and Salads

An Indian meal is not complete without the enhancing flavors of cooling, refreshing raitas and sweet, hot or sour chutneys. They are like punctuation marks in a text—small, but essential for success.

Raitas, which always contain yogurt and seasonings along with finely chopped vegetables, are served in small portions as a cooling contrast to the rest of a meal. Indians make yogurt for their raitas each night at home. I include a simple recipe for homemade yogurt, which I find tangier than store-bought, on page 5. There are no rules about choosing raitas to go with meals, except to avoid duplicating main ingredients: Don't serve the spinach raita with another spinach dish, for example. For very simple yet nutritious meals, I find nothing more satisfying than a comforting, well-seasoned dal, rice, and a raita.

A chutney is simply a form of relish used to balance flavors in other dishes. Chutneys can be made from any number of ingredients. They may be fruit-based and sweet, like the imported mango chutneys many people are familiar with, or they may be fiery and full of chiles. Indians often serve more than one chutney with a meal, balancing a very hot one with a sweet one, for example. Unusual ingredients, such as dried cranberries, often inspire some of my favorite chutneys, and I encourage cooks to experiment with their own combinations after they have become comfortable with the basic methods and seasonings.

The Bombay Cafe is famous for its chutneys. Of course, I serve them in the traditional manner, as an enhancement to "main dishes," but I also love using them unconventionally—with crisp crackers or poppadum as snacks, or dolloped on top of uttapams (griddle cakes) as appetizers, or with fried samosa wrappers, the way Mexicans serve chips and salsa. Although most Indian cookbooks present chutneys at the end, almost as an afterthought, I give them pride of place, both on my table and in this book.

Chutneys keep well in the refrigerator for weeks, as long as certain procedures are followed: Always spoon out just what is needed for a meal, using a clean spoon, and never put leftovers back into the jar. Again there are no rules as to which chutney to serve with a meal; I offer some suggestions throughout the book, but feel free to try different combinations on your own.

Green salads were unknown in India when I was growing up, probably because lettuce required too much irrigation to be a practical crop there. Usually we would serve a raita in place of a salad. The only exception was called "salat," a platter of cut vegetables drizzled with lemon juice. Now, however, as a Californian of twenty-nine years, I adore green salads as much as any native, and have created a few with an Indian flair, including the popular California Tandoori Salad. My delicious Cilantro-Cumin Dressing has become the house dressing at the Bombay Cafe; it may well become yours, too. Several of my other favorite salads, like the Black-Eyed Pea Salad, have a hearty, chopped-vegetable base, which makes them ideal for picnics or summer meals.

This chapter, in particular, offers cooks free rein to indulge their creative impulses, trying out their own favorite combinations for raitas, chutneys, and salads.

Tomato, Garlic, and Yogurt Relish
Tamatar Ka Raita

Every time I return to India, my friends and family vie to impress me with their latest gastronomic creations, hoping I'll take the recipe back and put it on the menu at the restaurant. This tangy raita is my aunt's recipe. I serve it frequently as a delicious accompaniment to Browned Lamb with Onions and Tomatoes and South Indian Green Beans (see pages 221 and 129), among others. This dish requires red, ripe, summer tomatoes to be at its best.

2 large, ripe tomatoes

2 cups plain yogurt,✳ store-bought or homemade (see page 5)

1 large clove garlic, minced

1 teaspoon salt

1 tablespoon vegetable oil

1 teaspoon mustard seeds ✳

8 to 10 kari leaves ✳

2 to 3 green serrano chiles, thinly sliced, lengthwise

1. Halve the tomatoes and force the cut side against the large holes of a grater set over a bowl, so that the grated flesh and juices are caught. Discard the skins.

2. Whisk the yogurt, garlic, and salt into the tomatoes.

3. Heat the oil over high heat in a small saucepan with a lid and tilt to form a pool. Add the mustard seeds and cover immediately. When they stop splattering, lift lid carefully and add kari leaves and chiles. Stir-fry until lightly blistered, about 2 minutes.

4. Add to yogurt mixture and mix well. Chill for several hours.

SERVES 6 TO 8

Potato and Yogurt Relish
Aloo Ka Raita

Cubes of tender potato in tangy, cumin-scented yogurt make this a substantial raita.
This was my father's favorite, and so my mother served it frequently, both to please him
and because all of the ingredients are easily available year-round. This traditional
Punjabi dish reminds me of my childhood.

2 medium red rose potatoes

2 cups plain yogurt,✳ store-bought
or homemade (see page 5)

1 teaspoon ground
roasted cumin ✳

1/2 to 3/4 teaspoon salt

1/2 teaspoon cayenne pepper

1. Boil potatoes until done, about 25 minutes, depending upon size. When they are cool enough to handle, peel them and dice into 1/2-inch pieces.

2. Place the yogurt in a bowl and fold in the potatoes, cumin, salt, and cayenne. Taste and adjust for saltiness and spiciness. Set aside in a cool place for 1 hour or refrigerate if made in advance. Remove from the refrigerator at least 1/2 hour before serving.

SERVES 6 TO 8

Spinach and Yogurt Relish
Palak Ka Raita

With its shredded spinach and chopped tomato, this dish seems almost like a mixed green salad with a tangy yogurt dressing. It goes well with Lamb Chops with Black Pepper and Vinegar (see page 216) or in a vegetarian meal with Baby Red Potatoes in a Tomato–Yogurt Sauce (see page 160), among other dishes.

$^{1}/_{2}$ pound spinach leaves
(about 1 small bunch)

$1^{1}/_{2}$ cups plain yogurt,✱
store-bought or homemade
(see page 5)

1 small tomato, seeded
and chopped finely

$^{1}/_{2}$-inch piece ginger, peeled and
minced

$^{1}/_{2}$ teaspoon salt, or more to taste

$^{1}/_{2}$ teaspoon cayenne pepper,
or more to taste

1. Remove and discard stems from spinach leaves. Julienne the leaves finely.

2. Mix all ingredients together, adjusting seasoning. Set aside in a cool place for an hour or refrigerate if made in advance. Remove from the refrigerator at least a $^{1}/_{2}$ hour before serving.

SERVES 6 TO 8

Banana-Yogurt Relish
Kela Ka Raita

The creamy sweetness of the banana in the cool yogurt balances
the spiciness of many Indian dishes beautifully. This is one of the most
popular raitas at the restaurant.

2 cups plain yogurt,✳ store-bought
or homemade (see page 5)

1 teaspoon ground
roasted cumin ✳

2 ripe bananas, peeled and sliced
into thin rounds

1 to 2 green serrano chiles, sliced
into thin rounds

1 tablespoon fresh cilantro,
chopped

1½ tablespoons sugar

½ teaspoon salt

¼ teaspoon cayenne pepper

1. Mix together all ingredients in a bowl.
Taste and add small amounts of sugar
or cayenne if desired. Set aside in a
cool place for 1 hour. Do not make
too far in advance, as the bananas
will turn brown.

SERVES 6 TO 8

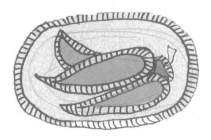

Cucumber and Onion Yogurt Relish
Kheere Ka Raita

This cooling cucumber condiment is perhaps the most widely known of Indian raitas among Americans. As simple and familiar as it is, however, I have rarely tasted a version here that is properly seasoned. The secret here (and for most raitas) is to use freshly roasted and ground cumin seeds.

2 cups plain yogurt,✳ store-bought or homemade (see page 5)

1 large cucumber, peeled, seeded, and finely chopped

1/2 small onion, finely chopped

1 green serrano chile, finely chopped

1 tablespoon fresh cilantro, chopped

1 teaspoon ground roasted cumin ✳

1 1/2 tablespoons sugar

1/2 teaspoon salt

1/4 teaspoon cayenne pepper

1. Mix all ingredients together and taste for seasonings. Add a little more sugar or chile, if desired. Refrigerate for about 1 hour and serve.

SERVES 6 TO 8

Variation: For a denser raita, more like a salad or relish, reduce the yogurt to 1 cup and increase the quantity of cucumbers to 3. Peel and seed the cucumbers as above, but grate them rather than chopping them. Squeeze out the cucumber juice by hand. Blend with the remaining ingredients.

Apricot Chutney with Nigella Seeds
Khurmani Chutney

This sweet-and-sour chutney goes well with tandoori meats and fish, or even Western-style grilled foods. Because it is such a favorite, I make it in large quantities to give as gifts. My friends report to me that they even enjoy this chutney on crackers or toast with a cup of tea.

1/2 pound dried apricots

1/3 cup plus 1 tablespoon white vinegar

1/4 cup sugar

1 1/2 ounces jaggery ✳

1 teaspoon nigella seeds ✳

1 heaping teaspoon cayenne pepper

3 to 4 whole cloves

1-inch piece cinnamon stick or cassia ✳

5 whole black peppercorns

1/2 teaspoon ground cinnamon

1. Soak dried apricots in 1 1/4 cups of hot water for six hours or overnight in the refrigerator.

2. The apricots will have absorbed all the water after soaking. Purée them in a blender or food processor and transfer into a nonreactive pan.

3. Add the remaining ingredients and 1 1/2 cups of water. Sir well.

4. Cook over low heat for about 30 minutes, stirring every so often to prevent sticking, until chutney resembles a thick preserve. Check for seasoning, adding more water or sugar as needed. Cool. (Traditionally, the whole spices remain in the chutney, but they may be removed at this point if desired.)

MAKES 3 CUPS

South Indian Red Onion and Tomato Chutney
Sagar's Pyaaz Ki Chutney

On a recent trip to India, I went to a little restaurant that serves typical South Indian food. I liked this pungent, sweet-and-hot chutney so much that I had to have the recipe for the Bombay Cafe. Even though I explained to the owner that my restaurant was in the United States, he would not relinquish his trade secret. Under intense coaxing, the waiter did reveal that the base was red onions and tomatoes. I figured out the rest on my own.

2 tablespoons oil

1 large red onion, coarsely chopped

5 to 6 red serrano chiles (see Note)

2 medium ripe tomatoes

1-ounce piece tamarind,✻ (size of golf ball), soaked in 1/4 cup hot water and then strained

2 tablespoons sugar

1 teaspoon ground roasted cumin ✻

1/2 teaspoon salt

1 teaspoon black salt ✻

1. Heat oil in a skillet over high heat. Add the onions and chiles, sautéing until the onions turn reddish brown. Add the tomatoes and continue to sauté, stirring frequently until they soften and cook down into a pulp.

2. Remove from the heat and add the tamarind pulp, sugar, cumin, and the two types of salt. Allow the mixture to cool a little and then purée in a food processor, scraping down the sides of the work bowl. Adjust the salt and sugar, if needed. The chutney should be slightly sweet. (You may substitute 2 tablespoons of prepared Tamarind and Date Chutney [see page 56], if you have it, for the tamarind, sugar, cumin, and salt.)

MAKES ABOUT 1 1/2 CUPS

Note: Red serrano chiles are sometimes available in the market or you can try leaving green ones on a sunny window sill, which often turns them red. If you cannot find red serrano chiles, you can use dried arbol chiles. Soak them in hot water to rehydrate for about 1/2 an hour, but discard the water, as it will be very hot.

Sweet Tomato Chutney

Meethi Tamatar Chutney

With the sweetness of the jaggery (a substance like brown sugar) and the heat of the chiles, this good, basic chutney brings out the flavors of almost anything. I even like it with the completely nontraditional corn chip! Based on a charred-tomato relish from Bengal, Sweet Tomato Chutney is one of the all-time favorites in the restaurant.

1 large can (29-ounce) whole, peeled tomatoes

1 tablespoon vegetable oil

1 tablespoon panch puran ✳

8 to 10 kari leaves ✳

2 to 3 green serrano chiles

¼ cup sugar

2 ounces jaggery ✳

1½ tablespoons white vinegar

1. Drain tomatoes. Coarsely chop in food processor.

2. Using a nonreactive 1-quart saucepan, heat the oil over high heat. Have a lid handy. Carefully add the panch puran, green chiles, and kari leaves and cover immediately to avoid splattering. Lift the lid after the sizzling subsides, about 30 to 45 seconds. Sauté until the chiles blister, about 1 minute.

3. Stir in the tomatoes, sugar, and jaggery. Cook over low heat until the jaggery melts and the liquid has reduced, about 25 to 30 minutes.

4. Cool, stir in the vinegar and refrigerate in a clean, airtight jar.

MAKES 2 CUPS

Tamarind and Date Chutney
Imli Ki Chutney

This sweet-and-sour traditional chutney makes the perfect partner for
Red Chile Chutney (see page 62). It can be made and kept tightly sealed
in jars in the refrigerator for several months.

½ pound tamarind pulp ✳

½ pound pitted dates

2 tablespoons ground roasted
cumin ✳

Pinch asafoetida ✳

2 teaspoons freshly ground
black pepper

2 teaspoons cayenne pepper

3 teaspoons black salt ✳

1 teaspoon salt

¾ to 1 cup sugar, depending on
the sweetness of the dates

6 ounces jaggery ✳

1. Pour 3 cups of boiling water over
   the tamarind pulp and allow to soak
   overnight. In another bowl, pour 1
   cup of boiling water over the dates
   and allow them to soak overnight
   also.

2. Break up lumps of soaked tamarind
   by kneading with fingers. Then force
   tamarind pulp through a fine sieve
   into a nonreactive saucepan. Scoop
   out the pulp remaining in the strainer
   and replace in soaking bowl. Knead
   again while adding a little hot water
   and repeat the straining procedure to
   get all the tamarind. Follow the same
   procedure with the dates.

3. Add remaining ingredients and cook
   over medium heat until the jaggery
   melts, stirring frequently. Reduce heat
   to low and simmer for about 10 minutes. Check seasoning and adjust for
   sweetness.

   MAKES 4 CUPS

Pear, Cherry, and Ginger Chutney

Sukhe Phal Ki Chutney

With the array of dried fruits available in this country, I can't resist creating interesting chutney combinations such as this one. Sweet-and-sour, with the zing of ginger, this one is great with parathas, whether plain or stuffed, or as an accompaniment to a simple meal of rice, dal, and a vegetable.

1/2 cup white vinegar

1/2 cup sugar

2 ounces jaggery ✳

2 bay leaves

5 to 6 whole cloves

1 1/2 teaspoons cayenne pepper

1/8 teaspoon turmeric

1-inch piece ginger, peeled and julienned

1 pound dried pears, cut into 1/4-inch strips

4 ounces dried cherries

1. In a nonreactive, medium saucepan, bring vinegar, sugar, jaggery, bay leaves, cloves, cayenne, turmeric, and 1 1/2 cups of water to a boil.

2. Cook over medium heat until a light syrup forms, about 8 to 10 minutes. Add ginger and cook for another 2 to 3 minutes.

3. Add pears and cherries and cook, covered, over low heat until the fruit softens and absorbs the flavors, about 25 to 30 minutes. If chutney becomes too thick, add no more than 1/4 cup water at a time. The chutney should resemble a thick preserve.

4. Remove bay leaves, cool, and pour into clean jars.

MAKES 3 1/4 CUPS

Dried Cranberry Chutney

I was once asked to bring a "cranberry chutney" to jazz up a Thanksgiving feast. Cranberries, of course, are not available in India, but this chutney came out very well despite its unconventional origins. Dried cranberries are available year-round now, so one doesn't have to wait for Thanksgiving to make this delicious accompaniment to Lamb Chops with Black Pepper and Vinegar or Rice with Ground Lamb, Green Beans and Garbanzo Beans (see page 216 or 226).

8 ounces dried cranberries

1/4 cup white vinegar

1 teaspoon cayenne pepper

4 whole dried red chiles

1/2-inch piece ginger, peeled and julienned

2 teaspoons nigella seeds ✳

1-inch piece cinnamon stick or cassia,✳ broken in half

6 to 7 whole cloves

2 bay leaves

6 to 7 black peppercorns

2/3 cup sugar

1. Place cranberries and 3 cups of water in a 4-quart nonreactive saucepan. Cook over high heat for about 4 to 5 minutes until the dried berries plump up and soften.

2. Add remaining ingredients and stir well. Lower heat, cover, and cook for about 30 minutes.

3. Check for seasoning, adding a little more water or sugar if necessary.

MAKES 2 CUPS

Mint Chutney
Pudine Ki Chutney

This lively chutney is one of the easiest to make (believe it or not, I have even made it on camping trips in India using wild mint and cilantro). For that reason, and because it enhances so many foods, such as tandoori meats, Lamb Kabobs with Sweet Tomato Chutney (see page 14), or stuffed parathas (see pages 92 to 99), it can be found frequently on almost every Indian table. Mint, which can turn black if handled improperly, will keep its bright green color if it is processed at the same time as other ingredients, such as cilantro.

1 tablespoon ground
roasted cumin ✳

1 small onion

2 to 3 green serrano chiles

3 to 4 tablespoons lemon juice

1/2 teaspoon salt, or more to taste

2 cloves garlic

1 cup fresh cilantro leaves

2 cups fresh mint leaves

1. Place all ingredients in a blender, in order, and blend, scraping down the container as necessary. Add spoonfuls of water or more lemon juice, to taste, if necessary to achieve a smooth consistency.

MAKES 1 1/2 CUPS

Yogurt Mint Chutney

Pudine Aur Dahi Ki Chutney

A variation of the preceding recipe, this chutney has a more saucelike texture because of the yogurt, making it perfect for dipping kabobs and breads, for example.

1 tablespoon ground
roasted cumin ✳

1/2 cup plain yogurt,✳ store-bought
or homemade (see page 5)

1 teaspoon dried ground
anardana ✳

2 cloves garlic

1/2 teaspoon salt

2 to 5 green serrano chiles

1 tablespoon lemon juice

1 cup packed fresh mint leaves

1/2 cup packed fresh cilantro leaves

1. Place all ingredients in a blender and process until smooth, scraping down the container as necessary.

MAKES ABOUT 1 CUP

Walnut and Yogurt Chutney
Akhrot Ki Chutney

Kashmiris, from the northern region of India, serve this rich chutney
frequently with highly spiced meat dishes. It also doubles as a good dip
for fresh vegetables. Any leftovers keep for several days, covered
tightly in the refrigerator, or the recipe may be halved.

---

2 cups walnut halves or pieces

2 cloves garlic

3 green serrano chiles

1 cup plain yogurt,✳ store-bought
or homemade (see page 5)

1/2 teaspoon salt, or more to taste

---

1. Place walnuts, garlic, and chiles in the
   bowl of a food processor and process
   until the mixture has the consistency
   of chunky peanut butter.

2. Add 1/2 cup of yogurt and blend. Taste
   for salt and adjust, if desired. Add
   remaining yogurt if a thinner consistency is desired.

MAKES 2 1/2 CUPS

Red Chile Chutney

Lal Mirchi Ki Chutney

My favorite street vendor, who sold delicious snacks from a cart in my neighborhood, always served them with a few of his special chutneys, including with this red-hot one. He was very proud to share his recipes with me when I told him I was opening a restaurant in Los Angeles. Pair this spicy chutney with a sweet one, such as Tamarind and Date Chutney (see page 56). The combination goes wonderfully with shrimp or fish. Though Red Chile Chutney is quite hot, my son even likes to add it to sandwiches.

2 teaspoons coriander seeds *

2 teaspoons cumin seeds *

12 large cloves garlic

14 whole dried arbol chiles

2 tablespoons cayenne pepper

1/2 teaspoon salt, or to taste

3 teaspoons lemon juice

1. Toast the coriander seeds and cumin seeds in a dry skillet over medium-high heat until they brown lightly.

2. Place the seeds, the garlic, whole chiles and cayenne in the blender. Adding 1/4 cup of water at a time (no more than 1/2 cup total), blend to a smooth paste. If there is too much liquid in the blender at this point, the resulting purée will not be smooth enough.

3. Add salt, lemon juice and about 1/4 cup more water and blend to make a sauce with the consistency of heavy cream.

MAKES 1 CUP

Note: This chutney is very hot and should be served by the teaspoon, with a sweet chutney, for contrast. If smaller quantities are desired, at step 2, the chile paste can be divided into 4 equal parts, frozen in plastic bags, and the chutney completed later, using 1/4 of the remaining ingredients for each packet of chile paste.

Green Chile Chutney

Hari Mirch Ki Chutney

Another traditional recipe from my favorite street vendor, this very spicy chutney should be served along with a contrasting sweet chutney, such as Pear, Cherry, and Ginger Chutney (see page 57), so that guests can choose from an array of flavors and heat.

12 to 14 coarsely chopped green serrano chiles

1/2 bunch fresh cilantro, chopped

1/2 bunch fresh mint leaves

1 tablespoon dalia ✳

2 tablespoons lemon juice

1 teaspoon salt

1. Place all the ingredients in the blender and purée, using a little water as needed. Adjust seasoning to taste, adding more lemon juice or chiles if desired. The chutney should be thick and very spicy.

MAKES ABOUT 1 CUP

Coconut Chutney
Naryal Ki Chutney

Used widely in the cuisines of the coastal regions, coconuts add a delectable richness to many curries and chutneys. This chutney is served with Uttapams (see page 11) and can enhance any light vegetarian meal such as Potatoes with Mustard Seeds and Kari Leaves, and Yogurt Curry with Daikon (see pages 156 and 135), along with Plain Basmati Rice (see page 78).

1 large coconut,* peeled and grated

2 tablespoons sour cream

3 tablespoons plain yogurt,* store-bought or homemade (see page 5)

1 teaspoon salt

2 tablespoons corn oil

1 teaspoon mustard seeds *

1 teaspoon cumin seeds *

1/2 teaspoon urad dal *

3 to 4 whole dried red chiles, broken in small pieces

4 to 5 kari leaves *

2 to 3 green serrano chiles, coarsely chopped

1. Place the grated coconut, sour cream, and yogurt in a blender and process, along with a little water as needed, to make a smooth paste. Add salt and remove to a small serving bowl. Set aside.

2. Heat the oil in a small saucepan with a lid, over high heat. Add the remaining ingredients and cover at once to avoid splattering. After the popping has subsided, about 30 to 45 seconds, lift the lid and sauté until the spices have finished sizzling, about 1 to 2 minutes. Stir this into the coconut mixture and serve. This keeps for about one week, in an airtight container in the refrigerator.

MAKES ABOUT 2 CUPS

Chopped Salad of Cucumber, Tomato, and Red Onions

Kachumber

Kachumber is an Indian term that describes simple, diced vegetables seasoned with nothing more than salt, pepper, and lemon juice. In traditional Indian cooking, this is the closest thing to a Western-style salad you'll find. This recipe is a classic combination; I often vary it by adding carrots, jicama, or any other vegetable I like.

1 small red onion, finely chopped

2 medium tomatoes, diced small

2 medium cucumbers or
1 English cucumber, peeled, seeded, and diced

2 tablespoons fresh cilantro, chopped

1 to 2 small green serrano chiles

1/2 teaspoon salt

1/2 teaspoon freshly ground black pepper

2 tablespoons lemon juice

1. In a bowl, toss all the ingredients together and set aside to blend the flavors for 30 to 45 minutes before serving.

SERVES 6

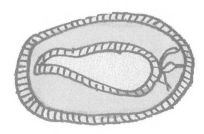

Carrot and Cilantro Relish

Gajjar ka Kutra

In this grated vegetable relish, the sweetness of the carrots is moderated by the zing of chiles and lemon juice. Although this type of relish is usually served along with an Indian meal, it can also be used as a simple starter by placing it on a bed of salad greens and garnishing it with cherry tomatoes or steamed baby beets.

3 to 4 medium carrots
(1½ pounds), peeled and grated

2 tablespoons fresh cilantro, chopped

1 large green serrano chile, minced

½ teaspoon salt

2 tablespoons sugar

2 tablespoons lemon juice

1 tablespoon vegetable oil

1 teaspoon mustard seeds ✳

8 to 10 fresh kari leaves ✳

1. Mix the grated carrots, cilantro, chile, salt, sugar, and lemon juice. Set aside.

2. Heat the oil over high heat in a small pan with a lid. Carefully add the mustard seeds and kari leaves and cover immediately to avoid splattering. When they finish sizzling, about 45 seconds, remove the lid and add the mustard seeds and kari leaves to the carrot mixture, mixing well. Set aside for at least a half-hour to blend the flavors. The relish can be made a few hours ahead, but refrigerate it so that the carrots don't wilt.

MAKES 2 TO 2½ CUPS OR SERVES 6

Variation I: Substitute an equal amount of grated jicama for half the carrots. Add ½ teaspoon cayenne pepper.

Variation II: Substitute an equal amount of grated daikon for half the carrots. Add ½ teaspoon of cayenne pepper.

Sweet and Sour Garbanzo Bean Relish

Chatpatta Channas

I love nutty-tasting garbanzo beans. They are very common in India, but
they are usually cooked in heavy curry sauces. This satisfying cold salad or
relish is the result of my desire to create a lighter, fresher dish featuring the goodness
of garbanzo beans. Usually I serve this as a refreshing counterpoint to a meal of
chicken curry and *Gobi Sabzi*, or Cauliflower with Ginger and Green Chiles
(see page 132) instead of dal. A more unconventional way of serving
this would be as a flavorful salad for a barbecue or picnic.

1 cup dried garbanzo beans
(about 1/2 pound)

1/4 teaspoon turmeric

1/2 teaspoon cayenne pepper

1/2 teaspoon black salt ✱

1/2 teaspoon salt

Juice of 1 lime

3 tablespoons Tamarind and
Date Chutney (see page 56)

1/2 cup red bell pepper,
finely diced

1/2 cup green bell pepper,
finely diced

1/3 cup (about 6) red
radishes, finely diced

1/2 cup green onions, finely
sliced, mostly white part

1. Place the beans in a large saucepan
   with about 5 cups of water and bring
   them to a full boil. Lower the heat,
   cover and cook for about an hour and
   15 minutes, until completely tender.
   Drain and place in a ceramic bowl.

2. Add the turmeric, cayenne, black salt,
   salt, lime juice, and chutney. Toss
   well to coat. Set aside to cool and
   absorb the flavors.

3. When the beans have cooled, add the
   diced vegetables and mix well. Check
   for seasonings, adding lime juice or
   chile as needed. Let the relish sit at
   room temperature for at least 30 minutes before serving. (The relish can
   be made several hours in advance.
   Refrigerate, but let it come to room
   temperature before serving.)

SERVES 6

Black-Eyed Pea Salad
Lobia Kachumber

This chopped salad centers on delicious black-eyed peas, punched up with red onion, cucumber and chiles. Cold dishes, other than raitas, are not at all traditional in Indian cooking, but as more and more younger Indians are exposed to the cuisines of other countries, salads such as this one are becoming popular. A friend in Delhi created this, complete with a secret ingredient, to test my palate. I successfully identified the slightly bitter dried fenugreek, much to his disappointment and my pleasure, because I have used the recipe successfully at the Bombay Cafe ever since.

1 cup dried black-eyed peas

1 cucumber, peeled, seeded and diced

1 small red onion, finely chopped

2 small tomatoes, diced

1 green serrano chile, finely chopped

1/4 cup fresh cilantro leaves, minced

1/4 cup dried fenugreek leaves ✻ (preferably Kastoori Methi)

1/2 teaspoon freshly ground black pepper

1 teaspoon salt

2 tablespoons lemon juice

6 to 8 radicchio leaves, cup-shaped, or other lettuce leaves (optional)

1. Place the peas in a small saucepan with 3 cups of water and a pinch of salt. Bring the water to a rapid boil, lower the heat and simmer, partially covered, for 15 to 20 minutes, until the beans are cooked through. Drain, rinsing the beans in cool water to arrest further cooking, and set aside until just cool.

2. Combine all the ingredients (except the optional radicchio or lettuce leaves) and check for seasoning, adding more salt or lemon juice as needed.

3. To serve, place a scoop of salad in each of the radicchio cups or mound in a bowl lined with lettuce leaves.

SERVES 6 TO 8

Sprouted Mung Bean Salad
with Daikon and Green Mangoes

Moongi Aur Mooli Ka Salat

With a little advance preparation to sprout the mung beans, this crisp and nutritious salad is easy to make. Mung beans are available in health-food stores. Sprouting beans before cooking them is a very common Indian way of obtaining the benefits of both legume and green vegetable in one. The sprouts are usually cooked with spices and served hot. Here, combined with the sweet daikon and tart green mangoes, they make a lovely summer salad.

3/4 cup green mung beans ✳

2 tablespoons lemon juice

1/2 cup red onions, thinly sliced

1 teaspoon salt

1 teaspoon freshly ground
black pepper

1 small green serrano chile,
finely chopped

1 cup daikon (about 1/2 pound),
diced small

1/2 cup raw, green mango,
diced small (about 1/2 mango,
or alternatively 1/2 cup tart,
green apple, diced)

1/2 cup fresh mint leaves, shredded

1. On the morning of the day before serving, pick over the mung beans, wash them until the water runs clear and soak in about 4 cups of hot water for at least 6 to 8 hours, until the beans split and soften. Drain and place in a bowl lined with a clean muslin cloth (not cheesecloth, as this is too porous). Loosely cover the beans, allowing room for them to breathe and sprout. Place in a dark, warm spot overnight. It is best to allow about 20 hours for them to sprout.

2. About 2 hours before serving, combine the lemon juice, onions, salt, pepper, and green chile and set aside.

3. Bring 4 cups of water to the boil in a saucepan and add the sprouted beans. Return the water to the boil and cook for two minutes. Drain and place the warm beans in a ceramic serving bowl. Stir in the lemon dressing, tossing well. Allow the beans to cool.

4. Add the daikon, green mango, and mint, toss well, and serve.

SERVES 6

Composed Salad of Tomatoes, Red Onions, Cucumbers, and Beets

Salat

Lettuce and other similar greens are not indigenous to India. For this reason, green salads as Westerners know them have not been a familiar part of the Indian meal. This "salat," composed of various vegetables in an artful arrangement, is what Indians think of as salad. It can be varied with whatever is on hand, but always with an eye to how the colors and shapes will look arranged on a platter.

> 2 medium beets, greens trimmed
>
> 1 small red onion
>
> 1 medium cucumber, preferably English
>
> 2 medium vine-ripened tomatoes
>
> 2 small green chiles
>
> 1/2 teaspoon salt
>
> 1/2 teaspoon freshly ground black pepper
>
> 2 lemons

1. Wrap the beets individually in plastic wrap and place in the microwave. Cook on high for 3 minutes. Let stand until cool enough to handle. Remove the plastic and peel the beets. Slice them into 1/8-inch rounds.

2. Cut the red onion into thin, round slices. Slice the unpeeled English cucumber into thin rounds (or peel, seed, and slice a regular cucumber into half-moons). Slice the tomatoes thinly and cut the green chiles into long, thin strips. Cut one lemon into thin wedges.

3. To serve, chill a large platter. Half an hour before serving, layer the vegetables on the platter, beginning with the onion. Arranging each layer in a circular pattern, place the beets on top of the onions. Sprinkle half the salt and pepper and half the juice of one lemon on top. Then layer the cucumber, the tomato, and the green chiles. Sprinkle the remaining salt, pepper and lemon juice over the top. Garnish with lemon wedges and set aside so flavors can blend.

SERVES 6 TO 8

Variation: Any number of sliced raw vegetables can be presented in this manner, such as radishes, daikon, jicama, sweet red peppers, or even tart green apples.

Cucumber and Peanut Salad

In this dish, crunchy peanuts are poised against buttery coconut, and the coolness of cucumbers contrasts with the fire of chiles in this interesting combination. I first encountered this in Bombay, where it is served as a relish, and sometimes instead of a chutney. Back at the restaurant, I tried serving it on a crisp bed of romaine lettuce and found out that it was really meant to be a delicious, memorable salad after all. Serve this with Ground Lamb with Peas and Fresh Spinach with Browned Garlic in Mustard Oil (see pages 219 and 165).

1 teaspoon cumin seed

1/2 cup raw peanuts

2 English cucumbers
(or 3 regular)

2 to 3 green serrano chiles,
finely chopped

1/4 cup fresh cilantro leaves,
minced

1/2 teaspoon salt

1 teaspoon sugar

2 tablespoons lemon juice

1/4 cup freshly grated coconut,✳
or dried unsweetened coconut,
reconstituted in warm water

Lettuce leaves for lining
the serving platter

1. Roast cumin seeds in small skillet, stirring frequently, until they brown, but do not allow them to darken too much. Transfer to a small plate, allow to cool, and then grind coarsely with mortar and pestle. Set aside.

2. Coarsely chop the peanuts and toast in a dry skillet over medium high heat, shaking a few times so that they roast evenly. Transfer to a small plate and set aside.

3. Peel cucumbers, cut in half lengthwise, and slice into thin half-rounds (if using regular cucumbers, peel and seed them before slicing).

4. Toss the cucumbers, chiles, cilantro, roasted cumin, salt, sugar, and lemon juice together in a bowl. Taste for seasoning, adding more lemon juice or salt as needed. Set aside for about 1/2 hour.

5. Just before serving, stir in half the roasted peanuts and the coconut. Place on a platter lined with lettuce leaves and sprinkle on the rest of the peanuts and coconut.

Serves 6 to 8

California Tandoori Salad

This completely nontraditional dish is what happens when you set an open-minded Indian cook—me—loose in salad-crazy California. Warm chunks of grilled, marinated tandoori-style chicken mingle with cubes of browned paneer and mushrooms, all unified by tangy Cilantro-Cumin Dressing. The mixture is served warm over a bed of crisp Romaine lettuce and sprinkled with crunchy, fried Indian noodles. It makes a wonderful lunch or light supper. Oddly enough, the dressing proved to be my biggest challenge—I worked hard to create something with plenty of bright Indian flavor, but not so much that it overwhelmed the salad greens. The result was so well received that it quickly became the "house dressing" at the restaurant.

FOR THE CILANTRO-CUMIN DRESSING:

3/4 cup fresh cilantro leaves and tender stems, tightly packed

1/2 cup lemon juice

3/4 cup vegetable oil

1 teaspoon ground roasted cumin ✳

1/2 teaspoon ground anardana ✳

1/2 teaspoon black pepper

1/4 teaspoon cayenne pepper

1/2 teaspoon salt

FOR THE SALAD:

1 tablespoon vegetable oil

12 medium white mushrooms, quartered

1/2 pound paneer,✳ cubed (1/2 recipe, see page 4)

6 pieces cooked Grilled Marinated Chicken (see page 198) or equivalent, boned and cut into bite-sized chunks

1 large head romaine lettuce, washed and torn into bite-sized pieces

2 small tomatoes, diced

1 cucumber, peeled and cubed

1/4 green or red bell pepper, sliced

6 green onions, sliced into thin rounds

1/2 cup sev, store-bought (see Note)

1. *Make the dressing:* In a blender, purée the cilantro and lemon juice until smooth, scraping down the sides as needed. With the machine running, slowly drizzle in the oil to emulsify the dressing. Add the seasonings and blend again for 30 to 45 seconds. This recipe yields about 1 1/2 cups. Reserve 1/2 cup for this salad and refrigerate the rest for another use.

2. *For the salad:* In a nonstick skillet, heat the oil over medium-high heat. Add the mushrooms and paneer cubes and sauté for about 2 minutes, browning them lightly. Add the chicken, continuing to sauté until the it is heated through. As you stir, the marinade clinging to the chicken should coat the mushrooms and paneer as well. Set aside to cool slightly.

3. Place the lettuce, tomatoes, cucumbers, peppers, and green onions in a large salad bowl. Add the warm chicken, and mushroom-paneer mixture.

4. Pour on the dressing and toss well to combine. Sprinkle with the sev and serve immediately.

SERVES 6

Note: Sev is a crisp, fried noodle made from besan (chick pea flour). They are easy to find in Indian markets, but if you are unable to find them, substitute crisp Chinese noodles.

Scallop and Paneer Salad

The mild flavor of scallops and homemade Indian cheese, or paneer, marries beautifully with the bright Indian flavors in this delicious dish—just as I had hoped when I created this handsome, warm salad. I have never seen scallops in India, but I have come to love them during my years in the West. This salad is perfect for a special lunch or a summer supper.

1/3 pound paneer ✱
(1/3 of the recipe, see page 4)

12 large sea scallops,
sliced in half horizontally

2 bunches green onions, white
and tender green parts, sliced

1 1/4 teaspoons cayenne pepper

1 teaspoon salt

1 tablespoon olive oil

1/2 tablespoon nigella seeds ✱

2 tablespoons lemon juice

2 teaspoons balsamic vinegar

1 tablespoon extra virgin olive oil

1/2 teaspoon salt

Freshly ground black pepper

Six handfuls (about 1 pound)
tender mixed lettuces

1. Slice the paneer horizontally into 1/4-inch-thick slices. Cut these into 1-inch squares. There should be about 18 pieces.

2. Sprinkle the sliced scallops with 1/2 teaspoon cayenne.

3. Over high heat, in a non-stick frying pan, sear the scallops, adding a few drops of olive oil if needed to prevent sticking. Cook, turning, for about 1 minutes, or until done. Remove to a platter and keep warm.

4. Sprinkle the paneer squares with 1/2 teaspoon cayenne. Using the same pan, over high heat, sauté the paneer until the squares are golden on both sides, about 1 minute. Remove to a platter and keep warm.

5. In the same pan, heat the rest of the olive oil over medium heat and add the nigella seed and green onions. Sauté until wilted, sprinkling with 1/2 teaspoon salt, 1/4 teaspoon cayenne, and the lemon juice.

6. Add the paneer squares and combine gently. Fold in the scallops. Reduce heat to very low or place pan in a low oven to keep warm while preparing the lettuces.

7. Toss dressing ingredients with the lettuces until just moistened. Divide the lettuces evenly among six plates.

8. Arrange 4 scallop pieces and three paneer pieces on each plate. Spoon the green onions and nigella dressing over all and serve immediately.

SERVES 6

Rice and Bread

Rice—and not just any rice, but flavorful, long-grained basmati rice—is an essential element in any Indian meal. Combined with dal, it forms a perfect—and very affordable—form of protein, and this also explains why it is the backbone of the Indian diet. Sometimes, on very simple occasions, this ubiquitous combination can form the entire meal. A hostess confronted with an unexpected guest for dinner, will use the saying, "Stay for dal chawal," which means, "Stay for dinner, even though it's only rice and dal." An American equivalent would be, "Stay for potluck."

Depending on what else is served with it, the rice might be served simply steamed or as an elaborate pullao (pilaf), with many additional seasonings and ingredients. Commonly, these pullaos are cooked with a little ghee (clarified butter), which adds buttery flavor as well as helping to keep the rice grains separate. Ghee, an important staple in Indian cooking, is easy to find ready-made in large markets or Indian grocery stores and it keeps very well.

Because rice is much more than a starchy side dish in Indian cuisine, it is not at all unusual to serve bread (and potatoes, too) at the same meal. Bread, in its various forms, offers a delightful difference in consistency to the other dishes surrounding it on an Indian table. Furthermore, in India, bread is an essential part of the meal because it is used in place of eating utensils, to scoop up the delicious, saucy vegetables and meat morsels. You may not adapt to that style of dining (although it is fun), but I think you'll enjoy adding these delicious breads, such as simple chapatis, naans, stuffed parathas, and crispy-fried puris to your repertoire. None of these breads require yeast, which makes the doughs themselves very quick to make. The more elaborate breads, such as the stuffed parathas, take time—but you'll be amply rewarded for your efforts.

Plain Basmati Rice
Chawal

Basmati rice has a nutty flavor all its own, which is particularly evident when it is served plain. This simple method, with a small amount of ghee, will always produce separate, fluffy grains. You can find basmati rice in the international section of large supermarkets. Some domestic growers are producing a type of basmati rice these days, but I think the imported kind is better.

1½ cups basmati rice ✳
2¼ cups warm water
1 teaspoon ghee ✳

1. Pick over rice, removing any stones. In a bowl, wash the rice in several changes of cold water until the water is clear.

2. Place rice in a medium saucepan and add the warm water. Soak the rice for at least 20 minutes but no longer than 45 minutes.

3. Bring rice and water to a rapid boil over high heat, add the ghee, and reduce heat to low. Cover and cook for 8 minutes.

4. Remove from heat and let stand for 2 or 3 minutes. Fluff rice gently with a fork and serve.

SERVES 6

Rice Pullao with Peas and Cumin

Mattar Wale Chawal

My grandmother served this rice dish almost every day to please my grandfather, who turned up his nose at plain rice. This pullao, though fancier than plain rice, is still simple enough so that it does not compete with flavorful curries.

1½ cups basmati rice ✳
1 tablespoon ghee ✳
1½ teaspoons cumin seeds
8 ounces frozen peas, rinsed with warm water
2¼ cups hot water
½ teaspoon salt

1. Pick over rice, removing any stones. In a bowl, wash the rice in several changes of cold water until the water is clear. Soak the rice in warm water to cover for at least 20 minutes but no longer than 45 minutes.

2. In a 10-inch skillet with a tightly fitting lid, heat the ghee over high heat. Tilt the pan and add the cumin seeds to the pool of ghee. When they sizzle, level the pan and add the drained rice. Mix gently so as not to break the grains.

3. Add the peas, hot water, and salt, stirring well. Bring to a full boil.

4. Immediately reduce the heat to low, cover tightly, and let cook for 8 minutes. Remove from heat and let stand, covered and undisturbed, for 5 minutes.

5. Uncover, fluff rice with a fork and serve immediately.

SERVES 6

Rice with Browned Onions
Bhuga Chawal

Plain rice may be fine for family and for some specific dals and curries, but when Indians entertain, a more festive version is usually required. Bhuga Chawal, with the added sweetness of the caramelized onions, is an easy choice, complementing especially meat and poultry dishes.

1½ cups basmati rice ✻

2 tablespoons ghee ✻

1 large onion, thinly sliced

4 black cardamom pods ✻
(6 to 8 green cardamom pods
may be substituted if black
is unavailable)

2 (1-inch) pieces cinnamon stick
or cassia ✻

2 bay leaves

6 whole cloves

2¼ cups hot water

½ teaspoon salt

1. Pick over rice, removing any stones. In a bowl, wash the rice in several changes of cold water until the water is clear. Soak the rice in warm water to cover for at least 20 minutes but no longer than 45 minutes.

2. Heat the ghee over high heat in a large saucepan. Add the onions and spices and sauté, stirring frequently, until the onions are dark brown, about 5 to 6 minutes.

3. Drain the rice and without stirring, add to the browned onions. Add 2¼ cups of water and the salt, stirring gently. Bring to a full boil and reduce heat to low. Cover and simmer for 10 minutes. Remove from heat and let stand, covered, for five minutes before serving.

SERVES 6

Rice with Onions, Tomatoes, and Chiles

Masala Chawal

Sweet, browned onions, tossed with chunks of fresh tomato
and lively ginger and chiles enrich this fragrant rice dish. Goes beautifully
with any light dal and Cornish Hens with Dried Mango Powder (see
page 212) or other grilled meat or fish dish.

1½ cups basmati rice ✳

3 tablespoons oil

1 teaspoon mustard seeds ✳

10 to 12 kari leaves ✳

1 teaspoon cumin seeds ✳

1 large onion, thinly sliced

½-inch piece ginger, peeled and
julienned

3 to 4 serrano chiles,
sliced lengthwise

2 small tomatoes, halved
and thinly sliced

2¼ cups hot water

1 teaspoon salt

2 tablespoons fresh cilantro,
chopped

1. Pick over rice, removing any stones. In a bowl, wash the rice in several changes of cold water until the water is clear. Soak the rice in warm water to cover for at least 20 minutes but no longer than 45 minutes.

2. In a 10-inch skillet with a lid, heat the oil over high heat. Tilt the pan so that the oil forms a pool and carefully add the mustard seeds and the kari leaves. Cover immediately to avoid splatters.

3. When the sizzling subsides, about 30 to 45 seconds, remove lid and add the cumin seeds. Let these sizzle for a few seconds and add the onions. Sauté over high heat for 2 to 3 minutes, until the onions are wilted and lightly browned.

4. Add the ginger, green chiles, and tomatoes and continue to stir-fry for another 2 to 5 minutes. Add the drained rice, water, salt, and cilantro. Stir gently so as not to break the grains. Bring to a full boil.

5. Immediately reduce the heat to low, cover tightly and cook for 8 minutes. Remove from heat and let stand, covered and undisturbed, for 5 minutes. Remove lid, fluff rice with a fork, and serve immediately.

SERVES 6

Rice with Paneer and Peas
Paneer Mattar Wale Chawal

The addition of the fresh Indian cheese, paneer, makes this pullao a balanced vegetarian dish. I like to serve it with richly flavored vegetables such as Okra with Red Onions or Eggplant with Cilantro and Chickpea Flour Stuffing (see page 149 or 138).

1½ cups basmati rice ✱

1 tablespoon vegetable oil

½ recipe (½ pound) paneer ✱ (see page 4), cut into small cubes

1 tablespoon ghee ✱

1 teaspoon cumin seeds ✱

1-inch piece ginger, peeled and cut into matchsticks

2½ cups hot water

8 ounces frozen peas, rinsed in warm water

½ teaspoon salt

1. Pick over rice, removing any stones. In a bowl, wash the rice in several changes of cold water until the water is clear. Soak the rice in warm water to cover for at least 20 minutes but no longer than 45 minutes.

2. Heat the oil in a nonstick skillet over medium heat. Brown the pieces of paneer, turning often. Set the paneer aside on paper towels.

3. In a 10-inch skillet, heat the ghee over high heat. Tilt the pan and add the cumin seeds to the pool of ghee. When they have finished sizzling, level the pan and add the ginger. Sauté for a minute.

4. Add the drained rice. Sauté for about a minute, stirring gently so as not to break the grains of rice.

5. Add 2½ cups of hot water, the paneer, the peas, and the salt. Mix well, bring to a full boil and reduce the heat. Cover tightly and simmer for 8 minutes.

6. Remove from heat and let stand, covered, for 5 minutes. Remove lid, fluff grains with a fork, and serve immediately.

SERVES 6

Rice with Mixed Vegetables
Sabzi Pullao

For a colorful complement to any nonvegetarian dish, I'll often choose this pullao. I created this in the early days of the Bombay Cafe, and it's been popular ever since. I like to use black cumin seeds here because they have a sweetness not found in other cumin. If you don't have it, you can substitute 2 teaspoons of regular Indian cumin.

1½ cups basmati rice ✳

2 tablespoons vegetable oil

1½ teaspoons black cumin seeds ✳

2 to 3 black cardamom pods ✳

2 (1-inch) pieces cinnamon stick or cassia ✳

2 bay leaves

4 to 5 whole cloves

3 to 4 green cardamom pods ✳

¼ pound green beans, trimmed and cut into ¼-inch pieces

½ cup fresh corn kernels (frozen may be used, rinsed in warm water first)

2 small carrots, diced

½ cup frozen green peas, rinsed in warm water

2¼ cups hot water

1 teaspoon salt

1. Pick over rice, removing any stones. In a bowl, wash the rice in several changes of cold water until the water is clear. Soak the rice in warm water to cover for at least 20 minutes but no longer than 45 minutes.

2. In a 10-inch skillet, heat the oil over high heat. Tilt the pan and add the cumin seeds to the pool of oil. When they finish sizzling, add the black cardamoms, cinnamon, bay leaves, cloves, and green cardamoms. Sauté for 1 minute.

3. Add the green beans and sauté for about 2 minutes. Add corn, carrots, and peas, and sauté for another 2 minutes. Add drained rice and sauté for about 1 minute, being careful not to break the rice grains.

4. Add the hot water and salt and bring to a full boil. Reduce heat to low, cover tightly and simmer for 10 minutes. Remove from heat and let stand, covered, for 5 minutes. Remove lid, fluff grains with a fork, and serve.

SERVES 6

Rice with Chinese Long Beans
Sem Pullao

These long, whiplike beans are not part of traditional Indian cuisine.
But when I first encountered them in the United States, I couldn't resist giving
them an Indian twist. Their crunchy, nutty flavor goes well with the
basmati rice and garlic in this dish.

1¹/₂ cups basmati rice ✳

2 tablespoons vegetable oil

1 teaspoon mustard seeds ✳

3 to 4 whole arbol chiles
(broken into pieces if more
spiciness is desired)

3 cloves garlic, sliced thinly

1/2 pound Chinese long beans,
trimmed and cut into
1/2-inch pieces

1 large tomato, diced

2¹/₄ cups hot water

1 teaspoon salt

1. Pick over rice, removing any stones. In a bowl, wash the rice in several changes of cold water until the water is clear. Soak the rice in warm water to cover for at least 20 minutes but no longer than 45 minutes.

2. In a 10-inch skillet with a lid, heat the oil over high heat. Tilt the pan so that the oil forms a pool and add the mustard seeds. Cover immediately to avoid splattering. When the sizzling subsides, about 30 or 45 seconds, lift the lid and carefully add the chiles and garlic. Stir-fry until the garlic is lightly browned, about 1 or 2 minutes.

3. Rinse the beans in a colander and add them, still slightly wet, to the garlic. Mix well, sautéing over medium heat for another 3 to 4 minutes, until the beans are halfway cooked.

4. Stir in the tomatoes gently, so that the cubes retain their shape as much as possible. Increase the heat and carefully stir in the drained rice, sautéing for a minute to combine all ingredients thoroughly.

5. Add the hot water and bring to a full boil. Stir in the salt, reduce heat to low, cover tightly and simmer for 10 minutes. Let stand, covered, for 5 minutes before lifting lid. Fluff the grains with a fork and serve immediately.

SERVES 6

Rice with Cauliflower

Gobi Pullao

Wholesome cauliflower is one of India's favorite vegetables. Sautéed with cumin, chiles, and ginger, you'd never mistake it for the bland vegetable many Americans know. This traditional Northern Indian dish was served very frequently when I was a child; for me, it is "comfort food." It is often served for lunch in winter, accompanied by a cucumber raita. For a more substantial meal, serve with Chicken Masala (see page 196).

1½ cups basmati rice ✱

2 tablespoons vegetable oil

1 teaspoon cumin seeds ✱

½-inch piece ginger, peeled and julienned

2 to 3 green serrano chiles, chopped

1 (2½ pound) cauliflower, trimmed and cut into small florets

1½ tablespoons ground coriander ✱

1 teaspoon cayenne pepper

¼ teaspoon turmeric

1 large tomato, diced

2¾ cups hot water

1 teaspoon salt

2 tablespoons fresh cilantro, chopped

1. Pick over rice, removing any stones. In a bowl, wash the rice in several changes of cold water until the water is clear. Soak the rice in warm water to cover for at least 20 minutes but no longer than 45 minutes.

2. Heat the oil over high heat in a 6-quart saucepan. Tilt the pan so that the oil forms a pool and add the cumin seeds, letting them sizzle.

3. Level the pan and add the ginger and chiles. Stir-fry to brown for 1 minute.

4. Rinse the cauliflower in a colander and add it, still slightly wet, to the pan. Sauté over medium heat until cauliflower is lightly browned, about 5 to 6 minutes.

5. Add the coriander, cayenne, turmeric, and tomatoes, stirring gently so that tomatoes retain their shape as much as possible. Add the salt, cover, and cook on low heat for 5 minutes, until the cauliflower is almost done.

6. Raise the heat to high and add the drained rice, hot water, salt, and cilantro, stirring gently so as not to break the rice grains. Bring to a full boil, cover tightly, and reduce the heat to low. Simmer for 12 minutes. Remove from heat and let stand, covered, for 5 minutes before lifting the lid. Fluff with a fork and serve immediately.

SERVES 6

Chapatis

An Indian meal is incomplete without some form of bread. Chapatis, or flat griddle breads, are the easiest to make and most common. Villagers take large, thick slabs out to their work in the fields while upper class households serve delicate, custom-made chapatis, one by one, just as they come off the griddle. Traditionally, chapatis are spread with a little ghee to keep the bread soft and add flavor, but the choice is yours. My father, for example, never adds ghee because he prefers his chapatis crisp. I always toast his a few seconds longer than usual.

2$^{1}/_{4}$ cups atta ✳
(soft whole wheat flour)

$^{3}/_{4}$ to 1 cup warm water

3 tablespoons ghee ✳ (optional)

1. Place 2 cups of the flour in a large mixing bowl, making a well in the center. Slowly work in 3/4 cup of water until the dough is no longer sticky. Continue to knead the dough with your hands and knuckles, sprinkling on droplets of water as necessary, until the dough is soft and pliable, about 15 minutes. Set aside, covered with a slightly damp kitchen towel, for at least 30 minutes. (The dough can be made several hours ahead of time, but should be tightly wrapped in plastic wrap and refrigerated. Bring the dough to room temperature before proceeding.)

2. To form the dough, break off chunks about 1 inch in diameter. Roll them into balls in the palm of your hand.

3. Put the remaining 1/4 cup of flour on a plate. Flatten a ball of dough into the flour on both sides and then remove to a work surface. Roll the flattened disk out into a circle about 5 to 6 inches in diameter, dredging in flour as needed to prevent sticking.

4. Heat a heavy griddle over medium heat. Place a chapati on the griddle and turn it when you see small bubbles or blisters on the surface, about 1 minute. Cook the other side for about 30 seconds.

5. Using tongs, remove the chapati from the griddle and hold it over an open gas flame for 20 or 30 seconds, until it puffs up. Turn over and repeat the process for about 10 seconds on the other side. (If no gas flame is available, finish the cooking process on the griddle as follows: Press down on the edges of the chapati with a folded kitchen towel or spatula for about 30 seconds, until the center puffs up. Repeat on the other side.)

6. Brush the chapati with a little of the optional ghee and set aside on a warm platter. Repeat the process with the remaining dough.

MAKES 16, OR 2 PER SERVING

Oven–Baked Breads with Nigella Seeds
Naans

Naans—those flat, warm breads redolent of the smoking charcoal of the tandoori oven—are without a doubt everyone's favorite Indian bread. Unfortunately for the home cook, they are very difficult to duplicate in a conventional oven. After weeks of experimentation—trying different doughs, different temperatures, different timings—I finally came up with the best possible homemade naan. The secret is a pizza stone and a very hot oven. Pizza stones are cheap and easy to find; buy one if you don't already have one, because they come in handy for many types of breads, pizza crusts, and of course, this irresistible naan.

1/4 cup plain yogurt,✳ store-bought or homemade (see page 5)

1 cup milk

3/4 cup water

1 egg

1 teaspoon baking soda

1 1/2 teaspoons baking powder

1 tablespoon sugar

1 teaspoon salt

1 1/2 teaspoons nigella seeds ✳

5 1/2 cups presifted flour

1/4 cup plus 2 tablespoons corn oil

1/4 cup melted ghee ✳

1. At least 4 to 5 hours before baking the naans, place the yogurt in a large mixing bowl and whisk in the milk, water, and egg. Add the baking soda, baking powder, sugar, salt, and the nigella seeds. Stir thoroughly and let stand for about 15 minutes.

2. Gently mix in 5 cups of the flour, kneading with your hands as the dough becomes stiffer. When all the ingredients have been well incorporated, knead in the 1/4 cup oil. The result should be a sticky dough. Cover with plastic wrap and let stand in a warm area for about 1 hour.

3. Line a cookie sheet with foil. Form dough balls the size of a tennis ball by dredging them in the remaining $1/2$ cup of flour (use more if needed) and rolling them firmly in the palms of your hands, making sure that there are no pockets of air in them. Place on the cookie sheet. When all the dough has been shaped into balls (about 10 to 12), with a pastry brush lightly coat the balls' surfaces with oil. Cover with plastic wrap and refrigerate for at least 3 hours.

4. Half an hour before you are ready to bake, remove the dough balls from the refrigerator and allow to come to room temperature. Put the pizza brick in the oven and preheat to 550 degrees. (You can use a heavy-duty cookie sheet if you don't have a pizza brick, but the results will not be quite as good.) It is important that the oven be really hot to approximate the tandoor.

5. To shape the naans, flatten one ball at a time on a board or other smooth surface. Press down with the palm of your hands, shaping the dough into a circle about 5 to 6 inches in diameter and pressing out any air pockets. Pick up the circle between your hands and, by using a flip-flop motion (almost like clapping), further stretch it into a larger one. (Or you can roll the dough out with a rolling pin, using extra flour to help. The dough is very pliable and difficult to roll, so use firm strokes, one at a time, in each direction.)

6. Once the naan has been either stretched or rolled out, open the oven and carefully place the naan on the center of the heated brick or cookie sheet. Bake for 2 minutes, until it puffs up and is lightly browned. (It may take about 30 seconds more on a cookie sheet.)

7. Remove the naan to a platter, brush with a little ghee, and serve. (To keep it warm while cooking the rest of the naans, cover the bread loosely with foil.)

MAKES 10 TO 12

Variation:

GARLIC NAANS
8 to 10 large cloves garlic, minced

$1/4$ cup fresh cilantro leaves, finely chopped

In step 5 above, sprinkle a teaspoon or so of the garlic and cilantro on the slightly flattened dough. Continue to flatten and stretch as for plain naans.

Layered Indian Griddle Bread
Parathas

Plain parathas puff up into airy layers when they are cooked. In fact, they resemble French puff pastry in the manner in which they are made. It is important to fold and roll the parathas in a specific manner, so that the ghee forms layers within the dough. Following this recipe for the plain version, you will find other types of paratha, filled with various stuffings. The term "paratha" can also refer to this type of bread; in this case, because the filling forms layers with the bread, it is not necessary to fold the dough so elaborately.

> 2^1/$_2$ cups atta ✳
> (soft whole wheat flour)
> 3/4 to 1 cup warm water
> 1/2 cup melted ghee ✳

1. Place 2 cups of the flour in a large mixing bowl, making a well in the center. Slowly work in 3/4 cup of water until the dough is no longer sticky. Continue to knead the dough with your hands and knuckles, sprinkling on droplets of water as necessary, until the dough is soft and pliable, about 15 minutes. Set aside, covered with a slightly damp kitchen towel, for at least 30 minutes. (The dough can be made several hours ahead of time, but should be tightly wrapped in plastic wrap and refrigerated. Bring the dough to room temperature before proceeding.)

2. Divide the dough into 8 equal pieces. Form them into balls in the palms of your hands.

3. Put the remaining ¹/₄ cup of flour on a plate. Flatten a ball of dough into the flour on both sides and then remove to a work surface. Roll the flattened dough out into a circle about 4 inches in diameter. Using a pastry brush, paint the circle lightly with ghee and roll it up, jelly-roll fashion. With the heel of your hand or the rolling pin, flatten this roll slightly, brush on a little more ghee, and roll up lengthwise like a snail. Lay the "snail" flat on the surface and press down upon it to flatten it. Roll it into a circle about 5¹/₂ inches in diameter, dredging in flour as needed to prevent sticking.

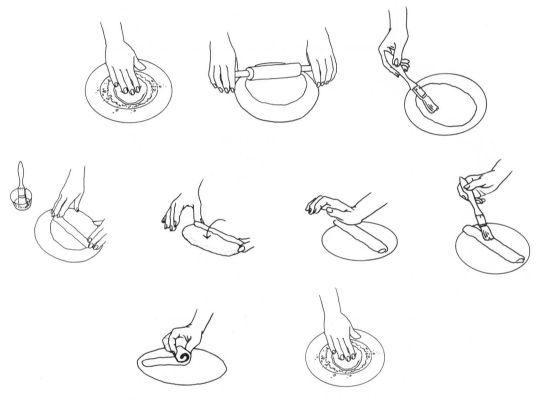

4. Heat a heavy griddle over medium heat. Place a paratha on the griddle and turn it after it begins to rise a little, about 1 minute. Lightly brush ghee on top and drizzle a little on the edges to help cook the underside. Turn the paratha again after about 30 seconds. Brush ghee on this side as well. The paratha will rise a little more and brown. Press down on it with a spatula for a few moments, turning once more to brown both sides, and remove to a warm platter. Repeat the process for the remaining dough.

5. Serve at once.

MAKES 8

Griddle Bread with Potato Stuffing
Aloo Parathas

These yummy stuffed parathas, along with plain yogurt, are a popular breakfast choice in India. Unlike many Americans, Indians prefer savory and even spicy things for their first meal of the day. However, you don't have to have these for breakfast if you don't want to, because they're wonderful with any meal. I especially like them with Cauliflower with Ginger and Green Chiles and Chicken Curry (see pages 132 and 192). The method for making parathas differs slightly when they are stuffed. There is no need for the layering of ghee and dough.

FOR PARATHAS:

2¹/₂ cups atta ✱
(soft whole wheat flour)

³/₄ to 1 cup warm water

¹/₂ cup ghee ✱

FOR STUFFING:

4 medium red rose potatoes,
peeled, boiled, and cooled

¹/₂ cup onions, minced

2 green serrano chiles, minced

¹/₄ cup fresh cilantro, chopped

³/₄ teaspoon salt

¹/₂ teaspoon crushed anardana ✱
(optional)

Lemon juice to taste

1. Place 2 cups of the flour in a large mixing bowl, making a well in the center. Slowly work in 3/4 cup of water until the dough is no longer sticky. Continue to knead the dough with your hands and knuckles, sprinkling on droplets of water as necessary, until the dough is soft and pliable, about 15 minutes. Set aside, covered with a slightly damp kitchen towel, for at least 30 minutes. (The dough can be made several hours ahead of time, but should be tightly wrapped in plastic and refrigerated. Bring the dough to room temperature before proceeding.)

2. Mash the potatoes in a mixing bowl. Add the other ingredients, mix well, and taste for seasoning, adding a little more salt or lemon juice if desired. Set aside.

3. Divide the dough into 8 equal pieces and roll them into balls between the palms of your hands.

4. Put the remaining 1/2 cup of flour on a plate and flatten a ball of dough into the flour on both sides. Remove to a work surface and roll the dough into a circle about 4 inches in diameter, dredging in flour as needed to prevent sticking.

5. Place about 2 tablespoons of the stuffing in the center of the dough. Pull the edges of the dough up around the stuffing, fully enclosing it, and forming another ball. Gently flatten this ball into the flour and carefully roll it out into a circle about 5 to 6 inches in diameter, making sure that the stuffing does not emerge. Dredge in flour again if necessary to prevent sticking.

6. Heat a griddle over medium-high heat. Place the dough circle on the hot griddle and cook until little air pockets begin to form at the edges, about 1 minute. Turn over, brush with ghee and drizzle a little on the edges to help cook the underside. After about 30 seconds, turn again and brush that side lightly with ghee. Continue to cook until both sides are lightly browned, about 1 minute more, flattening the paratha with a spatula to allow the steam to escape. Set aside in a warm place and repeat the process with the remaining dough.

Makes 8

Griddle Bread with Ground Lamb Stuffing
Keema Paratha

Parathas stuffed with this spicy lamb mixture are a favorite for
lunch, along with a raita and perhaps Black-Eyed Pea Salad (see page
68). Ask your butcher for lean ground lamb, preferably from the leg.
If the only ground lamb available is the fatty, preground sort in
the grocery meat case, substitute lean ground beef.

1 recipe paratha dough
(see Aloo Parathas, page 92)

2 tablespoons vegetable oil

1 small onion, minced

1/2-inch piece ginger, peeled
and minced

2 cloves garlic, minced

1/2 pound lean ground lamb

1 teaspoon ground cumin *

1 1/2 teaspoons ground coriander *

1 1/2 teaspoons turmeric

1/2 teaspoon cayenne pepper

1 medium tomato, peeled and
finely chopped

1/2 teaspoon salt

1 tablespoon fresh cilantro, minced

1. Follow the instructions for making the paratha dough in the recipe for Aloo Parathas, through step 1.

2. Heat the oil over high heat in a non-stick skillet. Add the onions and sauté until they are lightly browned, about 2 minutes. Add the minced ginger and the garlic.

3. Add the ground lamb and stir to break up lumps and incorporate well. Reducing heat to medium-high, continue to brown the mixture for 4 to 5 minutes, stirring frequently.

4. Stir in the cumin, coriander, turmeric, and cayenne, followed by the tomatoes and salt. Mix well and continue to cook until the tomato juices have evaporated. Remove from the heat and stir in the cilantro. Set aside to cool to room temperature before stuffing the parathas.

5. Divide the dough into 16 equal parts, rolling each into a ball.

6. Put the remaining 1/2 cup of flour on a plate and flatten the balls into it on both sides. Roll out 2 flattened balls into circles 4 to 5 inches in diameter, dredging in flour as needed to prevent sticking.

7. Spread about 2 tablespoons of stuffing on one circle, leaving the edges bare. Put the other circle on top and gently flatten with your palm to force out any air. Press down on the edges to make a firm seal. With a rolling pin, light roll the paratha out to a larger circle, 5 to 6 inches in diameter. Dredge again in flour to prevent sticking.

8. Place the dough circle on the hot griddle and cook until air pockets begin to form, about 1 minute. Turn over, brush with ghee and drizzle a little on the edges to help cook the underside. After about 30 seconds, turn again, and brush that side lightly with ghee. Continue to cook until both sides are lightly browned, about 1 minute more, flattening the paratha with a spatula to allow the steam to escape. Set aside in a warm place and repeat the process with the remaining dough.

MAKES 8

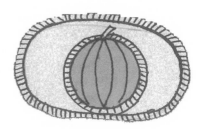

Griddle Bread with Daikon Stuffing
Mooli Ki Roti

During the mild winter months in India, lunches are often served
outside on terraces. Parathas stuffed with two favorite seasonal vegetables,
daikon and cauliflower (see following recipe), almost always grace
the tables. They're delicious served with plain yogurt.

FOR THE STUFFING:

1 large daikon (1 pound)

1 large green serrano chile, minced

1 tablespoon fresh cilantro,
finely chopped

1 teaspoon ground anardana ✳

1/2 teaspoon cayenne pepper

1 teaspoon salt

FOR THE DOUGH:

2 1/2 cups atta ✳
(soft whole wheat flour)

1 1/2 cups ghee ✳

1. Peel and grate the daikon into a bowl. Mix in the chile, cilantro, anardana, cayenne, and salt and set aside for 15 to 20 minutes.

2. Taking a small handful of the mixture at a time, squeeze firmly to extract the juices, letting the liquid fall back into the mixing bowl. Place the wrung-out daikon mixture in another bowl and continue by handfuls until all the daikon juices have been extracted. Set aside both bowls.

3. Place 2 cups of the flour in a large mixing bowl, making a well in the center. Slowly work in 3/4 cup of reserved daikon juices until the dough is no longer sticky. Continue to knead the dough with your hands and knuckles, sprinkling on droplets of the daikon juices as necessary, until the dough is soft and pliable, about 15 minutes. (Don't worry if tiny bits of daikon or cilantro get kneaded into the dough.) Set aside, covered with a slightly damp kitchen towel, for at least 30 minutes. (The dough can be made several hours ahead of time, but should be refrigerated. Bring the dough to room temperature before proceeding.)

4. Divide the dough into 16 equal parts, rolling each into a ball.

5. Put the remaining 1/2 cup of flour on a plate and flatten the balls into it on both sides. Roll out two balls into circles 4 to 5 inches in diameter, dredging in flour as needed to prevent sticking.

6. Spread about 2 tablespoons of stuffing on one circle, leaving the edges bare. Put another circle on top and gently flatten with your palm to force out any air. Press down on the edges to make a firm seal. With a rolling pin, lightly roll the paratha out to a larger circle 6 inches in diameter. Dredge the circles in flour again to prevent sticking.

7. Place the dough circle on the hot griddle and cook until air pockets begin to form, about 1 minute. Turn over, brush with ghee and drizzle a little on the edges to help cook the underside. After about 30 seconds, turn again and brush that side lightly with ghee. Continue to cook until both sides are lightly browned, about 1 minute more, flattening the paratha with a spatula to allow the steam to escape. Set aside in a warm place and repeat the process with the remaining dough.

MAKES 8

Griddle Bread with Cauliflower Stuffing

Gobi Parathas

1 recipe paratha dough
(see Aloo Parathas, page 92)

1 small cauliflower
(about 1/2 pound)

1/4-inch piece ginger, peeled
and minced

2 small green serrano chiles,
minced

2 tablespoons fresh cilantro,
chopped

1/2 teaspoon salt

1/2 teaspoon cayenne pepper

1 tablespoon lemon juice

1. Follow instructions for making parathas as in Aloo Parathas, through step 1.

2. Discard the leaves and inner core of the cauliflower. Place the florets and tender stems in a food processor and pulse rapidly until the cauliflower is finely chopped but not puréed. There should be about 1 1/2 cups.

3. Mix all the ingredients and set aside for half an hour. Squeeze out any liquid that may have accumulated.

4. Follow the rolling and stuffing procedure in Griddle Bread with Daikon Stuffing (see page 96).

MAKES 8

Griddle Bread with Cheese Stuffing

Paneer Ki Roti

These parathas are often served on special occasions or while entertaining. The paneer stuffing adds protein, which makes these parathas especially suitable for a vegetarian meal.

1 recipe paratha dough
(see Aloo Parathas, page 92)

3/4 pound paneer ✳ (see Note)

1 small onion, minced

2 small green chiles, minced

1/2-inch piece ginger, peeled
and minced

2 tablespoons fresh cilantro,
chopped

1/2 teaspoon salt

1/2 teaspoon cayenne pepper

1/2 teaspoon ground anardana ✳

1. Follow instructions for making parathas as in Aloo Parathas, through step 1.

2. Crumble paneer into a bowl and mix in the remaining ingredients, mashing with a wooden spoon to make a smooth stuffing.

3. Follow rolling and stuffing method for Aloo Parathas, using 2 1/2 table-spoons of stuffing per paratha.

MAKES 8

Note: See page 4 for recipe, but do not weigh cheese; instead, hang it in a muslin cloth to let the whey drain, but leave the cheese soft.

Griddle Bread with Onion, Chile, and Cumin

Kokis

These fragrant, Sindhi-style griddle breads were always the stars of Sunday morning, when the entire family would gather for a luxurious breakfast. Though they are a breakfast treat in India, I like to serve them for dinner with Scrambled Paneer with Peas (see page 154) or Railway Station Potato Curry (see page 158) and Lamb Kabobs with Sweet Tomato Chutney (see page 16).

5 tablespoons ghee *

1/2 teaspoon cumin seeds *

2 1/4 cups atta *
(soft whole wheat flour)

1 small onion, minced

1/4-inch piece ginger, peeled
and minced

2 small green chiles, minced

1 teaspoon salt

3/4 to 1 cup warm water

1. In a small saucepan, heat 2 tablespoons of the ghee over high heat and add the cumin seeds. Let them sizzle for a minute and remove from the heat. Set aside to cool.

2. Place 2 cups of the flour in a large mixing bowl. Add the onions, ginger, chiles, salt, and the cumin seeds, with their ghee. Work the mixture with your hands until it resembles coarse meal.

3. Slowly mix in the warm water. Knead well, adding droplets of water as needed to produce a smooth dough. Knead for 15 minutes. Set aside, covered with a damp towel, for half an hour.

4. Divide the dough into 12 equal pieces and roll them into balls between the palms of your hands. Place the remaining 1/4 cup of flour on a plate and flatten the balls into it on both sides. Roll the balls into circles 5 inches in diameter, dredging in flour as needed to prevent sticking.

5. Heat a griddle over medium-high heat until drops of water dance on it. Reduce the heat to medium and place one koki on the griddle. Cook for 1 minute, piercing the top of the koki with the tines of a fork in a few places. Turn the koki and pierce this side in a few places with the fork. Turn again and brush the top lightly with some of the reserved ghee. Quickly turn once more and brush the other side with the ghee. Press down with a spatula until both sides are lightly browned. Remove to a platter and keep warm. Repeat the procedure with the remaining dough. Serve hot.

MAKES 12

Puffed Whole Wheat Breads
Puris

Puris are delectable little rounds of bread, deep-fried until they puff up like clouds. They are an indulgence, but well worth it. They are always part of the special meal we serve at the Bombay Cafe to celebrate Diwali, the Indian New Year.

1 cup atta ✳ (soft whole wheat flour)
1/2 teaspoon salt
2 teaspoons vegetable oil
1/4 cup tepid water
Vegetable oil for deep frying

1. Sift the flour into a large bowl. Add the salt and slowly work in the 2 teaspoons of oil until the mixture forms large granules. Add water a little at a time, working it into the flour until it forms a ball. Knead the dough for 2 to 3 minutes, cover with plastic wrap, and set aside for about half an hour.

2. To fry puris, pour oil to a depth of about 2 inches in a small karhai,* or saucepan. Heat the oil over medium-high heat.

3. Divide the dough into 18 small balls about half the size of a walnut. Test the oil: Drop a small piece of dough in it and if the dough rises to the top immediately, it's hot enough. Lower the heat to medium (adjust heat as necessary to maintain the temperature).

4. Roll out one ball at a time into a $2\frac{1}{2}$-inch circle on a clean smooth work surface. (To keep the dough from sticking, use a little oil on the surface rather than flour; the excess flour will cause a burned residue in the frying oil.) Carefully slip the puri into the hot oil, using a slotted spoon. With the spoon, splash some hot oil on top of the puri. This will cause it to puff up. Flip it over to fry for about 30 seconds more, being careful not to burn. Remove from the oil and let drain on paper towels. Repeat with remaining dough. These are at their absolute best when eaten fresh from the pan, but if this is impossible, place them without crowding on a large, heatproof platter and keep in a warm place or in a turned-off warm oven for up to half an hour.

SERVES 6

Legumes (Dal)

Every Indian table offers a dal, or lentil dish, usually served in combination with rice to form a perfect protein. Dals may be thick and hearty or thin and brothlike, depending on the other dishes served. They may include other ingredients, rather like a vegetable curry (Pink Masoor Lentils with Onions and Tomatoes on page 118, for example), or simply consist of legumes and a few flavorings.

The preliminary cooking of the legumes is always simple; the artistry comes in at the end, in the finishing touch Indians call *tadka*.* Classically, this involves heating ghee along with various seeds and spices, and adding the hot, flavorful mixture to the cooked lentils just before serving. The tadka is essential to a good dal; however, I have developed a technique for adding the necessary flavors using only a tablespoon or so of ghee. This makes the finished dish lighter and fresher than usual.

Indian lentils, such as the tiny pink lentils and masoor lentils, are more flavorful and varied than ordinary lentils, and can usually be found in specialty markets (some dals, however, may be made with common brown lentils). I also use other legumes, such as mung beans and tiny chickpeas. Dals offer a cook a marvelous blank canvas for experimentation, because, once the basic techniques are understood, it is easy to substitute one legume for another—even Western ones such as pinto beans—or try different combinations of seasonings.

Aside from forming a nutritious basis for many meals, dals are comfort food for me, like mashed potatoes are to Americans. Some of my fondest childhood memories include Mercin's Lemon Lentils, a dish my nanny used to make for me, the recipe for which I include here.

Toor Lentils with Garlic and Tomatoes

Tamatar Aur Lasson Wali Toor Dal

This dal has a fresh, bright summery flavor, with its lemon, tomatoes, and garlic. Because the garlic is added at the end of the cooking, it retains its pungency. I like to serve this dal with vegetarian dishes, such as Green Beans with Onions and Tomatoes, and Plain Basmati Rice (see pages 127 and 78).

1½ cups dry toor dal *

⅛ teaspoon turmeric

½ teaspoon cayenne pepper

1 teaspoon salt

2 tablespoons lemon juice

2 medium tomatoes

1½ tablespoons ghee *

½ teaspoon mustard seeds *

1 teaspoon cumin seeds *

10 to 12 fresh kari leaves *

3 cloves garlic, minced
(or more, to taste)

2 to 3 serrano chiles,
sliced lengthwise

Fresh cilantro, chopped for garnish

1. Pick over and wash the lentils and let them soak in fresh water to cover for at least 30 minutes. Drain and place them in a large saucepan with 5 cups of water. Bring to a full boil, skimming off any foam that rises.

2. Lower the heat to medium and add the turmeric, cayenne, and salt. Cover partially and cook over medium-low heat for 35 or 40 minutes, until the lentils are very tender.

3. Mash the lentils with the back of a wooden spoon and continue to cook for another 5 minutes. Remove from heat and stir in the lemon juice. Taste for seasoning, adding more salt or lemon juice if needed. (The dish may be made ahead to this point. Reheat lentils before going on to step 4.)

4. Slice tomatoes in half and grate against the large holes of a grater until all the pulp and juice is forced through. Discard the skins. Set aside.

5. Heat ghee over high heat in a small skillet with a lid. Carefully add the mustard seeds, cumin seeds, and kari leaves and cover immediately to protect from splatters. When the sizzling stops, in under a minute, lift the lid, add the garlic and chiles and sauté for 2 minutes, until lightly browned. Add the grated tomatoes and juices and continue to sauté until the moisture has evaporated.

6. Stir this mixture (known as a *tadka,** or finishing touch) into the hot lentils and bring briefly to a simmer. Remove to warm serving bowl, garnish with chopped cilantro and serve.

SERVES 6

Green Mung Beans with Browned Onions

Hari Moong Dal

Mung beans resemble lentils in texture and flavor and are at their best
when they are fresh and bright green. This dal is good served with a paratha
and South Indian Chicken Curry with Fennel Seeds (see page 194).

1 cup green mung beans ✳

3 cloves garlic,
thinly sliced lengthwise

1/2-inch piece ginger, peeled
and thinly julienned

1/4 teaspoon turmeric

1 teaspoon salt

2 small tomatoes, quartered

2 1/2 tablespoons ghee ✳

Pinch asafoetida ✳

1 1/4 teaspoons cumin seeds ✳

1 teaspoon crushed red pepper

1 small onion, thinly sliced

Fresh cilantro, chopped,
for garnish

1. Pick over and wash the mung beans.
   Soak in hot water to cover for at least
   30 minutes. Drain, place in a large
   saucepan with 4 cups of water and
   bring to a boil. Remove the foam that
   rises.

2. Add the garlic, ginger, turmeric, and
   salt. Cover and cook over medium-
   low heat for 30 minutes.

3. Add the tomato wedges and cook for
   another 10 minutes. Add a little more
   hot water if the mixture seems too
   thick. Remove from heat. (Dish can
   be made ahead to this point; reheat
   before continuing.)

4. Heat ghee over high heat in a small
   skillet and add the asafoetida and
   cumin seeds. When the sizzling stops,
   add the red pepper and onions. Sauté,
   stirring frequently, for 4 to 5 minutes
   or until onions are dark brown. Stir
   the mixture into the hot beans.
   Remove to a warm serving bowl,
   garnish with chopped cilantro, and
   serve.

SERVES 6

Mercin's Lemon Lentils
Mercin Ki Khathi Dal

Fragrant with lemon and ginger, this dal is my "comfort food," because my childhood nanny used to make it for me frequently. It can be served as a soup, but I like it with Plain Basmati Rice (see page 78) and Cabbage with Garlic, Mustard Seeds, and Lemon (see page 131). Because it is light, it makes a good luncheon dish.

1¼ cups pink lentils ✳

1 medium onion, chopped

½-inch piece ginger, peeled and finely chopped

5 to 6 large cloves garlic, sliced

2 to 3 green serrano chiles, sliced into thin rounds

1 teaspoon salt

4 to 5 tablespoons fresh lemon juice

1 tablespoon ghee ✳

1 tablespoon mustard seeds ✳

2 sprigs fresh kari leaves (about 20 leaves) ✳

1 teaspoon nonfat milk

1. Pick over, wash, and soak the lentils in water to cover for about 15 minutes.

2. Drain the lentils and place in a large saucepan with 4 cups of fresh water. Bring to a boil, skimming off any foam as it rises. Add the onions, ginger, garlic, chiles, and salt.

3. Reduce heat to low and simmer, partially covered, for about 15 to 20 minutes, until the lentils are tender but not mushy. Remove from heat.

4. Add 4 tablespoons of lemon juice and taste, adding more lemon juice if desired.

5. Heat oil or ghee over high heat in a small saucepan with a lid. Carefully add the mustard seeds and kari leaves and immediately cover to prevent splattering. When the popping and sizzling has subsided, after about a minute, add the spice mixture to the lentils. Add the milk and serve immediately.

SERVES 6 TO 8

Brown Masoor Lentils with Tomatoes

Masala Wale Saabat Masoor Ki Dal

Unlike most dals, the lentils in this dish retain their shape. The ginger and chiles liven it up. I often serve Rice with Onions, Tomatoes, and Chiles and Fish Wrapped in Banana Leaves (see pages 81 and 176) with this dal.

1½ cups brown masoor lentils ✳ (ordinary brown lentils can be substituted if brown masoor lentils are unavailable)

2 tablespoons vegetable oil

1 teaspoon cumin seeds ✳

1 small onion, diced small

½-inch piece ginger, peeled and finely chopped

2 to 3 green serrano chiles, finely chopped

2 small tomatoes, diced small

1 tablespoon ground coriander ✳

½ teaspoon cayenne pepper

¼ teaspoon turmeric

1 teaspoon salt

½ tablespoon fresh cilantro, chopped

1. Pick over, wash, and soak the lentils in water to cover for at least 30 minutes.

2. Heat the oil over high heat in a 4-quart saucepan and add the cumin seeds. When they stop sizzling, add the onions and brown them lightly, stirring frequently for 3 to 4 minutes. Add the ginger and chiles and continue to brown for another 2 to 3 minutes.

3. Add the tomatoes and continue to cook, mashing the tomatoes with the back of a wooden spoon, for 2 to 3 minutes. Add the coriander, cayenne, and turmeric and mix well.

4. Drain the lentils and add them to the saucepan, along with 4½ cups of water and the salt. Bring to a full boil, reduce the heat and cover. Cook for 35 to 40 minutes, or until the lentils are tender. Using the back of a wooden spoon, mash some of the lentils so that the mixture forms a thick soup.

5. The dal can be made in advance. When ready to serve, heat through, and stir in the chopped cilantro.

SERVES 6

Brown Masoor Lentils with Sambar Spices
Saabat Masoor Aur Sambar Masala

Sambar is a typical South Indian spice mixture, based on ground roasted cumin, coriander, cayenne pepper, and other ingredients. Each household usually makes its own variation of sambar, but the ready-made powder is easily available in Indian markets. This aromatic dal is delicious with almost anything, but I particularly like to serve it with Lamb Chops with Dried Mango Powder and Eggplant with Cilantro and Chickpea Flour Stuffing (see pages 217 and 138).

1½ cups brown masoor lentils ✳
(ordinary brown lentils can be
substituted if brown masoor
lentils are unavailable)

1 small onion, thinly sliced

3 cloves garlic, thinly
sliced lengthwise

½-inch piece ginger, peeled and
finely julienned

2 tablespoons sambar powder ✳

1 teaspoon salt

1 tablespoon ghee ✳

1½ teaspoons cumin seeds ✳

3 to 4 whole red chiles,
broken in half

Fresh cilantro, for garnish

1. Pick over, wash, and soak the lentils in water to cover for 30 minutes.

2. Drain the lentils and place them, along with 4½ cups of fresh water, in a large saucepan. Bring to a full boil, skimming off any foam as it rises. Add the onions, garlic, ginger, sambar powder, and salt. Reduce the heat to low, cover the pan and cook for 35 to 40 minutes, or until the lentils are tender. With the back of a wooden spoon, mash some of the lentils until the mixture forms a thick soup.

3. The dal can be made in advance to this point. When ready to serve, reheat the lentils. While the dal is warming, heat the ghee over high heat in a small saucepan and add the cumin seeds and red chiles. When the sizzling stops, pour this *tadka,*✳ or final step, over the lentils. Garnish with chopped cilantro.

SERVES 6

South Indian Toor Dal

Sambar

Almost every South Indian household has a secret family recipe for sambar powder—roasted, ground coriander seeds, channa dal, cayenne pepper, and others—and each one is convinced theirs is the best. This dal uses store-bought sambar powder (available in Indian markets), and I don't think too many people could tell the difference. These lentils are the traditional accompaniment to *masala dosas,* crepes made of fermented rice and lentil batter, but it is also good served with rice and a simple vegetable such as South Indian Green Beans (see page 129).

1½ cups dry toor dal ✳

1 medium onion, chopped

1¼ teaspoons salt

4 tablespoons vegetable oil

Pinch asafoetida ✳

1 teaspoon mustard seeds ✳

8 to 10 kari leaves ✳

1 teaspoon cumin seeds ✳

3 to 4 whole arbol chiles,
broken into halves

3 tablespoons sambar powder ✳

1 teaspoon cayenne pepper

2 medium tomatoes, diced

⅓ cup desiccated coconut ✳

2 tablespoons lemon juice

Fresh cilantro, chopped, for garnish

1. Pick over, wash, and soak lentils in warm water to cover for 20 to 30 minutes. Drain, place in a saucepan with 5 cups of water, and bring to a full boil.

2. Skim off any foam that rises and reduce the heat to medium. Add the onions and cook for 30 minutes or so, until the lentils are completely disintegrated. Skim off the foam a few more times, as necessary, but be careful not to discard any of the onions or too much of the liquid. (Add up to 1 cup of hot water if necessary. The lentils should be liquid.) Add the salt and reduce heat to a low simmer.

3. To prepare the *tadka,** or finishing touch, heat 3 tablespoons of oil over high heat in a small skillet with a lid, tilting it to one side to form a pool. Carefully add the asafoetida, mustard seeds, and kari leaves, covering immediately to avoid splatters. When the sizzling subsides, after about 30 seconds, add the cumin seeds and arbol chiles. Stir-fry for another 30 seconds.

4. Add the sambar powder and cayenne. Sauté for 2 to 3 minutes, until lightly browned. Add the tomatoes and continue to cook until they exude some of their juices. Gently spoon the masala into the lentils.

5. Heat the remaining oil over high heat in the same skillet and sauté the coconut for 1 to 2 minutes, until golden brown. Add to the lentils.

6. Remove from the heat, add lemon juice, and serve immediately, garnished with chopped cilantro.

SERVES 6

Yellow Mung Beans
with Tomatoes and Cilantro
Tamatar Wali Moongi Dal

Yellow mung beans are simply green mung beans that have been husked and split. This light dal goes well with Plain Basmati Rice (see page 78) and any paneer and vegetable dish, or Chicken with Cardamom (see page 197).

1 cup yellow mung beans *

1 teaspoon salt

2 to 3 green serrano chiles, finely chopped

10 sprigs fresh cilantro, chopped

1 medium tomato, chopped

1 tablespoon ghee *

Pinch asafoetida *

1½ teaspoons cumin seeds *

1. Pick over, wash, and soak the lentils for 30 minutes in water to cover.

2. Drain the lentils and place in a large saucepan with 4½ cups of water. Bring to a full boil, skimming of any foam that rises. Add salt, chiles, and three-quarters of the cilantro, and cook, partially covered, for 20 minutes. Add the tomatoes and cook another 5 to 10 minutes. The lentils can be cooked in advance to this point.

3. When ready to proceed, heat the lentils to a quick boil. Make the *tadka,** or finishing touch, by heating ghee over high heat in a small saucepan. Add asafoetida and cumin seeds. Remove the lentils from the heat and immediately stir in the tadka. Garnish with the rest of the cilantro and serve.

SERVES 6

Simple Yellow Mung Beans

Saadi Moongi Dal

In this plain but delicious dal, the beans are simply seasoned with spices sautéed in ghee. Choose this quick dal when you want to serve a highly seasoned meat dish like Lamb with Puréed Spinach Curry (see page 228).

1 cup yellow mung beans ✳

¹/₄ teaspoon turmeric

1 teaspoon cayenne pepper

1 teaspoon salt

2 tablespoons ghee ✳

Pinch asafoetida ✳

1 teaspoon cumin seeds ✳

1 teaspoon coriander seeds, ✳ lightly crushed

1 teaspoon amchur ✳

Fresh cilantro, for garnish

1. Pick over, wash, and soak the lentils in water to cover for 30 minutes.

2. Drain the lentils and place in a large saucepan with 5 cups of fresh water. Bring to a boil, skimming off any foam that rises. Reduce heat to low and cook, partially covered, for 20 to 25 minutes. Dal can be made ahead to this point.

3. When ready to serve, bring lentils to a full boil and remove from heat. Meanwhile, heat the ghee or oil in a small pan or long-handled ladle. Add the asafoetida, coriander seeds, and cumin seeds. When they stop sizzling, remove from heat and add the amchur and cayenne. Add to the dal and serve immediately, garnished with cilantro.

SERVES 6

Yellow Mung Beans
with Tomatoes and Onions
Masala Wali Moongi Dal

A more richly seasoned and substantial version of the preceding dal,
this dish goes well with simple vegetable or paneer combinations, such
as Scrambled Paneer with Peas (see page 154).

1 cup yellow mung beans ✳

1 small onion, thinly sliced

2 green serrano chiles,
sliced in half lengthwise

2 to 3 cloves garlic, thinly sliced

1 teaspoon salt

1 large tomato, diced

1 tablespoon ghee ✳

Pinch asafoetida ✳

1 teaspoon cumin seeds ✳

1/2 to 1 teaspoon cayenne pepper

Fresh cilantro, for garnish

1. Pick over and wash the lentils several times. Soak for 30 minutes in water to cover.

2. Drain the lentils and place in a 4-quart saucepan with 4 cups of water. Bring to a full boil, skimming off any foam that rises. Lower heat to medium-low and add the onions, chiles, garlic, and salt. Partially cover and cook for 10 to 12 minutes, until the lentils start to split open. Add the tomatoes and continue to cook for another 8 to 10 minutes, until the lentils have almost disintegrated and the tomatoes are tender. The dal can be made ahead up to this point and refrigerated until needed.

3. Just before serving, bring the dal to a quick boil while you make the *tadka,*✱ (see Note) or final flavoring. Heat the ghee in a small pan and add the asafoetida and cumin seeds. When they stop sizzling, remove from heat and add the cayenne. Immediately add mixture to the lentils. Garnish with the cilantro.

SERVES 6

Note: The best method for making this tadka is to heat the ghee in a long-handled ladle and add the spices to this. Then, when the tadka is finished, the ladle goes right into the lentils, making sure every drop of it is used.

Pink Masoor Lentils
with Onions and Tomatoes
Masala Masoor Dal

Although this dish seems similar to Yellow Mung Beans with Onions
and Tomatoes (see page 116), pink lentils are lighter in flavor and texture.
I like to serve this dal in the summer, with a variety of seasonal vegetable
dishes such as corn, okra or opo squash, or with Spicy Tiger Prawns in
Fresh Tomato Sauce (page 189).

1½ cups pink lentils ✱

⅛ teaspoon turmeric

1 teaspoon salt

1 small onion, thinly sliced

2 to 3 green serrano chiles, sliced
into quarters lengthwise

2 to 3 small cloves garlic, thinly
sliced lengthwise

1 small tomato, cut into eighths

2 tablespoons fresh cilantro,
chopped

1½ tablespoons ghee ✱

Pinch asafoetida ✱

1¼ teaspoons cumin seeds ✱

1 teaspoon crushed red pepper

1. Pick over, wash, and soak lentils in
water to cover for at least 20 minutes.
Drain and place in saucepan with
4½ cups cold water. Bring to a boil,
skimming any foam that rises, and
add the turmeric, salt, onions, chiles,
and garlic. Cook over medium-low
heat, partially covered, for 15
minutes.

2. Stir in the tomatoes and continue
cooking for another 10 minutes.
Remove from heat and stir in the
cilantro. The dish may be made
ahead to this point.

3. To serve, bring lentils to a boil once
more as you make the *tadka,*✱ or
finishing touch. Heat the ghee over
high heat in a small skillet. Add the
asafoetida and cumin seed. When
they stop sizzling, remove from heat
and add the crushed red pepper.
Immediately pour the tadka over the
top of the hot lentils, scraping out
every drop. Serve at once, without
stirring the tadka into the lentils.

SERVES 6

Pink Masoor Lentils
with Browned Onions and Ginger

Masala Dal Aur Bhunna Pyaaz

The browned onions give this dal a hearty flavor, making
it a wonderful accompaniment to winter vegetables such as
cauliflower, daikon or mustard greens.

1½ cups pink lentils ✳

¼ teaspoon turmeric

1 teaspoon salt

2 tablespoons ghee ✳

Pinch asafoetida ✳

1½ teaspoons cumin seeds ✳

2 to 3 whole red chiles,
broken in half

1 small onion, thinly sliced

1-inch piece ginger,
peeled and julienned

1. Pick over, wash, and soak lentils in
   water to cover for at least 20 minutes.
   Drain and place in a saucepan with
   4½ cups of water. Bring to a boil,
   skimming any foam that rises, and
   add the salt and turmeric.

2. Cook, partially covered, over
   medium-low heat for 20 to 25 minutes, or until the lentils have almost
   disintegrated. The texture should be
   that of a thick purée. Remove from
   heat. Lentils can be cooked in
   advance to this point.

3. To serve, reheat lentils (if necessary)
   while you make the *tadka*,✳ or finishing touch. Heat ghee over high heat
   in a small skillet and add the
   asafoetida, cumin seeds, and red
   chiles. When the seeds stop sizzling,
   add the onions and ginger. Continue
   cooking over high heat for 4 to 5
   minutes, until the onions are dark
   brown. Do not stir in the tadka;
   instead pour it over the top of the
   lentils and serve immediately.

SERVES 6

Pink Masoor Lentils
with Tomatoes and Garlic

Lassoon Wali Masoor Dal

The garlic added at the end of cooking gives this dal a real kick. Serve it with Rice Pullao with Peas and Cumin and Grilled Marinated Chicken with Mint Chutney and Lime-Cilantro Onions (see pages 79 and 198).

1½ cups pink lentils ✻

⅛ teaspoon turmeric

1¼ teaspoons cayenne pepper

1 teaspoon salt

3 tablespoons ghee ✻

½ teaspoon mustard seeds ✻

1 teaspoon cumin seeds ✻

10 to 12 fresh kari leaves

3 small cloves garlic,
sliced into thin rounds

½-inch piece ginger, peeled and
finely chopped

2 small green serrano chiles,
sliced into thin rounds

2 small tomatoes, diced

Fresh cilantro, chopped, for garnish

1. Pick over, wash, and soak lentils in cold water to cover for 20 to 30 minutes. Drain, place in a saucepan with 4$\frac{1}{2}$ cups of water, and bring to a full boil. Skim off any foam that rises, reduce the heat, and add the salt, turmeric, and $\frac{1}{4}$ teaspoon of the cayenne.

2. Cover partially and cook on medium-low heat for about 15 minutes, until the lentils break but have not disintegrated. Remove from heat.

3. Heat the ghee over high heat in a small skillet with a lid, tilting it to one side to form a pool. Carefully add the mustard seeds and cumin seeds, covering immediately to avoid splatters. When the sizzling subsides, about 45 seconds, add the kari leaves, garlic, ginger, and green chiles. Stir-fry for about 1 minute, until the garlic just starts to color.

4. Add the tomatoes and the remaining cayenne. Stir-fry for 2 to 3 minutes, or until the tomatoes are cooked but still retain their shape. Immediately add this mixture to the lentils.

5. Over medium-high heat, cook the lentils for another 6 to 8 minutes, stirring so that the spice mixture is well incorporated and the lentils are heated through. Stir in the chopped cilantro and serve at once.

SERVES 6

Chickpeas with Opo Squash
Ghia Channa Dal

Popular in Northern India, these hearty legumes are often the focal point of a simple lunch, along with chapatis or rice. The tender opo squash contrasts nicely with the firm chick peas. If you can't find opo squash, substitute peeled zucchini.

1 cup channa dal ✳

1/4 teaspoon turmeric

1 teaspoon cayenne pepper

1 1/2 teaspoons salt

1 medium opo squash
(about 3/4 pound), peeled, seeded,
and cut into 1/2-inch cubes

2 tablespoons ghee ✳

Pinch asafoetida ✳

1 teaspoon cumin seeds ✳

2 small green serrano chiles,
finely chopped

1/2-inch piece ginger, peeled
and finely chopped

1 small onion, diced

1 medium tomato, diced

2 tablespoons fresh cilantro, chopped

1. Pick over and wash the chickpeas. Place them in a saucepan with 5 cups of water and bring it to a boil. Skim the foam that rises and stir in the turmeric, ½ teaspoon of the cayenne and salt. Cook, partially covered, over low heat for 25 to 30 minutes, until the chickpeas are halfway cooked. Add the opo squash and continue to cook for another 15 to 20 minutes, until the squash is tender and the peas are cooked through but still hold their shape. The peas should resemble a thick soup at this point. Add a little more water if all of it has been absorbed.

2. Prepare the *tadka,** or finishing touch, during the last 10 minutes of cooking. Heat the ghee over high heat in a small skillet and add the asafoetida and cumin seeds. When they stop sizzling, add the chiles and ginger, stirring well.

3. Add the onions and sauté until they are lightly browned, about 2 to 3 minutes. Stir in the tomatoes and the remaining cayenne. Continue sautéing for another 4 to 5 minutes, until the tomatoes soften.

4. Stir the tadka into the chickpeas. Cook for 6 to 8 minutes to let the flavors blend. Stir in the cilantro and serve at once.

SERVES 6

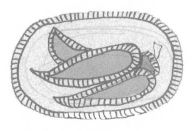

Vegetables

After years spent cooking and eating foods from around the world, I am convinced that Indian cuisine offers an unparalleled variety of—and yes, even passion, for—vegetable creations. There are many reasons for this, a prominent one being that most Indians have historically been too poor to include much meat in their diets. In addition to economics, there are religious strictures against eating meat (Hindus do not eat beef, and Muslims do not eat pork). Aside from this, it is my belief that the Indian preference for spices brings out the best in vegetables. Many people, for example, consider cauliflower bland and characterless, yet in the hands of a good Indian cook wielding chiles, ginger, cumin, and other seasonings, this favorite winter vegetable can take center stage. The same can be said of opo squash (similar to zucchini), spinach, or another staple, potatoes, cooked in so many different ways, with so many different combinations of seasonings and other vegetables that one can never tire of them.

One of the most popular entrées in my restaurant is the Vegetable *Thali,* or platter, a choice of two ever-changing vegetable selections along with rice and dal. Almost every Indian meal will include several vegetable dishes, and because there is such a rich

legacy of recipes from all over the country, this chapter is by far the longest. Almost all Indian vegetable dishes begin the cooking process the same way, by flavoring the heated cooking oil with spices. I find that using oil with a light hand keeps the flavors of the food brighter and lighter, so I have developed a simple technique: I tilt the pan to form a pool for the spices to sauté in, which allows me to use less oil than more traditional cooks do. This works best in a *karhai*, which is an Indian pan similar to a wok (a wok or deep skillet with a lid will suffice). Newcomers to Indian cooking should add the spices to the oil carefully, as many of them will splatter and some, especially mustard seeds and kari leaves, will pop.

Some of my most-requested recipes are my own creations, using non-Indian vegetables such as mushrooms and red peppers. I thrive on experimentation in my cooking and I encourage others to do so, too. I can almost guarantee that, by using these simple techniques and combinations of Indian spices, even unfamiliar vegetables (or those you thought you didn't like!) will become favorites.

Asparagus with Tomatoes

Though I adore asparagus now, I don't remember ever seeing it in India when I was growing up. However, as I was researching this book, Chandan, my family's long-time cook, told me that around his village it grows wild in the woods. This is his simple but delicious recipe. It makes a good luncheon dish, served with Brown Masoor Lentils with Tomatoes and Chicken Kabobs in Green Spices (see pages 110 and 200).

2 medium tomatoes

2 tablespoons vegetable oil

1 teaspoon mustard seeds *

1 teaspoon cumin seeds *

1-inch piece ginger, peeled and minced

2 green serrano chiles, minced

1/4 teaspoon turmeric

1 teaspoon cayenne pepper

1 1/2 tablespoons ground coriander *

2 pounds asparagus, tough ends trimmed, cut into 1 1/2-inch pieces

1 teaspoon salt

1 tablespoon fresh cilantro, chopped

1. Slice tomatoes in half and grate against the large holes of a grater. As the pulp is minced through the grater, you will be left holding an empty tomato skin, which should be discarded. Set aside tomatoes.

2. In a karhai,* wok, or skillet with a lid, heat oil over high heat. Tilt oil into a pool and add the mustard and cumin seeds. Cover immediately to prevent splatters and let sizzle for a few seconds. Add ginger and chiles, sautéing for a minute before adding tomatoes and their juices.

3. Add coriander, cayenne, and turmeric, mixing well. Continue cooking over high heat until all the liquid evaporates, leaving a thick paste, or masala.

4. To the masala add the asparagus, stirring well. If the spice mixture begins to stick, add 1/4 to 1/2 cup of water. Cover and cook on low heat for about 5 minutes, or until the asparagus is tender. Stir in cilantro.

5. Remove to a warm platter and serve immediately.

SERVES 6

Green Beans with Onions and Tomato

Sem Sabzi

The green beans common in India resemble Blue Lake beans and they are almost always chopped into small pieces before cooking so that they can be scooped up with bread at a meal. In Indian cooking, vegetables are always cooked until quite tender; this way, they absorb the flavors of the spices in which they simmer.

3 tablespoons vegetable oil

1½ teaspoons cumin seeds ✱

1 medium onion, chopped

1-inch piece ginger, peeled and finely chopped

2 green serrano chiles, finely chopped

2 medium tomatoes, chopped

½ teaspoon cayenne pepper

1½ tablespoons ground coriander ✱

1¼ pounds green beans, ends trimmed, chopped into ¼-inch pieces

½ teaspoon salt, or to taste

Fresh cilantro, for garnish

1. Heat a wok or karhai✱ over medium high heat and add oil. Add cumin seeds, onions, ginger, and chiles and sauté until onions brown slightly on their edges, about 3 to 4 minutes.

2. Mix in the tomatoes, cayenne, and coriander and stir-fry for 1 to 2 minutes.

3. Add the green beans, stir-frying for another 2 to 3 minutes. Add the salt and reduce the heat to low. Cover and simmer about 20 minutes, or until the beans are firm but tender.

4. Serve immediately, garnished with cilantro.

SERVES 6 TO 8

Bengali Green Beans
and Potatoes with Panch Puran

Bengali Sem Aur Aloos

In this light and quick dish, the spices all remain whole, imparting flavor to the mixture yet not merging into a thick sauce. Serve this with Chicken Kabobs in Tomato–Saffron Sauce (see page 206).

2 tablespoons vegetable oil

1 tablespoon panch puran *

4 to 5 dried arbol chiles

4 medium red rose potatoes (about 3/4 pound), unpeeled and cut into eighths

1 pound green beans, ends trimmed, and chopped into 1-inch pieces

1 teaspoon salt

1. In a karhai* or skillet with a lid, heat the oil over high heat. Add panch puran and chiles (if you desire more spiciness in the finished dish, break the chiles in half as you add them to the oil).

2. Add the potatoes and sauté for about 3 to 4 minutes. Add the green beans, stir well, and add the salt.

3. Cover and cook over low heat for about 15 to 20 minutes, or until the potatoes are done. Serve immediately.

SERVES 6

South Indian Green Beans
Dakshini Sem

Not all Indian food blends lots of flavors and spices in one dish. Many, like this simple South Indian dish, use mostly black pepper and small white lentils as seasoning. Lentils in this case are treated like a seed, for flavoring, and remain slightly crunchy.

1½ tablespoons vegetable oil

1½ teaspoons white urad dal ✳

2 pounds green beans, ends trimmed, and chopped into ⅛-inch pieces

1 teaspoon salt

1 teaspoon freshly ground black pepper

1. In a large skillet, heat the oil over high heat. Tilt the pan to one side to add urad dal to the oil. Allow to fry in hot oil for about 30 seconds.

2. Add green beans and stir rapidly. Reduce the heat to medium. Add salt and pepper. Continue to cook over medium-high heat, tossing pan or stirring frequently, for about 6 to 8 minutes, until beans are firm but tender. Serve immediately.

SERVES 6

Sautéed Mung Bean Sprouts with Marinated Onions

This dish, in which the mung beans serve as both a fresh green vegetable and a legume at once, is a traditional Gujerati recipe. I have given it my own twist by serving it for a first course as a warm salad on a bed of lettuce. This is also a good addition to a vegetarian meal made up of four or five dishes.

1 cup green mung beans *

2 tablespoons vegetable oil

4 to 5 cloves garlic, minced

3 to 4 green serrano chiles, finely chopped

1 tablespoon ground cumin *

1 tablespoon ground coriander *

1/2 teaspoon cayenne pepper

1/4 teaspoon turmeric

1 teaspoon plus a pinch salt

1 small onion, thinly sliced

2 tablespoons lemon juice

1 tablespoon fresh cilantro, chopped

1. On the morning of the day before serving, pick over the mung beans, wash them until the water runs clear and soak in about 4 cups of hot water for at least 6 to 8 hours, until the beans split and soften. Drain and place in a bowl lined with a clean muslin cloth (not cheesecloth). Loosely cover the beans, allowing room for them to breathe and sprout. Place in a dark, warm spot overnight. It is best to allow about 20 hours for them to sprout.

2. To cook, heat the oil over high heat in a large skillet with a lid. Add the garlic and chiles, sautéing for 1 minute. Add the sprouted beans, the spices and 1 teaspoon of salt. Stir in 1/2 cup of water, bring to a boil, reduce the heat and simmer, covered, for 30 minutes. Check from time to time to see if the water has evaporated. If so stir in 1/4 cup more. The beans should be tender and all the water absorbed at the end of cooking.

3. While the beans are cooking, toss the onions with the cilantro, lemon juice, the pinch of salt, and set aside.

4. To serve, arrange the hot beans on a platter and garnish with the marinated onions.

SERVES 6

Cabbage with Garlic, Mustard Seeds, and Lemon

Khatta Patta Gobi

Light and crisp, like a Chinese stir-fry, this dish was my favorite lunch in the late afternoons when I came home from college classes. Though it is usually served hot, I always ate it at room temperature, along with Mercin's Lemon Lentils and Plain Basmati Rice (see pages 109 and 78). It's delicious either way.

1 head (about 2 pounds) green cabbage

2 tablespoons vegetable oil

1½ teaspoons mustard seeds *

4 to 5 whole dried red chiles, broken into pieces

3 to 4 whole green chiles, sliced in half lengthwise

12 to 14 kari leaves *

6 large cloves garlic, minced

1-inch piece ginger, peeled and minced

½ teaspoon salt, or to taste

2 to 3 tablespoons lemon juice

1. Quarter, core, and slice the cabbage thinly. Rinse with cool water and set aside in a colander.

2. Heat a wok or karhai* over medium-high heat. Add oil and heat through. Keeping the lid handy, add mustard seeds, chiles, kari leaves, garlic, and ginger. Cover immediately to avoid splatters. Wait a moment and then cautiously lift lid. Sauté spices until garlic is lightly browned but not burned, about 2 minutes.

3. Add half the cabbage, mixing well, and then the other half. Heat through until the cabbage is lightly wilted. Add the salt and lemon juice and serve immediately.

SERVES 6 TO 8

Note: While the cabbage must be cooked at the last minute in this dish, the sautéing of the spices can be done up to 1 hour ahead of time. Do not brown the garlic all the way, as it will continue to cook when reheated. Reheat the spice mixture and proceed when ready to serve.

Cauliflower with Ginger and Green Chiles

Gobi Sabzi

Among the Punjabis of Northwest India, cauliflower is a particular favorite, appearing at almost every meal in the winter. My paternal grandmother served this dish frequently for lunch, with chapatis and sometimes a meat curry. Now, of course, cauliflower is grown in India, as it is here, all year round, so you can enjoy this any time. This cauliflower curry is also one of the traditional fillings for Frankies (see pages 34 to 35), delicious griddle-bread sandwiches. The only difference is that the filling should include 2 small diced tomatoes, added in step 4.

2 medium cauliflower

4 tablespoons vegetable oil

2-inch piece ginger, peeled and julienned

4 green serrano chiles, cut in half lengthwise

1 teaspoon whole cumin seeds ✱

2 tablespoons ground coriander ✱

1/2 teaspoon cayenne pepper

1/4 teaspoon turmeric

1 1/4 teaspoons salt or to taste

Fresh cilantro, for garnish

1. Discard the leaves and inner core of the cauliflower. Cut the florets and tender stems into 1 1/2-inch pieces. Rinse cauliflower and set aside in a colander.

2. Heat the oil in a karhai✱ or wok over medium high heat. Add cumin seeds, green chiles, and ginger and stir-fry for 1 minute.

3. Add cauliflower, mixing well. Reduce the heat to medium low and stir-fry until the cauliflower browns, about 10 to 12 minutes.

4. Add coriander, cayenne, turmeric, and salt (and tomatoes, if making the filling for Frankies). Continue to brown for another minute, blending all the spices thoroughly.

5. Cover and simmer for about 6 to 8 minutes, until the cauliflower is cooked through. If any liquid remains in the bottom of the pan, raise heat and rapidly stir until it evaporates.

6. Garnish with cilantro and serve immediately.

SERVES 6 TO 8

Cauliflower and Peas

Gobi Mattar Sabzi

Here, green peas add color and sweetness to cauliflower. This combination is another traditional Punjabi favorite, but I've given it a fresh twist by adding aromatic garam masala at the last minute.

1 medium cauliflower

3 tablespoons vegetable oil

2-inch piece ginger, peeled and julienned

4 green serrano chiles, cut in half lengthwise

1 teaspoon whole cumin seeds *

2 tablespoons ground coriander *

1/2 teaspoon cayenne pepper

1/4 teaspoon turmeric

1 1/2 teaspoons salt

1 (16-ounce) package frozen peas, rinsed in warm water

1/2 teaspoon Garam Masala II * (see page 3)

Fresh chopped cilantro, for garnish

1. Discard the leaves and inner core of the cauliflower. Cut the florets and tender stems into 1 1/2-inch pieces. Rinse cauliflower and set aside in a colander.

2. Heat the oil in a karhai* or wok over medium-high heat. Add cumin seeds, green chiles, and ginger and stir-fry for 1 minute.

3. Add cauliflower, mixing well. Reduce the heat to medium low and stir-fry until the cauliflower browns, about 10 to 12 minutes.

4. Add coriander, cayenne, turmeric, and salt. Continue to brown for another minute, blending all spices thoroughly.

5. Stir in peas. Cook, stirring, as cauliflower continues to brown, about a minute.

6. Cover and simmer for about 6 to 8 minutes, until cauliflower is tender. If any liquid remains in pan, raise the heat and rapidly boil it off. Stir in the Garam Masala.

7. Remove to a serving dish and serve at once, sprinkled with cilantro.

SERVES 6

+ Add Tomato Sauce to serve over rice

Fresh Corn with Red Onions
Makkai Aur Lal Pyaaz

Fresh corn is a summer delight in India, where it is usually sold as a snack by street vendors, who grill the cobs over hot coals and sprinkle them with lime juice, salt, and cayenne. Unfortunately corn season coincides with monsoon season, and it is a typical and funny sight to see the vendors tending their braziers under little umbrellas. Fresh corn kernels mingle with onion, chiles, cilantro, and lemon juice in this lively sauté; you can use frozen corn very successfully for this, too. This dish makes a wonderful companion to Lamb Chops with Black Pepper and Vinegar (see page 216), as well as Western-style meals.

1½ tablespoons vegetable oil

1½ teaspoons mustard seeds *

10 to 12 kari leaves *

1 small red onion (about ¾ cup), finely chopped

2 to 3 green serrano chiles, sliced into thin rounds

6 to 8 ears fresh, sweet corn, kernels sliced off cob (about 3 cups, or use frozen kernels)

2 tablespoons fresh cilantro, chopped

1 teaspoon salt

1 to 2 tablespoons lemon juice

1. In a karhai,* wok, or large skillet with a lid, heat the oil over high heat. Carefully add the mustard seeds and kari leaves and cover immediately to prevent splattering.

2. After the sizzling has subsided, about 30 seconds, lift the lid and add the green chiles. Sauté for a minute before adding onions. Cook, stirring frequently, until the onions are soft but not browned, about 2 to 3 minutes.

3. Add the corn kernels, cilantro, and salt, stirring well. Reduce heat to low and cook, covered, for about 8 to 10 minutes, or until corn is done. Do not overcook.

4. Season with lemon juice and serve immediately.

SERVES 6

Yogurt Curry with Daikon
Dahi Kari Aur Ki Mooli

This curry, like all of those from the northwestern region of Gujerat, is made with a yogurt base and remains rather liquidy. The crunchy, peppery daikon, or white radish, adds texture. Serve this with Plain Basmati Rice and Sweet and Sour Eggplant (see pages 78 and 140), or try it the way my husband does—as a soup.

2 cups plain yogurt * store-bought or homemade (see page 5)

2 tablespoons besan *

1 teaspoon salt

1/2 teaspoon cayenne pepper

1 teaspoon sugar

1 1/2 tablespoons ghee *

2 black cardamoms *

2 whole red chiles, broken in half

3 to 4 whole cloves

1-inch piece cinnamon stick or cassia *, broken in half

1/2 teaspoon mustard seeds *

1 teaspoon cumin seeds *

10 to 12 fresh kari leaves *

1/2-inch piece ginger, peeled and minced

2 green serrano chiles, minced

1 medium daikon or 8 to 10 white icicle radishes (about 1 pound)

1. Place yogurt in a mixing bowl and sift in the besan, whisking well. Add 2 1/2 cups of water, salt, cayenne, and sugar, blending well. Set aside.

2. Heat the ghee over high heat in a medium saucepan with a lid. Combine the cardamom, red chiles, cloves, cinnamon, mustard seeds, cumin seeds, kari leaves, ginger, and green chiles and add them all at once to the hot oil. Immediately cover the pan to avoid splattering. When the sizzling stops, remove from heat and whisk in the yogurt mixture.

3. Return to low heat and cook, uncovered, for 25 minutes. Stir occasionally as mixture comes to a slow boil.

4. Meanwhile, peel the daikon and cut into sticks about 2 1/2-inches long and 1/2-inch thick. Add the daikon to the yogurt mixture and continue to simmer for another 5 to 7 minutes, or until the daikon becomes just tender.

SERVES 6

Sautéed Daikon with Cayenne and Mustard Seeds

Mooli Ki Sabzi

Radishes are so easy to grow that almost every Indian garden has a patch set aside for them. Most people eat them raw, as part of a composed salad, but on the hillsides, the villagers cook native white radishes in simple but delicious curries like this one. Daikon is a good substitute for the white radishes of India, which are not available here.

3 daikons, about 12 to 14 inches long and about 1½ inches in diameter, preferably with their leaves

2 tablespoons vegetable oil

1½ teaspoons mustard seeds *

1 to 2 teaspoons cayenne pepper, to taste

1 teaspoon salt *

1. If the daikons have their leaves attached, remove them and discard any yellow or old stems. Wash the leaves and stems, chop them finely, and set aside.

2. Peel the daikons and cut them as you would a carrot: First, cut them in half lengthwise, and then in half widthwise. Taking one quarter at a time, slice it lengthwise in threes and then slice into even, ⅛-inch pieces.

3. In a karhai* or skillet with a lid, heat the oil over high heat. Carefully add mustard seeds and cover immediately. When the popping subsides, remove the skillet briefly from the heat, lift the lid, and add cayenne. Immediately add the daikon and their leaves and return to high heat.

4. Sauté, stirring well for about 2 minutes over high heat. Add salt, cover, lower heat, and cook for 15 minutes, until daikon is tender but holds its shape. Serve immediately.

SERVES 6

Smoked Eggplant Purée
Bharta

Roasting the eggplants, either on a charcoal grill or over a gas flame, lends them a delightfully smoky richness in this traditional Punjabi purée. This dish is at its best when cooked in ghee, but you may substitute oil if necessary.

2 medium, firm eggplants, preferably purchased the same day and kept at room temperature

3 tablespoons ghee or 3 tablespoons vegetable oil, plus a teaspoon or so to coat the eggplants

2 medium yellow onions, diced

2 to 3 green serrano chiles, finely chopped

1½-inch piece ginger, peeled and finely chopped

2 medium tomatoes, diced

1 teaspoon salt

¼ cup fresh cilantro, chopped

1. Wash the eggplants, dry them and rub them with a thin coating of vegetable oil. The oil gives the eggplants a smokier flavor and makes it easier to peel them.

2. Grill the eggplants over hot coals, turning occasionally until they are tender. (Alternatively, you can grill the eggplants over the flames of a gas stove. First, remove the grate and line the burner with foil. Replace grate, turn on a high flame and lay the eggplant directly on the grate. Turn occasionally until eggplant is tender. Set eggplant aside on a plate to cool. Carefully remove grate and foil and clean up juices immediately.)

3. When eggplants are cool enough to handle, peel and mash the pulp.

4. Heat the ghee or oil over high heat in a karhai* or skillet. Add onions, reducing the heat to medium, and sauté until golden brown, about 7 to 8 minutes. Add ginger and chiles, sautéing for another minute.

5. Add tomatoes, stirring well to combine. Sauté for 2 to 3 minutes. Mix in the eggplant and salt. Reduce heat to low, cover and cook for 30 minutes, stirring occasionally to prevent sticking.

6. Increase heat to medium-high and stir continuously to evaporate any excess moisture. The texture should resemble mashed potatoes.

7. Garnish with cilantro and serve.

SERVES 6 TO 8

Eggplant with Cilantro and Chickpea Flour Stuffing

Bharele Baingan

In India, as here, when eggplants are cooked whole, they are always stuffed with a spice mixture so that the flavors permeate the entire vegetable. The addition of the chickpea flour in this spice stuffing makes it a more substantial dish, adding not only body but a little protein as well. Eggplants usually absorb a lot of oil in cooking, but in this recipe, the small amount of oil lightly coats the skin at first and the eggplants steam in their own juices to complete the cooking.

1½ pounds eggplant (about 18 small Indian eggplants or 10 small, plump, not thin, Japanese eggplants)

2½ tablespoons sifted besan *

1-inch piece ginger, peeled and chopped

2 to 3 small green serrano chiles, chopped

½ cup fresh cilantro leaves, tightly packed

1 heaping tablespoon ground coriander *

1 teaspoon ground cumin *

¼ to ½ teaspoon cayenne pepper

1 heaping teaspoon amchur *

½ teaspoon salt, or to taste, plus a little extra for cooking

4 tablespoons vegetable oil

1. Wash eggplants and leaving caps intact, trim stems to 1/4 inch. Make a lengthwise slit in each eggplant, and then a crosswise slit, being careful not to cut all the way through to the end. Cover eggplants with water and let soak for 15 to 20 minutes.

2. Roast the chickpea flour in a heavy, dry skillet stirring frequently until it turns dark golden brown. Place in a small mixing bowl and set aside.

3. Place ginger, chiles, cilantro leaves, coriander, cumin, cayenne, amchur, salt, and about 1/4 cup of water in blender and purée until smooth. Add more water by the tablespoon if necessary.

4. Add mixture to the chickpea flour and set aside.

5. Remove eggplants from water and place on an absorbent kitchen towel. Pry open slits with fingers and spoon in about 1½ teaspoons of the spice mixture. Press closed firmly so that spices are evenly distributed in each eggplant.

6. In a wok or karhai,* heat the oil over high heat. Add any remaining spice mixture and eggplants. Gently stir eggplants to coat with the oil. Lightly sprinkle with salt. Reduce heat to low, cover and simmer until eggplants are tender, about 25 minutes. Turn eggplants from time to time to cook evenly.

7. Serve immediately, garnished with cilantro leaves.

SERVES 6 TO 8

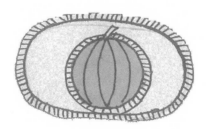

Sweet and Sour Eggplant
Khate Mithe Baingan

A few years ago, on a pilgrimage to the Tirupati Temple near Madras, my family and I picnicked along the way. One cousin brought this delicious dish, made with the freshest, small round Indian eggplant. These are often available in Indian or specialty markets and are well worth seeking out, as they have a delicious sweetness of their own. Small Japanese eggplants may be substituted. I serve this dish at room temperature, with Chapatis and Green Mung Beans (see pages 86 and108), or hot with Grilled Marinated Chicken with Mint Chutney and Lime-Cilantro Onions (see page 198).

2 pounds (about 12 to 18, egg-shaped
Indian or Japanese eggplant
2 medium tomatoes
2 tablespoons ground coriander *
1¹/₂ tablespoons ground cumin *
1 teaspoon cayenne pepper
¹/₄ teaspoon turmeric
1¹/₂ teaspoons amchur *
1 teaspoon salt
4 tablespoons vegetable oil
Fresh cilantro, chopped, for garnish

1. Trim off the tough end of the eggplant stems, leaving the caps intact. Make a crosswise slit halfway through the eggplants from the blossom end. Soak the eggplants in water to cover for at least half an hour to open the slits and remove any bitterness.

2. Cut tomatoes in half and rub the cut halves against the coarsest blades of a grater, set over a bowl, until only the skin remains. Discard the skin and set aside the pulp and juices.

3. In a bowl, mix all the ground spices with 1/2 teaspoon of salt.

4. Drain eggplants in a colander. Working over the bowl containing the spice mixture, pry open the slits with your fingers. Put about 1/2 teaspoon of spice mixture into each eggplant, letting any excess fall into the spice bowl, and push the slit closed to distribute the spices evenly.

5. Using a large skillet, heat the oil over high heat and add any remaining spice mixture. Add the eggplants, reducing the heat to medium, and turn them to brown as evenly as possible.

6. Add tomato pulp and remaining salt. Mix well and cover, reducing heat to low. Cook 15 to 30 minutes, depending on size and freshness of the eggplant. Eggplants should be tender when pierced by a fork, but remain intact.

7. Garnish with cilantro and serve immediately.

SERVES 6

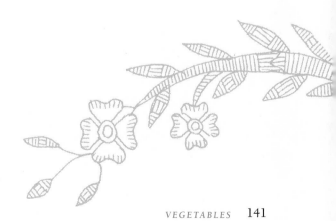

Sautéed Japanese Eggplant with Onions and Tomatoes

Baingan Sabzi

Similar to ratatouille, this dish complements Chicken with Cardamom and Rice with Mixed Vegetables (see pages 197 and 83). For a nontraditional treat, I love it cold, spread on thick whole-grain bread with a little lettuce to give it crunch.

8 to 10 medium, deep purple Japanese eggplants, about 6 inches long

3 tablespoons vegetable oil

1 teaspoon cumin seeds

2 medium onions, thinly sliced

1/2-inch piece ginger, peeled and julienned

2 green serrano chiles, chopped

2 large tomatoes, chopped

1 tablespoon ground coriander *

1/2 teaspoon cayenne pepper

1/4 teaspoon turmeric

1 teaspoon salt

Fresh cilantro, chopped, for garnish

1. Slice eggplants into 1-inch rounds and place in cold water to cover.

2. Heat oil over high heat in a karhai* or skillet with a tightly fitting lid. Add the cumin seeds and when they sizzle, add the onions. Reduce the heat to medium. Sauté, stirring frequently, until the onions are translucent and lightly browned.

3. Add ginger and green chiles, sautéing for a few minutes. Drain eggplants and add to skillet. Stir well and add tomatoes.

4. Add coriander, cayenne, turmeric, and salt. Stir well, reduce heat to low, cover, and cook for about 20 minutes, until the eggplants are tender but retain their shape.

5. Serve immediately, garnished with cilantro.

SERVES 6

Mushrooms and Green Peas
Khumbi Mattar

When I was growing up, mushrooms were only found growing wild
at the base of the Himalayas, and thus were not familiar to many Indians.
Recently, however, cultivated white mushrooms have become very popular.
The mild but distinctive taste of mushrooms harmonizes beautifully
with the Indian spices in this simple sauté.

2 tablespoons vegetable oil

1 teaspoon cumin seeds *

1-inch piece ginger, peeled
and julienned

2 to 3 green serrano chiles, coarsely
chopped

1 pound white mushrooms,
quartered

1 pound fresh green peas, or 1
(16-ounce) package frozen peas,
rinsed in hot water

1 tablespoon ground coriander *

1/2 teaspoon cayenne pepper

1/4 teaspoon turmeric

1 teaspoon salt

Fresh cilantro, chopped, for garnish

1. In a karhai* or skillet with a lid, heat
   oil over high heat. Add cumin seeds
   and after they have finished sizzling,
   add ginger and green chiles. Sauté for
   about 1 minute.

2. Add the mushrooms and the peas,
   if they are fresh. Sauté for about
   1 minute and add the coriander,
   cayenne, and turmeric, stirring well.

3. If you are using frozen peas, add them
   to the mushroom and spice mixture
   at this point. Stir in the salt, cover,
   and cook over low heat for 5 to 6
   minutes if using frozen peas and 8
   to 10 for fresh peas.

4. Sprinkle with cilantro and serve
   immediately.

SERVES 6

Eggplant Layered with Tomato Conserve and Ginger Yogurt

Baingan Deva

The smoky sweetness of the eggplant is complemented by the spicy tomato conserve and the tangy yogurt sauce in this delectable dish. Inspired by a dish popular in Hyderabad, a Muslim-dominated part of Southern India, I created this for my first restaurant, Chutneys. Years ago, when my partner David was a customer there, he wrote a magazine article singling out this dish, dubbing it "Deva" after my maiden name. Both the name and the recipe stuck—it is still very popular at the Bombay Cafe. I like to serve this either as a vegetable dish or as a first-course salad with Griddle Bread with Onion, Chile, and Cumin (see page 100).

8 to 10 deep purple Japanese eggplants, about 6 inches long, or 2 large, firm regular eggplants

1 cup vegetable oil

FOR THE CONSERVE:

1½ tablespoons vegetable oil

1 tablespoon panch puran *

½ teaspoon fennel seeds

8 to 10 fresh kari leaves *

1 (16-ounce) can whole, peeled tomatoes, drained and roughly chopped

¼ teaspoon cayenne pepper

½ teaspoon salt

FOR THE YOGURT SAUCE:

½ cup yogurt,* store-bought or homemade (see page 5)

1 clove garlic, minced

½-inch piece ginger, peeled and minced

2 tablespoons fresh cilantro, chopped, for garnish

1. If you are using Japanese eggplants, trim caps and, without peeling, slice lengthwise into three equal slices. For regular eggplants, trim caps, and slice into 1/2-inch rounds.

2. Heat the oil in a large skillet over high heat until hot but not smoking and fry the eggplant slices, without crowding, until they are brown and cooked through, about 5 minutes. Remove and set on several layers of paper towel to absorb excess oil. Set aside in a warm oven.

3. To make the tomato conserve, heat the oil over high heat in a 2-quart saucepan. Add panch puran, fennel seeds, and kari leaves and cover immediately to avoid splattering. Let cook for about 1 minute.

4. Add the tomatoes, cayenne, and salt; stir well, and reduce the heat to low. Let simmer for 15 minutes, uncovered.

5. To make the yogurt sauce, whisk yogurt with garlic and ginger. Set aside for 15 minutes.

6. To serve, arrange warm eggplant slices on platter. Over the slices, spoon the warm tomato conserve, covering all but the outermost edges of the eggplant. Drizzle yogurt over the tomato conserve, sprinkle with cilantro, and serve.

SERVES 6

Spicy Mixed Greens in Mustard Oil
Sarson Ki Bhurji

All over the northern plains of India, the winter fields are bright yellow because of the mustard plants. Even though Indians do not use prepared mustard as we know it, they use the seeds, both the reddish-brown and yellow ones, in cooking and in the preparation of pickles, and they treat the greens a little like spinach. The mustard greens sold in this country are a little different from those available in India. I have found that a combination of *rapini* (also known as broccoli rabe) and mustard greens almost exactly duplicates the Indian greens. The Punjabi tradition is to serve the greens doused with home-churned butter; you can add sweet butter if you're feeling indulgent.

---

2 bunches (1½ pounds)
mustard greens

2 bunches (1 pound) broccoli rabe
or rapini (see Note)

2 tablespoons mustard oil ✳

1½ teaspoons brown
mustard seeds ✳

5 to 6 dried arbol chiles

3/4 teaspoon salt

---

1. Wash greens in several changes of fresh, cold water to remove all the grit. Remove and discard the tough stems of the mustard greens and coarsely chop the greens. Peel the thick stems of the rapini and coarsely chop, along with the greens and florets.

2. In karhai✳ or wok with a lid, heat the mustard oil until it loses its yellow color. Carefully add the mustard seeds and cover immediately, to avoid splattering. When sizzling subsides, about 30 seconds, lift lid. Break chiles into halves and add to the hot oil, allowing them to turn dark brown, about 1 minute.

3. Add all greens, a handful at a time as they cook down, mixing well before each new addition. After all the greens have been tossed with the seasonings, add salt and cover. Cook over low heat for at least 30 minutes, checking occasionally to make sure the greens are not sticking. Add a little water if so. The greens are done when they resemble a purée.

SERVES 6

Note: This dish is best with both kinds of greens, but can be made with all mustard greens or all rapini if the other is unavailable.

Spicy Mushrooms with Red Bell Peppers
Khumbi Aur Lal Simla Mirch Ki Sabzi

Neither red bell peppers nor mushrooms are Indian vegetables, but they seem like naturals in this spicy sauté. The peppers add welcome color, an important consideration in an Indian meal. This goes well in a vegetarian meal with Okra with Red Onions and Railway Station Potato Curry (see pages 149 and 158).

1 red bell pepper

1 tablespoon vegetable oil

1 teaspoon cumin seeds *

3 to 4 long, green serrano chiles, julienned lengthwise

1½ pounds white mushrooms, thinly sliced

1 teaspoon coarsely ground black pepper

1 teaspoon salt

2 tablespoons fresh cilantro, chopped

1. Slice the red pepper into 6 equal wedges, remove the seeds and ribs, and slice the wedges crosswise, at an angle, into thin sticks.

2. In a karhai,* wok, or skillet, heat oil over high heat. Tilt the pan to one side and add the cumin seeds to the oil. When the seeds sizzle, add the green chiles and sauté about 1 minute, until their skin blisters.

3. Add the mushrooms and the bell peppers and continue cooking on high heat, mixing well. Add pepper and salt and sauté for about 2 to 3 minutes more.

4. Reduce heat to medium and stir in cilantro. Cover and cook for 3 to 4 minutes.

5. Spoon into a warmed bowl and serve immediately.

SERVES 6

Makhni Mushrooms and Paneer

Makhni Khumbi Aur Paneer

Rich Makhni Sauce is usually used as a popular addition to tandoori-style
chicken (see page 198). Here, I've used the classic, creamy tomato-saffron sauce
to enhance a combination of mushrooms and paneer. This makes a delicious
main dish for vegetarians, with Griddle Bread with Potato Stuffing
(see page 92) as the ideal complement.

1 tablespoon vegetable oil

1 pound mushrooms, quartered

**1/2 pound paneer,✱ cubed
(1/2 recipe, see page 4)**

1 cup Makhni Sauce (see page 207)

**Fresh cilantro, chopped,
for garnish**

1. Heat the oil over high heat and add
   the mushrooms and paneer. Sauté
   until lightly browned on all sides,
   about 2 to 3 minutes.

2. Add the Makhni Sauce and reduce the
   heat to low. Heat through, about 4 to
   5 minutes, being careful not to allow
   the sauce to boil, as the sour cream
   will separate.

3. Garnish with chopped cilantro.

   SERVES 6

Okra with Red Onions
Bhindi Sabzi

Okra is a favorite summer vegetable all over India, cooked in many different styles. In America, it is available year round, especially in Middle-Eastern or Indian markets with produce sections. The use of thickly sliced red onions in this recipe adds lovely color, texture, and sweetness. I often serve this with Potatoes and Paneer in Tomato Sauce and Chapatis (see pages 162 and 86).

1½ pounds okra

3 tablespoons vegetable oil

1 tablespoon cumin seeds ✳

Pinch asafoetida ✳

1-inch piece ginger, peeled and finely chopped

2 green serrano chiles, finely chopped

1 medium red onion, cut into ¼-inch slices

2 teaspoons ground coriander ✳

½ teaspoon cayenne pepper

¼ teaspoon turmeric

1 teaspoon salt

Fresh cilantro, chopped, for garnish

1. Prepare the okra pods in the following manner to prevent a slimy texture: Soak the okra in a bowl of water for a few minutes to remove any grit. Drain in a colander and spread out on paper towels to dry thoroughly. Trim stems from okra and cut into ½-inch rounds.

2. In karhai,✳ wok, or skillet, heat the oil over high heat. Add asafoetida and cumin seeds, sautéing until they sizzle, about one minute.

3. Add ginger, green chiles, and red onion and continue to sauté, stirring continuously, until the red onions are translucent and the edges are lightly browned, about 3 to 4 minutes.

4. Add okra and mix well. Stir in coriander, cayenne, and turmeric and continue to sauté for another 2 minutes. Add salt, lower heat, and cover. Cook for about 10 to 15 minutes, until the okra is tender and the slippery juices have cooked away.

5. This can be made ahead and reheated in the microwave at high heat for 2 or 3 minutes. Serve hot, garnished with cilantro.

SERVES 6

Baby Okra with Green Chiles and Black Pepper
Bhindi Aur Kali Mirch

This dish reminds me of my maternal grandfather, who adored okra and other vegetables—as long as they were prepared simply, so the fresh flavors could come through. Use the smallest okra pods available for this recipe. Serve with Simple Yellow Mung Beans (see page 115), rice, or, for a more elaborate meal, Fish Wrapped in Banana Leaves (see page 176).

1/4 pound small, tender okra

2 tablespoons vegetable oil

1 teaspoon ajwain seeds ✳

3 to 4 green serrano chiles, quartered lengthwise

1/2 teaspoon freshly ground black pepper

1/2 teaspoon salt

1. Prepare the okra in the following manner to prevent a slippery texture: Soak the okra in a bowl of water for a few minutes to remove any grit. Drain in a colander and spread it out on paper towels to dry thoroughly. Trim stems from okra and make a thin slit down one side of each pod. Do not slice all the way through. This allows the flavors to penetrate the okra.

2. In a nonstick skillet, heat the oil over high heat. Add the ajwain seeds and green chiles. Sauté until they sizzle, about one minute.

3. Add okra and mix well. Reduce heat to medium-low and add pepper and salt. Continue sautéing, stirring frequently, for about 5 minutes. Cover and cook on low heat for 10 minutes more, until tender and the slippery juices have cooked away.

4. This dish can be prepared ahead of time and reheated in the microwave on high heat for about two to three minutes. Serve hot.

SERVES 6

Crisp Okra

Karari Bhindi

You would never know you are eating okra when you taste these delicious, crunchy, spicy morsels. If you think of okra as that strange, fuzzy vegetable that can be disagreeably slimy when not cooked well—think again. Like french-fried potatoes, slices of okra are submerged in hot oil until all moisture is cooked away and what remains is the crispy essence of the vegetable. A frequent addition to meals at my mother's home, where it provided a textural contrast to thick curries or dals, Crisp Okra has now become a favorite of my husband and friends too. In fact, it's so crunchy and addictive that I often serve it as a snack with drinks. Note that this recipe requires a lot of oil for the deep-frying; the okra absorbs very little of it in the cooking process. The okra also requires a surprisingly long cooking time to become thoroughly, deliciously crisp.

3 pounds okra (young tender pods)

5 cups vegetable oil

1/2 teaspoon cayenne pepper

1 teaspoon amchur *

1/2 teaspoon salt

1. Thoroughly wash and dry the okra before cutting. Remove the stem end and slice pods into 1/2-inch pieces.

2. In a wide and deep saucepan, heat the oil over high heat. The oil should be very hot but not smoking. Using a spatula or large spoon, ease the okra into the oil, being careful not to splatter. Watch the pan, but do not stir for about 30 to 35 minutes, except if the okra near the edges of the pan seem to brown faster than those in the center; in this case, move them gently toward the center so the slices will cook evenly. During the last 5 minutes of the frying, stir gently a few times to ensure even frying. The okra will become dark brown when ready. Do not remove it from the oil when it is still slightly green, as this will leave it soggy, but do not let it blacken, either. The total frying will take approximately 40 minutes.

3. Quickly remove okra from the oil with a slotted spoon. Place it in an ovenproof bowl lined with paper towels to absorb excess oil. When all the okra is in the bowl, pull out the paper towels, allowing the crisp okra to fall back into the bowl. Sprinkle on the cayenne, amchur, and salt. Toss well to mix. Place the bowl in a warm oven until ready to serve.

SERVES 6 TO 8

Opo Squash with Tomatoes
Ghia Tamatar

Opo squash, or ghia, can sometimes be found in American grocery stores
that serve an Armenian clientele, or in Indian markets with produce sections.
They look like larger, paler, smoother zucchini, but must be peeled and seeded before
cooking. If opo squash are not available, peeled zucchini may be substituted.

2 medium opo squash
(about 3 pounds)

2 tablespoons vegetable oil

1 teaspoon cumin seeds ✳

1-inch piece ginger, peeled and
finely chopped

2 to 3 green serrano chiles,
finely chopped

1 tablespoon ground coriander ✳

1/2 teaspoon cayenne pepper

1/4 teaspoon turmeric

1 teaspoon salt

1 large tomato, diced

Fresh cilantro,
chopped, for garnish

1. Peel the squash and cut them in half
   lengthwise. Cut these halves into 4 or
   5 lengthwise slices, no more than 3/4-
   inch thick. Remove the inner core
   and seeds. Cut the squash sticks into
   1/2-inch pieces.

2. In a karhai✳ or skillet with a lid, heat
   the oil over high heat. Tilt the pan
   and add the cumin seeds to the pool
   of oil. After the seeds have stopped
   sizzling, add the ginger and chile and
   sauté for 1 minute.

3. Add the squash, coriander, cayenne,
   turmeric, and salt, mixing well after
   each addition. Gently stir in the
   tomato.

4. Reduce heat to low, cover, and simmer
   for 20 to 25 minutes, stirring once
   or twice. (When lifting lid, let moisture drop back into karhai to keep
   vegetables from drying out.) Squash
   is done when it is tender and rather
   translucent.

5. Place on a warm platter, garnish with
   chopped cilantro and serve.

SERVES 6

Opo Squash with Yogurt
Ghia Aur Dahi Ki Sabzi

Like any other type of summer squash, opo squash is rather bland and requires lively seasoning to be at its best. If opo squash is unavailable, substitute peeled zucchini. Pink Masoor Lentils with Onion and Tomatoes and Lamb Chops with Dried Mango Powder (see pages 118 and 217) are good accompaniments to this dish.

2 medium opo squash
(about 3 pounds)

2 tablespoons vegetable oil

1 teaspoon cumin seeds *

1-inch piece ginger, peeled and finely chopped

2 to 3 green serrano chiles, finely chopped

1 tablespoon ground coriander *

1/2 teaspoon turmeric

1 teaspoon salt

1/2 cup plain yogurt,* store-bought or homemade (see page 5)

Fresh cilantro, chopped, for garnish

1. Peel the squash and cut them in half lengthwise. Cut these halves into 4 or 5 lengthwise slices, no more than 3/4 inch thick. Remove the inner core and seeds. Cut the squash sticks into 1/2-inch pieces.

2. Heat the oil over high heat in a karhai* or skillet. Add cumin seeds and when they have stopped sizzling, add the ginger and chiles and sauté for a minute. Add squash, coriander, turmeric, and salt, stirring well after each addition.

3. Cover, reduce heat to low, and simmer for 20 to 25 minutes, stirring once or twice. (When lifting lid, let moisture drop back into pan to keep vegetables from drying out.) Squash is done when it is tender and rather translucent.

4. Remove from heat. Just before serving, stir in the yogurt. Remove to a warm platter, garnish with chopped cilantro and serve.

SERVES 6

Scrambled Paneer with Peas

Paneer Mattar Ki Bhurji

The combination of homemade cheese and peas is very common in Northern India. This version results in a dish a little like firm scrambled eggs, and is a favorite for brunch. I like to serve this along with Browned Lamb with Onions, Tomatoes, and Spices; Green Mung Beans with Browned Onions; and Griddle Bread with Daikon Stuffing (see pages 221, 108, and 96).

1/2 pound paneer *
(1/2 recipe, see page 4)

2 tablespoons vegetable oil

1 teaspoon cumin seeds *

1 medium onion, diced small

1-inch piece ginger, peeled and finely chopped

2 green serrano chiles, finely chopped

1 large tomato, chopped

1/4 teaspoon turmeric

1/2 teaspoon cayenne pepper

1 teaspoon salt

1 cup frozen peas, rinsed in hot water

2 tablespoons fresh cilantro, chopped

1. When making the paneer, do not allow it to set completely. Remove the weight after 15 minutes and crumble the paneer into a bowl. Set aside.

2. Heat the oil over high heat in a karhai* or skillet. Tilt pan to form a pool and add the cumin seeds. After they have finished sizzling, about 30 seconds, add the onions, sautéing for 3 to 4 minutes, stirring frequently until the edges are browned.

3. Add the ginger and chiles, mixing well. Add the paneer and sauté for 2 to 3 minutes, until the paneer is lightly browned.

4. Add the tomatoes, turmeric, cayenne, and salt, mixing thoroughly. Stir in the peas and the cilantro. Lower heat and cook, covered, for about 5 minutes.

SERVES 6

Sautéed Potatoes with Dried Mango Powder

Sukhe Aloo—Uttar Pradesh

In India, potatoes—either alone or combined with other vegetables such as peas—are always considered a vegetable rather than a starch, and they often appear at meals along with rice or bread. This simplest of potato dishes, a classic from the Uttar Pradesh province of India, consists of nothing but potatoes and spices. The dried mango powder adds a lemony tang, but more importantly, allows the potatoes to form their delicious brown crust.

1¼ pounds (6 to 8) small red potatoes

3 tablespoons vegetable oil

Pinch asafoetida ✳

1 teaspoon cumin seeds ✳

1 teaspoon coriander seeds, crushed in a mortar and pestle or with a rolling pin

2 green serrano chiles, halved lengthwise

½-inch piece of ginger, peeled and cut into matchsticks

2 tablespoons ground coriander ✳

1 teaspoon cayenne pepper

½ tablespoon dried mango powder ✳

1 teaspoon salt

Fresh cilantro leaves, chopped, to garnish

1. Place unpeeled, whole potatoes in a pan of cold water, bring to a boil, and cook until just tender, about 20 to 25 minutes. Drain the potatoes and allow to cool. Peel them and cut each into six wedges, lengthwise.

2. Heat oil in a large skillet. Add the asafoetida, cumin seeds, coriander seeds, green chiles, and ginger. Sauté until the skin of the chiles blister, 1 or 2 minutes.

3. Stir in the potatoes and add all the remaining ingredients. Cook, covered, over low heat for about 15 minutes, stirring once or twice to incorporate the spices. The potatoes should become slightly crusty. Garnish with cilantro. Serve immediately.

SERVES 6

Note: If made somewhat in advance, the steam from the hot potatoes will soften the crust. Reheat on high, tossing, until they become crisp again.

Potatoes with Mustard Seeds and Kari Leaves

Gujerati Sukhe Aloo

Another simple, well-spiced potato favorite from Bombay, this is traditionally served with deep-fried puris and Yogurt-Saffron Pudding, the sweetened, strained yogurt which I often serve as a dessert (see page 241). It makes a good companion for almost any meat or fish dish, as well, such as Tandoori Halibut (see page 179).

3 tablespoons vegetable oil

Pinch asafoetida ✳

1 teaspoon mustard seeds ✳

10 to 12 kari leaves ✳

1/2 teaspoon turmeric

1 teaspoon salt

2 tablespoons lemon juice

Chopped cilantro, for garnish

1. Heat oil in a karhai✳ or skillet with lid over high heat. Carefully add mustard seeds and kari leaves and cover for about 30 seconds to avoid splattering. Lift lid and add cumin seeds.

2. Add green chiles and sauté for 1 minute. Add potatoes and sauté for 2 to 3 minutes. Add turmeric and salt and cover.

3. Reduce heat to low and cook for about 25 minutes, until potatoes are done. Sprinkle on the lemon juice and stir.

4. Serve immediately, garnished with cilantro.

SERVES 6

Potatoes and Peas in Tomato Sauce

Rasedar Aloo Mattar

Potatoes and peas are a combination found everywhere in India. This version takes the place of a dal in a traditional meal and is wonderful served with Petrale Sole Fillets with Dried Mango Powder and Black-Eyed Pea Salad (see pages 174 and 68).

1 pound (5 or 6) red rose potatoes

3 tablespoons vegetable oil

Pinch asafoetida ✳

1 teaspoon cumin seeds ✳

1-inch piece ginger, peeled and minced

2 green serrano chiles, finely chopped

1½ tablespoons ground coriander ✳

½ teaspoon cayenne pepper

⅛ teaspoon turmeric

4 to 5 medium tomatoes, fresh or canned and well drained (about 1⅔ cups), chopped in food processor

3 cups frozen peas, rinsed in cold water

1½ teaspoons salt

2 tablespoons fresh cilantro, chopped, for garnish

1. Peel potatoes and cut into 1-inch dice. Place in a bowl of cold water.

2. Heat oil in a nonreactive saucepan over high heat. Add asafoetida and cumin seeds. As the seeds pop and sizzle, add ginger and green chiles. Cook for one minute.

3. Drain potatoes and add them, stirring well. Add coriander, cumin, cayenne, and turmeric, continuing to stir over high heat for about one to two minutes.

4. Stir in tomatoes, sautéing for 2 to 3 minutes to cook off some of the juices. Add peas, 2 cups of water, and the salt. Bring to a boil, reduce the heat, cover and simmer 25 to 30 minutes, or until the potatoes are done.

5. Remove to a serving dish, sprinkle with cilantro, and serve immediately.

SERVES 6

Railway Station Potato Curry
Taridar Aloo

Traveling back and forth to school by train, I loved to eat the "fast-food" served at almost every railway station. My favorite was this potato curry, popular as a quick, poor-man's lunch all over India. These days, I serve it with Griddle Bread with Ground Lamb Stuffing and maybe a Spinach and Yogurt Relish (see pages 94 and 50) for a complete meal.

2 pounds (10 to 12) medium
red rose potatoes

2 tablespoons vegetable oil

Pinch asafoetida *

1 teaspoon cumin seeds *

1 teaspoon coriander seeds,*
lightly crushed

3 to 4 whole arbol chiles

2 tablespoons ground coriander *

1/4 teaspoon turmeric

1 teaspoon cayenne pepper

1 teaspoon ground amchur *

1 teaspoon salt

Fresh cilantro,
chopped, for garnish

1. Place potatoes in a large kettle with water to cover and bring to a boil. Cook about 20 to 25 minutes, or until just tender. Drain and let cool. Peel the potatoes and cut into 1½-inch cubes.

2. In a large saucepan, heat the oil over high heat and add the asafoetida, cumin, and coriander seeds. When they finish sizzling, add the chiles (if a spicier dish is desired, break the chiles into pieces). Continue to cook the chiles over high heat, watching carefully as they begin to turn dark brown. Do not allow them to burn. This process allows the chiles to flavor the oil.

3. Add the potatoes, stirring well, and then the coriander, turmeric, cayenne, and amchur. Continue to toss and stir the potatoes to coat thoroughly with the spices and to allow the spices to brown, which gives them more flavor. Some of the potato slices will break up during this process, which serves to thicken the finished curry.

4. Add 5 cups of hot water and the salt to the pan and bring to a full boil. Cover, reduce the heat to low, and cook for 15 to 20 minutes. The result should resemble a thick soup with chunks of potato; if the sauce is too thick, add hot water by ¼-cupfuls.

5. Garnish with chopped cilantro.

SERVES 6

Baby Red Potatoes
in a Tomato-Yogurt Sauce
Dum Aloo

Dum Aloo, with its creamy yogurt and tomato sauce, often stars in festive dinners or wedding feasts, often along with the elaborate Lamb and Rice Casserole (see page 223). In India, the potatoes are deep-fried first. To make the dish lighter, I have eliminated this step with no loss of flavor at all.

1 large onion

$1^1/_2$-inch piece ginger, peeled

3 large cloves garlic

3 medium tomatoes

3 tablespoons vegetable oil

2 to 3 whole black cardamoms ✳

2 (1-inch) pieces cinnamon
stick or cassia ✳

5 to 6 whole cloves

2 bay leaves

$1^1/_2$ tablespoons ground coriander ✳

1 teaspoon ground cumin ✳

$1/_8$ teaspoon turmeric

$1/_2$ to 1 teaspoon cayenne pepper

18 baby red potatoes
(about $1^1/_2$ pounds), peeled

$1/_2$ cup plain yogurt,✳ store-bought
or homemade (see page 5)

3 serrano chiles, halved lengthwise

1 teaspoon salt

Fresh cilantro, chopped, to garnish

1. Mince onions finely in food processor. Set aside. Without cleaning the processor bowl, mince the ginger and garlic together. Set aside in a small bowl. Again without cleaning the processor bowl, chop the tomatoes coarsely.

2. Heat oil over high heat in a 4-quart nonreactive saucepan. Add whole black cardamoms, cinnamon stick or cassia, cloves, and bay leaves and fry until they splatter, about 1 minute.

3. Add onions and brown, stirring frequently over high heat for 2 or 3 minutes. Reduce heat to medium and continue to brown until dark golden, about 10 minutes.

4. Mix in ginger, garlic, and $1/4$ cup water. Increase heat and add coriander, cumin, turmeric, cayenne, and tomatoes. Continue to cook until liquid evaporates.

5. Prick each potato with a sharp skewer (this helps the sauce permeate the potato). Add potatoes to the pan and stir well. Reduce heat to low.

6. Let sauce cool for a few moments before adding yogurt and green chiles, salt, and about $1/2$ cup of water. Mix well, cover and cook on low heat until potatoes are done, about 30 minutes.

7. Garnish with cilantro and serve immediately.

SERVES 6 TO 8

Potatoes and Paneer in Tomato Sauce
Aloo Paneer Rasedar

The combination of potatoes and protein-filled paneer is a popular
one with Indian vegetarians. Our family cook, Chandan, created this
delicious variation, using a light, aromatic tomato sauce to bind the two together.
Spicy Tiger Prawns in Fresh Tomato Sauce and Rice with Browned Onions
(see pages 189 and 80) make perfect accompaniments to this.

1 pound (4 or 5) red rose potatoes

1-inch piece ginger, peeled

2 to 3 green chiles

3 tablespoons vegetable oil

1½ teaspoons cumin seeds *

2 tablespoons ground coriander *

⅛ teaspoon turmeric

1 scant teaspoon cayenne pepper

3 medium tomatoes,
puréed in food processor

3 cups whey from paneer *
(see page 4), or water

1 teaspoon salt

¾ pound paneer,* cut into
1-inch cubes (see page 4)

Fresh cilantro, chopped, for garnish

1. Peel and dice potatoes and set aside in a bowl of cool water.

2. Put ginger and chiles in the food processor and mince, scraping down the sides.

3. Heat a large sauté pan over medium-high heat and add the oil. When the oil is hot, tilt the pan to form a pool and add the cumin seeds carefully. Add ginger and green chiles to the pan, stirring well.

4. Drain potatoes and add to pan, sautéing for 1 minute.

5. Add coriander, turmeric, and cayenne, sautéing for 1 minute more, and then stir in the tomatoes.

6. Cook on high heat, stirring frequently, until the liquid from the tomatoes has evaporated somewhat, about 4 to 5 minutes. Add 2½ cups of whey or water and salt, and bring to a boil. Cover the pan, reduce the heat, and cook over medium-low heat for about 15 to 20 minutes, or until the potatoes are partially done.

7. Add paneer cubes and the remaining whey or water. Cover and cook for another 15 minutes, until the potatoes are done and the paneer has plumped up.

8. Serve immediately, garnished with cilantro.

SERVES 6 TO 8

Potatoes and Green Peas with Cumin
Sukhe Aloo Mattar

When the housewives of India are at a loss as to what to plan for the next meal, this combination of peas and potatoes always comes to mind. Everyone likes it and the ingredients are easily found in any larder. This quick and easy vegetable dish goes well with any almost any combination of meat and dal, along with rice or chapatis.

1¼ pounds (6 to 8) small or medium red rose potatoes

2 tablespoons vegetable oil

Pinch asafoetida *

1 teaspoon cumin seeds *

4 teaspoons ground coriander *

⅛ teaspoon turmeric

¾ teaspoon cayenne pepper, or to taste

2 cups frozen peas, defrosted

1 teaspoon salt, or to taste

1. Peel and dice the potatoes and set aside in a bowl of cool water.

2. Heat oil in a frying pan or karhai.* Tilting pan away, add asafoetida and cumin seeds, being careful to avoid the splattering oil.

3. Add potatoes, tossing well. Stir in spices, peas, and salt. Lower heat to a simmer, cover and cook for 20 to 25 minutes, or until potatoes are done.

4. Serve immediately.

SERVES 6 TO 8

Fresh Spinach with Browned Garlic in Mustard Oil

Palak Sarson Ke Tel Mein

Mustard oil, available in Indian markets, gives this vegetable combination a lively aroma. The oil, pressed from the seeds of the mustard plant that is widely grown in Northern India, is cheaper than other cooking oils and therefore popular among rural people. Because it has a distinct, mustard scent, it also allows the villagers to create flavorful combinations without adding many additional spices. The oil must be heated thoroughly before proceeding with the recipe to eliminate a raw taste.

3 tablespoons mustard oil ✳

4 to 5 large red dried chiles, broken into pieces (see Note)

4 cloves garlic, thinly sliced

1 cup shallots (3 to 4 shallots), thinly sliced

2 pounds spinach (approximately 4 bunches), stemmed and washed thoroughly

1/2 teaspoon salt, or to taste

1. Heat the mustard oil over medium-high heat in a karhai✳ or wok. As it heats, it will lose some of its deep yellow color, thereby losing its raw taste. When it just begins to smoke, add chiles and garlic, and sauté until the garlic is lightly browned. Watch carefully, as the garlic can burn very quickly if the oil is too hot.

2. Immediately add the shallots and spinach, a handful at a time, waiting until the spinach wilts before adding the next handful. Add salt, lower heat, and cover. Cook for about 20 minutes, allowing the spinach to absorb the flavors of the garlic and chiles.

SERVES 6

Note: If possible, use dried Kashmiri chiles from an Indian market. They have a slight sweetness not found in other dried chiles. Otherwise use widely available, dried arbol chiles.

Puréed Spinach with Homemade Indian Cheese

Palak Paneer

Beloved by Punjabis, this traditional dish combines two favorites—spinach (or similar leafy greens) and homemade cheese. Almost every Indian restaurant features a version of Palak Paneer, but it can often be heavy, in true Punjabi style. At the Bombay Cafe, I've devised a fresher, simpler version that makes a great starting point for a vegetarian meal. Palak Paneer is also wonderful with Tandoori Halibut, Potato and Yogurt Relish, and Layered Indian Griddle Bread (see pages 179, 49, and 90).

2 (15½ ounce) packages frozen chopped spinach, defrosted

5 to 6 medium cloves garlic

4 tablespoons vegetable oil

½ pound paneer,✱ cubed (½ recipe, see page 4)

1 small onion, thinly sliced

1-inch piece ginger, peeled and julienned

2 to 3 green serrano chiles, thinly sliced lengthwise

½ cup plain yogurt,✱ store-bought or homemade (see page 5)

1½ tablespoons ground cumin ✱

½ teaspoon cayenne pepper

1 teaspoon salt

1. Place the spinach and garlic in a saucepan. Add ½ cup of water and bring to a boil. Stir well, cover, and reduce heat to a simmer. Cook for 20 minutes. Remove from heat and allow to cool somewhat. Pour into a food processor and mince to a fine purée. Set aside.

2. In a nonstick skillet, heat 1 tablespoon of oil and sauté the paneer cubes until they are lightly browned on all sides. Set aside on paper towels to absorb excess oil.

3. In a large saucepan, heat the rest of the oil over high heat. Add the onion, ginger, and chiles and sauté until lightly browned, about 3 to 4 minutes. Reduce the heat to low and cook a minute more.

4. Add the yogurt, cumin, and cayenne, mixing well. Stir in the puréed spinach and salt. Cover and cook on low for about 10 minutes, to blend all the flavors. Add the browned paneer cubes, cover, and continue to cook for another 10 minutes.

SERVES 6 TO 8

Sugar Snap Peas with Cumin

Saabat Meethe Mattar

Sugar snaps are not available in India, but their sweetness reminds me of
the tender baby peas our cook, Chandan, used to serve at home. His method—a
quick sauté with green onions, chiles, cumin, and lemon juice—works just as well with
the sweet, crisp pods as it always did with peas. This is a wonderful choice for lunch,
accompanied with Brown Masoor Lentils with Sambar Powder (see page 111), or
even as a side dish with Western-style roast chicken.

1½ tablespoons vegetable oil

Pinch asafoetida ✱

1½ teaspoons cumin seeds ✱

1 cup (about 6) green onions, sliced, all white part and some of the green

2 to 3 green serrano chiles, sliced lengthwise into sixths

1½ pounds sugar snap peas, stem end and strings, if any, removed

½ teaspoon salt

1 tablespoon lemon juice

1. In a karhai,✱ wok, or skillet with a lid, heat oil over high heat. Tilt pan to one side and add asafoetida and cumin seeds to the pool of oil. Let them sizzle for a few seconds before adding the green onions and green chiles.

2. Lay the pan flat on the burner and stir-fry the onions and chiles for 2 to 3 minutes until wilted but not browned.

3. Add the sugar snaps and reduce heat to medium. Continue to sauté, stirring frequently, for another 1 to 2 minutes. Add salt, cover and cook for 2 to 3 minutes more, or until the sugar snaps are tender. Stir in the lemon juice.

4. Remove to a warm platter and serve immediately.

SERVES 6

Fresh Spinach with Homemade Indian Cheese

Kashmiri Palak Paneer

In many regions of India, this spinach and cheese mixture is puréed before serving. I prefer the Kashmiri version, in which the spinach leaves are left whole, adding more texture to the dish. Fold the paneer in gently, as it has a tendency to crumble when it has not been browned beforehand. This makes a wonderful vegetarian dinner served with Rice with Onions, Tomatoes, and Chiles and Sweet and Sour Garbanzo Bean Relish (see pages 81 and 67).

2 shallots, peeled and coarsely chopped

1/2-inch piece ginger, peeled

2 tablespoons plain yogurt,✱ store-bought or homemade (see page 5)

Pinch asafoetida ✱

1 tablespoon ground coriander ✱

1 teaspoon resham patti ✱ or cayenne pepper

1 1/2 teaspoons ground roasted cumin ✱

1 teaspoon cumin seeds ✱

1/2 teaspoon Garam Masala I ✱ (see page 3)

3 tablespoons mustard oil ✱

2 to 3 whole, red dried chiles (see Note)

2 to 3 cloves garlic, thinly sliced

2 pounds (about 4 bunches) fresh spinach, stemmed, and thoroughly washed

3/4 pound paneer,✱ cut into thin rectangular pieces (3/4 recipe, see page 4)

1 teaspoon salt

1. In a blender, process the shallots, ginger, yogurt, asafoetida, ground coriander, cayenne, ground roasted cumin, and Garam Masala, using a little water if necessary to form a smooth paste.

2. Heat the mustard oil in a large skillet over medium-high heat. The oil should be almost to the smoking point, until it loses its yellow color. This will eliminate the raw taste of uncooked mustard oil. Add the cumin seeds and then immediately add the red chiles and garlic. Sauté for about 1 minute, being careful not to burn the garlic.

3. Add the spice paste and sauté for about 1 minute.

4. Add spinach leaves, a handful at a time, stirring continuously as they wilt. Reduce heat, cover, and let simmer for about 15 minutes.

5. Add the paneer, season with salt, cover, and continue to cook for about 3 to 4 minutes.

Serves 6

Note: If possible, used dried Kashmiri chiles from an Indian market. They have a slight sweetness not found in other dried chiles. Otherwise, use widely available, dried arbol chiles.

Mixed Vegetable and Lentil Curry
Sindhi Curry

My grandfather's absolute favorite, Sindhi Curry appeared on my family's table every Sunday for lunch. With its complex mixture of vegetables, lentils, and spices, it seems daunting—but it is well worth a try. Rich and delicious, it easily forms a meal in itself, accompanied by Plain Basmati Rice (see page 78).

1 cup dry toor dal *

1/4 teaspoon turmeric

1 teaspoon cayenne pepper

3 teaspoons vegetable oil

Pinch asafoetida *

3 arbol chiles

1/2 teaspoon fenugreek seeds *

1/2 teaspoon mustard seeds *

1/2 teaspoon cumin seeds *

1/2-inch piece ginger, peeled and finely chopped

2 medium green serrano chiles, finely chopped

1/2 cup lightly packed besan *

1 tablespoon ground coriander *

2 small potatoes, peeled and cut into 8 pieces each

12 small kokum flowers * (if unavailable, substitute 1 large tomato cut into 6 wedges)

1 small (1/2 pound) cauliflower or the inner part of a larger one, about 12 medium florets

2 medium Japanese eggplants, cut in half lengthwise and then into 6 pieces each

6 green beans, trimmed, and cut into thirds

1 medium carrot, peeled and cut into 2 by 1/4-inch sticks

18 small okra, with ends trimmed

4 ounce piece tamarind * pulp, soaked in 1/2 cup hot water, then strained

1 1/2 teaspoons salt

1. Earlier in the day or the day before, pick over the dal, wash several times and then place in a saucepan with 8 cups of water. Bring to a boil and skim off the foam. Reduce the heat to low, stir in the turmeric and $1/2$ teaspoon of the cayenne. Cover partially and cook for 1 hour, mashing down the dal when it is tender. Strain the dal through a sieve, mashing lightly with the back of a wooden spoon. Reserve the liquid (there should be $5\frac{1}{2}$ to 6 cups) and discard the pulp.

2. Heat the oil over high heat in a large pot with a lid. Carefully add the asafoetida, red chiles, fenugreek seeds, and mustard seeds and cover immediately. When the sizzling subsides, about 30 seconds, add the cumin seeds, ginger, and green chiles. Sauté for 1 minute.

3. Reduce the heat to low and add the besan, stirring constantly to break down any lumps. Continue to sauté for about 1 or 2 minutes, until the besan turns a very light brown. Add the ground coriander and remaining cayenne and mix well.

4. Add the potatoes. At this point the mixture may be lumpy. Add the reserved dal liquid, stirring continuously to dissolve the lumps of besan. Bring the mixture to the boil.

5. Add the kokum flowers (wait to add the tomatoes if these are being substituted). Cook over low heat, covered, about 5 minutes.

6. Add the cauliflower, eggplant, and green beans. Continue to cook for another 5 minutes before adding the carrots.

7. Cook for 5 minutes more and then add the okra and the tomatoes, if they are being used. Cover and cook for 5 minutes.

8. Add the tamarind paste and salt and cook for 2 to 3 minutes. Serve hot with Plain Basmati Rice.

SERVES 6

Fish and Seafood

I have many fond memories of my visits to the tropical coastal region of Goa—the balmy beaches, ocean breezes and, without a doubt, the best seafood in India, always caught fresh and eaten the same day. I can still taste the rich, delectable Goan fish curry I had there. Goans love coconut as much as they love seafood, and their delicious fish specialties always include quantities of that rich and delicious ingredient.

Outside of the coastal regions, seafood was not very common when I was growing up, because of the scarcity of refrigeration throughout India. Here in the United States, however, fresh seafood of almost infinite variety is widely available as more and more people have come to appreciate it. It's quick and easy to cook, and best of all, it provides a perfect basis for my favorite flavor combinations. For example, like most Indians, I love tart tastes, so I included Petrale Sole Fillets with Dried Mango Powder, or *amchur;* anyone who has ever squeezed lemon juice on a fish fillet will enjoy amchur's lemony bouquet.

Most of the recipes in this chapter are my own creations, such as Spicy Tiger Prawns in Fresh Tomato Sauce, or adaptations of classics, such as Fish Wrapped in Banana Leaves. Because fish cooks so quickly, these recipes take very little time, which makes them perfect for either entertaining or family fare.

Petrale Sole Fillets
with Dried Mango Powder
Sindhi Machchi

The most common kind of fish found in Western India is the pomfret, similar to flounder, sole, or plaice. The mildness of this type of fish lends itself nicely to quick sautéing with spices. The *amchur,* or dried mango powder, adds a sour tang that enhances the fish just the way freshly squeezed lemon juice does in Western cooking. This simple fish dish goes well with the full-bodied Mixed Vegetable and Lentil Curry (see page 170) and Plain Basmati Rice (see page 78).

6 fillets (approximately 5 ounces each) of petrale sole or similar flat, white fish

1/2 teaspoon turmeric

1 1/2 teaspoons cayenne pepper

2 lemons

1 teaspoon salt

2 tablespoons vegetable oil

2 tablespoons ground coriander ✳

2 teaspoons amchur ✳

1/2 cup fresh cilantro, chopped

1. In a small bowl, combine the turmeric and 1/2 teaspoon of cayenne. Rub both sides of the fish fillets with the mixture and squeeze the lemon juice over them. Refrigerate for 1 hour.

2. To sauté, heat 1 tablespoon of oil over high heat in a nonstick skillet large enough to hold three fillets. Add one tablespoon of coriander and 1/2 teaspoon cayenne to the hot oil, mixing well until the spices start to sizzle. Be careful not to burn the cayenne.

3. Remove the fish fillets from the marinade, reserving any juices, and sprinkle both sides of the fillets with salt.

4. Add 3 fillets to the hot pan and sprinkle 1/2 teaspoon amchur and 1/8 cup of the cilantro on them. Turn the fillets carefully after about 1 minute and sprinkle with another 1/2 teaspoon amchur and 1/8 cup of the cilantro.

5. After about one minute, turn once more, being careful not to break the fillets. If the fish tends to stick to the pan, drizzle a little of the reserved marinade juices around the edges to help loosen them. Cook one minute more and remove to a warm platter.

6. Repeat the process with the remaining three fillets. Garnish with remaining cilantro and serve warm.

SERVES 6

Fish in Spinach Sauce

Palak Machchi

My aunt, famous in our family for her demanding standards, created this simplified version of a traditional Northern Indian dish. The lovely green spinach and cilantro sauce provides a colorful contrast to the white of the fish in this curry. The fish of choice in Bombay is pomfret, also known as plaice in the North Atlantic waters around England.

5 to 6 cloves garlic

1/2-inch piece ginger, peeled

2 to 3 green serrano chiles

1 tablespoon ground coriander ✱

1 1/2 teaspoons ground cumin ✱

1/8 teaspoon turmeric

3 tablespoons vegetable oil

1 bunch spinach (1/2 pound) stemmed, washed, and finely chopped

1 bunch fresh cilantro, leaves and tender stalks finely chopped

1 medium tomato, finely chopped

1 teaspoon salt

1 1/2 pounds halibut, red snapper, or orange roughy, cut into 1 1/2-inch cubes

Nonstick cooking spray

1. Place garlic, ginger, chiles, coriander, cumin, and turmeric in a blender and purée into a smooth paste, using a small amount of water if necessary. Set aside.

2. Heat 2 tablespoons of oil over medium heat in a large, shallow sauté pan. Add the spice paste and sauté for a minute or two, stirring continuously to avoid burning it.

3. Add the spinach and cilantro, mixing well, and continue to sauté over medium heat, stirring occasionally, until the liquid from the spinach has evaporated, about 5 to 6 minutes.

4. Meanwhile, heat the remaining tablespoon of oil in a skillet over medium-high heat. Add the fish pieces and sauté, turning to brown lightly on all sides.

5. Add the tomatoes to the spinach mixture and continue to cook for 2 to 3 minutes more.

6. Add the fish to the spinach mixture. Sprinkle with salt, cover, and cook over low heat for 5 to 8 minutes, depending on the thickness of the fish. Fish should be firm and cooked through. Serve immediately.

SERVES 6

Fish Wrapped in Banana Leaves

Patrel Nu Machchi

This dish is a favorite in Bombay. The fish of choice is pomfret, which is also known as plaice in the North Atlantic waters around England. The richness of the coconut counterbalances the spiciness of the chiles nicely. Look for banana leaves in Latin American or some Asian markets (or your neighbor's backyard, as I do!), but if they are unavailable, follow the same instructions using aluminum foil.

6 pieces of banana leaves,
8 by 6 inches

2 to 3 green serrano chiles

1-inch piece ginger, peeled

3 to 4 cloves garlic

1 bunch (about 1 cup) fresh cilantro,
with leaves and tender stalks

1/2 cup grated fresh coconut ✳

1 teaspoon Garam Masala ✳
(see page 3)

1/2 teaspoon cayenne pepper

1 teaspoon salt

6 fillets (5 to 6 ounces each)
orange roughy, halibut,
or red snapper

1 tablespoon vegetable oil
(for use in sautéing;
omit if steaming)

Lemon wedges for garnish

1. Heat the pieces of banana leaves over a gas burner or open flame of a barbecue grill, turning often to make them supple enough to fold into packets. The leaves will turn a black-green. Alternatively, blanch the leaves in boiling water for a few minutes. Set aside. If you don't have banana leaves, cut 6 pieces of aluminum foil, 8 by 6 inches, and set aside.

2. Place the chiles, ginger, garlic, cilantro, coconut, Garam Masala, and cayenne in the container of a blender, adding a little water, and process to a smooth, thick paste.

3. Place a fillet on a banana leaf or piece of foil. Sprinkle the fillet with a little salt and spoon 1 to 1½ tablespoons of the spice mixture on one side of the fish. Fold the leaf over to form a packet, making sure that the flaps tuck under the side of the fish without the spice mixture. If using the banana leaves, secure the flaps with a toothpick. Repeat for all the fillets.

4. The packets can be either steamed or sautéed. To steam, set in a Chinese basket or any kind of steamer over simmering water and cook for about 10 minutes, or until the fish feels firm to the touch when pressed through the packet. To sauté, heat the oil in a nonstick skillet, add the fish packets and cook over medium-high heat for 3 to 4 minutes on each side, depending on the thickness of the fish. Test for doneness by pressing on the packets to see if the fish feels firm.

5. To serve, remove the toothpicks and place the packets on a warm platter, flap side down. Make a crosswise slit on each packet and fold the corners back, revealing the fish. Garnish with lemon wedges. Serve at once.

SERVES 6

Halibut with Onions and Tomatoes
Sel Machchi

Cubes of firm, delicious fish in a fragrant, tomato-onion sauce—this dish
is a wonderful choice for entertaining because you can make the sauce ahead
of time and add the fish at the last minute. Rice with Chinese Long Beans,
Mercin's Lemon Lentils, and Sautéed Potatoes with Dried Mango Powder
(see pages 84, 109, and 155) make good accompaniments.

3 tablespoons vegetable oil

1 teaspoon cumin seeds ✳

2 medium onions, thinly sliced

2 to 3 green serrano chiles,
thinly sliced lengthwise

1-inch piece ginger, peeled
and julienned

3 medium tomatoes, thinly sliced

1/4 teaspoon turmeric

1/2 teaspoon cayenne pepper

1 tablespoon ground coriander ✳

1 1/2 pounds halibut, cut into
1 1/2-inch cubes

2 tablespoons fresh cilantro,
chopped

1 teaspoon salt

Lemon juice to taste

1. Heat the oil over medium-high heat
   in a large skillet. Tilt the pan to form
   a pool and add the cumin seeds.
   When they stop sizzling, level the
   pan and add the onions. Sauté until
   they are translucent, about 2 to 3
   minutes.

2. Add the ginger and chiles and continue to sauté for another minute.
   Add the tomatoes, turmeric, cayenne,
   and coriander and continue to cook,
   mixing well, for another minute.
   Sauce can be made ahead to this
   point.

3. Add the fish cubes and the cilantro,
   combining well. Sprinkle on the salt
   and about 1/2 to 3/4 cup of water.
   Lower heat and cook for 5 to 7
   minutes, until the fish is firm and
   cooked through.

SERVES 6

Tandoori Halibut
Tandoori Machchi

Technically, "tandoori" refers to a special clay oven in which tandoori dishes are cooked, and therefore it is impossible to recreate these delicious roasts at home. However, by using a charcoal grill and by seasoning the fish in the characteristic spicy yogurt marinade, it is possible to recreate the flavor of tandoori cooking very successfully. The tandoori marinade below works wonderfully with almost any kind of meat or seafood, or even grilled vegetables.

MARINADE:

1/2 cup plain yogurt,✱ store-bought or homemade (see page 5)

3-inch piece ginger, peeled

1 tablespoon Garam Masala I ✱

1 tablespoon ground coriander ✱

1 teaspoon cayenne pepper

1/8 teaspoon turmeric

1/4 cup vegetable oil or nonstick cooking spray

1 teaspoon salt

6 (5-ounce each) fillets halibut, 1/2-inch thick, skinned

Lemon wedges and cilantro sprigs, for garnish

1. Prepare a fire in the grill.

2. In a blender, process all the ingredients of the marinade to a smooth paste, using a little water if needed.

3. Sprinkle the salt on the fillets and then coat each side with the marinade. Set aside for 20 minutes.

4. Coat a fish-grilling basket with oil or spray it with cooking spray and set the fillets inside. Grill for 3 to 4 minutes on each side. Alternatively, grease a broiler rack or spray with cooking spray, arrange the fillets upon it, and place under a hot broiler for 4 to 5 minutes a side, until the fish is firm to the touch and cooked through. Garnish with lemon and cilantro.

SERVES 6

Coconut Curry with Yellowtail
Goan Machchi Ki Curry

On a visit to Goa, on the Western coast of India, we made a point of asking every taxi driver we encountered what his favorite meal was. Every one of them answered, "Fish curry and rice." The spices in a Goan curry vary from cook to cook, but you can be sure that each one will contain seafood of some sort and that enriching, tropical trademark, coconut. This is my adaptation of coastal India's most well-known dish, lightly sweet from the coconut and tart from the tamarind. I like to use *resham patti,* or ground red Kashmiri chiles, because they are sweeter and a little milder than cayenne pepper and because they impart the traditional red color to the sauce in this dish. Serve with Sautéed Potatoes with Dried Mango Powder and Black-Eyed Pea Salad (see pages 155 and 68).

1½ cups freshly grated coconut ✳

2 teaspoons resham patti ✳
or 1½ teaspoons
cayenne pepper

4 cloves garlic

¼ teaspoon turmeric

1½ tablespoons ground coriander ✳

1 teaspoon ground cumin ✳

3 tablespoons vegetable oil

1 small onion, thinly sliced

1 (12-ounce) can coconut milk
(see Note)

1 teaspoon salt

2 to 2½ pounds yellowtail tuna
or any other firm fish,
cut into 2-inch cubes

4-ounce piece tamarind ✳ pulp,
soaked in ½ cup hot water,
then strained

1. Place the coconut, red chile, garlic, turmeric, ground coriander, and ground cumin in a blender and purée with as much water as needed, up to a $1/2$ cup, to obtain a smooth paste. Do not overprocess, because the coconut oil will rise to the top. Set aside.

2. In a 4-quart saucepan, heat the oil over medium-high heat. Add the sliced onions and sauté until they are translucent, about 5 minutes. Add the coconut paste and sauté on high heat, stirring frequently to avoid burning. Cook for about 5 to 6 minutes, until all the moisture evaporates, leaving a dry "masala" in the pan.

3. Add the coconut milk and using the can as a measuring cup an additional 1 to 2 cans of hot water, depending on thickness of curry desired. When the mixture comes to a boil, add the salt. Reduce the heat to low, cover and simmer for 15 to 20 minutes to allow the flavors to blend. The dish can be made ahead to this point.

4. When ready to serve add fish and cook gently on low heat for 5 to 6 minutes until done. Add the tamarind pulp and cook for another 2 minutes. Serve hot with plain rice.

Serves 6

Note: Canned coconut milk is available in Indian and Asian markets.

Salmon Roll with Coconut Chutney and Cucumber Raita

At a recent party, the host served an elegant fillet of salmon wrapped around a leek stuffing and napped with a rich tarragon sauce. It was exquisite—but I couldn't help thinking how much better it would be with Indian flavors. When I got home I experimented for days until I came up with this delicious recipe. The salmon is rolled around a stuffing of leeks, chiles, and rich coconut chutney and garnished with cool Cucumber Raita. (Note that the recipe for this Raita here is slightly different from the Cucumber and Onion Yogurt Relish on page 52.) This Salmon Roll is a very impressive dish that looks more complicated than it is. Both the chutney and the raita can be made in advance. Serve it as a first course, with store-bought lentil poppadums, or as a light meal with Plain Basmati Rice (see page 78).

2 leeks, white and pale green parts only, thoroughly washed, halved lengthwise and julienned

2 to 4 green serrano chiles, minced

1^1/$_2$ tablespoons melted ghee ✳

3 pounds salmon fillet

1^1/$_2$ teaspoons salt

^{2}/$_3$ cup Green Coconut Chutney, strained (recipe follows)

1 tablespoon ajwain seeds ✳

1 tablespoon cracked black pepper

2 tablespoons plus 2 teaspoons corn oil

Cucumber Raita II (see page 184)

8 to 10 red radishes, minced, for garnish

1. Heat the ghee or butter in a skillet and sauté the leeks and chiles for 2 or 3 minutes, or until wilted. Do not brown the vegetables. Set aside.

2. With a sharp knife, butterfly the salmon fillet so that it opens flat, like a book. The fish may fall apart a little, but it will be easy to reassemble when it is rolled up. Place the butterflied salmon between two pieces of parchment or wax paper and, using a small, heavy skillet, pound the fillet as thin as possible.

3. Sprinkle the fillet with salt and place the leek and chile mixture across one long end. Fold the end over to start rolling. Spread the coconut chutney over the rest of the fillet and continue rolling as tightly as possible, using the wax paper for help if needed.

4. Place the salmon on a clean piece of wax paper and roll it into a tight package, twisting the ends of the paper to seal it. Refrigerate for at least 2 hours or up to 24.

5. Prepare two pieces of aluminum foil, each about 12 by 24 inches, by lightly coating one side of each with 1 teaspoon corn oil. The fillet will probably be too large to sauté in one piece, so after unwrapping the salmon from the wax paper, slice it in half, crosswise, with a sharp knife. Place each piece on a prepared sheet of foil and sprinkle each with half of the ajwain and cracked pepper. Once again, roll the foil snugly around the fillet, folding the ends under to make a neat package.

6. Heat a heavy skillet, adding 1 tablespoon of oil. Place one foil package in the hot skillet and sauté, turning often to ensure even cooking. Sauté for 8 to 10 minutes, until the roll feels firm. (If the fillet is thin or if you like fish lightly cooked, test after 6 minutes.) Remove from the skillet and sauté the second roll in the same manner. Let the roll sit for several minutes before slicing.

7. Using a sharp, serrated knife and leaving the foil on, cut the salmon rolls into 1¼-inch-thick slices. Remove the foil from the slices, place them on a serving platter and garnish with dollops of cucumber raita, and minced radishes.

SERVES 6 TO 8

Cucumber Raita II

1/8 teaspoon cumin seeds ✳

1 large cucumber, peeled, seeded, and grated

3/4 cup plain yogurt,✳ store-bought or homemade (see page 5)

1/8 teaspoon cayenne pepper

1 teaspoon sugar

1/4 teaspoon salt

1/2 tablespoon fresh cilantro leaves, minced

1. Roast the cumin seeds in dry skillet until they turn dark brown. Fold them in a piece of aluminum foil and crush them by rolling over them with a rolling pin.

2. Squeeze all the liquid out of the grated cucumbers with your hands. Place the squeezed cucumber in a mixing bowl with all the other ingredients and mix well. Check for seasonings, adding more sugar and cayenne to taste. Refrigerate for at least 30 minutes.

MAKES 1 CUP

Green Coconut Chutney

2 cups freshly grated coconut,✳ lightly packed (about 1 large coconut)

3 cloves garlic

4 to 6 green serrano chiles

1/2 cup fresh cilantro leaves, tightly packed

15 fresh mint leaves

4 tablespoons lemon juice

2/3 cup water

1 teaspoon salt

1. Place all the ingredients in a blender. Blend briefly on medium speed, scraping down the sides of the container once or twice. Then blend on high speed for 2 to 3 minutes, or until the chutney is fairly smooth. Remove to a small bowl and refrigerate if not using immediately. Chutney keeps about a week in the refrigerator, tightly covered.

MAKES ABOUT 2 1/2 CUPS

Rice with Shrimp and Tomato

Jhinga Pullao

This delectable combination of rice, shrimp, tomatoes, and spices is a favorite of co-writer, Helen. It's very important to use only large shrimp in this dish; smaller ones will cook too quickly and toughen up before the rice is done.

1½ cups basmatic rice ✳

2 tablespoons vegetable oil

1 teaspoon mustard seeds ✳

10 to 12 fresh kari seeds ✳

2 medium green serrano chiles, finely chopped

2 large tomatoes, diced small

½ teaspoon cayenne pepper

2 teaspoons ground coriander ✳

1 tablespoon fresh cilantro, chopped

1 teaspoon salt

24 large shrimp (just over 1 pound), shelled and deveined

1. Pick over the rice and wash it in a colander until the water runs clear. Soak it in warm water for at least 20 minutes but no more than 45.

2. Heat the oil over high heat in a large shallow saucepan with a lid. Tilt the pan to form a pool and carefully add the mustard seeds and kari leaves. Cover immediately to avoid splattering. When the sizzling subsides, about 30 seconds, remove the lid and add the green chiles and ginger. Mix well.

3. Add the tomatoes, coriander, and cayenne. Sauté, stirring, for 1 minute.

4. Stir in the rice, adding 2½ cups of hot water, salt, and cilantro. When the mixture comes to a full boil, stir in the shrimp, cover, reduce the heat, and simmer for 10 minutes. Remove from the heat and let stand for 5 minutes before removing the lid. Fluff the pullao with a fork and serve at once.

SERVES 6

Green Coconut Curry With Shrimp

Goan Jhinga Curry

You can always recognize a curry from Goa, the tropical region on India's
west coast, because it will contain seafood and coconut. Furthermore, you can tell
from across the room whether the curry contains fish or shrimp. Tradition decrees that
fish (such as the Coconut Curry with Yellowtail) be served in a red sauce and shrimp
in a green sauce. Here, the sauce gets its color and vibrant flavor from cilantro leaves.
This rich curry has a wonderful combination sweet, hot and sour flavors. I like to
serve it with Plain Basmati Rice and Crisp Okra (see pages 78 and 151).

1 tablespoon khus-khus ✳

1½ cups freshly grated coconut ✳

2 to 3 green serrano chiles

5 to 6 cloves garlic

1 cup fresh cilantro, chopped and
tightly packed

1 teaspoon cayenne pepper

1 tablespoon ground coriander ✳

3 tablespoons vegetable oil

1 teaspoon mustard seeds ✳

8 to 10 fresh kari leaves ✳

1 small onion, thinly sliced

1 (12-ounce) can coconut milk ✳

1 teaspoon salt

4-ounce piece tamarind ✳ pulp,
soaked in ½ cup hot water,
forced through a sieve,
discarding fiber and seeds

30 large shrimp, peeled and deveined

1. Grind the khus-khus in a clean spice grinder. Place the coconut, garlic, chiles, cilantro, ground khus-khus, cayenne, and coriander in a blender and purée with as much water as needed, up to a 1/2 cup, to obtain a smooth paste. Do not over-blend, or the coconut oil will rise to the surface.

2. In a medium saucepan, heat the oil over medium-high heat. Add the mustard seeds and cover immediately, as they will splatter. After about 30 seconds, when the sizzling subsides, add the kari leaves and the sliced onions. Sauté until the onions are translucent, about 3 minutes.

3. Add the coconut paste and sauté on high heat, stirring frequently to avoid burning. Cook for about 5 to 6 minutes, until all the moisture evaporates, leaving a dry "masala" in the pan.

4. Add the coconut milk and, using the can as a measuring cup, add an additional 1 to 2 cans of hot water, depending on thickness of curry desired. When the mixture comes to a boil, add the salt. Reduce the heat, cover and simmer for 15 to 20 minutes to allow the flavors to blend. Add the tamarind pulp and cook for another 2 to 3 minutes. The curry can be prepared a day ahead to this point. Refrigerate until ready to proceed.

5. When ready to serve, heat the curry mixture over medium heat and add the shrimp. Cook for 2 to 3 minutes, until the shrimp are done. Do not overcook. Serve immediately with plain rice.

SERVES 6

Aromatic Shrimp with Cilantro, Dill, and Tomatoes

Tamatar Aur Sua Jhinga

This is my aunt's version of a Sindhi dish. Dill, which is such a natural companion to shrimp, is actually rare in India. It appears often in Northern cooking, especially when combining with spinach. In this case, the fragrant dill and cilantro make a vibrant sauce for this quick sauté.

4 cloves garlic

1/2-inch piece ginger, peeled and coarsely chopped

1 cup fresh cilantro leaves and tender stems, tightly packed

1/4 cup fresh dill

2 tablespoons vegetable oil

1 teaspoon mustard seeds ✳

10 to 12 fresh kari leaves ✳

1 tablespoon ground coriander ✳

1/4 teaspoon turmeric

1/2 teaspoon cayenne pepper

1 large tomato, diced

1 1/2 pounds (about 45 to 60) small shrimp, shelled and deveined

1 teaspoon salt

1. In a food processor, mince the garlic, ginger, and chiles. Add the cilantro and dill, scraping down the sides of the bowl and processing finely. Use a little water if necessary.

2. Heat the oil over high heat in a 10-inch skillet with a lid. Tilt the pan to form a pool and carefully add the mustard seeds and kari leaves. Cover at once to avoid splatters. When the sizzling subsides, lift the lid and add the contents of the food processor and sauté for 1 minute.

3. Add 1/2 cup of water and the coriander, turmeric, and cayenne. Reduce the heat to low, stirring to blend the ingredients, and cook to reduce the liquid for about 5 minutes (see Note).

4. Add the tomato, cover, and cook for another 3 minutes. (Recipe can be prepared ahead to this point. Reheat spice mixture before proceeding)

5. Raise heat to medium-high and quickly add the shrimp, sprinkling them with the salt. Stirring and turning them frequently, cook the shrimp until they are pink and done, about 2 to 3 minutes.

SERVES 6

Note: This recipe produces shrimp coated thickly with the spicy sauce, but it is easy to turn it into a curry by adding another 1 1/2 cups of water to the spice mixture in step 3.

Spicy Tiger Prawns in Fresh Tomato Sauce

Jhinga Tamatar

I must have been under an Italian influence when I created this dish, because it reminds me of a lively, fresh pasta sauce. More traditional Indian cooks would simmer the tomatoes longer, but I think that the quick cooking adds to the vibrant flavor.

2 tablespoons vegetable oil

1 teaspoon mustard seeds *

10 to 12 kari leaves *

2 to 3 whole, dried arbol chiles

3 to 4 green serrano chiles, chopped

1-inch piece ginger, peeled and finely chopped

4 medium tomatoes, chopped

1/4 teaspoon turmeric

1 teaspoon cayenne pepper

2 teaspoons ground coriander *

18 large tiger prawns, shelled and deveined, leaving tails intact

1 teaspoon salt

Fresh cilantro, chopped, for garnish

1. Heat the oil over high heat in a karhai* or a large skillet with a lid. Tilt the pan to form a pool and carefully add the mustard seeds, kari leaves, and red chiles. Cover immediately to avoid splattering. When the sizzling subsides, about 30 seconds, add the green chiles and ginger and sauté for about a minute, until the chiles just begin to blister.

2. Add the tomatoes and sauté, stirring, for one minute.

3. Stir in turmeric, cayenne, and coriander. Reduce the heat, cover and cook for 5 to 6 minutes.

4. Uncover, add the prawns, and raise the heat to medium. Cook, stirring and turning, for 6 to 7 minutes, until the prawns turn pink and are cooked through. Be careful not to overcook the prawns, as they will toughen. Serve immediately, garnished with cilantro.

SERVES 6

Chicken and Poultry

When I was growing up, chicken was considered more of a delicacy than meat, reserved for honored guests or special occasions. The chickens available were small and flavorful, not like the large farm-raised ones sold in most markets here. For this reason, I sometimes substitute Cornish hens, which remind me more of the chickens at home.

Over the years, I have developed a huge repertoire of chicken recipes, for three reasons—almost everybody likes chicken; it's a healthy form of protein; and when cooked with Indian spices and techniques, there is surely nothing more delicious. Every night at the Bombay Cafe, I offer several different poultry specialties, from saucy curries to grilled, marinated kabobs, and they often sell out.

The rich curries that I remember so fondly from home always began with Chandan's slow caramelizing of the onions and spices in oil. My method produces results as delectable as Chandan's, but with much less oil. I always begin by mincing the onions in a food processor, a very unorthodox technique because it forces the onions to exude juices. In other styles of cooking, this is not desirable, because the wetness of the onions slows the browning process, but for my purposes it is ideal. The dampness of the onions makes it unnecessary to add large amounts of oil to keep them from burning during the slow browning process. I detail this technique in each recipe; it's important to follow the instructions. Indian recipes always call for the chicken to be skinned and almost always left on the bone, for both maximum health benefits and flavor.

Chicken Curry
Murghi Ki Curry

First, let's dispel some misapprehensions about curry, which is a basic
Indian style of cooking, or braising, with seasonings over low heat. Curry is not
a yellow spice bought in a jar from the market. Chandan and the cooking staff at the
Bombay Cafe have explained to me that the word *kard* in Hindi, from which "curry" is
derived, means "to cook over a long period of time," and it is the slow, careful browning of the onions that is the most crucial part of making a proper curry. Curry refers to
a dish which begins as a slow browning of onions (usually), ginger, garlic, tomatoes,
and ground spices, including cinnamon, cloves, bay leaves, cardamom, and black
pepper (or garam masala) as well as cumin, coriander, cayenne pepper, and turmeric.
The proportions of the spices vary from cook to cook. A curry can be a meat dish
with a thin sauce or a thick stew. The following mouth-watering chicken curry
recipe produces one of the most basic, popular curries in Indian cooking.

---

2 small yellow onions

5 to 6 cloves garlic

1/2-inch piece ginger, peeled

2 green serrano chiles

2 medium, ripe tomatoes

1/3 cup vegetable oil

2 black cardamom pods ✳

2 to 3 (1-inch) pieces cinnamon
stick or cassia ✳

1 to 2 bay leaves

4 to 5 whole cloves

5 to 6 black peppercorns

2 tablespoons ground coriander ✳

2 tablespoons ground cumin ✳

1/4 teaspoon turmeric

1/2 to 1 teaspoon cayenne pepper

1 1/2 teaspoons salt

2 (2 1/2 pound) chickens, cut into
8 pieces each and skinned

Fresh cilantro, chopped, for garnish

---

1. Finely chop the onions in a food processor. Set aside in a separate bowl. Without rinsing the workbowl, mince ginger, garlic, and green chiles together in the food processor and set aside in a separate bowl. Again without rinsing the workbowl, purée the tomatoes and set aside.

2. Heat oil in a large saucepan and add onions. Brown over medium-high heat, stirring frequently, until they turn a deep red-brown in color, about 12 to 14 minutes. Stir in 1 or 2 tablespoons of hot water, as needed, to arrest the browning and to make a paste.

3. Add the ginger, garlic, and chile mixture and sauté for a minute or so, adding a little more water if needed to prevent sticking.

4. Add all the whole and ground spices and continue to brown for another 2 to 3 minutes.

5. Add the puréed tomatoes and their juices and cook through until the solids separate from the oil, about 5 to 6 minutes, stirring frequently. This paste is called a "masala."

6. Add the chicken pieces and brown well on medium-high heat, about 5 minutes. Add the salt and about 1/3 cup hot water. Cover and simmer for 30 to 40 minutes, or until the chicken is cooked through. Add a little more hot water if needed during cooking. The curry should have the consistency of thick gravy.

7. Serve on a warm platter, garnished with chopped cilantro.

SERVES 6 TO 8

South Indian Chicken Curry with Fennel Seeds

Saunf Murghi

For a completely different flavor from the preceding chicken curry recipe, this dish eliminates the browned onions and garam masala in favor of fennel seeds and other Southern seasonings.

2 (3 pound) chickens, skinned and cut into 14 small pieces each (see Note)

1 teaspoon turmeric

4 tablespoons vegetable oil

8 to 10 whole red chiles, broken in half

1/2 tablespoon urad dal ✳

2 teaspoons mustard seeds ✳

2 teaspoons nigella seeds ✳

1 teaspoon fenugreek seeds ✳

2 tablespoons fennel seeds

2 sprigs fresh kari leaves ✳

4 medium onions, diced

1 teaspoon cayenne pepper

1 1/3 cups warm water with 1 1/2 teaspoons salt dissolved in it

1. Sprinkle the turmeric over the chicken pieces and set aside for at least 20 minutes.

2. Heat the oil over high heat in a karhai,* wok, or large saucepan with a lid. Add all the whole spices and kari leaves, covering immediately to prevent splattering. After the sizzling has subsided, about 30 seconds, lift the lid and add the onions.

3. Reduce heat to medium-high and sauté the onions until they are translucent and just beginning to brown, about 3 to 4 minutes.

4. Reduce heat to medium, add the chicken pieces, and sauté for 3 to 4 minutes. Add the cayenne and mix well.

5. Add 1/3 cup of the salted water, increase the heat to high, and continue cooking the chicken pieces, stirring frequently. As the water evaporates, add another 1/3 cup, in the same manner. Continue until all the salted water is used up, which should take about 10 to 12 minutes.

6. After adding the last 1/3 cup of water, cover the pot, reduce the heat to low, and cook for 10 to 15 minutes, until the chicken is very tender.

7. Serve immediately.

Serves 6 to 8

Note: Using a heavy cleaver, chop each thigh into two pieces; discard the lower, bony inch of each drumstick and cut the remaining piece in two; cut each half-breast into three pieces, leaving the wing "drumette" attached to one piece of breast.

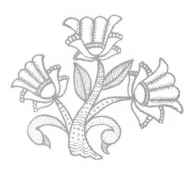

Chicken Masala
Murghi Masala

A quick and simple curry, this makes a great dish at buffets because the chicken is boneless and easy to eat. This recipe also makes a delicious filling for Frankies, irresistible "sandwich rolls" from Bombay (see page 34).

4 to 5 cloves garlic

1-inch piece ginger, peeled

3 medium tomatoes

3 tablespoons vegetable oil

2 medium onions, minced

1 tablespoon ground coriander ✳

1 teaspoon ground cumin ✳

1/2 teaspoon cayenne pepper

1/4 teaspoon turmeric

1 1/2 pounds boneless chicken, cut into 1-inch cubes (see Note)

1 teaspoon salt

1/2 teaspoon Garam Masala II ✳ (see page 3)

1/4 cup fresh cilantro, chopped

1. Purée the garlic and ginger in a blender, using as little water as necessary. Place in a small bowl and set aside. Without washing the blender, purée the tomatoes.

2. Heat the oil over high heat in a large saucepan. Add the onions and fry until golden brown, about 5 to 6 minutes. Add the puréed garlic and ginger and saute for another 2 minutes to blend the masala.

3. Add the tomatoes, coriander, cumin, cayenne, and turmeric. Continue to sauté the masala until all the liquid from the tomatoes has evaporated and the spice mixture pulls away from the pan, about 3 to 4 minutes.

4. Add the chicken, mixing well. Stir in the salt. Reduce heat to low and cook, covered, for 20 to 25 minutes. Remove from heat and mix in the Garam Masala and the chopped cilantro. Serve immediately.

SERVES 6 TO 8

Note: It is better to use a mixture of white and dark boneless chicken, rather than just breast meat. The cooking time in this recipe, which is necessary to blend the spices properly, will dry out the chicken if it is all white meat.

Chicken with Cardamom
Illaichi Murghi

This dish is simply "Mom's Chicken" to my family. It was the first Indian-flavored dish I served to my son when he was a baby (minus the green chiles, of course!). The sauce is light and goes well with plain rice and a simple vegetable such as Spicy Mushrooms with Red Bell Peppers or Eggplant Layered with Tomato Conserve and Ginger Yogurt (see page 147 or 144).

8 black cardamom pods ✳

32 green cardamom pods ✳

3 to 4 green serrano chiles

1-inch piece ginger, peeled

3 tablespoons vegetable oil

1 teaspoon black cumin ✳
(use regular cumin only if
black cumin is unavailable)

2 medium onions, finely minced

2 (2½ pound) chickens, cut
into 6 pieces each, skinned

1½ tablespoons ground
roasted cumin ✳

½ cup fresh cilantro, minced

1 teaspoon salt

½ to 1 teaspoon cayenne pepper
(optional)

1. Break open both types of cardamom pods, discarding husks, and grind the seeds in a spice grinder. Set aside.

2. Using a blender, purée chiles and ginger together, adding a little water as needed to create a smooth texture.

3. Heat oil over high heat in a large saucepan or Dutch oven. Add the cumin seeds and when they have stopped sizzling, add the onions and ground cardamom. Sauté over high heat until the natural juices have evaporated and the onions turn slightly brown, about 5 minutes. Add the ginger and chile purée and continue to stir-fry for another 2 to 3 minutes.

4. Add chicken and turn to brown lightly on all sides.

5. Add the cumin, cilantro, salt, and about 1½ to 2 cups of water. Add the optional cayenne, depending upon the degree of spiciness desired. Bring to a boil over high heat, cover, and reduce heat to a low simmer. Turn chicken after about 10 minutes, stirring up juices. If sauce becomes too thick, add a little more water. Cook for a total of 25 to 35 minutes, or until chicken is done.

SERVES 6

Grilled Marinated Chicken with Mint Chutney and Lime–Cilantro Onions

Shaan-Eh-Murgh

Without a special, high-heat tandoori oven, it is of course impossible to authentically recreate the taste of that beloved classic of Indian restaurants, tandoori Chicken. However, by using a similar marinade and cooking the chicken quickly on a hot barbecue grill, I have come up with this delicious approximation. The Mint Chutney and the marinated onions make mouth-watering complements to the simple grilled chicken. By the way, don't expect this tandoori-style chicken nor the tandoori chicken in the Bombay Cafe to have the ruddy, red color that you see in many restaurants. In the old days, the red appeared naturally from the use of saffron and sun-dried tomatoes; nowadays, it's usually food coloring, which I dislike.

MARINADE:

10 to 15 cloves garlic, to taste

4-inch piece ginger, peeled
and coarsely chopped

4 to 5 green serrano chiles

1 cup plain yogurt,✳ store-bought
or homemade (see page 5)

2 tablespoons Garam Masala I ✳
(see page 3)

1/2 to 1 teaspoon cayenne pepper,
to taste

1 teaspoon salt

2 (21/2 pound) chickens, skinned,
cut into 6 pieces each

1 tablespoon vegetable oil

Mint Chutney (see page 59)

Lime–Cilantro Onions (see next page)

1. Mince garlic, ginger, and chiles in a food processor. Remove to a bowl and stir in yogurt, Garam Masala, cayenne, and salt.

2. Using a sharp knife, score the chicken deeply with several cuts on each piece. Place the chicken in the marinade, turn to coat well and ensure that the marinade is rubbed into all the scores made in the chicken pieces. Let chicken marinate for at least 4 hours or overnight.

3. Add vegetable oil to chicken pieces before grilling. Cook chicken over hot coals on a grill, 8 to 10 minutes a side or until done.

4. Arrange chicken on a warm platter, garnished with the onions. Pass the chutney separately.

SERVES 6

Note: If the marinade is made in advance or if the chicken is placed in the marinade overnight, add the vegetable oil at that point to help prevent the marinade from drying out.

Lime-Cilantro Onions

1 medium onion, thinly sliced
1/4 cup fresh cilantro, chopped
Salt, to taste
Lime juice, to taste

1. In a bowl, toss all ingredients together at least an hour before serving, so that the lime juice can flavor the onions.

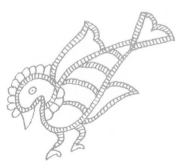

Chicken Kabobs in Green Spices

Mirch Masala Tikka

Tikka means "morsels of meat." These kabobs are cooked in a tandoori oven in the restaurant, but you can successfully approximate that great flavor by using this marinade and a barbecue grill. Because this dish is not saucy, it goes well with liquid dals, such as Chickpeas with Opo Squash (see page 122), and the stuffed bread, Griddle Bread with Potato Stuffing (see page 92). Cucumber and Onion Yogurt Relish and Mint Chutney are good accompaniments (see pages 52 and 59).

MARINADE:

10 cloves garlic

2-inch piece ginger, peeled and coarsely chopped

4 to 6 green serrano chiles, chopped coarsely

1 bunch fresh cilantro sprigs, tough stems discarded

1 tablespoon Garam Masala I ✳ (see page 3)

1 tablespoon ground coriander ✳

1 tablespoon ground roasted cumin ✳

1/2 teaspoon cayenne pepper

2 pounds boneless chicken breasts, skinned and cut into kabob-size pieces

1 teaspoon salt

1 tablespoon vegetable oil

Lime wedges, for garnish

1. To make the marinade, place garlic, ginger, chiles, and cilantro in a blender and process to a smooth paste, adding water by the spoonful as needed. Remove to a mixing bowl and stir in remaining spices. Set aside.

2. Place chicken in a large bowl and sprinkle with salt. Add the marinade and turn the chicken pieces to coat well. Set aside for at least half an hour at room temperature, or marinate for up to six hours in the refrigerator. Bring chicken to room temperature before proceeding.

3. When ready to cook, add the oil to the chicken pieces, stirring to coat well. Thread the pieces onto skewers and barbecue over hot coals or cook under a hot broiler for 6 to 8 minutes a side. Serve with lime wedges.

SERVES 6

Pepper Chicken
Kali Mirch Murghi

You may think black pepper is such an ordinary condiment that it can hold no interest. Wrong. This dish will show you what an intense flavor it can impart when it is allowed to take center stage. Black pepper is indigenous to India and this is one of the ways of handling it. Please note the two different techniques—coarsely cracked and finely pulverized—for treating the black peppercorns in this recipe.

2 (2½ pound) chickens, skinned and cut into 6 pieces each (or 3 small Cornish hens)

2½-inch piece ginger, peeled

10 cloves garlic

8 to 10 whole black peppercorns, plus 1 tablespoon whole black peppercorns

1 cup plain yogurt,✳ store-bought or homemade (see page 5)

1 teaspoon salt

4 small green chiles, sliced into quarters lengthwise

1½ tablespoons ghee ✳

1. Thinly slice a ½-inch piece of ginger and set aside. Mince the remaining ginger along with the garlic.

2. Crush the 8 to 10 black peppercorns in a mortar and pestle just until they crack in half. In a large nonreactive saucepan, place the chicken pieces, the minced ginger and garlic, crushed black pepper, yogurt, and salt. Set aside to marinate for 1 hour.

3. In the same pan, bring the mixture to a rapid boil and reduce the heat to low. Simmer for 40 minutes. Stir in the sliced ginger and chiles and remove to a warm serving dish.

4. Crush the remaining 1 tablespoon of black pepper thoroughly in a mortar and pestle. In a small saucepan, heat the ghee over high heat and add the pepper. Immediately pour over the warm chicken and serve.

SERVES 6 TO 8

Stir-Fried Chicken with Tomatoes
Karhai Murghi

This curry, stir-fried quickly in the *karhai*, or Indian wok, shows a Chinese influence. Because it depends more on tomatoes and not on browned onions for its sauce, the dish is lighter than many curries. The chicken is cut into small pieces, but it is important to leave them on the bone to give as much flavor as possible and to prevent them from drying out. Serve this with Chapatis and Sweet and Sour Eggplant (see pages 86 and 140).

2 (2½ pound) chickens, skinned and cut into 14 pieces each (see Note)

3 tablespoons vegetable oil

1½ teaspoons cumin seeds ✳

3-inch piece ginger, peeled and julienned

2 tablespoons coriander seeds,✳ freshly and coarsely ground

4 to 5 green serrano chiles, thinly sliced lengthwise

6 large tomatoes, chopped

1 teaspoon salt

½ cup fresh cilantro, finely chopped

½ teaspoon Garam Masala I ✳ (see page 3)

1. Using a heavy knife or cleaver, chop the chicken parts, through the bones, into pieces about 1 1/2 inches in size.

2. In a karhai,* wok, or large skillet, heat the oil over high heat. Add the cumin seeds and when they finish sizzling, add half the ginger and all the coriander. Sauté for one minute.

3. Add the chicken pieces and stir-fry for 4 to 5 minutes, tossing well to brown them evenly.

4. Add half the chiles and all the tomatoes, stirring to mix well, and sauté for about 2 minutes more. Add the salt, cover, and cook on low heat for 20 to 25 minutes, until the chicken is done.

5. Add the rest of the ginger, chiles and all the cilantro. Raise the heat to high and cook, stirring, for about 2 to 3 minutes, until the tomato juices are slightly reduced. Stir in the Garam Masala and serve.

SERVES 6

Note: Using a heavy cleaver, chop each thigh into two pieces; discard the lower, bony inch of each drumstick and cut the remaining piece in two; cut each half-breast into three pieces, leaving the wing "drumette" attached to one piece of breast.

Braised Chicken with Onions and Tomatoes

Sindhi Sel Murghi

My best friend's mother made the most delicious version of a Sindhi classic,
"Sel Meat," that I ever tasted when I was growing up. It had unique, rich flavor
that I had never encountered before and that I could not identify. Years later,
I pried it out of her that the secret ingredient was rum. I have adapted her
recipe, rum and all, for chicken, with delicious results.

3 tablespoons vegetable oil

4 large onions, thinly sliced

3-inch piece ginger, peeled and minced

8 cloves garlic, minced

2 to 3 green serrano chiles, chopped

2 (2½ pound) chickens, skinned and
cut into 8 pieces each

5 large tomatoes, coarsely chopped

3 to 4 black cardamom pods ✳

2 (1-inch) pieces cinnamon stick
or cassia ✳

5 to 6 whole cloves

6 to 8 whole black peppercorns

2 small bay leaves

3 tablespoons ground coriander ✳

2 tablespoons ground cumin ✳

1 teaspoon cayenne pepper

¼ teaspoon turmeric

½ cup plain yogurt,✳ store-bought
or homemade (see page 5)

¼ cup dark rum

1 teaspoon salt

Fresh cilantro, for garnish

1. Heat the oil over high heat in a large saucepan or Dutch oven. Add the onions and sauté for 2 minutes, until they begin to turn translucent. Stir in the ginger, garlic, and chiles.

2. Add the chicken pieces, a few at a time, and brown them lightly.

3. Add the tomatoes and all the remaining spices, the yogurt, rum, and salt. Turn the chicken and mix well to make sure each piece is well coated.

4. Reduce heat to low, cover and cook for about 45 minutes, until the chicken is done. If a slightly thicker sauce is desired, raise the heat and cook until some of the juices have evaporated. Serve at once, garnished with cilantro.

SERVES 6

Chicken Kabobs in Tomato–Saffron Sauce

Makhni Tikka

"Makhni Chicken" was the name of my favorite dish in the best tandoori restaurant, the Moti Mahal, when I was growing up in New Delhi. In my opinion, Makhni sauce is one of the most heavenly creations in any cuisine—golden, rich, buttery, with a touch of sweetness, redolent of saffron and roasted cumin. In my adaptation for home cooks, the yummy sauce cloaks grilled chicken kabobs. Luckily, there's always a little sauce left for mopping up with a Paratha.

1 recipe Chicken Kabobs in Green Spices (see page 200)

1 cup prepared Makhni Sauce (next page)

Fresh cilantro, for garnish

1. Make sure prepared kabobs are warm or at room temperature before proceeding.

2. Place Makhni Sauce in a skillet on low heat and add kabobs. Heat through, being careful not to let the sauce boil. Garnish with cilantro.

SERVES 6

Makhni Sauce

1/4 cup warm milk

1/4 teaspoon saffron threads

1/2 cup cream

1 cup half-and-half

1/2 stick (4 ounces) butter

1 (15-ounce) can tomato sauce, preferably with no added salt

2 small green serrano chiles, minced

1-inch piece ginger, peeled and minced

1/4 cup fresh cilantro, minced

1/2 teaspoon cayenne pepper

1/2 teaspoon Garam Masala I ✳

2 teaspoons ground roasted cumin ✳

2 tablespoons granulated sugar

1/2 teaspoon salt (less if tomato sauce has added salt)

1. To get the most flavor out of the saffron threads, dissolve them in the milk and set aside for about 5 minutes.

2. Place all the ingredients in a non-reactive saucepan over medium heat, stirring well. When sauce begins to boil, lower heat and cook until the sauce reduces by about one-third, approximately 1 hour. Remove from heat, cool, and refrigerate until ready to use.

MAKES 2 CUPS
RECIPE CAN BE DOUBLED EASILY

Rice with Chicken
Murghi Pullao

I look forward to eating this mouth-watering rice and chicken combination on all of my visits back home. In India, this dish is made with the local, small chickens that weigh no more than 1½ pounds. I like to use boneless, skinless chicken breasts, which makes this dish easy to eat and a great choice for a buffet dinner.

1½ cups basmati rice ✳

1 medium onion

1-inch piece ginger, peeled

4 cloves garlic

1 large tomato

3 tablespoons vegetable oil

2 to 3 black cardamom pods ✳

2 (1-inch) pieces cinnamon stick
or cassia ✳

4 to 5 cloves

2 small bay leaves

5 to 6 whole black peppercorns

1 tablespoon ground coriander ✳

2 teaspoons ground cumin ✳

¼ teaspoon turmeric

½ teaspoon cayenne pepper

1½ pounds boneless
chicken breasts, skinless
and cut into 2-inch pieces

2 medium green serrano chiles,
split in half

1¼ teaspoons salt

2½ cups hot water

Fresh cilantro, for garnish

1. Pick over the rice and wash it in a colander until the water runs clear. Soak it in warm water for at least 20 minutes but no more than 45 minutes.

2. In a food processor, mince the onions. Set them aside in a separate bowl and, without rinsing the workbowl, mince the ginger and garlic together. Set these aside and again, without rinsing the workbowl, process the tomato coarsely.

3. Heat the oil over medium-high heat in a large, shallow saucepan. Add the onions and sauté them, stirring, until they turn a light golden brown, about 3 to 4 minutes. Add a little water if the edges brown too quickly .

4. Add the garlic and ginger paste, mixing well, and continue to cook with the onions for a minute. Add the black cardamom, cinnamon or cassia, cloves, bay leaves, and peppercorns, stirring in a tablespoon or two of water to help blend the spices.

5. Add the ground coriander, cumin, turmeric, and cayenne. Mix well, continuing to sauté until the spice mixture pulls away from the pan. Stir in the minced tomato.

6. Raise the heat to high. Add the chicken pieces and green chiles, turning to coat with the masala, and brown well for 3 to 4 minutes, until the chicken turns opaque. Add the rice, salt, and water, stirring well to combine. Lower the heat to a simmer, cover, and cook for 15 minutes. Remove from the heat and let stand, covered, for 5 minutes. Open, fluff gently with a fork, and serve, garnished with cilantro.

SERVES 6

Chicken and Spinach Curry
Saag Murghi

It's the simple steps in cooking that make all the difference, I find. However, because they are time-consuming, many people—and many restaurants—eliminate them. In this case, it's essential to take the extra time to brown the chicken pieces for several minutes in the spicy "masala" mixture before adding the liquids. This simple technique pays off with rich flavor, color, and texture in the finished dish.

1 large onion

1/2-inch piece ginger, peeled

5 to 6 cloves garlic

2 medium tomatoes

1 (15 1/2 ounce) package frozen
spinach, defrosted

3 tablespoons vegetable oil

2 (1/2-inch) pieces cinnamon stick
or cassia *

5 to 6 whole cloves

4 to 5 whole black peppercorns

2 bay leaves

3 black cardamoms *

2 tablespoons besan *

1 1/2 tablespoons ground coriander *

1/4 teaspoon turmeric

1 1/2 teaspoons ground cumin *

1 teaspoon cayenne pepper

1/4 cup plain yogurt,* store-bought
or homemade (see page 5)

2 (2 1/2 pound) chickens, skinned and
cut into 8 pieces each

1 teaspoon salt

Ginger and green chiles, thinly sliced,
to garnish (optional)

1. In a food processor, mince the onions. Remove and set aside in a separate bowl. Without rinsing the workbowl, add the ginger and the garlic and process to a paste, adding a little water if needed. Remove and set aside. Then chop the tomatoes, remove, and set aside. Finally, purée the spinach with any liquid and set aside.

2. Using a 6-quart saucepan, heat the oil. Add the onions and brown on medium-high heat until they are a deep red-brown, about 5 to 6 minutes. Add a little water by table-spoons to slow the browning process and prevent burning.

3. Add the ginger and garlic to the onions, stirring well.

4. Add the whole spices and continue to stir the "masala" (mixture) over medium-high heat. Add the chickpea flour and sauté for about 2 minutes. If mixture becomes too dry, add 1/4 cup hot water.

5. Stir in the coriander, cumin, cayenne, and turmeric, again adding a little hot water to keep the consistency smooth.

6. Stir in the tomatoes and cook for 3 to 4 minutes. Reduce the heat to low and mix in the yogurt.

7. Add the chicken pieces and return the heat to high. Brown the chicken pieces on all sides, cooking for about 5 to 6 minutes. Stir in the puréed spinach and salt and let the mixture come to a boil. Reduce to a simmer, cover, and cook for 1 hour. Remove to a platter and garnish with the optional ginger and chiles.

SERVES 6

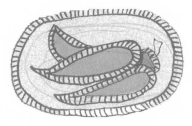

Cornish Hens with Dried Mango Powder
Sindhi Choosas

My mother came from the province of Sindh, now part of Pakistan, and loved the tangy specialties of that region. The flavors in this dish, especially the tartness of the dried mango powder, reflect her influence. The hens begin by poaching in cinnamon-scented stock (save the stock to make heavenly Chicken Soup with Spinach, Tomatoes, and Rice on page 42 later), and finish in a rich, spicy sauté. Melt-in-your-mouth delicious, this is one of the most popular dishes in the restaurant. I use Cornish hens here because they better approximate the small, flavorful chickens we have in India.

3 Cornish hens, skinned and quartered

2 medium onions, peeled and quartered

8 large cloves garlic, coarsely chopped

3-inch piece ginger, peeled and coarsely chopped

6 to 8 green serrano chiles, halved

8 black cardamom pods ✱

4 (2$\frac{1}{2}$-inch) pieces cinnamon stick or cassia ✱

1 teaspoon whole black peppercorns

$\frac{1}{2}$ tablespoon whole cloves

2$\frac{1}{2}$ teaspoons salt

3 tablespoons ghee ✱

3 tablespoons ground coriander ✱

1 teaspoon cayenne pepper

2 tablespoons amchur ✱

$\frac{1}{3}$ cup fresh cilantro leaves, chopped, to garnish

1. Place the hens, along with the onions, garlic, ginger, chiles, cardamom, cinnamon or cassia, peppercorns, cloves, and salt in a large pan. Add 2½ cups of cold water and bring to a boil. Reduce heat to low, cover and simmer for 45 to 50 minutes, or until hens are cooked through. Set aside. (The recipe can be prepared a day in advance to this point. Refrigerate until ready to proceed and then warm hens and stock before moving to the next step.)

2. Remove hens from stock, setting aside 4 tablespoons of stock. (Reserve the remaining stock for another use). Heat half the ghee over high heat in a large skillet. Add 1½ tablespoons coriander and ½ teaspoon cayenne. When the mixture bubbles, add half of the hens and 2 tablespoons of stock. Sprinkle ½ tablespoon mango powder over the hens. Turn the hens and sprinkle another ½ tablespoon mango powder on them. Remove the hens to a warm serving platter and repeat the process with the remaining pieces. The final cooking should take no more than 2 minutes per batch.

3. Sprinkle the chopped cilantro over the hens and serve.

SERVES 6

Meat

Kid—tender baby goat—is the meat of choice in India. There are no religious restrictions regarding kid, as there are on beef and pork, and goats are very easy to raise, not being particular about what they eat. They are the ideal source for meat in India, although I don't think the trend is going to catch on here. I use lamb in my cooking here, which has a very comparable flavor, and I occasionally use ground beef as well.

It is important to obtain lamb, especially ground lamb, from a good butcher. I always ask for ground shoulder or leg of lamb, all visible fat removed before processing. The preground lamb found in packages at the grocery stores is unacceptable for these recipes, because it is very high in fat and does not begin with a good cut of meat.

Although these recipes say that they serve six, an Indian hostess would not hesitate to prepare one of them for eight or even ten, and offer her guests a greater array of vegetable dishes, an elaborate rice creation, raitas, dals, and breads to complete the meal. This approach to eating meat—not as the centerpiece, but simply as one among many delicious offerings in a meal—is the healthiest there is.

Lamb Chops with Black Pepper and Vinegar

Kali Mirch Ke Champa

The combination of flavors of black pepper and vinegar—and the absence of more "typical" Indian spices like cumin—in these rich baby lamb chops from coastal Western India shows the heavy Portuguese influence. You'll find black pepper more commonly in the cuisines of the south and west, as opposed to the red chile peppers beloved in my home regions. Use small, tender lamb chops for this and trim the fat that encloses them, but be sure to leave a thin layer to keep the chops intact. Serve this as part of a meal with several other vegetarian choices, such as Rice with Mixed Vegetables and Tomato, Garlic, and Yogurt Relish (see pages 83 and 48).

18 small, rib lamb chops

1½ tablespoons coarsely ground black pepper

1 teaspoon salt

¼ cup white vinegar

3 tablespoons vegetable oil

2 medium onions, thinly sliced

2 tablespoons ground coriander ✳

¼ teaspoon turmeric

1 cup fresh cilantro, chopped

1. Trim the lamb chops of all visible fat but do not detach from the bone. Rub the chops with the salt and the pepper. Place them in a single layer on a baking sheet or large platter and sprinkle them evenly with the vinegar. Set aside.

2. Heat the oil over high heat in a large, deep skillet or a Dutch oven. Sauté the onions, stirring frequently, for about 6 to 8 minutes, until they are browned.

3. Add the lamb chops and their juices along with the coriander and turmeric. Brown the chops, turning them to color evenly, for about 5 minutes. Add one cup of water, lower heat, cover, and cook at a low simmer for 1½ hours. Check every 20 minutes, adding ½ cup of water toward the end if the liquids have cooked off. The lamb should be very tender. Mix in the chopped cilantro and serve at once.

SERVES 6

Lamb Chops with Dried Mango Powder
Sindhi Champa

Indians like their meats well done, even baby lamb chops, because
the long cooking allows them to absorb the flavors of the spices. The chops
begin by poaching in a fragrant stock (you'll recognize this method from the wonderful
Cornish Hens with Dried Mango Powder on page 212), and finish with a quick sauté
in *amchur*, or dried mango powder, a spice favored in Northern India. The amchur
gives the meat a delightful lemony flavor. I like to carry over that taste by
serving this with Mercin's Lemon Lentils, along with Potatoes and
Green Peas with Cumin (see pages 109 and 164).

18 small, rib lamb chops

2 medium onions, quartered

6 cloves garlic, coarsely chopped

2-inch piece ginger, peeled and
coarsely chopped

3 to 4 green serrano chiles,
coarsely chopped

6 black cardamom pods *

2 (2-inch) pieces cinnamon
stick or cassia *

2 bay leaves

8 cloves

8 to 10 black peppercorns

1½ teaspoons salt

3 tablespoons ghee *

3 tablespoons ground coriander *

2 teaspoons cayenne pepper
or more, to taste

4 teaspoons amchur *

½ cup fresh cilantro, chopped

1. Trim the lamb chops of excess fat, but do not detach them from the bone. Be sure to leave a thin membrane of fat to hold the meat together. Place the chops in a large, deep skillet with a lid or a Dutch oven, layering them with the onions, garlic, ginger, chiles, cardamom, cinnamon, bay leaves, cloves, and peppercorns. Sprinkle on the salt and add water to cover the meat (about 4 or 5 cups). Bring to a full boil, reduce the heat to low, cover, and simmer for about 1½ hours, until the meat is fork-tender. Remove chops from stock and reserve stock.

2. In a skillet large enough to hold half of the chops in a single layer, heat half the ghee over high heat. Tilt the pan to make a pool of the ghee and add half of the coriander and cayenne. Level the pan and stir in ¼ cup of the stock, making a paste of the spices.

3. Immediately add 9 of the chops. Sprinkle them with 1 teaspoon amchur, turn, and sprinkle the other side with another teaspoon amchur and half of the cilantro. Turn once more, just to wilt the cilantro, and remove to a warm platter. Keep warm while repeating the process for the remaining 9 chops. Serve at once.

SERVES 6

Ground Lamb with Peas
Keema Mattar

This dish is my husband's favorite, possibly because it reminds him
of the classic picadillo of his native Cuba. We often have it at home, with
Plain Basmati Rice and a Banana-Yogurt Relish (see pages 78 and 51), for a quick meal.
It is important to use lean ground lamb, from a good butcher, rather
than the preground, fatty lamb usually available at the market. You
can substitute lean ground beef, if desired.

2 large onions

4 medium tomatoes

5 to 6 cloves garlic

2-inch piece ginger, peeled

3 tablespoons vegetable oil

3 to 4 black cardamom pods ✻

2 (1-inch) pieces cinnamon
stick or cassia ✻

4 to 5 whole cloves

6 to 8 whole black peppercorns

2 small bay leaves

2 tablespoons ground coriander ✻

1 tablespoon ground cumin ✻

1 teaspoon cayenne pepper

1/4 teaspoon turmeric

1 1/2 pounds lean, ground lamb,
or lean ground beef

1 1/4 cups frozen peas, defrosted
by rinsing in hot water

1 teaspoon salt

2 green serrano chiles, halved
lengthwise (optional)

Fresh cilantro, for garnish

1. In a food processor, mince the onions and set aside. In the same bowl, mince the tomatoes and set aside.

2. In a blender, purée the garlic and ginger, using a little water to get a smooth paste. (This works best in one of the small containers that are sold as accessories to many blenders.) Set aside.

3. Heat the oil over high heat in a large, deep skillet with a lid or a Dutch oven. Add the onions and stir-fry until their liquid evaporates. Reduce the heat to medium and continue to cook the onions, stirring frequently, until they take on a dark, golden-brown color, being careful not to burn them. If they should start to burn, add a tablespoon or two of water to slow the process. This should take about 6 to 8 minutes.

4. When the onions are browned, increase the heat to high and add the garlic-ginger purée. Sauté for 2 minutes and add the cardamom, cinnamon, cloves, peppercorns, and bay leaves. Sauté for 1 minute and add the coriander, cumin, cayenne and turmeric. Mix this "masala" well, adding a little water if necessary to make a smooth, dry paste.

5. Add the ground lamb or beef, breaking up the clumps and mixing it into the masala. Continue to brown the meat for about 5 minutes.

6. Add the minced tomatoes and sauté until the tomato juices cook off. Add the peas, salt, and optional chiles, mixing well, and lower the heat. (If you prefer a finished dish with more sauce, you can add up to a cup of water at this point.) Cover and cook for about 25 to 30 minutes. Garnish with cilantro and serve.

SERVES 6

Variation I: To create a more substantial one-dish meal, in step 6, before adding the peas, add 2 medium red rose potatoes, cut in 1/2-inch dice. Serve with Layered Indian Griddle Bread or Plain Basmati Rice (see pages 90 and 78).

Variation II: For a slightly more elaborate version of this dish, do not add the optional extra water in step 6. Instead, after the dish has finished cooking, stir in 1/2 cup plain yogurt and 1/2 cup thinly sliced, sweet raw onions. Cover for five minutes to soften the onions and serve.

Browned Lamb with Onions, Tomatoes, and Spices

Bhunna Meat

My father's mother came from the Punjabi region of northwest India (now part of Pakistan) that was famous for its rich, meaty cuisine. Her table groaned with the most delicious dals swimming in butter and cream, yogurt raitas studded with deep-fried chick-pea-flour bits, and of course, the favorite, Bhunna Meat (usually prepared with tender kid). My mother, not being Punjabi herself, didn't relish the heavy cuisine as much as my father did, but to please him, she would serve many of his favorites at our home. What he never noticed was that she had lightened them considerably. I have followed her example in my version of this traditional Punjabi dish by eliminating the ghee. The lightness of the final product depends on the cut of lamb. Have a butcher cut the shank portion of a leg of lamb into 1½-inch cubes and remove all visible fat.

5 cloves garlic

1½-inch piece ginger, peeled

4 tablespoons vegetable oil

2 medium onions, chopped fine

3 to 4 black cardamom pods ✳

2 (1-inch) pieces cinnamon
stick or cassia ✳

5 to 6 cloves

6 to 8 black peppercorns

2 small bay leaves

2 tablespoons ground coriander ✳

2 tablespoons ground cumin ✳

1½ teaspoons cayenne pepper

¼ teaspoon turmeric

1¼ pounds lamb, cut into
1½-inch cubes

4 medium tomatoes, chopped

1 teaspoon salt

Fresh cilantro, for garnish

1. Process garlic and ginger together in a small blender jar or mini food processor, with a little water as needed to make a smooth paste. Set aside.

2. Heat the oil over high heat in a large shallow saucepan. Add the onions and stir-fry until their juices evaporate. Reduce the heat to medium and continue to sauté, stirring frequently, until the onions turn a dark golden-brown color. If the onions begin to burn, add a tablespoon or two of water to slow the cooking process. Browning the onions should take 6 to 8 minutes.

3. Add the garlic-ginger paste and the cardamom, cinnamon or cassia, cloves, peppercorns, and bay leaves. Continue to stir the spice and onion mixture, or masala, again adding a few tablespoons of water as needed.

4. Add the ground spices, continuing to stir and brown the mixture, adding a little water if needed. Cook for about 2 minutes, until the oil separates from the masala.

5. Add the lamb cubes and sauté for 6 to 8 minutes. Stir in the tomatoes, continuing to sauté until they are well-incorporated and the "masala" pulls away from the pan, about 5 minutes.

6. Add the salt and reduce heat to low. Cover and simmer for 1½ hours, stirring every 20 minutes and adding a little water if necessary to prevent sticking, until the lamb cubes are fork-tender. The mixture should be a thick paste, rather than a saucy curry. Garnish with cilantro and serve.

SERVES 6

Lamb and Rice Casserole

Shah Jahani Pullao

You'll think you're in heaven when you taste this delectable, creamy, layered lamb and rice casserole. It's time-consuming to make (although some of it can be done ahead), but the effort pays off in a memorable special-occasion meal. First, simmer up a delicious homemade stock from the lamb bones in which to cook the rice. Brown the lamb chunks in fragrant spices, and layer everything with yogurt and cream. Finally, lightly scent the casserole with *kewra,* the essence of an Indian pine tree, for its characteristic earthy and aromatic flavor. Kewra is easy to find in any Indian market. A perfect dish for entertaining, this pullao needs only a green salad to complete the meal.

3 pound shank portion of a leg of lamb

3 medium onions

3 (1-inch) pieces ginger, peeled

10 cloves garlic

9 green cardamom pods ✳

6 black cardamom pods ✳

2 (1-inch) pieces cinnamon stick or cassia ✳

6 whole cloves

6 black peppercorns

1 small bay leaf

3 tablespoons vegetable oil

1½ tablespoons ground coriander ✳

1 tablespoon ground cumin ✳

½ teaspoon cayenne pepper

¼ teaspoon turmeric

2 teaspoons salt

2 cups basmati rice ✳

1 tablespoon ghee ✳

2 small green serrano chiles

1 cup plain yogurt,✳ store-bought or homemade (see page 5)

1 cup cream, lightly whipped

1 tablespoon kewra essence ✳

1. *To make the stock:* The day before, bone the leg of lamb (or have the butcher do it for you). Cut the lamb into 1½-inch cubes, trimming away all visible fat. Set aside the meat in the refrigerator.

2. Place the lamb bones along with one onion, quartered; a 1-inch piece of ginger, chopped coarsely; 5 cloves of garlic; 4 green cardamom pods; 3 black cardamom pods; the cinnamon; cloves; peppercorns; bay leaf; and 5 cups of water in a large stockpot. Bring to a full boil, then reduce the heat to low. Cover and cook for about 2 hours. Strain the stock, discarding the solids, and refrigerate the stock overnight.

3. *To prepare the lamb:* Cut the remaining two onions in half and slice them into thin half-moons. Mince a 1-inch piece of ginger along with the remaining 5 garlic cloves.

4. Heat the oil over high heat in a large saucepan and add the onions. Sauté them for about 5 or 6 minutes, stirring frequently so as to brown them evenly. Reduce the heat to medium and continue to cook, stirring, for another 5 or 6 minutes, until the onions are a dark golden-brown. If necessary, add a few spoonfuls of water during this process to prevent burning.

5. Add the ginger and garlic and sauté for a minute. Add the lamb chunks and brown, stirring frequently, for about 15 to 20 minutes.

6. Add the ground coriander, cumin, cayenne, turmeric, 1 teaspoon salt, and ½ cup of water, mixing well. Reduce heat to low, cover and cook for 1½ hours. Check the meat every 20 minutes, stirring and turning to prevent burning. If necessary add ¼ cup of water at a time. When the meat is fork-tender, set aside. If preparing the lamb a day ahead, cool and then refrigerate. When ready to proceed, bring meat to room temperature.

7. *To prepare the rice:* Pick over the rice, removing any stones. Wash the rice until the water runs clear and soak it in fresh water to cover for at least 20 minutes.

8. Slice the green chiles into thin half-moons. Julienne the remaining 1-inch piece of ginger. Set these aside together.

9. Open the husks of the remaining green and black cardamom pods and scrape out the seeds. Set aside, discarding the husks.

10. Remove the stock from the refrigerator and discard the layer of fat that will have congealed on top.

11. Heat the ghee in a large skillet with a tightly fitting lid. Tilt the pan to one side to form a pool and add the seeds of the cardamoms. Level the pan and add the drained rice, sautéing for a minute. Add 1½ cups of stock and 1½ cups of water, along with the remaining salt, and bring to a full boil. Cover, reduce the heat to low, and simmer for 8 minutes. Remove from heat and let stand, covered, for 5 minutes before opening. Lightly mix in the green chiles and ginger, fluffing the rice as you do so. Spread rice in a larger casserole or baking sheet to prevent its getting sticky and allow it to cool before layering the pulao.

12. *Final assembly:* Preheat oven to 350 degrees. Using an 8 by 10 inch casserole dish with a cover, layer ¼ of the cooked and cooled rice on the bottom. Spread the lamb over the rice and cover that with another ¼ of the rice.

13. Whisk the yogurt lightly and spread it over the rice. Layer on another ¼ of the rice. Spread the whipped cream over that and finally cover it with the remaining rice.

14. Sprinkle the kewra essence over the top. (If kewra is not available, use 1 teaspoon of rose essence.) Cover and place in oven for 30 minutes. Serve at once.

SERVES 6 AS A MAIN COURSE, OR 8 IF THE PULLAO IS ONE OF SEVERAL DISHES. RECIPE CAN BE DOUBLED EASILY.

Rice with Ground Lamb, Green Beans, and Garbanzo Beans

Keema Channa Pullao

This is an American-style, meal-in-one casserole with lively Indian flavors that I developed for simple family meals. It remains a favorite in my home. I serve it, non-Indian style, with a green salad and plain yogurt. The ground lamb that is sold preground in markets is too fatty, so be sure to ask a butcher for ground leg of lamb, or substitute lean beef.

2 cups basmati rice *

1 medium onion

5 large cloves garlic

1½-inch piece ginger, peeled

2 small tomatoes

3 tablespoons vegetable oil

3 to 4 whole black cardamoms *

2 (1-inch) pieces cinnamon stick or cassia *

5 to 6 whole cloves

2 bay leaves

5 to 6 whole black peppercorns

1½ tablespoons ground coriander *

1 tablespoon ground cumin *

¼ teaspoon turmeric

¼ teaspoon cayenne pepper

½ pound lean, ground lamb

½ pound green beans, trimmed and cut into ½-inch pieces

1 (15-ounce) can garbanzo beans, drained and rinsed in cold water

2 to 3 green serrano chiles, sliced in half lengthwise (optional)

3½ cups hot water

1 teaspoon salt

Fresh cilantro, chopped, for garnish

1. Pick over the rice for any stones. Wash the rice until the water runs clear and soak it in warm water for 20 minutes.

2. Chop the onions finely in a food processor and set aside in a separate bowl. Without rinsing the workbowl, mince the garlic and ginger together and set aside. Again without rinsing the workbowl, purée the tomatoes and set aside.

3. Heat the oil in a large saucepan and add the onions. Sauté over medium heat until the onion juices evaporate and the onions start to brown. Reduce the heat to medium and continue to cook the onions, stirring frequently until they turn a dark golden brown. If the onions begin to burn, add hot water, a tablespoon at a time, to slow the process. This will take about 6 or 8 minutes.

4. Add the garlic and ginger to the onion mixture. Brown for 1 minute more.

5. Increase heat to high and add 1/4 cup of hot water, stirring to form a paste. Mix into this the cardamom, cinnamon or cassia, cloves, bay leaves, and black peppercorns, sautéing for another minute. If the "masala" becomes too dry, add another 1/4 cup of hot water.

6. Now stir in the ground coriander, cumin, turmeric, and cayenne. Mix well and continue to sauté until the "masala" starts to separate from the oil, about 2 minutes. Add the ground lamb, breaking up the lumps. Brown the meat well, about 5 or 6 minutes.

7. Add the tomatoes to the meat mixture. Cook on high until the tomatoes are thoroughly incorporated and the oil once again begins to separate from the "keema," or ground meat mixture.

8. Add the green beans and lower heat to medium. Cover and cook for about 2 minutes, until the beans start to become tender.

9. Stir in the drained rice carefully, so as not to break the grains. Add the garbanzo beans, sliced chiles, water, and salt. Bring to a full boil, cover, reduce heat to low, and let cook for 15 minutes. Remove from heat and let stand, covered, for 5 minutes before lifting lid. Fluff rice and serve, garnished with cilantro.

SERVES 6 TO 8

Lamb with Puréed Spinach Curry

Saag Gosht

Although this lamb curry is a familiar feature of many Indian restaurants, I add a personal signature to my version with dried fenugreek leaves, the hint of bitterness of which balances the richness of the lamb. Serve this with Potatoes and Peas in Tomato Sauce and Chapatis (see pages 157 and 86).

1 large onion

1½-inch piece ginger, peeled

5 to 6 cloves garlic

2 medium tomatoes

1 (15½-ounce) package frozen spinach, defrosted

4 tablespoons vegetable oil

2 (½-inch) pieces cinnamon stick or cassia ✳

5 to 6 whole cloves

4 to 5 whole black peppercorns

2 bay leaves

3 black cardamoms ✳

2 tablespoons besan ✳

1½ tablespoons ground coriander ✳

1½ teaspoons ground cumin ✳

1 teaspoon cayenne pepper

¼ teaspoon turmeric

1½ pounds lean leg of lamb, cut in 1½-inch cubes

1 teaspoon salt

¼ cup plain yogurt,✳ store-bought or homemade (see page 5)

½ cup dried fenugreek leaves ✳

Ginger and green chiles, thinly sliced, for garnish (optional)

1. In a food processor, mince the onions. Remove them and set aside. Without rinsing the workbowl, process the ginger and garlic together to form a paste, adding a little water as needed. Remove them and set aside. Process the tomatoes coarsely; set aside. Finally, mince the thawed spinach with its liquid.

2. Using a 6-quart saucepan, heat the oil. Add the onions and brown on medium-high heat until they are a deep red-brown, 5 to 6 minutes. Add a little water by tablespoons to slow the browning process and prevent burning.

3. Add the ginger and garlic to the onions, stirring well.

4. Add the whole spices and continue to stir the "masala" (mixture) over medium-high heat. Add the chick-pea flour and brown lightly for about 2 minutes. If mixture becomes too dry, add ¼ cup hot water.

5. Stir in the coriander, cumin, cayenne, and turmeric, again adding a little hot water to keep the consistency smooth.

6. Add the lamb pieces and brown them over high heat for 8 to 10 minutes, until the "masala" comes away from the sides of the pan.

7. Stir in the tomatoes, cooking for 3 to 4 minutes before reducing the heat to low. Add the yogurt, mixing well, and the puréed spinach and the fenugreek. Bring mixture to a slow boil, sprinkling on the salt, then cover, reduce the heat to low, and cook for 1½ hours. Garnish with the optional ginger and chiles and serve at once.

SERVES 6

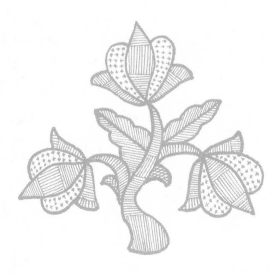

Desserts

A platter of fresh fruit, especially mangoes and melons, is my favorite way to end a delicious Indian meal—and the most customary in India, as well. Indian sweets are typically reserved for special occasions and are almost always made of reduced and thickened whole milk, often flavored with rose water. I was never particularly fond of these rich, heavy sweets growing up, and when I came here, I began to develop desserts more to my lighter tastes and the tastes of my customers. I include here my lighter versions of the Indian classics, such as *Phirni,* a cardamom-flavored custard lightly bound with cornstarch, and *Kheer,* which is traditional rice pudding.

The most popular desserts at the Bombay Cafe are my homemade sorbets and ice creams, made from mangoes, lime, and mint, or lemon and ginger. Their cool, fresh flavors are the perfect finale to Indian food, even if frozen desserts such as these do not exist at home (in India, desserts did not require refrigeration).

Candied Ginger

Ginger root is used all over India, but rarely as part of desserts. At the Bombay Cafe, we use it in our Ginger Ice Cream and as a garnish for Lemon–Ginger Sorbet (see pages 238 and 236). Although candied ginger is available in specialty markets, I have included this recipe because it is so easy to prepare.

> **2-inch piece ginger,
> as young and tender as possible,
> to avoid fibers**
>
> **3/4 cup sugar**

1. Peel the ginger and slice into thin rounds about 1/8-inch in thickness. Place in a saucepan with 1 1/2 cups of water and bring to a boil. Reduce the heat to medium and allow to simmer for 30 minutes.

2. Preheat the oven to a low heat (150 degrees). With a slotted spoon, remove the ginger from the syrup and place on a foil-lined cookie sheet. Put the ginger in the oven to dry for 10 minutes. Remove and allow to cool until just warm to the touch.

3. Put the remaining 1/4 cup of sugar in a bowl and add the ginger. Toss to coat well and set aside. Keeps well in an airtight container for several months.

MAKES 1/3 TO 1/2 CUP

Indian Cardamom Custard

Phirni

In India, Phirni is made with rice flour and then poured into clay bowls, taking on their earthy flavor as it firms up. Though we don't use the clay bowls here, it is still a family favorite. My version is a little lighter than traditional Phirni, because I use cornstarch to thicken it. The recipe can be doubled easily; refrigerate any leftovers, tightly covered with plastic wrap.

4 1/4 cups milk

6 pods cracked green cardamoms *

4 tablespoons cornstarch

4 tablespoons sugar

1/2 teaspoon ground cardamom *

Fresh grapes, seeded and halved, or fruit and nuts of your choice, for garnish (optional)

1. Rinse a medium saucepan and while it is still wet, pour in 4 cups of milk (this helps prevent the formation of a skin on the pan). Add the cardamom pods and bring to a boil over medium heat, stirring occasionally.

2. Dissolve the cornstarch into the remaining milk and set aside.

3. When the milk comes to a brisk boil, remove the pan from the heat and pour in the cornstarch mixture in a slow stream, whisking constantly to avoid lumps.

4. Return the custard to low heat, add sugar and continue to cook, stirring frequently, until the mixture comes to a boil again. Remove from heat.

5. Remove the cardamom pods and pour the custard into 6 serving dishes. Sprinkle with the ground cardamom and refrigerate until chilled and firm. Garnish with the optional grapes (or fruit or nuts of your choice).

SERVES 6

Cardamom Custard with Mango and Ginger Brandy Coulis

This simple variation on Phirni enhances the smooth custard with a tangy sauce.

1 recipe Indian Cardamom Custard (see page 232)

2 fresh mangoes (about 2 cups), peeled and diced

¼ cup sugar

2 tablespoons ginger brandy

6 fresh mint sprigs, for garnish

1. Prepare the Phirni, but pour it into a 9 by 9 inch pan. Refrigerate the custard while making the coulis.

2. Place the remaining ingredients in a food processor. Pulse a few times until the mangoes are coarsely chopped and the sugar is incorporated. Do not purée.

3. Spoon the coulis over the cooled Phirni and chill for several hours before serving. Cut into 6 pieces and place on dessert plates, garnished with mint.

SERVES 6

Mango Sorbet

There are about a thousand varieties of mango grown in India, but one variety, the Alphonso, is especially prized for its intense flavor and sweetness. Every year, we look forward to mango season with great anticipation, at least in part to see just how expensive the favored Alphonso mangos will be that year (they can cost three times as much as ordinary mangoes). Much of the Alphonso crop is bought to be canned for sale throughout the year. My favorite brand of these canned delicacies is Ratna; it is sometimes available in Indian markets. Sorbet made with these canned mangoes has a very vibrant flavor, but if canned Alphonso mangoes are not available, I recommend following the slightly different recipe for sorbet using fresh mangoes.

> *USING CANNED ALPHONSO MANGOES:*
>
> 3/4 cup sugar
>
> 1 3/4 cups mango pulp
>
> 1 tablespoon lemon juice
>
> 1/2 cup blueberries or raspberries, for garnish

1. Put the sugar and 1 1/2 cups of water in a saucepan. Bring to a boil over medium-high heat, dissolving the sugar. Let the mixture cool.

2. Stir in the mango pulp and lemon juice.

3. To freeze, use a 1-quart capacity ice-cream maker and freeze according to manufacturers' instructions. Or, pour into a 1-quart container suitable for freezing and cover tightly with foil.

Freeze for 1 hour, or until the edges seem to crystallize. Remove from the freezer and beat with an electric beat for 2 to 3 minutes. Return to the freezer for 30 minutes and beat again. Repeat the preceding step one more time and return to the freezer. The sorbet should be prepared one day ahead of time. Serve in small scoops, garnished with a few berries.

MAKES 4 CUPS

2 large, ripe mangoes
(about 2 cups diced)

3/4 to 1 cup of sugar
(depending upon the sweetness
of the mangoes)

1 tablespoon lemon juice

1/2 cup fresh blueberries or
raspberries, for garnish

1. Place the mangoes along with 3/4 cup of sugar, the lemon juice and 1 1/2 cups of water in a food processor or blender and process until it is a fine purée. Adjust for sweetness, if necessary. Force the purée through a sieve to remove any fibrous parts of the mango.

2. To freeze, use a 1-quart capacity ice-cream maker and freeze according to manufacturers' instructions. Or, pour into a 1-quart container suitable for freezing and cover tightly with foil. Freeze for 1 hour, or until the edges seem to crystallize. Remove from the freezer and beat with an electric beat for 2 to 3 minutes. Return to the freezer for 30 minutes and beat again. Repeat the preceding step one more time and return to the freezer. The sorbet should be prepared one day ahead of time. Serve in small scoops, garnished with a few berries.

MAKES 4 CUPS

Lemon-Ginger Sorbet

Remembering how much I loved my mother's homemade Lemon-Ginger
Fizz on hot days (see page 249), I appropriated the flavors for this zesty treat.
For me, the addition of the candied ginger as a garnish makes this more essentially
Indian, because it adds a note of sharpness to the sweet sorbet.

1½ cups sugar

Zest of 1 large lemon
(about 1 tablespoon), minced

1 cup (4 to 6 lemons) lemon juice

3-inch piece fresh ginger,
coarsely chopped

Candied Ginger, store-bought or
homemade (see page 231),
diced for garnish

---

1. Place the sugar, zest, and lemon juice in a nonreactive pan and bring to a quick boil over high heat. Reduce the heat and simmer for 5 minutes. Remove from the heat and set aside.

2. Place the fresh ginger in a blender with 3 to 4 tablespoons of water and process on high until ginger is pureed. Drape a clean muslin cloth (not cheesecloth, as the holes are too big) over a small bowl and pour the ginger-water into it. Wring the cloth tightly to extract the ginger juice and discard the pulp. Add the juice to the hot lemon syrup and let cool.

3. When the syrup is cool, add 2½ cups of water. To freeze, use a 1-quart capacity ice-cream maker and freeze according to manufacturers' instructions. Or, pour into a 1-quart container suitable for freezing and cover tightly with foil. Freeze for 1 hour, or until the edges seem to crystallize. Remove from the freezer and beat with an electric beat for 2 to 3 minutes. Return to the freezer for 30 minutes and beat again. Repeat the preceding step one more time and return to the freezer. The sorbet should be prepared one day ahead of time. Serve in small scoops, garnished with candied ginger.

MAKES 4 CUPS

Lime-Mint Sorbet

Even though sorbets are not part of Indian cuisine, I found that creating these cooling desserts from ingredients typical of India perfectly complements traditional meals. My partner, David Chaparro, originated this refreshing combination for the Bombay Cafe, where it remains very popular.

> 2 cups sugar
>
> Zest of 3 limes
>
> 1/2 cup fresh mint leaves, tightly packed
>
> 3/4 cup lime juice (about 8 or 9 limes)
>
> Fresh mint sprigs, for garnish

1. Place the sugar in a saucepan with 1 1/2 cups of water and the lime zest. Bring to a quick boil over high heat and remove from the flame. Add the mint leaves and set aside to steep for half an hour.

2. Strain the syrup and stir in the lime juice and 2 cups of water.

3. To freeze, use a 1-quart capacity ice-cream maker and freeze according to manufacturers' instructions. Or, pour into a 1-quart container suitable for freezing and cover tightly with foil. Freeze for 1 hour, or until the edges seem to crystallize. Remove from the freezer and beat with an electric beat for 2 to 3 minutes. Return to the freezer for 30 minutes and beat again. Repeat the preceding step one more time and return to the freezer. The sorbet should be prepared one day ahead of time. Serve in small scoops, garnished with mint sprigs.

MAKES 4 CUPS

Ginger Ice Cream

Adraki kulfi

Traditional Indian ice creams begin with long, slow cooking of milk,
until it becomes thick and condensed, to which flavorings are added.
While I love the familiar flavors, I prefer the texture of Western-style ice
cream. Voila! I married the two in this yummy Ginger Ice Cream.
Though similar in taste to the sorbet, it is obviously much richer.
It's one of my favorite desserts—and the customers of the
Bombay Cafe seem to agree.

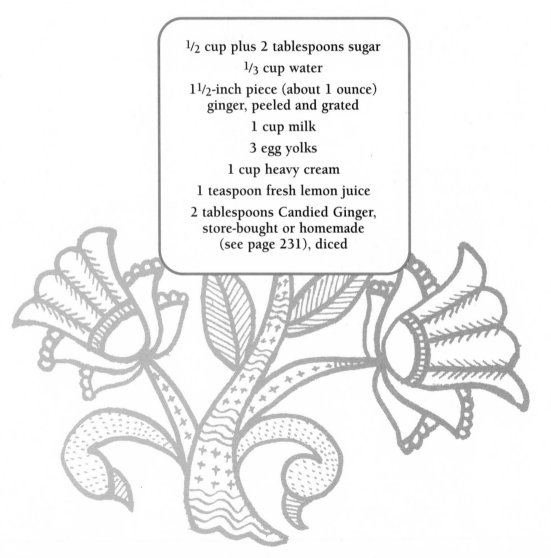

$1/2$ cup plus 2 tablespoons sugar

$1/3$ cup water

$1^1/2$-inch piece (about 1 ounce)
ginger, peeled and grated

1 cup milk

3 egg yolks

1 cup heavy cream

1 teaspoon fresh lemon juice

2 tablespoons Candied Ginger,
store-bought or homemade
(see page 231), diced

1. Combine ¼ cup of sugar with the water in a small saucepan and bring to a rapid boil. Add the grated ginger and reduce the heat to a simmer. Cook for 5 minutes, remove from heat, and strain into a small bowl. Reserve the cooked ginger in a separate bowl.

2. Over medium-high heat in a medium saucepan, combine the milk with 2 tablespoons sugar and reserved cooked ginger. When the milk comes to a boil, remove from heat, and pour in the ginger syrup. Set aside and allow the milk to steep for 30 minutes.

3. Whisk the egg yolks with the remaining ¼ cup of sugar until the yolks turn pale yellow.

4. Heat the ginger-infused milk once again, on low heat until hot. Pour the hot milk in a steady stream into the beaten egg yolks, whisking the whole time to avoid any lumps or scrambling of the eggs. Pour the custard mix back into the saucepan and cook on low heat stirring continuously for about 6 to 8 minutes until the custard thickens to coat a spoon.

5. Put a handful of ice cubes and a cup or two of water in a large bowl. Place a medium bowl in this ice bath. Remove the custard from the heat and strain it into the medium bowl. This cools the custard quickly. With a wooden spoon, press down on the candied ginger in the strainer to get any juices. When the custard has cooled through, stir in the heavy cream and the lemon juice. Pour into an ice-cream maker and add the candied ginger. Freeze according to manufacturer's instructions.

MAKES 1 QUART

Mango Ice Cream
Mango Kulfi

In sorbet, and in the following ice cream, mangoes make any dessert delicious.
With its lovely vibrant orange color, tropical flavor and rich creaminess, this nontraditional treat sells out at the restaurant every night. I make it at home, too,
when my father comes for a visit, as it is his favorite.

1 1/2 cups milk

1/2 cup sugar

3 egg yolks

1 1/3 cups canned mango pulp
(see Note)

1 tablespoon lime juice

1. In a medium saucepan combine the milk with 1/4 cup of sugar. Heat until hot but not boiling.

2. In the meantime, whisk the egg yolks with the remaining 1/4 cup of sugar until the yolks turn pale yellow. Pour the hot milk into the beaten egg yolks in a steady stream, whisking all the time to avoid any lumps or scrambling of the eggs.

3. Pour the custard mix back into the saucepan and cook on low heat, stir-ring continuously for about 6 to 8 minutes until the custard thickens enough to coat a spoon.

4. Put a handful of ice cubes and a cup or two of water in a large bowl. Place a medium bowl in this ice bath. Remove the custard from the heat and pour it into the medium bowl. This cools the custard quickly. When it has cooled through, stir in the mango pulp and the lime juice. Freeze in an ice-cream maker accord-ing to manufacturer's instructions.

MAKES 1 QUART

Note: Indian markets sell different brands of canned mango pulp. I look for the Ratna brand of "Alphonso" mango pulp, because it is by far the best. However, if that is not available look for another brand that uses the "Alphonso" mango.

Yogurt–Saffron Pudding
Shrikhand

In the state of Gujerat, where this pudding originates, sweets are served along with the rest of the meal, as one of many offerings in small bowls. I like to serve this pudding as an accompaniment to fresh fruit or by itself as a dessert. Although store-bought yogurt works well enough in this recipe, I prefer homemade. The saffron threads remain whole, imparting streaks of color and flavor throughout the smooth pudding.

5 cups plain yogurt,✳
store-bought or homemade
(see page 5)

1/4 teaspoon saffron threads

1/4 teaspoon (about 5 to 6 pods)
green cardamom,✳ freshly ground

2 1/2 cups confectioners' sugar

1 tablespoon (10 to 12 nuts)
raw green pistachios,
peeled and minced

1. Place a large muslin cloth over a bowl with the edges draping over the sides. Pour the yogurt onto the cloth and tie the corners of the muslin into a knot. Suspend the yogurt over the sink (tie the cloth to the faucet or drape the cloth over the edge of the sink, holding it in place with a heavy object) and let the yogurt drip for 24 hours.

2. Place the strained yogurt in a large mixing bowl. Whisk in the saffron threads and cardamom. The yogurt will be lumpy.

3. Whisk in the sugar, a 1/4-cup at a time, smoothing out the lumps at the same time. Spoon the mixture into a serving bowl or individual ramekins, sprinkle with the chopped pistachios and chill for at least 1 hour. Pudding can be made up to 1 day ahead; refrigerate, tightly covered with plastic wrap, until needed.

SERVES 6 TO 8

Carrot Pudding
Gajjar ka Halwa

Especially during the winter months, the carrots in India are a vibrant reddish-orange and so sweet that they are often used in this favorite dessert. The "pudding" consists of grated carrots slowly cooked in milk, until the milk has thickened and condensed, and flavored with almonds and raisins, which have been sautéed in clarified butter. Though we call it a pudding, the texture is not smooth and even, but cobbly and dense. It's best warm, with a dollop of whipped cream on the side.

6 cups whole milk

8 green cardamom pods,* split open

2 1/2 pounds carrots, peeled and grated

1/2 to 2/3 cup sugar

2 tablespoons melted ghee *

1 tablespoon slivered almonds

2 tablespoons raisins

1/4 teaspoon ground cardamom *

1/2 cup heavy cream, lightly whipped

1. Wash a large quart saucepan, but do not dry it completely (the moisture will prevent the milk from forming a skin as it boils). Pour in the milk and cardamom pods and bring to a boil. Reduce heat to medium and continue to boil slowly for about 15 to 20 minutes, until reduced almost by half.

2. Add the grated carrots and continue to cook for another 35 to 45 minutes, stirring occasionally and scraping down the sides of the pan. The time involved in cooking will depend on how much moisture was in the carrots. Once all the liquid has cooked away, add 1/2 cup of sugar, mixing well. Taste for sweetness and add more sugar, if necessary, depending, again, on the sweetness of the carrots.

3. The sugar will cause the carrots to exude more liquid. Continue to cook until it has dried up. Remove from heat and set aside.

4. In a small skillet heat the ghee and add the almonds. As they start to brown, add the raisins and sauté until they plump up. Remove from the heat and add the ground cardamom. Immediately pour the mixture into the pudding, mixing well. Serve warm. The dessert can be made ahead and warmed when needed by gently heating the desired amount in a nonstick skillet. Place in individual bowls and spoon a tablespoon or so of cream on it.

SERVES 6 TO 8

Indian Rice Pudding

Kheer

Kheer is one of India's favorite desserts. This pudding is usually served by itself, or garnished with nuts and raisins, but I think it tastes best as an accompaniment to fresh fruit. Many of my regular customers think it is best served warm—as does my father. Do not be confused by the low ratio of rice to milk; Indian Rice Pudding is less dense than its American counterpart.

2½ tablespoons basmati rice ✳

½ gallon milk

8 to 10 green cardamom pods,✳ split open

⅓ cup sugar

1 tablespoon slivered almonds (optional)

⅓ cup golden raisins (optional)

½ teaspoon ground cardamom ✳

1. Pick over rice for stones. In a bowl, wash rice in several changes of cold water until the water is clear. Soak in warm water to cover for at least 20 minutes but no longer than 45 minutes.

2. Rinse a 4-quart saucepan with cold water and while it is still damp, pour in the milk (this helps prevent a skin forming on the pan). Add the cardamom pods and bring to a full boil.

3. Reduce the heat to medium, add the drained rice, and stir well. Reduce heat to low and cook, stirring occasionally and scraping down the sides, until the mixture is reduced by about one-third. This will take 1 hour to 1 hour and 15 minutes.

4. Stir in the sugar, testing for sweetness. Add more if desired, keeping in mind that a chilled dish tastes less sweet than a warm one. If preferred, add the slivered almonds and/or raisins. Continue to cook for another 5 minutes, until the sugar has completely dissolved and the almonds have softened.

5. Let cool and remove the cardamom pods. Sprinkle with the ground cardamom. The pudding can be served warm, at room temperature or chilled.

SERVES 8

Variation: For a more festive, Indian-flavored dessert, add ¼ teaspoon saffron threads to the milk when the rice is added. Omit the almonds and raisins, adding instead ½ teaspoon of rose water. Garnish with a sprinkling of sliced raw, green, peeled pistachios (about 1 tablespoon, 12 to 14 nuts).

Drinks

This section includes classic recipes for Lassis, the nutritious and refreshing yogurt beverages that Indians sometimes drink as a pick-me-up, or even as a quick lunch substitute. As in the rest of their foods, Indians love cool Lassis in a wide range of flavors, from sweet and fruity to spicy and salty. Indians would never recognize another of my creations in this book—Spiced Iced Tea—but my customers at the Bombay Cafe love it. I also include a recipe for my childhood favorite, Lemon–Ginger Fizz, my mother's recipe for sparkling lemonade with a ginger twist.

Flavored Yogurt Drinks
Lassi

Indians love cool yogurt drinks (lassi) and serve them frequently with meals, as a between-meal snack, or even as a quick lunch-on-the-run. Both sweet lassis, flavored with fruit or vanilla, or salted lassis, redolent of cumin, are popular. My own favorite is Masala Lassi, because it is both sweet and spicy. The consistency of a lassi can be adjusted to suit your taste by increasing either the water or the yogurt.
Here are several variations, with a flavor for everyone.

Sweet Lassi

> 1/2 cup plain yogurt,✳ store-bought
> or homemade (see page 5)
> 1 1/2 tablespoons sugar
> 1/2 teaspoon rose essence ✳

1. Blend all ingredients together,
   along with 1/2 cup of cold water.
   Serve chilled.

MAKES 1 (16-OUNCE) SERVING

Salted Lassi

> 1/2 cup plain yogurt,✳ store-bought
> or homemade (see page 5)
> 1/4 teaspoon salt
> 1/2 teaspoon ground roasted cumin ✳

1. Blend all ingredients together,
   along with 1/2 cup of cold water.
   Serve chilled.

MAKES 1 (16-OUNCE) SERVING

Mango Lassi

1/3 cup plain yogurt,✳
store-bought or homemade
(see page 5)

1/4 cup canned mango pulp,
preferably from Alphonso mangoes
(see Note for Mango Sorbet)

1 1/2 tablespoons sugar

1. Blend all ingredients together
along with 1/3 cup of cold water.
Serve chilled.

MAKES 1 (16-OUNCE) SERVING

Note: If using fresh mangoes, increase
sugar to taste, depending on the
sweetness of the fruit. You may substitute strawberries, bananas, or the
fruit of your choice for the mangoes.

Vanilla Lassi

1/2 cup plain yogurt,✳
store-bought or homemade
(see page 5)

1 1/2 tablespoons sugar

1/4 teaspoon vanilla essence

1. Blend all the ingredients together,
along with 1/2 cup cold water.
Serve chilled.

MAKES 1 (16-OUNCE) SERVING

Masala Lassi

1/2 cup plain yogurt,✳
store-bought or homemade
(see page 5)

2 teaspoons sugar

1/2 teaspoon salt

1 teaspoon oil

1/8 teaspoon mustard seeds ✳

2 to 3 fresh kari leaves ✳

1/8 teaspoon cumin seeds ✳

1/2 medium, green serrano chile,
minced

1/8-inch piece ginger,
peeled and minced

1. In a blender jar, put yogurt, sugar
and salt with 1/2 cup of cold water.
Set aside.

2. In a very small saucepan with a lid,
heat the oil over high heat. Add the
remaining ingredients, covering
immediately. Allowing them to sizzle
for one minute. Pour this mixture
into the blender jar with the yogurt
and quickly blend with just one or
two pulses.

MAKES 1 (16-OUNCE) SERVING

Spiced Tea
Masala Chai

Just as Americans love coffee, Indians love tea (chai). It is served all over the country, even in the hottest months, in the belief that a steaming cup of tea somehow makes one feel the outside heat less. Tea is brewed in various strengths, depending on the quantity of tea leaves used and the length of time the tea is steeped. At roadside tea stalls, truck drivers will order their cups brewed to specific strengths according to how much mileage they intend to cover that day. Masala tea, a more flavorful version of the standard cup, offers a refreshing change of pace.

2 tablespoons Darjeeling tea leaves

4 to 5 green cardamom pods,✳ crushed open

½ teaspoon tea masala ✳

½-inch piece ginger, peeled and crushed

1 cup milk

1. Bring 2½ cups of water to a boil and add the tea leaves, cardamoms, tea masala, and ginger. Allow to simmer for 2 to 3 minutes.

2. Add the milk and bring to a boil again, being careful not to allow the tea to boil over.

3. Strain the tea into a warm teapot and serve with honey or the sweetener of your choice.

MAKES 3 CUPS

Spiced Iced Tea

Iced tea is unknown in India, but when I opened my first restaurant, I quickly realized how popular it is here in America. I created this refreshing Indian-flavored version for my customers, and they think it offers the best of both worlds. I serve this tea with sweetened milk, although it is very refreshing plain, as well.

> 1/4 cup Darjeeling tea leaves
>
> 1/2 teaspoon tea masala ✳
>
> 1/2 cup mint leaves, plus fresh mint sprigs for garnish
>
> 1 cup lightly Sweetened Milk (optional, see below)

1. Place 7 cups of water in a large saucepan and add all the ingredients to it. Bring it to a boil, reduce the heat to medium and allow to simmer for 10 minutes. Remove from the heat and let the tea steep for 30 minutes. Strain the tea into a pitcher or bottle and refrigerate. The tea will be strong.

2. Serve over ice in a tall glass, garnished with a mint sprig. Pass around sweetened milk with it.

MAKES 3 TO 4 (16-OUNCE) SERVINGS

Sweetened Milk

> 1 cup milk or half-and-half
>
> 1/2 cup sugar

1. In a nonreactive pan, heat milk and sugar together until sugar dissolves. Do not allow it to boil. Remove from the heat, allow to cool and store in the refrigerator.

MAKES 1 1/4 CUPS

Lemon–Ginger Fizz

Adraki Nimbu Soda

On a long, hot summer afternoon, Indians will often offer a cool glass of
sparkling lemonade to guests. But my mother maintained that lemonade alone
was not sufficient to quench thirst, so she added the spike of ginger to her special
variation. I use her recipe at the restaurant, with a variation of my own:
I mix the lemon-ginger syrup with sparkling water.

1½ cups sugar

1 cup (4 to 6 lemons) lemon juice

2½- to 3-inch piece ginger,
peeled and coarsely chopped

12 ounces club soda

1 thin slice lemon, for garnish

---

1. Place the sugar and lemon juice in a
   nonreactive pan and bring to a quick
   boil. Reduce the heat and simmer for
   5 minutes. Remove from the heat and
   let cool. Transfer to a bowl.

2. In a blender, purée the ginger with 3
   to 4 tablespoons of water. Drape a
   clean muslin cloth (not cheesecloth,
   which is too porous) over a bowl and
   pour the ginger mixture into it. Twist
   the cloth firmly, squeezing out all the
   ginger juice. Add the ginger juice to
   the hot lemon syrup and let cool.
   This recipe makes about 2 cups of
   syrup, which can be stored in the
   refrigerator for future use.

3. To make 1 (16-ounce) serving, stir
   together 1½ ounces of syrup, 2 to
   3 ice cubes, and 12 ounces of club
   soda. Either float the lemon slice on
   top of the drink or slit it and hang it
   from the side of the glass for garnish.

   **MAKES ABOUT 10
   (16-OUNCE) SERVINGS**

Variation:

"INDIAN COCKTAIL"

1 jigger vodka

1 ounce syrup

2 to 3 ice cubes

Sprig of fresh mint

1. Combine first three ingredients
   in a short glass and garnish with
   mint.

   MAKES 1 SERVING

Glossary

This glossary is a guide to unfamiliar terms and ingredients: what to look for, where to purchase them, and how they are used. Please refer to the "Bombay Basics" chapter (pages 2 to 7) at the beginning of this book for additional recipes featuring such frequently used basics of Indian cooking as the spice mixtures called garam masala, homemade cheese, and yogurt.

Ajwain (Carom) Resembling celery seed, ajwain is a relative of thyme and is used mostly in vegetarian cooking.

Amchur (Dried Mango Powder) Made from whole, dried, unripe mangoes, amchur adds tartness to chutneys, salads, and chicken dishes. Amchur is available in Indian markets and has a very distinct flavor, but in a pinch, 1 tablespoon of lemon juice may be substituted for 1 teaspoon amchur.

Anardana (Pomegranate Seed) The sun-dried seed of wild green pomegranate, this tart spice is available in Indian markets whole or crushed. The crushed seeds are preferable. If only the whole seeds are available, dry them out briefly in a low oven to remove any moisture and coarsely grind them in a spice grinder.

Asafoetida (Hing) A garlicky or oniony flavor, asafoetida comes from the resin of a tree grown in Nepal and Tibet. It is usually sold in powdered form.

Atta (Soft Whole Wheat Flour) Lighter than ordinary whole wheat flour, atta is essential in creating soft Indian breads. Atta is available in Indian markets, but if unavailable, substitute whole wheat pastry flour, found in gourmet stores. Ordinary whole wheat flour will not work.

Basmati rice (Chawal) A long grain rice indigenous to Northern India, basmati rice is widely used all over the world because it has a nuttier and more aromatic flavor than ordinary rice. Basmati rice is essential to Indian cooking, and is now available in many grocery stores and gourmet markets as well as Asian and Indian markets. Buy only basmati rice imported from India, Pakistan, or Iran, as this rice has been aged properly to give best results. Look for aged Indian brands such as "817" or "Lal Qila," as domestic versions are not as good. Do not substitute ordinary rice because it does not have the same flavor, nor does it cook in the same manner. It is necessary first to wash basmati rice thoroughly to remove the protective coating of starch and then to soak it for at least 20 minutes to obtain the correct texture.

Besan (Chickpea Flour) This is used as a thickening agent for vegetarian curries. Many traditional fried Indian snacks are made from a chickpea flour batter. There is no substitute. Do not confuse besan with garbanzo bean flour, which is used for making falafels.

Black Salt (Kala Namak) This salt, which is highly sulphuric, is pink in its powdered form but turns black when it touches liquid. It is more flavorful, but not as salty, as ordinary salt and there is no substitute. If it is not available, simply omit it and increase the regular salt slightly.

Cardamom (Illaichi) Cardamom comes in two varieties—green and black. Both types should be bought from an Indian market, because, although green cardamom can be found in supermarkets, it is not the right kind for Indian cooking. Green cardamom, either powdered or whole, is usually used for flavoring desserts, while black cardamom is an integral part of the spice mixture garam masala and is also used frequently to flavor Northern Indian meat or rice dishes.

Cassia (Dalchini) The bark of the cassia tree has a flavor similar to cinnamon, but not as sweet. Cinnamon may be substituted in equal proportions. Cassia or cinnamon is used in Indian cooking to flavor spice mixtures such as garam masala, but never in sweets as it is in the West.

Channa Dal This is a split and husked chickpea, from which chickpea flour, or besan, is made. The chickpeas used are much smaller than our ordinary garbanzo beans. Yellow split peas can be substituted for channa dal.

Coconut Buy fresh coconuts that do not have any fungus on their "eyes." They should have their water in them; shake them to see if you hear liquid inside. To open a coconut, first punch holes in their "eyes" and drain out the liquid. Crack them open with a hammer and pry away the hard shell. Using a vegetable peeler, remove brown skin. A coconut will yield anywhere from $2\frac{1}{2}$ to 3 cups of grated meat. Grated coconut should be frozen for later use. Though it is not as good as fresh, you can use desiccated coconut as a substitute. Look for it in Indian grocery stores; the dried coconut in ordinary markets is usually sweetened. Rehydrate the desiccated coconut in warm water, drain it, and let it dry out a little on absorbent paper before using in recipes.

Coriander (Dhania) The small, round coriander seeds available in grocery stores are passable substitutes, but the more oval, light green coriander seeds sold in Indian markets are preferable. Buy ground coriander only in small quantities, because it loses its flavor rapidly, or, better yet, grind the seeds as needed.

Cumin (Zeera) Probably the most widely used spice in Indian cooking, cumin seeds are available in any grocery store, although these are the Mexican variety. For Indian cooking, I feel the shorter, rounder Indian seeds available in Indian markets are far superior and well worth the effort to obtain them. There are two types sold: white, or ordinary cumin, and black, which is smaller, sweeter and rarer. Cumin is used whole or ground; roasting the seeds before grinding, required in some recipes, adds intensity and a little sweetness. To roast, put seeds in a small, dry skillet and set over high heat, shaking the pan continuously until the seeds toast to a dark brown. Once they begin to color, they can burn rapidly, so watch carefully. Let them cool for a minute or two. Grind in a clean spice grinder or pulverize in a mortar and pestle. One tablespoon of seeds yields about $1^1/2$ tablespoons of powder.

Dalia This is a small chickpea sold roasted, husked, and split in Indian markets. It is seasoned and eaten as a snack. It acts as a thickening agent in chutney.

Fenugreek (Methi) Dried fenugreek leaves (Kastoori Methi), aromatic and slightly bitter to the taste, are used as an herb in salads and to intensify spinach dishes. The seeds are part of the spice mixture called panch puran and are used to flavor some South Indian dishes. There is no substitute. Fenugreek is widely available in Indian or Middle Eastern markets.

Garam Masala Meaning "heat-creating mixture," this is the most widely known spice blend in Indian cooking, although exact recipes differ from household to household. It is possible to buy pre-made garam masala in an

Indian market, but it is easy to make and much better fresh (see recipes on page 3).

Ghee This is simply clarified butter. Classical Indian cooking relies heavily on ghee, but for our purposes it is used in small amounts to give flavor. It is essential in some dishes. It can be bought ready-made in Indian markets or gourmet stores. It comes in bottles and keeps indefinitely without refrigeration.

Jaggery (Gur) Jaggery, sold by weight in Indian markets, is solidified molasses. It has a caramel flavor important to chutneys. If necessary, substitute 1/4 cup brown sugar for every 2 ounces of jaggery.

Karhai A karhai is an Indian pan with wide sloping sides. It is similar to a wok and can be found in Indian or Middle Eastern markets. The advantages of a karhai are that it pools the oils and spices in the center and makes the initial frying of the spices much more efficient; and in deep-frying, it allows you to use much less oil than a conventional skillet. A wok may be substituted.

Kari Leaves (Sweet Neem) Although kari leaves are indigenous to Southern India, they are widely used throughout India now to add pungency and sweetness, usually to vegetarian dishes. Do not confuse "kari" with "curry." Kari leaves, either fresh or dried, are available in Indian markets.

Kashmiri Red Chili Powder, or Resham Patti Not as hot as cayenne pepper, this chili powder from Northern India adds brilliant red color and a hint of sweetness to food. Look for it in larger Indian markets; it is well worth a little effort to find. If you substitute cayenne pepper, reduce the amount by about one-quarter.

Kewra The essence of an Indian pine tree, kewra is used to make food more festive by adding a distinctive, aromatic flavor.

Khus-khus These white poppy seeds are usually used ground. Not to be confused with with "couscous," or black poppy seeds, they add tartness and thickness to spice mixtures. To use, grind them alone in a small spice grinder (the seeds are too small to be ground in a blender or food processor) and add them to the mixture. They are available in Indian markets.

Kokum The flower of the kokum tree, this is always sold dried. The dried blossoms resemble dark sun-dried tomatoes and add tartness to southern Indian cooking.

Masoor Dal The pink masoor dal are tiny, husked lentils available in Indian markets, although the larger red lentils may be substituted. The brown masoor dal are smaller than regular lentils, although they may be substituted too.

Mung Dal Green mung beans, or mung dal, are widely available in large grocery stores or health food markets; the yellow mung beans, or dal, which is the husked version of the green mung beans, can be found in Indian and Asian markets.

Mustard Oil An oil pressed from mustard seeds, it is a rich yellow in color and adds pungency to greens. Before proceeding in a recipe the oil must be heated until it lightens in color and hazes in the pan to remove a raw flavor. It is available in Indian markets.

Mustard Seeds (Rai) There are three types of seed available in the United States. Regular grocery stores carry the yellow variety, which is not normally used in Indian cooking but can be substituted in a pinch. Indian markets

Mustard Seeds *(continued)* carry both the black seeds, which are used for pickles and not called for in this book, and the small brown variety, which I prefer to use in my recipes.

Nigella (Kalonji) Sometimes referred as onion seed, nigella has nothing to do with onions. Necessary to panch puran and some chutneys, it imparts a sweetness to food. It is available in Indian markets. There is no substitute.

Panch Puran A combination of cumin seed, mustard seed, nigella, fennel seed, and fenugreek seed, and sometimes sesame seed, in equal proportions. Panch puran is readily available, pre-made, in Indian markets.

Paneer The only known form of Indian cheese, paneer is always made freshly at home. Like a farmer's cheese, paneer's only ingredients are milk and a curdling agent, such as buttermilk. No rennet or salt is used and it is never aged (see page 4 for recipe).

Resham Patti See Kashmiri Red Chili Powder.

Rose Essence The fragrant essence of rose petals, this adds a traditional aroma to some Indian desserts. It is easily found in health food stores, gourmet markets, or Indian and Middle Eastern markets.

Sambar Powder A delicate combination of toasted spices used in Southern Indian cooking, this is readily available in Indian markets.

Tamarind (Imli) The pulp of the ripe tamarind pods, used to add sourness to curries, is sold in cake form in Indian markets and must be soaked, as specified in the recipes. I look for tamarind from Thailand, because it is less stringy.

Tadka This refers to the final step in some recipes, in which spices are lightly fried in a small amount of ghee (usually) and stirred into the dal or other dish just before serving. Many Indian cooks accomplish this by heating the ghee and spices in the cup of a long-handled ladle. The tadka adds the essential bouquet to many dishes.

Tea Masala (Chai Masala) A ground mixture of such spices as green cardamom, cinnamon, cloves, and sometimes black pepper, chai masala is used for flavoring tea. It is sold loose in small packages in Indian markets.

Toor Dal Pale yellow or golden, these are husked, split Indian lentils. Do not substitute regular lentils, as toor dal has a denser texture and earthier flavor when cooked. When purchasing toor dal in Indian markets, make sure not to buy the oily variety, which has been treated with castor oil.

Urad Dal This tiny split bean is sometimes used as a spice in Southern Indian cooking. Buy them in Indian markets.

Yogurt Almost every Indian household sets aside milk each evening to culture into yogurt for use in the next day's raitas (relishes), marinades, drinks and desserts. Yogurt is an essential cooling element in Indian cooking. It also gives a wonderful, tangy contrast in flavor (see page 5).

Mail-Order Sources

India Bazaar
9133 East University Avenue, #107
Tempe, Arizona 85281
602-784-4442

VIK Distributors, Inc.
726 Allston Way
Berkeley, California 94710
510-644-4412

Bharat Bazaar
11510 West Washington Boulevard
Los Angeles, California 90066
310-398-6766

Commerce International
4201 34th Street
Orlando, Florida 32811
407-426-7098

Commerce International
4465-B Commerce Circle
Atlanta, Georgia 30336
404-699-0068

India Sweet and Spices
953 East Sahara Avenue, #A-20
Las Vegas, Nevada 89104
702-892-0720

India House
2501 Cerrillos Road
Santa Fe, New Mexico 87505
505-471-2651

KPM Corporation, Inc.
14 West 21st Street
Linden, New Jersey 07036
908-862-8629

India Palace
6963 South Lewis Avenue
Tulsa, Oklahoma 74136
918-492-8040

Dishaka USA Inc.
10854 Kinghurst
Houston, Texas 77099
281-495-9596

Northwest Trading
800 Maynard Avenue South
Seattle, Washington 98134
206-292-9230

Index

A

Ajwain. *See* Carom
Aloo. *See* Potato(es)
Alphonso mangoes, 234, 240
Amchur. *See* Mango powder, dried
Anardana. *See* Pomegranate Seed
Appetizers, 8–35
  carrot and cilantro relish, 66
  chutneys as, 47
  salmon roll, 182
Apples, 70
Apricot chutney with nigella seeds, 53
Arbol chiles, 54, 165
Aromatic shrimp with cilantro, dill, and tomatoes, 188
Asafoetida, 250
Asparagus with tomatoes, 126
Asterisk (✱) by ingredients, 2
Atta. *See* Whole wheat flour

B

Baby okra with green chiles and black pepper, 150
Baby peas, 167
Baby red potatoes in a tomato-yogurt sauce, 160–61. *See also* recipe on page 50
Baingan. *See* Eggplant
Banana leaves, fish wrapped in, 176–77. *See also* recipes on pages 110, 150
Banana-yogurt relish, 51. *See also* recipe on page 219
Basmati rice, 78–85
Beans. *See* Legumes
Beets with tomatoes, red onions, cucumber, 70
Bengali dishes, 55, 128
Besan. *See* Chickpea flour
Bhindi. *See* Okra
Bhunna meat, 221–22
Black-eyed pea salad, 68. *See also* recipes on pages 94, 157, 180
Black pepper. *See* Pepper
Black salt, 250
Blue lake beans, 127
Bombay Cafe house dressing, 47, 72
Bombay (city) dishes, 71, 175, 176
Braised chicken with onions and tomatoes, 204–5
Breads, 7, 76–77. *See also* Griddle bread (chapatis); Griddle bread (parathas); Griddle bread (rotis); Oven-baked bread; Whole wheat bread
  eaten with potato, 77
  used as silverware, 77
Breakfast dishes, 92. *See also* Brunch dishes
Broccoli rabe, 146
Brown common lentils, 105
Brown masoor lentils
  with sambar spices, 111. *See also* recipe on page 167
  with tomatoes, 110. *See also* recipe on page 126
Brunch dishes, 8, 11, 154
Buffet dishes, 8
Butter. *See* Clarified butter

C

Cabbage with garlic, mustard seeds, and lemon, 131
California tandoori salad, 72–73
Candied ginger, 231, 236, 238
Cardamom, 250
  chicken, 197. *See also* recipes on pages 114, 142
  custards, 232, 233
Carom, 250
Carrot
  cauliflower and ginger soup, 40–41
  and cilantro relish, 66
  pudding, 242
Casseroles, 223–27
Cassia, 251
Cauliflower
  carrot, and ginger soup, 40–41
  fritters, 26–17
  with ginger and green chiles, 132. *See also* recipe on page 92
  griddle bread stuffed with, 99
  and peas, 133
  relish for use with, 67
  rice with, 85
Cayenne, 136
  substitute, 180, 252
Chaat, 20
Chai. *See* Tea, hot
Channa dal, 251
Chaparro, David, 237
Chapatis. *See* Griddle bread (chapatis)
Chawal. *See* Basmati rice
Cheese. *See* Indian cheese
Cheesecloth, 4
Cherry, pear, and ginger chutney, 57
Chicken, 190–212
  braised, with onions and tomatoes, 204–5
  with cardamom, 197. *See also* recipes on pages 114, 142
  curry, 192–93. *See also* recipes on pages 67, 92
  curry with fennel seeds, 194–95. *See also* recipe on page 108
  fritters, 28–29
  kabobs in green spices, 200. *See also* recipes on pages 38, 126
  kabobs in tomato-saffron sauce, 206. *See also* recipe on page 128
  kabobs with saffron, 15
  marinated and grilled, with mint chutney and lime-cilantro onions, 198–99. *See also* recipes on pages 120, 140, 148
  pepper, 201
  preparing, 6
  with rice, 208–9
  roasted Western-style, 167
  soup with spinach, tomatoes, and rice, 42–43
  spiced (masala), 196. *See also* recipe on page 85
  and spinach curry, 210–11
  stir-fried with tomatoes, 202–3
  tandoori-style in salad, 72–73
Chickpea batter, 26–27
Chickpea flour, 6, 73, 250
  and cilantro stuffed eggplant, 138–39. *See also* recipe on page 111
Chickpeas, 6, 105, 251
  with opo squash, 122–23
Chiles. *See also* Arbol chiles; Green chiles; Kashmiri chili powder; Red serrano chiles
  chutneys with, 62, 63
  in lentil soup, 44–45
  shrimp with, 10
  in stuffed griddle bread, 100–1
Chinese long beans and rice, 84. *See also* recipe on page 178
Chips, samosa, 23
Chutneys, 46–47
  apricot with nigella seeds, 53
  coconut, 64. *See also* recipes on page 11, 30, 182
  cucumber and peanut, 71
  dried cranberry, 58
  green chile, 63
  green coconut, 184
  mint, 59. *See also* recipes on page 198, 200
  pear, cherry, and ginger, 57
  red chile, 62
  storing, 47, 184
  sweet tomato, 55. *See also* recipes on page 14, 59
  tamarind and date, 56
  walnut and yogurt, 61
  yogurt mint, 60
Cilantro, 138–39
  carrot relish with, 66
  and chickpea stuffed eggplant, 138–39
  cumin dressing, 72–73
  for green color, 186
  lime onions, with chicken, and mint chutney, 198–99. *See also* recipes on pages 120, 140, 148
  potato pancakes with, 16–17. *See also* recipe on page 100
  sauces, 175, 186–87
  shrimp with dill, tomatoes, and, 188

Cilantro (*continued*)
  yellow mung beans with tomatoes and, 114
Cinnamon, 251
Clarified butter, 76, 252
Coconut, 251
  chutney, 64. *See also* recipes on pages 11, 30, 182
  chutney, green, 184
  curry, with shrimp, 186–87
  curry, with yellowtail, 180–81
  milk, canned, 181
Coriander, 25
Cornish hens, 190
  with dried mango powder, 212–13. *See also* recipe on page 81
Corn with red onions, 134
Crackers, 37, 47, 182
Cranberry chutney, 58
Crepes, 30–33, 112
Crisp marinated shrimp, 12–13
Crisp okra, 151. *See also* recipe on page 186
Cucumber
  and onion yogurt relish, 52. *See also* recipe on page 200
  and peanut salad, 71
  with tomatoes, red onions, beets, 70
  yogurt raita, 182, 184
Cumin, 251
  black seed, 83. *See also* recipe on page 142
  griddle bread stuffed with onion, chile, and, 100–1. *See also* recipe on page 144
  potatoes and green peas with, 164. *See also* recipe on page 217
  in rice pilaf with peas, 79. *See also* recipe on page 120
  sugar snap peas with, 167
Curry, 2, 4
  chicken, 192–93. *See also* recipes on pages 67, 92
  chicken, with fennel seeds, 194–95. *See also* recipe on page 108
  chicken and spinach, 210–11
  coconut, with tuna, 180–81
  green coconut, with shrimp, 186–87
  lamb with puréed spinach, 228–29
  mixed vegetable and lentil, 170
  potato, 158–59
  yogurt, with daikon, 135. *See also* recipe on page 64
Custards, cardamom, 230, 232

D
Daikon, 70
  and green mango in sprouted mung bean salad, 69
  griddle bread stuffed with, 96–97. *See also* recipe on page 154

sautéed with cayenne and mustard seeds, 136
  yogurt curry with, 135. *See also* recipe on page 64
Dal. *See* Lentil dishes
Dalia, 251
Date chutney with tamarind, 56
Desserts, 7, 230–43
Dhania. *See* Coriander
Dill, shrimp with cilantro, tomatoes, and, 188
Dip, vegetable, 61
Dosas. *See* Crepes
Dried cranberry chutney, 58
Dried fruit, 57
Drinks, 244–49
Dumplings, 8, 22–25
  storing, 25

E
Eggplant. *See also* Japanese eggplant
  with cilantro and chickpea flour stuffing, 138–39. *See also* recipe on page 111
  fritters, 26–27
  layered with tomato conserve and ginger yogurt, 144–45
  purée, smoked, 137
  sweet and sour, 140–41. *See also* recipes on pages 20, 135

F
Fast foods, 20, 21, 22–25, 26–27, 34–35, 158
Fennel seeds, chicken curry with, 194–95. *See also* recipe on page 108
Fenugreek, 68, 228, 251
Festive occasions. *See* Food for celebrations
Fish, 173–89. *See also* recipe on page 81
  and chutneys, 62
  fritters, 28–29
  sauces to use with, 186
  in spinach sauce, 175
  wrapped in banana leaves, 176–77. *See also* recipes on pages 110, 150
Flavored yogurt drinks, 245–46
Flounder, 174
Food coloring, 198
Food for celebrations, 8, 99, 102, 160, 223–25
Frankies. *See* Sandwiches
Fritters, 8
  chicken, 28–29
  fish, 28–29
  vegetable, 26–27
Fruit, 7, 231. *See also* Dried fruit; names of fruit, e.g., Coconut, Mango

G
Garam masala, 2, 251
Garbanzo bean flour, 250
Garbanzo beans, 6
  relish, sweet and sour, 67. *See also* recipe on page 168
  rice with ground lamb, green beans, and, 226–27. *See also* recipe on page 58
Garlic
  cabbage with mustard seeds, lemon, and, 131
  oven-baked bread with, 89
  pink masoor lentils with onion and, 120–21
  shrimp with, 10
  spinach with mustard oil and browned, 165. *See also* recipe on page 71
  yellow lentils and tomatoes with, 106–7
  yogurt relish with tomatoes and, 48. *See also* recipe on page 216
Ghee. *See* Clarified butter
Ghia. *See* Opo squash
Ginger
  candied, 231, 236, 238
  cauliflower with green chiles and, 132. *See also* recipe on page 92
  ice cream, 238–39
  lemon sorbet, 236
  pear and cherry chutney with, 57
  pink masoor lentils with onion and, 119
  yogurt with eggplant and tomato conserve, 144–45. *See also* recipe on page 197
Goa dishes, 173, 180–81, 186–87
Gobi. *See* Cauliflower
Green apples, 70
Green beans. *See also* Chinese long beans
  with onions and tomato, 127. *See also* recipe on page 106
  and potatoes with panch puran, 128
  rice with ground lamb, garbanzo beans, and, 226–27. *See also* recipe on page 58
Green chiles
  baby okra with black pepper and, 150
  cauliflower with ginger and, 132. *See also* recipe on page 92
  chutney, 63
Green coconut curry with shrimp, 186–87
Green color of Indian foods, 186
Green mung beans, 252
  with browned onions, 108. *See also* recipes on pages 140, 154
Greens, spicy mixed, with mustard oil, 146

Green salads, 47, 223, 226
Griddle bread (chapatis), 7, 37, 86–87. *See also* recipes on pages 149, 202, 228
Griddle bread (parathas), 90–91. *See also* recipe on page 166
with cauliflower stuffing, 98
with cheese stuffing, 99
with daikon stuffing, 96–97. *See also* recipe on page 154
with ground lamb stuffing, 94–95. *See also* recipe on page 158
with onion, chile, and cumin, 100–1. *See also* recipe on page 144
with potato stuffing, 92–93. *See also* recipes on pages 148, 200
Griddle bread (rotis)
sandwiches with, 34–35, 132
Griddle cakes, 9. *See* Pancakes
with chutneys, 47
seminola, with coconut chutney, 11
Grilling fish and chicken, 179, 198
Ground beef, 219
Ground lamb
in griddle bread (parathas), 94–95
with rice, green beans and garbanzo beans, 226–27
Ground lamb with peas, 219–20. *See also* recipe on page 71
Gujerati dishes, 44, 130, 135

H
Halibut
with onions and tomatoes, 178
tandoori, 179. *See also* recipes on pages 156, 166
Hors d'oeuvres. *See* Appetizers
Hyderabad dishes, 144

I
Ice-cream
ginger, 238–39
mango, 240
Iced tea, 248
Indian cardamom custard, 232
Indian cheese, 4
griddle bread stuffed with, 99
homemade, with fresh spinach, 168–69
homemade, with puréed spinach, 166
and mushrooms in tomato-saffron sauce, 148
and potatoes in tomato sauce, 162–63. *See also* recipe on page 149
puffs stuffed with spinach, 18–19
rice and peas with, 82
and scallop salad, 74
scrambled, with peas, 154. *See also* recipe page 100
in tandoori salad, 72–73
Indian crisp crackers, 20
Indian dishes. *See* regions e.g., North, South, etc. and names of provinces,

e.g., Uttar Pradesh
Indian meals. *See* Meals
Indian pine tree, 223, 252
Indian rice pudding, 243
Indian street foods, 20, 21, 34

J
Jaggery. *See* Molasses
Japanese eggplant, 140
sautéed with onions and tomatoes, 142
Jhinga. *See* Prawns; Shrimp; Tiger Shrimp
Jicama, 70

K
Kabobs
chicken, in green spices, 200. *See also* recipes on pages 38, 126
chicken, in tomato-saffron sauce, 206–7. *See also* recipe on page 128
chicken, with saffron, 15
lamb, with sweet tomato chutney, 14
Kard, 192
Karhai. *See* Pans: Indian cooking
Kari leaves, 252
potatoes with mustard seeds and, 156. *See also* recipes on pages 38, 64
Kashmiri chili powder, 165, 180, 252
Kashmiri dishes, 61, 168–69
Kewra. *See* Indian pine tree
Kheer, 243
Khus-khus, 252
Kokum, 252
Kulfi. *See* Ice cream
Kurmura. *See* Puffed rice

L
Lamb
chops with black pepper and vinegar, 216. *See also* recipes on pages 50, 58, 134
chops with dried mango powder, 217–18. *See also* recipes on pages 111, 153
griddle bread stuffed with ground, 94–95. *See also* recipe on page 158
ground, with peas, 219–20. *See also* recipe on page 71
ground, with rice, green beans and garbanzo beans, 226–27. *See also* recipe on page 58
importance of lean lamb, 14
kabobs with sweet tomato chutney, 14
with onions, tomatoes, and spices, 221–22. *See also* recipes on pages 48, 154
with puréed spinach curry, 228–29. *See also* recipe on page 115
and rice casserole, 223–25. *See also* recipe on page 160
spiced, in sandwiches, 34–35
Lassis. *See* Yogurt drinks

Layered Indian griddle bread (parathas), 90–91. *See also* recipe on page 166
Legumes, 6, 104–23
Lemon
cabbage with garlic, mustard seeds, and, 131
ginger fizz (lemonade), 249
ginger sorbet, 236
juice substitute, 174
lentil soup with, 44–45
potato pancakes with, 16–17. *See also* recipe on page 100
Lentil dishes, 104–5. *See also* Mung beans; recipe on page 81
lentil soup with lemon and chiles, 44–45
Mercin's lemon lentils, 109. *See also* recipes on pages 178, 217
pink masoor lentils with onions and tomatoes, 118. *See also* recipe on page 153
with Sambar spices, 111. *See also* recipe on page 167
soups, 37, 44–45
substitutes for, 157
with tomatoes, 110. *See also* recipe on page 126
tomato-lentil soup, 38
yellow lentils, 112–113. *See also* recipe on page 30
yellow lentils with garlic and tomato, 106–7
Lentils
eaten with rice, 6
and mixed vegetable curry, 170–71. *See also* recipe on page 174
Lettuce, 70, 130
romaine, 71, 72
Lime-cilantro onions, 199
Lime-mint sorbet, 237
Low-fat cooking
desserts, 230
eggplant, 138
meats, 221
okra, 151
onions, 191
potatoes, 160
with vegetable oil, 5, 125
Lunch dishes, 96, 98, 109, 122, 126, 131, 170–71. *See also* Sandwiches

M
Machci. *See* Fish
Main dishes, 9. *See also* Dinner dishes
Makhni sauce. *See* Sauce(s): tomato-saffron
Mango. *See also* Alphonso mangoes
and cardamom custard, 233
green, and daikon in sprouted mung bean salad, 69
ice cream, 240
sorbet, 234–35
yogurt drink, 246

Mango powder, dried
  with cornish hens, 212–13. *See also* recipe on page 81
  with lamb chops, 217–18. *See also* recipes on pages 111, 153
  sautéed potatoes with, 155. *See also* recipes on pages 178, 180
  sole fillets with, 174. *See also* recipe on page 157
Marinades
  green spices, 200
  tandoori, 179, 198–99
Masala dosas. *See* Crepes
Masoor lentils, 105, 252
Mattar. *See* Peas
Meals. *See also* Breakfast dishes; Brunch dishes; Dinner dishes; Lunch dishes; Snack foods; Vegetarian meals
  courses, 9
  as sensory experiences, 7
Meat dishes, 6, 215–29. *See also* recipe on page 81
Mercin's lemon lentils, 109. *See also* recipes on pages 178, 217
Milk
  avoiding burning, 5
  avoiding skin on, 242
  sweetened, 248
  used for yogurt, 5
Mini potato pancakes with lemon and cilantro, 16–17
Mint
  chutney, 59. *See also* recipes on pages 198, 200
  lime sorbet, 237
  yogurt chutney, 60
Mixed vegetable and lentil curry, 170. *See also* recipe on page 174
Molasses, 55, 252
Mung beans, 105. *See also* Green mung beans; Yellow mung beans
  sautéed sprouts with marinated onions, 130
  sprouted, with daikon and green mango salad, 69
Mung dal. *See* Green mung beans; Yellow mung beans
Mushrooms, 7
  fritters, 26–27
  and green peas, 143
  and Indian cheese in tomato-saffron sauce, 148
  spicy with red peppers, 147. *See also* recipe on page 197
  in tandoori salad, 72–73
Mustard greens, 146
Mustard oil, 252
  spicy mixed greens with, 146
  spinach with browned garlic and, 165. *See also* recipe on page 71
Mustard plants, 146
Mustard seeds, 252
  cabbage with garlic, lemon, and, 131

potatoes with kari leaves and, 156. *See also* recipes on pages 38, 64
sautéed daikon with cayenne and, 136

N
Naans. *See* Oven-baked bread
Nigella seeds, 53, 88, 253
Noodles, 21, 72, 73
North Indian dishes, 122, 154, 175, 188. *See also* Kashmiri dishes; recipes on pages 100, 116
Northwestern Indian dishes, 44. *See also* Gujerati dishes, Punjabi dishes

O
Okra
  baby, with green chiles and black pepper, 150
  crisp, 151. *See also* recipe on page 186
  with red onions, 149
Onion(s). *See* Red onion(s)
  braised chicken with tomatoes and, 204–5
  browned, with rice, 80. *See also* recipe on page 162
  browned with green mung beans, 108. *See also* recipes on pages 140, 154
  browning technique, 4, 191
  cucumber yogurt relish, 52. *See also* recipe on page 200
  green beans with tomato and, 127. *See also* recipe on page 106
  griddle bread stuffed with chile, cumin, and, 100–1. *See also* recipe on page 144
  halibut with tomatoes and, 178
  lamb with tomatoes, spices, and, 221–22. *See also* recipes on pages 4, 8, 154
  lime-cilantro, with chicken and mint chutney, 198–99. *See also* recipes on pages 120, 140, 148
  mincing technique, 191
  pink masoor lentils with ginger and, 119
  pink masoor lentils with tomatoes and, 118. *See also* recipe on page 152
  sautéed Japanese eggplant with tomatoes and, 142
  sautéed mung bean sprouts with marinated, 130
  with tomatoes and chiles in rice, 81. *See also* recipe on page 168
  yellow mung beans with tomatoes and, 116–17
Opo squash
  chickpeas with, 122. *See also* recipe on page 200
  tomatoes with, 152
  yogurt with, 153
Oven-baked bread
  with garlic, 89
  with nigella seeds, 88–89

Ovens, tandoori, 6
  substitute for, 88, 179, 198

P
Pakoras. *See* Fritters
Pancakes. *See also* Griddle cakes
  potato with lemon and cilantro, 16–17. *See also* recipe on page 100
  storing and reheating, 17
Panch puran, 253
  green beans and potatoes with, 128
Paneer. *See* Indian cheese
Pans
  Indian cooking, 6, 125, 252
  preventing food sticking to, 14
Parathas. *See* Griddle bread (parathas)
Party foods. *See* food for celebrations
Patties. *See* Pancakes
Pattis. *See* Wrappers for dumplings
Peanut and cucumber salad, 71
Pea pods. *See* Sugar snap peas
Pear, cherry, and ginger chutney, 57
Peas
  cauliflower and, 133
  with cumin in rice pilaf, 79. *See also* recipe on page 120
  ground lamb with, 219–20. *See also* recipe on page 71
  mushrooms and, 142
  potato dumplings and, 22–25
  potatoes in tomato sauce and, 157. *See also* recipe on page 228
  potatoes with cumin and, 164. *See also* recipe on page 217
  rice and Indian cheese with, 82
  scrambled Indian cheese with, 154. *See also* recipes on pages 100, 116
Pepper
  baby okra with green chiles and, 150
  chicken, 201
  and vinegar with lamb chops, 216. *See also* recipes on pages 50, 58, 134
Petrale sole fillets with dried mango powder, 174. *See also* recipe on page 157
Phirni, 232, 233
Pilaf
  lamb and rice, 223–25. *See also* recipe on page 160
  with peas and cumin, 79. *See also* recipe on page 120
Pink lentils, 105, 118
Pink masoor lentils
  with browned onions and ginger, 119
  with onions and tomatoes, 118. *See also* recipe on page 153
  with tomatoes and garlic, 120–21
Pinto beans, 105
Pizza stones, 88
Plaice
  with dried mango powder, 174. *See also* recipe on page 157
  in spinach sauce, 175

wrapped in banana leaves, 176. *See also* recipes on pages 110, 150
Plain basmati rice, 78
Platter, vegetable, 124
Pomegranate seed, 250
Pomfret. *See* Plaice
Poppadum. *See* Crackers
Potato(es), 6
  baby red, in tomato-yogurt sauce, 160–61. *See also* recipe on page 50
  crepes stuffed with turmeric, 30–31
  curry, 158. *See also* recipe on page 147
  eaten with breads, 77
  fritters, 26–27
  and green beans with panch puran, 128
  and green peas with cumin, 164. *See also* recipe on page 217
  griddle bread stuffed with, 92–93. *See also* recipe on page 148, 200
  and Indian cheese in tomato sauce, 162–163. *See also* recipe on page 149
  with mustard seeds and kari leaves, 156. *See also* recipes on pages 38–39, 64
  pancakes with lemon and cilantro, 16–17. *See also* recipe on page 100
  pea dumplings and, 22–25
  and peas in tomato sauce, 157. *See also* recipe on page 228
  sautéed, with dried mango powder, 155. *See also* recipes on pages 178, 180
  soggy-crusted, 155
  yogurt relish and, 49
Poultry, 190–213
Prawns, 185. *See also* Tiger prawns
Pudding
  carrot, 242
  Indian rice, 243
  yogurt-saffron, 241
Puffed breads. *See* Griddle bread (parathas); Whole wheat bread
Puffed rice with crackers and crisp noodles, 21
Pullao. *See* Pilaf
Punjabi dishes, 49, 132, 133, 137, 146, 166, 221
Purée, smoked eggplant, 137
Puréed spinach with homemade Indian cheese, 166
Puris. *See* Whole wheat bread

R
Radishes, 70, 135, 136
Railway station potato curry, 158–59. *See also* recipe on page 147
Raitas. *See* Yogurt relishes
Rapini, 146
Red chile chutney, 62
Red color of Indian food, 180, 198

Red onion(s)
  fresh corn and, 134
  okra with, 149
  and tomato chutney, 54
  with tomatoes, cucumbers, beets, 70
Red bell peppers, 7, 70
  spicy mushrooms with, 147. *See also* recipe on page 197
Red serrano chiles, 54
Relishes. *See also* Chutneys; Yogurt relishes
  carrot and cilantro, 66
  cucumber and peanut salad, 71
  sweet and sour garbanzo bean, 67. *See also* recipe on page 168
Resham patti. *See* Kashmiri chili powder
Rice, 76–77. *See* Basmati rice
  with browned onions, 80. *See also* recipe on page 162
  with cauliflower, 85
  with chicken, 208–9
  with chicken, spinach, tomato soup, 42–43
  with Chinese long beans, 84. *See also* recipe on page 178
  eaten with lentils, 6
  with ground lamb, green beans, and garbanzo beans, 226–27. *See also* recipe on page 58
  with Indian cheese and peas, 82
  and lamb casserole, 223–25. *See also* recipe on page 160
  with mixed vegetables, 83. *See also* recipe on page 216
  with onions, tomatoes, and chiles, 81
  pilaf with peas and cumin, 79
  pudding, 243
  with shrimp and tomato, 185
Rose essence, 253
Rotis. *See* Griddle bread (rotis)

S
Saffron
  chicken kabobs with, 5
  chicken kabobs with tomato sauce and, 206–7. *See also* recipe on page 128
  maximizing flavor of, 15
  for red color, 198
  yogurt pudding, 241
Salad, 47
  black-eyed pea, 68. *See also* recipes on pages 94, 157, 180
  California tandoori, 72–73
  cucumber, tomato, and red onion, 65
  cucumber and peanut, 61
  for picnics, 67
  scallop and Indian cheese, 74–75
  sprouted mung bean, daikon, and green mango, 69
  tomatoes, red onions, cucumbers, and beets, 70
Salat. *See* Vegetables: in salads

Salmon roll with coconut chutney and cucumber raita, 183
Salt, 250
Sambar powder, 111, 112, 253
Samosas. *See* Dumplings
Sandwiches, 34–35
  and chutneys, 62
Sauce(s). *See* Curries
  cilantro, 186–87
  ginger brandy, 233
  spinach and cilantro, 175
  tomato, 189
  tomato-saffron, 206–7. *See also* recipe on page 148
  tomato-yogurt, 160–61
  to use for fish and shrimp, 186
Savories. *See* Appetizers
Scallop and paneer salad, 74–75
Scrambled Indian cheese with peas. *See also* recipes on pages 100, 116
Seafood, 173–89
Sem. *See* Green beans
Semolina griddle cakes with coconut chutney, 11
Sev. *See* Noodles
Shrimp
  and chutneys, 62
  cilantro, dill, and tomatoes with, 188
  crisp marinated, 13–14
  garlic and chiles with, 10
  green coconut curry with, 186–87
  rice with tomato and, 185
  sauces to use with, 186
Simple yellow mung beans, 115
Smoked eggplant purée, 137
Snack foods, 8, 20, 21, 22–25, 26–27, 47, 151
Sole fillets with dried mango powder, 174. *See also* recipe on page 157
Sorbet
  lemon-ginger, 236
  lime-mint, 237
  mango, 234–35
Soups, 37–45. *See also* Lentil dishes
  cauliflower, carrot, and ginger, 40–41
  chicken with spinach, tomatoes, and rice, 42–43
  lentil with lemon and chiles, 44–45
  stock for, 212
  tomato-lentil, 38–39
  yogurt curry with daikon, 135. *See also* recipe on page 64
South Indian dishes, 11, 30, 38–39, 54, 111, 112–13, 129, 194–95. *See also* Hyderabad dishes
Spiced iced tea, 248
Spiced tea, 247
Spiced yogurt drink, 246
Spices. *See also* Garam masala; Panch puran; Sambar powder; specific names, e.g., saffron
  adding to oil, 125
  in Indian cooking, 2, 3

Spicy chicken, 196. *See also* recipe on
 page 85
Spicy mixed greens in mustard oil, 146
Spicy mushrooms with red bell peppers,
 147. *See also* recipe on page 197
Spicy tiger prawns in fresh tomato
 sauce, 189. *See also* recipes on pages
 118, 162
Spinach
 with browned garlic in mustard oil,
 165. *See also* recipe on page 71
 in chicken, tomato, rice soup, 42–43
 curry and chicken, 210–11
 curry purée with lamb, 228–29. *See
 also* recipe on page 115
 fritters, 26–27
 with homemade Indian cheese,
 168–69
 in Indian cheese puffs, 18–19
 purée with homemade Indian cheese,
 166
 sauce, with fish, 175
 and yogurt relish, 50
Split peas, 6, 251
Sprouts. *See* Mung beans
Squash. *See* Opo squash
Starches, defined, 6, 155
Starters. *See* Appetizers
Sticking, preventing foods from, 14
Stir-fried chicken with tomatoes, 202–3
Straining liquids, 4
Street foods, 62, 63
String beans. *See* Green beans
Sugar, brown, 252
Sugar snap peas and cumin, 167
Summer squash. *See* Opo squash
Sun-dried tomatoes, 198
Sweet and sour eggplant, 140–41. *See
 also* recipes on pages 135, 202
Sweet and sour garbanzo bean relish, 67.
 See also recipe on page 168
Sweetened milk, 246, 248
Sweets, 7, 230–243
Sweet tomato chutney, 55. *See also*
 recipes on pages 14, 59

T

Tadka, 104, 253
Tamarind, 253
 and date chutney, 56
Tamatar. *See* Tomato(es)
Tandoori. *See* Ovens, tandoori
Tandoori halibut, 179. *See also* recipes
 on pages 156, 166
Tea, hot, 247, 253
Teatime, 8–9
Thali, 124
Tiger prawns
 spicy, in fresh tomato sauce, 189. *See
 also* recipes on pages 118, 162
Tomato(es)
 asparagus with, 126
 braised chicken with onions

and, 204–5
 brown masoor lentils with, 110. *See
 also* recipe on page 126
 chicken, spinach, rice soup with,
 42–43
 chutney, sweet, 55. *See also* recipes on
 pages 14, 59
 chutney, with red onion, 54
 conserve, with eggplant and ginger
 yogurt, 144–45. *See also* recipe on
 page 197
 garlic, and yogurt relish, 48. *See also*
 recipe on page 216
 green beans with onions and, 127. *See
 also* recipe on page 106
 halibut with onion and, 178
 lamb with onions, spices and, 221–22.
 See also recipes on pages 48, 154
 and lentil soup, 38–39
 opo squash with, 152
 pink masoor lentils with garlic and,
 120–21
 pink masoor lentils with onions and,
 118. *See also* recipe on page 153
 with red onions, cucumbers, beets, 70
 rice with shrimp and, 185
 and saffron sauce for chicken kabobs,
 206–7. *See also* recipes on pages 128
 sauce for potatoes and paneer,
 162–63. *See also* recipe on page 149
 sauce for spicy tiger prawns, 189. *See
 also* recipes on pages 118, 162
 sauce with potatoes and peas, 157. *See
 also* recipe on page 228
 sautéed Japanese eggplant with onion
 and, 142
 shrimp with cilantro, dill, and, 188
 stir-fried chicken with, 202–3
 yellow lentils and garlic with, 106
 yellow mung beans and cilantro with,
 114
 yellow mung beans with onions and,
 116–17
 yogurt sauce for baby red potatoes,
 160–61. *See also* recipe on page 50
Toor dal. *See* Yellow lentils
Tuna with coconut curry, 180–81
Turmeric, 30–31
 how to apply, 11

U

Urad dal, 253
Uttapams. *See* Griddle cakes
Uttar Pradesh dishes, 155

V.

Vanilla yogurt drink, 246
Vegetable oils, 5
Vegetables, 124–71. *See also* recipes on
 pages 118, 119
 cooking for Indian dishes, 127
 dip for, 61
 dumplings, 22–25

fritters, 26–27
 and lentil curry, 170–71. *See also*
 recipe on page 174
 pan for cooking, 6
 raw, 71
 rice with, 83. *See also* recipes on pages
 142, 216
 in salads, 47, 65, 70
 starchy, 6, 155
Vegetarian meals, 6, 50, 99, 147, 148,
 166, 168
 chutney to use with, 64

W

Walnut and yogurt chutney, 61
Western Indian dishes, 174, 216
White poppy seeds, 252
White radishes, 135, 136
Whole wheat bread, 102–3. *See also*
 recipe on page 156
 crisp, 20
 crisp, with puffed rice and crisp
 noodles, 21
Whole wheat flour, 150
Wrappers for dumplings, 22–25

Y

Yellow lentils, 253
Yellow mung beans, 115, 118, 252. *See
 also* recipe on page 150
 with tomatoes and cilantro, 114
 with tomatoes and onions, 116
Yellowtail with coconut curry, 180–81
Yogurt, 253
 curry, with daikon, 135. *See also*
 recipe on page 64
 eggplant with tomato conserve and
 ginger, 144–45. *See also* recipe on
 page 197
 homemade, 5
 mint chutney, 60
 opo squash with, 153
 saffron pudding, 341
 and walnut chutney, 61
Yogurt drinks, flavored, 245–46
Yogurt relishes, 46. *See also* recipe on
 page 94
 with banana, 51. *See also* recipe on
 page 219
 with cucumber, 182, 184
 with cucumber and onion, 52. *See also*
 recipe on page 200
 with potato, 49. *See also* recipe on
 page 166
 with spinach, 50. *See also* recipe on
 page 158
 with tomato and garlic, 48. *See also*
 recipe on page 216

Z

Zeera. *See* Cumin
Zucchini, 122, 152, 153